ONE LEG TOO FEW

Also by William Cook

Goodbye Again
Tragically I was an Only Twin

ONE LEG TOO FEW

The Adventures of
Peter Cook &
Dudley Moore

WILLIAM COOK

preface

Published by Preface 2013

2 4 6 8 10 9 7 5 3 1

The author and⎮ **NEATH PORT TALBOT** ⎮ ɔn granted to
reproduce the ⎮ **LIBRARIES** ⎮ s been made
to trace copyɪ ⎮ e publisher
apologises for a⎮ 2300073959 ⎮ rrections, will
make suitable ⎰ of this book.

Askews & Holts	10-Oct-2013
792.702	£25.00
GLY	

CONTENTS

This book is dedicated to Peter Cork and Peter Way

ACKNOWLEDGEMENTS

Biography is a team game, whichever name goes on the cover, and I am most grateful to all the following individuals and institutions without whose help this book would probably still have been written, but almost certainly by someone else:

Gillon Aitken
Nick Austin
Andrew Barrow
John Bassett
Alexandra Bastedo
Michael Bawtree
Francis Bennett
Michael Billington
Gaye Brown
Michael Burrell
Edward Cook
Elizabeth Cook
Judy Cook
Lin Cook
Sophie Cook
Thea Cook
Wendy Cook
Peter Cork
Brian Dallow
David Dearlove
Trevor Dolby
Eleanor Fazan
Rena Fruchter
John Gale

Lisolette Gale
Nicholas Garland
Patrick Garland
Georgia Glover
Vera Grigg
Andrew Gordon
Melanie Haselden
Jonathan Harlow
Amelia Harvell
Tony Hole
Barry Humphries
Bruce Hunter
Suzy Kendall
Andrew Kidd
Chris Langham
Roger Law
Ken Loach
Elisabeth Luard
Gillian Lynne
David Maclaren
Webster
Sally McLaren
Joe McGrath
Bob Miller

Amy Mitchell
Barbara Moore
Richard Morgan
Katherine Murphy
Mavis Nicholson
Michael Parkinson
Imogen Pelham
Robert Ponsonby
Peter Preston
Peter Raby
Linda Rhodes
Teresa Rudge
Clare Sargent
Sarah Seymour
Robert Smith
Barbara Stevens
Bernard Stevens
Mark Wareham
Elizabeth Way
Peter Way
Teresa Wells
Suzanne Westrip
Norma Winstone

Aitken Alexander Associates
Associated Newspapers
Billy Marsh Associates
Carr Design Studio
David Higham Associates

Martine Avenue Productions
Music for All Seasons
Radley College
Valence House

ONE LEG TOO FEW

'One of my favourite sketches I wrote very early on, when I was about eighteen. It was called "One Leg Too Few", about a one-legged man auditioning for the part of Tarzan. It's a bit alarming that I wrote it at eighteen. I don't think I've written anything better since.'

(*Peter Cook, Success Story*, BBC, May 1974)

PETER: Now, Mr Spiggott, you are, I believe, auditioning for the part of Tarzan.

DUDLEY: Right.

PETER: Now, I couldn't help noticing, almost at once, that you are a one-legged person.

DUDLEY: You noticed that?

PETER: I noticed that, Mr Spiggott. When you have been in the business as long as I have you get to notice these little things almost instinctively. Now, Mr Spiggott, you, a one-legged man, are applying for the role of Tarzan - a role which traditionally involves the use of a two-legged actor.

DUDLEY: Correct.

PETER: And yet you, a unidexter, are applying for the role.

DUDLEY: Right.

PETER: A role for which two legs would seem to be the minimum requirement.

DUDLEY: Very true.

PETER: Well, Mr Spiggott, need I point out to you where your deficiency lies as regards landing this role?

DUDLEY: Yes, I think you ought to.

PETER: Need I say with overmuch emphasis that it is in the leg division that you are deficient.

DUDLEY: The leg division?

PETER: Yes, the leg division, Mr Spiggott. You are deficient in it – to the tune of one. Your right leg I like. I like your right leg – it's a lovely leg for the role. That's what I said when I saw it come in. I said 'A lovely leg for the role.' I've got nothing against your right leg. The trouble is – neither have you . . .

Dudley Moore, Eleanor Bron and Peter Cook in *Bedazzled*.

INTRODUCTION

This is a book about an extraordinary relationship – a friendship, a partnership, almost, at times, a marriage. Like a lot of marriages it ended badly, but for twenty years, between the first date and the inevitable divorce, Peter Cook and Dudley Moore were the funniest thing on three continents. This is the story of that relationship, and the comedy that came from it.

Fifty years after they burst onto the British entertainment scene, in *Beyond the Fringe*, with Alan Bennett and Jonathan Miller, the comedy that Peter and Dudley originated together still feels fresh and vital. They remain the benchmark against which all the best double acts are measured. When their finest film, *Bedazzled*, was remade with Liz Hurley, it merely reminded everyone how much better it had been with Peter and Dudley in the leading roles. British comedy still resonates with the echo of their laughter. And, since they went their separate ways, it is their shared reputation that has grown.

Cook and Moore each created some wonderful comedy individually, but the stuff that will endure is the stuff they did together. Like Lennon and McCartney – whom they knew, and to some extent resembled – their combined talent was far greater than the sum of its parts. Like Paul McCartney, Dudley was a bit too sugary. Like John

Lennon, Peter was a bit too sharp. Together, however, their abilities seemed boundless. We loved them because we could see that they loved each other. And we loved them all the more because we could tell that their partnership couldn't last. *One Leg Too Few* is a sort of love story, the story of a doomed romance. It's the story of two men with a shared sense of humour that almost amounted to telepathy. The reason they made us laugh was because they could make each other laugh at will.

This empathy was all the more remarkable, considering how little they appeared to have in common. Physically, they could hardly have been less alike. Peter was over six feet tall, with the lithe frame of a natural athlete. Dudley was five foot two and a half, with a club foot to boot. Their backgrounds were different, too. Peter's father was in the Colonial Service – Dudley's dad was an electrician. Peter was raised in twee Torquay – Dudley in dreary Dagenham. Peter went to a top public school – Dudley went to the local grammar. Even their Oxbridge careers were poles apart. Peter went up to Cambridge as a matter of course and fitted in quite comfortably. Dudley's ascent to Oxford was so remarkable that his headmaster gave the entire school a half-day holiday. At Oxford, Dudley always felt like the odd man out.

When Peter and Dudley got together, it was Peter who was earmarked as a future film star. When he wasn't playing the piano, Dudley was frequently seen as Peter's stooge. When Gerald Scarfe drew the two of them, he depicted Dudley as Peter's glove puppet. Yet, behind the scenes, Dudley earned his joint writing credit. His realistic humour prevented Peter's comedy from floating off into space. When they joined forces Dudley was very much the junior partner, but by the time they split up the acolyte had eclipsed his master. In the 1960s it was Peter who was supposed to be the new Cary Grant. By the 1980s that accolade had become Dudley's.

Peter's humour was inspired, but on its own it felt aloof and alien. Without a humane foil, a little of his surrealism went an awfully long way. Dudley gave Peter's work the one thing it lacked – the human touch. People were in awe of Peter but they cared about Dudley. His comic acting had a naturalism that Peter's never achieved. Dudley never matched Peter gag for gag, even in the best stuff they wrote together. Yet Peter's writing tailed off pretty steeply after they stopped working together, and he never found another soulmate who could really bring his work alive. Peter's most famous sketch, 'One Leg Too Few', was written years before he met Dudley and was performed with countless other comics, but it wasn't until he did it with Dudley that it became a classic. It epitomised how they simultaneously helped and handicapped one another. Like partners in a three-legged race, they tripped each other up even as they spurred each other on. As long as Dudley was content to prop Peter up, everything was hunky-dory. As Dudley overtook Peter, though, Peter's comedy became more cruel.

Peter and Dudley's humour was a form of autobiography. All the fun, all the anger, was there for everyone to see. Most partners do their best to hide their differences. Peter and Dudley didn't. The friction was the thing that drove them. It drove them together, and then it drove them apart. Like a married couple, they knew too well how to hurt each other, because they knew each other so well.

For a while their lives ran in parallel, but it was never going to last. Dudley went off to Hollywood where he became, for a short while, one of the world's biggest movie stars. Peter retreated into Hampstead and a life of tipsy semi-retirement. Famously, he remarked that he much preferred watching TV to actually appearing on it. One of his many projects that never saw the light of day was a TV programme called *Peter Cook's London*, about the fifty yards of pavement between his local newsagent and his front door. Meanwhile Dudley's star rose and fell, from the world's most lovable drunk in *Arthur* (a role he modelled in part on Peter) to an elf in *Santa Claus*. The story of their double act almost feels like a modern fable, the tale of a man who left home to seek his fortune, and the man he left behind.

Eventually, Peter's third wife, Lin, helped to forge a cautious reconciliation between the two men who, more than any other duo, had turned comedy into an art form. Peter's ambition had been doused by alcohol, Dudley's film stardom had faded, and the two men were able to repair their friendship, though not their partnership. They could still enjoy each other's company but the laughter had gone for good. Peter died in 1995, aged 57, of a gastrointestinal haemorrhage brought on by his heavy drinking. Dudley died in 2002, aged 66, of progressive supranuclear palsy – a rare and aggressive form of Parkinson's disease that affects speech and balance, which gave those who did not know him the impression that he was often drunk.

When they look back, people tend to focus on the disparaging things that Peter said about Dudley. But Peter had always disparaged Dudley: it was the basis of their act. This sort of ritual humiliation is common to a lot of double acts, but in most other such routines it is more evenly spread. Hardy pours scorn on Laurel, but he suffers the most pratfalls. Dudley endured nearly all the abuse. The comedy that Cook and Moore made together was a timeline of their relationship. From the shared affection of Pete & Dud to the shared antagonism of Derek & Clive, it was a love affair laid bare.

Dudley's Hollywood success altered the dynamics of their double act. After this shift in status, even their timeless alter egos Pete & Dud were no longer quite the same. Peter and Dudley played father and son in several sketches, and Dudley's cinematic rise and fall contained something of the parable of the prodigal son. It was only when Dudley's Hollywood star had waned and he'd returned to his first love – music – that Peter and Dudley were reconciled. The wheel had come full circle – Dudley at the piano, Peter propping up the bar. When Dudley heard that Peter had died, the first thing he did was to phone Peter's answerphone. He wanted to hear his voice again. Peter's sudden death, on a slow news day, was marked by acres of effusive newsprint. Dudley's death, seven years later, was overshadowed by the death of the Queen Mum. It's a pity that Peter wasn't around to enjoy the joke. He would have found it hilarious.

It is tempting to portray Peter and Dudley as a rags-and-riches partnership – Dudley from the mean streets, Peter from the gentry. The truth is a bit more blurred. Dudley's family weren't paupers. They were respectable working class. Dagenham High was a good grammar school. Dagenham itself was no slum. The Moores had to count the pennies, but they always made ends meet. Peter enjoyed an upbringing that Dudley could only dream about, but the Cooks were comfortable rather than affluent. Maybe the two men had more in common than it appeared. Like millions of their fans, I still miss them even though I never met them. That was their illusion, the ultimate measure of their art. They reinvented the sketch show. They were the first comics to acquire rock-star status. They changed the British sense of humour. We shall not see their like again.

Peter and Dudley as Pete and Dud.

DUDLEY BY PETER

(Programme notes for *Behind The Fridge*, Cambridge Theatre, 1972)

Dudley Moore was born in Dagenham in 1935, which makes him some three years older than myself; despite the use of heavy make-up and yearly visits to a Swiss clinic, this age difference is readily apparent to the perceptive observer (namely me). He was educated (and I use the word in the loosest possible sense) at a local grammar school. Having failed in his attempt to become a pole-vaulting champion, he turned his attention to music; by diligent study, or possibly bribery, he won an Organ Scholarship to Magdalen College, Oxford. It was here, through mingling with his betters (not me, I was at Cambridge) that he acquired his somewhat effete upper-class accent.

At Oxford he divided his time between the serious study of his classical organ and the futile pursuit of women. It was for the latter reason that he took up jazz, his main influences being Oscar Peterson, Errol Garner and Mae West. In 1959 came his first stroke of real luck; he met me, and together with Jonathan Miller and Alan Bennett we wrote and performed **Beyond The Fringe**, which ran for four years in London and three years on Broadway.

Since returning from America in 1964, we have worked on several series of **Not Only ... But Also**. Out of a feeling of charity, I have also managed to secure him supporting roles with me in such films as **Bedazzled, Monte Carlo Or Bust** and **The Bed Sitting Room**.

Like many smallish men (Napoleon, Adolf Hitler, to name but two), Dudley has a superficial charm and warmth that deceive many. Underneath lurks a demented sadist, capable in private of unspeakable deeds. It is my personal belief that his secret ambition is to initiate World War Three. I can only hope that my unfailing modesty and tact may prevent this disaster for a few years to come.

Peter and Dudley in *The Bed Sitting Room*.

PETER BY DUDLEY

(Programme notes for *Behind The Fridge*, Cambridge Theatre, 1972)

Peter Cook was born in 1937. Two years later war broke out. Educated at Radley College, and Pembroke College, Cambridge. Here, ostensibly, he read French and German but, already driven relentlessly by a lust for power, he concentrated obsessively on seizing the Presidency of the Cambridge Footlights Club in 1959. Revue material gushed from his rancid pen. While still at Cambridge, he wrote two London revues – *Pieces of Eight* and *One Over The Eight*. Peter was thus the only real professional in the four-man cast of **Beyond The Fringe** when we performed it first in Edinburgh in 1959. He consequently received a fee of £110, as opposed to £100 allotted to the three amateurs. We learnt later that 10% of his £110 went in agent's fees, bringing his net earnings to £99. The meek shall inherit the Earth.

In 1962, Peter opened London's first satirical nightclub, The Establishment, and took over the magazine **Private Eye**.

Interesting facts. He would like to be Elvis Presley. He pretends to hate fashionable restaurants, and drives a battered Citroen with the front seats ripped out to show his simple tastes. He is a fanatical horse gambler and golfer. He uses me as a bank – £5 I lent him two years ago was returned recently on a cheque inscribed '£5 and not one penny more.' His solo films are *A Dandy In Aspic* and *The Rise and Rise of Michael Rimmer*. He was invited to be a poof in Fellini's *Satyricon*, and refused.

He pretends that under his glassy exterior is a heart of gold. The exterior is just the tip of the iceberg. Rumours that we have split up are true.

NOT ONLY...

Peter and Dudley in the back garden of Peter's home in Hampstead.

CHAPTER ONE

AD NAUSEAM

PETER COOK: What one has to wonder is why artists
                of the calibre of Cook and Moore should
                resort to material which basically could
                be done by—

DUDLEY MOORE: By me. [1]

On Friday, 8 September 1978, Peter Cook and Dudley Moore met
at the Town House Studios in Shepherd's Bush to record an album
called *Ad Nauseam*. Nobody knew it at the time, but it would be the
last time they'd work together. For nearly twenty years they'd been
the funniest thing on three continents. They were only in their early
forties, but their partnership had run its course.

Peter Cook and Dudley Moore were unlike any double act that
had come before them. Intelligent and dangerous, their humour
bridged the class divide. They'd transformed British comedy from a
harmless folly into something bold and virile. This was something
new. British punters weren't accustomed to comedians with sex
appeal. Morecambe and Wise were like jolly uncles, cracking jokes
at a family wedding. Peter Cook and Dudley Moore were more like
the Beatles or the Rolling Stones. Like the Stones they'd captured

the spirit of the age, inspiring countless imitators. They'd delighted and shocked a generation, and showed the next generation the way ahead. They'd been around the world, entertaining presidents and prime ministers. And this was where they'd ended up, in a recording studio on Goldhawk Road.

Goldhawk Road is one of London's bleaker thoroughfares. Most people tend to hurry through without stopping. For them it's simply somewhere on the way to somewhere else. Richard Branson's Town House Studios was a good deal grander than the surrounding buildings – the sad cafes and corner shops – but, despite its smart facade, the interior was dark and gloomy and so was the prevailing mood. The day before, Peter's close friend Keith Moon had died of a drug overdose, aged just 32. The Who had been among Peter and Dudley's biggest fans. Moon, their debauched drummer, was the champion of rock-and-roll excess. His death seemed like a signal that the party was over. Peter marked his friend's demise with a lurid impression of his death throes. It was a sordid, distasteful stunt. Moon would have loved it. This sick joke was actually one of this recording session's brighter moments. As Peter said, anyone who buys a record which comes with a free sick bag can hardly complain that they weren't warned.

By an odd coincidence, this recording studio was a few hundred yards from Sulgrave Boys Club, where Peter and Dudley had first donned flat caps and flashers' macs to perform their first sketch as Pete & Dud, their famous alter egos, thirteen years ago. Now they'd come full circle – but somehow, along the way, Jekyll had become Hyde. The characters they were playing today were a world away from those amiable idiots. Today they were Derek & Clive, the pictures in Pete & Dud's respective attics. And something else had shifted, too.

Back in 1965, just down the road, Peter had reduced Dudley to fits of helpless giggles. Now he could barely raise a smile. The laughter they had shared was spent.

After more than thirty years *Ad Nauseam* makes uneasy listening, like eavesdropping on a drunken quarrel or a violent domestic dispute. One of the out-takes from this recording session was called 'Rape, Death & Paralysis'. Its title summed up the ambience of the whole event. There was very little on this LP that was even remotely entertaining, but as the record of a divorce it exerted a ghoulish fascination. 'No wonder we're breaking up,' drawled Peter, as Britain's greatest double act fell apart in front of a few gobsmacked friends and liggers. 'Breaking up is so easy to do,' replied Dudley, knowing exactly where to stick the knife.

Yet even in his darkest hour Peter hadn't entirely lost his God-given talent to amuse. Through a fog of drink and misery, you could hear him groping for comic relief – and sometimes he could still find it. When he did, Dudley was still there to back him up, just as he used to do in Sulgrave Boys Club all those years ago. Back then, Peter used to conjure up something magical every few seconds. Now you had to wait, and wait – but, although obscured by booze and sorrow, some of that magic was still there. One gem amid the dross was a sketch called 'Endangered Species', about a man who finds a rare barking toad in his Y-fronts. 'Was it the Barking & Romford toad?' asks Dudley. 'No,' replies Peter. 'It's not called the barking toad because it lives in Barking. It's called the barking toad because it goes woof.' For a moment they could have been back in Sulgrave Boys Club, making each other corpse as Pete & Dud, but good gags like these were rare. Peter had always baited Dudley, but now that playful ribbing had toppled over into spite. Today, for the most part, Dudley simply sat and took it. When he tried to answer back, Peter would simply shout him down. Probably the lowest point was a misogynistic rant called 'Records', about Clive's attempt to produce the world's biggest bogey. When his wife Dolly foils his plans, Clive assaults her. 'I spread her legs apart, and I kicked her and I kicked her in the cunt for half a fucking hour until I was exhausted,' shrieked Peter, booting a blow-up doll between the legs. 'Then I said, "Dolly, will you get a Polaroid of that?" and the cunt wouldn't even get up.' Sulgrave Boys Club was a long way away, and now there was no way back.

One of the more successful sketches in this session was a skit called 'The Critics', in which two highbrow toffs deplore Derek & Clive's liberal use of bad language while praising Harold Pinter for using the same swear words 'as metaphysical punctuation' in his plays. 'A prick or a cunt in the hands of Cook and Moore, it's just a gratuitous prick or cunt,' says Peter, playing a smart-arsed critic to perfection. In the fallow months that followed, Peter would expand upon this theme. 'Because it's Pinter coupled with two very distinguished knights of the theatre, it's somehow tolerable,' he protested to a music hack from the *Melody Maker*, referring to Sir John Gielgud and Sir Ralph Richardson who had recently appeared on television in *No Man's Land*, Pinter's latest play. '"An arsehole is acceptable in Richardson's mouth," or "Sir John can handle a prick with delicacy and taste." Well, I think that's bullshit.' [2] However, what made *Ad Nauseam* so awful wasn't its Anglo-Saxon idioms. Peter and Dudley's first Derek & Clive LP had been awash with swear words, but the result had been quite different. That record had been a cheerful prank. This one was a howl of rage.

To compound the misery, on their second day in the studio Peter and Dudley were joined by a film crew under the direction of Russell

Mulcahy. This film was Richard Branson's idea and Peter had been happy to comply. Dudley knew nothing about it and when the cameras turned up he was aghast. Unlike Peter, Dudley was still trying to become a film star. A Derek & Clive movie was the last thing he needed. 'That was a very bad night for us,'[3] said Peter. Saturday, 9 September was the night when his partnership with Dudley fell apart.

Watching *Derek & Clive Get the Horn* (as this film was called, eventually) is a sobering experience, which is ironic – because throughout the day's filming Peter was very drunk. The movie that emerged from the wreckage has the compulsive appeal of a car crash – you don't want to look, but somehow you can't tear your eyes away. Incredibly, *Derek & Clive Get the Horn* is even grimmer than *Ad Nauseam* – partly because of the material (strangely, there's not much overlap between the two versions) but mainly because you can see their faces. Peter looks possessed, like a man on the brink of murder. Dudley looks like a man who wants to crawl away and die.

Recording studios tend to be claustrophobic places at the best of times, and as Peter set about Dudley this makeshift film set took on the manic intensity of a drunken cage fight. 'Afraid of your own homosexuality – yes, terrified of it,' Peter taunts Dudley, attempting to trap him in a boozy embrace. 'After all these years of slaving together – still not allowed to let the secret out.' 'Keep running, keep running, this is where the gold comes,' mutters Dudley, trying to maintain some semblance of normality. 'There's no gold here,' replies Peter. Dudley would never work with him again, and now he knew it. 'I want to marry you,' says Peter. 'No,' says Dudley. 'Why not?' asks Peter. 'You said you'd marry me.' 'No, I didn't,' says Dudley. Peter was sinking fast but Dudley was simply waving, not drowning. This film was Peter's forlorn attempt to take Dudley down with the ship.

When Peter and Dudley took a break, the camera crew followed them into the toilet. 'See how he reacts to a kiss,' says Peter, lunging at Dudley once again. 'Still doesn't like it.' 'Who would?' says Dudley. 'You think it's homosexuality I'm afraid of – it's your pongy gob, mate.' Peter, lost for words, for once, empties a packet of crisps over his head. 'There must be something here,' says Dudley, seeking refuge, as ever, at the piano. 'No, there's nothing here. Have you ever found that? You reach out and there's nothing there.'

One of the few 'routines' that made it onto both the LP and the film was Peter's 'cunt-kicking' assault on that captive blow-up doll. It's even more awful in the movie. 'That's how I feel about women,' says Peter, punching this inflatable woman in the face. 'Anybody who's watching this who's unhappily married, you see this silly smile, this sarcastic smile she's got on her face?' He hits her again. 'It's all getting out of hand,' says Dudley. Then the stripper arrives. As she peels off her clothes, Dudley seeks sanctuary behind the piano. 'I'm safe here for a bit,' he says. 'It's when she comes over and takes my knob out, that's the difficult bit. Oh, fucking hell. Oh, bloody hell. Can you play the piano, Peter?' 'He's my favourite,' the stripper tells Peter. 'You're a horrible man.' Peter pretends to strangle her. 'Now, dear,' Dudley tells her. 'You see what he did to the doll.' In the gallery Peter's second wife, Judy, looks on aghast.

A few joints are passed around, a welcome respite from the comedy. 'I don't smoke any of them but, just as I pass one to Peter, the front door opens and several police officers appear,' recalls Judy. 'They ask us what we are smoking and go round interrogating everyone. I glance at Dudley, who has quickly slipped a joint into his pocket. I can tell he is as terrified as I am.' [4] Only Peter keeps his cool. 'Well, that's the last time I play the Police Ball,' he says. At this point, Richard Branson appears. 'He is laughing his head off,' recalls Judy. 'It is one of his pranks.' [5] These police officers, it transpires, are actually accountants from Virgin Records. This so-called raid is Branson's idea of a practical joke. 'You know what's going to happen when we go to heaven?' predicts Dudley. 'We're going to have this tape played endlessly while we burn.' 'You don't burn in heaven,' says Peter. 'We will, mate,' says Dudley. 'That's how God'll have his revenge.' But this recording session was revenge enough. 'Has it come to that?' asks Dudley. 'Yes,' says Peter. 'It's come to that.' There was nothing else left to say. The studio was booked for a third day. Dudley didn't show up.

Dudley as a choirboy.

CHAPTER TWO

DAGENHAM

MICHAEL PARKINSON: Did you always want to be a comedian?

DUDLEY MOORE: No, it was never an ambition. It was a survival motive. [1]

You get off the Tube at Dagenham Heathway and turn left out of the station. Head down the high street, past the second-hand shops and burger bars. Turn left again along Parsloes Avenue, past some windswept playing fields. Fifth turning on the right, Monmouth Road, that was where Dudley spent his first few years.

Dudley's first house isn't there any more. It was flattened by the Luftwaffe. Bland and nondescript, these terraced houses were put up after the war. His second house, where he grew up, is about a mile away. As I set off towards it, through the backstreets, it starts to rain. These bleak boulevards stretch on for miles – no shops, no signs, no landmarks. Each street looks just the same. By now it's raining really hard and I'm bursting for a piss. I duck down a silent side street, looking for somewhere to shelter, praying for some place to take a slash. I pass a makeshift shack, like a rickety old Scout hut. The door is open. There are a few old-age pensioners inside, sitting round a trestle table. I peer in and ask them if I can use their toilet. A black woman with a dog collar and a big grin offers me a cup of tea. This sparse prefab is a church hall and she's the curate. It used to be the church, until they built a proper church next door. Talk about answered prayers.

The Church of England was Dudley's salvation when he lived in Dagenham. It was there that he learnt to play the organ, which took him to Oxford and beyond. Most of the OAPs in here today have lived in Dagenham since the war. They'd be about Dudley's age. Lots of people didn't want to move here, they say, as we drink our tea and dunk our biscuits. They didn't want to leave the East End. Sure, there were green fields here, but they didn't know anyone. Back in the East End, there was a pub on every corner, and the kids played in the road. None of them knew Dudley, but they all know all about him. Their faces light up at the mention of his name. Was he one of them? Not really, they say. He was always a bit different. But he was from Dagenham, a place where no one came from, and that was good enough for them. The rain has stopped rattling on the tin roof. I say goodbye and get up to go.

I wander on, down deserted avenues strewn with litter, hunting for the house where Dudley was raised. There are blue skies above the pylons. There are black puddles in the road. I remember the photographs I'd seen, of Dagenham in Dudley's day. In those old photos these streets looked plain and sombre. Today they seem both smarter and shabbier. There's a car in every drive. The grass verges are overgrown. I lose my way countless times as short cuts turn into cul-de-sacs. It's a place with no way in and no way out.

At last I find the house, on Baron Road, between Green Lane and Mayfield Avenue – why do plain streets always have pretty names?

There are net curtains in the windows. There's no one home. There's no plaque, which seems a shame – I've seen plaques to smaller stars on smaller houses. Rows of identical houses, squat and solid, stretch on for ever, as far as the eye can see. Until he went to Oxford, Dudley lived with his parents in this rented council house. As I walk on up the road, towards Chadwell Heath, to catch the train back into London, I marvel at how he managed to get away.

Dudley Stuart John Moore was born on Good Friday, 19 April 1935, at Charing Cross Hospital in London. Like a proletarian Lord Byron (with whom he shared his birthday) he was born with a withered leg and a club foot. The maternity nurse introduced him to his mother as her 'little hot cross bun.' [2] Dudley's mother, Ada, was aghast. 'This isn't my child,' she cried, when she first saw him. 'I don't want him. Take him away.' [3] It was a hard start in life, and an unlikely beginning for a comedian. 'I was a very serious, pompous child,' [4] recalled Dudley. You could hardly blame him. For the first few years of his childhood, he didn't have a lot to laugh about.

A few days after Dudley was born, his father came and took his wife and son back to Dagenham, where Dudley's sister Barbara was waiting. She was five. Years later Ada would tell Dudley that she'd never wanted another child. She'd only had him, she told him, to replace her beloved brother Billy, who'd died while working as a missionary in Africa. 'When she lost him, she longed to have someone to replace him,' reflected Dudley. 'But, instead of producing the perfect brother, she produced this leg.' [5] Later, much later, Ada told Dudley that when he was born she'd felt like killing him, to spare him the agony that awaited him. Most of all, however, she felt angry with herself. She knew that the pain he would suffer would be unbearable, but she knew she would suffer too. 'She was on trial for producing a hunchback,' [6] said Dudley, looking back.

Unlike most mothers of disabled children, Ada knew exactly what lay ahead. Her mother Bammy had also been born with a club foot – 'a green leg' as they called it in Dudley's family, or Talipes Equinovarus, to call it by its proper title (in later life, in therapy, Dudley drew his left foot as a horse's hoof). The condition can be hereditary. The foot points down, the heel turns in, the ankle is twisted. The only effective treatment is a series of painful operations. At best, these grim procedures merely mitigate the effects of this malaise. There was no time for Ada to dote on Dudley, no time to welcome her newborn son into the world. He returned to hospital for his first operation when he was only two weeks old.

Dudley's father John (aka Jock) bore these travails with stoical reserve. Born out of wedlock – his real name was Havlin – and raised in a Glaswegian orphanage, he was used to life's hard knocks. He worked as an electrician on the railways, a trade he'd learnt by correspondence course. He was always working, or so it seemed, even at weekends and in the evenings. He left the house before dawn, walking to the station to catch the train to work. After supper he'd sit and study the diagrams on his electrical drawing boards. In his spare time, he kept the books at St Peter's, his local parish church. Jock was a dutiful husband and a doting father, but he was a man of few words. Dudley was always sorry that he never got to know him better.

Dudley's mother Ada was a lot more highly strung. She'd had a breakdown as a teenager, but it was she not Jock who wore the trousers. David Russell, a reporter on the local paper, the *Dagenham Post*, who got to know her after Dudley became famous, found her quiet and sweet but very determined. [7] Clearly, those qualities were there right from the start. Ada was a regular churchgoer, like her husband, but her religious interests were more eclectic. Her father was a Welshman, a faith healer who wrote books about Christian Science. 'We used to have a lot of them in our front room that he hadn't been able to sell,' recalled Dudley. 'He was a very strict man, very frightening in many ways.' [8] Ada had eight brothers and sisters. She was a shorthand typist in the City. Her mother Bammy used to come round for her dinner once a week. Bammy walked with a stick, because of her bad leg. She promised Dudley a toy bus if he'd stop biting his nails. Her favourite grandson's 'green leg' – like her own – was never mentioned around the house.

Conditions in Dudley's childhood home were adequate but spartan. Number fourteen Monmouth Road was a modern council house, built in 1928. Jock and Ada were its first tenants. The rent was ten shillings a week. Their house was part of the Becontree Estate, the biggest council estate in Britain. It was erected in the 1930s for the deserving poor – skilled artisans, like Jock, but strictly blue collar all the same. Their estate comprised 26,000 new homes spread across 3,000 acres, built to house 90,000 people – all constructed in the same drab style from the same mud-coloured brick. It was like a maze. 'Every street and terraced house was exactly alike,' [9] recalled Dudley's friend and music teacher Peter Cork. Yet unlike the slums they'd replaced, at least these anonymous estates were fit for human habitation. Like most of the municipal houses that surrounded it, Dudley's home had two bedrooms, a drawing room, a kitchen and a bathroom – even an indoor toilet and a back garden, luxuries for most working-class people in those days.

For cockney tenants raised in the back-to-backs of London's East End, these modest mod cons and open spaces must have seemed like precious perks – but unlike the East End, Dagenham was incurably provincial. It was only a few miles from the metropolis but it might have been a hundred miles away. It felt more like an industrial town in the Midlands than a dormitory town on the edge of London. In 1931 Ford built a huge motor works in Dagenham, drawing its huge workforce from Becontree and the similar estates nearby. During the Depression this steady source of mass employment was a lifeline, but it was hardly pretty. It even lacked the sham romance of proper poverty. Fleet Street reporters used to joke that hell was covering a car strike on a rainy day in Dagenham.

Even by Dagenham's modest standards, Dudley's daily life was resolutely humdrum. A visit to the local cinema was a rare old treat. 'I remember seeing *Red River* at the Mayfair cinema in Dagenham,' said Dudley. 'It was so foggy outside that the fog came in and you couldn't see the screen.' [10] The highlight of Dudley's day was listening to *Children's Hour* on the radio at five o'clock every evening. The highlight of his year was two weeks' B&B in Clacton or Southend. Unlike most of her neighbours, Ada managed to save enough for a fortnight's holiday every summer (most folk made do with the odd day out, or a week away if they were lucky) but Christmas chez Jock and Ada was a particularly perfunctory affair – one present each, no tree, no turkey, and no decorations apart from the paper chains that Dudley and his sister Barbara made.

There was some respite from this dour repast at Bammy's home in Hornchurch, where they sang Christmas carols round the piano. Ada's family were all musical. Maybe little Dudley would also be that way inclined? Jock had bought an upright piano a few months before his son was born. It cost six pounds – a tidy sum in those days, a fortnight's wages for a working man. Dudley clambered onto the piano stool and began to muck about, hitting the notes at random. 'This makes a nice noise,' [11] he thought. He was eager to learn more, but his musical studies were rudely interrupted by the outbreak of World War Two.

Thanks to the huge Ford factory, Dudley's unassuming home town was now a prime target for German bombers. On 1 September 1939, two days before war was declared, Ada, Barbara and Dudley were evacuated. Only Jock remained at home. They rose before dawn and walked to Dagenham Dock, where they boarded a boat bound for Yarmouth. After a few nights in a noisy hotel, in a room shared with their next-door neighbours from Dagenham, they were packed off to a pretty Norfolk village called Plumstead. They sat together in the churchyard while the locals took their pick of the evacuees and were finally taken in by a kind and prosperous couple called Captain and Mrs Coltart. They moved into the servants' quarters and Dudley befriended the Coltarts' gardener, Herbert Harmer, with whom he collected eggs, chased rabbits and ate cheese rarebit in the greenhouse. It was a world away from dreary Dagenham. Hitler had given Dudley a glimpse of a better life elsewhere.

In April 1940, on his fifth birthday, Dudley enrolled at the local infant school, but in May, after eight months of the 'Phoney War' (during which time the Luftwaffe largely ignored London), he was allowed to return home with his mother and sister – just in time for the onset of the Blitz. As German bombers pounded London and the satellite towns like Dagenham that surrounded it, the Moores spent every night in a cold, damp bomb shelter in the back garden. One night they decided not to bother and Barbara and Dudley settled down to sleep in the front room. They were woken in the small hours by someone banging on the front door. It was a fireman. 'Don't light the gas!' he shouted. 'There's a leak!' A bomb had fallen through the roof and landed a few yards from where they were sleeping. Fortunately, it had failed to detonate, but the house was a write-off. 'We were very lucky,' said Dudley. 'It didn't really sink in at the time.' The family were rehoused in another council house, 146 Baron Road, on the north side of Dagenham, nearer Barking. Dudley lived there until he left home. Despite his subsequent attempts to buy them something bigger and better, his parents lived there until they died. 'They were very frightened of the world.' [12] he said.

Superficially, Dudley came to share some of their characteristics. He was reticent, like Jock, and fretful, like Ada. He looked a lot like both of them – slim and swarthy, more Celtic than Anglo-Saxon. He was short, like they were – both his parents were only five foot three. Like his parents, and his sister, he could have passed for Jewish, or even Romany. He inherited his mother's dark complexion and his father's elongated nose. In later life he bore some resemblance to Charlie Chaplin – the thick wavy hair, the piercing eyes.

Family life at 146 Baron Road was quiet – almost reclusive. There were hardly ever any visitors. There was no alcohol in the house – only Tizer and Lucozade. With few other distractions, the piano became Dudley's favourite pastime. If there'd been no music in the family, his talent might have been stillborn – but in the days before television, when the wireless was the only distraction, it was a lot more common for families to make music together. Ada's family was full of people who could carry a tune. She'd always sung songs around the piano. As an adult, she could play well enough to give lessons to local children. Crucially, she knew enough to recognise her son's talent. She knew enough to realise that it was infinitely greater than her own. She taught Barbara the basics, but she knew her limitations. She paid for Barbara's piano lessons – half an hour a week at a shilling a time. Despite the hardships of wartime, she did the same for Dudley. His life would have been very different if she hadn't been able to find that extra bob a week.

Barbara and Dudley's teacher was a nice lady called Irene Hoggard who had a stammer. She taught Dudley the piano for ten years, from six to sixteen. She was the only piano teacher he ever had. Dudley was fond of her and for ever grateful to her, but her abilities were finite. 'I thought she was a fairly useless old dear,' said Dudley. 'I didn't get any musicianship from her, merely the ability to read music.' [13] The fact that he still flourished was a sign of his vast potential. Barbara was a competent and conscientious pianist. Dudley was a lot less diligent, but he rapidly eclipsed his sister. When she couldn't master syncopation at the age of thirteen, Dudley showed her how to do it. He was only eight years old. 'I used to practise all week and he never used to practise,' she said. 'I used to get my knuckles rapped at the next lesson but he never did. He always whistled through the exams.' [14]

As well as playing the piano, Dudley loved going to church and singing hymns, and, mindful of his budding virtuosity, Dudley's devout parents transferred him from St Peter's, where he'd been an altar boy, to another local church, St Thomas's, which had its own choir. 'I dearly wanted to be in a choir,' said Dudley. 'I loved the sound of voices.' [15] Thursday choir practice and Sunday services became the high points of his week. When he won his first school prize he was allowed to choose any book he wanted. He chose *Hymns Ancient & Modern*. 'Dear Lord and Father of Mankind' was a particular favourite. Half a century later he could still remember the key – E flat – and even the page number. He loved carol singing too, especially when it snowed ('we used to be invited in for mince pies' [16]) but he had to be careful not to get his feet wet. The special boot he wore for his club foot cost a lot of money. His father would sit on a boot-blacking box in the kitchen, nailing new soles onto it. The thought of it made Dudley want to cry.

As well as joining the church choir, Dudley also started playing the church organ. He dismissed it as 'messing around' [17] but there was more to it than that. Soon he was playing at all the feasts and festivals – Christmas and Easter were the highlights. He liked sitting up in the organ loft, looking down on all the God-fearing congregants below. It was this instrument which would take him all the way to Oxford University, and ultimately into the orbit of a precocious Cambridge graduate called Peter Cook.

Meanwhile, however, Dudley had his crooked leg to contend with. It was a moot point which was worse – the condition or the cure. 'I had special boots, and – like Rumpelstiltskin – the only way I could express my rage was by stamping on the floor until it collapsed and gave way,' he recalled. 'It was my leg onto which I projected all my feelings of inadequacy and self-loathing.' [18] As well as the plaster casts and callipers, there were frequent operations, necessitating frequent stays in hospital, in wards full of wounded soldiers, often for weeks on end. These hospitals were sometimes on the other side of London, and the Blitz made it difficult for his family to visit him very often. 'I was in and out of hospitals until I was about seven,' recalled Dudley. 'My family used to appear at the bottom of the bed every two or three weeks, it seemed, and sat around shiftily.' [19] Dudley began to think he must have done something wrong to deserve such punishment. After numerous operations, his mother said, 'enough – no more,' yet his left leg remained a guilty secret. His mother warned him to keep it hidden. It became a ball and chain.

Despite these setbacks, Dudley always shone at school. At his first school, Fanshawe Infants, he came top of the class, even though he'd spent much of the year in hospital. Ada was proud of him, but she was sparing with her praise. 'She wasn't one for putting her arms around us,' [20] said Barbara, but although Ada didn't go in for hugs and kisses she was fiercely loyal to her only son. When the headmaster of Dudley's new junior school, Green Lane, said that Dudley ought to go to a special school instead, Ada talked him out of it. 'My mother came with me into the classroom and was standing at the front, very protective and anxious,' [21] Dudley told his biographer Barbra Paskin, recalling his first day at Green Lane.

Ada's brusqueness and Jock's reticence seems fairly typical of those buttoned-up times. There was a war on, and with a crippled child to contend with they could be forgiven for being a bit uptight. However, Dudley craved something more. 'I don't know that either of them could express love very well, either to each other or to us,' [22] he told Paskin. Clearly, he could have done a great deal worse, but he never lost the sense that something was missing from his upbringing – something more passionate than the practical stability which Jock and Ada worked so hard to provide. His most vivid childhood memory was when a nurse kissed him goodnight in hospital one Christmas, when he was seven. This moment of intimacy with a stranger, more sensuous than anything he'd shared with his mother, made such a deep impression on him that, nearly half a century later, he tried to track her down – without success. This kiss was Dudley's Rosebud, his emotional *raison d'être*, and none of the many liaisons of his adult life ever entirely matched it, even though, in a quest to recreate it, he would seduce some of the most glamorous women in the world. 'I've looked for that tenderness ever since – it haunts and sustains me,' he reflected, in his fifties. 'In many ways my entire life is based on recapturing that single moment of affection.' [23] Plenty of people have been raised by similarly matter-of-fact parents without suffering such a sense of loss (Dudley's sister Barbara seems to have survived entirely unscathed) but not that many people are born with a touch of genius AND a club foot. Dudley's creativity and his disability were the two things that made him special. Together they created a craving for affection and affirmation which neither Ada nor any other woman could ever quite fulfil.

At the age of eleven, Dudley started at Dagenham County High School (now Sydney Russell Comprehensive). Ada told the headmaster, Mr Grainger, that her son should be taught to stand on his own two feet. 'She insisted that, as far as possible, he was to be treated as an ordinary boy,' said Dudley's headmaster. 'She was very possessive, very proud of her son, but at the same time I felt that she was rather conscience-stricken.' [24] He had a sense that she felt responsible for Dudley's crippled leg.

Like all the other pupils at this school, Dudley had passed the eleven-plus exam to get in, but there was still an element of good fortune about his arrival at the only grammar school in the district. Built in 1936, Dagenham County High was chronically over-subscribed, and a lot of local kids who passed the test ended up at Beverley, the local secondary modern. If he'd been one of those unlucky children, Dudley's life could easily have taken an entirely different course. Unlike the secondary moderns and the comprehensive schools that followed, Dagenham County High, like most other grammar schools, was run like an ersatz public school: four streams, commencing after the first year; four houses, named after old local manors now buried under the cul-de-sacs of the Becontree Estate. It was co-educational, but there were separate playgrounds, separate dining rooms, even separate staffrooms. Girls were called by their Christian names, boys by their surnames. For anyone who was diligent and able, it was a rare and precious opportunity to make the great escape, from lumpenproletariat to bourgeoisie.

Like a lot of grammar schools, Dagenham County High was an odd mix of academic excellence and adolescent hurly-burly. Dudley was an avid reader, devouring several books every evening. He loved his schoolwork and soon emerged as one of the best scholars in the class. However, with his withered left leg (cruelly exposed in schoolboy shorts) he was easy prey for bullies, who mocked his appetite for learning. 'It was as if I'd been caught doing something vile,' said Dudley. 'Everybody hated me for enjoying work.' [25] They pulled his trousers down. They called him Hopalong. 'I couldn't believe the hostility,' he said. 'I shall always remember that haunting refrain.' [26] As he entered his teens, he learnt that the best way to appease these bullies was by playing the fool. 'Comedy was something I did on a day-to-day basis, trying to keep myself away from kids my own age who were going to beat the shit out of me,' [27] he said. 'I guess if I'd been able to hit somebody on the nose, I wouldn't have been a comic.' [28]

For a lot of nascent comics, the discovery that they can amuse their classmates is a liberation. For Dudley, it was a capitulation. His schoolwork suffered as a consequence, which he bitterly resented. 'I was top of the class at most things and wanted to become a maths teacher,' [29] he said. 'I stopped reading when I started clowning – it stopped me learning and developing. I decided to abandon the academic life and make them laugh before they laughed at me.' [30] Even in his fifties, the thought of it still made him angry. Unlike a lot of comics, he would always harbour mixed feelings about his ability to raise a laugh.

Thankfully, out of school, Dudley persevered with his music – and with no bullies to mollify he prospered. Aged twelve, he wrote his first composition, a haunting piece for piano called 'Anxiety' ('mysterioso sostenuto' – mysterious and sustained – he wrote at the top of the first page). This precocious magnum opus was no flash in the pan. At the local Stratford Music Festival he won first prize for composition, for a carol he'd written – Barbara brought him the news because he was in bed with flu. Money was always tight – Dudley could recall this parents standing outside the local butcher's shop, debating whether they could afford three rashers of bacon or merely two – yet as well as continuing to fund his piano lessons they also somehow saved up to buy him a violin, a gift he cherished. Dudley was always disparaging about his abilities as a violinist, but he played the violin well enough to win not one but two music scholarships – to the Royal Academy of Music and the Guildhall School of Music, London's top two music schools. Pragmatically, Ada opted for the Guildhall, marginally the less prestigious of the pair, because it was easier to get to by public transport. Located in Blackfriars (it moved to the Barbican in 1978) it was a direct Tube ride from Dagenham. The Royal Academy required a change. On such mundane decisions are reputations made.

Dudley travelled to the Guildhall by Underground every Saturday morning to study violin, piano, composition and organ, playing the left-foot pedals with an improvised boot adapted from one of Ada's old shoes. For a boy whose greatest ambition was to own his own bicycle (his parents couldn't afford to buy him one) this was a godsent opportunity. But an equally formative influence was his music teacher, Peter Cork.

Peter Cork met Dudley in 1950, when he was 23 and Dudley was 15. It was Cork's first teaching job, after Goldsmiths College, National Service (in the RAF) and a year at the Royal College of Music, studying composition, like Dudley. He'd hoped to make a living writing film music, but after a lean year as a freelance composer he was forced to get a steady job, and reluctantly became a music teacher. Thankfully, he enjoyed teaching far more than he'd expected, for right at the start of his career he encountered a bona fide prodigy. 'He was already a brilliant pianist,' [31] recalled Cork. 'There were only a few years between us and I often think Dudley taught me just as much as I taught him. Even then, Dudley was an exceptional sight-reader and could play at sight the most complex Bach Fugue, something way beyond my powers.' [32] Dudley became Cork's friend as well as his pupil. He'd visit him in his digs, where they'd play duets together on his landlady's piano.

By the time Cork met him, Dudley had blossomed, leaving the barren years of his early childhood far behind. 'It is often said that Dudley was unhappy and bullied at school,' observed Cork. 'This may have been the case before I met him, but I can only say that by this time he was surely the most popular boy in the school.' [33] So what had changed? Well, his music, for one thing. Unlike a lot of grammar schools, Dagenham High took the performing arts just as seriously as sport or academic studies, and with its choir, orchestra and music festivals there were ample opportunities for Dudley to show off his ample skills. 'He was the accompanist for my school choir, which was wonderful because he could sight-read anything,' [34] said Cork. Together they tackled big, ambitious choral works like Handel's *Messiah*.

Music also gave Dudley scope for his emerging comic talent. As well as serious compositions, he started writing musical parodies – 'Baa Baa Black Sheep' in the style of Beethoven, and suchlike – which he'd perform on the piano, singing along in a shrill falsetto, a trick which would become his hallmark in the show that made him famous, *Beyond The Fringe*. His favourite radio show was no longer *Children's Hour*, but *The Goon Show*, with Spike Milligan, Peter Sellers, Harry Secombe and Michael Bentine. He also enjoyed *Around the Horne*, with Kenneth Williams and Kenneth Horne. He appeared in school plays, playing Tony Lumpkin in *She Stoops to Conquer*. His headmaster was ambivalent about Dudley's amateur dramatics. He felt Dudley was always clowning around. 'They wouldn't let me be head boy because I was too much of a comic,' [35] said Dudley. He was made vice head boy (or head of vice, as Dudley said) instead.

After the physical constrictions of his early childhood, Dudley began to bloom. His creativity didn't stop at the school gates. He still went to the Guildhall every Saturday, devouring musical scores like detective novels, impatient to see what happened next. He played the organ in St Thomas's on Sundays, earning a guinea a time for weddings – more than two weeks' rent for the Moores. He joined the local jazz-record club, where he discovered Oscar Peterson, Fats Waller and his favourite, Erroll Garner, who became a formative influence on his own emerging style. Once he'd heard his first Garner record, 'The Way You Look Tonight', he was hooked. 'After that I chased Garner records all over the place, and spent hours and hours trying to play like him, copying his style quite slavishly,' [36] he said. 'It wasn't so much the technique as the feeling that knocked me out.' [37] With so many strings to his (violin) bow, the only question seemed to be not whether he'd become a musician, but what sort of musician he'd become.

Another factor in Dudley's transformation was his growing confidence with girls. Dagenham High's co-ed status gave him more access to girls than most grammar-school boys had, and despite his club foot and diminutive stature he had no shortage of girlfriends. The first time he fondled a girl's breasts, in the yard behind her house, he had to stand on a pile of bricks in order to reach inside her bra. Yet despite his keen interest in the fair sex, it was a while before he strayed further south. 'As a teenager, I found the idea of intercourse completely frightening.' [38]

Dudley's first proper girlfriend was a French exchange student called Marie Jose. He met her in Dagenham (she was staying with a friend) and managed to win an invitation to visit her at her parents' house near Paris. In Dagenham their relationship hadn't progressed much beyond some energetic snogging, but on home turf Marie Jose had other ideas. After the usual preliminaries ('She had a little garden house, where we'd go and I would venture to insert part of my disgusting body into her') [39] Marie Jose purloined some of her stepfather's condoms and dangled them under Dudley's nose. A prolific masturbator from an early age ('I used to wank myself to death over my father's magazines – he had quite a collection' [40]), Dudley was nevertheless still a virgin, and despite his energetic overtures he was too shy to go through with it. 'I was terrified that her stepfather would count them and find some missing so I made her put them back.' [41] His first true love, Marie Jose always held a small place in a quiet corner of his heart. Some thirty years later, in a letter to Peter Cork, he remembered being 'moonstruck' by her. 'I can't say that I swoon over her name now, but I do feel my heart twinge!' [42]

If Dudley had broken his duck there and then, there probably would have been no stopping him, but he returned to Dagenham still chaste and continued with his studies. He got eight O levels and went on to take three A levels – in Latin, French and Music. But it was Peter Cork and Mr Grainger who really put him on the right track, by entering him for two Oxbridge organ scholarships. Dudley took the Cambridge test first, but he was a bag of nerves and didn't do himself justice. 'I was so frightened, I couldn't move my hands. My hands were frozen. I didn't know what to do.' [43]

This proved to be a blessing. When the Oxford test came around he didn't have any expectations of success. 'I'll never get this, so I'll just have a bit of fun,' [44] he thought. Consequently he was able to relax and enjoy it, and his natural showmanship shone through. The Oxford test was at Magdalen, one of the university's oldest and grandest colleges (uniquely, it even had its own deer park) but this time Dudley was unfazed. 'Will you excuse me?' he told the examiners. 'I just have to put this contraption on.' [45] He strapped an old high-heeled shoe of his mother's onto his club foot (so his withered left leg could reach the pedals), climbed the stone stairs of the spiral staircase that led up to the medieval organ loft, and gave a virtuoso performance for the benefit of the dons below. 'I modulated and transposed and improvised and all the things you were supposed to do.' [46]

Three days later, the letter arrived. Ada took it up to his bedroom, where Dudley was waiting, as nervous as she was. His hands shook as he opened it. 'We are pleased to announce that you have won a McKinnon Organ Scholarship to Magdalen College,' read the letter. 'I couldn't quite believe it,' [47] said Dudley, reliving the moment when his life changed for ever. Ada grabbed the letter and ran out into the street. 'My son's going to university!' she shouted, while Dudley hid upstairs, squirming with embarrassment. 'I don't think it impressed too many people there,' [48] he said. But as she ran down the road, brandishing this precious piece of paper, Ada wasn't really shouting to the neighbours. She was shouting to herself. Her crippled son had won a scholarship to one of the poshest colleges at the oldest university in the country. All the years of hardship, all that hard work, had finally paid off.

A few months later I went back to Dagenham to see Linda Rhodes, the archivist at Valence House. Valence House is a fifteenth-century manor house, a fragment of medieval history amid this twentieth-century suburban sprawl. Before the Becontree Estate was built, this grand old house would have presided over a vast estate – a country estate, not a council estate. Now it's a quaint old curio in a pretty park, a historic building boxed in by municipal buildings on all sides. Today it's a cultural centre – a museum and a library. Linda never knew Dudley but she grew up round here and so she knows plenty of people who did. She's laid out the entire Dudley Moore archive in preparation for my visit – books, newspaper cuttings and other curios. 'I remember using this library when I was a boy,' writes Dudley, in a letter to the library, 'often making two or even three trips back and forth to get books, which I read avidly. As an undergraduate student at Oxford, I also remember that the reference library was of great use to me too in my search for truth of all sorts.' That's from 1988. Then

I see a later letter. 'It's totally mysterious, the way this illness attacks and eats you up, and then spits you out,' he writes. 'I did get angry. But there's not much point feeling angry. There's always this feeling of, "Why did it hit me?" And I cannot make peace with it because I know I am going to die from it.'

Before I head for home I take a wander around the old house, now a local history museum. I try to imagine Dudley here, and his mother, and his sister, but my imagination fails. All I can think of are those two quotes – bookends of a life lived in the world's gaze. This place was Dudley's solace during the days before his talent made him public property. This would have been his refuge from the drab monotony of home. In a little anteroom there's a film running – silent, with no commentary. It's called *The Seeds of Time – A Day in the Life of the Becontree Estate*, by the Dagenham Film Society. It's from the late 1940s, I reckon, so Dudley must be in here, somewhere. There's even footage of his old school but I can't see any sign of him. For the first time in his life, and the last time, he's lost in the crowd. How smart they all look, these boys and girls, how dignified, how dapper. You can tell they're not well off, but their school uniforms are faultless. They look happy, too – more carefree than the kids you see on these streets today. The second film is called *Scenes from the Festival Month* – the Festival of Britain in 1951, when Dudley was sixteen. But this isn't shot on London's South Bank, where the Festival of Britain took place. This is Dagenham's festival, a proper street party that didn't cost these people a penny. There are carnival floats and brass bands and boxing competitions, and an outdoor concert by the church choir (with communal prayers) and an indoor concert by Max Bygraves. There's a historical pageant and a display by the famous Dagenham Girl Pipers. And as the film ends I realise that I've changed my mind about Dagenham. Sure, Dudley couldn't wait to get away, but that didn't mean he was unhappy here. 'When I was living at home in Dagenham I felt very threatened by the place,' he told the journalist Mavis Nicholson, half a lifetime later. 'I wanted to get out, but I now find it a very nice, cosy, friendly place.' [49]

Peter with his sister Sarah.

CHAPTER THREE

RADLEY

MICHAEL PARKINSON: What do you remember about public school?

PETER COOK: Trying to avoid buggery.[1]

You get off the train at Radley, the only passenger, and walk up a leafy lane towards the village. Cross the little bridge that straddles the river and walk on, past the post office. When you reach the church, turn right and head towards the Real Tennis courts. You'll see Peter Cook's old school soon enough.

Straight away, you can tell this is no bog-standard comprehensive. With its long drive and sweeping lawns, it looks more like a stately home. Signposts point the way to the stables and the golf course. It's nearly lunchtime and there are lots of boys about. The older boys are clad in well-cut suits, the younger boys in blazers. Peter was renowned for his languid gait, and now I see where he got it. These boys don't quite saunter, but there's something supremely self-assured about them. I'm given directions by a suave teenager with more poise than I've acquired in half a lifetime. I resist the urge to doff my cap.

The way into Radley College is through a Memorial Arch inscribed with the names of the school's heroic dead. There are an awful lot of names, from both World Wars. I try to count them, but there are so many that I soon give up. Inside are photos of fresh-faced old boys, killed in action in Afghanistan. I walk down pristine polished corridors to the dining room, adorned with coats of arms and portraits of stern schoolmasters. In the book about Radley that I've brought along [2] there's an old photograph of this vast vaulted hall, full of boys in gowns and suits and ties at long trestle tables. It was taken in 1956, Peter's final year. I try to find him in the photo, but he's lost in the Brylcreem crowd.

I'm here to meet Clare Sargent, Radley's Head of Library and Archives. That sounds like rather a grand job title for a school librarian, but as soon as I see her library I realise it's not too grand at all. The place is a bibliophile's paradise, full of beautiful books, beautifully presented. In the gallery above are shelves and shelves of files, the archives of the lives that made this library, and hidden in these archives are the teenage years of Peter Cook.

The first piece of paper in Peter's file is his New Boy's Form, filled out in 1951 when he first arrived. His handwriting is tidy and tentative. Surname: COOK. Christian names in full (write in block capitals): PETER EDWARD. Social: Thompson's. Social is Radlese for boarding house, named after the resident housemaster or Social Tutor. Peter's Social Tutor was J.N.P. Thompson. Anyone important seemed to have three initials in those days. Date of birth: 17 Nov 37. Place of birth: Peter leaves this blank. Prep. School: St Bede's, Eastbourne, Sussex. Nationality of Parents: English. Parent's name and address (exactly as you would address an envelope): A.E. Cook, The Aloes, Europa Rd, Gibraltar. Father's Christian names in full: Alexander Edward. If he has military rank, give it and the regiment. If he is dead, give his last place of residence. Peter leaves both spaces blank.

Peter's Leaving Form, filled out in 1956, is a bold contrast to that timid entry. Here his handwriting is fluent, so different from his New Boy's Form, five years before. His achievements seem unexceptional: School Prefect in his final year, but not Senior Prefect. The Birt Speech Prize in 1955, but no academic awards. The spaces for 1st XV (rugby), 1st XI (cricket) and 1st VIII (rowing) are all blank. The real point of interest is PLANS FOR FUTURE (Give full details, such as names of firms, etc.). Here Peter has written, in his firm and florid hand: 'Study for three months at the Sorbonne, with another nine months spent abroad. University: Cambridge; Pembroke, 1957. BBC, Films, TV, Sherry.' It's that last word which marks him out as a future comic. It's also curiously prophetic. As I retrace my steps towards the station the boys are outside, playing cricket. The playing fields are immaculate, a glorious expanse of green stretching away into the distance. The boys look beautiful in their whites.

Peter Edward Cook was born at St Chad's nursing home in Torquay on 17 November 1937. He was the first child of Alexander Edward Cook and his wife Margaret. Alec Cook was not present at the birth. He was thousands of miles away, working for the Colonial Service as a District Officer in Nigeria. Alec had followed in the colonial footsteps of his own father, Edward Cook, Traffic Manager for the Malay States Railway. In 1914, when Alec was eight and at boarding school in Windsor, Edward went out into his garden in Kuala Lumpur and shot himself. Apparently he was worried about his imminent promotion to Acting General Manager. His suicide remained a secret. Alec's mother never told him how his father really died. Alec became captain of his public school (an austere establishment called

Imperial Service College, which churned out patriotic young men to serve the Empire) and won a scholarship to Pembroke College, Cambridge. It was only after Alec passed away that Peter discovered that his grandfather had killed himself.

Unlike Dudley's mother, two years earlier, Margaret Cook was presented with 'the most beautiful baby that ever happened.' [3] As she wrote to her husband, absent in Nigeria, 'He has quantities of mouse-coloured hair, lovely deep blue eyes set quite far apart, quite long eyelashes and the beginning of eyebrows which he lifts rather cynically at the world.' [4] Cynical is a strange word to choose to describe a newborn baby, but Margaret's assessment was apposite. It would be hard to conjure up a better description of Peter's face, even as an adult. This child was the father of the man.

Alec Cook's career was demanding, stimulating – and terribly solitary. He'd sailed out to Nigeria in 1928, a callow youth in his early twenties, to take charge of a hundred square miles of territory, of which he was the de facto ruler. It was a respectable job, prestigious but not glamorous – the Colonial Service, not the Diplomatic Service: a life of dutiful self-sacrifice. 'District Officers are in my experience obscure people,' he wrote in his unpublished memoirs. 'There is a lot to be said for decent obscurity.' Alec obeyed his own dictum. He was decent but obscure.

'They were tremendously alarming circumstances to live in,' Peter told the journalist and author John Hind, 'to have to reach moral or judicial decisions over a society about which, at least when you arrived, you knew absolutely nothing.' [5] Without any understanding of the local languages, Alec was at the mercy of his Nigerian interpreters. Trekking through the bush, 'arbitrating on everything from land disputes to problems of male impotence,' [6] he could have slotted straight into a comic novel by Evelyn Waugh. [7] As Peter was well aware, it was a quietly heroic occupation – yet, with its Wavian echoes of *Black Mischief*, it contained an element of the absurd. A man needs a sense of humour to survive such isolation. 'The average bout of malaria is no worse than a bad cold,' wrote Alec in his memoirs. 'It is the mind and not the body that is most severely tried.'

Alec generally only saw another Englishman once a month or so, but every 18 months he came home for four months' leave and in 1936, while holidaying in Eastbourne with the family of his best friend from Cambridge, he fell in love with a solicitor's daughter called Margaret Mayo. They married that summer. Less than two weeks later, they sailed to Nigeria together. A few months after she'd arrived Margaret sailed back to England, alone. Not that she wanted to be parted from Alec, whom she adored. But she was pregnant and the official procedure was that wives should give birth back in Blighty. She went to live with her mother, in a 'substantial and slightly gloomy' [8] house in Torquay. This was Peter's childhood home.

When Peter was three months old, his father returned home on leave and saw his son for the first time. Alec noticed that Peter had inherited his large, uneven ears. Alec spent four months in Torquay and then returned to Nigeria with Margaret, leaving Peter with his maternal grandmother, Granny Mayo. Margaret found these separations heartbreaking. Granny Mayo did a sterling job ('the years roll back as I look at his dear little face, and I am a mother again, with a small son to whom I was the world' she wrote to her daughter in Nigeria) but she could never be a substitute for Peter's mother. Peter's first birthday party was attended by a plethora of adoring adults, but only one other child. When Alec and Margaret returned home again, over a year later, they inevitably found Peter somewhat estranged. Alec made some home movies of his son, playing in the garden, but it is telling that in these silent films the focus of Peter's attention is the gardener – he can be seen copying his spadework with a toy trowel. 'Peter's male role model at the time was the gardener, following him with a wheelbarrow,' confirmed his sister Sarah, 'picking up leaves and all sorts of horrible things – bugs and things that crept.' [9] Shadowing the gardener in his duties, Peter developed a fascination with insects. One his favourite books was *Ruthless Rhymes For Heartless Homes* ('very weird, very funny, very strange' [10] says Sarah – not a bad shorthand for Peter's humour) which featured a poem about a woman who was stung to death by vicious bees. Creepy-crawlies would become one of Peter's perennial motifs.

Alec and Margaret's home visits were further curtailed by the outbreak of the Second World War. Margaret became a governmental cypher clerk in Lagos. Her contract specifically stated that she was not entitled to home leave. Peter didn't see his mother again until 1943. Thankfully, Torquay was not a prime target for the Luftwaffe, unlike Dudley's industrial Dagenham. The most dramatic incident of Peter's war (suitably surreal, given his comic calling) was when a woman from down the road was blown clean out of her house by a doodlebug while bathing. Safe within her bathtub, she survived the blast unscathed.

While Peter's parents were far away, Granny Mayo did her best to entertain him. A trip to the pantomime was not a success. 'I had to be bound and gagged,' recalled Peter. 'It was almost as bad as folk dancing.' [11] He had more fun at Plainmoor, home of Torquay United, where his grandmother's housekeeper took him on match days. 'I became a complete fanatic,' he recalled. 'I used to queue up an hour and a half beforehand to get in the front row by the halfway line. By the time the players came out I had to rush off to the gents so I always came back to find I'd lost my place.' [12] Watching football (and sport in general) remained a lifelong pleasure. 'Men must amuse themselves,' he told Hunter Davies. 'That's the prime purpose of sport, and of life.' [13]

In 1944 Peter's mother returned home, pregnant again, leaving Alec alone in Nigeria. In January 1945 she gave birth to a baby girl called Sarah. Once the war was over Alec came home, leaving Nigeria behind for good. 'I didn't quite know who he was and I was told he was my father,' recalled Peter. 'He was a total stranger to me.' [14] Unfortunately, Peter didn't have long to get to know his dad. Later that year Alec was posted to Gibraltar. His wife and daughter went with him, while Peter was packed off to an Eastbourne boarding school called St Bede's. 'Foreign parts weren't considered safe for children and so there were a lot of separations,' [15] said Sarah. Peter cried and cried when he was sent away.

At least he had school holidays in Gibraltar to look forward to. Despite the demands of his post as Financial Secretary, Alec made time for his children. With his fondness for P.G. Wodehouse, he was a wry conformist – a supporter of the status quo who could also see the funny side. 'His was the signature on the pound notes,' wrote Sarah, 'yet he made no objection to holding my hand and skipping to school every morning on the way to the office. When a ship carrying ammunition blew up with a huge bang he told me that everyone at the Secretariat had hidden under the table, playing bears.' [16] During school holidays, Peter also got to spend some quality time with his father – going fishing and playing golf and tennis (his interest in golf would last a lifetime). Despite an age gap of more than seven years, he played happily with Sarah, too. 'I never felt bossed, teased, patronised or merely tolerated by him,' she wrote. 'Not then, not ever.' [17] In Gibraltar, Peter cultivated his interest in tiny creatures. He kept a praying mantis in a shoebox; he made a pond for terrapins in the garden; he tried to sneak a tortoise across the border in a teapot. He was similarly enthralled by a *Reader's Digest* feature about killer bees.

All too soon, however, it would be time to return to school. It's revealing that Geoffrey Willans's Molesworth books were among Peter's favourite childhood reading. Nigel Molesworth may be a comic creation, but Willans's portrait of boarding-school life is unremittingly dark and cruel. Peter had a tough time at St Bede's. He was bullied, but he learned to fend off the bigger boys with wit and sarcasm. 'From a very early age, on my reports it used to say, "He's a very cynical little boy,"' said Peter. 'I always used to think "cynical" was their way of saying I was being realistic.' [18] In the classroom, his idiosyncratic intelligence shone through. 'Originality of thought and a command of words give him a maturity of style beyond his years,' was the verdict of his final school report. 'In speech or essay he is never dull and his work should always be interesting.' His headmaster predicted a 'very promising future at Radley'.

Peter's father had chosen Radley College because of its connections with the Colonial Service. French, the diplomatic lingua franca, was the main foreign language taught here, not Latin. Founded in 1847 to educate 'Christian scholars and Christian gentlemen', it was a bit more liberal and benign than some schools he could have chosen – but not much. It had always attracted boys from middle-class families, not just members of the gentry. It had always taught mathematics, modern history and modern languages, in an age when most public schools still filled the timetable with rote learning of Greek and Latin texts. Yet although Radley's origins were more progressive than some of its older rivals, it was essentially conventional and conservative. By the time Peter arrived, in 1951, it had evolved into a very traditional public school.

Like most public schools, Radley had its own obscure vocabulary, virtually incomprehensible to outsiders. Its eccentric customs were designed to reinforce the rigid hierarchy of the school. First-years had to wear their blazers buttoned up, second-years were allowed to undo one button, third-years could undo two buttons, and so on. New boys had to commit vast tracts of school trivia to memory, and then endure a bizarre (and obliquely kinky) initiation ceremony, in which a jug of ice-cold water was poured down their trousers.

Prefects had countless petty perks, symbolic of their position at the top of the pecking order. They could shut the toilet door while they took a shit – lesser mortals had to leave theirs open. They could walk past the clock tower – lesser mortals had to run. Fagging was obligatory, and prefects as well as Dons (as Radley called its teachers) were allowed to dole out corporal punishment as they saw fit. In Peter's day, the prefects thrashed the boys more often than the teachers did. For smaller offences, younger boys administered their own form of rough justice, whacking the luckless culprit with hockey sticks while chasing him round a table-tennis table. 'I hated it for two years,' said Peter. 'I was bullied – not excessively, but enough. This started off a defence mechanism, of trying to make people laugh so they wouldn't hit you.' [19] However, he was far too reserved and sensible to become the class clown. By and large, he kept his head down. 'In those first years he was not especially distinguished,' recalled Jonathan Harlow, his best friend at that time. 'He was neither a promising nor a keen games player. He was not picked out for accelerated academic progress. He did not act in plays.' [20] As Harlow put it, 'His gift was slow to emerge.' [21]

Daily life was spartan. Boys rose at quarter to seven for a cold shower. The only respite from lessons was chapel straight after breakfast, physical jerks in the morning, team sports in the afternoons and prep before bed. Peter suffered from asthma, and some nights, in the big dorm, he used to bang his head against the wall in sheer frustration. His secret solace from this gruelling regime was *The Goon Show*. Peter was enchanted by this bizarre radio show: Spike Milligan, Peter Sellers, Harry Secombe (and, initially, Michael Bentine) climbing Everest from the inside, drinking Loch Lomond dry or tracking down the Dreaded Batter-Pudding Hurler of Bexhill-on-Sea ... Peter used to feign illness every Friday so that he could listen to the series in the sanatorium ('I had an understanding with the matron' [22]). He was sufficiently inspired to write a *Goon Show* script of his own and send it to the BBC. Peter's pastiche was good enough to elicit an encouraging reply from a BBC executive called Peter Titheridge, who later worked with John Cleese. Peter subsequently earned four guineas for a contribution to *Punch*, but his comedy remained mainly private, something to be shared with a few friends behind closed doors.

Even by public-school standards, Radley was particularly sporty. In 1952, the year after Peter arrived, *The Field* awarded it the accolade of top sports school in the country. Peter was an avid sports fan, but he was not a natural sportsman, and his favourite sport, Association Football, was considered far too plebby for a posh school like Radley. [23] Neither a 'dry bob' nor a 'wet bob' (as Radley's cricketers and rowers were called) he particularly disliked rugby.

'I spent the whole time avoiding the ball,' [24] he said. Peter's nemesis was Radley's cricket captain, 'Lord' Ted Dexter [25] (so called because of his aristocratic air of innate authority, on the cricket field and elsewhere) who went on to captain Cambridge University, Sussex and England. The Headmaster (aka Warden) regarded Dexter as the best schoolboy athlete he'd ever seen. 'I was always envious of him,' said Peter. 'He was Head Boy, good at every sport, and he beat me for drinking cider at Henley Regatta. [26] OK, you weren't allowed to drink cider at Henley Regatta, so perhaps I deserved to be beaten. What I thought was a little unfair was that I'd seen him coming out of the pub with a bottle of Scotch.' [27]

For the most part, however, Peter was quite happy to toe the line. The ethos of the school was overwhelmingly conformist – pupils went to chapel every day, Grace was said in Latin before and after every meal, the Combined Cadet Force trained every week in preparation for the Third World War to come – and Peter played along, with no more than a wry smile. Initially, at least, his subversion was entirely secretive. During CCF manoeuvres he would hide in hedges with his friends and make fun of his commanding officers, but only behind their backs. 'Not only were these rituals unchanging, but there was no sense that their continuation was even open to review,' recalled Harlow. 'The student body was insular, poorly informed and largely Conservative. [28] Peter was no more left-wing than any of us.' [29] Peter's conformist attitude was reflected in his (prize-winning) essay, advocating the chemical castration of the unintelligent working class. 'People say I've got more reactionary in my old age,' reflected Peter. 'In fact, I've moved to the left from my very solidly Nazi position at the age of sixteen.' [30] Tellingly, the only politician who got his goat was a Labour MP, Lieutenant Colonel George Wigg.

'Peter could deliver a shrill fantasia on the man's name in an ecstasy of scorn,' [31] remembered Harlow. Gradually, Peter's mimicry found new targets closer to home – the Warden, the Chaplain, all the usual suspects. Initially, his impressions were much the same as anyone else's. They only became unusual – and infinitely funnier – when he would veer away from straight impersonation into surrealism. As Harlow recalled, 'He could spin a whole fantastic web of absurdity from the merest thread of an idea or phrase.' [32]

Peter's richest inspiration was Arthur Boylett, a Pinteresque figure 'like some waiter in a Hungarian nightclub,' [33] who served as a butler at Radley's High Table during meals. Despite these pretensions of grandeur, Boylett's shabby appearance and downbeat demeanour made him unwittingly absurd, and his shuffling assistance at these august occasions often teetered on the edge of farce. On one occasion, he swept all the breadcrumbs off the dinner table into a prefect's lap. The prefect was indignant. 'Well, they were your crumbs,' said Boylett.

Boylett's speciality was his supernatural pronouncements. He thought he saw stones that moved and sometimes tried to sell them. If even half of what Peter said about him was true, he must have been very strange indeed. He was a familiar comic figure and many of the boys made fun of him, but only Peter had the wit to engage him in conversation, teasing out these superficially profound (but fundamentally banal) statements and working them up into a comic character with a life of its own. 'The more pathetic and simple the poor man was, the more Peter saw in him an absurdist superhero,' [34] reflected another close friend at Radley, Michael Bawtree. 'I thought I saw it move,' became Peter's catchphrase. Boylett gradually mutated into Peter's comic alter ego, first as Mr Grole at Cambridge and ultimately as E.L. Wisty on TV. In a way, you could say that Arthur Boylett was the greatest inspiration of Peter's life.

Slowly but surely, Peter found his creative voice. In 1953 he made his stage debut, playing a socialist duchess in *Stuck in a Lift*. In March 1954 he dragged up again, playing the prostitute Dol Common in Ben Jonson's *The Alchemist*. The school magazine, *The Radleian*, praised the gusto of his performance. In November he appeared in a production of *The Love of The Four Colonels*, Peter Ustinov's modern fairy tale in which Sleeping Beauty is wooed by officers from the four victorious Allied powers. Peter played the Wicked Fairy, the part originally played by Ustinov, and dominated the production with his energy and comic timing. It was an oddly prophetic performance. At that time Ustinov was widely regarded as the funniest man in the world, an accolade that clung to him until Peter became famous. 'The weight's off my shoulders now,' said Ustinov when he saw Peter perform, years later. 'The accolade, for what it's worth, belongs to him. It's a vast relief.' [35]

That Radley was such a dramatic hotbed was largely due to a remarkable English teacher called Peter Way, a Radley schoolboy who'd won the Newdigate Prize [36] for poetry at Oxford before returning to Radley as a Don. Gentle, intelligent and gifted, Way gave Peter an essential platform for his nascent talents. Way didn't simply put on a school play at the end of every year, but also organised an annual inter-house drama contest, of which *The Love of The Four Colonels* was just one entry. Peter's crowning glory as a schoolboy actor came in 1956 as the swashbuckling Spaniard Don Adriano in Shakespeare's *Love's Labour's Lost*, a flamboyant performance which stayed just the right side of send-up. 'A wonderful display of virtuosity,' raved *The Radleian*. 'A delightful creation,' concurred his school report.

As well as acting, Peter was also starting to write his own material. In 1955 he wrote a spooky yarn called 'Bric-a-Brac', which won the school's Medrington short-story trophy. A spine-chiller about a young woman babysitting for a sinister couple who run a junk shop, it was not so much a comic composition as a study in suspense that anticipated some of Peter's professional sketches, particularly his later, darker work with Dudley. He also started to write (and perform in) his own revues. The most memorable of these was *The Gold Mine Revue*, in December 1955. Its highlight was a brilliant spoof of that year's inter-house drama competition. Radley usually invited an eminent thespian to judge the contest, but due to a slight cock-up they'd invited two judges that year (actors Geoffrey Keen and Desmond Llewelyn) and the result was a bit of a dog's dinner. With a boy called Paul Butters as his foil (the first time Peter had performed in a double act) Peter delivered a superb send-up of their well-meaning but muddled efforts at adjudication. It brought the house down, and laid down a marker for Peter's famous parodies to come.

Peter's *Gold Mine Revue* demonstrated his talent for controlled chaos. He loved to take the piss, but he knew where to draw the line. 'He wasn't a rebel,' said his friend Peter Raby. 'He was unclassifiable.' [37] His humour was a textbook example of the old schoolmaster's adage, 'A joke's a joke but don't go too far.' At the end of that term, he was duly rewarded for his (slightly tongue-in-cheek) conformity when he became a prefect and Head of House. 'I had a life of complete luxury in my last year,' he recalled. 'I had two fags. I had breakfast in bed. I used to go to the pictures and fish for trout in the lake.' All his friends were also prefects. 'I wormed my way into power,' he said. 'We were vaguely reforming.' [38] Peter's approach to school reform was a model of diplomacy. 'At that time, prefects were still allowed to beat boys for any offence,' he recalled. 'All of which we got rid of, not by overt rebellion. We didn't go to the masters and say, "This is a ridiculous system." We didn't demonstrate in any way. We just didn't enforce the rules.' [39] Peter's attitude to sport was similarly canny. Instead of rebelling against rugger, he organised illicit (and highly popular) soccer matches of his own. But although he was well liked by his peer group and the younger boys in his care, Peter's friends all sensed a certain distance, a detachment from those around him. Everyone enjoyed his company, but no one knew him really well.

Maybe Peter could have poured his heart out to a sympathetic girlfriend, but girls at Radley were in extremely short supply. Just about the only chance he had to meet the 'opposite number' was at a sixth-form dancing contest against the local girls' school. Radley never won. This event took place once a term, and although Peter enjoyed a few furtive fumbles in the organ loft it was all pretty puerile stuff. His classmates compiled a list of Top Ten Tarts, ranking each other (rather than the girls) on the basis of their sexual prowess. Peter generally came second, and although he laughed it off in later life there was something rather sad about these sixth formers sniggering together after these school-sanctioned dancing sessions, instead of behaving like normal teenagers and going out on proper dates. Radley made a man of Peter in most respects, but sexually he was still a child.

In most boarding houses there was at least some platonic female company, but Peter's Social Tutor J.V.P. Thompson (nicknamed Rutch, for some unknown reason) was unmarried, and so there were no wives or daughters in his Social ('Thompson's') to alleviate the testosterone-ridden atmosphere. By now, Peter had a baby sister, Elizabeth, whom he adored, and her absence, along with that of his other sister Sarah (who'd also been packed off to boarding school) can't have helped at all. Starved of female contact, some boys turned to one another. When *Playboy* asked Peter how he lost his virginity at school, he answered 'At what end?' Maybe that was just a joke, but at the very least he had to fend off a few amorous advances, though even Peter seemed unsure whether they were entirely unwelcome. 'I was quite a pretty boy – I was number three in the charts,' he told Michael Parkinson, recalling the attentions of a prefect whom Peter took good care not to name. 'He came into my cubicle, sat on the bed, put his hand up the back of my pyjamas and started stroking my back. He said, "Do you mind that, Cook?" I said, "Yes," and he went away. In fact I didn't mind at all. It was a very pleasant sort of feeling.' [40]

The peak of Peter's dramatic career at Radley was a puppet show, of all things, produced with his good friend Michael Bawtree. It was another example of the vibrant creativity beneath Radley's rugger-bugger veneer. As well as a thriving drama department, run by Peter Way, Radley also boasted a Marionette Society, founded by the art master, Chris Ellis. Like Way, Ellis was no ordinary schoolmaster. A round-the-world yachtsman who'd won the George Medal during the Blitz for removing an unexploded bomb from St Paul's Cathedral, he ran this little troupe with extraordinary verve and flair. Under his guidance, the boys performed puppet versions of *The Magic Flute*, *The Beggar's Opera* and *The Pirates of Penzance*. In 1956 Ellis decided it was high time his puppeteers staged an original musical. He asked Peter to write the words and he asked Bawtree to write the music. The musical they came up with was called *Black & White Blues*.

Black & White Blues was a jolly romp about a missionary called Mr Slump, who takes a jazz band to darkest Africa to stop the natives eating one another, narrowly escaping the cooking pot for his pains. Of course, such a politically incorrect plot would probably be frowned on today, but these were less enlightened times, and though the vocabulary was cringeworthy, the actual sentiment behind Peter's coy allusions to interracial sex was really quite right-on:

> 'We've cocked a snoot at the colour bar
> Hurrah for the female darkie
> Black and white will always mix
> Who cares if the kids are khaki!'

With manic enthusiasm, Peter organised virtually everything: auditions, costumes, rehearsals, making posters, selling tickets. He even made some of the puppets, but his most impressive contribution was cajoling so many other people to muck in. For the first time he revealed the organisational flair that would later make him famous, persuading all sorts of people to perform all sorts of unpaid favours by sheer force of personality. He didn't bully them. He charmed them. It was a sign of things to come.

Performed over three nights in March 1956, *Black & White Blues* was a huge success and Peter was the star turn. Peter was self-deprecating about the show, but Peter Raby remembers his monologues as 'amazingly assured and sophisticated'. [41] They still sound assured and sophisticated today. Peter narrated both the leading roles, Mr Slump and the cannibal chief (an Old Etonian, like the Warden) though he recited rather than sung his lines – despite his gift for foreign languages, his tin ear wasn't up to carrying the simplest of tunes.

The staff were suitably impressed by the show's superb production standards, while the boys loved Peter's satirical sideswipes at the staff – which went largely unnoticed in the staffroom – especially his subtle ragging of the Warden, W.M.M. Milligan, who 'seemed to regard schoolboy interest in the theatre with a kind of horror'. [42] Against this disapproving backdrop, Peter's gentle ribbing was rather daring, even if it was mainly confined to aping Warden Milligan's favourite turn of phrase, 'Not a scrap!' *Black & White Blues* was such a hit that the cast went into Oxford and cut a 78rpm disc, selling all 500 copies around the school. It was Peter's first hit record. 'It was diabolical,' said Peter, years later, 'but people still come up to me and say, "That thing you did at Radley was the best bloody thing you ever did."' [43]

Peter's first challenge when he left Radley was avoiding National Service. During the 1950s, able-bodied young men born before 1 October 1939 were required by law to enlist for two years in the armed forces when they reached the age of eighteen. The only exemptions were for miners, farmers and merchant seamen, none of which were really Peter's cup of tea. After five years of half-hearted square-bashing in Radley's cadet corps, Peter had no illusions about what these two years would entail. Dudley had escaped on account of his club foot. Peter required a stroke of luck. 'I had been allergic to feathers and I had grown out of it, but it was still on my medical record. They asked me if I would sneeze if I was in a barrack room full of feather pillows – an unlikely situation, I thought.' [44] But Peter saw his chance and seized it. 'Yes,' he said. He was duly turned down on medical grounds. With admirable sangfroid, he feigned jingoistic disappointment. 'If there's a real crisis,' he pleaded, 'will you take me on?' [45]

Released from this patriotic chore, Peter enjoyed eighteen months of freedom. He'd won a place at Cambridge to read French and German at Pembroke, his father's old college, but he wasn't due to start there until October 1957. Until then he was free to brush up his French and German in France and Germany, rather than behind a desk at Radley. First, he went to Paris, where he saw Edith Piaf and *The Threepenny Opera* and tried his hand at oil painting. At the Cité Universitaire, he acquired his first girlfriend, with whom he hitch-hiked to the South of France. On his return to England he wrote a play for Thompson's, his old Social (which they performed at the Radley Drama Festival) about some respectable Martians who are scandalised by the lurid private lives of suburban earthlings.

That summer, Peter teamed up with four Radley chums – Michael Bawtree, Jonathan Harlow, Peter Raby and Noel Slocock, for an ad-hoc camping trip. It was an idyllic interlude, untainted by childhood constraints or adult cares. Peter's pals all kept photos of this trip, and 55 years later these faint grey snapshots still glow with the simple happiness of lost youth. In glorious sunshine, they criss-crossed the country, more or less willy-nilly, in a little Hillman Husky, kindly lent to them by Noel's dad. From Studley Priory in Oxfordshire (which Bawtree's parents were running as a hotel) they drove through the Cotswolds, the Forest of Dean and the New Forest. They visited Noel's grandmother in Devon and Jonathan's parents in Northumberland, winding up in Swanage a few weeks (and a few hundred miles) later.

In October 1956, Peter set off for Koblenz, 'in an attempt to achieve sexual emancipation and to learn to speak fluent German.' [46] He was sorely disappointed. Koblenz is a pretty spot, where the Mosel meets the Rhine, but it's never been renowned for raucous nightlife, and when Peter arrived it was still picking up the pieces after the devastation of the Second World War. Badly bombed by the Allies and rebuilt in a hurry, it was a pleasant but provincial place, more of a market town than a metropolis. Peter's host family were kindly yet conventional, and their hillside home on the edge of town offered little in the way of teenage kicks. After six months of daily German lessons from an old woman in the neighbourhood, Peter wangled a transfer to Berlin.

Peter only spent three weeks in Berlin, but on his last night in this ruined city he had an evening out that changed his life – and changed the course of British comedy. He went to the Porcupine Club, renowned for its political cabaret. He thought the show was awful, but he loved the concept. 'Why on Earth don't we have such a place in London?' [47] he wondered. From Berlin, he travelled to Hamburg, where he saw his first production of Goethe's *Faust*.

In May 1957 Peter left Germany, making the long train journey to Tours to join a French language course for English students, where he acquired another girlfriend. In July he returned home, in time for the Henley Regatta. France had given Peter the sexual emancipation he craved, but Germany had given him his comic inspiration. The Porcupine Club and Goethe's *Faust* were two ideas which would grow and grow.

Dudley in his school uniform about to go up to Oxford.

CHAPTER FOUR

OXFORD

PETER: The thing that is bothering me is the fact
that I have a very boring job. Do you realise I
have to get up every morning and deliver the
identical lectures that I have been delivering
for the past thirty years? They never vary, not
by a word, not by a jot, or a tittle. And that is
bothering me.

DUDLEY: Oh sir, I enjoy your lectures. I find them
terribly interesting.

PETER: That's because you're hearing them for the
first time.

('Dean of University', BBC2, 1974)

Dudley went up to Magdalen College in October 1954, on a McKinnon Organ Scholarship, to read for a Bachelor of Arts degree in Music. The contrast with Dagenham County High could scarcely have been more stark. Magdalen was one of Oxford University's most beautiful and ancient colleges. Even its so-called New Building dated back to 1733. 'I thought I had died and gone to heaven,' said Dudley. 'I found myself in the most beautiful place I could imagine.'[1]

Magdalen wasn't just an august group of buildings. It was also an august group of people, past and present. The Prince of Wales (subsequently Edward VIII) had been an undergraduate here. More recent students included John Betjeman and C.S. Lewis. Its alumni ranged from Cardinal Wolsey to Oscar Wilde.

Dudley's room was in Saint Swithin's Quad, at the top of a narrow, winding staircase. He had an upright piano and a record player, and a porter (or scout) who made his bed and brought hot water for him to wash in. For the vast majority of his fellow freshmen, who'd arrived here from boarding school, this was a familiar progression from the life they'd known before. For Dudley, it was another world. Even the name of the place seemed designed to trip up outsiders (it was pronounced 'Maudlin'). 'It was, at that time, a very aristocratic college,' [2] he said. 'I felt dwarfed, if you'll pardon the expression, by the social ease of the people who'd come from public schools. I couldn't stand the sound of their voices – they seemed so in charge of themselves.' [3] Are you a Wykehamist?' [4] his fellow undergraduates would ask him. 'No, I'm actually from the County High School of Dagenham,' [5] he'd reply. Dudley tried to imitate his fellow students ('I didn't have the courage to be myself' [6]) but he found his Dagenham vowels hard to lose. 'I was absolutely terrified of the place,' he said. 'When I first went there I couldn't open my mouth. Everybody was frightfully suave and in control and I couldn't really say a thing. I found that my voice started doing very peculiar things. When my parents came up I think we were all terrified that we'd do the wrong thing.' [7] 'I can understand perfectly why Dudley would have felt solitary or out of place,' says the *Guardian*'s theatre critic, Michael Billington, who went up to Oxford in Dudley's final year, from a fairly modest background in the Midlands. 'I remember being appalled by the class barriers that existed then.'

Not everyone at Oxford was a toff (recent graduates included Kingsley Amis, John Wain and Philip Larkin) but grammar-school boys remained a minority, and the authorities made little effort to make these interlopers feel at ease. At one college function, coffee was served. Dudley was asked if he wanted black or white. He didn't know the difference. 'We never had coffee in our place – never ever,' [8] he recalled. 'Black,' he said, bluffing frantically. He was handed a cup of black coffee. 'Can't I have some milk?' [9] he asked. Port was a complete mystery. Even eating soup before a main course was unfamiliar. Yet a lot of people found his naivety charming rather than crass or clumsy. At the age of eighteen, he got drunk for the first time on Pimm's ('a wonderful experience' [10]) and fell into the river. Some people on the bank asked him to fall in again, so that they could take some photographs. Dudley was happy to oblige.

The college chapel was especially grand. As one of its nineteenth-century organists, Sir Walter Parratt, put it, 'Even a sneeze sounds beautiful in Magdalen.' [11] But here, where Dudley had some expertise, he felt a bit more at ease. For £80 a year, he played the organ at daily services in one of Oxford's architectural wonders. 'There I was, this club-footed wanker, playing this beautiful organ in this stunning chapel. I felt I really didn't deserve to be there.' [12] Despite his enduring feelings of inadequacy, by all accounts he did very well. Having improvised with a high-heeled ladies' shoe at his audition, he had a special boot made for his left foot, with a platform heel, so that he could reach the pedals.

On top of his religious duties, Dudley read for his BA in Music. Unlike some of his posher peers, he studied fairly hard, under his tutor, Bernard Rose. Rose regarded Dudley as the only genius he ever taught. The only problem was trying to get him to focus on one discipline. 'It was obvious from the word go that he was a very talented musician,' said Rose. 'It was also extremely difficult to know which way he was going to turn.' [13] As well as playing the organ in the college chapel, Dudley was increasingly in demand at student parties. He'd often arrive to find the other guests sitting round the piano, waiting for him to begin. Yet like a lot of grammar-school boys (and girls) of his generation, Dudley felt stranded in no-man's-land, a stranger to both worlds. Oxford had changed him – an old school friend who came to visit him was amazed to see so many books in his room – but among his new friends, he was still painfully aware of what he called his 'sloppy suburban accent.' [14] The one place where he felt entirely comfortable was onstage. He played Enobarbus in *Antony and Cleopatra* and Autolycus in *The Winter's Tale*. Like a true Shakespearean clown, he wasn't afraid to ad-lib, but it was playing a deaf mute in *The Changeling* that unlocked his gift for comedy. He subsequently stole the show in an open-air production of *Bartholomew Fair*, in what was barely a walk-on part. 'Apples, apples, who'll buy my lovely apples?' he'd cry, walking across the stage between scenes, with a basketful of fruit. He'd stop and take a bite and pull a face. 'Pears, pears,' he'd cry. 'Who'll buy my lovely pears?' His contemporaries could see that he was destined for bigger things. Patrick Garland, who became an eminent stage and screen director, said that Dudley was the funniest man he met at Oxford. Peter Preston, who went on to become editor of the *Guardian*, described him as 'an instant star.' [15]

Soon he was writing musical sketches of his own. At Oxford's Experimental Theatre Club he played a hilarious version of Little Miss Muffet, as performed by Benjamin Britten and Peter Pears. Only a musician as good as him could have parodied Britten's chord sequences so acutely. Only a comic as good as him could have sent up Pears's nasal singing with such aplomb. This number later resurfaced in *Beyond The Fringe*, entitled 'Little Miss Britten'. Dudley subsequently chose it as one of his selections on *Desert Island Discs*. However, his most important discovery during his time at Oxford was jazz.

Dudley had been a jazz fan since his schooldays but he'd never played jazz with other people. That all changed when he met a fellow undergraduate called John Bassett, who ran his own jazz band, called the Bassett Hounds. 'Dudley loved jazz, but didn't really know a thing about it,' [16] said Bassett. 'He cracked the code in five seconds flat. [17] He never needed a chord book, because he could pick up the chords straight away by ear. In fact, within a chorus or two, he'd be finding delicious substitution chords, which is what real jazz musicians do.' [18] In this lively genre, which married composition and improvisation, Dudley had found a new way to express himself. When a school friend, Tiefon Griffiths, came to visit him, and went to evensong to hear him play, Dudley told him to listen out for 'Blowing Wild', a popular ballad by Frankie Laine. Sure enough, Griffiths heard Laine's melody float discreetly into Dudley's organ playing and discreetly out again. Dudley also discovered that jazz brought added glamour to his social life. 'It got the girls' eyes sparkling sooner than preludes and fugues,' [19] he said. Playing Oscar Peterson and Erroll Garner was a better way to impress women than playing Bach.

Dudley sat his Finals in the summer of 1957 and graduated with a Second Class degree. 'He certainly could have got a First,' [20] said Rose, but by now his interests went way beyond baroque music, his special subject. He was playing the piano at parties, revues, even screenings by the Film Society. In the circumstances, it was remarkable that he even managed to get a Second. After three years at Oxford, he'd decided he wanted to be a performer. 'I was intoxicated by the audience's reaction and the applause,'[21] he said. He decided to stay on for another year and take a Bachelor of Music degree in composition, but his jazz playing (and the fringe benefits that came with it) left him little time for study. For his Bachelor of Music degree, he had to write a string quartet – no mean undertaking. He finally got around to it a mere fortnight before the deadline. Somehow he managed it, knocking out a major composition in two weeks flat.

That summer Dudley went to the Edinburgh Festival with the Experimental Theatre Club. 'Dudley was the musical linchpin,' said Denis Moriarty, who directed him in Oxford and Edinburgh, and went on to become a TV director. 'He was a great star in cabaret.'[22] In Edinburgh, Dudley met the woman who relieved him of his virginity. He was already 23, she was a few years older, and when he told her that he was still a virgin she offered to help him out. After the festival she returned to London and he returned to Oxford, but not before they'd agreed to meet up again in Oxford to do the deed. Aptly, this red-letter day was touched with an element of farce. Dudley was due to meet her off the train at midnight, but she missed the last train from London and arrived at six a.m., on the milk train. They booked into a hotel as Mr and Mrs Moore but, like a lot of first-timers, Dudley didn't feel the Earth move. 'It was disastrous,'[23] he recalled. For her, it was just a one-night stand. He would have preferred something more enduring. Even so, the dam was burst. 'After that,' he said, 'I began making up for lost time.'[24]

Dudley was awarded his second Bachelor's degree the following summer, but his real graduation was Magdalen's grand Commemorative Ball in June 1958, at the end of Trinity term (summer term to you and me). The star turn was John Dankworth's jazz band, featuring Dankworth's fiancée, the singer Cleo Laine. For Dudley, Dankworth was something of a kindred spirit. He was born in Chingford, Essex, not a million miles away from Dagenham, and had trained at the Royal Academy of Music, where his interest in jazz was rather frowned upon. Only eight years older than Dudley, he was now a rising star. Having performed until the small hours, Dankworth and Laine were tucking into a well-earned buffet breakfast when they were intrigued to hear some amazing jazz piano booming out from the next room. 'The sound we heard was not student jazz,' remembered Dankworth. 'It was mature, impressive and expertly executed.' [25] At first they thought it was a record, it was that good, but eventually they realised it was live, and after listening for about 15 minutes they went next door to discover the identity of this mystery jazz pianist. It was Dudley, doing his party piece – jazzing up the coda of a Beethoven sonata. 'Next time I need an accompanist, that's the boy for me!' [26] Cleo told Dankworth. 'If you're ever short of a job, let me know,' [27] Dankworth told Dudley. However, Dankworth had no job to offer him, so nothing came of it, for now.

In July, Dudley was offered a very different sort of job by his tutor, Bernard Rose. Rose invited him to become the organist of Queen's College, and its choirmaster, and a tutor too. He surely would have ended up a Don, maybe even a Dean, at least a Fellow. For Dudley's mother, who'd always fantasised about him playing the organ in a cathedral, it would have been a dream come true. Dudley asked Rose for five minutes to think about it. He left the room. He returned five minutes later. 'I don't think this would be the life for me,' [28] he told his disappointed tutor. Dudley wanted to be a performer. What sort of performer, he still wasn't sure, but he knew academia wasn't for him. Some years later, Rose was clearing out the organ loft when he found a strange contraption beneath a pile of rubbish. It was Dudley's left-footed organ shoe – he didn't need it any more.

It was bold of Dudley to turn down Rose's offer, for he had nothing else lined up. He was now 23 years old, and despite his two degrees he wasn't really qualified for anything apart from playing the piano. However, after Oxford he felt hopeful. Surely something would come up. He didn't want to go back to Dagenham. He wanted to live in London. He didn't have any money, but thankfully his guardian angel John Bassett came up trumps. Bassett's mum lived in a block of flats in Hampstead. Bassett introduced her to Dudley, and she found him a bedsit in the same block. It was only a small single room, but he soon won over his kindly landlady and she allowed him into her flat to use her phone – and her piano. The rent was ten shillings a week, the same as that for his parents' council house in Dagenham.

For any freelance entertainer, charm and chutzpah are just as important as talent. Dudley had always been diligent about his music. Oxford had given him the self-confidence to go with it. He wheedled his way into numerous auditions, and soon found a job playing the piano in the Cafe des Artistes on Fulham Road. It paid ten shillings a night – his weekly rent. It wasn't much, but it was a start. Unlike most aspiring jazz musicians, he was now gainfully employed. He also played the piano at Ronnie Scott's jazz club in Soho, but not all his early bookings were quite so salubrious, especially up north. In a working men's club in Manchester, he had to follow a striptease artiste. Inevitably, his Mancunian audience weren't all that interested in his Britten and Schubert parodies. Thankfully, there were plenty of places in London where the performers kept their clothes on. He hooked up with John Bassett and his jazz band, the Bassett Hounds, gigging at posh London hotels like the Dorchester and the Savoy. He teamed up with a Footlights veteran called Joe Melia, in a comedy and music double act called *The Moore The Melia*. Some of these workaday gigs spawned some enduring friendships. While working as an accompanist at the ITV studios in Holborn he met a talented young pianist, composer and singer called Barbara Moore.

Barbara Moore had been booked to make a demo tape of an old standard called 'Stranger In Paradise', for an actress to use to learn a song. 'Against one wall was a small upright piano,' she recalled. 'Seated at it was an equally small and upright chap.' [29] 'Hi, I'm Dud,' [30] he said. 'I'm Barb,' [31] she said. They shook hands and he began to play. However, he played the song too straight for her liking, so she asked him to jazz it up a bit. To her absolute amazement, he proceeded to play it in a dozen completely different styles. Entranced by his virtuosity, she sang along to every version in a different style, each more outrageous than the last. They ended up in fits of laughter, but the producer didn't find it quite so funny. 'Call yourselves professionals?' [32] he yelled at them. So they did a straight version, just to keep him happy. Finally they made their getaway, into the sunlit street outside. 'My name's Dudley Moore,' [33] said Dudley. 'And I'm Barbara Moore,' [34] said Barbara. 'Good God!' he said. 'That's my sister's name. We're going to be friends.' [35] One of the few musicians who could compete with him, she became a lifelong confidante. Divorced with a young daughter, Barbara was living with her mother in a large house on Ealing Common. Dudley started going round there on Sundays to play her grand piano. While he was there he'd demolish a traditional Sunday roast – a welcome break from the endless bowls of cornflakes he survived on in his Hampstead bedsit.

Dudley's ambitions weren't confined to music. Anthony Page, who'd directed him in *Antony and Cleopatra* at Oxford, had got a directing job at the Royal Court Theatre, working for the great director George Devine. He got Dudley an audition. For once, Dudley overreached himself – Devine told him that he had a lot to learn – but he got a job as the Royal Court's resident composer, writing incidental music for £5 per week. The first play Dudley worked on turned out to be a modern classic. Directed by Lindsay Anderson, who went on to make seminal movies like *This Sporting Life*, *Serjeant Musgrave's Dance* was a powerful anti-war play by the radical playwright John Arden. As usual, Dudley procrastinated until the last moment, and Anderson had to ask Page to stand over him to make sure that he delivered. Thanks to Page, Dudley met his deadline and Anderson was delighted with the result. This sparse Brechtian drama wasn't an instant hit, but it has since been acknowledged as a landmark in the history of the English stage.

Despite this *coup de théâtre*, Dudley's main interest was still jazz, and when John Dankworth heard that fellow bandleader Vic Lewis was looking for a pianist, he put in a good word for him. Dudley went to call on him, at his mansion flat in Bloomsbury. 'Mr Lewis, sir – I believe you're looking for a piano player, sir,' [36] said Dudley. 'Don't call me sir, I'm only a jazzman,' [37] replied Lewis. 'Very well, sir,' [38] replied Dudley. Lewis invited him along to a band rehearsal the next week. 'You play very well,' said Lewis. 'But you don't play like that all the time, do you?' [39] 'What do you mean?' [40] asked Dudley, nonplussed. Lewis explained that Dudley was playing like a soloist. That was fine when it was his turn to do a solo, but when the other band members did their solos he needed to take a back seat. Dudley heard him out, and then carried on regardless. Dudley was a born soloist. He found it impossible to just play the chords. Lewis could see he was no rhythm player, but even so he took him on. Sure enough, some of the other musicians got fed up with him, and weren't afraid to tell him so, but his natural charm won them over. 'If he'd been a nasty little character he wouldn't have lasted long,' said Lewis, 'but everyone loved him.' [41]

For the next few months Dudley toured the country with the Vic Lewis Orchestra, playing seaside resorts like Morecambe and Blackpool for £40 a week. Vic's band had played with stars like Nat King Cole, and a few years earlier they would have been booked up virtually every night. However, Big Band music had been eclipsed by Rock & Roll, and by the time Dudley joined the band they were only playing three or four nights a week. Even so, it was a great apprenticeship. After a good deal of trial and error, Dudley learned to be a team player. He would always be a natural soloist, but Vic taught him how to knock out the chords if needs be.

Vic Lewis wasn't just a bandleader. He was also a wheeler-dealer, and with the American bandleader Stan Kenton he broke the long-standing embargo on British Big Bands touring the USA. For over twenty years, thanks to union regulations, British Big Bands had been unable to cross the Atlantic. Lewis and Keaton set up a reciprocal arrangement between the Musicians' Union and the American Federation of Musicians, whereby twenty musicians from the UK travelled to America while twenty US musicians toured the UK, all performing for the same fees. In 1956, the British bandleader Ted Heath went to America while Kenton came to Britain. In 1959, Count Basie came to Britain and the Vic Lewis Orchestra was booked to tour the States.

Travelling to America was a much bigger deal in those days, and
for Dudley it was a great adventure. They flew there (a rare treat back
then – most people still went by boat) and on the plane Dudley broke
the ice with his fellow jazzmen, some of whom were still wary of this
Oxbridge upstart, with his penchant for playing fancy solos during
their star turns. The saxophonist Roy East had been particularly cool
towards him, but during the flight Dudley made him laugh and they
were friends by the time they landed. Dudley's charm and humour
had paid off, yet again.

Dudley adored every minute of his US odyssey. It wasn't the
most glamorous assignment. The venues were fairly workmanlike,
mainly military bases, in Long Island, New Jersey and Connecticut.
They played Boston, Massachusetts, which was a bit better, but
they never ventured further west. They arrived in February, and the
weather along the eastern seaboard was biting. But Dudley wasn't
complaining. 'I was in a constant state of happiness,' [42] he said. The
wages were very good indeed (£100 a week, worth about £2,000
nowadays) and there was no shortage of hospitality – or friendly
female company.

The tour wound up in New York and, like countless Brits before
and since, Dudley fell in love with Manhattan. He loved the sight,
the sound, the smell of it – particularly the plumes of steam that
wafted up through the sidewalks, like dry ice in the theatre. When
the tour finished, in March, and the band went back to Blighty,
Dudley stayed on in New York with Vic Lewis. They shared a room
at the Forest Hotel, just off Broadway, and went to jazz clubs every
night. Dudley saw great jazz pianists like Dwike Mitchell and blind
Lennie Tristano. For a jazz fan like Dudley, this was the centre of the
universe. Vic went home after two weeks, but Dudley stayed on for

another fortnight, full of vague plans of becoming a Stateside star, on TV or in the theatre. There were far easier pickings back in Britain, but New York had seduced him and he couldn't tear himself away.

Dudley moved into the YMCA and did the rounds of auditions. The New York jazz scene was booming and there was no shortage of openings for musicians, but there was no shortage of musicians either and Dudley had no takers until he turned up at a Greenwich Village nightclub called the Duplex, recommended to him by John Bassett's mum. Here he got a gig playing piano in the basement bar. It was an awful old piano – completely out of tune – but Dudley still made it sing, and on his last night Ahmet Ertegun dropped in and heard him play. Ertegun wasn't just a jazz fan. He was the founder and president of one of America's most important record labels, with jazz icons like Ray Charles and John Coltrane on his books. 'My God, you are terrific,' he told Dudley. 'Come to my office. I'm the head of Atlantic Records and I'd like to make an album with you.' [43] This was fairy-tale stuff, but Dudley bottled it. He was returning to England the next day, he said.

Turning down Ahmet Ertegun might have gone down as one of the worst career moves in showbiz history (Ertegun went on to work with the Rolling Stones and Led Zeppelin, and put the Young in Crosby, Stills, Nash & Young) but talent makes its own luck and Dudley's luck was in. On his return home, he learned that John Dankworth's pianist had left the band. Dankworth asked Dudley to take his place and soon he was gigging several times a week, for £10 a time. He still found it hard to be an ensemble player, and his fellow musicians still found him hard to play with. 'They felt it was impossible to solo against me,' recalled Dudley. Dankworth agreed. 'Dudley was a soloist from the start,' he said. 'He wasn't meant to be a rhythm-section pianist.' [44] Yet Dankworth stuck with him and Dudley won over the other musicians with his clowning. He was enjoying a growing reputation as a pianist, but he could also play the fool.

As well as playing in Dankworth's band, Dudley formed his own jazz trio, with Hugo Boyd on double bass and Derek Hogg on drums. With no brass or woodwind to compete with, Dudley could take centre stage, playing solos to his heart's content while Boyd and Hogg supplied the bass line and the back-beat. The Dudley Moore Trio rehearsed at Barbara Moore's house in Ealing, and played the Cafe des Artistes, earning £2 a night between them. 'It was a right dump,' recalled Barbara, 'but we had a good time.' [45]

Dudley was also in demand as a composer and arranger. In the spring of 1960 he returned to the Royal Court as the musical director of *Song in the Theatre*, starring Albert Finney. This ensemble of theatrical songs was a big hit, and Dudley's musical direction was singled out for fulsome praise in *The Times*. Advertising director Francis Megahy hired him to write jingles for Pepsodent and Persil commercials, and when Megahy directed his first film, *Just One More Time* ('a day in the life of a Chelsea layabout'), Dudley wrote the score. Meanwhile, Vic Lewis had realised that Big Band music was on the way out, and had decided to set himself up as a showbiz agent (he went on to manage stars like Shirley Bassey and Matt Monro). Dudley was his first signing, and Lewis wasted no time getting him a string of bookings, at jazz clubs like the Blue Angel and the Cool Elephant, where he soon attracted an avid following. He was even asked to cut a record, called 'Strictly For The Birds' (a jazz version of a lullaby he'd first performed in Oxford, in a student production of *The Birds* by Aristophanes). The producer who cut the record was none other than George Martin, who, just a few years later, went on to produce the Beatles.

Dudley was now well on his way to becoming an established jazz pianist, and his flair for clowning might well have remained a mere youthful aberration if John Bassett hadn't got back in touch and asked him to appear in a late-night revue at the Edinburgh Festival. Dudley was keen to go, but he was still working for John Dankworth. He asked Dankworth if he could do it. He said he'd only need three weeks off. Dankworth said yes, but he could tell that Dudley wouldn't be coming back.

Peter and his sister Elizabeth in Lyme Regis.

CHAPTER FIVE

CAMBRIDGE

'I could have been a judge but I never had the Latin, never had
the Latin for the judging. I just never had sufficient of it to get
through the rigorous judging exams. They're noted for their rigour.
People come staggering out saying, "My God, what a rigorous
exam." And so I became a miner instead – a coal miner. I
managed to get through the mining exams – they're not very
rigorous. They only ask one question. They say, "Who are you?"
And I got 75% for that.'

(Peter Cook, 'Sitting On The Bench')

Oxford catapulted Dudley into a different world. For Peter, Cambridge
was familiar territory. His college, Pembroke, had been his father's
college in the 1920s. His student lodging in Pembroke's New Court [1]
wasn't all that different from his boarding house at Radley. Founded
in 1347, Pembroke was one of Cambridge University's oldest colleges.
Much of its architecture was medieval. A grammar-school boy like
Dudley might have been intimidated by such grand surroundings,
but Peter was used to these educational establishments. He'd been
living in them for half his life.

Another thing he was accustomed to was the absence of women.
There were no co-ed colleges at Cambridge then, and only four female

colleges. The other twenty, including Pembroke, were all male, and so Peter had to search far and wide for female company. Emboldened by fond memories of his year abroad, he focused his amorous attention on visiting Continental students, but his attempts proved unsuccessful. 'I remember so many futile treks to places in Cambridge where Swedish, French and German girls were studying English,' he recalled. 'I remember so many foul ham-salad lunches, trying to strike up a conversation, in various faltering tongues.' [2]

With women so few and far between, and so unaccommodating when he found them, Peter turned, briefly, to the last refuge of the sexually frustrated undergraduate – student politics. He joined the Cambridge Union, but packed it in after just one speech. 'I can do this,' he thought, 'but I don't want to do this.' [3] With his flair for thinking on his feet, he would have been a brilliant debater, but his innate aversion to pomposity made it impossible for him to contemplate any sort of political career. 'I remember people like Leon Brittan at 22, running round like a 44-year-old, making the same sort of debating points they're still making,' [4] he reflected. 'It's a bit distressing when you find them running the country. They were all so self-important at twenty that you would have thought they'd have grown out of it.' [5] Fat chance. Brittan eventually became Conservative Home Secretary, as did two of Peter's other Cambridge contemporaries, Michael Howard and Kenneth Clarke. The fact that they were all Tories didn't make much difference. Peter generally found Socialists just as irritating. The Liberals were the only mainstream party who ever won his backing, and even that support was fairly ironic and half-hearted. Seeing these apprentice politicians at close quarters and realising how arrogant they seemed was just as influential, in its own way, as his visit to the Porcupine Club in Berlin. Peter had far more fun playing on the left wing for his college football team. He was modest about his abilities ('I was the worst kind of player – too flashy' [6]) but his teammates remembered him as a competent footballer – funny, on and off the field, but never a figure of fun.

Peter amused his teammates but it was back in Halls, where he ate his meals, that his natural wit shone through. During his first evening, over dinner, he left his fellow freshers in stitches, with a performance which set the tone for his entire undergraduate (and postgraduate) career. Peter's mealtime turns weren't all that different from his riffs at Radley, latching onto a mundane remark and building it up, bit by bit, into an absurd, rambling monologue – on one occasion he spent an entire evening discussing gravel.

If anyone else had tried it, it would have been awful, like being cornered by the worst sort of saloon bar bore, but somehow Peter got away with it. He was so charming and self-effacing that no one seemed to mind. For someone so funny, he was strangely selfless – Roger Law, a student at the local art school (and future co-creator of *Spitting Image*) found him 'pleasantly diffident,' [7] a rare quality in a comic. Peter needed other people to bounce off – his humour abhorred a vacuum – but although he invariably ended up centre stage, he never seemed to hog the limelight. Creativity flowed through him, like a virtuoso musician. 'It was effortless,' said Roger Law. 'It was almost as if he'd arrived with his talent intact.' [8]

Bolstered by his successful table-talk, Peter joined the Pembroke Players – the biggest student drama society in Cambridge, and the country, after the illustrious ADC [9] – and in November 1957, less than a month after he'd arrived at Cambridge, he made his theatrical debut in a dramatisation of Thomas Love Peacock's *Nightmare Abbey*. He also started performing his own sketches at Pembroke Smoking

Concerts, quaint cabaret evenings where students in dinner dress took turns to try out comic routines. Peter stole the show with his Arthur Boylett monologues. Within a few weeks, 'I thought I saw it move' had become a college catchphrase.

Unusually, Peter was also an assiduous student of foreign comedy. He bought comedy LPs from America by mail order – a laborious and expensive process in the 1950s, and a sign of his growing enthusiasm for humour in all its forms. A firm favourite was the clever Canadian stand-up Mort Sahl, whose keen interest in current affairs marked him out from most trad comics on both sides of the pond. Peter's earlier influences, like the Goons, had all been other-worldly. Sahl's humour was rooted in the real world.

Despite his growing sense of vocation, Peter kept on top of his studies, swotting fairly diligently for his Modern Languages degree. In his end-of-year exams he got an Upper Second in French and a Lower Second in German – respectable but nothing special. However, even dry academia couldn't hide his flair for comedy. One of the highlights of his first year was his brilliant spoof of Racine's biblical tragedy *Athalie*, featuring a young Queen Elizabeth and the Shadow Chancellor, Harold Wilson (later, as Labour Prime Minister, the butt of many of Peter's best jokes at *Private Eye*).

Having passed his first-year exams, Peter was free to join the Pembroke Players' trip to Germany, where they performed Shakespeare's *Merchant of Venice* for German students in Bielefeld and Cologne. Peter played Launcelot Gobbo (a role generally played by the clown of the company in Shakespeare's day) and almost stole the show, camping it up something rotten. Although it was a fairly small part, Peter didn't really learn his lines – and, having got away with it, this lack of preparation became a habit. On this occasion, it wasn't a problem (Shakespeare's clowns used to busk it, and these foreign audiences were none the wiser) but failing to commit his part to memory would eventually cost him. At the time, however, none of this mattered in the slightest. Peter was on a roll. After the tour, he returned home to his family in Torquay. A photo from this happy holiday, taken on an outing to Lyme Regis, shows him strolling down the prom, relaxed and elegant in slacks and deck shoes, leading his little sister Elizabeth by the hand, grinning from ear to ear.

In October 1958, a year after he arrived at Cambridge, Peter finally plucked up sufficient courage to introduce himself to the President of Footlights. Founded in 1883, the Cambridge Footlights Club had an illustrious history (one of its early presidents was W.S. Gilbert) but lately it had hit a purple patch and its stock had never been higher. The 1954 and 1955 Footlights revues had both transferred to London's West End, and the 1957 revue, *Share My Lettuce* (largely written by Bamber Gascoigne), had been recast as a professional production. Peter had seen it in the West End, starring Maggie Smith and Kenneth Williams.

The President of Footlights was Adrian Slade, who subsequently became a Liberal politician and a lifelong friend of Peter's. In 1958 he was sitting in his room at Trinity – an even grander college than Pembroke – when 'a long, thin, hesitant person with dashing darting eyes' [10] knocked on his door and asked if he could join the Footlights. Slade didn't know Peter. He'd never seen him perform. He hadn't even heard of him. 'Have you ever written anything?' [11] asked Slade. Yes, said Peter, and produced a script about two Antarctic explorers called 'Polar Bores' which he would eventually perform with Dudley. Slade read it. He liked it. He suggested they perform it together at the next

Footlights Smoker (an informal cabaret evening, like a Pembroke Smoking Concert but on a considerably bigger scale). 'Have you got any more?' asked Slade. 'Yes,' said Peter. 'Quite a few.' 'Then what have you been doing in the past year?' asked Slade. 'Playing football,' said Peter. They talked and talked, the way students do, and two hilarious hours flew by.

Slade found Peter rather shy at first but as Peter chatted about his past he opened up – especially when he started impersonating Arthur Boylett. 'Why not do that at the Smoker?' suggested Slade. 'Do what?' 'Mr Boylett.' 'But it's not a sketch,' said Peter. 'And anyway, why would anyone think it funny?' 'Well, I do,' said Slade. 'What would we call it?' asked Peter. '"Mr Boylett Speaks",' said Slade. At the next Smoker, Slade and Peter performed 'Polar Bores' together, but it was Peter's Boylett monologue that brought the house down. Dressed in a battered trilby and a flasher's mac, he droned on and on about bees and ants in a nasal whine, and a Footlights legend was born. 'All over Cambridge at that time I would hear young men talking with oddly depressed vowels,' recalled Roger Law. 'I was relieved to meet the originator of this strange voice. I was beginning to fear it might be contagious.' [12]

Unlike most professional comics, Peter never hoarded his humour for a paying public, and some of his funniest routines are remembered only by those few friends who were lucky enough to be with him at the time. 'His normal voice was deep and resonant, but could switch in the blink of an eye to the weird, surrealistic, back-of-the-throat drone he'd developed at Radley,' [13] recalled his new Footlights pal, Peter Bellwood. Strange new characters emerged from these impromptu sessions, like Colonel Rutter, a dirty old man who liked looking up women's dresses. Rutter became a Footlights staple, but other creations simply vanished into thin air. There was a riff about a man who believed that Soviet spies had hidden a camera in his bathtub, which would have made a splendid sketch but never saw the light of day. Peter's imagination was so fertile that he could afford to squander new material. Even the small proportion which ended up onstage was vast by anyone else's standards.

One of the many students wowed by Peter's Footlights performances was a King's College postgrad called John Bird. 'I've just met the funniest man in England,' [14] he told Eleanor Bron (a Modern Languages undergraduate at Newnham College) after visiting Peter in his rooms Pembroke. Bird was a budding theatre director, and although his postgraduate subject was the history of naturalistic drama – Chekov, Ibsen and suchlike – his theatrical interests were more absurdist. He'd already directed Ionesco's *The Bald Prima Donna* for the ADC. Now he wanted to tackle N.F. Simpson's *A Resounding Tinkle*. This surrealist drama had premiered at the Royal Court Theatre in 1957, but only in a shortened one-act version – the Royal Court regarded the full two-act version as unstageable. Bird wanted to stage the play unabridged, and he wanted Peter and Bron to play the leading roles.

The full-length version of *A Resounding Tinkle* received its world premiere at the ADC in January 1959. The show was a hit, playing to 'full and enthusiastic houses' (as Peter reported, in a letter to his parents). The critics were sniffy about the script, but they were polite about the production. The Royal Court invited the cast to give a Sunday-night performance at their Sloane Square theatre (Peter's London debut) and subsequently gave Bird a job, as an Assistant Director. 'I later discovered I'd directed the play in a manner entirely at odds with the intentions of Simpson and his director at the Royal

Court, William Gaskill,' recalled Bird. 'They wished it to proceed at a grave and stately pace, with long pauses, whereas Peter and Eleanor complained that the only direction I ever gave them was "faster!"' [15] 'They couldn't believe it could be done so fast,' confirmed Bron. 'It went at a tremendous lick.' [16]

In March 1959 Peter mounted his own revue at Pembroke with Eleanor Bron. It was called *The Jolly Good Show Involving (To A Considerable Extent) Music With Some Richly Comic Interspersions by the Merry Pembroke Players (Theatrical People) and Some Women Too (Two) Revue*. It was a show that changed his life. It included an Arthur Boylett routine called 'Interesting Facts', which would become one of his most celebrated sketches. It featured an impression of the Prime Minister, Harold Macmillan, which would make Peter famous. And sitting in the audience was a man called Donald Langdon, his first agent.

Mindful of the comedy that was cascading out of Cambridge, Langdon had hit upon the smart idea of hiring a student talent scout. The student he hired was Tom Rosenthal, who went on to become an eminent publisher. When Rosenthal saw Peter at a Footlights Smoker, he telephoned Langdon and persuaded him to come and see Peter's Pembroke revue. Langdon liked what he saw. Straight after the show, he introduced himself to Peter and asked if he could represent him. Peter said yes. To protect Arthur Boylett's privacy, he renamed his alter ego Mr Grole.

Peter was wise to preserve Boylett's anonymity, for by now his reputation had spread way beyond Cambridge. In May, alongside Adrian Slade, he was invited to perform at Woburn Abbey, the Duke of Bedford's ancestral seat. 'It was a marvellous dinner, with more liveried footmen than guests,' wrote Peter to his parents. The guest list was equally impressive. One of the Duke's guests was Bernard Braden, who ended up giving Peter his first break on TV. Another was Peter Sellers. Only a few years before, Peter had feigned illness to listen to Sellers on the radio in the school sanatorium. Now the Goon star was in the audience, listening to him. The opening act that night was Cyril Fletcher, best remembered nowadays for his cosy monologues on the BBC's *That's Life!* Fletcher was already in his mid-forties, old enough to be Peter's father, and the contrast between Fletcher's muted reception and the raucous laughter that greeted Peter's turn was telling. As Slade observed, it was a sign of the new direction in which British comedy would soon be heading. In that room that night, and around the country, there was a growing appetite for a new type of humour, in tune with the new generation who'd grown up since the war. All it needed was a dynamic young comic to lead the vanguard. That comic was already in the room.

Peter's comedy was now branching out in all sorts of new directions. He started writing a comic strip for the *Spectator* with his Footlights colleague Timothy Birdsall (a gifted cartoonist, who sadly died of leukaemia a few years later, aged just 24). In June 1959, Birdsall appeared alongside Peter in the Footlights revue, *The Last Laugh*, directed by John Bird. Peter contributed ten of the 28 sketches in the show, including his Scott of the Antarctic skit, 'Polar Bores', a hunting satire called 'For Fox Sake', and another classic Grole sketch, with Birdsall as his feed. A notable feature of the show was the participation of Eleanor Bron – the first woman ever permitted to appear in a Footlights revue, thanks to a tireless campaign by Peter and John Bird.

Peter's sketches were the comedic highlights of the show, but Bird wrote most of the material – and it was his writing, more than

Peter's, that reflected the earnest spirit of the age. The Cold War was escalating and the Campaign for Nuclear Disarmament was growing, with marches to Britain's Atomic Weapons Establishment at Aldermaston and rallies in Trafalgar Square. Left-wing students like Bird were preoccupied by the gathering threat of nuclear Armageddon. *The Last Laugh* encapsulated this aura of impending doom. The show opened with an atomic explosion, each sketch ended with an execution, and the closing number was a gloomy ditty called 'Goodbye World'.

Looking back, Bird admitted that Peter's sketches were the only ones that were actually funny – but, unlike Peter, he wasn't merely seeking to amuse. John Osborne's play *Look Back In Anger* had shaken up the English stage, a spate of kitchen-sink novels had done much the same to English literature, and Bird was keen to do something similar to the cosy world of university revue. 'It was time to break from the camp tradition of Footlights,' he declared. 'It felt absolutely imperative that this creaky, old, outmoded political structure, with a self-serving ruling class, should be attacked.' [17] This didactic attitude was a world away from Peter's languid scepticism. The ruling class had actually served him rather well.

Bird's Footlights revue wasn't just ideologically daring. It was technically audacious, too. Set in a nuclear bunker, it featured a ten-piece jazz band and a series of suitably apocalyptic back-projections. There was no proper dress rehearsal, and the opening night was chaos. 'It was a complete disaster,' remembered Bird. 'The first night ran about four and a half hours. I was told it was the first Footlights revue to be booed on the first night.' [18] The local paper gave it a bad write-up, but as luck would have it Alistair Cooke (of *Letter From America*) happened to be in Cambridge and had taken along some

American friends, keen to show them a Footlights revue. Delighted to see something so different from the shows of his own student days, Cooke wrote a review in the (*Manchester*) *Guardian*, championing Peter and John Bird, and their co-stars Geoff Pattie and Patrick Gowers, and singling out Eleanor Bron for some particularly gushing praise. 'They have got themselves a very fetching dish,' cooed Cooke. 'She has a wolf-whistle figure, a confident pout, and needs only to practise singing in pitch.' [19] (The mind boggles at the thought of the *Guardian* running such a lascivious write-up today).

Armed with this rave review ('the whole show is acted with never a fumbling line or gesture,' [20] wrote Cooke) Donald Langdon persuaded two young producers to travel up from London to see the show. One of these men was Michael Codron – still only 29 but already an important producer (he'd taken Bamber Gascoigne's 1957 Footlights show, *Share My Lettuce*, into the West End). The other was Willie Donaldson, better known today as Henry Root. Donaldson had just graduated from Magdalene College, Cambridge, and had recently inherited a large sum of money from his father. Donaldson's father had owned a big slice of the family shipping firm, Elders & Fyffes, and had left about half a million pounds, split between Willie and his sister. Today, a quarter of a million is a handsome sum. In 1959, it was a fortune. Aged just 23, with his inheritance burning a big hole in his pocket, Donaldson had set himself up as a theatre producer – but he was the first to admit that he didn't know the first thing about it. 'I was a complete prat at it,' he confessed. 'I didn't have the faintest idea about anything.' [21] Astutely, Codron bought Peter's sketches. Rather less astutely, Donaldson bought the rest.

Today Donaldson is best remembered as a literary prankster. In 1959, however, his enthusiasms were more highbrow. At Cambridge he'd founded a classy literary magazine called *Gemini*, which published poems by Malcolm Bradbury, C. Day Lewis, Sylvia Plath and Ted Hughes. Although his inability to sign up Peter was the first in a long line of heroic failures, his enthusiasm for Bird's work was utterly sincere. 'I didn't rate Cook at all,' he recalled, 'but I thought John Bird was a genius.' [22] He was half right, at least. *The Last Laugh* was a groundbreaking show. It tackled serious subjects that no one had previously thought fit to tackle in a university revue, paving the way for *Beyond The Fringe* and a generation of English satirists. Unfortunately, like a lot of innovative shows, it was terribly unwieldy. Like a lot of innovators, John Bird was just a bit too far ahead of his time.

With some new sketches by Bird replacing Peter's more apolitical material, Donaldson mounted a professional production of *The Last Laugh*, starring Sheila Hancock, with music by John Dankworth and Cleo Laine. Renamed *Here Is The News*, it opened in Coventry – where it died a spectacular death, earning an honourable mention in Donaldson's book *Great Disasters of the Stage*. On the first night, there wasn't even any proper lighting – Bird thought the designer, Sean Kenny, was doing it, Kenny thought Bird was doing it, and Donaldson was such a novice that the thought hadn't even crossed his mind. *Here Is The News* stumbled on to Oxford, where it actually got some good reviews, but paying customers were less forgiving. Laine and Hancock were chased down the street by a group of irate punters. Hancock later called it 'the angriest reaction from an audience I ever had.' [23] Bird fell ill and the transfer to London's Cambridge Theatre was unceremoniously cancelled. *Here Is The News* never made it to the West End.

Luckily for Peter, Michael Codron proved to be a far safer pair of hands. Codron was mounting a West End revue called *Pieces of*

Eight, as a vehicle for Kenneth Williams, and he reckoned that Peter's sketches would be ideal material for the camp co-star of *Hancock's Half Hour* and *Round the Horne*. It wasn't a perfect fit – Williams's style was uptempo, Peter's was more downbeat – but it was close enough for Williams, and for Peter it was a huge break. The female lead was Fenella Fielding (a rising star renowned for her husky, seductive voice) and the show was earmarked for the Apollo, one of London's leading theatres. Passing up the chance to return to Germany with the Pembroke Players in a production of *Julius Caesar*, Peter returned to Torquay to work on the script. By mid-August it was finished. Two weeks later, after a fortnight's rehearsal, his new show hit the road.

Like *Here Is The News* – and most other West End shows, then and now – *Pieces of Eight* set off on a short regional tour, to give the performance some polish before its London opening. Peter went too, paid to tag along in case these provincial previews revealed the need for urgent rewrites. The show opened on 1 September at the New Theatre, Oxford, to good houses and good notices. A week later it transferred to Liverpool's Royal Court, where it got even better reviews, including raves from the *Daily Mirror* and the *Daily Mail*. After another successful week, at Brighton's Theatre Royal, *Pieces of Eight* opened at London's Apollo Theatre on 24 September 1959.

Pieces of Eight was a traditional revue, with none of the strident satire of *The Last Laugh*, but Peter's sketches gave it something new. The only blemish, as Adrian Slade observed, was that they would have been even funnier if Peter had been performing them. 'Snail Reform' (about the Society for the Prevention of Snail Racing) gave fresh vent to Peter's preoccupation with creepy-crawlies, but the pick of the bunch was 'If Only', in which Williams moaned about the many ways in which life had passed him by. This maudlin sketch was positively

ONE LEG TOO FEW

Pinteresque, which was fitting, since several other sketches in the show were actually written by Harold Pinter, still waiting for his first big hit after the failure of *The Birthday Party*. Pinter's sketches, like his plays, were notable for their long pauses, which worked out rather well for Pinter since royalties were paid according to the time that each sketch took to perform. 'I eventually submitted a sketch to Michael Codron which consisted almost entirely of significant pauses,' recollected Peter. 'But he knew perfectly well what I was up to, and it was rejected.' [24] There was no need to worry. When the London critics saw the show it was Peter, not Pinter, who was singled out for praise. *The Illustrated London News* called him 'the sort of writer that hunts for haddocks' eyes among the heather bright' – an astute allusion to Lewis Carroll, one of Peter's favourite authors. Not all the reviews were positive (*The Times* said the show 'tried desperately hard' – a comment more applicable to Williams's flamboyant acting than to Peter's deadpan prose) but the paying public didn't care. *Pieces of Eight* ran for more than 400 performances. 'I loved that revue,' recalled Peter. 'It was old-fashioned revue, which was eventually killed off by *Beyond The Fringe*.' [25]

Peter returned to Cambridge for his final year on a retainer of £100 a week – a small fortune for a student in 1959. Having inherited £2,000 the year before, on his twenty-first birthday, compared to all but the poshest undergraduates he was now very well off indeed. He bought himself a sports car and a tape recorder (for improvising sketches) and learned to play the horses. Roger Law recalls, 'If he had a keen interest, other than the horse-racing pages of the national newspapers, I never noticed what it was.' [26] However, his keenest interest was comedy. Peter's comedy wasn't a pastime – it was a lifestyle, a way of looking at the world that was always slightly askance. Elected President of Footlights, he was called upon to propose the toast at the first Footlights dinner of the new term. 'The Queen,' he said, solemnly. 'The Queen,' repeated his fellow diners, loyally. 'And all who sail in her,' added Peter. Was he mocking the monarchy, or the republican pretensions of his friends? With Peter, you could never tell, but it was terribly funny either way.

A lesser entertainer might have been happy to sit back and bask in this adulation, but comedy was in Peter's blood and he carried on writing and performing at an almost hyperactive rate. Jonathan Miller, star of the 1954 and 1955 Footlights revues, came to see one of Peter's Smokers and was instantly transfixed. 'I remember his first line when I was shot upright in my seat by him. He was playing some person in a suburban kitchen concealed behind a newspaper. He didn't say a word. But all eyes were drawn to him. Then he rustled the newspaper and simply said, "Hello, hello. I see the *Titanic's* sunk again." One knew one was in the presence of comedy at right angles to all the comedy we'd heard.' [27] Peter went on to recite a new monologue about a miner who could have been a judge if only he'd had the Latin, which would become one of the most famous sketches in *Beyond The Fringe*. 'I was immediately struck by the absolutely extraordinary peculiarity of this performer,' [28] recalled Miller. 'I realised immediately that I was in the presence of a really peculiar and original imagination.' [29]

After the show, Miller introduced himself to Peter and asked him if he'd ever worked with schizophrenics. 'No,' said Peter, nonplussed. 'Why?' 'Because you've perfectly reproduced the schizophrenic speech pattern,' said Miller. In later years Peter laughed off this observation. 'I wasn't aware of it at all,' he said. 'It doesn't make me a schizophrenic.' [30] Yet Miller's observation was perceptive. Peter hadn't worked with schizophrenics and he hadn't tried to reproduce their speech patterns, but there was something almost autistic about his distracted stage persona.

On 8 October, in the 1959 General Election, Harold Macmillan's Tories were re-elected with a huge majority, giving Peter's Macmillan impression a new lease of life. It was the third Conservative victory in a row and left-wing students were aghast. Peter wasn't one of them. By depicting Macmillan as complacent and out of touch, Peter would ride a rising tide of dissatisfaction with the Prime Minister and his party, but Peter was amused, rather than outraged, by Macmillan's patronising manner. He enjoyed mocking authority figures, but he was never an Angry Young Man. 'I don't think he wrote it out of any sense of indignation about the patrician complacency of Harold Macmillan,' argued Jonathan Miller. 'I think he found him rather adorable, really.' [31] Peter bore this out. 'My impersonation of Macmillan was in fact extremely affectionate,' he said. 'I was a great Macmillan fan.' [32] For him, Supermac was mainly a figure of fun.

Peter stayed on in Cambridge for most of the Christmas holidays, and it was here that he got together with the woman who became his first wife. Wendy Snowden was a student at the Cambridge School of Art. They'd actually met six months before, when Wendy was asked to pose for a (rather naff) photo with Peter, in evening dress, to illustrate a profile of him in *Varsity*, the student newspaper. Wendy wore a strapless ball gown (borrowed from her friend Penny – she didn't have a ball gown of her own) but, although they were both dressed to kill, it was hardly love at first sight. 'I thought Peter was incredibly full of himself,' [33] she recalled. 'I could see he was dynamic but he wasn't the sort of person I would have fallen for.' [34] And he had acne. She was glad when it was over. She was pleased to get two ball tickets out of it, but she didn't go with him. She took her friend Penny instead.

When they met again, six months later, Peter was just as cocky – but this time Wendy warmed to him. She was working as a waitress in a local coffee shop when Peter came in with his Pembroke friend Jack Altman. Even in her nylon uniform, Wendy looked stunning, with her hair piled high like Brigitte Bardot and her tight belt showing off her tiny waist. 'Are you going to buy me a coffee?' [35] Peter asked her. Wendy had plenty of admirers, so she was gobsmacked by his cheek. It worked a treat. She bought him a coffee out of her wages. As he was leaving, he asked her, 'How would you like to take me to the pictures tomorrow?' [36] She already had a steady boyfriend, her first true love, but she said yes. 'I was bewitched by his sense of humour,' [37] she said.

The movie wasn't a great success. Without any preamble, Peter put his hand down the front of her dress. Wendy was unimpressed. 'I grabbed his hand and held it so he couldn't get up to more mischief,' she recollected. 'Did he think that I was some kind of tart, just because I was an art student, and had allowed myself to be photographed lying across him?' [38] Yet when they left the cinema Peter cracked a joke, which broke the ice. They went on to a Greek restaurant, where he kept her laughing all the way through dinner. She told him she was already seeing someone but Peter was undeterred, and her conversations with her boyfriend, Barry, seemed mundane by comparison thereafter. Peter sent her letters, and even flowers. He was already quite a celebrity around Cambridge, and despite her best intentions Wendy was flattered. When she told Barry what was happening, he behaved like the perfect gentleman. 'You must do what you think is right,' [39] he said.

With her dark doe eyes and dark bobbed hair, Wendy was a natural beauty, but she was more than just a pretty face. She'd cultivated her love of art during childhood bouts of tuberculosis and bronchitis, painting and drawing to while away the months in bed. Her art-school friend Roger Law remembered her as 'a bunch of trouble,' [40] but beneath her flirty, fun-loving exterior she was spiritual and intense. She made her own clothes, and she encouraged Peter to swap his tweedy outfits for more fashionable threads. Peter more or less moved out of his student digs and into Wendy's place – a former pub called the Prince of Wales, owned by an enterprising postgrad, where she lived with numerous other students. The communal atmosphere was pleasantly convivial and chaotic. The parties in the dilapidated bar downstairs often ran on right through the night.

The Prince of Wales (or the PoW, as its student occupants all called it) was only a bike ride away from Pembroke College, but for Peter it was another country. At Pembroke, and all the other Cambridge colleges in those days, the sexes were strictly segregated, and overnight guests were forbidden. At the PoW, it was quite common for boyfriends and girlfriends to stay the night. However, it wasn't a seedy knocking shop – steady relationships were the norm, not one-night stands. Wendy went steady with Barry for a year ('I don't think that I could have had a more caring partner' [41]) until she met Peter, nearly a year later.

As Wendy soon discovered, Peter was sexually rather gauche. 'Women were still strangers to him,' [42] she reflected. She felt a lot more comfortable when he stopped putting on an act and confided in her about his heartfelt ambition – to set up a satirical nightclub in London, like the one he'd seen in Berlin. 'I was caught up in his idealism,' she recalled. 'Here was a young man who was going to make a difference, and I was going to be by his side, helping him to do it.' [43] This sincerity was something Peter never revealed to his male friends. 'He seemed very worldly and cynical,' [44] said Roger Law, but behind this caustic front Peter was a lot less worldly-wise. 'Underneath it all Peter had a deep idealism,' concluded Wendy. 'His confidence, though, was a total facade.' [45]

When he wasn't ensconced in the Prince of Wales, Peter found time to appear in one last Pembroke College revue. He didn't write much of this revue (called *Something Borrowed*) but one of the sketches he supplied would become the most celebrated sketch of his career. 'I don't think I've ever written anything better,' [46] he said. That sketch was 'One Leg Too Few'. Today, this droll two-hander about a one-legged man auditioning for the role of Tarzan is rightly regarded as a comic classic (Jonathan Miller called it one of the most masterly sketches of the twentieth century) but it wasn't an instant success. The BBC rejected it (along with a host of other sketches that Peter sent them) and Kenneth Williams poo-pooed it. For the sketch to click the one-legged man needed to be lovable, and no one Peter had met so far had really met the mark. For all his Footlights triumphs, Peter was still working in isolation. To make his comedy complete, he needed to find a sympathetic foil.

Peter had found his comic voice, but this voice came at a cost. Already, his humour was something he was finding increasingly difficult to switch off. It was partly insecurity, but it quickly became a habit. 'Eventually he monopolised the conversation,' recalled his Pembroke friend Peter Lloyd. 'He would go into one of his characters, monologues or styles of speech almost as soon as he saw you.' [47] 'Because he was so funny people expected him to be funny, so he was always on parade,' [48] said Christopher Booker. 'Wherever he was in Cambridge, he would be surrounded by a group of people falling about with laughter. It was so powerful and so funny that a lot of people copied it and no one more touchingly and one might say amateurishly than a young man who came up a year after us called David Frost.' [49]

Peter's attitude to David Frost has become enshrined in the nickname he gave him, 'the bubonic plagiarist,' but their relationship at Cambridge was actually quite complex. 'There was never a lot of point in knowing Frost if you already knew Cook because he would retell all Cook's jokes,' [50] said Roger Law. Yet in this regard, Frost was merely first among equals – at that time, virtually every young man at the university seemed to be imitating Peter Cook. 'It was the first time in my life I was ever conscious of meeting a genius,' [51] said Frost. 'He was the spirit of Cambridge. He was seminal to everybody's sense of humour.' [52] Frost's imitation was a form of flattery – and initially Peter was happy to indulge him. As Adrian Slade observed, other people got much more cross on his behalf. It was only later, when Frost's career eclipsed Peter's, that it really began to grate.

For now, however, Peter could afford to be magnanimous. He had more than enough celebrity to share around. He performed with Frost in Footlights Smokers, and in cabaret at the Cambridge Corn Exchange. Yet on a symbolic level, there was a sense in which Frost was Peter's nemesis. Peter had the talent but Frost had the ambition, and Peter recognised Frost's professionalism long before his Footlights peers. 'They all thought in Footlights that David couldn't tell jokes,' said Peter. 'He was a very bright lad, and we didn't know it.' [53] Frost lacked Peter's comic gifts, but his skills were more resilient – drive, dedication and indestructible self-belief.

*

With a West End show, a glamorous girlfriend and money in the bank, life could hardly have been better, but that Easter Peter suffered a serious setback which would return to haunt him in years to come. Peter's father had been posted to Libya, taking his mother and his younger sister, Elizabeth, with him, and at the end of term Peter flew out to spend some time with them and cram for his Finals, only a few months away. He didn't do much of either. His mother flew back to Britain to be by her dying father's bedside, and his sister Sarah, who should have flown out with him, stayed in England to attend the funeral. Soon after Peter arrived he fell ill with jaundice and was bedridden throughout his stay. He was still a sickly yellow when he returned to Cambridge for his final term. Wendy nursed him back to health but the disease weakened his liver, leaving it vulnerable to the effects of alcohol. This didn't matter much at the time – Peter wasn't a heavy drinker (yet) – but in later years, it would help to destroy his health.

For the time being, however, Peter had more pressing matters on his mind – his final exams, and his final Footlights revue. He swotted furiously for his Finals, spreading Eleanor Bron's lecture notes across his bedroom floor in a frantic attempt to memorise them. He eventually emerged with a Lower Second, an adequate but unremarkable degree. Actually, it was quite a feat for him to get any sort of degree at all. All his writing and performing had left little time for studying and he'd done hardly any academic work since he'd joined the Footlights, eighteen months before.

Peter's final Footlights revue, on the other hand, was a euphoric tour de force. Called *Pop Goes Mrs Jessop*, it is commonly regarded by those who saw it as one of the funniest Footlights shows ever staged. His fever hadn't dampened Peter's creativity – indeed,

Wendy believed it may even have heightened his imagination. Of the 29 sketches in the show, Peter wrote 16 and co-wrote a further seven, several with the show's director, John Wood, better known nowadays as John Fortune. 'Interesting Facts' got another airing, but most of the sketches were brand new. Among the highlights were 'Ornithology' (about a madman feeding ducks) and 'Second Flood', about a suburban couple confronted by a biblical deluge. Unlike *The Last Laugh*, the mood was unashamedly upbeat. There were several songs, such as 'Wha Hae', which made fun of drunken Scotsmen, and only two political sketches, presenting opposing points of view. One of them, 'Whose Finger on What Button?' (which ended up in *Beyond The Fringe*), was predictably apocalyptic. The other, less predictably, mocked the platitudes of anti-nuclear protesters: 'Do we want worldwide complication and suffering, with women and children being knocked down by a hydrogen bomb? Certainly not! Do we not want peaceful coexistence with us all living happily together and having no worries at all? Yes, we do!' It was a sign of Peter's political independence that he was willing to satirise the sympathies of his audience, and a sign of his comic skill that he could go against the grain and still raise a laugh.

'Cambridge seemed to be the hub of the world,' [54] said Peter, and after three idyllic years he was in no hurry to come down. *Varsity*, the student paper, named him as one of the Twelve Golden Boys of the Future, but despite his Footlights and West End hits Peter was far from confident about his ability to make a living out of comedy. Secretly, he went for a few interviews and (rather incongruously) got a job as a junior copywriter in an advertising agency, to start that autumn. At the end of term, he went for a walk with an old Pembroke pal called Martin Page. Over a few pints beside the Mill Bridge, they discussed their plans. Page was torn between academia and the law (he eventually opted for academia). Peter told Page about his office job. Page was surprised. Hadn't Peter thought of trying to pursue a career in show business? 'Good heavens, no,' said Peter. 'Far too insecure. You shouldn't allow your hobby to turn into a job. You would lose the fun of it.' [55] In fact, Peter had just one more date in his diary before he became a copywriter. Six months earlier, against the advice of his agent, he'd agreed to take part in a small revue at that summer's Edinburgh Festival. The other members of the cast were Jonathan Miller, Alan Bennett and Dudley Moore.

Peter at a Cambridge Smoker.

CHAPTER SIX

BEFORE THE FRINGE

'I was sort of blown into show business. I didn't really have any ambition to learn my craft as a performer. If it had involved any hard graft, I'd have given up very early on.'

(Peter Cook)

The man who brought Peter Cook and Dudley Moore together (and changed the course of British comedy in the process) was Dudley's old Oxford pal, John Bassett. After graduating in 1958 he got a job as assistant to Robert Ponsonby, Artistic Director of the Edinburgh Festival. Without this fortuitous appointment, and the events that flowed from it, it is quite possible that Peter and Dudley never would have met. Bassett almost didn't get the job – it was a dead heat between him and another candidate. Ponsonby didn't know who to choose, so he asked his three secretaries (important people like Ponsonby used to have several secretaries in those days). 'You've got to choose Mr Bassett,' they told him. 'The other man wears suede shoes, and we can't stand them.' [1] Ponsonby telephoned Bassett and told him he'd got the job, and invited him out to lunch to celebrate, without telling him what had swung it. Bassett turned up wearing a pair of suede shoes.

Founded in 1947, as an antidote to the austerity of the post-war years, the Edinburgh International Festival of Music and Drama had quickly become the summer highlight of the British artistic calendar. Yet by the time Ponsonby took charge, in 1956, this annual programme of highbrow plays and recitals, performed in Edinburgh's grand old theatres, was being overshadowed by a growing band of theatrical gatecrashers. These uninvited guests mounted more informal shows in smaller halls around the city, a spontaneous outpouring of creative vigour – and sometimes even talent – that became known as the Festival Fringe. Since the official Festival shut up shop around last orders every evening, late-night Fringe revues were particularly popular. In 1960 Ponsonby decided to mount a professional revue that would put their amateur efforts to shame.

Robert Ponsonby was an Old Etonian and former Guardsman (and a future Controller of Music for the BBC) but, despite his conservative credentials, he was open to new ideas. In 1959 he booked Flanders and Swann, [2] whose erudite revue, *At the Drop of a Hat*, had run for two years in London's West End. In 1960 he tried to book Louis Armstrong, but Armstrong's agent couldn't find any other British dates to make the transatlantic trip worthwhile, so Armstrong cancelled, leaving a gap in the programme. In need of a quick replacement, Ponsonby turned to his new assistant. 'Let's put on our own revue,' he told Bassett, mindful of the Fringe performers who'd been upstaging them. 'Let's beat them at their own game.' [3]

Britain in 1960 was arranged along strict social lines, and nowhere was this caste system more rigidly enforced than in the class-bound world of comedy. With a variety theatre in every town, British comedy was booming. You could see a first-class revue, with several fine comics on the same bill, virtually anywhere, on virtually any night of the year. The appetite for revue was so vast, and the venues so numerous, that many artistes spent the whole year travelling around the country, performing the same short set twice nightly in a different theatre every week. They'd work through the winter in pantomime, and spend the summer by the seaside in Summer Season, and every spring and autumn they'd simply start all over again. Ponsonby could have had his pick of these seasoned performers – acts like Tommy Cooper, Frankie Howerd or Morecambe & Wise [4] – but in 1960, British comedy, like British society, was divided into gentlemen and players. These jobbing comics were the players. Ponsonby wasn't bothered about the players. He wanted to beat the gentlemen, those 'clever undergraduates from Oxford and Cambridge', [5] whose amateur revues had become the talk of the Festival and its emerging Fringe. Hence, when he asked Bassett to assemble this comic supergroup, Bassett looked no further than Oxbridge. The first person he thought of asking was his old friend from Magdalen, Dudley Moore. Dudley was contracted to John Dankworth, and Vic Lewis was getting him all the solo gigs he needed. This was just a few weeks away in Edinburgh, more of a paid holiday than anything. Dudley was happy to tag along, but he didn't set much store by it. Bassett asked him to suggest someone else from Oxford. Dudley recommended a young historian called Alan Bennett.

Bookish, bespectacled and shy, Bennett was ostensibly very different from Dudley, with his amorous adventures in Soho jazz clubs, but classwise they actually had quite a lot in common. A butcher's son, born in Leeds in 1934, Bennett grew up in comparable circumstances – 'not poor, not well off' [6] as he put it. When the Bennetts went away on holiday, to seaside boarding houses, they took their own food, packing tins of corned beef among their bathing costumes. When they went to cafes they'd smuggle in their own bread and butter, to pad out the tea and cake. This was the world that Dudley knew, a world of keeping up appearances and making do. Bennett's parents were intelligent and sensitive but socially insecure, and the genteel austerity of Bennett's childhood would inform his later writing. What informed his early comedy, however, was religion.

Bennett wasn't a particularly funny schoolboy. He read *Doctor Dolittle* as a child, and he liked George Formby, but he was more keen on classical music and even keener on Christianity. He joined the Crusaders, an evangelical club for teenage boys which met every Sunday afternoon for Bible study at the local Congregational chapel. Having become an ardent Anglo-Catholic in his later teens, he assumed he'd become a clergyman. That he became a comic, and then a writer, was due to his stint in National Service. An unlikely soldier, Bennett called these two years 'the happiest time of my life'. [7]

Bennett's spell in uniform was the making of him as a performer. He was lucky. While the rest of his platoon was packed off to Korea, he was chosen for the Joint Services Russian Course, designed to train smarter soldiers to speak the language of Britain's latest foe. Some of these clever conscripts (like the budding playwright Dennis Potter) were sent to work in the War Office as translators, but the brightest of the bunch (including Bennett) were sent to the School of Slavonic Studies in Cambridge. Here Bennett met another future playwright, Michael Frayn. Together, they started writing sketches for mess-room cabarets – not so different from the Smokers of Peter's Cambridge years. They didn't actually collaborate – they each wrote separately – but budding comics need kindred spirits, and they egged each other on. One of Bennett's best sketches was a monologue by a pompous cleric (sending up his own teenage piety, rather than any clergyman in particular) which eventually formed the basis for his sermon in *Beyond The Fringe*.

Bennett already had a place at Cambridge and was due to go there once he'd finished his National Service, but during his Slavonic sabbatical he developed a 'hopeless crush' [8] on a fellow cadet, who was bound for Oxford. Bennett won a scholarship to Exeter College, Oxford, the cadet on whom he had a crush went to Brasenose (a much more boisterous and sporty college) and, despite having followed him to Oxford, Bennett's crush remained unrequited. 'I'd always been in love with guys,' he revealed, 'but always unhappily. They were always straight and it was always totally unfulfilled.' [9] Free from amorous distractions, he focused on his studies, spending three quiet yet contented years reading for a degree in Medieval History. Owlish and self-effacing, it's hard to imagine a less likely comedian.

Bennett was far too introverted to consider joining the Oxford University Drama Society or the Experimental Theatre Club so, unlike Dudley, he never took part in a proper OUDS or ETC production. He didn't even perform in a college Smoker until his third and final year. Finally, encouraged by his college friend (and future broadcaster) Russell Harty, he dusted down the ecclesiastical monologue he'd performed so successfully at Cambridge. Here at Oxford it received even greater acclaim. Heartened by this warm reception, he worked up several other monologues, including a parody of the Queen's Christmas Broadcast. Nowadays, parodies of the Queen are commonplace but in the 1950s Bennett's gently risqué jokes felt quite daring. By his own admission, the actual content was pretty tame – but the idea of doing it at all seemed almost sacrilegious, in an age when Her Majesty was still regarded with quasi-religious awe.

In his Finals, Bennett took a First, which enabled him to stay on as a Junior Lecturer while doing postgraduate research on Richard II. 'I wasn't very good at research,' he said. 'I never got a fellowship and I don't think I ever would have done.' [10] However, as a postgrad he finally found the courage to perform outside his college, at OUDS Smokers, and here he really shone. 'Every line was perfect,' recalled John Wells, then a fresher at St Edmund's Hall, reading Modern Languages, and later a leading contributor to *Private Eye*. 'When Alan came to do a Smoker, the whole room went quiet.' [11] Fired up by this triumph he joined the Oxford Theatre Group's trip to Edinburgh, with their 1959 revue *Better Never*, written and directed by an American postgrad called Stanley Daniels. Bennett reprised his popular atomic-scientist sketch (called 'At Home With The Atom') but Daniels couldn't – or wouldn't – find room for his comic sermon, which had become his party piece. On the last night Bennett did it anyway, without telling Daniels. 'There was a tremendous row about it,' recalled Bennett, 'but it was a great success.' [12] Indeed, such was its success that when Bassett asked Dudley to recommend another Oxford comic, Bennett was the first name he thought of, even though he'd never met him.

Bassett had his Oxford duo. Now he needed a pair from Cambridge. The brightest comic to come out of Cambridge during the last few years was Jonathan Miller, the undisputed star of the 1954 and 1955 Footlights Revues *Out of The Blue* and *Between The Lines*, both of which had transferred to the West End. Reviewing *Out of The Blue*, Harold Hobson of the *Sunday Times*, probably the most important theatre critic in the country, called him 'A mimic the like of whom has never before been seen in the Charing Cross Road.' [13] One instance of Miller's mimicry was his impression of Bertrand Russell, which eventually resurfaced in *Beyond The Fringe*, but Miller's talents weren't confined to impersonating Nobel Prize-winning philosophers. Reviewing *Between the Lines*, the *Daily Telegraph* called Miller the 'Danny Kaye of Cambridge'. 'His range of expression equals the variety of his imagination,' reported the *Telegraph*. 'His timing has acquired a polish that makes a critic regret that he is dedicated to the noble art of medicine.' [14] After graduating in 1956, Miller had put his West End triumphs behind him and gone to University College Hospital in London to complete his medical training. He planned to specialise in neuropsychology, but comedy kept calling him back. He appeared on ITV's flagship variety show *Sunday Night at the London Palladium*, reprising his spoof of Bertrand Russell. He appeared on BBC TV's *Tonight*, sending up the death of Nelson. He also went on the radio, and appeared in hospital revue, but these were just distractions. Medicine was his main aim.

Miller had just got married to a fellow medical student called Rachel Collet. [15] Collet had been at school with Bassett. This gave Bassett an introduction. He found Miller hard at work in the casualty department and persuaded him to take a few weeks off from medicine. Mindful of how poorly paid junior doctors were in those days, Miller was attracted to the idea of a short break that would also earn him some extra money. 'It was going to be a holiday,' said Miller. 'I knew how many people crucify their families on the unremitting demands of junior medicine. So I was therefore very vulnerable and susceptible to the appeals of the theatre as an alternative.' [16] Little did Miller know this 'holiday' would occupy him for several years and across two continents. Bassett asked Miller to recommend another Cambridge comic. Miller recommended a man he'd seen in a Footlights Smoker called Peter Cook.

*

Peter and Dudley first met in an Italian restaurant in London on 14 January 1960. The address of this restaurant remains a mystery. Miller thought it was on Warren Street, Bennett thought it was on Goodge Street and Peter thought that it was in Swiss Cottage. 'The main thing I remember was the food,' said Peter. 'It was revolting.' [17] Of the four performers who met for lunch that day, only Peter and Dudley really wanted to be there. Bennett and Miller had both supposedly forsaken comedy – Bennett to become an academic, Miller to become a doctor. Indeed, the location was chosen because of its close proximity to University College Hospital, so that Miller, who was working in the pathology department, could nip out in his lunch hour. Miller was extremely reluctant to revive what, for him, had been a student pastime – something he'd enjoyed, but which he now wanted to put behind him. 'I still fiercely regret the distraction,' he confirmed, years later. 'I think that was a bad thing I did. Much better to have been a very funny comic undergraduate and forget about it. But I got onto this terrible treadmill.' [18]

Initially, the atmosphere was wary – as it often is among funny people meeting for the first time (especially when they've been thrust together, and told they'll get on famously). 'We were all very suspicious of each other,' [19] recalled Dudley. Only one person really seemed at ease – and that was Peter. 'I was a Jew and the other two were proles,' said Miller. 'He was already in show business.' [20] However, it wasn't just his showbiz pedigree that set Peter apart. As soon as they sat down to lunch he started talking. And talking. Even a man as talkative as Miller found it impossible to compete. 'This flow of uncontrollably inventive stuff came out of him,' recalled Miller. 'You couldn't actually participate. There was no room for anyone to get in. You simply had to be an audience. [21] Things spoke through him – he became them.' [22] He almost seemed like a ventriloquist's dummy.

'Peter was very funny and, to my alarm, very fluent,' [23] recalled Bennett. 'It was alarming to see him produce this wonderful stream of stuff, seemingly without any effort, really. It just spilled out of him.' [24] It wasn't just Peter's conversation that overawed him. It was his clothes. Peter had money to spend and Wendy had dressed him in the latest fashions. 'He was wearing a shortie overcoat, a not quite bum-freezer jacket, narrow trousers, winkle-picker shoes and a silk tie with horizontal bars across it,' recalled Bennett. 'Most of the people I knew dressed in sports coat and flannels.' [25] But the biggest clues to Peter's personality were the things he was carrying – an armful of newspapers, and a book on racing form. Bennett began to feel he was there under false pretences – 'a feeling that never really left me.' [26] This was a million miles away from his Bible classes back in Leeds.

Dudley, if anything, felt even more overawed. 'I remember feeling very small, figuratively and physically,' he recalled. 'Peter Cook seemed to me a very urbane, relaxed, sophisticated young chap.' [27] When Dudley finally found the courage to pipe up, demonstrating a mime about a violin that cried like a baby, Peter poured scorn on it, anticipating the master–servant relationship that would define their double act for years to come. 'I felt completely mute in front of these intellectual giants,' [28] said Dudley. But while Peter's verbal invective vanished into the ether, it was Dudley who performed the comic turn that reduced everyone to stitches, following the waitresses into the kitchen and out again, like Groucho Marx, with bent knees and stooping gait.

Despite their various reservations, this meal encapsulated all the elements which made *Beyond The Fringe* so special. Peter was the star turn and Bennett and Miller were the supporting players, but it was Dudley's clowning that saved the whole thing from disappearing up its collective arse. Dudley's antics broke the ice, and when Bassett took them back to his West End office to meet their new boss, their initial sangfroid had melted. 'I could see we were onto something, because they were sparking each other off just in conversation,' [29] said Ponsonby. Bennett and Miller were still undecided but Peter and Dudley were both keen to do it, so the other two agreed to go ahead.

The title was Ponsonby's idea. None of the performers liked it and nor did Bassett, but they couldn't agree on an alternative. Peter's suggestion, *One Of The Best Revues For Some Time – Bernard Levin*, was considered too wayward, which was a pity (Levin, who subsequently wrote a rave review of the show, was at that time the theatre critic of the *Daily Express*). By *Beyond The Fringe*, Ponsonby meant a show produced by the official International Festival which was beyond the capabilities of anyone on the unofficial Festival Fringe. This convoluted in-joke was lost on everyone apart from a handful of Edinburgh insiders, and it became completely meaningless once the show transferred to London and then to New York. No matter. Ponsonby's title, though incomprehensible, was memorable and catchy – a far more important requirement than telling the audience what the show was actually about.

So what was *Beyond The Fringe* about? Well, nothing in particular. 'We just wrote about things which amused or annoyed us,' [30] said Peter. Bassett suggested that they all do their best solo material, so the show was mercifully free from any overarching central theme. Bassett also suggested that they get together during the next six months and create some new ensemble sketches to complement their individual routines. They met up, off and on, sometimes at Bassett's office in St James's Street, more often at University College Hospital where Miller was working, performing surgical operations. They improvised, which suited Peter and Jonathan in particular. 'Peter bends words and twists them,' said Dudley. 'Jonathan juggles with them.' [31] Alan mainly wrote his contributions in advance. They wrote the ensemble sketches together, so it's hard to assess exactly who wrote what, but Dudley reckoned Peter wrote about two-thirds of the script while Jonathan and Alan wrote the remaining third between them. Dudley contributed nothing to the text, concentrating solely on the music. 'I felt totally constricted and overpowered,' [32] he said. And no wonder. 'Apart from his musical contributions, Dudley's suggestions were treated with benign contempt by the rest of us,' wrote Peter in *Esquire*. 'He was in awe of Jonathan's spectacular ability to speak at length on everything under the sun. Alan Bennett also inhibited Dudley, mainly with his scholarly demeanour. And I wore a cloak of precocious urbanity, which did little to encourage friendships.' 'I didn't contribute a word to the writing, because I was so intimidated by them,' confirmed Dudley. 'Psychology, philosophy and current events weren't up my alley, so how could I contribute in those areas? What did I know?' [33]

Acutely aware of his lack of input, Dudley played down his part in *Beyond The Fringe*. Even 25 years later, looking back on the most successful and influential revue of the last century, he dismissed himself as 'a rehearsal pianist' [34] – an absurdly modest self-assessment. In fact, he sorely underestimated his contribution, not only behind the piano but also onstage. His music gave this cerebral show an emotional dimension, and his acting gave these clever sketches the human touch. Peter and Jonathan were intense and wordy. Alan was dour and downbeat. All together, on the same stage, they could be terribly forbidding. Dudley was someone you warmed to, someone audiences could relate to. Without him, it would have been a very dry revue indeed.

Not only did Dudley bring something special to the show. It also gave him something special, which would stand him in good stead in years to come. Anyone who came up with a funny line tended to keep it for themselves, and since Dudley came up with virtually nothing he was left with little to say. 'I was a mildly mute person onstage while the others flourished their wares shamelessly,' [35] he said. Yet with few gag lines of his own, he had to work on his reactions. Reacting is the basis of good acting, especially on TV and in the movies. The other three remained mainly monologists, particularly Peter. It's no coincidence that Dudley was the only one to become a star on the big screen.

Even so, in rehearsal there was no doubt that Dudley was the odd man out. 'You can't do that,' [36] he kept saying, whenever someone came up with anything remotely shocking. Scandalised by their lack of inhibition and anxious not to cause offence, he felt completely out of place. 'I was always terrified that we'd get arrested,' Dudley told his biographer, Barbra Paskin. 'I was very timid. And Jonathan, Alan and Peter treated that fear with total scorn.' [37] Peter wasn't as timid as Dudley, but as an established West End scriptwriter, he erred on the side of caution. His contributions were more surreal than satirical. It was Alan and Jonathan, more than anyone, who gave the show its cutting edge. Unlike Peter or Dudley, they had no plans to pursue a career in show business. Unlike Peter or Dudley, they had nothing to lose. Yet there was something about Peter's humour that was inherently alarming. 'Peter resisted anything which might seem to be offensive,' said Jonathan. 'In some odd way, however, some of the things that he did and said as a performer were much more upsetting than those things where we explicitly set out to be satirical.' [38]

Before they could perform the show, they had to submit the script to the Lord Chamberlain, the official censor of all public performances in Britain until 1968. Absurdly, the only objection was to an unspoken stage direction: 'Enter two outrageous old queens.' This was altered to 'Enter two aesthetic young men,' presumably to save the cast and crew from Sodom. At the beginning of August, with the Lord Chamberlain's blessing, the four of them set off from London by car at 6:30 a.m., arriving in Edinburgh eleven hours later. When they returned to London, a few weeks later, their young lives had entirely changed.

Sarah, Peter, Elizabeth, Margaret and Alec Cook, and Candy the Labrador.

CHAPTER SEVEN

EDINBURGH AND AFTER

'I think at about this juncture it would be wise to point out to those
of you who haven't noticed – and God knows, it's apparent
enough – that Jonathan Miller and myself come from good families
and have had the benefits of a public school education, whereas
the other two members of the cast have worked their way up from
working-class origins. And yet Jonathan and I are working together
with them in the cast and treating them as equals, and I must say
it's proving to be a most worthwhile, enjoyable and stimulating
experience for both of us.'

(Peter Cook, *Beyond The Fringe*)

In the opening sketch of *Beyond The Fringe*, at Edinburgh's Lyceum
Theatre, Peter complained that the Festival had put up the cast in
the world's smallest bungalow, forcing them to share their digs with
a 138-piece orchestra. In fact, they were accommodated in a fairly
spacious fourth-floor flat on Cornwall Street, right opposite the
Lyceum. It belonged to a Mrs Grosset – the sort of name that Peter
might have invented. It didn't have a 138-piece orchestra, but it did
have its own piano.

This was just as well, as there were no rehearsal facilities at the
Lyceum. The Old Vic were performing Chekhov's *The Seagull* on the

same stage earlier in the evening and wouldn't let them in until five minutes before curtain-up on the first night. 'There is a great deal of rehearsal to be done,' wrote Peter to his mother, after a sleepless night at Mrs Grosset's. Not that they did much rehearsing. On Thursday, 18 August, the journalist Alan Brien came to interview them and found it hard to believe they'd be ready to open by Monday. They couldn't even get into the Lyceum to do a dress rehearsal. They did the dress rehearsal, as best they could, at Mrs Grosset's. Ponsonby came along to see what his four protégés had been getting up to. He wasn't impressed with what he saw. The cast got the giggles – usually a sure sign of an unfunny show – and as he watched them corpsing Ponsonby feared the worst. 'Oh my God, this is the worst sort of amateurism,' [1] he thought. 'This is going to be a shambles and I shall be blamed for putting it on.' [2] However, the cast were quietly confident. As Jonathan said, 'We knew that it was funnier than anything we had ever seen.' [3]

Wendy came up to Edinburgh to keep Peter company and do the cooking. She was seduced by the rugged beauty of this dark, dramatic city – the winding alleys of the medieval Old Town, the wide boulevards of the Georgian New Town, and the craggy castle that towered above them, like a scene from a Gothic fairy tale. Dudley, on the other hand, wasn't so interested in seductive architecture. He'd started seeing one of Ponsonby's several secretaries, and tended to spend his nights elsewhere. The night before they opened, he returned to Mrs Grosset's and sat up writing a brand new composition – 'The Colonel Bogey March' (from the classic war movie *Bridge On The River Kwai*) rewritten in the style of a Beethoven sonata. This last-minute magnum opus, with its elongated closing cadence, became one of the highlights of the show and Dudley's lifelong curtain call.

On the first night [4] the auditorium was only one-third full. The publicity was scant, and none of the cast were names outside Oxbridge. While the others waited in the wings, Dudley dashed off to the toilet. The backstage lavatory was right at the top of the building, and by the time he returned the other three were already waiting for him onstage. The curtain went up at a quarter to eleven. By the time it came down, around midnight, they were already rising stars. 'For the first ten minutes, nobody in the audience knew quite what to expect,' [5] recalled Ponsonby. But then the show took off. 'You knew you were in the presence of something extraordinary,' [6] said Michael Billington (who, having acted with Dudley at Oxford, had come to Edinburgh as a student critic). 'We'd seen nothing like this before.' [7] It felt like a shock, a slap in the face, but mostly he felt exhausted, physically sick from so much laughing. For Billington, British theatre didn't change with *Look Back In Anger*. It changed with *Beyond The Fringe*.

Even the performers were surprised to receive such a rapturous reception. 'It wasn't simply like a good Footlights revue,' said Miller. 'Something rather special had happened. [8] It was as if the audience was waiting for that sort of thing, although they didn't know what they were waiting for.' [9] *Beyond The Fringe* was a speculative venture, with no idea what it would consist of, or whether it would work at all. But, by bringing together these four performers, Bassett had conjured up something far greater than the sum of its disparate parts.

So what was so special about *Beyond The Fringe*? 'We'd never seen names named on the stage,' said Michael Billington. 'We hadn't seen Prime Ministers lampooned, by name.' [10] Richard Ingrams agreed. 'It was the first time in my memory that someone had actually got up in public and ridiculed the Prime Minister,' [11] he said. But there was more to this show than Peter's impression of Harold Macmillan. What was really radical was the removal of that invisible barrier, between what people joked about among themselves, and what they joked about onstage. 'We dealt with things that young people made jokes about in private but never publicly, like politics and the monarchy,' [12] concurred Bennett. No revue had ever before dared to break down that divide.

Conventional revues (like Peter's *Pieces of Eight*) were generally performed by professional comedians (like Kenneth Williams) and their green-room jokes had little relevance beyond the gossip columns of *The Stage*. *Beyond The Fringe* was not part of this self-referential show-business establishment. 'It absolutely cut through all the showbiz rubbish,' [13] said John Wells. 'It was exactly as if the curtain, the proscenium and the audience weren't there, and you were sitting in somebody's rooms in Oxford or Cambridge. [14] They were fooling about on the stage in exactly the same way as they fooled about off it.' [15] In 1962, when *Beyond The Fringe* was a huge hit in the West End, Peter was still describing it – quite correctly – as 'an amateur revue'. [16] Proper amateurs are people who do it for the love of it, and this description fitted this cast perfectly. They didn't need to please a theatre manager to pay their way, so they laughed at the things their audience laughed about, from the Church of England to the Battle of Britain. 'Nothing was sacred,' recalled Eric Idle. 'Not the Queen, not the Army, not the schools, not the Church, not the City, not advertising, not the Prime Minister, not the late war, not even the impending nuclear holocaust we were all sure was coming.' [17] Until now, there'd been an unspoken understanding that there were certain things you simply didn't talk about in public. *Beyond The Fringe* asked 'Why not?' And there was no answer. There was no reason why not, not any more, and British comedy – and British culture – was never quite the same again.

Having written most of the show, Peter got the most laughs, particularly for his Mr Grole monologue, 'Sitting on the Bench', which often ended up running for fifteen minutes rather than the allotted five. Bennett had to follow this tour de force with a monologue of his own. 'I would be handed an audience so weak from laughter I could do nothing with them,' [18] he remembered. But he had lots of other opportunities to shine, and so did Jonathan and Dudley. They were all very different, but they complemented each other perfectly. As Wendy put it, 'It was a kind of alchemy of incompatibility.' [19] Despite his feelings of inadequacy, Dudley more than held his own. Richard Ingrams saw the show in Edinburgh and was blown away by Dudley's musicianship. 'I thought he was the star of the show,' [20] he said. Peter Preston concurred. 'The other three needed Moore most of all,' he observed. 'He was the natural clown.' [21]

Most of the monologues in this show had already been aired in university revues – but university revue was a private world. *Beyond The Fringe* transported an Oxbridge Smoker into the public realm, and the general public had never seen anything quite like it. Even for punters familiar with the Footlights, this was a cut above the usual fare. '*Beyond The Fringe*, like rock and roll, was perceived as something fresh and new and dangerous,' recalled Michael Palin. 'It was shocking and thrilling, but it was done with such skill and intelligence that it could not easily be shot down, dismissed or shaken off.' [22]

And the stagecraft was inspired. The show began with Dudley playing the National Anthem (still a standard curtain-raiser in the theatre in 1960) and, dutifully, the audience all stood up, as they'd been trained to do. Only then did it dawn on them that Dudley's rendition of 'God Save the Queen' was actually part of the opening sketch, 'Steppes in the Right Direction', and that Dudley was playing a Russian musician, performing at the Festival. 'I do wish he wouldn't keep coming in and playing "God Save the Queen",' was Alan's killer line. 'It's probably because they get so little chance to play it over there.' The resultant confusion was sublime: should the audience remain standing for a rendition of the National Anthem which was within a sketch, and therefore essentially a work of fiction? No one seemed to know.

The next sketch, 'Royal Box', was equally ingenious and subversive: Dudley masqueraded as a member of the audience, telling Peter (playing a fellow punter) how he'd attended the same show 497 times in the vain hope of spotting a member of the Royal Family, crouching in the royal box. 'Do you mean to say you spend twelve and sixpence every night just on the off chance you may catch a glimpse of the Royal Family?' asked Peter. 'Well, they're not worth the fifteen shillings,' replied Dudley, to rapturous applause. Such a joke may seem mild by modern standards, but this was an age of deference, when the Royal Family were revered in a way that would seem absurd today. *Beyond The Fringe* reflected changing attitudes but it helped to change them, too. During one hour in the Lyceum, traditional revue was rendered virtually obsolete.

It wasn't just the script that was radical. The (almost non-existent) set and costumes also made it visually avant-garde. The motivation for this stark approach was actually purely practical. The total budget for the show was £100, which left no spare cash for any extras. Dudley's bass player, Hugo Boyd, was recruited for the Edinburgh run, but that was just about the only outlay. The cast even bought their own costumes – everyday grey suits and V-necked pullovers, white shirts and plain dark ties. *Beyond The Fringe* was minimal by default rather than by design ('We'd have been delighted to have had a hundred chorus girls dancing about' [23] said Peter) but this penny-pinching house style turned out to be inspired. It made the show look cutting edge. It made the cast look cool and nonchalant. They didn't look like actors. They looked like they'd stepped out of the stalls.

This Brechtian staging suited the production perfectly. It was fashionable – Brecht's Berliner Ensemble had played the Festival a few years before, delighting trendy critics like Kenneth Tynan – yet it was essentially a happy accident, the sort of lucky synergy that attends every successful show. Miller was right to tell *The Times* that they'd abandoned gaudy decor to let the script speak for itself, but they'd made a virtue of a necessity. The penury (or parsimony) of the producers had been a blessing in disguise.

Without a technical run-through or a proper dress rehearsal, there were a few first-night hiccups – the lights went out during Bennett's sermon, plunging him into darkness – but the amateur aesthetic of *Beyond The Fringe* meant that these cock-ups hardly mattered. 'It was an amazing atmosphere – absolutely electric,' [24] said Barbara Moore, who'd travelled up to Edinburgh for the first night. The next night was a sell-out, and every night thereafter. The queue for returns stretched round the block.

Like all the best Edinburgh shows, it was word of mouth that sold the tickets, rather than reviews. In fact, most of the posher papers completely missed the mark. *The Times* was only mildly enthusiastic. The *Sunday Times* was complimentary, but extremely brief. The *Observer* called it an 'average-level undergraduate revue.' [25] It was left to Peter Lewis of the more proletarian *Daily Mail* to deliver the first outright rave – the first of many. After half a century, it is still the best (and, by virtue of being the first, by far the bravest) summary of what made *Beyond The Fringe* so special. 'Behind this unpromising title lies what I believe can be described as the funniest, most intelligent, and most original revue to be staged in Britain for a very long time,' wrote Lewis in the *Mail*. 'It is the creation of four mobile, deadpan young men of Oxford and Cambridge extraction who are in private life a doctor, scriptwriter, historian and musician. They take the stage for ninety minutes with grey sweaters, four chairs and a piano, and proceed to demolish all that is sacred in the British way of life with glorious and expert precision. Disregarding all the jaded trimmings of conventional sketches, production numbers, dancing and girls, they get down to the real business of intimate revue, which is satire and parody ... These four high priests of parody make most professional comedians look ham-handed and vulgar. If the show comes to London I doubt if revue will ever be the same again.' [26] The *Mail* asked Lewis to track down the cast and find out some more about them. 'Of course, I'm only doing this as a summer holiday from medicine,' [27] said Miller. 'My subject is Richard II,' said Bennett. 'I'm going back to that.' [28] Lewis went on to play an active part in the 'satire boom' he helped to foster, working on the TV show that brought satire into people's living rooms – *That Was The Week That Was*, presented by Peter's Cambridge disciple, David Frost.

On the morning of Wednesday, 24 August, the day Lewis's review appeared in the *Mail*, the four new stars gave a press conference. Billington went along. 'What are you really attacking?' he asked them. 'What's your gripe?' [29] Complacency, they told him. Yet they were far from complacent about the show, despite Lewis's rave review. Jonathan even requested criticism, a rare show of humility for a comic in a hit show. Billington told him he didn't really like their sketch that poked fun at charities that give clothes to refugees. He was gratified when this sketch was dropped ('possibly the only time in my life any criticism of mine may have had some effect' [30]) but not half as gratified as Bennett, who'd played an (unclothed) refugee in this sketch and had been required to undress onstage.

Lewis's rave, and those that followed, brought a flood of journalists up to Edinburgh. Within a few days, *Beyond The Fringe* had become the height of fashion. The *Edinburgh Evening News* (an important player on the Fringe, second only to its sister paper, *The Scotsman*) called it 'the hit of the festival'. The paper even printed excerpts. It was obvious that *Beyond The Fringe* was ripe for a West End transfer. Agents and producers started sniffing round, eager for a slice of the action. Bassett and Ponsonby had never imagined the show would be such a hit. They'd made no contractual arrangements to ensure they got a say in any subsequent transfer or revival. Consequently, the cast soon had offers from fourteen different managements on the table. It was all rather overwhelming. Onstage, they were peerless, but when it came to the business side of show business their sudden success had swept them way out of their depth.

Meanwhile, down in London, Peter's agent, Donald Langdon, went to see his friend and colleague, Willie Donaldson. 'His contribution to *Beyond The Fringe* was to try to persuade Peter Cook not to do it,' claimed Donaldson. 'He didn't even go up to the opening – he'd never met the other three at all. When it opened to triumphant reviews, everybody rushed to Edinburgh to see it except him.' Well, not everybody. Donaldson still hadn't seen it either. 'It looks like a success,' Langdon told him. 'I'd better go up and see it, and I'll get it for you.' [31] 'You'll be lucky,' [32] said Donaldson. 'Considering I'm the only impresario in London who's not up there, and considering

I'm the only impresario in London who's just had a huge flop, I couldn't be a worse candidate.' [33] Langdon was undeterred. He flew up to Edinburgh to meet the cast. Within twenty-four hours he'd persuaded them to entrust the West End transfer to Donaldson. 'It was extraordinary,' said Donaldson. 'This was a sure-fire hit, and they'd given it to this bloke in London the same age as themselves, who knew nothing, who'd just had a flop, who was obviously an idiot, who was teetering on the edge of bankruptcy, and who was the only person who hadn't been bothered to go up and see them!' [34]

Well, that was Donaldson's version of events. However, as author of the Henry Root letters and various other works of semi-fiction, he was never averse to adding a comic gloss to his reminiscences. This was the way the tale played best, so this was the way he chose to tell it. In fact, it rather suited Donaldson to portray himself as a complete nincompoop – partly because it made a funny story (Donaldson had a lifelong love of funny stories) and partly because it offered some protection against the accusation (which he eventually more or less admitted) that he had ripped off the cast, depriving them of their rightful share of the spoils. In Terence Blacker's biography of Willie Donaldson [35] the chapter about Donaldson's involvement in *Beyond The Fringe* is called 'Fleecing the Fringers'.

In fact, in his handling of *Here Is The News*, Donaldson had proved himself to be a sensitive producer, something which Langdon was acute enough to realise. He'd been impressed by Donaldson's commitment to John Bird (whom he also represented). 'I thought he would be the ideal producer for another show that was about to open in Edinburgh with equally inspired content but much simpler in concept. It needed a producer who would allow the same complete freedom of expression to the authors as had been given to Bird, and its very simplicity was proof against the problems that had beset its very complicated predecessor.' [36]

Actually, the first question wasn't who they'd do the deal with but whether they'd do a deal at all. Peter and Dudley were both keen, but Alan and Jonathan were 'perpetually struggling with their consciences,' [37] as Peter put it. Alan was open to persuasion, as a temporary respite from academia, but Jonathan was reluctant to abandon medicine for this 'frivolous pursuit'. [38] Holed up in a bedroom at Mrs Grosset's, he thrashed it out with his wife Rachel, while Alan and Dudley took turns to listen at the keyhole. Eventually, he decided to do the London show – for a while. 'Medicine was becoming boring,' he told Wendy. 'And we had no money.' [39] Looking back, he has mixed feelings. 'It changed my life completely. It didn't change Peter's life because that is what he was going to do anyway. Yet it was a sort of catastrophe for me, although I enjoyed it in many ways.' [40]

The other three were delighted – as Wendy observed, it would have been unthinkable to do the show without Jonathan – and enthused by this celebratory atmosphere, Peter and Wendy decided to get engaged. It wasn't an entirely impetuous decision – they'd been together for a year – but there was a pragmatic element to the timing. Peter's mother and his two sisters were on their way up to Edinburgh to see the show (Peter's father was in Tripoli) and Peter and Wendy were living together, a much bigger deal for an unmarried couple then than it is today. They bought a silver-and-agate engagement ring, and Peter hired some fishing tackle and drove Wendy to the nearest loch, where he taught her the rudiments of fly-fishing. They caught some trout, which they ate for supper. Life was good.

Wendy got on well with Peter's mother, and really hit it off with Peter's sisters. Sarah and Elizabeth loved the show, even though

Sarah was only fifteen and Elizabeth barely eight (she celebrated her eighth birthday in Edinburgh with a trip to the Military Tattoo). That they both enjoyed *Beyond The Fringe* was an indication of its broad appeal. Elizabeth especially enjoyed Dudley's clowning. Thankfully, the joke about Dudley 'playing with himself' went over her head.

The deal with Donaldson was done at the end of August, in a West End restaurant called the White Elephant. Donaldson's trump card (indeed, his only card) was that he promised not to interfere with the show in any way – by his own estimation, he was just about the only person in London who still hadn't seen it. Reassured that he'd give them a free hand, the four performers agreed to do the West End run for a flat rate of £75 a week. [41] Its London backers, by comparison, made almost half a million pounds. Peter's biographer Harry Thompson called it 'one of the greatest rip-offs in the history of show business.' [42] 'Nothing seems to have alerted us to the fact that play our cards right and there was a fortune to be made,' rued Alan. 'In the worldly-wisdom department we tended to look to Peter. He had already had material in West End revues and besides he wore pointed shoes and had a tailor in Old Compton Street. It followed that he must know what he was doing.' [43]

After the meal, outside the restaurant, Miller flagged down a taxi and offered Bennett a lift. It was the first time that Bennett had ever been in a black cab. As they sped through Mayfair, Miller enthused about the contract. 'It's ten times what I'd be receiving as a junior doctor,' [44] he said. Bennett said nothing, but he was less enthusiastic. 'It was fifteen times what I'd be receiving as a medieval historian but something told me even then that this was not really the point.' [45] Donaldson had seduced them, but, looking back, Bennett was sanguine. 'Even if we had been told he was going to rip us off, he was so gentle and funny that it would have been difficult to change.' [46] Miller was less forgiving. 'He had the charm that is associated with that sort of trickster. We were innocents abroad and he was simply a confidence trickster. He was a crook.' [47]

Peter and Dudley with Alan Bennett and Jonathan Miller beneath Brighton Pier.

CHAPTER EIGHT

BRIGHTON OR BUST

'Satire is not a social dynamite but it is a social indicator.
It shows that new men are knocking at the door.'

(Jacob Bronowski) [1]

As it turned out, no West End theatre was free until the following spring – so, while Willie Donaldson went about his business, the cast of *Beyond The Fringe* went back to their day jobs. Jonathan went back to medicine, Alan went back to academia and Dudley went back to music. Despite the triumph of the Edinburgh run and the prospect of a West End transfer, *Beyond The Fringe* still seemed like a brief divertissement, a pleasant distraction from his real career. Indeed, while he was in Edinburgh Dudley even auditioned for the vacant post of conductor of the Edinburgh Festival Ballet. He didn't get the job, but it showed where his main interests lay.

Back in London, as well as playing jazz, Dudley wrote more music for the theatre, and when the BBC's leading arts strand, *Monitor*, decided to make a documentary about two young composers, one of the composers they chose was Dudley. The film drew a bold contrast between Dudley's bohemian lifestyle – shuffling around Soho jazz clubs, sleeping on friends' floors – with the more austere routine of

Peter Maxwell Davies, who combined composing with a respectable day job as a teacher at a grammar school. 'I wasn't popular at school, being a very serious boy,' revealed Dudley in the programme. 'I wanted to be less unpopular, which is why I started to fool around.' This was a surprising confession for someone who was still regarded as a musician rather than a comedian, but what Dudley's family found most surprising was the squalid state of his accommodation – especially as he was now earning £100 a week, a sum it had taken his parents twenty years to save. Despite his newfound wealth, he still lived in a one-bedroom flat over a shop in Kilburn High Road, festooned with record sleeves and empty milk bottles. It was chaotically untidy and freezing cold – he used his dad's old overcoat as a blanket. No wonder he often slept elsewhere.

Peter was also busy, writing a sequel to *Pieces of Eight* (called *One Over The Eight*) for Kenneth Williams and Sheila Hancock (who'd replaced Fenella Fielding as the female lead). The script was due by the end of September, barely a month away. Peter delivered on time, but Williams wasn't happy with the writing. In his diary he described Peter's new material as mediocre, which was bizarre since it was in much the same vein as *Pieces of Eight* and was arguably even better. As well as fresh sketches like 'Chez Malcolm' (with Williams as a camp hairdresser) Peter also incorporated several Cambridge favourites, including 'One Leg Too Few' which, ironically, Williams identified as the weakest of the bunch. In retrospect, Williams's criticism of this classic sketch seems absurd, after all the success it brought Peter and Dudley, but the fact that he had such trouble with it was telling. Williams's stage persona, like Peter's, was essentially unsympathetic. It needed a sympathetic character, like Dudley, to make this classic sketch come alive.

His work done and Williams (temporarily) appeased, Peter returned to Cambridge with Wendy, to a house in Park Street, not far from the Prince of Wales. With typical generosity, Peter let Roger Law and his art-school partner Peter Fluck use the ground floor rent free. Fluck and Law used these premises to run a ragged arts collective called East Anglian Artists. It never did much business but it was the forerunner of *Spitting Image*, making it the first in a long line of creative ventures in which Peter had a hand.

Another frequent visitor to Park Street was David Frost, who was now Secretary of Footlights and editor of *Granta*. A manic bundle of activity, he'd drop in to use the telephone – still a rarity in student circles in those days. When Wendy was upstairs and Frost was downstairs, it sounded to her as if he had half a dozen secretaries buzzing round him. Peter's attitude to Frost remained ambiguous and contradictory. On the one hand, he wrote a cutting sketch for *One Over The Eight* called 'Critic's Choice', about a playwright called David Frost who, through highly selective quotation, transforms awful reviews of his latest play into outright raves. On the other hand, he was quite happy to collaborate with Frost on a (rather good) spoof sports report for *Granta*. 'He was a strange, pushy little character,' [2] recalled Christopher Booker, who went on to become the inaugural editor of *Private Eye*. However, at that stage, before he became a star, Frost's obvious ambition provoked more amusement than irritation, and his flattering imitation of Peter was too blatant to be taken seriously. 'Recipe for a bad joke,' ran a gag of Booker's. 'De-Frost and leave to Cook for ten minutes.' [3]

At Christmas, Peter took Wendy to Torquay to meet his father, who was home from Libya. They got on well but, despite the undoubted affection that flowed between them, Wendy detected a certain distance between Mr and Mrs Cook and their son. 'It was as if Peter's parents were almost encountering him for the first time each time they met.' [4] After Christmas, Peter limbered up for the impending West End run with a few previews of Beyond The Fringe, at Bennett's Oxford College, Exeter, and the Dorchester Hotel in London. At the Dorchester, Peter brought the house down by repeating his new catchphrase, 'Good Evening,' over and over again. Most comics spend half a lifetime learning how to conjure laughter out of nothing. At the age of only twenty-three, Peter had already reached that stage.

In March, Peter and Wendy left Cambridge and moved to London, lodging for a short while in the spare bedroom of John Bassett's flat in Hampstead before moving into a large mansion-block flat in Battersea, on Prince of Wales Drive, which they shared with their Cambridge pals Roger Hammond, Peter Bellwood, Colin Bell and Ian Davidson. Bellwood was working in advertising, Colin and Ian were both just starting out as journalists, and Wendy had a place at the Central School of Art. However, Peter wasn't keen for her to take it up (he was worried that they'd never see each other) so she turned it down. At first, she didn't miss it all that much. Without a college course to occupy her energy and creativity, she set about turning their bachelor apartment into a proper home, hunting for antique furniture on the Portobello Road. The 1960s were just beginning, Victoriana was back in vogue, and Wendy discovered a flair for interior design. Looking back, though, it was a decision she regretted. Peter wasn't short of money, but she was now financially dependent on him and never had the chance to develop her own career.

Even after he left Cambridge, Peter's influence endured. The 1961 Footlights Revue (starring David Frost) even took its title from

Peter's old Radley catchphrase, *I Thought I Saw It Move*. 'His spirit lurked everywhere in the funny voices he had left behind,' [5] said Eric Idle, who arrived at Pembroke College as an undergraduate that autumn. As Auden said of W.B. Yeats, he'd become his admirers. Even today, at Pembroke, the ghost of Peter Cook (and Arthur Boylett) lives on.

One Over The Eight opened at the Duke of York's Theatre on 5 April 1961. The *Evening Standard* described it as 'snappy and gay' but the *Daily Mail* wasn't quite so keen. 'The trouble with this revue is that its chief author, Peter Cook, has failed to find real targets for his satire,' [6] wrote the *Mail*'s critic, Robert Muller. It was the second time that the *Mail* had cited 'satire' in a review of Peter's work, praising its inclusion in *Beyond The Fringe* and bemoaning its absence from *One Over The Eight*. In fact, Peter hadn't set out to be satirical in either show. Like *Beyond The Fringe*, *One Over The Eight* was written purely to entertain. 'The Ephemeral Triangle', about a dissatisfied customer in a music shop, anticipated Monty Python. 'Hand Up Your Sticks', about an incompetent bank robber, wouldn't have looked out of place in an episode of *The Two Ronnies*. Yet it was a sign of the zeitgeist that Peter was now being judged as a satirist, not just as a humorist. After ten years of Tory rule, the times were changing. Whatever Peter's intentions, satire was in the air.

On 4 April, the day before the opening night of *One Over The Eight*, the cast of *Beyond The Fringe* reassembled for a rehearsal in the stalls bar of the Prince of Wales Theatre. Those rave reviews now seemed like ancient history. Seven months after Donaldson had snapped it up, *Beyond The Fringe* didn't seem like such a hot ticket. Donaldson needed to raise £8,000 to mount this new production, but after blowing so much money backing *Here Is The News*, he could only find £1,000. To his eternal regret, he was forced to lay off the remaining £7,000 to a variety of other investors, most notably the eminent impresario Donald Albery who bought a half-share and assumed effective control.

Albery was a tough old bird and Donaldson was no match for him. He came from a long line of theatre proprietors (his father and grandfather had both been big names in show business) and the string of West End theatres that he managed made him one of the most important players in London's theatreland. He had a nose for new talent (he'd championed Samuel Beckett, John Osborne and Brendan Behan) but, like all the best impresarios, he was shrewd and unsentimental. Like Donaldson, he'd never seen the show before and when he came to the Prince of Wales to see a run-through he didn't much like what he saw. He was particularly unimpressed with Alan Bennett. 'The blond one will have to go,' he told Donaldson. Donaldson won that battle, but Albery remained lukewarm. He refused to book the show straight into one of his London theatres. It would have to prove its worth in the provinces before he'd even consider bringing it into the West End.

Donaldson hired Eleanor Fazan, a dancer and choreographer turned director, to knock the show into shape. He told her it would be a small job since the show had already been a hit in Edinburgh. On this basis, Fazan accepted a flat fee of £20 per week. Yet when she saw the show for the first time, in rehearsal, she realised that Donaldson had sorely underestimated the size of her task. She'd directed several West End revues by Footlights veterans, including Bamber Gascoigne's *Share My Lettuce*, and she knew how much work it took to transform a university revue into a successful commercial show. The Edinburgh show was only an hour long. The new show would need to be much longer, and not all the Edinburgh material was up to scratch. 'The show was badly put together and their attitude was typically undergraduate,' she concluded. 'To reach any sort of London standard, they would have to work hard.' [7] Fazan realised the cast's rebellious nature was integral to the show, but she wondered whether such free spirits would be willing to put in the necessary hard graft. She needn't have worried. The cast worked hard. Rehearsing in her flat in Eaton Place, in Belgravia, they started to knock the show into shape.

Fazan proved accomplished at balancing these four powerful, competing egos, and she found Donaldson to be a supportive and sympathetic producer. He was happy to sit in on rehearsals, but only when invited. 'He'd give an intelligent and sensitive appraisal that was always encouraging. He seemed almost embarrassed to intrude.' [8] Bennett bears this out. 'Willie was never condescending as Albery invariably was and seemed as much at sea in the world of show business as we were.' [9] Donaldson was a friend, albeit an unreliable and inconstant one. Albery was aloof and domineering. As Fazan recalls, he could reduce Donaldson to 'a stuttering schoolboy'. [10] On one occasion, at a meeting with Donald Albery and Donald Langdon, Bennett enraged Albery merely by using his Christian name. Bennett had in fact been addressing Langdon. Albery had assumed that Bennett was talking to him, and was outraged that a mere performer had the audacity to address a producer by his first name. It would have made a fine sketch in *Beyond The Fringe*.

Thankfully, these spats had scant impact on rehearsals. Incredibly, the cast came up with sixty sketches, which were whittled down to thirty-five. Of the twenty sketches in the Edinburgh show, only twelve survived. Among the new sketches were 'The Sadder and Wiser Beaver' (Peter's left-wing dig at the hypocrisy of liberal journalists on Lord Beaverbrook's conservative newspapers) and 'Black Equals White' (Peter's right-wing dig at the hypocrisy of African independence leaders). Peter was always happy to mock both left and right.

The new version of the show opened at the Arts Theatre in Cambridge on 21 April. The curtain went up at eight p.m. It didn't come down until after midnight. 'It was riotous,' [11] remembered Bassett. The show went well all week. Many of the people who saw the show at the Arts Theatre were Cambridge undergraduates, like John Cleese, then a 21-year-old student at Downing College. 'It remains the funniest show I've ever seen in my life,' [12] he said. 'It just seemed the natural content of comedy, the sort of things that you would make jokes about.' [13] Another future comic who saw the show at the Arts Theatre was Tony Hendra, who went on to play 'Ian Faith' in the spoof rockumentary *Spinal Tap*. 'When I went up to Cambridge University in the early 1960s it was to complete my studies as a Benedictine monk,' he recalled. 'But then I bought a ticket for *Beyond The Fringe*. I went into the show a monk, and I emerged having completely lost my vocation. I didn't know things could be so funny. I didn't realise that authority was so absurd. The next day I went round to the Footlights Club and asked if I could join.' [14] Clearly, this was a show with the power to change the course of people's lives. Yet for Peter in particular, it was merely preaching to the converted. Cambridge was his home crowd. Brighton would prove a stiffer test, and a better indicator of the show's prospects. Would their student humour play so well in the real world?

As professional performers, accustomed to appeasing paying punters, Peter and Dudley were reluctant to perform the show's more controversial sketches in Brighton. They were wise to be wary. Back then, Brighton was a lot more prim and proper than it is today. It had a strong conservative streak that was at odds with its kiss-me-quick image, and one of its bastions of conservatism was the Theatre Royal. 'Its Victorian theatre has always been a notoriously difficult place to play in,' wrote Ronald Bergan in his history of *Beyond The Fringe*. [15] 'The audiences usually consist of retired people or holidaymakers desirous of seeing a bedroom farce starring some mediocre TV personality.' As Alan Bennett put it, 'One of the chief pleasures of going to the theatre in Brighton is leaving it.' [16]

With respectable day jobs to fall back on, Alan and Jonathan were less timid than Peter or Dudley. However, their confidence was confounded on the first night [17] and throughout the week that followed. 'The seats were going up like pistol shots throughout the performance,' recalled Bennett. 'Come the curtain, there were scarcely more people in the audience than there were on the stage.' [18] The sketch that inspired most walk-outs was 'Aftermyth of War', a send-up of patriotic British war films. By modern standards it was pretty tame, the sort of skit you might see performed by Armstrong and Miller, but only fifteen years after the Second World War it inevitably felt a lot more raw. Someone started a slow handclap, and Bennett was roundly hissed for his stiff-legged impersonation of Douglas Bader, the fighter pilot who lost his legs in the Battle of Britain. 'You young bounders don't know anything about it,' [19] yelled an indignant heckler on his way out. 'We were not mocking anybody who'd been brave during the war,' said Peter. 'It was just the movies.' [20] Still, even their cinematic satire touched a nerve. 'No doubt I shall be told that their real target is the films about the battle,' wrote the theatre critic from the *Brighton & Hove Herald*. 'My answer is that most of those who endured the battle overhead thought the films were a worthy tribute to the "Few" who won it.' [21] 'I look back on it with some guilt,' conceded Miller. 'It was funny at the time, but looking back I can understand why people who had fought in the war, or who had relatives who had laid down their lives, were upset.' [22]

It wasn't just that sketch which roused the *Herald* critic's ire. 'If you think that four bright young university men on the stage without feminine assistance, scenery, change of costume or an orchestra would find it hard to keep me amused for a whole evening with material they have written themselves,' he wrote, 'you would be right.' [23] It was a succinct and comprehensive summary of all the things that made *Beyond The Fringe* so special, but for Brighton it was a bridge too far. 'The satire has as much sting as a blancmange,' [24] concluded the *Herald*'s answer to Kenneth Tynan. Fittingly, it transpired that this theatre critic was a Tory, a Boy Scout leader and a leading light in Brighton's Civil Defence – hence his disparaging remarks about Peter's inspired send-up of the Four-Minute Warning: 'Some people have said, "Oh, my goodness me! Four minutes? That is not a very long time!" Well, I would remind those doubters that some people in this great country of ours can run a mile in four minutes.' In the theatre critic of the *Herald*, *Beyond The Fringe* had found an archetypal bogeyman. The fact that it could annoy this sort of person was actually a good sign.

It didn't seem that way at the time. Albery's interest in *Beyond The Fringe* had always been pragmatic. When the show had been the toast of Edinburgh he'd been keen to buy a slice of it. Now that it was stiffing, he was quite prepared to cut his losses. There would be no West End transfer – not to any of *his* theatres, at any rate. Fortunately, help was at hand in the unlikely shape of Anna Deere Wiman, an

American who owned the Fortune, one of London's smaller West End theatres. She came down to Brighton to see the show with her lawyer, David Jacobs, who also did some business as a showbiz agent and promoter. Jacobs expressed an interest. He represented Bernard Cribbins, who'd been playing the Fortune Theatre since October in a revue called *And Another Thing*. The show was due to close for a few weeks and then reopen with new material. Committed to renting the theatre in the interim, Jacobs was looking for a cheap show (no stars, small cast, no costly sets or costumes) to mitigate his overheads until Cribbins was ready to return. *Beyond The Fringe* fitted the bill, but that wasn't much of an endorsement. 'He thought the show was so bad it would keep the Fortune warm,' said Donaldson. 'He thought it would run for about six weeks.' [25]

At least they'd got a West End transfer (of a sort) and earned the show a brief reprieve but, battered by their week in Brighton, the cast were nervous about the prospect of even this modest London run. Donaldson brought the photographer Lewis Morley down to Brighton to take some publicity photos. He took a moody shot of them beneath the pier, looking suitably pensive. Even this single photo demonstrates what a different sort of show this was. Dressed in dark suits and framed against a grid of girders, glaring rather than grinning at the camera, fifty years later it still looks avant-garde, more like a still from *Reservoir Dogs* than a promo for a theatrical revue. The cast look like a pop group rather than a cabaret troupe. The similarities with Astrid Kirchner's arty photos of the Beatles are uncanny. Back in London, Morley took some more photos of the cast, including a wonderful shot in London Zoo, below a sign that read The British Owls. Peter, Dudley and Jonathan are all doing decent owl impressions (Dudley's is especially good). Only Alan declined to join in. They finished up on a derelict industrial site in Acton ('appropriately stark and gritty,' [26] wrote Alan). These weren't conventional publicity shots for a conventional revue. This was something new.

Morley's photos set the tone for the publicity that followed, but there was still time for one last cock-up, when the cast appeared on the BBC TV programme *Tonight* to do an interview and perform an extract from 'Aftermyth of War'. Bennett wondered why his stiff-legged Douglas Bader impression received such a muted reception, until the interviewer appeared – Kenneth Allsop, who'd lost a leg serving in the RAF during the war.

After the dress rehearsal, on Tuesday, 9 May, Donaldson treated the cast to a blue movie – a rather more risqué enterprise in those days than today. [27] He took them to a brothel in Bond Street. John Bassett, Wendy and Jonathan's wife Rachel all came along. The middle-aged 'maid' who answered the door was reluctant to let them in – she was shocked by how young Alan Bennett looked although, ironically, he was actually the oldest member of the party. But eventually she relented, and they were escorted upstairs (she had to tell them to keep the noise down – their nervous laughter was putting the previous punter off his stride). Finally, they were led into a pink greaseproofed boudoir containing a bed, a dressing table and a French prostitute. She set up an ancient film projector and showed them a black and white porn film. Bassett thought it was made in Egypt. Wendy thought it starred a Frenchman. Jonathan thought the participants were Cubans. After half a century, he could still recall that they kept their socks on.

Bassett claimed Bennett was so embarrassed that he crawled under the bed – a claim Bennett denied (Wendy says he merely stuffed a hanky into his mouth to stifle his shrieks). The Millers provided a running commentary – 'If he does that again, he'll certainly do damage to the *symphysis pubis*' [28] – which kept Peter and Dudley in stitches. Shocked and horrified, Wendy hid her face. After the show was over, they were asked to leave one by one, so as not to arouse suspicion.

It sounds like an excruciating – and thoroughly unerotic – experience. With admirable honesty, Wendy admitted that she found the whole thing deeply upsetting. 'I wouldn't let Peter touch me for some days afterwards,' she recalled. 'I thought it so utterly cheap and denigrating of an act I thought was a very private affair.' [29] It's a revealing illustration of what a different world we all lived in before *Beyond The Fringe*. Britain was about to become less censorious and less innocent. For better or worse, the moral climate was about to change. Arriving midway between the advent of the contraceptive pill and the birth of Beatlemania, [30] *Beyond The Fringe* would be a catalyst for this explosion. The next day, Wednesday, 10 May, the cast reassembled in the Fortune Theatre to find a telegram from Donaldson. 'Good luck tonight, girls,' cabled their producer. 'You may not be good but at least you are cheap!'

Peter and Dudley with Alan Bennett and Jonathan Miller in *Beyond The Fringe*.

CHAPTER NINE

BEYOND THE FRINGE

'Beyond The Fringe first fell upon London like a sweet refreshing rain on 10 May 1961. It must have been St Jonathan's Day, because it rained satire thereafter, day and night, harder and harder, spreading outwards from London to cover the whole of the British Isles in one steady downpour of soaking jokes, until, as Peter Cook said, the entire realm seemed about to sink sniggering beneath the watery main.'

(Michael Frayn, *The Complete Beyond The Fringe*)

Brighton had been a false alarm. The first night was a triumph. The next morning, the *Daily Express* ran an ecstatic review by Bernard Levin. 'The theatre came of age last night,' he wrote. 'On the tiny stage of the tiny Fortune Theatre erupted a review so brilliant, adult, hard-boiled, accurate, merciless, witty, unexpected, alive, exhilarating, cleansing, right, true and good that my first conscious thought as I stumbled, weak and sick with laughter, up the stairs at the end was one of gratitude.' [1] Yet it was what Levin said about satire which set the tone for the show's enduring reputation. 'Satirical revue in this country has been, until now, basically cowardly,' he argued. 'First, it has picked on easy targets. Second, however hard it hit the targets (and it rarely hit them at all, let alone in the middle), it left its audience alone, to leave the theatre as fat and complacent as it came in. This sorry tale went on for so long that some of us began to despair of the form itself. We believed that satirical revue was impossible in this country. And now we know we were wrong.' [2] The satire in *Beyond The Fringe* was 'real, barbed, deeply planted and aimed at things and people that need it.' [3] Among the things that needed it (and here Levin provided a helpful hit list) were patriotism, capital punishment, Shakespeare and the clergy. *Beyond The Fringe* put all of these sacred cows to the sword. Peter's impression of Macmillan was singled out for special praise, as 'one of the most diabolically clever pieces of political comment ever created.' [4] Even the paying punters weren't spared. 'The final target, the real victim, the ultimate object of the whole proceedings, is the audience,' concluded Levin. 'It is they who feel the final punch, the last twist of the knife.' [5] Half a lifetime later, Levin's passion remained undimmed. 'It was not just a string of jokes,' he said. 'They'd moved laughter onto another plane.' [6]

Levin's rave review was no surprise. His shrieks of laughter on the first night were so loud and penetrating that they threatened to disrupt the performance – during the interval, the cast even discussed whether there was anything they could do to shut him up. The other critics weren't quite so raucous, but their reviews were almost as enthusiastic. The *Evening Standard*'s Milton Shulman called the show 'provocative and uncompromising'. Felix Barber of the *Evening News* called it 'the perfect revue'. *The Times* and the *Telegraph* were both complimentary, but the most illuminating review came from the *Guardian*'s John Rosselli, who likened *Beyond The Fringe* to the 'Miscellany' column in the *Guardian*. The author of 'Miscellany' was Alan Bennett's old National Service comrade (and comic collaborator) Michael Frayn.

Frayn went to see the show on the second night, and subsequently described it as 'the official opening of the Satirical Sixties'. [7] One memory stood out. Sitting in front of him that night were a young couple whom Frayn took for Tories. They laughed and laughed until Peter started his Macmillan sketch. 'I say!' whispered the young man to his girlfriend, clearly horrified. 'This is supposed to be the Prime Minister!' [8] They watched the rest of the show in silence. Clearly, this was shocking stuff. 'I predict it will cause a sensation,' wrote Pearson Phillips in the *Daily Mail*. 'Between them they carve up a clutch of sacred British institutions – the National Anthem, the "Few", Civil Defence, Mr Macmillan and the Church of England. And then suddenly they stifle our laughter, stuffing it down our throats with some vicious sweep of wit which has the audience gasping.' [9] Phillips was right. This was a show that would divide the country, into Britain old and new.

The divisive potential of this brave new revue was encapsulated in two contrasting notices in the Sunday papers, written by the two most influential theatre critics in the land. Harold Hobson and Kenneth Tynan could hardly have been less alike. Hobson was in his late fifties, cultured and conservative. Fittingly, he wrote for the cultured and conservative *Sunday Times*. Tynan was in his mid-thirties, young enough to be Hobson's son. His weekly column appeared in the more liberal *Observer*. For anyone under forty, it was required reading. 'He writes about acting and the theatre as if he were a sports commentator,' [10] wrote Simon Callow, who should know.

Having seen *Beyond The Fringe* in Edinburgh, Hobson had dismissed it in four words of (rather muted) approval. Now, writing at greater length, he was similarly restrained. 'Four young men, till recently undergraduates in Oxford,' he wrote (inaccurately) 'give an entertainment securely founded in their conviction of their natural superiority to all that they discuss, attack or caricature. Their cleverness is such that not once does it occur to us to ask if this feeling of superiority is justified.' [11] Hobson devoted the rest of his review to praising Jonathan Miller, whom he'd praised when he made his West End debut in *Out of The Blue*, seven years before. Then he'd been on the money. Now he was behind the times. It was Tynan, not Hobson, who was the voice of the *Beyond The Fringe* generation. Five years before, Tynan had heralded a revolution in British theatre by declaring (pretentiously, but memorably) that he could never love anyone who hadn't seen *Look Back In Anger*. Would he now herald this revolution in British revue?

He would indeed. 'Future historians may well thank me for providing them with a full account of the moment when English comedy took its first decisive step into the second half of the twentieth century,' wrote Tynan. 'It has no slick coffee-bar scenery, no glib one-line blackouts, no twirling dancers in tight trousers, no sad ballets for fisherwomen clad in fishnet stockings.' [12] Tynan praised Dudley's piano playing (spotting the similarity to Erroll Garner) and Peter's park-bench monologue (spotting the similarity to Harold Pinter). He also spotted something that had escaped the other critics – the show was subversive, but it wasn't really all that radical. It ridiculed the powers that be, but it didn't set out to overthrow them. '*Beyond The Fringe* is anti-reactionary without being progressive,' concluded Tynan. 'It goes less far than one could have hoped, but immeasurably farther than one had any right to expect.' [13] It was the headline above his review which attracted most attention: 'English Satire Advances Into The Sixties.'

As satire became that year's buzzword and then, rapidly, that year's cliché, the cast were at pains to point out that they weren't actually trying to be satirical. 'None of us approached the world with a satirical indignation,' said Miller. 'We had no reason to. We were all very comfortably off, and doing very nicely. Alan was all set to be an academic at Oxford, Dudley was doing very well as a jazz musician – and Peter and I came from professional middle-class families anyway, and had nothing to complain of.' [14] Miller said *Beyond The Fringe* was merely 'mildly cynical'. [15] He said Tynan had shoved a satirical banner into their hands.

In fact, Tynan never mentioned the word 'satire' in his revue. Its sole appearance was in the headline, written by an anonymous sub-editor. If anyone had shoved a satirical banner into their hands, it was that nameless sub-editor, or maybe Bernard Levin. Whoever started it, Miller was quite right that 'the satire boom' was a largely journalistic construct, an umbrella term for various irreverent attitudes, few of which were truly satirical in the strict sense of the word. But, as the certainties of the Second World War receded, after ten years of Tory rule, there was clearly an appetite for satire, and an appetite for discussing it. Miller subsequently added his twopennyworth to the debate, writing a provocative article for the *Observer*, entitled 'Can English Satire Draw Blood?'

Satire or no satire, the cast could sense that they were onto something. 'There was an intensity of laughter which made us feel that something strange and rather special had happened,' [16] said Miller. Suddenly they were celebrities. A new door had opened onto a different world. A reporter from the *Daily Herald* took them to the Caprice, London's most fashionable showbiz restaurant, to interview them for the paper. They'd been told there'd be a Rolls-Royce waiting to collect them afterwards, but they couldn't quite believe it. 'Gosh!' yelled Miller, when they emerged. 'It really is a Rolls!' [17] Their daily lives didn't change overnight. Bennett was still lecturing at Oxford, and Miller still rode his Lambretta to hospital every morning to perform his post-mortems. However, the show had now acquired its own momentum, which would soon sweep medicine and academia away.

Alerted by the rave reviews, the rest of the media were quick off the mark. Only a week after the first night, Parlophone did a recording at the Fortune and brought out a *Beyond The Fringe* LP, produced by George Martin (who'd produced Dudley's first jazz record, *Strictly For The Birds*). The advantage (or disadvantage) of this record was that it enabled pub bores to learn the entire show off by heart. Michael Billington recalled how people would recite whole sketches, word for word, at parties. Like The Goons, *Beyond The Fringe* had acquired the true mark of comic greatness – it had spawned its own comedy nerds.

The LP spread the word to a younger generation who were unable to get along to the Fortune to see the show in person. 'To find ourselves laughing at things like the clichés of war heroism was an illicit pleasure to boys for whom the style, and indeed syllabus, of their education was firmly rooted in the past,' remembered Michael Palin, who was then a sixth-former at Shrewsbury School (a few years behind Christopher Booker, Richard Ingrams and Willie Rushton – the three Salopians who started *Private Eye*). 'With *Beyond The Fringe*, comedy came in from the end of the pier and out of the chummy comfort of the BBC studios and sank its teeth hard and deep into the fleshy buttocks of the British establishment.' [18] As Palin observed, the show's subversive power stemmed from its establishment credentials. The kitchen-sink plays that shook up the theatre were written by outsiders. Unlike *Look Back In Anger*, *Beyond The Fringe* came from the inside. 'At my boarding school, the authorities didn't quite know what to do when the show became a bestselling record,' recalled Christopher Hitchens, who was then a pupil at the Leys, a public school in Cambridge. 'The players were Oxbridge types, after all, and the Edinburgh Festival was "culture."' [19] Hitchens and Palin soon became 'Oxbridge types' themselves. Hitchens carried the irreverent intelligence of *Beyond The Fringe* into journalism, Palin carried its absurdism into television and the movies. Before the decade was out, *Monty Python* fans would be reciting Palin's sketches, word for word.

Back at the Fortune, *Beyond The Fringe* was selling out every night. Though the show had ended up here quite by chance, this venue was its ideal home. The Fortune was big enough and grand enough to feel like a proper West End theatre – in a more informal space, their iconoclastic sketches wouldn't have seemed so daring. Yet in one of Albery's bigger theatres, the show wouldn't have felt so immediate. With just 440 seats, the Fortune was small enough to feel compact and confidential – essential ingredients for such an intimate revue.

Still, even 440 seats eight times a week soon adds up to an awful lot of money. Belatedly, the cast realised that their paltry £75 each only amounted to a small slice of the weekly take. 'Albery and myself were pocketing £2,000 every Friday,' [20] recollected Donaldson. The cast asked Donaldson for a better deal. He said the matter was out of his hands. They wrote to Albery, requesting a meeting. Albery invited them to tea. 'Over seed cake and Earl Grey he patiently explained the economics of the theatre,' recalled Donaldson. '"Difficult times, rising costs, laundry, bricks and mortar, the successes have to pay for the flops. Review the situation when I return from Juan les Pins in late September. Have another cup of tea."' [21]

By now, *Beyond The Fringe* was not just the show to see but the show to be seen at – a rather awkward accolade for a satirical (or even mildly cynical) revue. The Home Secretary, Rab Butler, and his fellow cabinet minister, Iain Macleod, both came to see it, closely followed by the target of Peter's 'TVPM' monologue, the Prime Minister, Harold Macmillan. The performance passed off without incident, until 'TVPM'. Even as it stood, Peter's Prime Ministerial spoof was considered very daring. To perform it in front of the Prime Minister himself was audacious indeed. But Peter went one further. 'When I've a spare evening, there's nothing I like better than to wander over to a theatre,' he ad-libbed, pointing out Macmillan in the audience, 'and sit there listening to a group of sappy, urgent, vibrant young satirists with a stupid great grin spread all over my silly old face.' [22] 'Macmillan buried his face in his programme, and the audience, out of embarrassment, gradually froze,' recalled Bennett. 'Peter has a kind of madness on stage. His performance would often be quite dangerous, on the edge of embarrassment.' [23] That evening his performance went right over the edge and disappeared into the abyss, but Peter didn't seem to mind. Indifferent to the stunned silence that had fallen over the auditorium, he ploughed on without a care. 'We were standing in the wings, absolutely horror-struck by his peculiar suicidal bravery,' [24] said Miller. 'Is Peter Cook the best Prime Minister we've got?' [25] asked the press. Macmillan subsequently said he'd much enjoyed 'TVPM' – though, cannily, he claimed he hadn't heard much of the actual content. The ease with which he was able to appropriate Peter's lampoon and exploit it as an example of his good sportsmanship was one more instance of a common problem that has confounded generations of English comics. Less enlightened nations torture satirists. England embraces them, and smothers them. 'Castration by adoption,' [26] as Miller put it in his *Observer* polemic, 'Can English Satire Draw Blood?'

Within a year of its West End opening, *Beyond The Fringe* had become a favourite pastime of the very people it set out to mock. 'Each night, before curtain-up, sleek Bentleys evacuate a glittering load into the foyer,' [27] rued Miller. For a politician, to go along and laugh at it was seen as proof that you didn't take yourself too seriously. 'Long before the end of its run it had suffered the inevitable fate reserved in England for rebels,' concluded Bernard Levin, 'namely affectionate absorption into the bosom of the Establishment that they are supposed to be out to destroy.' [28] Levin was slightly overstating things, as usual. Nobody in *Beyond The Fringe* was out to destroy the Establishment (least of all Dudley, who was terrified of offending anyone) but providing PR opportunities for the PM and his cronies wasn't quite what they had in mind. This paradox reached its surreal climax when the Queen came to see the show, unwittingly participating in a bizarre *coup de théâtre* when Dudley played the National Anthem (as part of the opening sketch, 'Steppes In The Right Direction') and then speculated about the possible presence of royalty in the auditorium (as part of the subsequent sketch, 'The Royal Box'). The Queen was accompanied by Sir Alec Douglas Home, the Tory laird who would soon succeed Macmillan as Prime Minister. What had started out as a ragbag of amateur skits, performed for student friends at college Smokers, was now being seen by the most eminent people in the land.

Forewarned of Her Majesty's impending visit, the show's management asked Bennett to cut a line from his sketch about corporal punishment which featured the word 'erection.' 'I priggishly refused,' he recalled. 'I cringe to think of it today. I suppose I must be one of the few people who have said "erection" in front of the Queen. I wish I hadn't. I don't suppose either of us profited from the experience.' [29] Bennett was too modest. Far from being priggish, his refusal to censor his performance to save the monarch's blushes was actually rather noble, and just as fearless, in its own quiet way, as Peter's more voluble assault on the Prime Minister. The Queen 'laughed heartily' [30] at *Beyond The Fringe*, particularly at 'TVPM'. 'It proves we haven't been doing our job properly,' [31] said Miller, but it was quite an accolade, nonetheless. *Beyond The Fringe* changed British theatre. It even changed British culture. However, the visit of the Prime Minister and Head of State to the best satirical revue in living memory was proof (if any further proof was needed) that no satire, however clever, could ever trouble the status quo.

Dudley, on the other hand, was completely indifferent to these conundrums. He was far too busy enjoying himself, onstage and in the wings. Miller marvelled at his 'Pan-like capacity to enchant the ladies.' [32] As Bennett recalled, 'his performance on the stage was often merely a perfunctory interruption of the more prolonged and energetic performance going on in his dressing room.' [33] Thankfully, not all his liaisons were quite so fleeting. He went steady for a while with Anna Leroy, who was appearing in the chorus line of Lionel Bart's *Oliver!* But he was utterly incapable of settling down. 'The ability to enjoy your sex life is central,' he declared. 'I don't give a shit about anything else. My obsession is total. What else is there to live for? Chinese food and women. There is nothing else.' [34]

But there was something else. There was music. Despite performing every evening, he somehow still found time to write the music for four more stage shows: a Royal Court production of *The Fire Raisers* by Max Frisch, an RSC production of Bertolt Brecht's *The Caucasian Chalk Circle*, a ballet called *The Owl and The Pussycat* (based on the nonsense poem by Edward Lear) and *England Our*

England, a new revue by Keith Waterhouse and Willis Hall. *England Our England* was especially gruelling. The show was set to open up north, prior to a West End transfer, and after the curtain came down on *Beyond The Fringe*, Dudley would sometimes drive as far as Hull or Wolverhampton to meet up with the cast. He'd write and rehearse there the next morning, making last-minute changes to the score, then drive back to London in time for curtain-up that evening. *Beyond The Fringe* had become his day job. Playing the fool was fun, but music was still where his passion lay.

Yet despite his best efforts, none of these shows was a great success. Working on *The Fire Raisers*, he fell out with the director, Lindsay Anderson. Despite their happy associations in the past, they never worked together again. Working on *The Caucasian Chalk Circle*, he felt unloved by the director, William Gaskill. 'Gaskill didn't like anything I wrote, and kept asking me to change it,' [35] he said. Despite some success up north, *England Our England* flopped in the West End. *The Owl and The Pussycat* was a modest hit, but nothing to compare with *Beyond The Fringe*.

The Owl and The Pussycat and *England Our England* were both collaborations with Gillian Lynne, a dancer turned choreographer who went on to mastermind hit shows like *Cats*. Half a lifetime later, with a string of blockbusters behind her, she still described Dudley as the most important influence in her life. 'I think of Dudley as a quite brilliant composer,' [36] she said. 'All my grasp of jazz phrasing I learned from Dudley. It was a tragedy that he stopped composing and became a star.' [37] Yet, like writers of every ilk, Dudley was always glad of any excuse to put off the job in hand. 'I'd have to sit him down and make him write,' [38] said Lynne. 'Can't we just go to the pictures?' [39] he'd ask her, when they were up against a deadline. Yet when the chips were down he'd put the hours in, even though he always left it until the last moment.

On top of all this, Dudley was still performing with his jazz trio – not only in jazz clubs but also on TV in a weekly variety series called *Strictly For The Birds* (after his first jazz record). The series was made by Southern, the ITV broadcaster based in Southampton, and he had to drive down there every Friday night to record the show, after performing in *Beyond The Fringe*. He'd drive back to London in time for the Saturday matinee the next day, do another show that evening, and then drive over to Dagenham to see his parents for Sunday lunch the next day.

This roller-coaster ride came to an abrupt halt when Hugo Boyd, Dudley's bass player, was killed in a car crash in the South of France. This accident affected Dudley deeply. Boyd was just 26, the same age as Dudley. Dudley played the organ at the funeral, at Golders Green Crematorium, revealing a spiritual side which rarely surfaced in his daily life. 'I felt he was there as I played,' said Dudley. 'Hugo had gone but his spirit was with us.' [40] Dudley reformed the trio, with Peter McGurk on double bass, but Boyd's death had shaken him, and it left a shadow on his memory. A lot of Dudley's contemporaries sailed through the 1960s on a wave of optimism, but his childhood had taught him to be more pessimistic. This was a reminder, rather than a realisation, of just how fragile life could be.

Signed off from *Beyond The Fringe* for three weeks, suffering from acute exhaustion, Dudley flew out to Portofino for a much-needed break, handing over his role to the musical actor Robin Ray. In the lounge at Heathrow he was buttonholed by John Gielgud, who'd seen him in *Beyond The Fringe*. In a small but significant way, it felt like a transforming moment. Dudley was no longer a mere civilian, a short-arsed wannabe from Dagenham. He was now a fully paid-up member of the freemasonry of famous luvvies. Like being an Old Boy of a major public school, membership of this clique would open doors. When Gielgud found out where Dudley was going, he gave him a letter of introduction to his old friend, the German actress Lilli Palmer, who lived in Portofino. Flattered to have been recognised by one of the great actors of the age, Dudley said goodbye to Gielgud and boarded the plane. On board, Dudley's curiosity got the better of him. He opened Gielgud's letter. 'Darling Lilli,' Gielgud had written. 'This is to introduce the brilliant young pianist from *Beyond The Fringe*, Stanley Moon.' It was a timely reality check. Dudley was famous, but he wasn't all that famous. Dudley kept Gielgud's note as a memento, but he never called on Lilli Palmer. He was too embarrassed to admit to her that Gielgud had got his name wrong.

Dudley was happy to retell this story, but Peter found it particularly funny and adopted Gielgud's malapropism as Dudley's new nickname. Like a lot of his jokes about Dudley, it was first cracked in affection but repetition made it grate. As it turned out, the incident had a curious prophetic quality. Dudley's character in *Bedazzled*, Peter and Dudley's finest film, was christened Stanley Moon, but the movie wasn't the big hit that it should have been. Conversely, when Dudley was reunited with Gielgud in *Arthur* (an inferior movie) both men triumphed. It was a triumph that Peter would never share, but *Beyond The Fringe* had a more lasting legacy. It changed a lot of people's lives. 'It made me want to be a comedian,' said Eric Idle, speaking for countless others like him. 'I never realised before that you could laugh at everything that oppressed you.' [41]

Peter outside The Establishment.

CHAPTER TEN

THE ESTABLISHMENT

RUSSELL HARTY: What would you like to be when you
grow up?

PETER COOK: A little boy. [1]

Peter had wanted to open a satirical nightclub ever since his visit to the Porcupine Club in Berlin. 'I thought it was a pipe dream,' said his friend from Cambridge, Nicholas Luard. 'I never thought it would happen.' [2] For Peter it was no fantasy, but he feared someone else would get it together long before him. 'It seemed such an obvious idea,' [3] he said, but all the best ideas seem obvious to the people who are bright enough to think of them. Four years after his gap-year trip to Germany, *Beyond The Fringe* had given him the resources to realise his ambition. Pleasantly surprised to find the coast still clear, he started scouting around for premises.

Peter soon found somewhere suitable – a bankrupt strip club called the Tropicana which had shut down after a police raid. It was seedy and derelict. It stank of stale beer. For Peter, it was perfect. He sent a telegram to Luard who was on holiday in Mexico. 'Have premises,' cabled Peter. 'Come home.' Luard came home. Initially, he didn't share Peter's enthusiasm. Littered with used condoms and discarded G-strings, they were the least appealing premises he'd ever seen. However, the place was cheap and empty, and its location, on Greek Street, in the heart of Soho, was ideal. Then as now, Soho was a seductive blend of style and sleaze. Cafes and restaurants, clip joints and knocking shops – from delis to dirty bookshops, all human life was there. Its spivs and prostitutes gave it a whiff of danger. Its artists and piss artists gave it an air of run-down glamour. It was a bohemian enclave, a refuge from conformity and, conveniently, it was just a short walk from the Fortune Theatre. This was a place where Peter could come and let rip after hours.

Unlike the Fortune Theatre, Peter's venue would be a private members' club, putting it beyond the reach of the Lord Chamberlain who maintained the right to censor anything and everything presented on the public stage, even the angle of a ladder. 'Until one could escape his bloodshot gaze, there was no real hope of putting the last edge on the satirical scalpel,' [4] wrote Jonathan Miller in his *Observer* essay, 'Can English Satire Draw Blood?' Behind closed doors, free from these restrictions, performers at Peter's new club could go much further than *Beyond The Fringe*. 'European satire thrived best under the old-fashioned, indolently repressive regimes in which offensive comment was punished by short terms of imprisonment rather than by execution,' [5] wrote Miller in the *Observer*. Peter faced little danger of imprisonment, let alone execution, but the financial perils were real. He had to stump up a hefty premium to insure the club for libel. Yet by the end of June he'd already taken up residence, posing for photographers in the street outside. Dressed in a smart and sombre suit, he looked more like a prosperous young stockbroker than a nightclub proprietor.

'All Girl Strip Revue,' read the sign above the door. A new sign soon replaced it. 'London's first satirical nightclub.'

The name that Peter chose for his new club was inspired. Peter told Clive James it was the only good title he'd ever thought of. 'The Establishment' was a phrase popularised in 1955 by the *Spectator* columnist Henry Fairlie to describe the invisible web of contacts which ensured that a small unelected cabal – mainly upper-class men from the same families, public schools and Oxbridge colleges – maintained control of the most powerful institutions in the country. To appropriate this term as the title of a satirical nightclub was a joke that worked on several levels. Soho was a world away (yet just a short walk away) from posh gentlemen's clubs like White's where members of the Establishment would gather. Incognito, many members of the Establishment were no strangers to fleshpots like the Tropicana. Would the audience – and the performers – at Peter's club be Establishment insiders or outsiders? Was Peter (Radley and Cambridge) a poacher or a gamekeeper? A bit of both, which was what made it such a good idea.

Peter's business partner Nicholas Luard had been the treasurer of Footlights. Luard was a public schoolboy, like Peter, but his background was a good deal grander. He'd gone to Winchester (like Willie Donaldson) and had done his National Service as an officer in the Coldstream Guards in Germany. In Germany and in France (where he'd spent a year in Paris, at the Sorbonne) he'd seen some political cabaret, like Peter. Like Peter, he could sense The Establishment was an idea whose time had come. 'The post-war world we'd grown up in was breaking down,' recalled Luard. 'Sotheby's and Christie's belonged to the world of street-corner pawnbrokers. The great merchant banks, like Barings, were incompetently run moneylenders, loan sharks masquerading under fine names. We looked at our world, we found it comic and grubby – we thought we might change it a bit.' [6] Luard was not a comic, but he was a kindred spirit. He and Peter formed a limited company, Cook & Luard Productions. 'I imagined he was a financial wizard,' said Peter. 'He also had a bit of money.' [7] Twenty thousand pounds, to be precise – his inheritance from a trust fund.

As it turned out, Peter's confidence in Luard's financial wizardry was rather over-optimistic, but initially that didn't matter. Audaciously, Peter advertised membership of the club at two guineas a year in advance, three thereafter or twenty guineas for life. The Establishment was still a hollow shell, but 7,000 people signed up – more than half of them before the club opened, which pretty much paid for all the building work. Members ranged from high-minded luminaries like Isaiah Berlin, Graham Greene, Somerset Maugham, Yehudi Menuhin and J.B. Priestley to showbiz figures like Lionel Bart (creator of the hit musical *Oliver!*) and Brian Rix and Ben Travers (authors of farces, old and new). Clearly, Britain's fresh thirst for satire ranged from highbrow to middlebrow, and all points in between. Every new member was rewarded with a complimentary poster of Harold Macmillan. Peter really should have given him free membership after all he'd done to promote Britain's newest industry, the satire boom.

Sean Kenny, the Irish stage designer who'd designed the set for *Beyond The Fringe*, was recruited to redesign the interior in a similarly spartan style. He replaced the thick drapes and plastic chandeliers with bare wood, glass and steel. In September Peter presented The Establishment to the press, posing for photographers in a Harold Macmillan mask. The humour wouldn't be left-wing, he explained, but since the Tories were in power they were bound to be the main target. 'Attacking the Labour Party at the moment seems a bit like robbing a blind man.' [8] There would be an hour's cabaret every evening at nine-thirty, performed by members of the resident company: John Bird and John Fortune (the directors of Peter's 1959 and 1960 Footlights revues) plus three regular thespians – Jeremy Geidt, David Walsh and Hazel Wright. They were soon joined by John Wells, who'd been the star of the Oxford Revue at the Edinburgh Festival that summer, and was now working as a schoolmaster at Eton. Peter heard about his success in Edinburgh and sent him a telegram inviting him along to The Establishment. When Wells arrived it was still a building site, full of people sawing and hammering. Peter was a year younger than Wells (to the day – they shared the same birthday) but to Wells he seemed a lot older. 'He was wearing a suit, while everybody else wore sweaters and gym shoes,' [9] recalled Wells. 'I remember the formal way he shook hands, very English and polite.' [10] Despite his scholastic duties, Wells agreed to play the opening night.

Peter planned to come along every night after he'd finished at the Fortune, to try out new material in an impromptu late-night show. He wanted the other three to join him ('The boys will come in from *Beyond The Fringe* to perform at half past midnight,' [11] promised the *Evening Standard*, prematurely) but Alan and Jonathan didn't fancy it. However, Dudley agreed to play the piano in the basement with his jazz trio. 'We paid him a ludicrously small wage,' said Peter, 'but he was surrounded by the best-looking birds in London.' [12] Jonathan agreed to appear in a couple of short films (to be shown between live sketches) including a superb parody of a cigarette commercial, playing a chain-smoking surgeon operating on a patient with lung cancer, puffing on a filter tip through his surgical mask. Only Alan played no part – as well as performing at the Fortune, he was still holding down a postgrad job at Oxford. 'Alan Bennett is really behind the catering,' [13] Peter told the press. Working flat out, Peter got the club ready just in time for the grand opening in October but belatedly he realised that, having sold advance subscriptions to more than four thousand people, he was powerless to prevent them all turning up on the first night. Having drummed up heaps of publicity, Peter was left in the absurd position of trying to dissuade people from coming. Gamely, he told the press that he hoped some punters would be small enough to stack in tiers.

Behind the scenes there were more pressing problems to deal with. 'The Kray Twins came round when we were just about to open,' remembered Peter. 'They said, "It's a very nice place you've got here ... It would be dreadful if the wrong element came in and started smashing the place up. We're willing to put people on the door to keep those types of element out because we know these elements and we can keep them out." I knew very well that they were indeed the element that I didn't want to have in and so I said, "Thank you very much, very kind of you, but the police are just round the corner. If there's any trouble we'll call them and I'm sure they'll do their best." We never saw them again.' [14] Peter's bravery was admirable, and so was his diplomacy. If he'd been more aggressive and less polite, he might have come a cropper. His public-school etiquette proved to be a surprisingly effective defence.

On Thursday, 5 October 1961 John Wells finished his day's teaching at Eton and then sneaked away to catch the train to London. By the time he arrived Greek Street was packed with people, like a crowd outside a football match. Journalists were interviewing anyone they could find, or, if all else failed, each other. Arc lights lit up the street as TV crews filmed the assembled throng. Wells finally found his way inside, but by nine p.m. the club was so overcrowded that the staff felt compelled to shut the doors for fear that they'd lose their licence, leaving an indignant pack of paid-up members stranded in the cold outside. Alan Bennett had come along to see the show and just about managed to get in, leaving Patrick Leigh Fermor on the doorstep, pleading to be let in. Inside, the place was packed and the noise was deafening. Bennett spotted Ian Gilmour (owner and sometime editor of the *Spectator*) in the audience, and the Warden of All Souls. Harold Hobson had a gammy foot, and there was no room for him among the narrow tables, so the theatre critic of the *Sunday Times* was seated on the stage. Wells was struck by the number of posh young partygoers. 'Satire was in, and they were damned if they were going to miss a second of it,' [15] he recalled.

For Wells, the atmosphere was reminiscent of a Berlin cabaret club in the 1930s (one of those clubs that did so much to prevent the rise of Adolf Hitler, as Peter put it, drolly). 'The harsh wooden decor, the clusters of spotlights, the little stage, the wooden tables, the committed cast running through their lines for the last time. The only thing that was missing, it seemed, was the harsh clatter of the fascist jackboots.' [16] As Wells observed, the boots that clattered on this floor weren't jackboots but elasticated Chelsea boots. The 1960s had arrived. 'Ludicrous parodies of pressmen lurched and belched about the bar. Somewhere in a corner, far away above the heads of the crowd, vainly trying to compete with the roar of conversation, the actors moved through their entertainment.' [17] Yet for those who could hear it, this first-night show was full of good things. The opening sketch was a parody of the crucifixion (anticipating *Monty Python's Life of Brian* by nearly twenty years) with John Fortune as an upper-class Jesus and John Bird and Jeremy Geidt as two working-class thieves. 'Forgive them, Lord, for they know not what they do,' said Fortune. 'They bloody well know what they're doing all right, mate,' said Bird.

Fortune also played Harold Macmillan, along much the same lines as Peter, wondering what had become of that funny Austrian chap he met at Munich, the one with the silly moustache. Geidt played Iain Macleod, the Tory Party Chairman, advocating replacing the electoral system with market research – a theme that would resurface a few years later in Peter's feature film, *The Rise and Rise of Michael Rimmer*. The Foreign Secretary (Alec Douglas Home) and Home Secretary (Rab Butler) also got a ribbing, but there was a lot more to this show than poking fun at politicians. Peter had wanted to set up a club where performers were free to be more outrageous than they could be on the West End stage. This performance realised his ambition. Many of these sketches would have been impossible to perform in *Beyond The Fringe*. The Lord Chamberlain would have banned them. Here, in a private members' club, he was powerless to intervene.

In one such sketch, John Bird played a businessman taking a doctor (John Fortune) out to lunch in the hope of procuring an abortion – still illegal in 1961. The hinge of the joke was Bird's pretence that he was procuring this operation on behalf of two unfortunate friends. 'Of course they'd love to be able to have the baby, but they just can't afford it,' said Bird. 'So they're willing to spend anything to get rid of it.' It was the sort of thing that people talked about all the time in private, but it was a subject that was never discussed with such candour onstage.

Ironically, the only sketch that might be seen as shocking today was widely regarded as completely harmless at the time. In this politically incorrect (but highly amusing) number, John Bird impersonated the

African statesman Jomo Kenyatta (shades of Miller's 'Black Equals White' sketch in *Beyond The Fringe*). Jeremy Geidt played a sports reporter, trying to interview Kenyatta about a forthcoming football match between Spurs and Burnley, only for his every question to be met by a diatribe about black power. 'Would you like to stick your neck out and make a prophecy, Jomo?' asked Geidt. 'Yes,' replied Bird. 'Ah shall be perhaps de first Negro man to be Queen of England.' Of all the sketches that evening, this was the one that got most applause. The show overran, and Wells finally went on around midnight. He missed the last train home and spent the night on a chaise longue at Bennett's London flat. He had to get up at five o'clock the next morning to travel back to Eton in time for school, breaking a window to get inside, changing into white tie and tails in time for the first lesson at half past seven.

Kenneth Tynan reviewed the first night in the *Observer*. He didn't think the satire went far enough. 'Such teeth as the script has are engaged more in nibbling than in biting,' he wrote. 'No political cabaret can be accounted a success unless at least a quarter of the audience walks out.' [18] Having watched the show from his makeshift perch upon the stage, Harold Hobson seemed more concerned with the seating arrangements. 'The Establishment will certainly be more comfortable when it is less crowded,' he wrote in the *Sunday Times*, 'a state of affairs there should be no difficulty in bringing about if it continues with its present programme.' [19]

Hobson's opinion didn't matter. The club had acquired its own momentum. Even Tynan's blessing wasn't crucial any more. 'The atmosphere at The Establishment crackled with electricity,' said Christopher Booker. 'It was *the* place to be that autumn.' [20] Confounding Hobson's sour prediction, the show continued to sell out night after night, and the streets outside were gridlocked. 'There were queues in Greek Street every night,' recalled John Bird. 'Socialites, cabinet ministers, fashion models, intellectuals fought to get in.' [21] Regular guests included Rudolf Nureyev, Michael Caine, Peter O'Toole, Terence Stamp, Lucien Freud, Francis Bacon and Arnold Wesker. The only time Bird saw an empty seat, it turned out that it belonged to a man who'd just been rushed to hospital with a heart attack. His seat was swiftly filled. Over the next few months, The Establishment established an awesome reputation, not only as a fashionable night spot but as a unique forum for polemic. Roger Law became The Establishment's official artist, painting a new picture every week, like a gigantic comic strip, on the wall opposite the bar. Subjects ranged from Sir Roy Welensky, Prime Minister of Southern Rhodesia to Saint Francis of Assisi being eaten alive by a flock of crows.

Like *Beyond The Fringe*, The Establishment's success inevitably attracted a well-heeled, well-connected crowd. Writing in the *New Statesman*, Malcolm Muggeridge carped about the air of affluence ('One looks around instinctively for Princess Margaret, or at any rate the Duke of Bedford') but Peter was unperturbed. 'Most of the Establishment have joined and I'm glad to have them,' he said. 'They'll be in here every night and we can get at them.' [22] The fact that the audience was the target was what gave the show such a frisson. They weren't preaching to the converted, something that Peter relished from the start, and the upper-class clientele merely made the cast more determined to be shocking. John Fortune played Sir Basil Spence, the architect of Coventry's new cathedral ('we owe an enormous debt of gratitude to the German people for making this whole project possible in the first place') and the Bishop of Norwich in a satirical assault on capital punishment. A particularly blinkered cleric had said that criminals welcomed the death penalty because it gave them an opportunity for repentance. Geidt played a criminal who refuted this thesis in no uncertain terms. It made the same sort of point as the capital punishment sketch in *Beyond The Fringe*, but in a more robust idiom:

JOHN FORTUNE: Good evening, I am the Bishop of Norwich.
JEREMY GEIDT: Why don't you fuck off, you stupid old cunt.

Ironically, conservative satire proved a lot more controversial. 'What really annoyed people were attacks on the liberal left,'[23] claimed Peter. As he said, the real sacred cows weren't Macmillan or the Church of England but people like Pat Arrowsmith, one of the founders of CND. 'That's not what you're here for!' protested a woman in the audience when the cast performed a send-up of Ms Arrowsmith, and she hit Peter on the head with her handbag. As Peter said, this was the only time that English satire drew blood.

In January 1962 Kenneth Tynan revisited The Establishment and was more enthusiastic. 'Its attitude is one of radical anarchism,'[24] he wrote. He was full of praise for Bird and Fortune, and Jeremy Geidt, but he still felt there was something missing. 'Something is wrong with the show, some essential is lacking,' he argued. 'One misses that *sine qua non* of successful revue: a gripping, outgoing central personality for whose every entrance one waits and on whose every word one devotedly hangs.'[25] That gripping personality was Peter. Unless he was there to play the compère, it felt like *Hamlet* without the Dane. Yet Peter was no longer just an entertainer. He was now an impresario, and in addition to the resident troupe of comics he brought several distinguished guest stars to The Establishment, the most notable of whom was the American comic Lenny Bruce.

'Lenny Bruce was a revelation,' said Peter. 'I watched him every night for four weeks and I never got over it.' [26] Bruce was a groundbreaking comic, one of the first performers to liberate stand-up comedy from its straitjacket of hand-me-down one-liners. Jonathan Miller called him a secular preacher. His act was part sermon, part confession, a brutally honest examination of human relationships and human weakness. His routines were laden with swear words and frank sexual references – standard practice nowadays, but virtually unheard-of back then. Yet it was the content that was most remarkable. Thanks to his enduring influence, autobiographical stand-up is familiar fare today, but in the early 1960s it was revolutionary. One of the many taboos he discussed with fearless candour was his heroin addiction – a habit he'd acquired after being prescribed opiate-based painkillers as a wounded sailor during World War Two.

In his own way, Bruce was doing something similar to *Beyond The Fringe*, taking things that people talked about offstage and putting them onstage, where people had previously considered them unmentionable. Of course, the content was completely different (Bruce's New York background was a world away from Oxbridge) but the philosophy was much the same. From politics to pornography, nothing was off limits. 'Hands up who's masturbated today,' he'd ask his audience as an icebreaker, but he was more than just a shock jock and his best gags, though daring, were wonderfully well-crafted. 'My mother-in-law broke up my marriage,' he'd say, lulling his punters with the false promise of a trite one-liner. 'My wife came home early from work and found us in bed together.'

These iconoclastic attributes naturally made Bruce a Fleet Street bogeyman, and Peter could only obtain a work permit from the Home Office by assuring them that Bruce's heroin addiction was in the past. This optimistic assurance was shot to pieces a few days after Bruce arrived, when the comic was evicted from his hotel on account of the used syringes found in his toilet (and the prostitutes found in his bedroom). Peter took him in, but Bruce arrived in Battersea in dire need of drugs. Peter did his best to get some. Peter was clueless about drugs in those days, so clueless that he turned to Dudley, hopeful that one of Dudley's jazz contacts might know where he could 'score'. Dudley proved equally naive. 'He only had junior aspirin, which I didn't think would satisfy Lenny's craving,' [27] quipped Peter. Armed with Bruce's dodgy prescription, and a list of supposedly sympathetic medics, Peter wandered around town until the small hours, trying to find an obliging doctor, without success. Defeated, he returned to Battersea, expecting to find Bruce in the throes of cold turkey, but Bruce seemed unperturbed. 'I'm terribly sorry,' said Peter. 'I couldn't get hold of any heroin.' 'That's cool,' replied Bruce. 'I'd like some chocolate cake.' [28] 'I got quite cross,' recalled Peter. 'I said, "I'm willing to traipse all over London at three in the morning to look for heroin but chocolate cake is out of the question." This was of course in 1962, when chocolate cake was not so freely available.' [29]

Peter played these tales for laughs, but the reality of Bruce's heroin addiction was inevitably pretty grim. 'He had got hold of some prescribed narcotic which I remember him heating in a silver tablespoon over a candle as I watched, hypnotised,' recalled Wendy. 'At that point he was like a marionette whose strings had been cut. He applied a tourniquet and injected himself and within moments became like Superman. Somehow we thought it all rather glamorous, but looking back it was tragic.' [30] It was a similar story onstage. When Bruce told his audience to wait a minute while he went backstage to jack up, everyone howled with laughter, unaware that it was no joke but a simple statement of fact.

Bruce was an amiable soul, so long as he got his daily fix. He was popular with the other comics and keen to see them succeed. He advised John Bird and John Fortune not to treat their posher punters with such hostility. 'These people have come to see you, and whatever they're like, you have to assume that they're on your side,' [31] he told them. 'You've got to believe that everybody in the room is sharing your opinion. It may be true that they don't, but if you play it as if you're all in agreement, you'll come over better.' [32] Despite his shocking subject matter Bruce was still a showman at heart. Bird and Fortune went down a lot better after they followed his advice.

Kenneth Tynan saw Bruce's first night at The Establishment and made a list of the provocative opinions he espoused, from 'Smoking of marijuana should be encouraged because it does not induce lung cancer' to 'Children ought to watch pornographic movies – it's healthier than learning about sex from Hollywood.' [33] 'Ninety minutes later there was little room for doubt that he was the most original, free-speaking, wild-thinking gymnast of language our inhibited island has ever hired to beguile its citizens,' [34] concluded Tynan. Jonathan Miller was also there that night. After the show, Tynan and Miller compared notes. If Beyond The Fringe was a pinprick, they concurred, Bruce was a bloodbath.

Not everyone was so approving of Bruce's linguistic gymnastics. 'Scarcely a night passed without vocal protests from offended customers,' [35] recalled Tynan. Predictably some people walked out when he used the F-word, but some of the subjects that people found shocking seem utterly bizarre today. 'A very upper-class couple were there with their daughters,' remembered Peter. 'They sat through every four-letter word in the world and suddenly Lenny mentioned the word "cancer", whereupon, "Fiona, Caroline, Deborah! Cancer! Out!" And they all stormed out.' [36] 'What they'll probably do, the ad companies, is make it hip to have cancer,' said Bruce. One of the most vocal protests came from the fiery Irish actress Siobhan McKenna. McKenna was attending the show with her (much) younger boyfriend, when, rather the worse for wear, she heckled Bruce, offended by his foul-mouthed (yet eloquent) anti-religious ranting. 'If you don't like it, you must leave,' retorted Bruce. 'And take your son with you.' [37] Peter was usually happy to indulge such spats, mindful that controversy made great publicity, but when McKenna started shouting he ushered her towards the door. She grabbed his tie and punched him on the nose. 'These are Irish hands and they're clean,' [38] she said. 'This is an English face, and it's bleeding,' [39] said Peter. Peter paid for her taxi home, and the next day the cast delivered a polite note of regret to London's Comedy Theatre where McKenna was starring in a hit production of *The Playboy of The Western World*. But Bruce had the last laugh. He'd tape-recorded the entire fracas, and played it back onstage the following night. Despite his difficulties scoring heroin (or chocolate cake) he thoroughly enjoyed his month at The Establishment. 'I had a lot of fun in England,' he recalled, 'although I didn't get laid once.' [40]

Peter's other special booking was completely different, but equally inspired. Earlier that year, the four Fringers had gone along to the *Evening Standard* Drama Awards at the Savoy to collect an award for *Beyond The Fringe*. The award was presented by Peter Sellers, and the evening's entertainment was provided by Frankie Howerd, another of the comedians Peter had grown up with, listening to the radio at boarding school. 'He just sent the whole thing up so marvellously,' [41] recalled Peter. 'He was still an enormous star and I felt very shy about approaching him.' [42] After downing a couple of stiff drinks Peter plucked up the courage to introduce himself, unaware that Howerd had needed to polish off half a bottle of Scotch before he could perform. Unbeknown to Peter (or anyone else at the Savoy that evening) Peter's offer was a lifeline. Although Peter still saw him as a star, Howerd's career had hit the buffers. He had no more bookings in his diary. He'd decided this show would be his final bow before he packed it all in to run a pub.

Peter was sticking his neck out by booking Howerd for The Establishment. Within the BBC, and elsewhere, he was widely regarded as a has-been. Nick Luard wasn't the only one who saw him as an end-of-the-pier turn. Peter's club was a bastion of youthful irreverence. Howerd was forty-five (though he pretended to be forty). Most of Peter's colleagues were young enough to be his children. Age wasn't the only issue. It was also a matter of style and class. The Establishment was moneyed and intellectual. Howerd was working class, a comic from the wrong side of the tracks. He was intelligent and cultured, but he was also devout and patriotic, and like a lot of autodidacts he hid his learning behind a self-deprecating mask. The army had been his stage school and his university. All in all, he was pretty much the last comedian you'd expect to see at The Establishment. Only Peter had the wit to realise how well this contrast would play. Peter was aware that The Establishment had almost become too fashionable. 'We were a pretty snotty little club at that time and I thought we needed somebody to send it up,' [43] he said.

By the time his first night came around, Howerd had enlisted the help of three of Britain's best comedy writers: Ray Galton and Alan Simpson ('Hancock's Half Hour') and Johnny Speight ('Till Death Us Do Part'). Shrewdly, they advised him to focus on the incongruity of this booking. This approach went down a treat. 'I'm a humble Music Hall comedian,' he told this trendy crowd. 'I'm not usually associated with these sophisticated venues.' He told them how Peter had come to book him. 'This young lad came over to me. Quite a presentable boy, you know. Quite a nice lad. Quite a nice type. And he said, "I was wondering if I could introduce myself. I'm Cook." I said, "Oh! It was a lovely meal!" He said, "No, I'm Peter Cook!" I said, "I still enjoyed the meal." Then, of course the penny dropped. I suddenly realised he's that chap who runs this place, or fronts it, or whatever it is he does.'

Howerd went on to satirise The Establishment itself. 'Peter Cook has made it very clear. He said, "You must be satirical. You must have a go. You must be bitter. They must leave here angry. Otherwise they won't be satisfied. Knock the Establishment!" I said, "I've done nothing else since I've been here!" He said, "No, not this place – the people! The Establishment – the faceless ones!" It was a battle of wits from now on. I said, "Whom had you in mind?" He said, "The Government. Macmillan. The Establishment. The Civil Service." I said, "Make them angry? But these are your audience. These are the people who come here. You don't want to make them angry. They think it's all rather sweet! They enjoy it! It's water off a duck's back! After all, the whole place is only a snob's *Workers' Playtime*, let's face it. Instead of making jokes about the foreman we make jokes about Harold Macmillan. It's the same thing."' Howerd stormed it. Peter had resurrected his career.

*

Dudley, meanwhile, was busy with his jazz band. With Peter McGurk replacing the late Hugo Boyd on bass, and Australian Chris Karan taking over from Dudley's old drummer Derek Hogg, the new Dudley Moore Trio cut their first LP, *Theme From Beyond The Fringe And All That Jazz*. The title track was Dudley's composition, but the rest of the record consisted of new arrangements of American classics like 'I Get A Kick Out of You'. However, this was no simple rehash of old standards. Dudley's interpretation was inspired. Half a century later, the elegance and invention of his piano playing is still astounding, and in McGurk and Karan's selfless accompaniment he'd found the perfect foil. 'Neither Pete nor Chris is particularly interested in solo work,' explained Dudley. 'Their satisfaction comes from playing time and they really lay down the kind of beat which I find most congenial and relaxing for my own improvising. When you have this groove to fit into, the music follows by itself.' [44] Over the next six years Dudley would make four more albums with McGurk and Karan, and it was only another tragic death which would prevent this partnership from lasting even longer.

Dudley was also enjoying himself at The Establishment where, as Peter had predicted, his late-night piano playing was a magnet for an endless succession of gorgeous women. Yet when he finally fell for someone, it was Dudley who did the running. One night at The Establishment, he saw a tall blonde woman dancing (the first of many tall blonde women) and was instantly smitten. He recognised her face. It was Celia Hammond, a model he'd seen in *Vogue*. Not sure how to approach her, he eventually sent her a telegram. She was already going out with the photographer Terence Donovan, but Dudley swept her off her feet. 'Dudley had a vulnerability about him which to me was utterly endearing,' remembered Hammond.

'I watched him play at the nightclub and I fell in love with his music.'[45] Still shy in person, Dudley had a unique ability to communicate through his piano playing. 'I felt he was talking to me when he played,' she said. 'He was irresistible.' [46] She wasn't the last woman he'd woo this way, but this was no cool, calculating conquest. Dudley had never dreamed he could attract her and, when he did, he was ecstatic. 'It was the most extraordinary experience,' he recalled. 'I was so turned on to her that I couldn't think of anything else.' [47] Hammond was taken aback by the squalor of Dudley's flat, but this merely made her want to mother him – she even cleaned the mouldy food out of his larder. She was more upset by Dudley's habit of wearing a sock in the bath, to hide his club foot. They couldn't see enough of each other, but a new development conspired to separate them. *Beyond The Fringe* had already conquered the West End. Now the cast had been invited to take the show to America.

CHAPTER ELEVEN

ON BROADWAY

DUDLEY: I thought I'd better brush up on my Star-Spangled Banner.

ALAN: Well, of course you have to. You have to be able to play it. Otherwise, they won't give you a visa. They're terribly sticky about that. Toscanini waited for years and years.

PETER: Mind you, I can see their point of view. If they didn't have these sort of regulations, any old riff-raff could get in.

JONATHAN: They've got a lot of old riff-raff in there already.

(Home Thoughts From Abroad, *Beyond The Fringe*, 1964)

With keen competing interest from David Merrick and Alexander Cohen, two of America's top producers, this time the four Fringers managed to cut themselves a better deal. They signed up with Cohen for £750 a week (a tenfold increase on their initial West End rate) plus a percentage of the gross. At last it looked as if they might actually make some decent money.

Before they left for America, they needed four performers to replace them. Initially, they'd wanted to wrap up the West End show when they went. 'This is not the kind of show which even the most experienced professional could step into,' [1] announced Peter, prematurely, but the prospect of residual fees trumped any creative reservations. Donaldson's favoured substitutes were John Wells for Bennett, Joe Melia for Miller, Richard Ingrams for Dudley and David Frost for Peter, but Wells, Frost and Ingrams were all vetoed by the cast. Peter was particularly reluctant to see Frost cracking his jokes onstage. 'Over my dead body,' he told Donaldson. Donaldson said Frost and Ingrams were 'desperate' to take over from Peter and Dudley, and it's fun to wonder what might have become of them if they had. 'That would have been the end of Frost, and the end of Ingrams,' [2] predicted Donaldson. This seems unlikely. Frost and Ingrams surely would have climbed the greasy pole one way or another, but if they'd ended up deputising for Peter and Dudley, in a show that ended up running for four more years, their subsequent careers might well have taken a very different course.

Peter wanted to hand over his role to the Australian actor Barry Humphries – a punter (and subsequent performer) at The Establishment. 'I went to the theatre and auditioned,' said Humphries. 'I did a very expressionist party turn of mine, in which I played a psychiatrist and an idiot having an interview. It was a two-hander which I played by doing both characters and then slowly going insane.' [3] Peter watched him from the stalls. 'You've got the job,' [4] Peter told him, straight afterwards. Humphries was thrilled. He already had a job, appearing in the original cast of *Oliver!*, but the show's producer, Donald Albery (yes, him again), had promised to let him go if he found something better. But when it came down to it Albery declined to release him from his contract. Humphries was gutted but this setback was probably a blessing. Peter's role went to Terence Brady, while Robin Ray, who'd stood in for Dudley during his recuperative trip to Italy, replaced him on a permanent basis. Jonathan Miller had wanted Bill Wallis to play his part, but Donaldson held out for Joe Melia. Wallis took over Alan Bennett's role instead. It was the kind of steady gig most jobbing actors dream of getting but it was a bit of a cul-de-sac. All four replacements forged successful careers but none of them became household names.

On 28 September 1962, the four Fringers set sail for New York on the SS *France*. They could have gone by plane, but John Bassett thought a week at sea would give them a chance to work up some new material for the US show. He was wrong. They didn't rehearse any new sketches, and life aboard this 'luxury liner' wasn't as luxurious as they'd supposed. They'd assumed they'd be sitting at the captain's table but the crew were all French and had never heard of them. There was no room for them in the main dining room. They had to eat in the nursery. Nobody asked them to perform – not even in the talent contest. To all intents and purposes, they were travelling incognito. At least the food was good (Peter had caviar for breakfast) but it was a timely reminder that there was a world beyond the West End, full of people who knew nothing about *Beyond The Fringe*. Peter wrote to his parents that he was 'bored stiff' on this 'vulgar floating hotel'. [5]

Things looked up when they docked in New York. Alexander Cohen put them up in the Algonquin Hotel, and then in his mansion in Connecticut, and the show was a smash hit. They opened in Washington on 6 October, and went on to Boston and Toronto, playing to full houses at every turn. Wendy flew into Boston, and while the show went to Toronto she went on ahead to New York with Peter's PA, Judy Scott-Fox, to find somewhere for them to stay during the Broadway run. She found a bohemian basement flat in a brownstone house in Greenwich Village, decorated in pseudo-Arabian style, like a Bedouin tent. Dudley, meanwhile, found himself a large two-bedroom apartment on East 63rd Street. He moved in with John Bassett, who'd travelled to America to oversee the Broadway show.

Beyond The Fringe opened in New York on 27 October, at the John Golden Theatre on Broadway. Alexander Cohen could hardly have chosen a worse time to launch a new comedy revue. America was in a state of panic, as the Cuban Missile Crisis threatened to plunge the planet into a full-scale nuclear war. A lot of New Yorkers were packing their cars and fleeing the city. Alan Bennett was so concerned that he moved out of his own apartment and went to stay with Dudley and John Bassett. 'If we were going to be blown up,' said Bassett, 'it would be better to be blown up together.' [6] The producers held an emergency meeting to discuss whether to delay the opening. The cast said the show must go on.

All sorts of celebs turned up on the first night, from Jean Shrimpton and Terence Stamp to the General Secretary of the UN, but inside the theatre the atmosphere was uneasy. The sound of a police siren in the street outside was enough to kill the laughter. 'The audience went absolutely dead,' recalled Alan Bennett. 'You couldn't do anything with them.' [7] As it turned out, these punters were quite right to feel so jumpy. Unbeknown to the general public, an American spy plane had been shot down over Cuba that afternoon, rendering the Broadway opening of *Beyond The Fringe* arguably the most perilous evening in human history.

Despite such awkward circumstances, the critics loved it. 'There is hardly a review this morning that is less than delirious,' reported Alistair Cooke, revisiting the show he'd seen two years before in

Edinburgh. 'This tumult of acceptance is a puzzle to many shrewd theatre men here who deplored the quartet's decision not to adapt their material to American themes, or their strangulated tripthongs to the ears of a people to whom a vowel is a vowel is a vowel. But they make no concessions, a British trick Oscar Wilde discovered before them. In a way, their success is a reprise of the old, and most popular, visiting lecturers, who pitied their audience, said so, and made a mint.' [8] Peter agreed: 'Alexander Cohen took the absolutely correct view that it would become an immensely chic show in the States, and the fact that it was English and we hadn't altered a word would be a sort of built-in snob merit.' [9] Alan Bennett was more blunt. 'It had snob appeal because they couldn't understand it,' [10] he said. Sure enough, stars like Bette Davis and Noel Coward flocked to see the show and meet the cast. President Kennedy's people got in touch to request a special performance at the White House. 'We're not some fucking cabaret,' said Peter, audaciously. 'He can come to the theatre.' [11] As he wrote to his parents, 'it would have made us seem rather like performing seals.' [12]

Having successfully transferred *Beyond The Fringe* from the West End to Broadway, Peter now proceeded to do the same thing for The Establishment. He found a similarly run-down venue – a nightclub called the El Morocco on East 54th Street. Cast and crew were recruited with almost supernatural ease. Nicholas Garland was already in Boston, directing Peter Ustinov in his play *Photo Finish*. Peter hired him to direct The Establishment show in New York. The London cast of The Establishment were already in Chicago, playing the prestigious comedy club Second City, while the Second City cast played The Establishment in London – an inspired exchange which Peter had arranged before he set sail for the States.

The only problem was publicity. As if the threat of nuclear Armageddon wasn't enough of a nuisance, New York was also in the throes of a newspaper strike. Rival producer David Merrick wasn't afraid to voice his opinion that without press coverage The Establishment's chances of success would be hampered. Of course he was quite right, but talking down a show's prospects is often a self-fulfilling prophecy, and since Merrick had lost out to Cohen in his bid to bring *Beyond The Fringe* to Broadway his pessimism smelled of sour grapes. In 1961 Merrick had revived an ailing musical by eliciting rave reviews from anonymous punters who shared the names of New York theatre critics. Peter decided to beat Merrick at his own game. In the Philadelphia phone directory he found a postman called David Merrick and took him to a rehearsal at The Establishment. This postman said it was the best Broadway show he'd ever seen (it was actually the *only* Broadway show he'd ever seen) and Peter reprinted his endorsement on several thousand flyers, which were handed out around town. Wendy and Judy Scott-Fox marched up and down Broadway, past the theatres where Merrick's shows (*Tchin-Tchin*, *Stop The World* and *Oliver!*) were playing, wearing sandwich boards plastered with Postman Merrick's praise.

It was obviously just a joke, with no attempt to hoodwink the paying public. Peter's flyer even bore a photo of Postman Merrick, who was black (unlike his theatrical namesake). Still, the speech bubble on the flyer was guaranteed to get Producer Merrick's goat. 'I think The Establishment is the most brilliant show in New York,' proclaimed Postman Merrick. 'It is better than *Tchin-Tchin*, *Stop The World* and *Oliver!* all rolled into one. I wish I had a piece of it.' Flyers tied to helium balloons were released on the street beneath Merrick's office. Peter even put Postman Merrick on the radio and broadcast his endorsement from a loudspeaker van, driving up and down Broadway. There was nothing producer Merrick could do about it. Peter had put him in his place and generated some great publicity at the same time.

The opening of The Establishment was put back a month, in response to the newspaper strike, and by the time the show opened, on 23 January 1963, the presses were rolling again. Christened The Strollers Theatre Club (the plan was to cohabit with a straight theatre company, producing straight plays) this new venue was smarter than its London counterpart, but the new show was even more daring, and the papers showered it with praise. Like its London counterpart, it quickly became the show to see – and the show to be seen at. Film stars like Laurence Olivier, Kirk Douglas and Rex Harrison, jazz legends like Miles Davis, Oscar Peterson and Nina Simone ... Anyone who was anyone dropped in. Even Salvador Dali paid a visit. Once again, Peter had struck gold.

The Beyond The Fringe quartet were now moving in the most elevated social circles. Jonathan Miller became friends with Susan Sontag, and met Norman Mailer and Philip Roth. He attended chic soirées hosted by George Plimpton, alongside literary lions like Gore Vidal and Truman Capote. Peter and Wendy were invited to parties where Noel Coward played the piano, and to dinner at a secluded country club with Bobby Kennedy and a dozen hand-picked guests. Peter enjoyed this social whirl but he didn't lose sight of its absurdities, and he found a kindred spirit in Joseph Heller whose first novel, Catch 22, had recently become a bestseller, propelling him onto the same party circuit. 'Peter was being lionised at the same time and in the same way,' said Heller. 'We both found it funny when we discovered that neither of us knew the host or hostess.' [13] Peter and Wendy became good friends with Heller and his wife Shirley, and amid the self-conscious stars and socialites they met several other down-to-earth celebs. Joan Collins cooked them supper, wearing fluffy carpet slippers. Peter Ustinov visited them for dinner and proved to be one of the few people who could compete with Peter as a raconteur.

Even Peter's head was turned by America's First Lady, Jackie Kennedy, whom he met at a dinner given by the Vice-President, Lyndon Johnson. Two days later she turned up at The Establishment, unannounced, to see the late show. Peter sat with her and plied her with champagne. 'She was very sweet and she spoke in a voice like Marilyn Monroe,' wrote Peter, in a letter to his parents. 'She kept shrieking with delight, and saying how naughty it all was, and how Jack would never allow her up to New York again.' [14] Three days later, Jack and Jackie arrived at the John Golden Theatre to see *Beyond The Fringe*. This time there was some advance warning. The President's security staff searched the theatre beforehand and set up a special red telephone backstage, just in case JFK decided to nuke Russia during 'The Aftermyth of War'. Straight-faced security men mingled with the audience, and everyone was watching the President rather than the performance. Peter left a replica pistol in his dressing room to test JFK's security team (they ignored it) and dropped a cheeky reference to JFK into his Macmillan monologue. During the rest of the show Kennedy laughed along, but during Peter's impression of the British Prime Minister he assumed a perfect poker face.

The world's most famous couple came backstage to meet the cast, and Alan Bennett detected some electricity between Peter and the First Lady. 'I think he may have seen something of Jackie Kennedy,' speculated Bennett. 'I have a vision of the presidential party in the Green Room having drinks in the interval, with Mrs Kennedy absently stroking Peter's hand as they chatted.' [15] Shortly after this Presidential visit, Peter offered to send Wendy on a two-week holiday to Puerto Rico, with Nicholas Garland's wife Harriet. Wendy and Harriet accepted the offer, but bored and uncomfortable in a luxury hotel in the midst of abject poverty, they returned to New York on an earlier flight. That evening Wendy went along to The Establishment to see Peter. 'Arriving at the club I noticed a buzz in the air,' she recalled. 'Peter caught sight of me and momentarily looked a little ruffled, but then greeted me with a hug and a kiss and broke the news that Jackie Kennedy had come that evening.' [16] Peter introduced them, but as the two women shook hands Wendy trod on the hem of her backless dress and snapped a shoulder strap, leaving her holding her dress up with one hand while she tried to extricate her other hand from Jackie's grasp. 'I did suspect there had been something going on,' reflected Wendy. 'It may have been only a flirtation, but even that was going to be a hard act for me to follow.' [17]

Whatever went on with Jackie Kennedy, there was no doubt that Peter's showbiz lifestyle was putting a huge strain on his relationship with Wendy. In Boston he'd had a brief fling with a Playboy Bunny whom he nicknamed Kitty Nisty. In New York, though he lived with Wendy, they were rarely alone together. Peter's daily routine was nocturnal, and he was surrounded by colleagues and admirers virtually everywhere he went. During his frequent absences Wendy eventually found solace elsewhere. At the Royale Theatre in Greenwich Village, while watching a show by Chicago's Second City, she met a (married) actor called Benito Carruthers and began a passionate affair. When Carruthers asked her to run away with him, Wendy came clean to Peter. Peter advised her to return to London to decide between them.

Wendy went back to Blighty to think things over, leaving Peter (and Carruthers) in New York.

Barry Humphries got a job in the Broadway run of *Oliver!* and met up with Peter in Manhattan. He was surprised to find Peter wearing tracksuits and trainers, rather than his usual suits and ties. 'He went to a lot of baseball matches,' said Humphries. 'He was very interested in every form of sport, and not much in any other thing. He read the papers, he knew exactly what was happening, and could immediately interpret current events comically, but he didn't go to concerts. As far as I could tell he didn't really read books. He had no interest in art.' [18] Eventually, Peter's constant wisecracking began to pall. 'I was a bit put off by his studied philistinism, as I was by this barrier of humour that he erected,' said Humphries. 'He disguised what may have been shyness or diffidence or insecurity with compulsive jocularity. He was always putting on a voice, putting on a performance – invariably hilarious, but at the same time it was a barrier, and it was occasionally rather daunting and depressing.' [19] For Peter, comedy wasn't a sword but a shield.

The success of *Beyond The Fringe* also opened lots of new doors for Dudley. He was in great demand at jazz clubs like the Village Vanguard, the Blue Angel and Michael's Pub. He was similarly popular between the sheets. Starved of physical affection as a child and still racked with insecurity about his club foot, like a schoolboy in a sweetshop he was incapable of passing up any opportunity for confirmation of his lovability that his fame and charm provided. Having sowed his wild oats in the West End, he sowed some more on Broadway. Talent and modesty is a rare, seductive combination, and to the leggy blondes who were the focus of his amorous attentions his impish wit made a nice change from the usual bores and macho men. He listened to them, he made them laugh, he was shy and self-effacing, yet he had a sparkle which lit up every room. He liked women and women liked him back.

Despite his numerous liaisons, Dudley missed Celia Hammond desperately and wrote her countless love letters. Even his letters to his friends back home were full of his feelings for her, often to the exclusion of any other news. The apartment he shared with John Bassett had two bedrooms, but rather than taking a bedroom each Dudley shared a room with Bassett and kept the other room pristine for Hammond. When Hammond set a date to fly to New York, he asked Bassett to move out. Dudley eventually relented after they'd tested the soundproofing. Bassett sat in one bedroom, Dudley went into the other and let out a series of loud orgasmic groans. Could Bassett hear anything? No? Then he could stay. If anyone else had done this, it would have felt crude and chauvinistic, but when Dudley did it, it simply seemed sweet and funny. Maybe that was the secret of his success.

Dudley was ecstatic when Hammond arrived. She went down well with the other Fringers. Alan Bennett remarked that she was the only one of Dudley's girlfriends who actually talked to them. The couple spent lots of time alone together, visiting jazz clubs and walking in Central Park. Dudley was smitten, but monogamy was an anathema. As Wendy says, 'Dudley was capable of love, though not fidelity or commitment.' As well as his various New York flings, he was also conducting another long-distance romance with another English model, Cynthia Cassidy. Yet when Hammond returned to her old boyfriend, the photographer Terry Donovan, Dudley was devastated. Broken-hearted, he sought consolation in a series of energetic one-night stands, but even this didn't cheer him up. Eventually, he decided to see a psychiatrist. 'I told him I couldn't work,' said Dudley, 'but I also wanted to find out about myself.' [20] As Dudley poured his heart out, his psychiatrist sat and listened, filling and refilling his pipe. 'Why don't you bloody well say something?' asked Dudley. 'Why does that make you annoyed?' replied his shrink. Dudley would remain in psychoanalysis for much of his adult life.

Dudley threw himself into his work, writing the score for a new ballet called *Collages* which his good friend Gillian Lynne was mounting at the Edinburgh Festival. 'The only cure for my depression,' he wrote in his diary, 'is activity. Once I get into my work, the pressure of LIFE is taken from me and I am able to think clearly and without obstruction. Work makes me able to cope with my reality and fight off the cloying fingers of fatalism and resignation. Not that I could ever let myself resign from my constant struggle to discipline myself. It has to be a victory for my soul – there is no alternative. Thus my true self – or at least my better self – will emerge.' The man that emerges from such extracts is anxious, earnest – and utterly unlike Peter. 'I don't know why Dudley took so long to find himself,' he'd say. 'I found him years ago.' [21] Later in life, Peter would dabble with psychotherapy, but like most aspects of human existence he found it hard to take it seriously. Publicly, he treated Dudley's passion for psychoanalysis with amused disdain.

Peter and Dudley's contrasting attitudes to therapy reflected their contrasting attitudes to America. As Peter's old school friend Michael Bawtree pointed out, for English people in those days to say they were seeing a psychiatrist was an extraordinary, even shameful admission. 'Any kind of psychotherapy was looked on with considerable scorn,' said Dudley. 'People preferred to tell you to pull yourself together. [22] Here in

New York, however, psychiatry wasn't taboo, an attitude that Dudley relished. As Wendy said, virtually everyone she met in Manhattan seemed to have a shrink. This was one of the many differences that eventually drew Dudley back to let-it-all-out America, and eventually drew Peter back to buttoned-up Britain.

Despite his navel-gazing self-absorption, Dudley proved to be a considerate and generous friend. When *Collages* ran short of funds, he bought costumes for the production and put them on a plane to London. He paid for Lynne to fly to New York to discuss the show. He lent her £800 and refused to let her repay him. She sent him several cheques but he tore them up and sent them back. *Collages* was a hit. Melvyn Bragg made a film about it for the BBC, and Binkie Beaumont and David Merrick (the producer, not the postman) flew to Edinburgh to see it. Its success transformed Lynne's career. She went on to work on three movies and a Broadway play, all in the following year. Dudley was similarly generous towards his parents. His father was due to retire and could only look forward to a modest pension. Dudley sent him a cheque for £200 and set up a weekly standing order. 'Thanks to you, I shall look forward to happy times without worry,' [23] replied his dad.

While Peter and Dudley threw themselves into show business, Jonathan and Alan remained adamant that their Broadway run was just a sabbatical. 'When the show closes I shall return to medicine,' Miller told the *New York Times*. 'I'll work three hours every morning on my thesis, which will become a book, the history of Richard II,' Bennett told the paper. Miller was married, with a baby on the way, but Bennett was all alone in New York, so he saw a lot more of Dudley. Virtually every evening, before the show, they'd dine together at an

Italian restaurant on 46th Street called Barbetta's. Dudley ordered the same meal every night: gazpacho, fettuccine and chocolate mousse. The Italian doorman always welcomed them with the same greeting. 'Meester Cook! Meester Moore! Be'ind The Fri'ge!' Dudley remarked to Alan that this sounded like a good title for something. It would eventually re-emerge as the title of Peter and Dudley's two-man stage show.

Wendy returned to New York keen to forget about Ben Carruthers and make a go of things with Peter. They rekindled their relationship on Fire Island, a beach resort off Long Island. 'It was a really special weekend, with all other distractions banished,' recalled Wendy. 'Peter even desisted from reading all the newspapers for two whole days!' [24] Wendy yearned to become a mother and by the end of this romantic break she could sense that her wish had been fulfilled.

To escape the summer heat, Alexander Cohen gave the Fringers the run of his summer home in Fairfield, Connecticut, chauffeuring them into town for the show every night. This clapboard house was spacious, and the cast had fun around the outdoor pool, with guests like John Bird and Jeremy Geidt. Wendy was glad of the chance to spend more time with Peter and avoid Carruthers. Then they were joined by David Frost.

While the cast of *Beyond The Fringe* had been busy in America, David Frost had become a TV star in Britain. Peter was particularly aggrieved about the way this had come about. Before the invitation had arrived to take *Beyond The Fringe* to Broadway, Peter had approached the BBC, alongside John Bird, with an idea for an Establishment TV series. They'd been to see Donald Baverstock, an executive in the Current Affairs Department, and the Controller of

Programmes, Stuart Hood. It sounded as if the Beeb were keen (they'd even asked for sample scripts and formats) but then they suddenly went cold on the idea. Without knowing anything of Peter's previous plan, Ned Sherrin, then a young producer in the BBC's Current Affairs Department, had been along to The Establishment and had submitted a proposal for a similar satire show. Naturally, Hood and Baverstock preferred the internal option. Sherrin was given the go-ahead, knowing nothing of the rival bid. Neither Peter nor John Bird were told why their idea had been shelved.

Blissful in his ignorance, Sherrin got in touch with John Bird and asked him to become the presenter of the BBC's new satire show. Nobody at the BBC had done anything untoward, least of all Ned Sherrin, but Bird felt uncomfortable about the similarity between Sherrin's show and the concept he'd hatched with Peter. He'd also agreed to go to Chicago, to perform with The Establishment at Second City. If he accepted Sherrin's offer, he'd be letting Peter down twice over. Honourably, Bird turned down Sherrin's invitation, though he agreed to appear in the pilot. He also suggested a possible title – *That Was The Week That Was*. With *Beyond The Fringe* bound for Broadway, and The Establishment en route to Chicago, Sherrin needed to cast around for other candidates. Bird suggested that he should pay a visit to the Blue Angel nightclub to see a satire show featuring his flatmate, David Frost.

Although Bird shared a flat with Frost, he hadn't seen Frost's Blue Angel act – he was working at The Establishment every night. Still, what he'd heard confirmed the qualities which would make Frost famous. 'He's someone with complete self-belief,' said Bird. 'He'd come home from the Blue Angel, and I'd ask how it had gone, and he'd say, "Oh, fine," and then he'd describe what to me sounded like a nightmare.' [25] Frost seemed unaffected by such setbacks. 'David always saw himself as coming out of any situation triumphantly, and I envied him for that.' [26]

Frost's act featured an impression of Macmillan, including questions from the floor. Impersonating Macmillan was Peter's party piece, and some of Peter's friends felt Frost's act was a bit too close for comfort. Of course, once Peter had started impersonating the Prime Minister it was inevitable that other performers would want to do their own impressions, and even specific jokes weren't considered quite so precious in those days. Trad stand-ups would often 'borrow' jokes from other comics, who'd often 'borrowed' them from someone else. On the Oxbridge circuit, things weren't quite so laissez-faire, but authorship could be a hazy matter, especially as sketches were frequently written *en ensemble* and continued to evolve onstage. Peter had written some of his early sketches in isolation, but much of his later work was created together with other comics, including Frost. Nobody ever doubted that Peter wrote the bulk of it, but there were usually other people involved. The same issue would resurface when Peter began to write with Dudley. To Peter it seemed preposterous that Dudley demanded a joint writing credit, but though Peter wrote the lion's share he found it hard to write alone. Nobody knew quite where to draw the line, but there was a feeling among some of Peter's friends that Frost had overstepped it. The success of *That Was The Week That Was* (or *TW3*, as it became known) turned this resentment into something more acute.

Sherrin was impressed by Frost's Blue Angel act, particularly his ad-libs. He was well-versed in current affairs and could think on his feet. Initially, Sherrin only saw him as a useful member of the supporting cast, but then the two men lunched together and Frost emerged triumphant as co-presenter of the pilot, alongside the more seasoned broadcaster Brian Redhead. For Frost, it was a big break. After graduating from Cambridge he'd joined Associated Rediffusion as a trainee, but he'd only done a smidgeon of presenting, fronting a cheesy series about the latest dance sensation, called *Let's Twist*. But this apprenticeship had given Frost the opportunity to learn the mechanics and techniques of television, and he took to *TW3* as if he'd been doing it all his life. 'He was tirelessly inventive and energetic in helping to shape and colour the programme,' [27] recalled Sherrin. The pilot was recorded on 15 July 1962. John Bird took part, as promised, alongside his Establishment colleagues Eleanor Bron, John Fortune and Jeremy Geidt. Peter declined to appear, but his comic voice was omnipresent. This wasn't plagiarism. It was a tribute to his influence. In 1962 it was actually quite hard to crack a joke without sounding like Peter Cook.

When Sherrin's superiors saw the pilot tape, their first impressions were pretty tepid. Grace Wyndham Goldie, Head of TV Talks & Current Affairs, found it 'tendentious and dangerous'. [28] The idea might never have got any further if Frost's employers, Associated Rediffusion, hadn't heard about it and decided to make their own satire show, with Frost as the presenter. It was this rival plan which prompted the BBC to proceed. Donald Baverstock didn't like The Establishment sketches but he thought Frost was a winner. Frost parted company with Associated Rediffusion and threw in his lot with the BBC. A second pilot was recorded on 29 September, the day after the Fringers set sail for America. This pilot was deemed a success, Frost proved himself a TV natural, and the BBC commissioned twenty-three weekly episodes, due to begin transmission on Saturday, 24 November.

Nobody expected *TW3* would be anything more than a cult hit. The singer Millicent Martin, contracted for the first series, regretted having to turn down a pantomime booking in Bromley. Even Sherrin predicted that his creation would merely be 'late-night ghetto television which would probably only attract a fringe metropolitan audience'. [29] The BBC were hoping for half a million viewers but when the first episode was broadcast more than one and a half million tuned in. The papers loved the show, and the second episode was watched by five million. By the end of the first series, on 27 April 1963, these ratings had more than doubled. A second series was commissioned for the autumn. By the time Frost arrived in Connecticut, *TW3* had become a national institution, and Frost had become a superstar. 'He had a gift for the telly,' said Christopher Booker, who wrote with Frost for *TW3*. 'It was the one place where he really could be fully himself.' [30]

Peter had been following the progress of *TW3* with growing irritation. In public, he spoke through gritted teeth. 'I would have liked to see the programme,' he told the student paper *Varsity*. 'There was a lot of my material in it.' [31] In private he was less oblique. 'Peter would be on the phone at the stage door on the Saturday night being told what *TW3* had done that week,' recalled Alan Bennett. 'A lot of it was stuff he had written himself, or co-written. He wasn't benign about this at the time.' [32] Yet, when Frost finally appeared, Peter was scrupulously polite. He asked Frost if he'd like to cool off in the pool. Frost changed into his trunks and plunged in. 'I was and still am a pathetic swimmer,' [33] said Frost. As Frost put it, he started making 'odd, gulping noises,' and, as Jonathan Miller, who was there, recalled, 'sank as he has subsequently risen – without a trace.' [34]

'I suddenly saw him struggling in the water and I thought, "Ho, ho,

David is making a satirical attack on drowning,"' said Peter. 'Then he went under. When he went under for a third time, I decided he was serious and pulled him out.' [35] John Bird thought at first that Peter was trying to murder him. Frost had no doubt that Peter's prompt action made all the difference. 'He saved my life.' [36] Alan Bennett maintained that this heroic act was the only regret of Peter's life. Frost maintains that this was just Bennett's joke, that Peter was proud to have saved his life. It seems fitting that the most famous story about Peter's relationship with Frost is so ambiguous and contradictory. It sums up the ambiguous and contradictory nature of the relationship itself. Ned Sherrin likened it to the fable of the hare and the tortoise, but Christopher Booker put it best. Frost, he said, marketed Peter's genius for a mass audience. For Peter, it was a salutary lesson about the omnipotent power of television. Playing to full houses every night for four years, on the West End and then on Broadway, *Beyond The Fringe* was probably seen by about half a million people. At its peak, nearly fifteen million people saw *TW3* every week.

On 28 October 1963 Peter and Wendy got married. Wendy wanted a church wedding, so Peter's American agent, Janet Roberts, introduced them to the pastor of her Episcopalian church, the American equivalent of the C of E. 'I am not prepared to marry you just to give this child a name,' he told them. 'You must understand that marriage is for life.' [37] For Wendy, it was a wake-up call. Even her fiancé was subdued. 'Few people could have reduced Peter to a spirit of such deference, but this pastor was a real man of God,' she recalled. 'I was a child in many ways and unprepared for the life that was about to unfold.' [38] She was twenty-three. Peter was twenty-five.

Peter's parents flew over for the wedding. Peter and Wendy showed them the sights – fine art at the Guggenheim, opera at the Met. They dined at the Four Seasons and went on the Staten Island Ferry. Wendy's parents couldn't make it at such short notice, so Wendy and Peter's friend, Nathan Silver, gave her away. As a respected academic, Wendy felt he was the best substitute for her father. Judy Scott-Fox was maid of honour. Peter's friend from Cambridge, Peter Bellwood, was the best man.

The wedding took place at St Luke's in Greenwich Village. The chapel was a sea of flowers. Wendy had designed a blue silk wedding dress – three months pregnant, she felt that a white wedding would be inappropriate. Alan Bennett came along, as did John Bird, John Fortune and Jonathan and Rachel Miller. Dudley played the organ. The reception was at The Establishment. Since Peter was performing in *Beyond The Fringe*, they couldn't go away on honeymoon, so they went to see *The Man With The X-Ray Eyes* in a cinema on Times Square. 'I think the idea was to be cool,' said Nathan Silver, 'but I don't think it quite came off.' [39] The happy couple moved out of their basement flat and into a more conventional apartment, on the first floor of an old brownstone on West 9th Street. Wendy's wedding ring was an antique, a hundred years old exactly, with October 1863 engraved upon it. 'I loved this notion,' she reflected. 'In hindsight I wondered how good an idea it had been to wear somebody else's ring.' [40]

A month later, on 22 November, President Kennedy was assassinated. The Establishment shut out of respect, but back in Britain *TW3* mounted a heartfelt tribute. The programme was shown on NBC, an LP of the broadcast became a big seller, and the cast were invited to New York to reprise the show as part of a big glitzy event at Madison Square Garden, sandwiched between a succession of international cabaret artistes. Christopher Booker had written the bulk of the original show, and was proud of what he'd written. However, the sincerity of the original had been spontaneous and immediate. Booker regarded this reheated requiem as the most embarrassing thing he'd ever been involved with. Peter and Wendy thought it would be fun to go along. They soon regretted it. In a letter to her parents, Wendy called it 'the most nauseating, revolting display that is ever likely to happen in the history of mankind'. [41] Peter was only slightly less damning. 'He thought it was the most appalling thing he'd seen in all his life,' [42] said Willie Rushton, but the audience lapped it up. As far as Britain and America were now concerned, the new king of satire wasn't Peter Cook but David Frost.

By now, creative tensions weren't confined to Peter's relationship with David Frost. Performing the same show night after night, the cast of *Beyond The Fringe* were beginning to get on each other's nerves. They hadn't got together of their own accord but had been thrust together like 'an intellectual boy band' [43] (as Wendy put it) and, after several years together, the cracks were beginning to show. Things came to a head between Bennett and Miller during the interval one evening. 'There was a round table in a sort of Green Room where we used to sit and eat the most disgusting institutional sandwiches, which were brought up from some hideous cemetery underneath the theatre,' recalled Miller. 'I remember tipping the table up and racing out in high dudgeon – or trying to race out in high dudgeon, because what happens is you always forget that the door opens the opposite way to the one you think it's going to.' [44]

Miller also fell out with Dudley. 'They didn't get on,' revealed Bennett. 'Jonathan, if he didn't like the audience, or they didn't respond immediately, wrote them off and didn't work at it. Dudley was much more of a trouper. He would go out and try to win the audience over. He would mug away and do all sorts of outrageous things, while Jonathan couldn't be bothered.' [45] Dudley also did his best to make Bennett and Miller corpse, fooling around in the wings while they were doing their double act as two philosophers. When they turned the other way to avoid him, he'd scamper around the back of the set and reappear on the other side. 'Nurse! Nurse!' he'd cry. 'The screens! The screens!' Sometimes he'd blow raspberries. At one point, a rubber penis made an unscheduled appearance, fired across the stage.

Peter was even more creative. One night Rachel Miller was backstage with the Millers' newborn son. Peter picked him up and carried him onstage. 'Excuse me, sir,' he said. 'Your wife's just given birth to this.' 'Just put it in the fridge,' said Miller, a brilliant ad-lib which brought the house down. But at the interval, Miller reprimanded him. 'You might have dropped him,' he said. 'Never having wittingly dropped a baby in my life I felt a little aggrieved,' recalled Peter. 'He was the one who was clumsy with props.' [46] During a subsequent performance, Peter carried Dudley onstage. 'I've discovered this man in bed with your wife and so I shot him,' [47] said Peter. As Alan and Jonathan grew apart, Peter and Dudley were growing together. 'I loved performing with Peter in the latter years of *Beyond The Fringe*,' [48] said Dudley. Initially, Jonathan and Peter had seemed more alike – extrovert and middle class – while Alan seemed more like Dudley – working class and introverted. Yet in this long-running stage show, their truer natures surfaced. Alan and Jonathan were thinkers – Peter and Dudley were entertainers. 'We were the two performers in *Beyond The Fringe* who had no qualms about doing it,' said Peter. 'Jonathan thought he should be a doctor. Alan thought he should be teaching history at Oxford University. Dudley and I just had a ball.' [49]

Peter had become tired of repeating the same lines night after night, and in Dudley he'd found someone with the same improvisational flair. 'As the show went on I began to enjoy the digressions more than the written text,' he reflected. 'I particularly looked forward to Dudley interrupting the civil defence sketch. The barmy ad-libbed questions and answers, usually nothing to do with the subject, were the highlight of the evening for me. I think it was this kind of daft random backchat that led to the two of us working together on television.' [50] This shared appetite for improvisation was equally evident offstage. When Dudley went to Peter and Wendy's place for Christmas Day, Peter and Dudley had everyone in stitches, riffing off-the-cuff about the Dead Sea Scrolls.

Alan and Dudley eventually fell out over Dudley's attempts to spice up the script, precisely the sort of ad-libbing which Peter most enjoyed. 'We had a sketch which Peter rather unkindly called the Boring Old Man sketch, where Alan was interviewed by all of us in turn,' said Dudley. 'One night I played it a little differently, to try and get something out of the audience. And it worked, or so I thought.' [51] Alan disagreed. 'I think it's the worst performance we've ever given,' [52] he said afterwards. Dudley said they hardly spoke to each other after that. 'I guess he thought I'd tampered with his words, but I found it difficult to believe the way he reacted.' [53] In fact, Alan soon forgot about it. It was Dudley who let it fester.

Usually these sorts of pranks are the sure sign of a poor show – performers entertaining one another, rather than the audience. Yet this time the audience were in on the joke, and so the more the performers mugged and corpsed, the more the audience enjoyed it.

'I think this was partly because they knew that the show belonged to us entirely,' explained Miller. 'I think they felt we were in on some sort of secret.' [54] Yet Miller was becoming increasingly unhappy onstage. His stammer returned. He even went to see a doctor about it. 'It was surely a form of stage fright,' writes his biographer, Kate Bassett, 'almost as if he were gagging at being a gagman.' [55] Miller left the show at Christmas, six months ahead of schedule. 'It was a great relief,' said Bennett. 'He and I really got on each other's nerves.' [56] Apart from an appearance in the film *One Way Pendulum* in 1964, Miller never acted again.

Miller was replaced by Paxton Whitehead, an English actor based in America who'd appeared in American sitcoms. Physically, he was similar to Miller, but inevitably the show wasn't the same. What made *Beyond The Fringe* special was that the performers were cracking their own jokes, rather than reciting someone else's. 'Mr Whitehead,' wrote the *New York Times*, 'reminds you of a man who isn't there.' However the new show included some new material, most notably 'One Leg Too Few'. Peter had been batting this sketch around for several years, with several different co-stars, but it was only when Dudley did it that it clicked. 'I think Alan tried the part first, but he made it too maudlin,' [57] revealed Dudley. 'Jonathan could play Mr Spiggot, the unidexter artiste, but he never really got his essential optimism. [58] My boundless optimism was the key.' [59] As an added bonus, Dudley really was 'deficient in the leg division'. This sketch would become their calling card.

The new show also featured some good gags about America ('I gather the Negroes are sweeping the country – it's one of the few jobs they can get') but the buzz was gone. *Beyond The Fringe* closed in April 1964, after 669 performances. The London show, with its replacement cast, trundled on until 1966. 'Beyond The Fringe took nearly five years of our time and made £400,000 profit for the backers in England and America,' said Peter. 'If only we had put up the money ourselves we could have had that profit. As it was we got £75 a week each in London and £500 a week each in America.' [60] Dudley was similarly aggrieved. 'We could have made a lot of money except that we believed everything we were told about financial terms and felt that it was grubby to be interested in the commercial side,' [61] he said. Neither of them would make the same mistake again.

Dudley with his mum and dad, Jock and Ada.

CHAPTER TWELVE

HOMEWARD BOUND

'What I do in the future rather depends on what Cook does.
Write that down and I'll get lots of letters of sympathy.'

(Dudley Moore, *Sun*, 1 March 1965)

To avoid paying two sets of taxes, Peter and Dudley had to stay in America until April. Wendy went home, with Judy Scott-Fox. Her baby was due in May. Peter had been offered a job doing stand-up in casinos in Las Vegas, but though the money was good he couldn't face it. 'I didn't have the nerve,' [1] he said. He didn't want to stay in America yet he was dreading his return to England. Even at a distance of three thousand miles, he could sense that the satire bubble was about to burst. 'The whole of England is overwhelmed by satirists,' he said. 'The whole island is going to sink, giggling, into the sea.' [2] He even talked about retiring, and although this was clearly just a joke, for the first time since he'd left Cambridge he didn't quite know what to do next. *Beyond The Fringe* was finished, the four performers had gone their separate ways, and, while he'd been busy setting up The Establishment in Manhattan, back in Soho the original Establishment Club had collapsed.

The first sign of trouble had come in April 1963, when Nicholas

Luard booked Lenny Bruce for a return trip. Bruce's first visit had been a big success, but the British press whipped up one of their prurient moral panics, and when he arrived at Heathrow on 8 April he was detained, strip-searched, and put on the next plane back to New York. The Tory Home Secretary Henry Brooke denounced him as an undesirable alien and a threat to public order. He said that Bruce's visit was not in the public interest, due to his 'sick jokes and lavatory humour' (a catchphrase which subsequently adorned the masthead of *Private Eye*). Peter tried to find a way of smuggling Bruce into England, by flying him to Ireland and putting him on a ferry to Wales, but for once his efforts were in vain. Bruce had been paid most of his fee up front, and the legal costs were considerable. The affair left Peter about £2,000 out of pocket.

In the same month that Bruce was deported, Peter's cultural magazine *Scene* ceased publication. Launched in September 1962, when The Establishment was riding high, *Private Eye* called it *Scone* ('the new all-hip weekly paper devoted to all branches of the catering trade') but the idea was a good one, anticipating the success of *Time Out*. But *Time Out* started as a single listings sheet. *Scene* was an expensive glossy. Within six months it had run out of cash. The company behind it, Nicholas Luard Associates, went bankrupt on 28 June 1963. Its sole claim to fame was that it employed the future playwright Tom Stoppard as its first – and final – theatre critic.

'We were naive enough to do everything under the same company, so when *Scene* came down, it brought down The Establishment,'[3] said Peter. This was true enough, but the club itself was also in deep trouble. Peter's absence left a void onstage, and Chicago's Second City were no substitute for the joyous anarchy of the original British cast. 'They were immensely talented,' reflected Luard, 'but they were a little too earnest, a little too rigid and contrived.'[4] However, the biggest problem was financial. Like a lot of bright new businesses, The Establishment had expanded far too fast. The *Observer* calculated that more than sixty people were employed at 18 Greek Street in one way or another, and running such a big concern didn't just require creative flair – it needed cold economic nous. 'Neither Peter nor Nicholas knew the first thing about stock control,' reflected Wendy. 'At least half the goods moved out of the back door as soon as they came in the front.'[5] Peter was three thousand miles away, and Luard was no match for the vultures that descended on the club, sensing easy pickings. According to John Wells, 'the staff turned out to be fiddling the management blind.'[6] Willie Rushton reckoned most of the waiters were on the take. To try and keep the club afloat, Wendy sold two diamond brooches (inherited from her grandmother) for £1,200. Elisabeth Luard also pawned some jewellery, but it was too little too late. On 23 September 1963, Cook & Luard Productions went into voluntary liquidation. Peter thought he'd be a millionaire by the time he was thirty. Instead he found himself £75,000 in debt. His personal liability was £10,000. At the bankruptcy hearing, the accountant who went through their books was blunt. 'The directors have acted in a stupid, foolhardy way,'[7] he said. Their own solicitor described them as 'utter fools'.[8] They'd lost nearly £27,000 of their own money and left over a hundred suppliers more than £24,000 short. A tough Lebanese businessman called Raymond Nash stepped in and did a deal with the creditors, on the condition that Peter and Luard maintained their association with the club. Nash promised Peter that nothing would change, but though the *Guardian* claimed that The Establishment would continue 'in the same old satirical way' Peter wasn't fooled. 'We all knew he'd wreck the place,'[9] he said.

Nash persuaded The Establishment cast to leave New York and return to London. They came home and performed a new show, but the ambience had changed. Now the atmosphere was seedy and rather menacing. There was gaming on the first floor, singers were encouraged to show more cleavage. The Establishment was never the same again.

'I lost interest in business as soon as I went out of business,' [10] said Peter. Still, the one thing he salvaged from the wreckage was his majority share in *Private Eye*. He'd wanted to start a satirical magazine for almost as long as he'd wanted to start a satirical nightclub, so he was gutted when Christopher Booker, his friend from Cambridge, arrived at The Establishment with the first issue of *Private Eye*. 'It pissed me off no end,' [11] he said. Swallowing his frustration, Peter told Booker how much he admired his new magazine and offered him a useful tip. Peter had seen an American magazine called *Sick* which appended satirical speech bubbles to photos of public figures. Why didn't Booker do something similar on the cover of *Private Eye*? Booker adopted this device, which remained the hallmark of the magazine thereafter. Despite doing the *Eye* this favour, Peter wasn't spared. The sixth issue included a cartoon by Willie Rushton, about a young wag called Jonathan Crake who cracks some jokes at Cambridge, appears in a topical revue called *Short Back & Sides*, opens a satirical nightclub in Fulham and becomes a drunken Midas, unable to ask the way to the Gents without everyone collapsing in fits of laughter. Rushton's lampoon was to prove eerily prophetic.

Private Eye quickly acquired cult status but its circulation remained modest, and in 1962 its majority owner, Andrew Osmond, decided to sell up. Cook & Luard Productions offered him £1,500 for 75 of his 99 shares. Osmond had put in £450, so he was glad to accept this offer. As a parting gesture, he gave half his profits to Willie Rushton, Christopher Booker and their colleague Peter Usborne. He felt bad about abandoning them. He feared the *Eye* wouldn't survive. In fact, Luard ended up buying Osmond's shares in his own name, something Peter didn't discover until Cook & Luard Productions went bust. Peter wasn't best pleased about this revelation (to put it mildly) but, as it turned out, this was actually a stroke of luck. These shares weren't swallowed up by the bankruptcy, but remained Luard's own property. Mortified by his failure to keep The Establishment afloat in Peter's absence, Luard gave his shares to Peter and went away to Spain. Despite the collapse of Cook & Luard Productions, the Cooks and Luards remained on good terms. After the Luards went to Spain, and Peter and Wendy returned from America, they moved into their vacant flat near Hyde Park.

Peter was pleased to be the *Eye*'s new owner. Fascinated by the press, and delighted by its absurdities and hypocrisies, he was perfectly suited to his new role as the proprietor of a satirical magazine. 'Wherever he went, he carried huge bundles of newspapers,' [12] said John Fortune. Despite his literary education, his friends could hardly recall him reading anything else.

Private Eye moved into The Establishment and produced several issues from the waiters' changing room. This was hardly ideal. Not only did the writers have to share the room with changing waiters, but the only way in or out was across the stage so anyone still in there at six p.m. was stuck there until the show was over. There were other problems, too. Despite their shared enthusiasm for satire, *Private Eye* and The Establishment were poles apart. *Private Eye* was boozy, irreverent and conservative. The Establishment was sober, liberal and intellectual. The Establishment were Roundheads in black polo necks. *Private Eye* were Cavaliers in scruffy tweeds. 'Taking oneself too seriously was a major crime in *Eye* circles,' wrote Harry Thompson in his biography of Richard Ingrams. '*Private Eye* disapproved of the Establishment Club in much the same way that it disapproved of the establishment.' [13] A series of working lunches only made things worse. 'We never spoke to each other,' said Rushton. 'We viewed each other with intense suspicion.' [14] The rival camps even sat on opposite sides of the room.

Although he'd gone to Cambridge, like Bird and Fortune, rather than to Oxford, like Paul Foot and Richard Ingrams, Peter was no Roundhead, and he bridged the gap between these two sides. His input had a dramatic effect. *Private Eye* became funnier – and more hard-hitting, too. Incredibly, it ended up breaking the inside story of the Profumo scandal when one of the chief protagonists, the society osteopath Stephen Ward, walked into the offices and spilled the beans after seeing a cryptic cartoon in the *Eye* which led him to assume (quite mistakenly) that they knew all about the affair. Sales doubled and then quadrupled. Yet by the time Peter returned from America, the circulation had withered from 95,000 to less than 20,000. The magazine had missed his dynamic influence, and the tide of history had turned. Macmillan had resigned, robbing Peter of his favourite target, and *TW3* had saturated the satire market. It had appropriated a lot of the *Eye*'s best writers, and TV had gobbled up their best material. Topical humour was no longer edgy or alternative. David Frost had made it mainstream, and now it felt like old news.

Peter reinvigorated the *Eye* with his mere presence, but he provided practical help as well. With Richard Ingrams, he toured the North-

East, galvanising distributors in far-flung outposts like Darlington and Middlesbrough. He also put his money where his mouth was, stumping up £2,000 and coaxing £100 contributions from celebs like Jane Asher, Dirk Bogarde and Peter Sellers. He hatched the idea of *Mrs Wilson's Diary*, a spoof journal supposedly written by the wife of the new Prime Minister. With Barry Fantoni, he created Neasden FC (a useless football club) and The Turds (satirical cousins of The Beatles). Peter also brought new blood into the magazine. 'He was a great promoter of talent,' said Ingrams. [15] Peter introduced Barry Humphries to Nicholas Garland, and encouraged them to collaborate on *The Adventures of Barry McKenzie* (Garland drew the pictures, Humphries wrote the words). Described by Peter as an 'Australian Candide,' [16] and by Humphries as 'a kind of early version of Crocodile Dundee,' [17] this innovation was an example of Peter's fine disregard for prevailing fashion. When Humphries was still largely unknown, Peter had hired him to play The Establishment for the princely fee of £100 per week, and hadn't seemed remotely bothered that he'd died on his proverbial arse. 'He was convinced I would be a big success in London,' [18] recalled Humphries. 'I died an incredible death. [19] He never saw the show, fortunately, since he was still working in New York when I opened – and closed.' [20] 'Nobody knew what on Earth he was talking about,' said Peter. 'Dame Edna in those days was rather dowdy, just a Melbourne suburban housewife.' [21] Humphries's comic strip, conversely, became a massive hit, repaying Peter's faith in Humphries, launching Garland's new career as a cartoonist, and eventually spawning two feature films. 'That, at the time, was the most popular feature we had in *Private Eye*,' [22] said Ingrams. The magazine was rejuvenated, the circulation recovered and *Private Eye* remained the one constant in Peter's career, long outliving The

Establishment – and even his partnership with Dudley.

In the meantime, Peter had become a dad. His daughter Lucy was born at Charing Cross Hospital on 4 May 1964. Peter had asked to be present at the birth, still an unusual request at that time. Heroically, Wendy kept her false eyelashes on throughout the labour. With the Luards due to return to London, the new family moved to another rented flat, in Knightsbridge, while Wendy started looking for a family house. As ever, bringing up a baby brought new challenges to the marriage. 'Although Peter was a doting father, he never volunteered to change a nappy and when he was working he expected a decent night's sleep,' [23] remembered Wendy. Not that he was doing that much work. *Private Eye* kept him busy, but one reason he had so much time to devote to it was because, since his return from America, his performing career had gone quiet. Jonathan Miller was working for *Monitor*, the BBC's arts strand. Alan Bennett was working with Eleanor Bron, John Bird and John Fortune on a new television series starring David Frost, called *Not So Much A Programme, More A Way of Life*. Peter had discussions with the BBC about a role on their TV show *Tonight*, but it never came to anything. He'd never been an outright satirist (his humour was more surreal than satirical) yet as the founder of The Establishment he was seen as the voice of satire – and satire was now seen as last year's thing.

Peter got back together with Alan Bennett and Jonathan Miller to try and write a film. The idea was inspired (the Prussian Kaiser plans to destabilise the British Empire with a battalion of Queen Victoria lookalikes) but their writing sessions confirmed that they were incapable of working together again. 'We sat round the table simply destroying each other's stuff,' recalled Peter. 'I don't know if it was successful but it made us all take up smoking again.' [24] Another brilliant idea – a film of Evelyn Waugh's journalistic satire *Scoop*, co-written with John Bird – hit the buffers on account of the dramatic differences in their writing styles. Bird's scenes were full of detailed camera directions, while Peter wrote reams of dialogue. Looking back, it seems a shame that they chose to write their contributions separately, rather than together. As Wendy observed, Peter was most productive when there was someone else around to act as a sounding board for his ideas.

Peter was rescued from the wilderness by the Canadian broadcaster Bernard Braden. Peter had met Braden when he was performing with the Footlights. Now Braden was presenting his own Saturday-night series on ITV called *On The Braden Beat*. He invited Peter to reprise his Mr Grole character on the programme. A light-hearted blend of current and consumer affairs, a sort of forerunner to *That's Life*, *On The Braden Beat* wasn't the most obvious forum for Peter's surrealist talents. But it was a hit show with a big audience, and Braden was a clever, cultured man who understood Peter's sense of humour. He gave Peter four weekly slots as Grole – 'a man on a park bench who talks endlessly about everything and knows nothing,' [25] as Peter put it. Renamed E.L. Wisty, but still wearing Grole's crumpled mac and battered trilby, Wisty mesmerised the nation and four episodes turned into twenty. Successful spin-offs included an LP and a series of radio and TV commercials for Watneys Ale.

As E.L. Wisty became a household name, Peter took good care to conceal the character's original inspiration. 'I've never met the man,' he told reporters. 'He came out of me.' [26] This was partly an act of kindness, to protect Mr Boylett from the attentions of Fleet Street, but by now this white lie had some substance. What had started out as straightforward mimicry had escaped its schoolboy origins, and had grown into something more abstract. 'I'm terrified I shall become some sort of Wisty figure,' [27] said Peter, but, in a way, he was already. Wisty was the voice within him, an autistic alter ego running 24/7 inside his head. Every Wednesday, Peter would talk into a tape recorder for up to five hours as E.L. Wisty, then distil the contents into a compact monologue, which was copied onto cue cards ready for recording on Thursday. Since Wisty stared straight at the camera, reciting his lines as if by rote, this technique worked a treat. It increased Peter's reliance on the autocue, which hampered his performance when he came to play less static, stilted roles, but for now that hardly mattered. Up and down the country, viewers imitated his nasal whine, as they had done at Cambridge and Radley. The difference was that now, instead of entertaining hundreds (as his Boylett had done at Radley) or thousands (as his Mr Grole had done at Cambridge), E.L. Wisty commanded the attention of millions of unseen fans.

Of the four Fringers, Dudley remained in New York the longest, playing jazz at the Village Vanguard. He made a recording with Dizzy Gillespie, but his main project was collaborating with playwright and director Ben Shaktman, writing the score for a musical version of Eugene O'Neill's play, *The Emperor Jones*. The show was due to premiere in August at the Boston Arts Festival, starring James Earl Jones, and Dudley rented a house on Cape Ann, near Boston, and set to work on the score. It wasn't all work and no play. Peter Bellwood came to stay. An enormous house next door bore a wrought-iron nameplate that read 'Tranquillity', so they made a makeshift wooden sign which read 'Anxiety'. It was just a joke, of course, a harmless stunt to tease the neighbours, but it was also the title of Dudley's first childhood composition. Shaktman perceived a conflict in Dudley, between popular entertainer and serious classical musician. It was a tension that he would never resolve. Anxiety, rather than tranquillity, would remain his leitmotif.

Dudley worked hard on *The Emperor Jones*. He even flew over to London to record his score with a full orchestra, bringing a recording back to America to use in rehearsals. The first night in August at the Boston Public Garden was attended by more than four thousand people. 'In conception, a masterpiece; in execution, not far below,' reported *The Harvard Crimson*. 'It will be a shame if this Emperor Jones dies at the end of the week.' [28] Sadly, it did just that. O'Neill's widow wouldn't allow Shaktman to take the show elsewhere, and so Dudley's score was never played again. The only other job offer on the horizon was an invitation from the BBC to film *Beyond The Fringe* for TV. Feeling homesick, Dudley decided to return to Blighty. Peter, Alan and Jonathan had all bought houses with the money they'd made in America – Peter in Hampstead, Alan and Jonathan in Camden. Dudley didn't buy a house. He moved in with his friend George Hastings in Hastings's flat in Shepherd's Market.

Unlike Peter, Dudley had no trouble finding work. His talents were broader, and less closely shackled to the satire boom. The Dudley Moore Trio took up residence at the Cool Elephant Club, and Dudley appeared in a musical series called *Offbeat*. He did so well that the BBC offered him his own Variety special. It was a 45-minute pilot, to do with as he wanted. Dudley got in touch with Peter and asked if he'd like to be in the show.

Peter and Dudley with Peter Sellers on the set of *Not Only ... But Also*.

CHAPTER THIRTEEN

NOT ONLY ... BUT ALSO

DUDLEY MOORE: 'Where did you strat your work?

SIR ARTHUR STREEB-GREEBLING: I think it can be said
of me that I have never, ever strated my work.
That is one thing I have never done. I can lay
my hand on my heart, or indeed anybody else's
heart, and say I have never strated my work,
never strated at all. I think what you probably
know is when I started my work. You've misread
completely the question.

('Ravens', *Not Only ... But Also*, BBC2, 1965)

Dudley's invitation to Peter to join him on *The Dudley Moore Show* marked the beginning of the best double act in the history of British comedy, but it didn't seem like that at the time. Peter was only one of several special guests. He wasn't even the biggest name. His billing on the programme was eclipsed by the presence of John Lennon, who was at the height of his Beatlemania phase of fame. Landing a star as big as Lennon was a fantastic coup but it made the billing a bit awkward. Dudley was now headlining a programme whose supporting cast included someone far more famous than the show's supposed star. Sensibly (and sportingly) Dudley suggested that the

BBC should change the title, from *The Dudley Moore Show* to *Not Only* (Dudley Moore) *But Also* (John Lennon, Peter Cook & Co). It was a logical decision, and the title that Dudley proposed was excellent – enigmatic yet memorable, much like *Beyond The Fringe*. Even so, it was a suggestion which betrayed a lack of confidence. There aren't many TV stars who'd suggest removing their name from the title of their own show.

The show's producer and director was Joe McGrath, a jovial and talented Glaswegian who'd worked with Dudley before. 'My first job as a director was at ABC television,' recalls McGrath. 'During a technicians' strike I was asked to put together a short show – a sort of trainee directors' exercise. I contacted Dudley and he agreed to take part. He duly played the piano, accompanying a cartoon by Bob Godfrey about Aristophanes' *The Birds*. He also sang in his well-known falsetto and did a couple of numbers with his trio. He did all this as a favour to me. Years later, when I contacted him about doing *The Dudley Moore Show*, which became *Not Only ... But Also* he agreed to appear and asked me, "Will I get paid this time?" He certainly did!'[1]

Now at the BBC, McGrath was keen to break into the movies. Rather than producing a standard studio-based programme, he wanted to shoot a lot of *Not Only ... But Also* on film, on location, to show prospective producers what he could do. There would be music, of course (this was still supposed to be Dudley's show, despite the new title) and poetry, too – Lennon had agreed to recite two poems from his illustrated book of nonsense verse, *In His Own Write (And Draw)*. Lennon's poetry recital was filmed on Wimbledon Common, with the Beatle perched on a children's swing – a subtle send-up of the arty style of Jonathan Miller's *Monitor*. Dudley was assigned to push him, but he pushed him a bit too hard. One of Lennon's contact lenses flew out and was lost for ever in the long grass. Lennon's modest fee was less than the cost of his new lenses, but he didn't bear a grudge. Afterwards, he joined them for dinner at a local Chinese restaurant. 'I really dig what you're doing,' [2] he told them. Lennon got up and danced on the table. The owner said he'd never let him in again.

Joe McGrath had planned to write most of the script, with his writing partner Bob Fuest, but he was more than happy to let Peter write a couple of sketches. Naturally they'd need to feature Dudley, but within these confines Peter had a free hand. He came up with two of the finest sketches of his career. 'Ravens' marked the debut of Sir Arthur Streeb-Greebling, a stupid but supremely self-assured toff who's wasted his life trying (and failing) to teach ravens to fly underwater:

DUDLEY: Sir Arthur, is it difficult to get ravens to fly underwater?

SIR ARTHUR STREEB-GREEBLING: Well, I think the word 'difficult' is an awfully good one here. Yes, it is. It's well-nigh impossible. The trouble is, you see, God, in his infinite wisdom and mercy, has designed these creatures to fly in the air, rather than through the watery substances of the deep. Hence they experience enormous difficulty, as you said, in beating their tiny wings against the water. It's a disastrous experience for them.

Peter's other sketch owed quite a bit to E.L. Wisty, but two things compelled him to turn Wisty into something new: E.L. Wisty was otherwise engaged on ITV, and a monologue was out of the question, since he needed to find a role for Dudley. Rather than a loner, spouting nonsense on a park bench, Peter created something more familiar, a philosophising pub bore. Dudley played his acolyte, hanging on his every word. They called their characters Pete & Dud. They soon became their alter egos. 'Pete is the informed idiot and Dud is the uninformed idiot,' said Peter. 'They're both idiots, but Pete is always slightly superior. In fact, he knows nothing either.' [3]

The masterstroke was locating this sketch (and all its sequels) in Dudley's native Dagenham. This grounded Peter's flights of fancy, and allowed Dudley to create a character who was more than just a stooge. 'I drew my own character from various inoffensive men I'd known, including myself,' [4] he said. A particular inspiration was a congregant from his parish church. 'I never knew his name,' said Dudley. 'He almost made me cry because he was so pathetic and didn't know anything about anything,' [5] Dudley peppered his responses with prosaic childhood memories – a perfect counterpoint to Pete's autodidactic gibberish. 'I used to build my humour by elaborating on things that had happened to me,' said Dudley. 'Peter's came out of left field.' [6] It was this combination which gave Pete & Dud such staying power. 'They discuss the same lofty subjects as E.L. Wisty,' [7] said Peter. Yet unlike E.L. Wisty, Pete & Dud were rooted in the real world.

Pete & Dud's first sketch, subsequently known as 'Film Stars', was based on one of Peter's many private jokes. At the end of a perfectly friendly phone conversation, he'd yell, 'Goodbye for ever!,' slam down the phone, and tell whoever else was in the room, 'That was that bloody Sophia Loren again.' Peter stretched this one-liner into a shaggy-dog story, as Pete & Dud swapped tall tales about being pestered by a succession of sex-starved movie starlets, whom they would rebuff with withering contempt:

PETE: I was just about to drop off when suddenly – tap,
        tap, tap at the bloody window pane. I looked out.
        You know who it was?

DUD: Who?

PETE: Bloody Greta Garbo, stark naked, save for a
        shortie nightie, hanging on to the windowsill
        – I could see her knuckles all white – saying,
        'Peter, Peter.' You know how these bloody Swedes
        go on. I said, 'Get out of it!' She wouldn't go. I
        had to smash her down with a broomstick.

Ironically, by now the idea of Peter and Dudley being courted by female film stars wasn't actually so far-fetched, but in their Dagenham personae it was a marvellous conceit. Yet when they did a read-through, at Sulgrave Boys' Club on Goldhawk Road, the characters fell completely flat. Pete & Dud only came to life when they put on their costumes. 'They arrived fully formed,' [8] said Peter. Kitted out in flat caps and flashers' macs, their estuarial alter egos had acquired personalities of their own.

Pete & Dud moved up another gear when they went into the studio to film the sketch in front of a live audience. Much like *Beyond The Fringe*, the set and props were minimal – just a table and two pints of bitter. Members of the audience weren't being asked to suspend their disbelief. This was just Peter and Dudley, mucking about. As Dudley said, 'We were very relaxed with each other and that feeling transmitted itself to the box.' [9] A sketch that had run for less than three minutes in rehearsal now ran to nearly twelve. One reason it went on so long was because Dudley was trying not to corpse, and Peter was trying to make him. 'Peter's delight was to make Dudley corpse,' said Alexander Games, the author of a perceptive biography of Peter and Dudley. 'He could make anybody corpse but I think he got a special thrill out of seeing Dudley unable to control his hysteria. It was almost sexual.' [10] At one point during 'Film Stars', Peter corpsed himself, banging the table in an attempt to regain his composure. By rights, this should have come across as the worst sort of self-indulgence but, just as in *Beyond The Fringe*, Peter and Dudley were having so much fun that their shared enjoyment was infectious. It was joyous and unpretentious, and it had everyone on the studio floor in fits.

'Peter kept a lot of lines up his sleeve to see what effect they had on Dudley,' said McGrath. 'He was like a matador with a bull.' [11] 'I'm just getting off to kip, when suddenly I feel a hand on my cheek,' said Dudley. 'Which cheek was that?' asked Peter, poker-faced. 'Come on! Which cheek was it?' 'The left upper,' spluttered Dudley, trying desperately not to laugh. McGrath was watching from the gallery, alongside Tom Sloan, the BBC's new Head of Light Entertainment, and Michael Peacock, the new Controller of BBC 2. McGrath found these ad-libs hilarious, but Sloan was not amused. 'Aren't you going to pick up all those fluffs?' he asked McGrath. 'They're not fluffs,' said McGrath. Sloan wanted McGrath to reshoot the sketches, without Dudley corpsing. Thankfully, Frank Muir and Denis Norden were there too. They told Sloan to leave it. 'If this is Light Entertainment, I'm in the wrong business,' [12] he said. 'I think you're in the wrong business,' [13] said Michael Peacock, the new Controller of BBC2. 'I want six of these,' [14] he told McGrath.

The next morning, Peter, Dudley and McGrath went to the BBC's TV Centre for a meeting with Michael Peacock. Peacock commissioned a series, and stipulated that Peter should be in all the episodes. *Not Only Dudley Moore But Also Peter Cook* had become *Not Only Dudley Moore & Peter Cook*. It might well have happened without him, and many people played a bigger role, but in a sense Peacock was the originator of their double act. Peter, Dudley and Joe McGrath left Peacock's office in high spirits. After the setbacks of the previous year, Peter was particularly happy. It was like being back at university, he told McGrath, but with bigger grants. 'No running in the corridors!' said Peter, sternly, then sprinted off down the hall.

The pilot was broadcast on BBC2 on 9 January 1965. Six further episodes (each lasting 45 minutes, like the pilot) were scheduled to go out once a fortnight, commencing a fortnight later. Still less than a year old, BBC2 was very much the junior partner to BBC1, but they were grateful for a low-profile launch, giving the show time to find its feet. The title was changed yet again, from *Not Only Dudley Moore & Peter Cook* to *Not Only Peter Cook & Dudley Moore*, after Dudley rearranged the billing in alphabetical order to avoid upsetting Peter. 'Dudley felt slightly in awe of Peter,' said McGrath. 'They started off equal, but Peter was more equal than Dudley.' [15] Dudley described their double act as a partnership between a know-all and a yes-man. As he said himself, he followed Peter around like a chihuahua.

The papers all loved the show, from the *Sun* to *The Times*. Peter and Dudley had bridged the class divide. Their Oxbridge humour had become universal. 'Surely no two people have ever before united so many talents so successfully, the verbal wit, the songs, the visual fantasies ...' [16] raved Margaret Drabble in the *Daily Mail*. Recordings were like first nights, with a studio audience of five hundred. Wendy would go along with a big group of friends, all dressed up for the occasion. The show didn't go out live but it was virtually shot as such, and McGrath's direction heightened the sense of theatricality. Keeping cutaways and retakes to a minimum, he homed in on the performers' faces, highlighting every grin and giggle. Small budgets and tight schedules meant there wasn't much in the way of costumes or scenery but, like *Beyond The Fringe*, *Not Only ... But Also* made a virtue out of a necessity. This informality made the audience feel part of something special, at home and in the studio. Even the technical crew looked forward to it all week.

By far the biggest attraction was the chemistry between Peter and Dudley. 'They would just sit down and start doing Pete & Dud when they came into the office, or during rehearsals, or in the BBC canteen,' said McGrath. 'It didn't stop. It just went on. They could have gone on doing Pete & Dud for the rest of their lives.' [17] Like a happily married couple, you couldn't imagine them apart. 'There was nothing to indicate it was going to happen,' said Jonathan Miller. 'Yet when it did happen it seemed quite natural. Once you saw what they were doing together, it seemed inevitable.' [18] Their physical disparity was intrinsically funny, but they also complimented one another temperamentally, in virtually every way. Peter was middle-class, Dudley was working-class. Peter was verbal, Dudley was visual. Peter was high-status, Dudley was low-status. Peter was the clever-clogs, Dudley played the fool. They completed one another, like missing pieces in a jigsaw puzzle. Now the audience had someone to feel sorry for, and someone to admire. 'There was a sort of sweet, proletarian, cuddlesome quality about Dudley,' said Miller. 'It's very hard to imagine the success of the show without Dudley's talent as a performer.' [19] For the first time, Peter was up against someone who was his equal – not an outright competitor, but someone with a completely different set of skills. 'I view them as equals,' said Richard Ingrams. 'I know Peter plays the dominant characters, but when you look at them performing together, Dudley's actually the one who makes me laugh more.' [20]

Dudley didn't go head-to-head with Peter – he was happy to defer to him, for now – but his warmth and musicality were talents that Peter could never hope to duplicate. Even when his input seemed paltry, the sketches played far better when he was supplying the feed lines. Peter knew what an asset Dudley was, even if it was hard to quantify. 'Martin and Lewis were a hilarious act together, but most people thought Jerry Lewis was the funny one,' he said. 'What does Dean Martin do? The answer is he makes Jerry Lewis funny.' [21] Like all successful partnerships, it was a reciprocal arrangement. Dudley had found a writer with boundless energy and imagination. Peter had found the perfect foil for his weird other-worldly wit.

Even their acting methods were complementary. When they were filming Pete & Dud, Peter relied on idiot boards or the teleprompter, giving him free rein to improvise. Yet the only reason he could get away with this loose approach was because Dudley stuck to the script, having memorised his lines word for word by copying them out in longhand. The way they wrote together was a similar blend of inspiration and hard graft. They'd ad-lib into a tape recorder for hours on end, then edit the results. Dudley provided the structure. Peter provided the spontaneity. Like a lot of the most creative endeavours, it scarcely felt like work. 'We used to sit around and giggle a lot,' said Peter, 'which was a nice way of working.' [22] 'And then we used to listen to it,' added Dudley, 'and giggle even more.' [23] Peter had used the same technique to write his E.L. Wisty monologues, but it worked even better in tandem. Dudley reckoned Peter had seventeen ideas for each one of his but, even though the invention was predominantly Peter's, the discipline was mainly Dudley's. His contribution wasn't something you could measure by the yard. In most writing partnerships, one partner strides around the room, extemporising to their heart's content, while the other sits hunched over the typewriter, trying to give the thing some sense of shape. In this instance, their modus operandi was a tape recorder, not a typewriter, but the principle was the same. Peter found it hard to be creative in a vacuum. He needed someone more matter-of-fact to bounce off. Dudley acted as an editor, bringing Peter's conceptual leaps back down to Earth.

One illogicality Dudley tried hard to curb was Peter's misguided belief that he could sing. 'He always wished he'd been a pop star,' said Dudley, 'but he had no musicality in him.' [24] 'He was tone deaf,' [25] agreed McGrath. 'He couldn't sing a note.' But music was Peter's blind spot. Despite his flair for mimicry, he could barely sing the tune to 'Happy Birthday', yet he was forever trying to find an excuse to air his awful Elvis Presley impersonation. Of course Peter was just joking around, but McGrath was determined not to let this particular joke end up on camera. The one concession he made was allowing Peter to muck in on the signature tune. This proved to be a masterstroke, despite Peter's tin ear. McGrath suggested they do a farewell number in the same sort of style as the nostalgic musical *The Boyfriend*. With the same casual elan that Peter brought to his sketch-writing, Dudley sat down at the piano and rattled off the chorus to 'Goodbyee'. Singing along with Peter, almost drowning him out with a shrill falsetto, Dudley just about managed to carry his tuneless partner along. Indeed, such was the song's success that Decca released it as a single that summer. It reached number eighteen in the hit parade – a lot of sales in those days – making Peter a kind of pop star for a brief time after all.

Each episode was put together in a fortnight – five days writing, two days filming, then rehearsals and recording – and then they'd start all over again. It was a pretty gruelling schedule, and Peter and Dudley invariably wrote up to the wire. 'We were always late on deadlines,' said Peter. 'We always had enough material for the show, but practically inevitably we'd change it. We'd become dissatisfied with the stuff we'd written, and do something at the last minute.' [26] As it turned out, this did the show no harm at all, making the material fresh and vital, and giving the BBC designers no time to construct their usual elaborate (and restrictive) sets. Nearly fifty years later, these sketches still retain the same abstract, ad hoc quality, enhanced rather than restricted by being filmed in black and white.

Sadly, not much remains of this seminal series, due to the BBC's parsimonious policy of recycling old mastertapes. *Not Only ... But Also* wasn't singled out for destruction (countless other classic series were wiped) but its eradication was indicative of the BBC's casual attitude to comedy at that time. While banal news broadcasts were preserved with almost religious devotion, comedies that are revered today were obliterated without a care. Eventually the BBC saw sense, but their change of heart came too late to save Peter and Dudley's masterpiece. One shudders to think what twaddle was taped over it. They even threw away the scripts. That even a sample of their work survived was thanks to Joe McGrath, who ran off his own illicit copies of the first three episodes using a device known as telerecording – an extremely grand name for an extremely rudimentary procedure (you simply pointed a film camera at the TV screen while the programme was being transmitted).

McGrath's blurry muffled bootlegs contain several of the funniest sketches ever broadcast by the BBC, including 'Tramponuns' (featuring Peter as Mother Superior of the trampolining Order of

Saint Beryl) and 'At The Art Gallery', in which Pete & Dud ate a packed lunch at the National Gallery while discussing the finer points of fine art. Their analysis of Rubens was priceless:

PETE: He does all the fat ladies with nothing on. Great big fat ladies, naked except for a tiny little wisp of gauze that always lands on the appropriate place, if you know what I mean. Always, the wind blows a little bit of gauze over you know where, Dud.

DUD: Course, it must be a million to one chance, Pete, that the gauze lands in the right place at the right time, you know.

PETE: Course it is.

DUD: I bet there's thousands of paintings that we're not allowed to see where the gauze hasn't landed in the right place – it's on their nose or something.

PETE: But I suppose if the gauze landed on the wrong place, Dud – you know, landed on the nose or the elbow or somewhere unimportant, what Rubens did was put down his painting and go off to have lunch or something.

DUD: Or have a good look.

This gloriously uninformed debate was further enhanced when Dudley corpsed, spitting his half-eaten sandwich straight at Peter. 'The laughter in the Pete & Dud sketches was never rehearsed,'[27] said McGrath.

These opening episodes proved so popular that, in a reversal of conventional showbiz protocol, Peter Sellers rang up and asked if he could be on the show. He duly appeared in the penultimate episode and Eric Sykes appeared in the finale, but both these episodes were destroyed, along with virtually everything from episode four. Ironically, one of the few routines that wasn't erased was a sketch which was cut – Dudley blacked up, in the shower, singing 'Old Man River', his Al Jolson accent fading as the make-up disappeared down the plughole. Today such a routine might be regarded as rather dubious, but it wasn't pulled for reasons of political correctness. According to McGrath, Peter axed it because Dudley did it alone. 'I think it's wonderful,' Dudley told McGrath, 'but he doesn't want to use it.' [28] *The Dudley Moore Show* had become *Not Only Peter Cook But Also Dudley Moore*.

A lot of great double acts feature a bully and a victim. In this respect, Peter and Dudley were really no different from Laurel and Hardy. Like Stan Laurel, Dudley was usually the dogsbody. Yet unlike Stan Laurel, he rarely had the last laugh. Even when Peter played the underdog, he invariably turned the tables. Even when Dudley played the authority figure, he invariably ended up as the fall guy. Some of the sketches were incredibly cruel. In a sketch called 'Pseudolene', Dudley played an earnest young scientist who's left his job and moved his young family to London, on the understanding that he's been given a new job by Peter, playing a pompous tycoon. Over dinner in a posh restaurant, Peter gradually withdraws the job offer, while pouring all three courses over Dudley's head.

Dudley spent every Sunday back at his childhood home in Dagenham. His account of these visits was pure Pete & Dud, with just a dash of Harold Pinter. 'First I have two helpings of roast lamb. Then I have some beer, and my father has orangeade. Then

I have jelly with fruit in it. Then we all sit in armchairs, and after fifteen minutes my mother says, "What about a cup of tea?" Then we have the tea, and we walk round the garden. Then I have a packet of liquorice allsorts. Then some more tea. Then it's time to go.' [29] Dudley bought his parents a TV set, so they could watch their son on the telly. 'I'm only a little fellow,' he told his mother. 'You'll need a large screen.' [30] 'You put me right off to sleep, dear,' Ada told him, approvingly. 'It was lovely.'

Away from sleepy Dagenham, Dudley's life was considerably more exciting. His second LP with Chris Karan and Pete McGurk, *The Other Side of Dudley Moore*, became the top-selling jazz album in Britain that year. He made numerous TV appearances: *Juke Box Jury*, *On The Braden Beat*, *Billy Cotton's Band Show* ... His love life was just as varied. For a few months he went out with the actress Shirley Anne Field, but he still kept a list in the back of his diary, entitled 'Girls To See Again'. In the spring of 1965 he turned thirty, but he showed no sign of settling down. Yet that summer at the Cool Elephant, while playing the piano with his jazz trio, he met a young woman called Suzy Kendall, and his life changed completely.

A middle-class girl from Derbyshire, Suzy Kendall (born Frieda Harrison) had been to convent school and then art college in Derby, done a bit of modelling (she fell off the catwalk on her debut) and was now working as an actress. She would go on to star in two of the classic movies of the 1960s, *Up The Junction* and *To Sir With Love*. She'd been married before, for just six months, to a jazz musician she met in Italy. She hadn't seen *Beyond The Fringe* or even *Not Only ... But Also*. She didn't know that Dudley was a comedian. Aged twenty-one, she was nearly ten years Dudley's junior. A petite five foot five, she was only a few inches taller. Dudley moved out of his flat and into hers (they both lived in Chelsea). With his black Maserati Mistrale and her yellow E-type Jag – a gift from Dudley – they seemed like the quintessential 1960s couple. Yet behind this glamorous facade, their private life was very simple. It seemed that Dudley's roving days might be over.

Peter and Dudley's partnership was also going from strength to strength. Only a month after the end of its first run on BBC2, *Not Only ... But Also* was repeated on BBC1, introducing them to a much broader audience. 'With an eye on repeats, we never mention anyone over fifty years old in case they die,' [31] said Peter. Their show was timeless, unlike *That Was The Week That Was*. Invitations followed from two bastions of the showbiz establishment, *Sunday Night At The London Palladium* and the Royal Variety Show. In both programmes they appeared as Pete & Dud in two brand new sketches. 'By Appointment', written for the Royal Variety Show, was an indication of their conventional aspirations. The sketch was full of funny lines, but although they mocked the aristocracy, ripping the royal piss out of *Burke's Peerage*, they only poked gentle fun at the monarchy, in deference to the show's guest of honour, the Queen. Three years after she'd seen *Beyond The Fringe*, she would have found this show far tamer. When Macmillan came to see *Beyond The Fringe*, Peter tore into him without mercy. Performing for Her Majesty, they were careful to mind their P's and Q's:

DUD: Her Majesty has the chance to meet some interesting people.

PETE: The trouble is, you see, although they're very interesting, when they get round the Palace they're so nervous they become boring. They're overawed by the occasion. Now the other day, Albert Einstein, the bloke who invented gravity, went round to collect his OBE.

DUD: His what?

PETE: His OBE for inventing the gravity – a very interesting person and a fine mind. The Queen was looking forward to meeting him and asking him a few questions, you see. So Einstein was waiting there, all tense, waiting for his medal. Her Majesty come up and stuck one on him and said to him, 'Hello, Mr Einstein, how does all this gravity business work?' And Einstein was so nervous his teeth dropped out on the floor. Mind you, Her Majesty passed it off very nicely and said, 'Aha, Mr Einstein, I see gravity is at work today.'

It might have been slightly cheeky, but it wasn't satirical in the slightest. Even the most ardent royalist would have struggled to find any cause for offence. Tellingly, Peter reserved his fiercest rhetoric for the Queen's new PM, Harold Wilson. 'Being a socialist, he's fascinated by all the trappings of royalty,' said Pete. 'Before becoming Prime Minister, the grandest building he'd ever seen was the Hampstead Golf Club.' Peter described the Labour leader sniffing around Buckingham Palace, fingering the gold lamé curtains. If anyone had mistaken Peter for a rabid lefty, they were left in no doubt now.

In fact, the script had been given a discreet trim before Her Majesty saw the show. The producer Bernard Delfont demanded several cuts, in particular a (very amusing) reference to the Queen's brother-in-law, Antony Armstrong Jones (Lord Snowdon) being forced to run from Land's End to John O'Groats in a wet suit to get his weight down before he was allowed to marry Princess Margaret. It was precisely the sort of gem which would have sparkled in *Beyond*

The Fringe but Peter acquiesced without a murmur. 'By Appointment' concluded with a chorus of 'Rule Britannia'. The satire boom was over. Peter and Dudley had become mainstream.

Daisy, Wendy, Peter and Lucy in their home in Church Row, Hampstead.

CHAPTER FOURTEEN

THE WRONG BOX

PETER: Making films is all a matter of illusion. Remember *Ben Hur*? All those battles, with thousands of soldiers ...

DUDLEY: Running about.

PETER: To and fro.

DUDLEY: Hither and thither.

PETER: Ants. Ants dressed in uniform. They make these thousands of tiny uniforms and dress the ants in them. Then they tell them to go out and have a battle, and they photograph them, and blow it up big.[1]

Peter and Dudley now had an ideal place in which to write. Wendy had found a handsome Georgian town house for sale in Church Row, one of the most attractive streets in Hampstead. Peter bought it at auction for £24,000. Back in 1965, £24,000 was a lot to pay for any property and Alan Bennett feared they'd never make their money back. He needn't have worried. Similar houses now sell for several million pounds. It was a beautiful building, which had once been owned by H.G. Wells. Spread across five floors, it was the perfect family home. Wendy supervised the extensive renovation, knocking down interior walls and opening up old bricked-up windows. She stripped the woodwork, put up William Morris wallpaper and filled the interior with Victorian antiques. It was fashionable and stylish – the height of 1960s chic. On the top floor was Peter's study, with a wonderful view across the rooftops, where he and Dudley would conjure up their routines. 'You could hear them screaming at the top of the house,' [2] said Wendy. She'd take up a tray of coffee and home-made biscuits and they'd share their latest ideas with her. Their exuberance was exhilarating. 'Being with them was like being a bubble dancing around the surface of a glass of champagne.' [3] Dudley and Suzy subsequently bought their own Georgian house in Hampstead, just around the corner, on Heath Street, and decorated it in a similar style, with stripped pine and William Morris wallpaper. They filled the house with art nouveau lamps. Dudley installed a piano on the first floor and a Hammond organ in the basement. They bought five Persian cats – one named Ada, after Dudley's mum. 'We were inseparable,' recalled Suzy. 'I couldn't stand being apart from him for a day, never mind a week.' [4]

Peter's attic was his workshop, but the heart of his house was the basement kitchen, festooned with copper pots and pans. A superb hostess and an excellent cook, Wendy threw countless dinner parties around the big pine table, as often as two or three times a week. The list of dinner guests reads like a *Who's Who* of the 1960s: John Lennon and Paul McCartney, Peter Ustinov, Alan Bates, Joan Collins, Christopher Logue, Claude Cockburn and Malcolm Muggeridge... 'It was not that Peter had a nose for the centre of things,' observed Elisabeth Luard. 'He *was* the centre of things.' [5] These celebrities had sought him out, rather than the other way around.

It was useful for Peter's career, of course, but it wasn't merely networking. Although most of the guests were showbiz types, there were a few 'civilians' (including the local vicar and the cleaning lady) and the seating plan was deliberately eclectic – Bernard Levin was sat beside the cockney boxer Terry Downes. 'Peter gives the finest parties I've ever been to,' said Downes. 'He looks after everybody, especially the women – gives them that little bit of extra attention. My bird's knocked out by Peter.' [6] Dudley was a frequent guest but he was notably abstemious. He never smoked (even though most people in those days puffed away like chimneys) and rarely drank more than a single glass of wine. At the head of the table, surrounded by this new aristocracy, sat Peter, 'spinning word pictures like candyfloss'. [7] His comic riffs ranged from current affairs to classical mythology, from John Profumo and Christine Keeler to Leda and the Swan.

For their guests this was terrific fun, but Wendy felt there was something almost pathological about her husband's endless need to entertain (Dudley's Hampstead get-togethers were much quieter affairs). 'I never knew what he really felt about anything,' she said. 'Humour was his way of keeping the world at bay.' [8] She wasn't the only one who felt this way. As Christopher Booker said, 'because he was so funny, people expected him to be funny, so he was always on parade.' [9] Michael Bawtree said that when Peter was at a party, any party, he felt compelled to perform from the moment he arrived. Alan Bennett thought this avalanche of jokes was actually a sort of shyness. 'I never wanted to be alone in a room with Peter because he would then go on and on,' he told Wendy. 'It was always better to have three of you there.' [10] John Bird believed it was a form of self-defence. If you couldn't get a word in edgeways, you couldn't ask him what was on his mind. Clearing up after their guests had gone, Peter and Wendy's differences would surface. A wartime baby raised on rationing, Wendy didn't like seeing good food go to waste. 'Why don't you wrap it up and send it to the Chinese?' [11] retorted Peter, as she scraped away the leftovers. As Wendy observed, it was just a joke, but it revealed a widening gulf between them.

These are the sort of tensions that test any normal marriage, but there was nothing normal about Peter's superhuman wit. Arguing with him was like sparring with a brilliant boxer. He had the ability to fell you with one punch. 'I met Muhammad Ali once, and you got the feeling that he had the physical power to destroy you absolutely,' said Peter's *Private Eye* colleague Barry Fantoni. 'Peter had that in an intellectual sense.' [12] Peter could reduce virtually anyone to fits of laughter. Dudley could charm virtually any woman into bed. These were enviable gifts, but it made matrimony a challenge. In their own ways, both men were blessed and cursed with the same Midas touch. Peter was determined that fame wouldn't wreck his family life. 'It'll never ruin me,' he told Jay Landesman. 'I can handle it.' [13] But stronger marriages have been weakened by celebrity's corrosive force.

Wendy was a warm-hearted woman with a healthy sense of fun, but she was essentially rather earnest. In tune with the changing times, she had an interest in various New Age ideas, ideas that Peter found difficult to take seriously. Despite his surreal imagination, he was a rationalist at heart. He was cynical about alternative therapies, the paranormal and suchlike, and could hardly help but mock them. Ever since Boylett and his stones that moved, sending up the supernatural had been a feature of Peter's humour. Now it was his wife who bore the brunt. 'I was good material for his sketches,' she says. Her sincerity and his scepticism made her the inevitable butt of numerous jokes. 'To begin with it was probably quite healthy to be made fun of,' she told Peter's biographer, Harry Thompson, 'but eventually it began to erode my self-confidence.' [14] As Dudley also discovered, what was amusing at a dinner party wasn't quite so funny day in, day out.

In the summer of 1965 Peter and Dudley signed up with Columbia to make three feature films together. Peter was keen to use this opportunity to resurrect two of his own screenplays: the adaptation of Evelyn Waugh's *Scoop* that he'd been writing with John Bird, and the script about Prussian Queen Victoria lookalikes which he'd been working on with Alan Bennett and Jonathan Miller. Both projects were merely works in progress (without much recent work, or progress) but either might have made a super movie. However Columbia weren't interested. They wanted Peter and Dudley to appear in a film called *The Wrong Box*.

Adapted from a novel by Robert Louis Stevenson and his nephew, Lloyd Osbourne, *The Wrong Box* was a complex (and confusing) farce about a tontine, a lottery in which the pot goes to the last surviving entrant. John Mills and Ralph Richardson were cast as the last two survivors. Peter and Dudley played Richardson's fiendish, foolish nephews, who are determined to ensure that their uncle wins the loot. Initially Peter had a far larger part, until Dudley said he wouldn't appear at all unless his role was fleshed out to match Peter's. It was a sign of Dudley's growing confidence that he was willing to call Columbia's bluff. It was a sign of how far Peter and Dudley had both come that Columbia acquiesced. Another indication of their growing status was the advance publicity. Despite the presence of stars like Peter Sellers and Michael Caine, it was Peter and Dudley, making their film debut, who excited the most interest. 'These are big names to brandish at the box office,' announced the *Sunday Times*, 'but there's no doubt that Cook and Moore are the ones which matter most.' [15] In high spirits they set off for a fortnight's filming in Bath, chosen for its splendid Georgian architecture.

At first, they relished the novelty of making a proper feature film on location. 'We laughed ourselves sick,' said the film's director, Bryan Forbes. 'It was a very happy film.' [16] Forbes was a fine director, with films like *Whistle Down The Wind* among his credits, and he was thrilled to be working with two of the hottest comics in the country. 'They were great exponents of black humour and I thought they'd be marvellous,' [17] he said, but little of that humour made it onto the big screen. Neither Peter nor Dudley had done any conventional acting since they were at university, and their sketches had always relied a good deal on improvisation. 'They weren't straight actors and they had to learn a new technique,' [18] said Forbes, but Dudley didn't welcome his attempts to teach them. 'I disagreed with Bryan Forbes a great deal about his approach to comedy,' said Dudley. 'He used to act it all out all the time. He used to do it for you.' [19] Despite these creative differences, the two men became firm friends, and it says a lot for Dudley's diplomacy (or duplicity) that Forbes was amazed to discover, some thirty years later, that Dudley had been unhappy during the shoot. 'Peter was more at ease in front of the camera than Dudley,' [20] said Forbes. He was certainly more pliant, but whether this made for a better performance was debatable, to say the least.

Peter and Dudley did nothing wrong but, speaking someone else's lines, they simply didn't come across as that funny. For Peter in particular it was an uncomfortable revelation, the first indication that his talents might be finite. They might have done better with a better script, but not even Larry Gelbart and Burt Shevelove (who wrote the book for *A Funny Thing Happened On The Way To The Forum*) could breathe much life into this labyrinthine plot. 'I've seen the film a few times and I've never been able to understand quite what goes on in it,' [21] admitted Dudley. Peter Sellers showed these young upstarts how to do it, with a brilliant cameo as a seedy doctor skulking in a cat-infested attic. His single scene (with Peter as his feed) was the only time this lumbering movie really came alive, even though he barely had a decent line to work with. Peter and Dudley had shown they were masters of the sketch show, but as movie actors they still had an awful lot to learn.

Peter was also upstaged by the arrival of his second child, who was born at Charing Cross Hospital on 10 September 1965, midway through the shoot. Peter had known the shoot would clash with Wendy's due date, and Wendy had been anxious that he might miss the birth. However, having 'wined and dined and flattered' [22] them, Forbes secured Peter's presence on the set by promising he'd release Peter as soon as Wendy went into labour. 'By now I was aware of the persuasiveness of showbiz people when they want something,' [23] reflected Wendy. 'I had to queue up to speak to him at parties and it began to pall.' [24] Now that motherhood was her priority, Peter's glitzy lifestyle had lost some of its old sheen.

Thankfully, Forbes kept his word, and Peter dashed back to London just in time. Peter and Wendy named their second daughter Daisy Clementine. After a few days ('just long enough for "happy family" pictures for the press', [25] recalled Wendy) Peter had to return to Bath. This enforced separation from his newborn baby might have accounted for his unusually scathing comments about actors in an interview that he gave a few weeks later. 'The good thing about a university background is, it keeps you from getting as conceited as most actors,' he told the *Sun*. 'Unlike them, you have a period of intellectual activity. You get curious and then you stay curious. This means you're less likely to become enthralled with yourself than the actors and actresses with no cultural or intellectual background. Suddenly they're thrust into prominence. Suddenly they're told they're so important. Everything they do is reported. Usually they just get drunk. They can't cope.' [26] These blunt comments betrayed a distinct unease about the new world he had entered. Peter had felt at home at the BBC, and even in the theatre, but this was an alien environment, one that he could not control. Like those actors he had railed against, from now on a good deal of what he did would be reported, and though he never became conceited or self-enthralled, his intellectual curiosity was scant use to him in his coming battle with the bottle.

Dudley was similarly uneasy about *The Wrong Box*, even declining to turn up for the premiere, leaving an empty seat between Forbes and his wife, Nanette Newman, who'd played the romantic lead opposite Michael Caine. 'I thought my performance was hideous and I was very embarrassed about it,' [27] said Dudley, by way of explanation. They were both quite right to feel awkward – the critical reaction was extremely mixed – 'opulent but overblown,' said the *Daily Mail* – yet Peter and Dudley escaped more or less unscathed. Kenneth Tynan summed up the mood in the *Observer*, applauding their 'unique brand of unadulterated lunacy' (actually conspicuous by its absence in this movie) yet regretting that this script gave them no room 'for the kind of improvised comedy on which their genius thrives.' It was a perceptive critique, which identified a fundamental problem. Peter's extemporisation was the hallmark of his humour. Even in a more experimental movie, the ad-libs which enlivened his head-to-heads in *Not Only ... But Also* would have been impossible to replicate on a film set. There were simply too many other people involved. In the United States, the critics were more enthusiastic, if less astute. 'A farce so fantastic and explosive that it virtually pops right out of the screen,' raved the *New York Times*. But the film didn't do great box office on either side of the Atlantic. Onstage, and on television, Peter and Dudley had proved they were comedians without equal. Whether they could transfer that magic to the big screen remained to be seen.

With *The Wrong Box* in the can, Peter and Dudley immediately embarked on a second series of *Not Only ... But Also*. They'd already written the scripts, while they were shooting *The Wrong Box*. They shot all the location footage in advance, over Christmas. Joe McGrath had left the BBC to make movies and had been replaced by Dick Clement, best known today as the co-writer of two of the BBC's greatest sitcoms, *Porridge* and *The Likely Lads*. Commendably, Clement didn't try too hard to put his own stamp on the programme. He let Peter and Dudley steer the show and shot the second series in much the same style as the first, with Peter and Dudley working on the hoof. 'We used to go off and film on the Monday and we didn't even have a finished script,' said Clement. 'They'd just improvise, and it was brilliant.' [28] Even the finished sketches were enlivened by Peter's games of cat and mouse. 'If Dudley made a mistake, Peter would instantly pick up on it and home in on it,' said Clement. You can see Dudley desperately trying to hold it in and failing, and that became part of the act.' [29]

The title sequences were even more audacious than they had been in Series One. The first series had begun with Dudley playing a piano in a car wash. The second series began with Peter and Dudley playing a piano while being lowered into the Thames. This ambitious sequence nearly ended in disaster, when one of the steel cables holding the grand piano became entangled round Dudley's neck. Clement feared that when the cable was pulled taut, Dudley would be decapitated, but the crane driver was out of earshot so there was no way that he could warn him. Mercifully, the cable unravelled of its own accord, and what Clement called 'the moment which nearly ended Dudley's career – and mine as well' [30] came to nothing.

The rest of the series enjoyed a similarly charmed life. Peter and Dudley were at the peak of their powers, and their relationship had never been better. 'It was a very, very happy partnership,' said Clement. 'Peter was very cerebral and slightly cold whereas Dudley was extremely warm. You put that together and you got a very potent combination.' [31] Since the first series there'd been a slight improvement in the BBC's tape-retention (or non-retention) policy: the Corporation had now decided to keep the first and final episodes of every series, to give future generations some idea of what they were missing. However, there were no pirate copies this time so only two episodes survived, one less than Series One.

The first of these surviving episodes contained several classic sketches, most notably 'Facts Of Life', in which Peter played an awkward father attempting to teach his son Roger (played by Dudley, looking almost prepubescent in school uniform) about the so-called 'opposite number'.

PETER: Roger, in order for you to be brought about, it was necessary for your mother and I to do something. In particular, it was necessary for your mother to sit on a chair – a chair which I had recently vacated and which was still warm from my body.

And then something very mysterious, rather wonderful and beautiful happened, and sure enough, four years later, you were born. There was nothing unhealthy about this, Roger. There's nothing unnatural. It's a beautiful thing in the right hands, and there's no need to think less of your mother because of it. She had to do it, she did it, and here you are.

DUDLEY: I must say it's very kind of you to tell me. One thing, actually, slightly alarms me. I was sitting in this very chair yesterday, sir, and I vacated it, and the cat sat on it while it was still warm. Should we have it destroyed?

PETER: It's a lovely chair, Roger.

DUDLEY: The cat, sir.

PETER: Destroyed? Oh no, Roger, you don't understand. This thing of which I speak can only happen between two people who are married, and you're not married.

DUDLEY: Not yet anyway, sir.

PETER: Not to the cat, in any case.

In episode two Dudley played the winner of the Most Boring Man In The World contest:

PETER: Was there any time during the proceedings that you felt in danger of losing the title?

DUDLEY: Well, yes. I had a very nasty moment in the second minute, when one of the judges showed a flicker of interest, so I quickly changed the subject of what I was talking about.

PETER: What do you normally talk about?

DUDLEY: Carpets, and how difficult it is to park in London.

In episode three, Pete and Dud discussed the rudiments of music:

PETE: D'you know, I often wish my mother had forced me
          to learn the piano when I was young.

DUD: Yeah, me too. If only she'd forced me to play,
          forced me to be a genius.

Even in a comic sketch, in character, this was a significant exchange. Dudley was willing to defer to Peter about most topics, but music wasn't one of them. His musicality was something close to genius. It was a gift that Peter never could have matched, even if he'd been forced to practise day and night. Another sign of Dudley's growing confidence was the reinstatement of his 'Old Man River' sketch, which Peter had removed from the first series. The chihuahua was beginning to bite back.

Sir Arthur Streeb-Greebling made a welcome return in the fourth episode, in a sketch called 'The Frog & Peach' which became one of Peter's most famous turns. Sir Arthur is the proprietor of a hopeless restaurant hidden in the wilds of Dartmoor which only serves two (equally revolting) dishes:

SIR ARTHUR STREEB-GREEBLING: There's frog à la pêche,
          which is frog done in Cointreau, with a peach
          stuffed in its mouth. And then of course there's
          pêche à la frog, which is really not much to write
          home about. A waiter comes to your table, he's
          got this huge peach, which is covered in boiling
          liqueur, and then he slices it open to reveal
          about two thousand little black tadpoles. It's one
          of the most disgusting sights I've ever seen.

The fifth episode featured two excellent sketches, both reflecting Dudley's own experiences – of psychiatry and family life. In 'The

Psychiatrist', Dudley played an impotent patient whose psychiatric sessions have proved so successful that he has embarked on a passionate affair with the psychiatrist's wife:

PETER: You're in love with my wife Stephanie?

DUDLEY: Yes.

PETER: Well, this is a perfectly understandable thing, Roger. She's a very attractive woman. I married her myself. I don't see why you should feel upset about that.

DUDLEY: But she's in love with me.

PETER: Well, this again is perfectly understandable, Roger. I mean, you're a perfectly attractive human being, as I've told you over the last few weeks. There's nothing repulsive about you, is there? There's no reason why a highly sexed woman, such as Stephanie, shouldn't fall in love with you. I must explain to you, Roger, that I'm a very busy man. I have many, many patients to see. I see rather less of my wife perhaps than I should, and I think it's very understandable that she should seek some sort of companionship outside the marriage. I don't think that's unreasonable at all.

DUDLEY: But she's not seeking anything outside marriage, doctor, and nor am I. We want to get married.

PETER: Well, this again, I think, is perfectly understandable. After all, you're two young people in love. You want to manifest your love feelings, within the confines of a bourgeois society, through marriage.

And so on.

In 'Father & Son', Dudley played a working-class father (borrowing some biographical details from his dad) failing to exert any authority whatsoever over Peter as his self-confident, successful son:

DUDLEY: I've got a good mind to give you a good hiding. I've got a good mind to take my belt off to you.

PETER: I wouldn't do that, father. Your trousers will fall down.

The highlight of the sixth episode was 'The Music Teacher', with Peter as an arrogant self-made man who's just bought his own orchestra and expects Dudley to teach him to play Beethoven's Fifth Symphony on the piano in a fortnight, even though he cannot play a note. As Dudley protests, raising all sorts of practical objections, Peter simply raises the price:

DUDLEY: It doesn't really matter if you've got the Welsh National Philharmonic in the back yard. It's not a piano concerto – it's a symphony. There's no piano in it.

PETER: If it's my orchestra, I would have thought I could come in with what instrument I like at what time I like. I'm sure they'll see it my way. We can put a piano in just like that.

The series concluded with a musical number, 'Bo Duddley', in which Peter and Dudley played two earnest middle-class Englishmen analysing (and entirely misunderstanding) a lusty black American blues number:

PETER: You don't think any of these lyrics could be in any way connected with making love or sex?

DUDLEY: Good Lord, no! And anyway, I wouldn't sing garbage like that.

Pete & Dud finished up in the afterlife, a fitting end to a triumphant series.

DUD: Is this heaven, Pete?

PETE: Bloody hell. Is this what I've been good for all my life?

DUD: Is this what the Reverend Griffin promised us, Pete?

PETE: It's very vulgar, isn't it? It's more like Liberace's bedroom.

'It was about the most creative three-month period of my life,' said Clement. 'I'd just give it an incredibly light touch on the tiller and that was it. Those studio tickets were the hottest tickets in town. It was like a party. Everyone wanted to be there.' [32] The viewing public loved it too and the BBC were keen to commission another series, but Peter and Dudley weren't interested. 'We're bored of doing quick little sketches on television,' [33] said Dudley. Peter felt the same. They'd conquered the small screen. Now they wanted to crack the movies. The most they would agree to do was a one-off Christmas special. In the opening sequence, Dudley played a nervous first-timer at a posh fox hunt. Peter played the Master of Hounds. Peter persuades Dudley to dress up as a fox, and then chases him across the moors with a pack of hungry hounds. It was extremely amusing but there was something of the schoolyard about it, the self-assured prefect ragging the clueless new boy with the club foot. For Dudley, this sketch felt like a step too far. 'There was an element of sadism,' [34] he said. He didn't find it all that funny.

Peter and Dudley's relationship was affectionate, but it was also a tug-of-war. They both had sisters, but neither of them had a brother.

Their mutual friend, the actress Gaye Brown, likened them to Cain and Abel. The title of Peter's (unwritten) autobiography was *Tragically I Was An Only Twin*. This sibling rivalry fuelled some of their funniest routines. It also spilled over into their private lives. 'After dinner, Dudley would sometimes play the organ, and he was brilliant and very amusing,' said the film director Francis Megahy, recalling an evening at Dudley's house in Hampstead. 'And then Peter would get into a competitive frenzy and stand up and do his Elvis Presley imitation, which was embarrassing because it was so terrible.' [35]

Wendy maintained that Peter's humiliation of Dudley was just an act, that Dudley was far more confident than his pathetic screen persona. Suzy Kendall agreed. Dudley was merely playing a part, she said. 'He was very strong,' she said. 'Dudley was not shoved around by anybody.' [36] Yet even if there was no truth in Gerald Scarfe's depiction of Dudley as Peter's glove puppet, this public perception was bound to grate. 'Peter's sarcasm was detrimental to the relationship,' [37] said Dudley. Like Wendy, he was beginning to tire of being the butt of Peter's jokes. 'Peter was brilliant, but he would probe until he'd found your weak spot.' said Dick Clement. 'On his own he was slightly cold. He needed Dudley's warmth.' [38] What Peter didn't realise was that he needed Dudley more than Dudley needed him.

Peter and Dudley with Raquel Welch on the set of *Bedazzled*.

CHAPTER FIFTEEN

BEDAZZLED

DUDLEY: What about Debussy's *La Mer*?

PETER: Lovely. I can just see her. Sitting there all calm and beautiful, the lamplight on her hair. 'Come in, son,' she says. 'Come in and have a cup of tea.'

DUDLEY: And Bach.

PETER: He was deaf in one leg.

DUDLEY: And Handel. There's a success story. Unknown in 1949, then he wrote the *Water Music* at 11 p. m. at night ...

PETER: Now he's driving an Alfa Romeo round Beirut. [1]

The second series of *Not Only ... But Also* did what *The Wrong Box* had failed to do: it gave Peter and Dudley the opportunity to write their own film script. Suitably impressed by their latest small-screen success, Twentieth-Century Fox contracted them to write and star in their own feature film. Audaciously, Peter opted for a comic version of Goethe's *Faust*.

The idea for a film of *Faust* had originally come from Wendy. She'd first suggested it to Peter back in 1964, on their return to London from New York. It was a subject that had intrigued Peter ever since his gap year, when he'd seen a production of the play in Hamburg, but, living in a rented flat with a new baby, he hadn't made much progress. Now, with his own house to write in and the incentive of a film deal, this smart idea acquired fresh momentum. With Wendy, Lucy and Daisy, and Suzy Kendall, Peter and Dudley flew out to Grenada to write the script.

At least, that was what Dudley thought they'd be doing. When they arrived, however, Peter seemed strangely reluctant to get started. 'I waited a week and nothing ever happened,' [2] said Dudley. Having changed his prior vacation plans, he was understandably rather miffed. Eventually, he lost his temper. 'You brought us out here for no good reason,' he told Peter. 'What the fuck is going on?' [3] 'I've told Wendy it's a holiday,' said Peter evasively. In fact, Peter had resolved to write this screenplay alone, regardless of the contract. This was his biggest break so far, and he wanted to take sole responsibility for the script ('screenplay by Peter Cook, based on a story by Peter Cook and Dudley Moore,' read the eventual writing credit, rather sheepishly). When Peter's true intentions became clear, Dudley was even more annoyed, but as far as the writing was concerned, you might have thought it wouldn't make much difference. Peter had written the lion's share of *Beyond The Fringe* and virtually everything of any note in *Not Only ... But Also*. Yet although Dudley's contribution to the writing process was elusive, his mere presence was a potent influence. Peter worked best when he was bouncing ideas off other people. Without Dudley, his writing lacked the human touch.

By the time Peter finished writing his screenplay (long after his return from Grenada) he'd also acquired a top director, Stanley

Donen. This was quite a coup. Donen had directed Hollywood classics like *Singin' In The Rain*. Now he lived in London, where he'd become a big fan of *Not Only ... But Also*. 'I remember watching it religiously and thinking it was the funniest, cleverest, most pointed material I'd seen,' [4] he said. 'Bowled over' by this series, he got in touch with Peter and Dudley and told them he'd love to make a film with them. 'It was the first time I'd called any performer to say I liked them so much that I wanted to work with them,' [5] he said. Wendy had been similarly bowled over by Donen's latest movie, *Charade* (a stylish thriller starring Cary Grant and Audrey Hepburn) and had implored Peter to try and get Donen to direct his Faust film. As luck would have it, a few weeks later Dirk Bogarde invited Peter and Wendy to dinner. The other guests were David Niven and his wife, and Stanley Donen. Peter and Donen hit it off, but there was an awkward moment over dinner when Wendy (rather admirably) tore into Mrs Niven for boasting that she'd had to hire an extra suite at Claridge's, simply to accommodate the couple's copious Christmas presents. Peter acted as peacemaker, and the two women parted on friendly terms, but it was another sign that for Wendy the novelty of Peter's showbiz lifestyle had worn off.

Peter worked hard on his screenplay, turning down virtually all engagements for a year or more. He reckoned writing it cost him £50,000 in lost wages. The only jobs he accepted were the *Not Only ... But Also* Christmas Special and the role of the Mad Hatter in Jonathan Miller's haunting adaptation of *Alice In Wonderland*. Miller was pleased with Peter's performance but his shrewd assessment didn't bode well for Peter's future as a film star. 'Peter was mainly a solitary performer,' he told Peter's biographer, Harry Thompson. 'He found it very difficult to meet people's eyes.' [6]

Peter's *Bedazzled* brought the Faust legend bang up to date. Dudley was cast as a suicidal short-order chef called Stanley Moon, hopelessly infatuated with Margaret Spencer, a shallow waitress in the Wimpy Bar where he works. Like Goethe's Faust, Moon sells his soul to the Devil for seven wishes, each of which he squanders in a futile attempt to win her heart. Assisted by the Seven Deadly Sins (including Barry Humphries as Envy and Raquel Welch as Lust) Peter's debonair Devil, aka George Spiggott, delights in finding a loophole in each of Stanley's wishes. In his bids to woo Margaret, he becomes an intellectual, a tycoon and a pop star – all to no avail. The monikers that Peter chose for him and Dudley were both in-jokes: George Spiggott was the unidexter from 'One Leg Too Few'; Stanley Moon was the name that John Gielgud had mistakenly ascribed to Dudley. Though the result lacked Dudley's bonhomie, it was still a super script, brimming over with brilliant bons mots, worthy of Oscar Wilde. 'You realise suicide's a criminal offence?' Peter's Devil tells Dudley. 'In less enlightened times, they'd have hung you for it.'

The casting was similarly inspired, with Eleanor Bron as a wonderfully unappealing Margaret, and Raquel Welch suitably seductive as Lillian Lust. Peter and Dudley were keen to call the film *Raquel Welch*, so the posters would read Peter Cook & Dudley Moore in *Raquel Welch*. Sadly, Twentieth Century Fox were unwilling to play along. They settled instead on *Bedazzled* – a catchy enough name, but one which broke the first rule of movie titles: tell the punters what the film's about. Yet this movie was so full of good things that the name seemed almost incidental. 'What worked very well in that film was Donen's more classical approach,' says Humphries. 'He wasn't imposing visual jokes upon the text so we could hear the dialogue.' [7] And what dialogue! 'What rotten sins I've got working for me,' grumbles Peter's Devil. 'It must be the wages.' Appropriately for a character called Envy, Humphries only had a small part, but he grabbed his fair share of glory in a scene-stealing cameo inspired by Kenneth Tynan. 'I put all the envy I could muster into it,' [8] he recalled. Humphries's only regret was that he didn't manage to purloin the green silk pyjamas (with an E for Envy embroidered on the breast pocket) that had been specially made for him in Savile Row.

Meanwhile Peter's marriage was beginning to unravel. 'He'd always been in structured situations – prep school, public school, university,' says Wendy. 'Everything was provided. He was the most impractical person. He couldn't open a can of beans.' Wendy provided a practical structure, with the context of a loving family. But although she'd made the ideal home, she was more than just a homemaker. Peter's work took him away a lot, and in his abscence Wendy fell in love with the actor and writer Simon Gough. For Wendy, this was the fruition of a close friendship during which Gough had become a regular house guest. He had also become friends with Peter, who remained ignorant of the affair. 'God, I envy you, Simon,' Peter told him. 'What could I possibly have that you envy?' replied Gough. 'You are anonymous,' said Peter. 'You can go into any porn shop in Soho and nobody will know you.' [9]

Feeling the need to clear her conscience, Wendy owned up to Peter. They'd both had affairs before and he'd remained civil when she'd told him about Ben Carruthers, so she expected him to take the news quite calmly. Yet now they were married with children, his reaction was very different. 'He hit me and kicked me down the stairs in a fit of rage,' recalled Wendy. 'The front doorbell rang. It was Simon. Peter immediately, without a word, punched him in the jaw, breaking it in two places.' [10] 'If you come here again, I'll kill you,' [11] Peter told him. Simon left. Wendy was left with two black eyes. Thankfully, the children slept right through it.

Peter apologised profusely, Wendy agreed to end her romance with Simon Gough, and Peter and Wendy decided to try and make a go of things. As a parting gesture, Simon Gough gave Wendy a letter of introduction to his great-uncle, the writer Robert Graves, who lived on Majorca. Wendy took Lucy and Daisy out there and fell in love with the island. Peter joined them for a fortnight's holiday. When he returned to England, to film *Bedazzled*, Wendy and the children stayed on in Majorca. Wendy found a run-down farmhouse that took her fancy, and Peter agreed to buy it. 'It represented something very deep to him,' she says. 'He was always looking for home.' By renovating it, she hoped to repair their relationship. 'It was an attempt to save the marriage,' she says.

However, back in London, out shopping in the West End, Peter bumped into Judy Huxtable, an actress he'd met a few years before at The Establishment. There had been a spark between them back then, but Peter had already been engaged to Wendy and Judy was going steady with Sean Kenny (the designer of The Establishment and *Beyond The Fringe*) so nothing came of it. Judy was now married to Kenny but she wasn't happy. He had been violent, drunken and unfaithful. The stage was set for the great love affair of Peter's life.

A few days later, Judy's friend, the actress Gaye Brown (who'd originally introduced Judy to Sean Kenny) invited Judy to a dinner party. She told her that Peter would be there. 'He's going through a bad time right now with his marriage,' [12] she told Judy. Kenny was away. Judy didn't usually go to parties, but she decided to go along.

When she got there, she found that Gaye had sat her next to Peter. They talked all evening. They really hit it off. When Judy drove home, around midnight, Peter went back with her for a nightcap. They talked until the small hours. 'I gave him whisky after whisky and he seemed quite happy,' [13] she said. Judy didn't drink.

Peter stayed the night but they didn't sleep together. He slept in Judy's bed – she slept on the sofa (she'd always been faithful to her husband). In the morning, she made him breakfast. A few days later Peter invited her to Church Row for dinner. He made her smoked salmon and scrambled eggs. After watching Spurs on television (Peter's team, since he'd forsaken Torquay United) they went to bed together, and began a passionate affair.

Peter fell head over heels in love with Judy and she fell in love with him. Seeing him with his children merely heightened the attraction. 'He was bathing them and making them laugh and put their knickers on their heads because they'd lost their bath caps,' [14] she said. Judy was still only in her early twenties, but five years with Sean Kenny had left her feeling like a battered housewife. No wonder she was smitten. 'Here is this bright, intelligent, witty, sexy man, and it's ridiculous – he is nice too,' [15] she thought. She didn't tell Sean Kenny. She worried what he'd do if he found out.

Peter didn't tell Wendy about Judy, but he introduced her to Dudley and Suzy. Judy realised straight away that she would need to be friends with Dudley if she wanted to be with Peter. This wasn't a problem. She took to Dudley (and Suzy) immediately. After a few months Judy fell pregnant. Judy and Peter both knew without a doubt that it could only be their baby. They were both devastated. Peter felt terribly guilty. She decided to have an abortion – a decision she later regretted. 'I thought I had no choice,' she said. 'We were still married to other people.' [16]

Peter hadn't tried to talk her into it. He hadn't tried to talk her out of it. He told her they'd have a child of their own some day.

Despite the upheavals in Peter's marriage, Peter and Dudley spent a happy summer on location. To maximise their finite resources ($600,000 – hardly a fortune for a feature film, even in 1967), Peter, Dudley and Stanley Donen all agreed to waive any advance wages – a particularly generous concession on Donen's part, since he'd turned down *Hello, Dolly* to make this film, forgoing a fee bigger than *Bedazzled*'s entire budget. This shared self-sacrifice helped to create a healthy sense of solidarity on the set. 'I only had fun on one movie in my life and that was *Bedazzled*,' [17] recalled Donen. From a man who'd directed feel-good films like *On The Town* and *Seven Brides For Seven Brothers* this was quite a compliment. This heady air of *joie de vivre* was encapsulated in a location report by Movietone News,[18] which Peter and Dudley hijacked, improvising an impromptu duologue between Dudley (as an unctuous TV reporter) and Peter (as the Devil) which was far funnier – and more revealing – than a conventional po-faced preview:

DUDLEY: Good afternoon. I'm speaking to you from the gardening centre, Syon House, Brentford, Middlesex, England. I should like to ask this gentleman a question or two. First of all, who are you?

PETER: My name is George Spiggott.

DUDLEY: What do you do?

PETER: I'm the Devil and I tempt people, mainly – during the daytime, and during the night-time.

DUDLEY: I see. Are you the only devil? Do you have any other partners?

PETER: I've got a few hobgoblins, sprites, minor evil bodies around the place, bad fairies of one kind and another. And trolls, small trolls which jump around and throw spinach in people's eyes, but they're rather boring. I'm the main devil. I'm the most evil person in the world.

DUDLEY: What are you in fact doing here at this very moment?

PETER: Being interviewed, at the moment.

DUDLEY: Being interviewed, yes, that's certainly true. But before you were being interviewed, was there anything you were up to at all?

PETER: I was preparing to be interviewed, and getting myself in the frame of mind to talk.

DUDLEY: What sort of work are you involved in?

PETER: Tempting, mainly. Tempting people to do horrible things, on the whole.

DUDLEY: That is very interesting. What sort of tempting do you do? What sort of things do you do to tempt people?

PETER: Nasty things. For example, if I was tempting I'd probably size you up, see you being of a portly build - forgive me saying that.

DUDLEY: Of course not. How very nice.

PETER: I'd come up to you with a cream bun and say 'why don't you eat that?' Thus tempting you to eat the bun and get fat and fall into the sin of gluttony. It's tremendous work.

DUDLEY: Obviously it has a tremendous satisfaction for you.

PETER: None at all. Absolutely none at all. No satisfaction. I've been tempting since way back.

Eve was the first one I tempted. Slid down the tree. Remember that?

DUDLEY: Eve slid down the tree?

PETER: Well, she did slide down the tree – but not on this particular day. It was one of her innocent pastimes before she fell. Before the Fall, she was always sliding down trees. And after the Fall, of course, she couldn't slide as well as she used to. But I slid down the tree on that day, in serpent's guise – lovely costume – and gave her this apple, what God had said, 'Don't eat this, please. Above all, do not eat this apple.' So I come down and said, 'Eat it.'

DUDLEY: And of course, as we all know, she ate it, didn't she?

PETER: Yes, it really was a success. A wonderful day for me. Not much good for her, of course, being cast out.

DUDLEY: Yes, of course.

A week before *Bedazzled* was released Peter gave a more serious interview to Bernard Braden, the Canadian broadcaster who'd introduced E.L. Wisty to the nation. This interview was part of a remarkable series which Braden shot on spec, at his own expense, for a prospective TV show called *Now & Then* (the idea was to interview and re-interview the same celebrities over several years, creating an evolving set of portraits). Incredibly, Braden filmed interviews with 330 celebs, including stars like Tom Jones and Sean Connery – but no broadcaster took the bait, and these pilots languished unseen for 40 years until the BFI acquired them in 2008, after the death of Braden's widow (and fellow film-maker) Barbara Kelly. [19] Seen today, after all those years, Peter's interview with Braden makes intriguing viewing, for it captured him at a unique point, at the summit of his powers.

Peter had turned thirty a fortnight earlier and here he looks extremely well on it – less gawky than he was in his early twenties, but still slim, with bright eyes and a clear complexion. His face is neatly framed by a thick thatch of hair, tinged with grey around the temples. He's conservatively dressed, in a sober jacket, shirt and tie. Answering Braden's questions with quiet courtesy, he looks calm and confident, as well he might be. Virtually everything he'd touched so far had turned to gold. A positive reception for this film would propel him into the big league, leaving his stage and TV work far behind. After eighteen months writing, shooting and editing what he had every right to expect would be his masterpiece, he looked like a man waiting to reap the rewards his talent and hard work had brought him. His twenties had been spectacular. His thirties surely promised even more.

'It was a very enjoyable year and a half,' Peter tells Braden, looking back on this cinematic marathon, for which he'd worked for longer (and far harder) than anything else in his career. 'It wasn't that much of a sacrifice. I was doing exactly what I wanted.' Braden asks if it's hard to strike a balance between work and family. 'I think I've probably spent too much time with my family for their own good,' says Peter. 'I've been hanging about the house so much, moping around and worrying whether the film was going to be made, and drooping up and downstairs in a rather desultory way when I've not been writing or can't think of anything. I think it'd be good for me to be out of the house a great deal more.'

'There's a quality you have which I seem to have noticed through the years, which is – the moment a subject gets serious, in any form of conversation, under any circumstances, you tend to go into character,' says Braden. 'I think I do that less now and I'm glad I do it less,' replies Peter. 'It's a very easy way, if you have voices, to get out of any personal responsibility in an argument. That's what I've always used it for. Often, I think it's a very good way of making points. It's not always a cop-out. But I can often be heard talking in what I conceive to be my own voice these days, which is roughly similar to the one I'm using now.'

The conversation turns to politics, and it's here that this interview really comes alive. Talking about himself, Peter is modest and self-effacing. Talking about politicians, he's far more assertive. 'Politicians who go on television and make party points are just boring the audience stiff and making the public despise them,' says Peter. 'I would hope a few of them would see the good sense in being honest and straightforward. It would be the most captivating thing for any major politician to actually tell the truth.' Peter also showed he was an astute political pundit. He predicts that Harold Wilson, the Labour Prime Minister, will survive to fight the next election, but will lose to Edward Heath. (This was remarkably prescient. Heath did indeed beat Wilson in the 1970 General Election, but for most professional commentators, the result was a big surprise.) Not that Peter was hoping for a Tory victory – far from it. 'Whenever I really go off a Labour government, I only have to think of those faces and voices of the Conservative Party,' he tells Braden, 'and I think, "Oh well, whatever happens I prefer this bungling lot to the others."' Yet despite his healthy scepticism, the overriding impression is one of quiet contentment. 'I'd rather live here than anywhere else,' he says.

Braden describes him as a definitive amateur, and Peter seemed happy with this description. 'I think I shall go on getting more and more amateurish as I go on,' he says.

There was nothing amateurish about *Bedazzled*, which opened in December 1967. Donen's adroit direction provided the perfect counterpoint to Peter's fluent wordplay, and Dudley was the ideal foil for his cruel wit. Dudley's score was sublime, and Peter was a convincing Devil – aloof yet curiously likeable. Eleanor Bron revelled in her role as Dudley's grumpy muse and Raquel Welch was so gorgeous that Dudley had to wear three pairs of pants in the bedroom scene, to try and prevent himself from rising to the occasion. Suave and erudite, fashionable yet universal, the critics should have loved it, but somehow this clever film never quite caught fire. Peter and Dudley flew to New York for the US premiere, to be met by withering reviews. The man from *Time* magazine said they'd 'failed to grasp the basic difference between a four-minute skit and a 107-minute movie' – a harsh critique of a film with a conventional and perfectly coherent plot. The *LA Times* called it the most infuriating film of the year, 'because the best of it is so deliciously inventively good and the worst of it so appallingly, distastefully awful' – an odd reaction to a movie with nothing appalling or distasteful in it whatsoever, a film which maintained the same tone throughout.

Peter and Dudley flew back to London for the British opening a week later, only to be greeted by similarly mixed reviews. 'Funny – but what went wrong?' asked the *Daily Mail*, in a polite but tepid notice that summed up the prevailing mood. 'Despite some brilliant flashes, a full-length film seems to have overtaxed a pair who are accustomed to getting their laughs in short, sharp bursts.' [20] On the Continent, where Peter and Dudley were virtually unknown, *Bedazzled* fared much better. In Germany it was called *Mephisto 67* – a far better title than *Bedazzled* – and in Italy it became one of the year's most popular movies, generating (completely unfounded) stories in the Italian tabloids, coupling Peter with Raquel Welch. 'I saw it in Rome, dubbed into Italian,' recalled Peter. 'It was fabulous in Italian. I had the most beautiful voice.' [21] With its philosophical humour, *Bedazzled* was actually a very Continental film, but the main reason for its European success was that European audiences weren't expecting *Pete & Dud – The Movie*. Still, betraying the lack of confidence that bedevilled all the films they made together, Peter and Dudley both took this criticism to heart. 'I think we were too overawed,' said Peter. 'I don't think we relaxed enough in performing and we did takes which we weren't satisfied with which were too tight.' [22] 'There wasn't the same ease as on TV,' agreed Dudley. 'I think we lost a lot by appearing on film, because there was no improvisation. Just a script and a rehearsal and then we had to stick to it. [23] I can see why people objected to the film. It's gauche, it's awkward, it's not as flowing as our other work.' [24] Yet the main problem was the medium. No mainstream movie could have incorporated the spontaneity of their TV appearances. Dudley was learning to adapt his talents to this larger, more unwieldy format. Peter had yet to learn that the cinema was entirely unsuited to his skills.

The critics were barking up the wrong tree as usual but, though none of them identified the real culprit, they'd sensed an endemic weakness in this film that would become increasingly apparent in the years to come. What no one spotted at the time was Peter's intrinsic unease with moviemaking. His best performances had always had an audience, just as his best writing had always had a sounding board.

In this movie, he had neither. With its sparky but wordy dialogue, *Bedazzled* would have made a wonderful stage play. The script was full of people saying funny things, rather than doing funny things – fine in the theatre, but always a problem in the cinema. The episodic structure was also more theatrical than cinematic. Onstage it would have worked a treat. Onscreen, it seemed stilted. Joe Orton, a writer whose witty epigrams bore more than a passing resemblance to Peter's, suffered from the same problem when his plays transferred from stage to screen.

Dudley's subtle input might have given Peter's script a bit more warmth, but it was their contrasting performance styles that really revealed the growing differences between them. In *The Wrong Box*, confined to a brief double act, they'd both looked out of sorts. Here, in the starring roles, their acting moved in opposite directions. Dudley was naturalistic and self-assured. Peter was remote and other-worldly. Cast as the Prince of Darkness, this wasn't such a problem. However, what no one else had yet discovered was that this was pretty much the only film role he could play. 'Peter wasn't really a very good actor,' said Barry Humphries. 'He couldn't be other people very successfully.' [25] As Eleanor Bron surmised, he was essentially a solo turn. Onstage or on television, he could hold an audience spellbound, but like a lot of the best comedians (Tony Hancock, Eric Morecambe) his acting was far too mannered for the big screen. As Dudley said, he was too self-aware. Dudley had built a bridge between Peter's imagination and his audience. In the aftermath of *Bedazzled*, that bridge began to crumble. 'British actors fail because they still do not understand that movie acting is not about disguising but about revealing oneself,' [26] wrote Quentin Crisp. He could have been talking about Peter and Dudley. In *Bedazzled*, for the first time, Dudley revealed something of himself, something intimate and vulnerable. For Peter, acting was always a form of disguise. In a sketch show, this didn't really matter. In a feature film, as he was to learn, it mattered very much indeed.

Fired up by the fun they'd had together on location, Peter and Dudley had already started to plan a second film with Stanley Donen, provisionally called *The Whack*. A musical about alternative medicine, starring Peter and Dudley as quack doctors, the subject was topical and potentially very funny, but the box-office takings for *Bedazzled* knocked that project on the head. It took $5 million in the United States – not too bad, but not good enough for Twentieth Century Fox to contemplate a sequel. This flawed but brilliant film would come to be regarded as a cult classic, but Peter and Dudley weren't all that interested in posterity. Onstage and on TV, they'd already done more than most entertainers dream of doing in a lifetime. Yet as far as their film careers were concerned the future looked sketchy, to say the least.

Like the 'crickets' (as Peter called them) Wendy also had mixed feelings about *Bedazzled*, but for rather different reasons. She was spooked to discover that some of the scenes were uncomfortably close to home. In these scenes, Peter's character always seemed to be portrayed in a sympathetic light, especially in the (hilarious) sequence about an adulterous wife (played by Eleanor Bron) whose husband (played by Peter) is so saintly that she's unable to enjoy her secret liaisons with her lover (a similarly guilt-stricken Dudley). Wendy was also disconcerted by what she perceived to be a deep vein of sadism in the movie. It was only make-believe, of course, but she couldn't help feeling that this revealed an unpleasant aspect of Peter's personality.

She was particularly troubled by his closing monologue, in which he rails against the Almighty, promising to swamp the world with space-age rubbish:

'I'll fill it full of concrete runways, motorways, aircraft, television and automobiles, advertising, plastic flowers and frozen foods. I'll make it so noisy and disgusting that even you'll be ashamed of yourself. No wonder you've so few friends. You're unbelievable.'

It was an irrational reaction. Peter was supposed to be playing Lucifer, after all, and his petty practical jokes were virtually the mildest form of evil you could imagine. Likewise, his virulent soliloquy about the modern world was a stirring critique of commercialism, which, in happier times, might have struck a chord with Wendy. Yet she was quite right to detect an underlying cynicism in *Bedazzled*, especially regarding love and marriage. The only character with any compassion is Stanley Moon, who's portrayed as a pathetic loser. Every other character is intrinsically selfish. Yet Peter's comedy was ever thus. It was his relationship with Wendy that had changed. Before, he'd been in her tent, pissing out. Now he was outside, pissing in.

For Wendy, Majorca represented an escape – from modern life, from showbiz and from Peter. In January 1968 she moved out there on a permanent basis, driving all the way to Spain with as many of her possessions as she could carry. Peter flew out with the children, but returned to London a fortnight later, leaving Lucy and Daisy in Majorca with their mother. 'How much time I spend on the farm is something Peter and I have got to work out,' said Wendy. 'It will mean being parted at times but that is nothing new. Peter's work often takes him away.' [27] Wendy told the press they'd both divide their time between London and Majorca, but this was surely wishful thinking. For Peter, Majorca was never more than a holiday home and Wendy had fallen out of love with London, even if she still loved Peter. 'I'm tired of living in London,' she said. 'It's a ghastly scene at the moment – like living in a goldfish bowl.' [28] The long-term nature of this new plan was confirmed when Lucy and Daisy enrolled at the local school, the only English children in a class full of Spanish youngsters.

To all intents and purposes, Peter was now living alone at 17 Church Row (except when Judy spent the night there). His happy family life there had lasted less than three years. On 27 January he travelled to Old Trafford with a group of friends to see Tottenham Hotspur play Manchester United in the third round of the FA Cup. Bravely or foolishly – foolishly, as it turned out – Peter chose to stand in the Stretford End, the terrace where the most fervent home supporters gathered, and heckled the home team throughout the game. When Tottenham scored a late equaliser, some Man Utd fans failed to see the funny side. Afterwards, outside the ground, Peter was cornered by about a dozen adolescent boys, who kicked the proverbial shit out of him. Peter ended up on the pavement, curled up like a hedgehog. He later laughed off the incident ('I shall certainly continue to wear my Spurs rosette to away games,' [29]) but he went home without his two front teeth. It was an unpleasant foretaste of further troubles to come.

Peter, Dudley and Suzy Kendall.

CHAPTER SIXTEEN

GOODBYE AGAIN

PETER: Didn't you used to be a lot taller?

DUDLEY: Yeah, I use to be six foot four. But as I can't stand upper-class gits, I went on a crash diet and got myself down to five nothing.

PETER: Ah, bless me, that reminds me of when I was your age. My father was five foot one. I couldn't stand the way he looked or anything about him. Got myself stretched up to six foot two.

('That Rebellion Thing', *Goodbye Again*, ATV, 1968)

Dudley's response to Peter cutting him out of the scriptwriting for *Bedazzled* had been to make a movie of his own. The invitation came from Joe McGrath, who'd made such a good job of the first series of *Not Only … But Also*. Since then, Joe had been working on the Beatles' second feature film, *Help!* The Beatles' film producer, Walter Shenson, subsequently invited him to direct his own film for Columbia. All Joe had to do was find a story. He turned to Dudley and together they came up with *30 Is A Dangerous Age, Cynthia* – a quasi-autobiographical yarn about a jazz musician called Rupert Street who plays the piano in a London nightclub – no prizes for guessing where Joe and Dudley got their inspiration.

The plot concerned Rupert's frantic attempts to write a hit musical before his impending thirtieth birthday. Dudley, who was now 32, had experienced a similar crisis of confidence shortly before he turned 30, prompting his first visit to a psychiatrist – absurdly, he felt he should have achieved far more by the grand old age of 29.

Shenson said he was willing to put up £500,000 to make this movie, but only if it also featured Rupert's frantic attempts to find a wife. Dudley wasn't keen on this development. 'I really wanted it to be a simple story about a man who wants to compose music,' he protested. 'It seemed to me irrelevant that he got married.' [1] But Shenson was reluctant to devote half a million pounds to a touching tale of artistic angst. He brought in John Wells to write a more romantic (and commercial) outline, and Dudley, mindful that money talks and bullshit walks, reluctantly acquiesced.

Dudley and Joe McGrath collaborated with John Wells on the script, and though the storyline was adapted to satisfy Shenson's demand for a love interest, the resultant screenplay still had Dudley's fingerprints all over it. The heroine was called Louise Hammond, after two of Dudley's old girlfriends, Celia Hammond and Louise McDermott. Rupert Street was a street around the corner from The Establishment. The character of Mrs Woolley (played by Patricia Routledge) was familiar to fans of Not Only … But Also as the mainstay of many a Pete & Dud routine. Dudley was happy to admit that much of this material was directly drawn from his own experience. 'My mother always sent me my laundry through the mail, just like Rupert's does,' he revealed. 'And like Rupert's, she always included a sack of lemon drops and some bread pudding in the package.' [2]

The object of Rupert's affections was an artist from Belper in Derbyshire, just like Dudley's live-in girlfriend, artist turned actress Suzy Kendall, but even Dudley stopped short of casting Suzy as his wife. 'Dudley had actually written the story around us, but he didn't try to get me cast for it,' said Suzy. 'He never even mentioned me.' [3] Joe McGrath had no such qualms. 'Why can't we use Suzy?' [4] he asked. Suzy Kendall was cast as Louise Hammond, the love of Rupert's life. John Wells also joined the cast, alongside his fellow Establishment veteran John Bird.

Dudley had enjoyed working with Joe McGrath on *Not Only ... But Also*, and was delighted to be reunited with his old director. McGrath was aware that Dudley had felt constricted by Bryan Forbes's direction in *The Wrong Box*, and did his best to give Dudley a freer rein. 'The worst thing you can do with some comedy actors is show them what to do, because then you destroy their vision and their instinctive way of working, so I just let Dudley get on with it,' [5] he explained. Dudley relished this new-found freedom. Indeed, he was almost too relaxed. One of McGrath's most enduring memories was Dudley's chronic flatulence on set. 'He got into a habit of farting before each take,' recalled McGrath. 'Even if he wasn't in the scene but was on the set he'd run across and fart before we slated.' [6] John Wells, on the other hand, remembered a more po-faced Dudley, a man torn between his gift for clowning and his growing interest in psychoanalysis. 'Once, during the shooting, he sat in the middle of a group of cameramen telling them that the reason he had trouble producing scripts was because of potty training. Nobody laughed at all, as it was done with the utmost seriousness. I think that's what Peter teased him about most.' [7]

The thing that really distinguished this idiosyncratic film was Dudley's music. Dudley's role allowed him to show off his musical skills on camera, sending up Handel, Mozart, Beethoven and Noel Coward. The Dudley Moore Trio played much of the incidental music. Dudley also composed the orchestral score. Determined to get it right, he spent so long on it that eventually Walter Shenson told him to call a halt, saying they'd run out of money. 'I'll pay for the rest of it,'[8] said Dudley. He was still composing, in the car, when Suzy drove him to the recording studio, where a full symphony orchestra sat waiting to record it. 'He was always like that, doing everything at the last second,' said Suzy. 'It was never good enough, until finally time ran out and he had to go with whatever he'd done.'[9] For Dudley, conducting this orchestra, playing his own music, was the highlight of his creative life. He had such a good time doing it that, once the score was safely recorded, he asked the orchestra if they could run through it together one more time, this time for the sheer fun of it. Comedy had become his day job, but music was still his passion. His score was well received, prompting comparisons with Delius and Elgar.

Dudley and Suzy flew to New York in March 1968 for the US premiere. The American critics were ecstatic. *Esquire* called it 'one of the best films ever made'. Yet back in Britain the reaction was quite the opposite. Dudley took his mum and dad to the London premiere, in October, along with a life-size cardboard cut-out of Suzy (who was away filming in Belgrade) but this time the reviews were dire. *The Times* said it felt like they'd made it up as they went along. 'We had the worst press in the world,' said Joe McGrath. 'The feeling was, "Who does he think he is?"'[10] It was a question that Dudley was increasingly asking of himself. Sadly, this film didn't provide him with any answers. Columbia marketed it as a 'Swinging London' movie, an image at odds with Dudley's intentions. 'The film took a direction I didn't want it to take,' he said. He'd struck out on his own, without Peter, only to find the public were still far more interested in Pete & Dud.

In between the US and UK premieres Dudley did something he swore he'd never do. He got married. He and Suzy were already living together, in Bentham House in Hampstead. It was here that he put a colander on his head, went down on his knees and said to Suzy, 'Will you marry me?' Suzy said yes. They set a date for a few weeks hence and she invited two friends to come along that day, but she didn't tell them she was getting married. 'If we don't do it then it won't matter and they'll just have a nice day in London,' she told Dudley's biographer, Barbra Paskin. 'I wasn't terribly sure even then that we were going to do it.' [11]

When the big day dawned, on 14 June 1968, Dudley got up early and went out. 'OK, he's forgotten,' thought Suzy. 'Never mind.' [12] However, he'd gone out to buy a ring, and when he got back Suzy still wasn't dressed. She still thought he'd forgotten all about the wedding. 'It was all quite amusing,' she told Paskin. 'We'd almost done it so many times.' [13] This time, though, they went through with it, at a discreet ceremony at Hampstead Register Office. No one else knew anything about it, apart from Suzy's two friends. Suzy looked stunning and very stylish in flowing white trousers and a big floppy hat. Sadly, a few days later tragedy intervened when Pete McGurk, the double-bass player in the Dudley Moore trio, killed himself after his girlfriend left him for the band's drummer, Chris Karan. McGurk had joined the band after the death of Dudley's previous bass player, Hugo Boyd, who'd died in a road accident seven years before. Dudley became tormented by the idea that his band was somehow cursed, and that whoever he appointed to take McGurk's place might also perish. Thankfully, McGurk's successor, Peter Morgan, suffered no such mishap, but it was a sign that marriage hadn't exorcised the demons in Dudley's head.

Peter Cook, meanwhile, had also been appearing in a movie on his own. *A Dandy In Aspic* was an adaptation of a thriller by Derek Marlowe, starring Laurence Harvey as a British spy in Berlin. Unfortunately, the director, Anthony Mann, died midway through the shoot, leaving Harvey to complete the task. Peter played Harvey's Foreign Office minder. He did OK, but it was only a small part, and it was hardly the sort of performance (or the sort of film) to set the box office alight. 'A mad decision,' reflected Peter. 'Luckily, not that many people saw it.' [14] Peter's attempts at straight acting had been barely mediocre. For the time being, at least, his future lay with Dudley.

Peter and Dudley were reunited in a most peculiar movie called *The Bed Sitting Room*. The film's American director, Richard Lester, had planned to make a completely different movie, *Up Against It*, written by the hip young playwright Joe Orton, whose slick black comedy, *Loot*, had been a West End hit the year before. Paul McCartney had enjoyed *Loot* – he told Orton it was the only play he hadn't wanted to leave before the end – 'the only thing I get from the theatre,' he said to Orton, 'is a sore arse' [15] – and had subsequently commissioned Orton to write the screenplay for the Beatles' latest movie. Orton's manuscript depicted the Fab Four in women's clothes, in prison and in flagrante. It portrayed them committing murder and adultery. To nobody's surprise, Brian Epstein turned it down.

Richard Lester (who'd directed the Beatles' first two movies, *A Hard Day's Night* and *Help!*) thought Orton's script might work as a vehicle for Mick Jagger. He arranged to meet Orton for lunch in Twickenham to discuss the idea. Unfortunately, when the chauffeur arrived at Orton's flat in Islington to take Orton to Twickenham, he couldn't rouse the playwright or his partner, Kenneth Halliwell. Inside the flat, the police found two corpses. Halliwell, it transpired, had taken a fatal overdose of tranquillizers, after beating Orton's brains in with a hammer. 'If you read his diary,' read Halliwell's suicide note, 'all will be explained.' [16]

That might have been that, but for the fact that Lester's backers, United Artists, had already earmarked one million dollars to make a British movie. With the funds in place but no film, Lester cast around for a replacement and bought the rights to *The Bed Sitting Room*, a play by Spike Milligan and John Antrobus that had been treading the boards, in various guises, since 1962. It was currently enjoying a West End revival, but it was still a bold – or foolhardy – choice for a million-dollar feature film. Its main selling point was the erratic brilliance of its star, Spike Milligan, who ad-libbed to his heart's content, resulting in a different play every evening – heady stuff for seasoned theatregoers, but hardly the best template for the cinema. The play's bleak, surreal subject matter also presented a stiff challenge, for actors and audiences alike. Set in the aftermath of a brief but catastrophic nuclear war ('two minutes and 28 seconds, including signing the peace treaty') it featured a series of absurd transmogrifications, as humans morphed into animals and even inanimate objects. As Milligan himself admitted, in a TV interview with Bernard Braden, 'Nobody ever got the point about what it was about.'

Nevertheless, on its first run it received a rave review from Kenneth Tynan, who'd done so much to champion *Beyond The Fringe*. 'Mr Milligan and his partner have imagined England as it might be three years after the next war, which is referred to as "the nuclear misunderstanding,"' reported Tynan. 'The play draws its title from a peer of the realm who undergoes an inadvertent metamorphosis into a Paddington bedsitter ("No coloureds," he sternly insists). Stethoscope to the wall, the doctor examines him for dry rot. We are deep in Goon country, where the fifth and basic freedom is that of free association.' [17] The play was full of funny lines – 'the great task of burying our 40 million dead was carried out with cheerfulness and goodwill' – but not even Tynan had suggested it might make a successful motion picture (he foresaw a bright future for this eccentric curio at that bastion of experimental theatre, the Royal Court). United Artists were undeterred. On the face of it, they were buying a West End hit, adapted by a commercially astute director. If they'd bothered to find out a bit more about the play beforehand, it's a fair bet that this bizarre movie might never have been made.

'Abstract terrain will form a mournful escarpment against the sky,' wrote the film's designer, Assheton Gorton, in the pre-production notes, describing the kind of scene he intended to conjure up. 'Black broken tree roots char a white sea of lava; bleached clay pits jut against the sky with a jagged starkness; half a mile of chipped blue and white pottery is scattered over an empty, echoing wasteland.' Lester found no seas of lava in his search for suitable locations, but there were clay pits aplenty, and lots of similarly desolate settings. 'The really awful thing is that we were able to film most of these without faking it,' said Lester. 'All that garbage is real. We spent weeks driving around England ignoring all the beauty spots and then stopping enraptured in front of some hideous vista of industrial squalor.' [18] *The Bed Sitting Room* was filmed in the summer of 1968, mainly in a disused quarry in Surrey. 'It was not so much its theme of nuclear annihilation that interested me,' said Lester. 'It was a way of saying something about the whole fragmentation of society.' [19]

With United Artists' backing, and the kudos of its stage success, Lester was able to assemble an impressive cast, including Arthur Lowe, Roy Kinnear and Michael Horden, all billed in ascending order of stature. 'In a moment of abstraction, I said I'd feature these actors in reverse order of their height,' said Lester. 'The minute I said it, it became the Tablets of Moses, divine law, and the lawyers have been wrestling with the language.' [20] 'The company shall have final decision as to how high each actor is,' read the resultant contract. As the second-smallest member of the cast, Dudley was billed second-top, behind Rita Tushingham. As the second-tallest, Peter was billed second-bottom, just above Ralph Richardson. Sadly, this was one of Lester's better jokes. Good gags in the script were few and far between.

Peter and Dudley were cast as two mysterious, slightly sinister plain-clothes policemen, surveying the blighted scene below from a burnt-out police car attached to a hot-air balloon. On the final day's filming, disaster struck. 'It was very windy,' said Peter. 'We really shouldn't have gone up, but it was the last day at that particular location.' The balloon expert was up there with them, crouching out of shot. 'I wouldn't go up on a day like this,' he told Peter and Dudley. 'But you *are* up on a day like this,' said Peter. 'What d'you mean?' 'Well, it's just for Mr Lester,' said the balloon expert, 'but I wouldn't normally go up – we're at the mercy of the winds.' 'Whereupon,' recalled Peter, 'we fell violently to the ground.' [21] The car fell about a hundred feet. Peter was taken to the Nuffield Hospital for an emergency operation on his knee. He'd planned to go to Majorca for four weeks, to see Wendy and his daughters. Instead, he spent a month in hospital. In a metaphor for their future film careers, Dudley emerged from the wreckage unharmed.

Dudley might have walked away physically unscathed, but – not for the first time – he was dissatisfied with the direction he'd received. Faced with another big-screen flop, it was tempting to shift the blame. 'Dick Lester never seemed to know what he wanted,' complained Dudley, whose performance (in a smaller role than Peter's) was rather perfunctory but otherwise entirely sound. 'He gave peculiar instructions, which were hard to follow. He wanted different opinions but rejected them all, which was disconcerting. [22] He wasn't prepared to let us be ourselves.' [23]

Even Lester sounded doubtful about *The Bed Sitting Room*'s ability to entertain. 'It's a sad film, even though I didn't feel sad at the play,' he told Bernard Braden that autumn. 'I hope, though, that it'll be as funny as the original, as well. But the more surrealist it is, the more bizarre the images, the more serious and dedicated I think we have to be not to go for an easy gag. And being so busy keeping those away, I'm not able to tell whether it's funny any more.' [24] Hardly a ringing endorsement for a film that boasted some of Britain's finest comics, including Jimmy Edwards, Harry Secombe, Marty Feldman (as the National Health Service) and Peter's childhood hero, Spike Milligan. Lester had created an art-house film of stark Beckettian beauty, but it was the antithesis of a blockbuster. United Artists could have done with a few of the easy gags that Lester was so eager to avoid.

Inevitably, Lester's paymasters were less than ecstatic when they saw the final cut. 'How long is this shit going to go on for?' asked an irate executive at a private screening. Postponed for more than a year and finally released in 1970, *The Bed Sitting Room* was mauled by the critics and largely ignored by the public. 'I don't consider post-nuclear mutation a funny joke, a clever joke, a bitter joke or indeed a joke at all,' opined Penelope Mortimer, rather piously, in the *Observer*. Critical reaction in America was similarly grudging. 'One laughs from time to time,' wrote Pauline Kael, in the *New Yorker*, 'but, as in so much modern English far-out satire, there's no spirit, no rage, nothing left but ghastly, incessant sinking-island humour.'

The box office returns were predictably dire. The film fared so poorly in Anglophone countries that it was scarcely released elsewhere, and Lester had to wait nearly five years for his next outing as a director. But just because *The Bed Sitting Room* was a critical and commercial flop, that didn't make it a bad movie. Shot in eerie sepia, capturing the apocalyptic gloom that had replaced the shallow euphoria of the early 1960s, it's now rightly regarded as a cult classic, 'the missing link between *The Goon Show* and *Monty Python's Flying Circus*,' [25] according to the BFI curator Michael Brooke. As with *Bedazzled*, Peter and Dudley were simply ahead of their time. One of the highlights of this underrated film was Peter's closing speech, to which he added a few trademark flourishes of his own invention, promising a brighter future for all of Britain (or what was left of it) under his benign dictatorship. 'All in all, I think we're in for a time of peace, prosperity and stability, when the Earth will burgeon forth anew,' declared Peter, clinging to a rope ladder, suspended from his doomed balloon. 'The lion will lie down with the lamb and the goat give suck to the tiny bee. At times of great national emergency you'll often find that a new leader tends to emerge. Here I am, so watch it.' As an allegory of Cold War angst, *The Bed Sitting Room* is a fascinating period piece, but Peter and Dudley didn't want cult status – they wanted mainstream success. Yet again, their breakthrough movie had somehow passed them by.

At least *The Bed Sitting Room* was a heroic failure, a brave attempt to try something new. Peter and Dudley's next movie was a sideways step, back to the nostalgic flimflam of *The Wrong Box*. Paramount had asked the director Ken Annakin to make a sequel to his hit film *Those Magnificent Men In Their Flying Machines*. Annakin's follow-up was a 1920s Trans-European road race caper, called *Monte Carlo Or Bust*. A Franco-Italian co-production, filmed in Italy and Sweden, Peter and Dudley were hired on account of *Bedazzled*'s popularity in Italy. Their roles, however, were considerably more restrictive. They played a pair of stiff-upper-lipped English army officers, racing across the Continent against various other nationalistic archetypes, including Tony Curtis as the triumphant Yank and Gert Frobe as the beastly Kraut. Dudley's trailer was equipped with a piano, and he whiled away his waiting hours at the keyboard. Suzy joined him on location in Italy, but Annakin heard mutterings that they weren't getting on so well.

The critics were fairly kind, but the film was not a commercial success – and for anyone who'd seen *Not Only ... But Also*, it felt like a waste of Peter and Dudley's talents. Dudley was as competent as ever, though his role gave him no real chance to shine, while Peter's stilted performance merely added to the mounting evidence that he was not a natural movie actor. 'I always felt that Dudley was a more obviously brilliant talent than Peter,' [26] said Annakin, diplomatically. Dudley was more blunt. 'Peter acted terribly,' he said. 'He couldn't deliver other people's stuff at all.' [27]

Peter and Dudley were rescued from what Peter called 'the twilight world of films' [28] by an offer from Lew Grade, the charismatic boss of ATV, to make another series of their sketch show. Peter and Dudley had turned down the BBC, saying they wanted to concentrate on making movies. Grade succeeded where the Beeb had failed by employing the simple but effective strategy of offering them a lot more money. Called *Goodbye Again*, to distinguish it from its BBC prototype, three hour-long episodes were broadcast on ITV during the summer of 1968. Like a lot of comedy programmes poached by ITV from the BBC it was perfectly competent, but something was lost in translation.

On TV, sixty minutes is a lot of time to fill, even including ad breaks. As a consequence, some of the sketches were rather ragged. The director, Shaun O'Riordan, opted for realistic sets rather than the minimal settings favoured by Joe McGrath and Dick Clement. This constrained the action – Peter and Dudley worked far better with a few basic props to set the scene. It was also confusing, since the main set for each episode, which doubled as a general backdrop, was built to stage each week's Pete & Dud sketch – a prison in episode one, a hospital in episode two, and a gymnasium in episode three. This wouldn't have been quite so bad if Pete & Dud had kicked off every episode, but they didn't actually appear until the second half of each show. Even so, each episode contained several gems, and after their forgettable film cameos it was a welcome return to what they did best.

The most memorable sketch in the first episode was 'Long Distance', set in a fashionable bachelor pad, featuring Peter and Dudley as two cocksure men about town. Dudley is on the phone to his girlfriend, Penny, who's modelling swimwear on a photo shoot in Mexico. While she's abroad Dudley has been playing the field. He's phoning her to reassure her, and to check that she's not been up to any mischief of her own. With Peter beside him, taking the piss, Dudley tells Penny how much he loves her, only to overhear another voice in her hotel room. Suspecting her of infidelity, Dudley hangs up in a huff, just in time to welcome two women whom Peter has invited over for the evening. For once, Dudley's character was completely unsympathetic. For once, Peter's acting was entirely naturalistic. It was hard to believe it was the same man who'd seemed so awkward in the movies. Speaking his own lines, rather than someone else's, he seemed utterly at ease.

Wendy had returned from Majorca to escape the summer heat, and came along to the recording. This sketch made her feel particularly uncomfortable, and rightly so. Queasily compulsive, despite being curiously bereft of laughs, it reeked of real life, like the clandestine recording of a private conversation. Even though Dudley was playing the adulterer, not Peter, it still felt too close to home. Wendy could sense that Peter had been unfaithful but she was still in the dark about Judy. This suave, sardonic sketch was a sign that something was awry.

The standout sketch of the second episode, 'Aversion Therapy', also alluded to Peter's private life. Again, Dudley played the philanderer, but the personal details were all Peter's. Dudley is torn between his wife, Mary, with whom he has two children, and his secretary, Jane, with whom he's having an affair. Peter, playing a psychiatrist, trains Dudley to associate Mary with pleasure and Jane with pain, by giving Dudley Turkish Delight whenever he sees a photo of Mary, and giving him an electric shock whenever he sees a photo of Jane. It was highly amusing, but not for Wendy.

The highlight of the third show was a new father-and-son sketch called 'That Rebellion Thing', with Peter as a posh father and Dudley as his streetwise son – noticeably less servile than the parts he'd played in *Not Only ... But Also*. Dudley has decided to get married, with or without his father's consent, and reluctantly introduces his fiancée to his parents. The twist is that Dudley's fiancée is stuck inside an enormous box, and so is his mother, yet both Peter and Dudley behave as if nothing is amiss. It was a wonderfully absurdist flourish (positively avant-garde compared to most of ITV's peak-time output) but there was something disconcerting and vaguely misogynistic about it. 'Several new sketches on the subjects of both psychiatry and marital fidelity seemed to me to be overtly flagging up our domestic situation,' wrote Wendy. 'I found the imagery in Peter's work more and more sexualised, and even violent.' [29] It was a sign of things to come.

Before Christmas, Judy finally broke up with her husband, Sean Kenny. She moved out of the house they shared and into a rented flat. As Judy had feared, Kenny took the break-up badly. He went round to her new home at night, hammered on the door, and shouted through the letter box, threatening to kill her. He started tampering with her car at night, so that it wouldn't start. Once he even hot-wired it and drove it away. Judy was too scared to tell Kenny about Peter. She was too scared to have Peter over to stay. By now, Peter had been seeing Judy behind Wendy's back for eighteen months. When he went to Majorca for Christmas, Peter decided it was time to come clean. 'I have something to tell you,' he told Wendy. 'I've fallen in love with Judy Huxtable.' [30] Wendy was numb with shock. She guessed that Peter had been seeing other people, but this was something she was not expecting. 'We had better get a divorce, then,' [31] she replied. Now it was Peter's turn to be shocked.

'It's not like that,' he said. 'I just need time. It's probably just the fantasy of a lonely husband.' [32] Peter loved Judy, but he loved his family too. The thought of losing them terrified him, just as much as the thought of losing Judy. He hadn't really thought things through. 'He probably wanted it all,' [33] said his daughter Lucy, but that was never a realistic option. They talked it over in Majorca but Peter returned to London in the New Year with things still up in the air. Judy was upset to learn that he'd told Wendy about the two of them without discussing the matter with her first. She decided she couldn't sleep with him until the situation had been resolved. Peter was so rattled that, for the only time in his life, he followed Dudley's example and went into psychotherapy. 'I wanted to talk to someone who wasn't involved and who had no bias, so I could talk about how unhappy I felt without being a burden on friends,' he said. 'From my experience, most people I've known going through a difficult time in a relationship only want you to say, "Yes, you're right, how could she do that, isn't it awful?" I didn't want to burden my friends with that.' [34] He kept it up for six months.

Dudley, meanwhile, seemed to be enjoying married life. His weekends with Suzy soon fell into a familiar pattern. On Saturdays they'd wander down the King's Road, nosing around the boutiques and the antiques market, stopping off for a plate of cottage pie along the way. In the evening they'd go dancing at a trendy nightclub called Aretusa. On Sundays they'd go to Dudley's parents' place in Dagenham, where Dudley's mum always made them exactly the same Sunday Lunch – roast lamb with gravy, and jelly that had been left to set the night before. At home in Bentham House, he relished playing Bach sonatas with his good friend, the violinist Robert Mann, when he came to

Britain from New York with the Juilliard Quartet. The two men had met in Edinburgh when Mann went to see *Beyond The Fringe*. Mann had been so amazed by Dudley's musicality that he went backstage to introduce himself. It was the beginning of a lifelong friendship and music was at the heart of it.

Suitably impressed by his haunting score for *Bedazzled*, Stanley Donen commissioned Dudley to write the music for his next movie, *Staircase*, starring Richard Burton and Rex Harrison as a couple of homosexual hairdressers. Dudley's composition was subtle and discreet, supplementing the action rather than trying to fill each scene with false emotion. 'He wrote the most fabulous score, which was a perfect fit for the film,' [35] said Donen. A beautiful, talented and loving wife, a wonderful historic home, writing music, playing music, appearing on TV and in the movies – it sounded like a blissful existence, but Dudley still wasn't happy. An extraordinary entry in his diary outlined his inexplicably despondent state of mind:

> 'There is the predictable confusion, depression, the indecision,
> the paralysis of mind, the lack of purpose, lack of faith, lack
> of enthusiasm – in short, the feeling of life rushing by like
> an express train while one stands powerless on a windy
> platform ... The futility of my life and of every sort of activity is
> overwhelming. The knowledge that the way out of this impasse
> is hidden from me is intolerable ...'

And so on. Inevitably, the strain of Dudley's melancholia began to bear down on Suzy. 'Dudley always had angst,' she explained. 'He couldn't exist without it.' [36] But that didn't make it any easier to live with. When Dudley and Suzy went to Francis Megahy's flat for dinner, Megahy's wife found Dudley such miserable company that she swore she'd never let him in her home again. To outsiders it must have seemed ridiculous but depression is never rational.

Like Peter, Dudley needed constant validation, but whether onstage or in the bedroom the thrill of reassurance never lasted. 'You can have all the proof in the world, but if you don't feel it in your heart and soul then it doesn't count,' [37] said Suzy. Like Peter, Dudley seemed to have achieved everything that most people can only dream about. Within a few years, like Peter, he would have thrown it all away.

CHAPTER SEVENTEEN

POETS CORNERED

DUD: Fantasy can trigger off fact.

PETE: I don't catch your gist.

DUD: Like when a dream comes true. You dream you're
going along to the bathroom and then you wake
up and find that you haven't been to the bathroom
- except that you have, in a manner of speaking.
Not that it's ever happened to me, but a friend
told me about it.

PETE: He was incontinent.

DUD: No, it happened right here in England.

('Dreams', *Not Only ... But Also*, BBC2, 1970)

Peter and Wendy kept up appearances, for the next few months at
least. There was no phone at the Majorcan farmhouse, but Peter
sent frequent letters. He flew out for a few weeks in the spring, to
celebrate Lucy's birthday. They were joined by Peter's parents, who'd
arranged to come and stay for a week. Wendy was apprehensive
about entertaining her in-laws in such awkward circumstances, but
Alec and Margaret Cook had already booked their flights before Peter
told Wendy about Judy, and, since Peter had yet to tell his parents,

their visit passed off smoothly. Whatever their marital troubles, Peter could still rely on Wendy to be a superb host.

However, a marriage of convenience was never on the cards, and with Judy in the picture this holiday detente couldn't last. Soon after Peter's parents departed, Wendy started having trouble with her left knee and needed to return to England for treatment. She spent some time in a London clinic, receiving a series of painful steroid injections, then went to Church Row to convalesce. Peter had told Wendy he was about to give up Judy but, back in Hampstead, Wendy realised this was not the case. She found a bill from a taxi company, listing his numerous visits to Judy's flat. Wendy confronted him. He denied it, which she found particularly upsetting. Not surprisingly, in such strained circumstances, Peter's writing didn't prosper. 'I try and try, but I can't think of anything funny any more,' [1] he said.

Wendy decided to start divorce proceedings. She could see no way to save the marriage. 'I was a bit hasty' she says today. 'If we'd been a bit wiser, I think we could have worked through it.' Peter rented a flat in central London, where he stayed whenever Wendy was at Church Row, but he hated being there alone and rang Judy every night, begging her to come round. Judy still didn't feel ready to resume their sex life, so they just lay on his bed and cuddled. Clearly, this was no casual fling. In June 1969, Judy bought a two-up two-down in Ruston Mews, off Ladbroke Grove. Six weeks later, Peter moved in.

Peter and Judy relished living together, but it was a traumatic time for both of them, and for their respective spouses too. Soon after Judy moved in a solicitor's letter arrived, addressed to Peter. Peter's Swedish au pair was claiming that Peter had made her pregnant. He hadn't, in fact, but he did admit to Judy that they'd had a brief affair. Judy was upset, but she decided to let it go. More ominously, soon after Peter moved in Sean Kenny turned up late at night, blind drunk, and started hammering on the front door, threatening to kill them. He was thumping the door so hard that Judy feared he might break it down. Peter was just as terrified as Judy. They lay in bed, in silence, too scared to speak. At last, after what seemed like hours, the noise finally abated. Peter phoned Dudley. 'We need a bed,' [2] he said.

When the coast seemed clear, they drove to Dudley's house in their pyjamas. When they told Dudley what had happened, he thought it was hilarious. Peter did his best to laugh along, but he found it hard to see the funny side. Kenny had been a friend of his. Dudley made them a cup of tea and put them up in his spare room. 'When I woke up in the morning it was really spooky because the room was identical to Wendy and Peter's house,' said Judy. 'The house was a complete replica of Peter's, down to the same William Morris wallpaper.' [3] The furniture and bric-a-brac in both houses were extremely similar. Dudley even had an antique pram, like the one in Church Row. For the first time, Judy was struck by the extent of the sibling rivalry between them. 'I have observed it professionally, but this is different,' she reflected. 'Whatever one has in his life the other wants it too.' [4]

Despite mounting evidence to the contrary, Peter still believed his future lay in the movies. It was a woefully misguided notion, but he was merely obeying showbiz convention. The cinema was where the money was, so it was only natural that the biggest comedians would gravitate towards the big screen. In fact, these two genres were completely different. To become a movie star, he'd have to abandon the quick-fire format that had served him (and Dudley) so well, and learn to hold an audience for an hour or two – quite a challenge for someone who said that most of his ideas were only worth about five minutes. Peter was bored of making sketch shows. The only career progression was making feature films. It was a hierarchy based on status rather than any creative logic, and Peter's next movie would test this preconception to destruction. The tragedy of his career was that his humour was so original that the perfect forum for his comedy had yet to be invented.

The movie that Peter settled on was *The Rise And Rise of Michael Rimmer* – a film devised, ironically, by David Frost. Back in 1967, Frost had paid John Cleese and Graham Chapman to write the script during a three-month sabbatical in Ibiza – nice work if you can get it. Peter was lined up to play the lead, but raising sufficient funds took time so the project had been put on the backburner. Finally, Columbia-Warner agreed to stump up the necessary cash. They already had Peter under contract, to do three films for them. *The Wrong Box* and *A Dandy In Aspic* were the first two. *The Rise And Rise of Michael Rimmer* would be the third. With Cleese and Chapman, and the film's director, Kevin Billington, Peter set about rewriting the script. He worked hard on the screenplay, as he had done on *Bedazzled*. Fatally, Dudley was conspicuous by his absence – not only from the writing process this time, but also from the film itself.

As befitted a man with an innate understanding of the zeitgeist, Frost had come up with a topical and intriguing plot. Michael Rimmer is an opinion pollster who rises without a trace (as Jonathan Miller said of Frost) to become Prime Minister, by replacing normal parliamentary procedure with an endless series of referenda. As Rimmer foresees, the electorate love this idea at first but soon grow tired of being asked their opinion about absolutely everything and are eventually relieved to vote away their democratic rights, appointing him as their supreme dictator. It was pure fantasy, of course, but it addressed a real worry. Opinion polls were still a novelty and there was some concern that they might become a self-fulfilling prophecy. Frost's idea was pertinent and potentially very funny. Peter had every right to believe it would secure his status as a movie star.

Michael Rimmer was a fictional character in a fantastical story, but the character that Peter created bore more than a passing resemblance to the film's executive producer, David Frost. These resemblances were confined to Frost's suave mannerisms, rather than to any of Rimmer's dastardly deeds. Like Rimmer, Frost welcomed friends and colleagues by saying 'Super to see you.' Unlike Rimmer, he hadn't pushed the Prime Minister off a North Sea oil rig. Yet these superficial traits were similar enough to prompt some probing questions from the press, which Peter parried with a (fairly) straight face. 'There are obviously similarities with someone who gets on very successfully, like David, in the character of Michael Rimmer, but I think it would be odd if there weren't,' he said. 'Honestly, the film isn't really supposed to be about anyone.' [5] Peter's protestations of innocence were delivered tongue-in-cheek, with a nod and a wink to anyone who was in the know. Frost didn't say 'Super to see you' any more, explained Peter. He said 'Gorgeous to see you' nowadays. Fuelled by such flimsy and inflammatory rebuttals, these rumours persisted, prompting Frost's film company, Paradine Productions, to issue a public denial.

For insiders it was just a jolly jape, but these rather juvenile in-jokes showed how the balance of power had altered. At Cambridge Peter had been the master and Frost had been his pupil. Now Peter was the naughty schoolboy, scribbling rude words on the blackboard while the teacher's back was turned. Peter couldn't resist a poke at the man who'd usurped him as the King of Satire, but he wasn't too proud to take Frost's shilling. He needed this film too badly to walk away. A decade later, once the dust had settled, Peter was far more frank about the similarities between Frost and Rimmer. 'He got quite paranoid in that he thought that we were mirroring his career – which to an extent we were,' said Peter. 'Some of the character was based on David. The ultimate irony was that the set designer, who had never seen David's living room, and which we'd never talked about to her, produced an almost exact replica of David's room.' [6] The ultimate irony, however, was that Peter, who felt Frost's early work had imitated his own a mite too closely, had ended up imitating Frost in a film of Frost's own making.

Rather than taking the piss out of David Frost, Peter would have been wiser to have created a character with more of Frost's impressive social skills. All the best baddies are likeable, despite their evil stratagems. Even Peter's Devil in *Bedazzled* had a certain droll Satanic charm. Rimmer, on the other hand, was completely unappealing, with no redeeming qualities whatsoever. His only character trait was his insatiable lust for power. To engage an audience in such a loathsome role would have tested far better actors. Fleshing out this heartless villain was too much for Peter's finite acting skills. Peter sleepwalked through the film, like a patient under sedation. As an antidote to conventional acting, it had a certain strange allure. Peter Sellers might have pulled it off (as indeed he did, doing something similar in *Being There*) but Sellers was a brilliant actor. *The Rise And Rise of Michael Rimmer* was a star vehicle without a star.

Kevin Billington attempted to beef up the movie with an array of seasoned character actors, such as Arthur Lowe and Denholm Elliott, yet the roles they were assigned were equally unsympathetic. The film cried out for Dudley, but Dudley wasn't there. With no one nice to root for, the film felt nihilistic, and the sly digs against David Frost added to the sense of alienation. The essence of an in-joke, after all, is that most people don't get it. Despite its satirical tone it was hard to work out what point the movie was making, apart from reiterating the trite old truism that most politicians aren't terribly trustworthy, and that swapping democracy for dictatorship probably isn't such a good idea.

With the benefit of hindsight, it's easy to see why Peter wasn't cut out to be a film star. Most of his creations were stock archetypes, rather than real people. His most successful movie role was as a supernatural apparition. His funniest characters were idiot savants, with no connection with the real world. Even the stagecraft of his sketches betrayed his limitations as an actor. He acted from the neck up. His body was an awkward appendage. Fundamentally he was a one-man band, rather than an ensemble player. Only Dudley could intrude on his hypnotic trance-like state. 'I belong to the school of acting which consists of doing nothing in particular,' said Peter. 'The variety of my expressions between shock, joy and terror are very hard to define.' [7]

'Cookie was the best sketch actor that I ever saw, but I don't think he was anything like as good when he was trying to be absolutely real and portray real emotion,' [8] confirmed John Cleese. 'I would suspect that it was something to do with the fact that he wasn't very comfortable with his emotions, and as an actor you have to be able to access your emotions.' [9] Portraying real emotion was an anathema to Peter, but it was what the cinema required. On TV, in short sketches, he could conceal these handicaps. Playing the lead in a full-length feature film, they were exposed for all to see. 'He was a terrible actor,' said Dudley. 'He was very awkward with other people's lines.' [10] In the right context, playing to his strengths, Peter was a performer without equal. In *The Rise And Rise of Michael Rimmer*, he was as wooden as a flat-pack wardrobe. His career as a leading man was over.

The one thing that *The Rise And Rise of Michael Rimmer* really had going for it was its extraordinary power of prophecy. It predicted the outcome of the next general election – a shock win for the Tories, which took even the most seasoned pundits by surprise. It even foresaw the sacking of Enoch Powell. In more general terms, it anticipated the way in which public relations would reshape party politics, promoting style over substance, leading ultimately to smooth operators like David Cameron and Tony Blair. A general election was imminent. If the film premiered ahead of polling day, its news value might mitigate its many weaknesses. Peter realised the importance of releasing the film before the election. He suggested they stage three simultaneous premieres, in the constituencies of the three party leaders – Huyton (Harold Wilson), Bexley (Edward Heath) and North Devon (Jeremy Thorpe).

Catastrophically for the film (and for Peter's stuttering film career) the studio decided to delay *Michael Rimmer*'s release until after the general election. They felt it would be irresponsible to screen it during an election campaign. It was a fatal blow. *Rimmer*'s only trump card was its topicality. Everyone involved was devastated, particularly Peter, but he was powerless to intervene. Ironically, a similar fate had befallen *That Was The Week That Was* (the series that had made Frost a star – eclipsing Peter) when the BBC decided to axe the weekly satire show so as not to offend any politicians during the run-up to the 1964 election. The difference was that the Beeb's decision to cancel

TW3 enabled Frost to go out in a blaze of glory. Columbia's decision to postpone *Rimmer* meant that Peter's movie would be stillborn.

At least Peter's relationship with Judy was prospering. One day she returned home to Ruston Mews and found an enormous circle drawn on the wall. Inside the circle, in huge letters, were two words. 'Marry Me.' Underneath it she wrote 'Yes.' They were still both married to other people but, to all intents and purposes, Peter and Judy were now effectively engaged.

Dudley had also landed a leading role – not in the cinema, but on the West End stage, in Woody Allen's *Play It Again, Sam*. He'd seen the show on Broadway the year before, with Allen in the starring role, and thought it was the funniest play he'd ever seen. When Peter's old Broadway rival David Merrick offered him the lead in a West End transfer, Dudley turned him down. He was overawed by Allen's performance and didn't think he could match it. Eventually he changed his mind and agreed to take on Allen's role in an anglicised version of the play, substituting fish fingers for TV dinners and suchlike. After a try-out in Cambridge in August, the show opened at the Globe in London in September. The critics weren't all that keen but Dudley received better notices than the play itself. Most of the criticism was directed at the anglicisation of Allen's script, which transferred the play's location from Manhattan to Swiss Cottage. In *The Times*, Irving Wardle called it 'yet another instance of the folly of trying to anglicise American comedy.' This was Dudley's doing as well as Merrick's – he'd changed numerous jokes 'to make them more meaningful to English audiences.' [11] Yet despite tinkering with Allen's gags, and turning his central character into a Gentile Englishman, Dudley managed to avoid the blame. In *Tatler*, Sheridan

Morley said he made the best of a rather uninspired comedy. In fact, as Dudley had recognised when he saw the play on Broadway, Allen had written a masterpiece. If anything made it uninspired, it was stripping the play of its Jewish shtick and its New York locale. Yet Allen's work wasn't so well known in Britain then, which worked to Dudley's advantage. 'Relying on the cuddly appeal of a small furry animal, Dudley Moore looks appropriately hunted and haunted,' wrote John Barber in the *Daily Telegraph*. Onstage for the best part of two hours, Dudley showed he could be a leading man and not just a supporting player. He enjoyed himself in the role, and his enjoyment was infectious. For all its faults, it was a performance that showed he could make it on his own.

Peter and Dudley got back together to record a *Goodbye Again* special with Anne Bancroft. Like the rest of *Goodbye Again*, it wasn't quite up there with *Not Only ... But Also*, but it contained some decent sketches, including 'Plunger Jarvis', in which Dudley played an inept trapeze artiste auditioning for Peter's circus (reminiscent of 'One Leg Too Few') and 'Insurance Salesmen', in which Peter and Dudley teamed up as a couple of charming conmen trying to flog Bancroft a useless insurance policy. On the back of this qualified success, in December 1969 Peter contacted the BBC. Would they like another series of *Not Only ... But Also*? Of course they would. There were only two problems – Dudley was still appearing in *Play It Again, Sam* and the series was scheduled to begin transmission in mid-February, only a couple of months away. It was terribly tight, but Peter and Dudley were at their best when they were up against a deadline. In the New Year they set to work.

*

By now, Peter and Judy had moved out of Judy's little house in Ladbroke Grove. Peter thought it was too small. He wanted to live in a house he owned. He bought a sixteenth-century farmhouse called Kenwood Cottage, beside Highgate Ponds. Peter and Judy both adored it. Peter even did a bit of DIY, stripping away the plaster to reveal some old oak beams and knocking down a wall. 'I never thought I'd become the owner of a Black & Decker,' [12] he said. Dudley gave them a table-tennis table as a housewarming present. The location was ideal, close to Hampstead Heath. Peter was resigned to leaving Church Row, but Hampstead was his home. It was here that Peter and Dudley wrote the third series of *Not Only ... But Also*. It was the last TV series they wrote together.

Dudley was always punctual, which was a blessing considering what a short time they had to write the show. Peter would rise early and have a shower, keen to be alert and ready to start writing when Dudley arrived. They'd sit at a coffee table, Dudley in jeans and a black jumper, Peter in jeans and a black T-shirt, Peter chain-smoking and glugging copious quantities of black coffee. A notebook and a tape recorder were set out in front of them. Dudley brought his own provisions – fashionable health foods like dandelion tea and seaweed biscuits. He was trying to lose weight. Judy sat and listened, often for hours on end, making them tea and coffee and opening the windows when the room became too smoky. She was happy to be a captive audience, but she couldn't relax completely. If she didn't laugh, they'd assume that what they'd written wasn't funny. If she laughed too much it broke their flow. As always, there was a competitive element to their partnership. When Peter became aggressive during their role-playing sessions, it reaped rich creative dividends, but Judy noticed a cruel streak too. She felt it was an inherent trait rather than something calculated or deliberate. One running joke was calling Dudley 'a walking example of Preparation H.' Preparation H was a popular brand of haemorrhoid lotion. Peter thought Dudley was anally retentive. Dudley's riposte, calling Peter 'a long streak of piss,' lacked the same savage ingenuity. Even when they took a break, to play table tennis, the sparring didn't cease. They were both determined to win. When Dudley won, Peter cried foul and kept demanding replays until he triumphed. Whenever Judy joined in they gave no quarter. She didn't stand a chance.

Peter might have maintained the edge at table tennis, but the writing process was becoming a more even contest. 'Gradually, Dudley developed far more of a role in the writing,' reflected Peter, a decade later. 'I tend to flutter off very quickly and improvise and ignore illogicalities. I'd rather get through a whole sketch quickly and then come back and deal with whatever is wrong. Dudley began, when we had an idea, to examine what was logically incorrect, right at the beginning. I would regard this as pernickety, and he would regard it as logical. So the writing process became slower.' [13] However on Dudley's firmer foundations, they could now construct longer sketches. 'Peter has this extraordinary seam of invention he can draw on, an area of fantasy derived from Edward Lear and Lewis Carroll,' said Dudley. 'I perhaps have a slightly stronger feeling, though, for the architecture of a sketch.' [14] Dudley now calculated that his contribution to the writing was around 30% – a lot more than the first series, when he'd said Peter had seventeen ideas for every one of his.

One distraction they could have done without was Peter's preoccupation with horse racing. He bought a copy of *The Sporting Life* every morning, and then phoned Ladbrokes to place his bets. Judy didn't ask him how much he'd wagered, or how much he won or lost, but it must have mounted up. He'd keep the TV on while they were working, and stop work to watch each race. Dudley kept telling him to turn it off but Peter took no notice. He'd cheer on his chosen horses, often urged on by Joyce the cleaning lady, and mourn or celebrate accordingly at the end of every race. 'He loved horse racing – he was always betting,' [15] said Dudley. Was he hooked? Maybe, maybe not, but Judy thought there was an element of compulsion about it. Peter was also drinking more. He'd sometimes start late in the afternoon, after Dudley left, and just keep going. He wasn't drinking huge amounts, but it was becoming something that Judy noticed. 'Hang on,' she'd sometimes tell him. 'Do you realise you had a whole bottle of wine and fell asleep?' [16]

Dudley wasn't distracted by booze or horses, but he was still appearing in *Play It Again, Sam* six nights a week, plus Wednesday and Saturday matinees. Sunday was his only day off, and despite his and Peter's best efforts there simply wasn't time to write enough new material. Their director, Jimmy Gilbert, didn't think there was much point trying to direct them until they'd learnt their lines, but often there were barely any lines to learn. 'They always left everything to the last minute,' he said. 'They'd start each fortnight with nothing.' [17] Gilbert shut them in a room at TV Centre with a tape recorder and gave the tapes to his secretary for transcription, but even then they came up short. They'd always liked to leave things until the last minute, but this was later than ever. Their funniest work had always been a blend of preparation and inspiration. Now that delicate balance was in danger of being lost.

Peter saved the day with a new idea called 'Poets Cornered'. Every week, the show would finish with Peter and Dudley and a special guest sitting on stools above a large tank of sludge. They'd improvise a poem, all providing a line each in quick succession. As each contestant dried, they'd be tipped into the sludge. It was very funny, and it also served a useful function. It needed no preparation (a godsend in a show with such scant rehearsal time) and Gilbert could easily control the duration of the contest. If the show was overrunning, he could cut things short by plunging contestants into the sludge at the slightest hesitation. If the show was running short, he could just as easily spin it out. 'It was completely arbitrary,' said Peter. 'None of us knew when we were going to go. Jimmy would press a button and we'd fall into the foam.' [18] Spike Milligan was the first guest, followed by Willie Rushton, Barry Humphries, Frank Muir, Ronnie Barker, Denis Norden and Alan Bennett.

The first episode was distinguished by one of the best Pete & Dud sketches of the series – 'one of the strongest,' said Gilbert, 'because they'd written it far enough ahead to be able to rehearse it.' [19] It was a send-up of Freud's *Interpretation of Dreams*, with a friendly dig at Dudley's enduring faith in psychoanalysis. Dud was the fall guy, as usual, persuaded by Pete to undergo a rebirthing exercise by climbing in and out of a wardrobe – representing his mother's womb – but it was telling that Dud had some of the best punchlines:

PETE: I don't know if you're familiar with the works of Freud?

DUD: I do have a cursory knowledge of his theories. I recently skimmed through his lectures to the students of Heidelberg on the phallic interpretation of the penis.

PETE: An interesting if superficial study. Did you read it in the original German?

DUD: No, I read it in précis form on the back of a box of Swan Vestas.

The highlight of the second show was 'The Scriptwriter', one of Dudley's favourite sketches. Dudley played a working-class scriptwriter (clearly modelled on Johnny Speight) haggling with the BBC's Head of Light Ent (played by Peter) about the number of tits and bums he can mention in his latest sitcom. The premise seemed absurd, but it was remarkably realistic. As the creator of *Till Death Us Do Part*, featuring East End bigot Alf Garnett, Speight had endured similar showdowns with the BBC as the Beeb tried to trim the number of 'bloodys' and 'buggers' in his scripts. Peter and Dudley had also had comparable tussles with the Corporation. Like Speight, they employed an age-old haggler's ruse, peppering their scripts with superfluous swear words, so that the compromise solution actually contained the amount of 'industrial' language they really wanted. 'The sketch was based on an actual meeting,' confirmed Dudley. 'Peter loved it when we got away with things.' [20]

Despite these bureaucratic victories, Peter was feeling jaded. 'All my best work was done before I was eighteen, or before I was twenty anyway,' [21] he told Gilbert. This was a bit of an exaggeration – Peter didn't do *Beyond The Fringe* until his early twenties, and he was already in his late twenties when he and Dudley became a double act. Nevertheless, it was quite true that Peter now had a lot less creative energy than he'd enjoyed in his late teens. His talent had not deserted him, but he no longer had that demonic drive which had once carried all before him. As Gilbert observed, he still loved performing but he no longer relished the hard graft of writing. The filmed sequence in episode two, a nonsense poem called 'The Glidd of Glood', was from a book of children's verse which Peter started but never finished. It only found its way into *Not Only ... But Also* because Peter had failed to come up with anything new. At Cambridge, sketches had poured out of him. Now he was having to dredge them up from a deeper well within him. The results were often just as good, if not better (a lot of the Footlights sketches that Peter recalled so fondly haven't worn so well) but the making of them was becoming harder all the time.

Peter's 'Glidd of Glood' is one of the few film fragments that survives, and, watching it again today, it seems a shame that Peter's book of children's verse remained unfinished. The debts to Lear and Carroll are obvious, but it's still an original and accomplished piece, delivered in rhyming couplets against the bleak backdrop of Bodiam Castle, a windswept ruin on the south coast. The poem's storyline and setting reflected Peter's maudlin mood. Peter's Glidd is a miserable old miser who's robbed by Dudley's Sparquin, a court jester. Formerly the constant fall guy, Dudley was now frequently coming out on top.

This melancholy tone continued in episode three. 'In The Club' featured Peter and Dudley as two elderly toffs getting absolutely shitfaced. Bereft of proper punchlines, but engrossing all the same, the sketch had a malevolent flavour reminiscent of Harold Pinter, which anticipated Peter's darker work to come. Whereas Dudley always used to corpse, Peter was the one who cracked up during this recording. It was another sign of the slow but steady transfer of power from Peter to Dudley. 'Dudley had gone from being a subservient little creep, a genial serf, to become an obstinate bastard who asserted himself,' [22] reflected Peter. This shift in status even showed up in Pete & Dud. Now that Dud was beginning to answer back, it wasn't quite so funny. As Dudley said, Dud had become 'too intelligent, too well read.' [23]

In the fifth episode, Dudley took centre stage, playing a cross between Tom Jones and Ludwig van Beethoven, performing an orchestral arrangement of 'Delilah' before an audience of adoring fans. In keeping with the last-minute nature of the series, Dudley didn't deliver his score to Gilbert until the day they were due to film it, but the sketch still passed off very well. Peter played William Wordsworth, an effective but subsidiary role. Dudley had told the press he was fed up with being regarded as Peter's cute sidekick. Like all the brightest pupils, he was beginning to break away.

Thankfully, the final episode went out with a flourish. The most ambitious sketch was 'The Making of A Movie', a satire that reflected Peter's bitterness about the film industry. Peter played a pretentious film director – Dudley played a moronic film producer. The two men also played two hammy actors. It was funny stuff – especially their cod Shakespearean repartee in the BBC canteen. Still, the satirical content was rather undercut by the fact that the movie they were sending up, Robert Bolt's *A Man For All Seasons*, was neither moronic nor pretentious but an undisputed masterpiece. Peter and Dudley continued this send-up after the recording, at the wrap party, jumping up onto two adjoining tables in a crowded restaurant, improvising iambic pentameters before an audience of amazed but delighted diners. Like so many of Peter's finest performances, this impromptu turn was just as funny as anything they'd written or recorded – maybe even funnier – but it was only seen by a handful of people as it vanished into thin air. 'My greatest tragedy is that I haven't got a Boswell,' Peter told Gilbert as the evening wound down, 'I really need a Boswell to write it all down.' [24]

Wendy came along to some of the recordings, but inevitably she didn't enjoy the show as much as she had done before. Against the dark backdrop of their disintegrating marriage, even an identical

311

set of sketches would probably have felt quite different. But Wendy also noticed a change of tone, and some uncomfortable similarities between her personal circumstances and Peter's humour. In 'The Piano Tuner', Dudley played a randy pianist who goads a prim Latin teacher (played by Peter) with a lascivious description of his wife's attire ('thigh-length boots, micro skirt, see-through blouse, Indian headband') which Wendy took to be an unflattering reference to her own wardrobe:

PETER: I've never seen her in a see-through blouse.

DUDLEY: Well, maybe she's keeping it as a surprise for you – or someone else.

Dudley subsequently speculates that Peter's wife might have 'fallen under a West Indian'. As in numerous other sketches in this series, Dudley was the victor, as opposed to Peter – but the changing dynamics of their double act weren't uppermost in Wendy's mind. 'I was getting paranoid,' she reflected. 'I wondered what Peter would do for material once I wasn't so prominent in his life.' [25] One sketch which she found especially wounding was 'The Lunch Party', a Pinteresque depiction of a boozy get-together, similar in tone and content to 'In The Club'. Booze was becoming a recurring motif in Peter's comedy, reflecting its growing importance in his life, and the mood of this sour sketch, like several others in this series, was markedly more decadent than anything in series one or two. There was one line in 'The Lunch Party' that Wendy found particularly hurtful. 'Verity and I have a very honest relationship,' says Dudley. 'She knows perfectly well that from time to time I may have a bit of a fling – but she also knows that I'll never get seriously involved with another woman. I mean, I've never got involved with her.' From

Cambridge to Edinburgh, from the West End to Broadway, Wendy had been the bedrock of Peter's most creative years. Now the end of their relationship was being played out before a TV audience of millions.

Despite the acute time shortage, Jimmy Gilbert had maintained the tradition (begun by Joe McGrath and continued by Dick Clement) of presenting the opening credits for each week's show in a series of surreal and spectacular settings. With time-lapse photography, he'd spelled out the title in sprouting flowers (planted by Sir Arthur Greeb-Streebling) and in the final episode he surpassed himself, painting *Not Only ... But Also* in enormous letters across the deck of the Royal Navy aircraft carrier HMS *Ark Royal* – three days' work for the ship's crew. For the closing credits, a piano and two dummies dressed as Peter and Dudley were catapulted off the ship into the sea. It was a suitably flamboyant finale for one of the most brilliant comedy series ever broadcast by the BBC but, ominously, it also contained a note of tragedy. Shortly afterwards, one of the *Ark Royal*'s planes crashed into the sea in the same spot, killing both of the plane's pilots. Spookily, the plane's wreckage became entangled with the wreckage of the piano. Meanwhile, Wendy had a bad car accident in Majorca. She escaped without serious injury but the car was a write-off and she needed twelve stitches in a head wound. She was understandably very rattled and returned to England to recuperate. Back in Church Row, she was rushed into hospital for an operation to remove a gallstone and spent a month in the Royal Free Hospital in Hampstead. Returning to Church Row, Wendy was upset to find that Peter had taken the Tiffany lamp which he'd given to her. He'd taken it to Kenwood Cottage, where he was making a new home with Judy. 'It was the most moveable and valuable item,' says Wendy.

And yet it wasn't just a portable piece of bounty. This lamp was Peter's Rosebud, what Wendy calls his Maltese Falcon. 'It's assumed such symbolic proportions,' she says. When he died he left it to Dudley.

While Peter was moving out of Church Row, Dudley was moving out of Bentham House. His marriage to Suzy, which seemed so full of promise, had run aground against two insurmountable obstacles. Suzy wanted to have a baby (Dudley didn't) and Dudley felt trapped by being married. He still saw Suzy for dinner. They still went to Dagenham together to see his parents. He still loved her. He still cared about her. Yet he was now living with his friend George Hastings and his wife in Camden Town, rather than with the woman he still loved in a lovely house in Hampstead. To outsiders, it seemed unfathomable. 'Dudley always had angst,' Suzy told Dudley's biographer, Barbra Paskin. 'He couldn't live without it.' [26] Living without angst was harder for him than living without Suzy.

Peter and Judy.

CHAPTER EIGHTEEN

WHERE DO I SIT?

PETE: You don't think that your lack of acting
experience might stand in your way?

DUD: I've acted. I played the part of a troll in the Wood
Lane Primary production of *Peer Gynt.*

('Double O Dud', *Not Only ... But Also*, BBC2, 1970)

The third series of *Not Only ... But Also* ran from February to May
1970 on BBC2. Jimmy Gilbert then trimmed each 45-minute episode
to 30 minutes, and the series was repeated, in this shorter form, on
BBC1 that autumn. Gilbert was especially pleased with these leaner
repeats. However, the press reaction was surprisingly tepid. The
Daily Mail called the series 'a disappointment.' [1] This assessment was
rather mean. The third series wasn't quite as good as either of the
first two series, but it was significantly better than *Goodbye Again*
and streets ahead of any other TV sketch show in 1970. Having
showered them with praise for their early work before they'd really
found their feet, the critics were growing tired of Peter and Dudley
just as they were starting to hit their peak.

Like the critics, Peter and Dudley couldn't quite agree on whether
the series had been a success or not. Peter described it as 'textually

messy.' [2] Dudley regarded it as some of the best work they did. In fact, they were both right. The text was a mess because they hadn't had time to write enough material, or enough time to rehearse it thoroughly. Yet though these sketches were more hit-and-miss, they were also more ambitious. John Wells described their Greta Garbo skit (in which Peter dragged up as the reclusive film star) as almost expressionistic. With its sense that anything was worth a try, it was a show that stretched the boundaries of TV comedy, inspiring *Monty Python* and *The Goodies*. There were fewer punchlines and more surprises. And Dudley was now emerging as a comedian in his own right.

Meanwhile, Peter's divorce from Wendy dragged on. It was a difficult time for both of them. Their separation was announced in May 1970, but that was only the beginning. Peter insisted that the children should go to school in London, so Wendy had to remain in Hampstead rather than returning to Majorca. Until a financial settlement could be thrashed out, her bank account was frozen. She had to sell some of her family silver to make ends meet. Both of them wanted to keep matters on a friendly footing. 'I hope we will be one of the few couples of this or any century who will do this without bitterness,' [3] Peter told the press. 'Peter has said we must be civilised about this and I agree entirely,' concurred Wendy. 'I don't regret our years together at all.' [4] Even today she says she doesn't blame him. But once the lawyers got involved, the process inevitably became more brutal.

Peter wanted custody of the children, and Wendy duly received a legal letter, implying that her psychotherapy sessions with Doctor Sidney Gottlieb meant she might not be a stable parent. This was a nonsensical suggestion, on several counts. Visiting a respectable psychiatrist like Dr Sid Gottlieb was no more a sign of instability than visiting the dentist – particularly in Hampstead, the adopted home of Sigmund Freud. Moreover, Gottlieb was a family friend who accompanied Peter to numerous football matches. His therapeutic role in the Cook household was more that of agony aunt than shrink. To top it all, Gottlieb had also been treating Peter. If consulting Gottlieb was a sign of instability (which it wasn't) the charge applied to Peter as much as it did to Wendy.

Wendy was an excellent mother, and there was never any serious doubt that she would manage to retain custody of the children. Nevertheless, this letter was a signal that the gloves were off. The man she was now dealing with was no longer the creator of E.L. Wisty and Sir Arthur Streeb-Greebling, but a wealthy, well-connected Old Radleian with plenty of powerful and influential contacts. Most of their mutual friends took sides, and the more famous they were, the more likely they were to side with Peter. Wendy could be forgiven for feeling the cards were stacked against her. 'I was devastated by the shallowness of the thing showbiz people call friendship,' [5] she said.

Peter was keen to get divorced as soon as possible, so he could marry Judy. The easiest way to get a quick divorce was for one party to cite adultery. Peter asked Judy if she'd be willing to be named as the guilty party. Judy agreed, though she later regretted it. Wendy hired a private detective, and Peter and Judy prepared to be photographed being suitably adulterous together. After a false start, when the detective took some photos of Judy paying an innocent visit to a blameless neighbour, the private eye finally got some incriminating snaps of Peter and Judy coming home together. They left the curtains open, so he could get some shots of Peter inside.

*

In November 1970, *The Rise And Rise of Michael Rimmer* was finally released, nearly six months after the shock Conservative victory it had so astutely (and fruitlessly) predicted. In a forlorn attempt to give the movie some illicit cachet, it was billed as 'the film they wouldn't let us show until after the election' – vaguely implying that it had been banned by some unseen arm of the establishment, rather than being shelved by its own distributors. Not that this ruse did *Rimmer* any good. The punters didn't care either way. Even worse than outright hostility, which might at least have lent it some notoriety, *The Rise And Rise of Michael Rimmer* was merely received with mild disdain. 'Too many cooks spoil the Cook,' [6] ran the headline in the *Daily Mail*, a telling reference to the surfeit of celebrity cameos (a sure-fire sign of a film in trouble) which had failed to prop up Peter's somnambulistic performance. Driving home from the premiere, Peter was stopped by the police and charged with drink-driving. He went to court to contest the charge, claiming he was on Valium, which had made him seem drunk and skewed the alcohol levels in his bloodstream, but he was fined £25 and banned from driving for a year. 'Does that disqualify me from driving a power-assisted pedal cycle or a lawnmower?' [7] he asked the judge. He hadn't lost his old pizzazz, but his drinking was now becoming a more public affair.

Peter was treading water, unsure what to do next. He turned down an offer from the BBC to make another series of *Not Only ... But Also*. Still, the failure of *Michael Rimmer* had put a stop to any more movies. In December he appeared as E.L. Wisty in a cheesy Yuletide variety show called *Holiday Startime* on ITV. The script and the performance were as good as anything he'd done in *On The Braden Beat*, but the studio audience didn't really get it. He was playing second string to trad comics like Les Dawson, Ted Ray and Reg Varney (all further up the bill) and there was an air of ennui about reviving a character that he'd killed off six years ago.

The details of Peter and Wendy's decree nisi hit the press in December 1970. Judy's parents were upset to see their daughter named in a divorce case. Judy felt bad about upsetting them. Wendy had admitted adultery too, but as the so-called 'guilty party' it was Judy who ended up in the papers for sleeping with a married man. The case came to the Old Bailey in January. Wendy went along, accompanied by her friend Caroline Silver who'd been divorced a few weeks before. Caroline suggested they should arrive early and sit in on a few other cases. She thought it'd be good preparation for the ordeal ahead, but she hadn't anticipated the bizarre nature of the preceding case. An Irishwoman was divorcing a one-legged octogenarian for physical cruelty (shades of 'One Leg Too Few'). 'Just read through this statement and tell me if everything in it is true,' the judge told her. 'Are there any words in that statement that you don't understand?' [8] 'I don't know what sodomy means,' she replied. 'Is it the one with the mouth?' [9] Wendy and Caroline had to stuff their gloves into their mouths to prevent themselves from laughing.

The outcome of Wendy's divorce case wasn't quite so funny. She felt Peter's lawyer had 'conjured up a picture of an artiste practically on the breadline.' [10] She was awarded alimony of £200 a month (hardly a fortune, even in 1971) and the Majorcan farmhouse – which, under Spanish law, she couldn't own outright in any case. She got custody of the children, with 'reasonable access' granted to Peter. Peter wasn't there to hear the judgement. He had flown to Australia, with Judy and Dudley.

*

The invitation had come from ABC, the Australian Broadcasting Commission. *Not Only ... But Also* had become a big hit in Australia and ABC wanted two special editions, to be shot Down Under. There were a few new sketches – one with the England cricket team, who were in Australia for the Ashes, and one in which Sir Arthur Streeb-Greebling tries (and fails) to teach the Australian funnel-web spider to swim. Yet the bulk of these two shows consisted of new recordings of old favourites. Some of these favourites were very old indeed. As well as Dudley's Colonel Bogey variations from *Beyond The Fringe*, they reprised 'Balance of Trade', the shirt-shop sketch which Peter had written for *Pieces of Eight* in 1959. The sketch worked well with Peter as the smug shopkeeper (a part originally played by Kenneth Williams) and Dudley as his irate customer, but it was a sign of Peter's shrinking inspiration that he needed to revive material that he'd written when he was at university. In one respect, however, this increasing reliance on old standards was a blessing. One of the sketches they rerecorded in Australia was 'Pseudolene', one of the finest items from the first series of *Not Only ... But Also*, which had been wiped by the BBC.

For Peter and Dudley (and Judy) the trip Down Under was a welcome break. They swapped midwinter for midsummer, marital strife for foreign travel, and a carping British press for an Australian media who welcomed them with open arms – literally, in Dudley's case. In Sydney, he fell head over heels in love with a tall blonde journalist called Lyndall Hobbs. She was the first woman he'd felt anything for since his marriage had broken down, and though she was initially resistant to his elfin charms, he managed to win her over. For Peter and Judy, it was a relief to be on the other side of the world, far away from the turmoil of their respective marriages – they were in Sydney when Peter's divorce from Wendy was announced. They couldn't remarry just yet, since Judy's divorce from Sean Kenny was proving to be a more protracted process (Kenny wasn't responding to her solicitor's letters – always an effective tactic) but Peter told the press that he intended to marry Judy. In the public eye, at least, they were now practically man and wife.

In Australia, Peter and Dudley resumed their working relationship with Barry Humphries, a perennial figure in their work together, from the first series of *Not Only ... But Also* to *Bedazzled*. 'It was an extraordinary friendship those two men had,' marvelled Humphries. 'It was impossible to get a word in.' [11] Humphries appeared in a couple of new sketches and accompanied Peter on several enjoyable and entertaining road trips. Peter delighted in riffing about the unfamiliar shop signs and billboards that flitted past, revelling in the daft vagaries of the Australian dialect. Professionally and personally, it had been a successful assignment – far more pleasant (and productive) than their daily lives back in Blighty. True to form, the two shows were very well received when they were broadcast in Australia in February, but damned with faint praise when they were repeated by the BBC a few months later. In Australia they could do no wrong, it seemed – in Britain, little right. Dudley kept in touch with Lyndall Hobbs, talking into the small hours on the telephone, and flew back to Sydney to see her only a week after he'd returned to London. For both men, Australia had become their Great Escape.

Back in Britain, Peter did precisely what he'd said he didn't want to do, and returned to television. He'd turned down numerous offers from the BBC, but this latest invitation was something else. Michael Mills had become the BBC's new Head of Comedy, and in his eagerness to land a big name he told Peter he could do virtually anything he wanted. It was the televisual equivalent of a blank cheque. Peter decided he didn't want to do anything topical or political. He didn't want to do anything with Dudley. He wanted to front a chat show. He'd interview a few guests, do some sketches, and sing a pop song every week.

It was this weekly pop song that should have sounded the alarm bell. It was a sign that Peter was running wild, without the restraining influence of good advice. Wisely, Dudley had always put a stop to Peter's pop-star aspirations, confining his dubious singing skills to their comic curtain call, 'Goodbyee'. But this time Dudley wasn't around to save him, and Mills was happy to give him enough rope to hang himself. 'I'd love to be able to sing,' Peter told the writer Ray Connolly. 'I think if I get into the right state of mind I can.' [12] Peter gave Connolly a demonstration. 'Suddenly he jumps up from his settee and gives me a very lively and unselfconscious version of a complete verse of "All Shook Up", complete with voice tremor, sneering lip and a rotating movement in his left leg,' [13] wrote Connolly. At least he was the only witness to this spectacle. Mills was about to share it with the nation. The show was called *Where Do I Sit?* The producer was Ian MacNaughton. MacNaughton was best known for zany shows like Spike Milligan's *Q5* and *Monty Python's Flying Circus*, but Peter could already do zany. What he really needed, in this unfamiliar format, was someone who could keep him in check.

With rigorous rehearsal and ruthless editing, Peter might just about have got away with it. However, he was determined that the show should go out live. 'There's so little live TV,' he told the

BBC. 'People will enjoy disasters if they happen.' [14] As he said to Russell Harty, 'I wanted to restore that embarrassing element that there used to be on television, when sets fell over and people forgot their lines and things went wrong.' [15] His wish was granted. Mills found Peter so persuasive that he didn't even request a pilot. He commissioned a dozen live shows, to be screened at peak time on Friday evenings on BBC2. Some sketches were filmed in advance, but even these lacked Peter's usual verve. In a lacklustre stunt that sounds like an unsuccessful out-take from *Beadle's About* (or some similarly dreadful hidden-camera show) Peter dragged up as Cilla Black and hung around outside a petrol station in Batley, accosting bemused motorists and asking them, in a shrill voice, if they knew who he was. Some did. Some didn't. Some told him to get lost. In another item, Peter lay across a stream as Judy clambered over his prostrate frame. This scene was filmed to accompany Peter's rendition of Simon and Garfunkel's 'Bridge Over Troubled Water'. In this instance, the BBC's policy of recycling old mastertapes was probably a blessing.

For the opening episode, to be broadcast live on Friday, 11 February 1971, Peter's first guest was the American humorist S.J. Perelman. Peter was a big fan of Perelman's work but Perelman was a writer, not a performer, and like most writers he saved his best bons mots for the page. Having made his name before the Second World War, he was now well into his sixties and most British TV viewers had no idea who he was. Willie Rushton met him at a dinner party a few days before the show went out and was aghast to hear that he'd been booked to appear on Peter's new chat show. 'He just sat there yawning heavily and dropping off,' said Rushton. 'He was not a very amusing man.' [16]

In front of the cameras Perelman was no better ('almost mono-syllabic,' [17] remembered Judy) and Peter compounded the problem by failing to prepare any questions or do any research. 'His strength is instant repartee,' [18] maintained Judy, which was quite true, but Peter's repartee had always flourished within some sort of framework. Without it, he was liable to wander off down a comic cul-de-sac. Peter's other guest, Auberon Waugh (a witty interviewee, but hardly a household name) called the show 'an unmitigated catastrophe'. [19] It played no better at home. Rushton watched it and saw his worst fears confirmed. Peter's Johnny Cash impression was the nadir of the first episode. 'It was the worst thing he ever did,' said Rushton. 'Nobody knew whether he was joking or not.' [20] The critics didn't pull their punches, but there was no relish in their reviews. 'Dismally embarrassing,' wrote Chris Dunkley in *The Times*. 'A sad disappointment.' [21] Dunkley also recognised a growing imbalance in Peter's work. 'Peter Cook seemingly will persist in the belief that his ad-lib material is better than the rehearsed sections,' he argued, astutely. 'Unfortunately the precise opposite is the case.' [22] Dunkley was right, and the big difference was Dudley. When Dudley was around, Peter's ad-libs were constrained and channelled, bolstered by an established script which Dudley learned by heart. Without Dudley's patient preparation, his improvisation was inclined to veer way off course. What worked so well around a dinner table simply didn't work on live TV. 'I wanted to take it off after the first show,' [23] said Bill Cotton, the BBC's Head of Light Entertainment. It might have been kinder if he had. Instead, like a punch-drunk boxer, Peter staggered on. The talking point of the second show was a sketch with Peter and Spike Milligan as two tramps, which actually contained at least one good joke:

PETER: I'm God.

SPIKE: Oh Christ! Oh dear. I'm sorry. He's your son, isn't he?

This sketch prompted Mary Whitehouse to ask the police to prosecute Peter for blasphemy, which could have put the show on the side of the angels, had Peter not asked the studio audience if any of them had been offended. A polite young man voiced a tentative objection, whereupon Peter tore into him. This might not have been quite so bad if the show hadn't been going out live. 'I have a feeling that fame has gone to Cook's head,' [24] observed the *Daily Mail*.

The man from the *Mail* was wrong. What had gone to Peter's head wasn't fame, but a cocktail of drink and prescription drugs. After the critical reaction to the first episode, he was understandably nervous ('a gathering sense of panic' [25] was how he put it) and imbibed a bit too much before the second show. This only made things worse, of course. After the second show, one viewer, a Mr Wentworth, wrote to the BBC, accusing Peter of being a drug addict. Peter's response was to phone Mr Wentworth during the third show, to have it out with him on air. Even with proper preparation this would have been a risky stunt, but Peter made the call completely blind. Mrs Wentworth answered the phone and summoned her husband, only to discover that he was in the bath. A more prudent presenter would have cut his losses and hung up straight away. Instead, a torpid interlude ensued as Mrs Wentworth turned on the telly, waited for the set to warm up, and shouted repeatedly to her husband to come to the phone. Meanwhile, Peter sat and waited, the cameras rolling, a butterfly impaled upon a pin.

Eventually, Mr Wentworth emerged from his bathtub and batted away Peter's accusations with an accomplished ease that suggested he could have fronted a decent chat show of his own. 'You said I was a drug addict,' said Peter. 'I can't linger now because I'm dripping wet,' said Mr Wentworth, 'and I'd like to watch the rest of the show.' In a sense, Peter was ahead of his time (you can imagine Chris Evans or Jonathan Ross performing a similar stunt today, albeit with a bit more polish) but in a programme where every other element was so erratic it merely added to the sense of mayhem. Ned Sherrin, a guest on the show, witnessed the carnage at close hand. 'It was chaos,' said Sherrin. 'Being a chat-show host is pretty negligible compared with being a comic genius, but it does require certain skills.' [26]

On Monday morning, Peter and Ian MacNaughton were called into Bill Cotton's office. With nine episodes still to run, Cotton had decided to cancel the show, to protect Peter's reputation and the reputation of the BBC. 'He tried to sue us, but it came out in a meeting with the lawyers that he'd spent the money, so we came to an agreement,' [27] said Cotton. *Where Do I Sit?* was subsequently voted the worst TV show of the year, by TV critics and TV viewers alike (quite an accolade). Peter was replaced by a young journalist called Michael Parkinson.

Sherrin believed that Peter's desire to crack the chat-show format was partly driven by a deep-seated desire to beat David Frost at his own game ('If Frost can do it, I can do it better' [28]). It was a battle Peter was bound to lose. In fact, anyone who'd pondered the dynamics of Peter and Dudley's double act should have realised that the qualities which made Peter such a super chat-show guest would make him an awful host. A chat-show host is the straight man in a double act, supplying the feed lines and keeping the star turn on track. This had always been Dudley's role, not Peter's.

In the aftermath of this fiasco, Peter was his own sternest critic.

'I was no good at talking to people on TV,' he said. 'I realised that I was not going to be interested in anything the guests said.' [29] This was a tad too harsh. Unlike a lot of other comics (including Dudley) Peter wasn't self-obsessed. He didn't really like to talk about himself. He far preferred talking about other people. Yet whenever he was performing, he was primarily a monologist. His humour was compulsive, with no connection with the world around him. 'It was obviously a great gift, but it was almost an affliction,' [30] said John Bird. The only person who could really share a stage with him was Dudley.

Dudley, meanwhile, was being battered by a crisis of a more fundamental kind. After his brief return trip Down Under, to renew his intimate acquaintance with Lyndall Hobbs, he resolved to give his marriage another go and invited Suzy on a trip to Fiji. The holiday passed off pretty well, and they flew on to Hong Kong together. They were en route to Bangkok when an urgent message reached them. Dudley's father, Jock, was gravely ill. He had cancer of the colon. He had only a few weeks to live. They took the next flight home. Dudley went straight to Dagenham to support his mother and be near his father, who was in hospital. Staying in his childhood home, Dudley had trouble sleeping, awaking horrified at the thought of the 'terrible hole' [31] that would open up within him when his father died. Yet when the call came from the hospital, saying that Jock was about to slip away, Ada was in no rush to go. 'Please don't let's hurry,' she told Dudley. 'I don't want to see him struggle.' [32] It was a strange reaction but Dudley felt the same way. Jock was already dead by the time they arrived. The last thing he'd said to Dudley was, 'Don't let it pass you by.' [33] It was an odd thing to say to someone who'd already crammed more into half a lifetime than Jock ever could have dreamed of, but Dudley's biographer, Barbra Paskin, saw this statement in another light. 'He had seen the sadness in him after all.' [34]

Jock's death hit Dudley hard. He wished he'd done more to help him. He wished he'd spent more time with him. It was an understandable reaction, but an illogical one. Dudley had been a model son – supporting his parents financially without ever making them feel in thrall to him, and visiting them regularly, even at the height of his new-found fame. In fact, Dudley's sense of separation from Jock (and Ada) wasn't due to any dereliction on his part. It was the result of the success he'd striven for, on their behalf. He'd fulfilled their dreams for him, and in doing so he'd become a different person. A child of the new Welfare State, Dudley's progress from council estate to Oxbridge and beyond personified the new egalitarianism of the post-war years, an era with far more social mobility than the present day. Millions of other grammar-school boys (and girls) felt much the same way. Dudley played the organ at Jock's funeral, at St Peter's church in Dagenham. Suzy came too. Dudley was inconsolable. As he played 'Jesu Joy of Man's Desiring', the tears streamed down his face. 'I was dreadfully upset and I just couldn't stop sobbing,' he said. 'I wish we'd talked more. I wish I could have found out who he was.' [35]

Peter was soon faced with a far graver problem than his failure to emulate David Frost as a successful chat-show host. For several months Judy had been becoming increasingly unwell, with mounting pelvic pain. At first she thought it was the result of stress. Then she feared she might have cancer. Her stomach swelled up. She couldn't bear anyone to touch her. After trying to nurse her back to health with bowls of soup and nips of brandy, Peter phoned Judy's mother. She flew over from Jersey and insisted that Judy should see a doctor. Judy went for tests but walked out, too scared to find out what was wrong with her. Her condition became worse and worse. Her weight dropped from seven-and-a-half stone to just five stone. In May she collapsed and was rushed into London's King Edward VII Hospital. She lost consciousness and ended up in intensive care. Tragically, after her abortion, Judy had been fitted with a coil which had pierced the lining of her womb and caused a serious infection. Mercifully, Judy's mother found her a first class gynaecologist called Tom Lewis, who diagnosed peritonitis. Judy feels sure his quick thinking saved her life. Eventually, Judy returned home to convalesce. Peter was the perfect nurse, feeding her up on scrambled eggs and taking her on recuperative trips to Ladbrokes. Slowly she recovered, but the effects of the infection lingered on.

In July 1971 Peter put the Church Row house on the market for £45,000 – nearly twice what he'd paid for it some six years before. It sold quickly – so much for Alan Bennett's fear that Peter would never recoup his money. Lucy and Daisy were now attending Gospel Oak Primary School, so Wendy and her daughters needed to find somewhere nearby where they could live. Bizarrely or pragmatically (depending on your point of view) they moved into Peter and Judy's new house, Kenwood Cottage, and Peter and Judy moved out, packing all their belongings into Judy's terraced house in Ruston Mews. Moving into Peter and Judy's home felt strange at first, but Wendy made the best of it. She liked the rural setting, but she missed the farmhouse in Majorca, which had been put out to rent.

Dudley, meanwhile, gave Bentham House to Suzy. Their respective Hampstead idylls had lasted for only a few years.

In the midst of these domestic upheavals, a return visit to Australia became an increasingly attractive prospect, and when Peter and Dudley were offered a five-month tour Down Under they were happy to accept. They got together to write some new sketches and spent a week at Champneys, a posh health farm in Hertfordshire, to get into shape (Dudley stuck to the special diet – Peter didn't). In September 1971, Peter, Dudley and Judy flew to Sydney. It was the first leg of a marathon that would keep them occupied for three years.

CHAPTER NINETEEN

DOWN UNDER

DUDLEY MOORE: Sir Arthur, what is the porpoise of your
visit to Australia?

SIR ARTHUR STREEB-GREEBLING: There is no porpoise
involved in my visit to Australia. I've never got
involved with a porpoise. One of my strictest
rules – never get involved with a porpoise.
Whatever you may have read in the sensational
tabloids, I have never become involved with a
porpoise. What I think is happening is you're
misreading the word 'purpose.'

('The Funnel-Web Spider', *Not Only ... But Also,* Australian Broadcasting Commission, 1971)

The title of their Australian show was Dudley's idea, harking back
to his pre-show suppers with Alan Bennett at Barbetta's in New
York, and the Italian waiter who'd been unable to pronounce the
title of their Broadway show. It was a clever conceit, but it invited
comparisons with past glories. A decade later, would their new show
match up to *Beyond The Fringe*?

Behind The Fridge comprised twelve new sketches and three new
musical numbers, padded out with a few old routines from *Beyond
The Fringe*. Given the fraught circumstances in which Peter and

Dudley wrote it, the quality of the material was remarkably good. But the writing had been hard going. Often they could only think of anything after several fruitless hours together, when they'd both had enough and were about to call it a day. 'Sometimes we used to fall about endlessly,' said Dudley. 'Sometimes it used to be miserable.' [1] That misery seeped into some of the material. One item, 'Mini Drama', was more like a scene from a horror film. Dudley played a pompous politician, with Peter as his malevolent chauffeur, driving him to parliament for a late-night sitting. As Peter motors through the night, responding to increasingly sinister instructions on the car radio, Dudley becomes convinced that he's about to be murdered. It was a compelling and disturbing sketch, reminiscent (like much of their later work) of Harold Pinter – riveting, but virtually bereft of laughs. Peter and Dudley were nudging at the boundaries of a new art form. This was unlike any previous revue. Calling them sketches was quite inadequate. 'I wish there was another word to describe them,' said Peter. 'Perhaps we should call them scenes.' [2]

Other sketches (or scenes) showed the strain of recent family travails. In 'On Location', Peter played a callous movie star, returning home from a foreign film shoot too late to attend his mother's funeral. Dudley played his star-struck father, pathetically in awe of Peter's glamorous career:

DUDLEY: I told her every time I went to that bloody
hospital, I said, 'Ada, you can't expect a film
company to stop a multimillion-dollar production
in Yugoslavia just because you're feeling a bit
under the weather, dear.'

PETER: You know, Dad, I tried to get away, but we were
shooting this snow sequence and the snow was
melting, and the director just refused to release me.

DUDLEY: Of course he refused to release you. I would have refused to release you. I kept on saying to your mother, I said, 'Ada, what is Mr Omar Sharif going to say if his co-star – our only son – suddenly does a midnight flit out of Yugoslavia just to see his mother?'

As Dudley told the journalist Mavis Nicholson, 'On Location' was a direct response to his father's recent death (he even used his mother's real name). 'It was a way of exorcising the event,' [3] he said, but it was clear from this sketch that his father's ghost hadn't yet been laid to rest.

Thankfully for Australian audiences, who'd come to see some comedy rather than a spine-chiller or a kitchen-sink drama, the rest of the show was more upbeat. The opening sketch, 'Hello', was a shrewd lampoon of English etiquette. Peter and Dudley played smarmy strangers exchanging empty pleasantries, assuming they must know each other though they've actually never met. The best sketch in the show was 'Gospel Truth', in which Dudley played Matthew, a tabloid reporter on the *Bethlehem Star* ('you may have heard of me and my colleagues – Mark, Luke and John') interviewing a shepherd (played by Peter) for an 'in-depth profile' of Jesus Christ:

DUDLEY: What was the atmosphere like amongst the members of the Holy Family?

PETER: Well, in one word – tense.

DUDLEY: Tense? You surprise me.

PETER: Joseph in particular. He was sitting in the corner of the stable, looking very gloomy indeed.

DUDLEY: Well, he might have been feeling a bit disgruntled, not being the real father.

This friendly send-up of the Nativity may seem mild today, but in 1971 (nearly a decade before *Monty Python's Life of Brian*) it was really rather daring:

DUDLEY: Was the Holy Ghost there?

PETER: Hard to say. He's an elusive little bugger at the best of times.

After their arrival in Australia, to publicise *Behind The Fridge*, Peter and Dudley performed 'Gospel Truth' on Australia's Channel Nine, in a special edition of *The Dave Allen Show*. Mindful of the sketch's potential to cause offence, Channel Nine took the precaution of running it past a panel of Australian clergymen before transmission. Two of the most controversial lines were subsequently cut from the broadcast version, but hundreds of outraged viewers still phoned the station to complain.

Instead of defending their special guests against this pious protest, craven TV bosses did what craven TV bosses often do and ignored the silent majority, siding with the noisy minority instead. Clyde Packer, Managing Director of Channel Nine, called the show 'offensive and irresponsible.' [4] His father, Sir Frank Packer, another TV bigwig, called it 'a vulgar programme in bad taste.' [5] Allen had cracked some Jewish jokes, which had been (wrongly) construed as anti-Semitic. Peter and Dudley had said 'piss' and 'bum' – still regarded as rather shocking on Australian TV back then. The chairman of the Australian Broadcasting Control Board said he'd never seen such a 'blatantly offensive reference to homosexuality and masturbation' [6] (he'd clearly led a sheltered life). Peter and Dudley and Dave Allen were barred from performing live on TV or radio in Australia. The ban applied to every station, with immediate effect.

Peter and Dudley were gobsmacked. Extensive broadcast coverage was crucial if they were going to sell the show. They tried to sidestep the furore by putting out a statement, blaming Allen for letting the programme go 'beyond the bounds of decency' [7] – which was a bit shabby, to say the least. Yet, as countless entertainers have discovered, a broadcast ban is often the best form of publicity. *Behind The Fridge* became a cause célèbre, and Peter and Dudley were cast as champions of free speech. Christians picketed the theatres, which only increased the pair's rebellious kudos. A week after they'd been prohibited from appearing live on TV, they appeared on live TV – in a charity gala for famine relief, broadcast by Channel Nine, the station which had transmitted 'Gospel Truth'. *Behind The Fridge* was now a sell-out. Peter sent the Australian Broadcasting Control Board a suitably grateful telegram.

The stage show opened in Canberra to a rapturous reception, from press and public alike. 'We'd hit a peak,' said Dudley. 'I couldn't think of anything being more enjoyable. It was such tremendous fun.' [8] Reunited with Lyndall Hobbs, having parted amicably from Suzy Kendall, he was coping pretty well with the end of his first marriage. Even their hotel ('like a drab motel from a B movie' [9] recalled Judy) didn't dampen Dudley's high spirits. Peter, on the other hand, was finding this Antipodean trip more trying. As the father of two young children, his divorce was bound to be more difficult than Dudley's. Judy was the love of his life but he missed Lucy and Daisy terribly.

Things came to a head when the show reached Melbourne. On 2nd October, the day they were due to open, Peter got a telegram from Wendy. Daisy had had a bad asthma attack and had had to go to hospital. Daisy had always suffered from severe asthma, but this latest attack was especially acute. Wendy was simply doing the decent thing by letting Peter know that his daughter had been to hospital. However worried about Daisy's health, and feeling guilty about being so far away, Peter hit the bottle, and ended up walking into the hotel pool with all his clothes on. The hotel staff had to haul him out. 'He felt terrible about it,' said Dudley. 'To my mind, he became an alcoholic from that moment on. After that, it seemed like he was drunk every night.' [10]

Remarkably, Peter made it through the first night without a hitch. The *Melbourne Herald* called it a 'supremely well-worked evening.' The *Melbourne Sun* called it 'brilliant,' but Dudley wasn't so pleased. 'What's the matter?' asked Peter. 'You're drunk!' replied Dudley. 'Getting the show into shape has been something of a headache,' he wrote to Suzy, from their hotel in Melbourne, 'especially when Peter was consistently throwing wine, spirits, champagne and Valium down his throat at a rate that showed up onstage. I had a large and pretty extended argument with him about this and told him I didn't think I could face this tour with the real possibility of him being bombed out of his head every time we went onstage.' [11]

Normally, Dudley would never touch a drop before a show, but one night, to prove a point, he got drunk before he went on. 'That's the worst performance you've ever given,' [12] said Peter afterwards. 'I didn't know what to do.' [13] 'Well, now you know what it's like to play opposite someone who's inebriated,' [14] replied Dudley. 'Now you know what it's like, you cunt.' [15] This practical demonstration didn't have much effect. On 21 October the show transferred to Sydney, for a four-week run. 'In Sydney I think he was drunk for a whole week,' said Dudley. 'I thought, "I can't stay onstage with this guy for two hours."' [16] But, with no understudies, he had no choice. 'Dudley was literally holding Peter up and propelling him around the stage,' [17] said Michael Parkinson, who saw the show in Sydney. 'If Peter couldn't grab the furniture he'd grab Dudley. He was pissed all the time.' [18] With no co-stars to support him, the strain on Dudley was immense. 'Peter's drinking was destroying the relationship,' [19] said Parkinson. 'Dudley didn't want to see that happen to anybody.' [20] It was at this time, for the first time, that Dudley decided he wanted out. He told Parkinson that he and Peter needed to go their separate ways. He told him he couldn't go on any more because he loved Peter too much. In Sydney, Peter and Dudley went to dinner with Lewis Morley, the photographer who'd worked with them on *Beyond The Fringe*. 'The other guests at the party were a little confused,' recalled Morley. 'They had expected an evening of jollity.' [21] But Peter and Dudley were in no mood for cracking jokes. Dudley recited some John Betjeman poems and burst into tears. 'Things have changed,' murmured Peter, sadly. 'Things have changed.' [22]

At least the accommodation was an improvement. After putting up with motels and motor inns in Canberra and Melbourne, they'd been booked into a superb hotel overlooking Sydney Harbour. The Australian cricket team were staying in the same hotel, and Peter was pleased to join them for a few drinks. He was drinking at lunchtime, and with his pre-show supper – something Dudley never dared to do – plus about a bottle and a half of wine every evening after the show came down. 'He had always drunk rather a lot but suddenly it turned the corner,' [23] said Dudley.

Peter and Dudley's relationship had always been intense. In London this intensity had been diluted by a metropolis full of people. In Australia it was distilled by isolation. Cooped up in the same hotels, doing the show together every night, their partnership became a pressure cooker. Peter's boozing and Judy's beauty added petrol to the mix. Dudley would phone Peter's suite every afternoon, to ask how he was and what he'd been up to, even though he'd usually seen him only a few hours before. He wanted to know if Peter and Judy had had a row. He wanted to how much Peter had been drinking.

Often, Peter would be sleeping off his lunch, so Dudley would talk to Judy. They'd become good friends back in England, but on the other side of the world, in constant contact, with no other close friends to distract them, their friendship acquired an added frisson. Dudley would come over to their suite and sit and talk to Judy in the sitting room while Peter slept in the adjoining bedroom. Dudley didn't spell it out, but Judy knew what he was thinking: 'Why are you with him when he's drunk and you could be with me and I'm sober?' [24] Dudley became flirtatious. He sent her notes from the honeymoon suite, saying he was in the whirlpool and he wished she was there with him. Meanwhile, a few feet away, Peter slumbered on.

For Judy, it was a no-win situation. She didn't want to lead Dudley on, but she couldn't afford to fall out with him. He was the only person she could talk to about Peter's drinking – she didn't dare speak to anyone else about it, for fear it might end up in the papers. Any bad publicity, any bust-up would be disastrous for the show. She found Dudley very attractive – she'd even grown to love him, as a friend – but she didn't want to betray Peter. Dudley's amorous advances confirmed what Peter had already told her – that Dudley could be very crafty. 'What could be more devious than working with and loving someone and all the while waiting for an opportunity to whip his girlfriend away and make love to her, knowing you are stealing everything he cares about?' [25] she wrote. She already knew that Dudley was a sexual predator ('Not Safe In Taxis', as her girlfriends used to put it) but this was something else. Whatever Peter had, Dudley wanted – from a house in Hampstead with William Morris wallpaper to the woman in his life. It was an unpleasant aspect of Dudley's personality. His angst was real but it doubled as a clever ploy for talking women into bed.

Dudley loved the thrill of the chase, but what he really craved was variety. A constant stream of short-term girlfriends (or 'meaningful one-week stands' as he liked to call them) gave Judy some respite from his romantic overtures. He wanted Judy but in the end he wanted everyone. His sexual appetite was uncompromising and insatiable. As he said himself, from the age of eleven he'd been a 'prisoner of sex.' [26] It was addiction just as powerful as Peter's addiction to alcohol.

By now, Peter was topping up his tipple with various uppers and downers. He took slimming pills before the curtain went up to pep himself up, Valium afterwards to mellow out and sleeping pills at bedtime. His sex life with Judy suffered. His performance with Dudley suffered, too. Speed made him seem sober onstage, but Dudley wasn't fooled. As Peter's drinking increased, his performances became increasingly erratic. Dudley had always stuck to the script, Peter had always improvised, but previously his ad-libs had been brief divertissements. Now they threatened to overwhelm the show. Dudley was prone to corpsing, Peter could keep a straight face, so when a routine fell apart as a result of his tipsy impro it was Dudley who ended up looking like a fool. Australian audiences were forgiving – maybe too forgiving – and, even in this addled state, outright cock-ups were surprisingly few and far between. Peter often still got away with it (he was that good) but the price he paid was far higher than tepid applause. Dudley soldiered on but, watching from the wings, Judy could tell that Dudley wasn't enjoying it any more. 'Some days, he can take it in his stride,' she reflected. 'Other days he looks as if he'd like to murder Peter.' [27]

After the show finished in Sydney, Peter and Dudley took a well-earned break from one another. Dudley spent Christmas in London with Suzy – they were much better at being friends than they were at being man and wife. Peter and Judy flew to Fiji and then returned to Sydney to spend Christmas in a rented apartment on Bondi Beach. It wasn't as enjoyable as it should have been. Judy often had to stay inside to protect her fair skin from the summer sun. Peter didn't burn so easily. He preferred to stay outdoors, by the pool or on the beach. Peter was drinking steadily, at lunchtime as well as dinner time. For a father separated from his children, Christmas was bound to be the worst time of year.

In the New Year Dudley returned and the show travelled on, to New Zealand. This extension of the tour, to Auckland and Wellington, was another source of strife. Dudley was angry that Peter had arranged it without discussing it with him beforehand. Peter was now acting as his own agent, which took a lot of time and effort. He drove a hard bargain, but Judy saw it as a manifestation of his growing addiction to gambling.

When they arrived in Auckland the simmering tension between Peter and Dudley very nearly bubbled over. They reached their hotel on a Sunday night. As soon as they checked in, Peter ordered two bottles of wine, polished them off in record time and crashed out in his hotel room. Judy was annoyed that they hadn't made more use of this evening off. She went down to the foyer, where Dudley was playing the piano, and ordered a glass of milk from the bar. 'Where's Peter?' [28] asked Dudley. 'Out for the count,' [29] replied Judy. 'Come and sit beside me,' [30] said Dudley. He asked her what she'd like him to play. She requested Mendelssohn's Wedding March, but as he played she saw the lights above the lift going up and down and up and down. She guessed that it was Peter, struggling to find the right button for the ground floor. Finally, Peter staggered out, wearing a pair of underpants and nothing else. He strode across the foyer towards them, his anger rather undermined by his immodest attire. He asked Judy what she was doing. 'She came down to get a glass of milk,' [31] said Dudley. 'Come back upstairs,' [32] said Peter. Judy followed him upstairs. Peter went straight back to sleep. None of them referred to Dudley's nocturne again.

A more prudent man might have backed off, thankful that no lasting damage had been done, but a couple of days later Dudley booked Peter onto a sightseeing trip in a small plane. Peter was thrilled. He assumed that Judy would be coming too. But Dudley had only bought one ticket. It was a shameless ruse to get Peter out of the way so that he could be alone with Judy. Peter didn't go. The tour finished in February 1972. Peter and Judy returned to London. Dudley stayed on in New Zealand to play some dates with his jazz trio. It was a relief to spend some time apart, but there was more trouble to come.

CHAPTER TWENTY

BEHIND THE FRIDGE

DUDLEY: The whole point of calling it *Behind The Fridge*
was to disassociate it from *Beyond The Fringe*.

PETER: I've never been able to follow your reasoning on
that.

DUDLEY: No, neither have I. [1]

At the end of his Antipodean jazz tour, Dudley followed Peter back
to London. Alexander Cohen, who'd produced *Beyond The Fringe*
on Broadway, wanted to take *Behind The Fridge* to America. Peter's
old agent, Donald Langdon, wanted to put it on in the West End.
Peter missed his daughters. He wanted to do the show in London.
However, *Behind The Fridge* wasn't due to open in the West End until
the autumn. In the meantime, Peter and Dudley had the best part
of a year to kill. As usual, the BBC were keen for them to do another
series of *Not Only ... But Also*. As usual, Peter wasn't interested. He
hated to repeat himself. He couldn't see that great artists often make
endless variations on the same themes.

Instead of doing another TV series with Dudley, Peter returned
to the cinema in *The Adventures of Barry McKenzie*. The movie was
a tribute to his talent as an impresario. He had conceived of Barry

McKenzie as a cartoon for *Private Eye* and, having brought Barry Humphries and Nicholas Garland together to create it, their comic strip had proved so popular that it had now inspired a feature film. On the shoot, Peter was reunited with Humphries, who was playing Edna Everage in the movie, plus a couple of other roles. Humphries was looking forward to renewing a collaboration that straddled several of Peter's greatest hits. However, when Humphries met Peter on the set, in Soho, he was shocked to find him drunk. Humphries had recently won his own battle with the bottle so he was especially upset to see his old friend in such a state. 'I was absolutely horrified,' he said. 'I was quite shaken and distressed.' [2]

Peter was only playing a cameo, as a TV producer, yet even this small part provided further proof that his idiosyncratic talent didn't translate to the movies – drunk or sober. 'He wasn't really an actor,' recalled Humphries. 'He did everything with a half-smile and a curiously writhing movement of the head and shoulders.' [3] Onstage it wasn't such a problem. Even on TV Peter usually got away with it. In the cinema there was nowhere to hide. His limbs seemed too long. His body seemed too big. You couldn't take your eyes off him, but for all the wrong reasons. It's no coincidence that many of the most successful movie stars have been short-arses – like Dudley Moore.

The reviews were awful, but just as the Australian Broadcasting Control Board had come to the aid of *Behind The Fridge* by banning Peter and Dudley from live broadcasting, the Australian Film Development Corporation (who'd financed the film) gave *The Adventures of Barry McKenzie* a helping hand by making a futile attempt to temper its Rabelaisian obscenities. With the wind of controversy in its sails, the movie became a (complete and utter) cult, making a five-fold return on its investment and spawning a (less successful) sequel. The Australian Film Development Board's worries proved unfounded. Far from portraying Australia in a bad light, as they'd feared, the film helped to foster an image of Australians as friendly, fun-loving and unpretentious. Like a lot of innovators, Peter never shared in the spoils. His initial contribution was forgotten. His 'midwifery' (as Humphries put it) remained unknown to all but a handful of industry insiders. His fleeting appearance had no bearing on the film's critical mauling, nor on its commercial triumph.

Gradually, the word began to get around that Peter was on the sauce. At a farewell lunch for Paul Foot, who'd decided to leave *Private Eye* after an ideological dispute with Richard Ingrams, Peter got 'totally legless' [4] and ended up outside in the gutter. Some of his other lapses were a lot more public. In March 1972 he was invited to a lavish bunfight at London's Grosvenor House Hotel, staged by the *Sunday Times* to celebrate the tenth birthday of their groundbreaking colour supplement. Peter was asked along (together with Alan Bennett, Jonathan Miller and several hundred others) as someone who'd made the news in the 1960s. In the 1970s, he was making headlines of a rather different sort.

As is often the case at such events, writers and celebrities were far outnumbered by advertising executives and various other men in suits. Kenneth Tynan, who'd also been invited, reckoned there were about 2,000 men there that day and less than 20 women. Tynan had pestered Thomson, the paper's publishers, to let him bring his wife, Kathleen. Peter, like most of the other guests, had been commanded to come alone. As the meal dragged on, and the wine flowed freely, Judy's absence began to grate. 'As the guests are departing, Peter Cook mounts the speakers' podium,' wrote Tynan in his diary, 'and begins a drunken harangue, attacking the Thomson organisation for their "fucking stupidity and rudeness" in refusing to allow the guests to bring their wives and mistresses.' [5] Ten years before, in *Beyond The Fringe*, Peter's fearlessness had been a priceless asset. Now, his judgement blurred by booze, it was becoming a costly handicap. The only consolation was that the microphone on the podium had been switched off and Peter hadn't thought to switch it on again. 'Sad to see Peter so incoherent,' reflected Tynan. 'One had heard rumours that he had become a lush.' [6]

What on Earth had happened? How did this man, who bestrode the 1960s like a colossus, fall so far, so fast? 'To my mind it was just a straightforward case of alcoholism,' said Richard Ingrams, with the cold, clear eye of a reformed drinker (he turned teetotal in 1967). 'Peter was a very, very nice and kind person who when drunk would become vicious and unpleasant. And he took it out particularly on Dudley and broke up the partnership.' [7] That partnership still had some way to travel, but Peter's drinking (and Dudley's philandering) had put it on the downward slope.

Why did Peter become an alcoholic? Nature or nurture? Bad luck or predisposition? As with any alcoholic, the answer remains a mystery. You can search and search for explanations, only to find countless other people who tick all the same boxes yet never sink more than one pint in the pub or one glass of wine with dinner. None of Peter's school or college friends remember him as a heavy drinker. Even Wendy seemed surprised. 'The strange thing is, I seldom remember him being drunk in all our years together,' she recalled. 'He just could not bear to be out of control in those days.' [8]

More work might have helped to moderate Peter's intake – particularly with Dudley, whose abstemious self-discipline, honed by the hard graft of classical music, had previously given Peter some sort of structure, a routine to shape his days (Dudley had never been a big drinker – women were his drug of choice). But neither of them wanted to spend much time together. Their Australian tour had pushed their relationship to its limits.

Dudley's love life was as complicated as ever – he was still seeing Lyndall Hobbs, had a brief affair with Lynsey de Paul, and had also become involved with Lysie Hastings, the wife of George Hastings, one of his closest friends. When Dudley introduced Lysie to Peter and Judy over dinner they both warmed to her, but their friendship was complicated by the fact that Dudley was still coming on strong to Judy. When Peter had to go to Rome to do an interview, Dudley was on the phone to her almost as soon as Peter had departed for the airport. He went to see her in Ruston Mews that evening and invited her back to his basement flat, where they ended up kissing and cuddling. He told her that he had trouble reaching an orgasm. He told her it was bound up with the way he looked. He told her he needed physical and mental stimulation to help him overcome it. Judy was sympathetic. She saw it as a cause of his inconstancy. A less sympathetic person might have seen it as a cunning gambit for talking gullible women into bed.

Judy dashed home before midnight – she was expecting a call from Peter. In the morning she felt awful. When Dudley phoned, she told him not to say anything about the kisses and cuddles. She told him to back off. She knew he'd never remain faithful to anyone, and she didn't want to hurt Peter. When Peter and Dudley met up the next day to do some advance preparation for the London run of *Behind The Fridge*, Judy sensed a new distance between her and Dudley. 'I believe he wants to destroy our relationship,' she reflected. 'He is just jealous of anything good that Peter has.' [9]

With another joint project on the horizon, which would tie them together like partners in a three-legged race, Peter and Dudley both chose to work apart until the West End opening of *Behind The Fridge*. Yet these solo turns merely confirmed that they still worked best together. A role for Peter as an adulterous dentist in a TV play called *Mill Hill* sounded promising. His co-star was Geraldine McEwan and the author was John Mortimer, who'd written *A Voyage Round My Father* and had acted as defence counsel for *Oz* magazine in his day job as a barrister. Sadly, *Mill Hill* wasn't one of his better efforts. Judy described it as a 'weak farce.' [10] Like a gambler on a losing streak, Peter's instinct for picking winners had deserted him. Judy wasn't sure whether he was depressed or simply exhausted. Either way, his attempts at self-medication simply made things worse. Alcohol and prescription drugs is rarely a productive combination, and Peter often exceeded the prescribed dose. Judy felt as if she was living with three Peters: the professional Peter, high on adrenalin; the real Peter, loving and sensitive; and Peter the depressive drunk.

Dudley was spending his evenings playing jazz in a Knightsbridge restaurant, but his attempts to find a dramatic hit proved as elusive as Peter's. He played the Dormouse in a lavish feature film of *Alice's Adventures in Wonderland*, amid a superb array of comedians (Spike Milligan as the Gryphon, Peter Sellers as the March Hare) and classical actors (Michael Hordern as the Mock Turtle, Roy Kinnear as the Cheshire Cat, Ralph Richardson as the Caterpillar and Flora Robson as the Queen of Hearts). However, the elaborate costumes constricted the characters, hiding their facial expressions behind heavy make-up and false whiskers, and the film didn't really click, either with the critics or at the box office. Tellingly, while Jonathan

Miller's earlier film of Alice (with Peter as the Mad Hatter) still feels daring and avant-garde, this florid movie now seems terribly tired and dated.

Fiona Fullerton, who played Alice, remembered Dudley with fondness, as a considerate and caring friend, but she could also sense some sadness in him. 'He said I must be careful in this business because relationships are put under strain and you must be very careful to make time together,' she said. 'He said he and Suzy had spent too much time apart.' [11] It was a wise warning, which could just as easily have applied to Peter. Dudley and Suzy were divorced on 15 September. Incompatibility, not adultery, was the grounds for the divorce. Dudley collected Suzy from the hearing in a chauffeur-driven Rolls-Royce, consoling her as she sobbed on his shoulder. It was a chivalrous gesture which spoke volumes about the love they still shared. They remained firm friends for the rest of his life. It was merely marriage that he couldn't stand. 'We should never have got married,' said Suzy. 'We were just so happy the way we were before.' [12]

Dudley's attempts to forge a solo TV career were similarly unimpressive. He made a series for the BBC with Lulu, shamelessly entitled *Not Only Lulu But Also Dudley Moore*. They got along well together, and the musical element posed no problems, but when Dudley was required to write a sketch he realised how dependent he'd been on Peter. 'I hated it,' [13] he said. 'I didn't want to be funny any more.' [14] Like it or not, they both needed one another. Neither of them had found a way to make it on their own.

That summer, Peter and Judy moved again, into a large Victorian house on Denbigh Terrace, just off Portobello Road. Wendy and the girls were still living in Kenwood Cottage, and Judy's house in Ruston Mews was too small. This house was a lot bigger. It was detached, spread over four floors, with a roof terrace and a large basement – big enough for Peter and Dudley's table-tennis table. Dudley duly arrived, to prepare for the West End run of *Behind The Fridge*. Judy made the coffee and listened to their routines, as she'd done many times before, but this time she could tell that Peter's heart wasn't really in it. Though the two men were living only a few miles apart, a good deal of the writing ended up taking place by post. Dudley was understandably unhappy with this new way of working, which he attributed to Peter's growing apathy rather than to any artistic considerations. 'It's harder to become colloquial from a written script than it is to keep it natural by continually improvising it,' [15] he complained. He was right to feel frustrated. Their best work had always evolved out of a combination of writing and improvisation. Now that unique blend was in danger of becoming lost. Peter was similarly indifferent to practical demands like staging. Dudley protested that he simply sat around and left him to do all the work. But Peter seemed blithely confident. He demanded that the production company book them into a big theatre. 'The bookings will be good, regardless of what the "crickets" say,' he predicted. They'll be coming from north of Watford in coachloads. It's not just the West End we're talking about.' [16]

Peter was absolutely right – the show sold out months in advance – but Dudley wasn't merely bothered about reviews or ticket sales. He wanted to put on a decent show, something more polished than the erratic performances they'd done Down Under. He asked his old friend Joe McGrath, who'd produced the first series of *Not Only ... But Also*, to direct the West End run. McGrath was happy to oblige, but when he met up with Peter and Dudley he noticed a dramatic shift in the dynamics of their double act. Last time he'd worked with them,

Peter had had the upper hand. Now Dudley was the one in charge. When McGrath shot several short films, to be screened between the live sketches, it was telling that a couple of them were written (and performed alone) by Dudley. Peter's presence was still a spur (look how hard Dudley had found it to write a sketch for Lulu) but Dudley no longer found it quite so hard to write new material on his own.

Peter and Dudley also came up with several new sketches. There was a skit about the Ugandan dictator Idi Amin, and a spoof soul song about the Conservative Prime Minister, Edward Heath. Pick of the bunch was a routine called 'Resting' about a camp actor (Dudley) cleaning the house of a posh barrister (played by Peter). This sketch was inspired by Peter's experience of hiring resting actors as his cleaners, only to discover that they far preferred to stand around gossiping about the theatre rather than doing any cleaning. Dudley's limp-wristed luvvie talks Peter into rehearsing a scene from *Othello* and ends up throttling him, in an overenthusiastic display of method acting. It was a funny and accomplished sketch, which showed that when Peter was sober and Dudley wasn't trying to get off with Judy the impact of their double act was still greater than its increasingly disparate parts.

Thanks to McGrath's wise stewardship and Peter and Dudley's irrepressible talent, the London producers were rewarded with a remarkably strong script. Yet, as the first night drew near, Peter began to get stage fright. Despite his bravado about 'the crickets', he was always more nervous about reviews than Dudley. This time, it wasn't just the fear of bad notices that made him jumpy. The management had followed his instructions and had booked one of the West End's biggest venues – the Cambridge Theatre, which held over 1,200 seats. This art deco auditorium was an architectural gem but Peter didn't like it. He thought it had no atmosphere. He thought it was too big. He was probably right. With its stark modernist design, the Cambridge Theatre was large and airy, far better suited for glitzy musicals. With hindsight, Peter and Dudley might have felt more comfortable in a smaller theatre like the Fortune, where *Beyond The Fringe* had thrived. Still, hiring a big venue had been Peter's idea. It was too late for second thoughts.

Joe McGrath also had his reservations about the theatre. The stagehands kept on changing, for one thing. 'They never got the lighting cues right,' he said. 'We rehearsed for days before the first night, and half an hour before curtain-up a new group of stagehands came on, who hadn't even seen it.' [17] There was worse to come. On 21 November, as Peter and Dudley were about to start their dress rehearsal, just a few hours before the press night, Eamonn Andrews turned up at the theatre, disguised as a traffic warden, and spirited Dudley away for a surprise appearance on *This Is Your Life*. Meekly, Peter accompanied Dudley to the Thames TV studios – there was little else he could do. Dudley asked McGrath to come too, but he said no. He was far too cross. 'I'm not going!' he said. 'This is a first night! I'm not leaving this theatre until we go up!' Eventually, hours later, Peter and Dudley returned to the theatre, where McGrath had been waiting for them. By now it was too late for any sort of run-through. And that wasn't the only problem. While Dudley had been doing *This Is Your Life*, Peter had been in the green room, with the drinks trolley. He was completely pissed.

As the audience started to arrive, Peter went backstage and passed out. At seven o'clock, with the show due to start, he was still out cold, with a full house, packed with celebs and critics, out front. 'I thought we weren't going to get the curtain up at all,' said McGrath.

'I was in the dressing room, slapping him. Dudley was screaming and swearing at him, pouring water and coffee down him.' [18] The audience grew restless. A slow handclap ensued. 'Somebody has to tell them,' [19] said Dudley. 'I'm not,' [20] said McGrath. 'Neither am I,' [21] said Dudley. Eventually the house manager went out and announced that there'd been a problem with the projection equipment. McGrath peeped through the drapes and saw Sean Connery in the front row. Behind the curtain, Dudley started to lark around onstage. 'It doesn't really matter,' he sang. 'It's really not important.' [22] But it was. 'Why are we waiting?' sang the audience. Dudley grabbed hold of McGrath and started waltzing round the stage. 'I'll tell you why we're fucking waiting,' he sang. 'Because the cunt is drunk. Because the cunt is drunk.' Hidden behind the curtain, Dudley dropped his trousers and mooned at the unsuspecting punters a few feet away in the stalls.

McGrath poured Peter into his costume, and walked him round and round the dressing room in circles until he was deemed sufficiently sober to go on. 'You dry, you bastard, and I'll fucking kill you,' [23] Dudley told him. The curtain finally went up half an hour late. Peter and Dudley walked on, to rapturous applause. They went straight into the opening number, 'Hello'. They were due to walk on from opposite wings, as if to greet each other centre stage, walk straight past without stopping, and then walk on again from opposite wings. Their first entrance got a big laugh, but when Dudley made his second entrance, he found himself alone onstage. Peter was still in the wings. 'I can't do this,' he told McGrath. 'I can't fucking do this.' [24] And then he burst into tears. McGrath turned Peter around and pushed him back onstage. Incredibly, he proceeded to deliver a faultless performance. At least, that's how it appeared. Dudley knew better, of course, and so did Joe McGrath. 'Peter was like a zombie onstage,' [25] said McGrath. 'Dudley was cueing Peter all the time beneath his breath. Peter would walk into the wings and I'd tell him the next line and he'd walk back onstage.' [26] It was a testament to Dudley's talent that nobody else suspected. Well, almost nobody. Afterwards, McGrath had a much-needed drink with his fellow Scotsman, Sean Connery. 'A wee bit of trouble with half of your cast, eh, Joe?' said Connery. 'Yes Sean,' said McGrath. 'I thought so,' said Connery. 'He saw it,' said McGrath. 'He knew.' [27]

The reviews were a mixed bag. *The Times* called the show 'original and intelligent.' The *Daily Express*, *Daily Mail* and *Daily Telegraph* weren't so keen. One of the best reviews was in *Time Out*, London's hip new magazine for turned-on twenty-somethings. *Punch* was less enthusiastic. 'There is a terrible dearth of punchlines,' wrote Sheridan Morley. 'Sketches are prolonged far beyond their natural life, occasionally bolstered by irritating fits of giggling.' Ironically, a couple of write-ups praised Peter's performance while criticising Dudley's first-night nerves. Dudley, who'd been preoccupied with propping up his partner rather than focusing on his own performance, was justifiably furious. 'I've had it,' he told McGrath. 'I'm getting out of this. It's driving me up the fucking wall.' [28] For Dudley, it was no longer a matter of whether they'd break up, but when. 'I've got to make my own future,' [29] he told McGrath. It was a future without Peter. But for the time being they were still bound together, like quarrelling conjoined twins. Peter's drinking undoubtedly made life very difficult (and sometimes virtually impossible) for Dudley, but it was a symptom, not just a cause, of the endemic problems in their partnership. As Judy said, 'If Peter hadn't got drunk, the arguments would have been about something else.' [30]

As Peter had predicted, the punters didn't really care what the critics had to say. *Behind The Fridge* sold out months ahead despite mixed reviews, confounding the producers, who had worried it might be too dark for West End tastes. Even after it had opened they still wanted to cut 'Mini Drama', until Harold Pinter came to see it and said it was the best thing in the show. Dudley hadn't forgotten the fiasco of the first night, but it made financial sense to make the most of it. After his divorce he was feeling the pinch, having given his Hampstead house to Suzy. If he could keep Peter on the straight and narrow there was some serious money to be made. Peter agreed to moderate his drinking, and for the rest of the London run he remained relatively sober, at least until the curtain came down every evening. After the show it was a different story. Sometimes he drank so much that he found it a struggle to get his trousers off at bedtime, which Judy thought was very funny. Sometimes he suffered from brewer's droop, which she found less amusing.

In January 1973, Judy took over as the show's dresser (she already knew the show inside out, having seen it countless times in Australia) and generally managed to limit Peter to half a bottle of champagne, mixed with orange juice, during the course of each performance. With his comic faculties restored, Peter reverted to the sort of pranks which had characterised the later days of *Beyond The Fringe* – swapping Dudley's trousers for his own backstage, blowing cigarette smoke into his face onstage. Yet Dudley wasn't quite so willing to be Peter's plaything any more. He kept up appearances, and the audience were none the wiser, yet McGrath could see that his hysterical laughter was no longer spontaneous but contrived. Offstage, they hardly saw each other. When Dudley came round for lunch, in the New Year, Peter drank a bottle of wine, while Dudley didn't touch a drop. After Dudley left, he drank another bottle, plus three vodka miniatures. Drink was replacing Dudley as the other half of the double act. A few weeks later, Judy's divorce from Sean Kenny came through. Kenny cited her adultery with Peter, who was ordered to pay the costs. She was now free to marry Peter.

Several months into the run, in April 1973, Peter and Dudley gave an interview to the journalist Mavis Nicholson, on her ITV chat show *Good Afternoon*.[31] It was a remarkably revealing discussion, especially for daytime TV. Peter and Dudley both opened up to an extraordinary degree. 'I'm very jealous, I'm very – superficially – arrogant,' said Peter. 'You mean underneath there's this tremendous humanity?' said Dudley. 'Probably lurking, if you bother to look,' parried Peter. 'I think we are terribly opposite, actually – opposite to the point where it becomes difficult to communicate,' said Dudley. 'Sometimes, when we're working, it's disastrous,' concurred Peter. 'It's like the worst kind of polite marriage. Neither of us is really very good at coming out with what we really think.' 'I remember just recently I had a couple of things I wanted to say about the show and I just couldn't say them and it built up and up in me like a sort of terrible tumour,' added Dudley. 'I was going mad with it.' Interviewing comedy double acts is a notoriously tricky business. Wisely, Nicholson asked a few leading questions, and then left Peter and Dudley to interrogate each other.

PETER: I can be very, very sarcastic, and very bitchy, in an almost feminine way.

DUDLEY: You say this isn't really you, but it's something you've done or felt for years, so does that mean you've hidden your real self for years?

PETER: Yes, I should think I probably have, but this thing about the 'real self' implies that you know what your real self is. I'd hesitate to say that I knew what my real self was.

DUDLEY: I think one has an inkling. You get the idea that
you're living some sort of a lie ... that you are
against yourself in some way.

Egged on by Mavis, Dudley expanded on his enthusiasm for
psychoanalysis. 'You don't go to an analyst to find out who you are,'
he explained. 'It's to find out how to get to what you know you are.'
Peter looked nonplussed. 'You don't have the courage to get to it,'
Dudley told him. 'You don't have the courage to display it.' Yet such
a concept was utterly alien to Peter. In any relationship, however
close, there is usually one important subject about which two people
disagree. For Peter and Dudley, that subject was psychoanalysis.
For Dudley it was a kind of religion, part of what freed him up as
a performer. Dudley's comedy was revelatory. Peter's was all about
concealment. Despite his sporadic attempts to embrace the faith, he
remained an unbeliever.

The interview shed fresh light on their contrasting working
methods. 'I can only work from my direct experience in life,' said
Dudley. 'I feel there's an endless vat of material there, but I think
Peter probably works in a different way.' 'I think mine is more fantasy,'
said Peter. 'I started writing at school and that couldn't have come
from experience. The early formation of the character E.L. Wisty, the
man on the park bench who talks endlessly about everything and
knows nothing, that wasn't based on anybody I'd met – it came from
inside me. I've written a lot of stuff which is fantasy, which you could
say was along the same lines as Lewis Carroll or Edward Lear. I don't
think I use my background as much as Dudley does with his writing.'

But writing was one thing. Performing was another. For Dudley,
the memory of Peter's drunken first night, and Dudley's self-
defeating efforts to (literally) prop him up still smarted. 'I tend to

drink too much,' admitted Peter. 'Why?' asked Mavis. 'I don't know,' said Peter. 'I think it's a symptom of boredom, really.' That was as close as he ever came, in public, to an admission of his addiction and the possible reasons for it. A deep, abiding fear of boredom was what drove Peter on – and, eventually, what stalled him. 'I get bored very easily,' he said. 'I tend to get up late. I read the newspapers, then I sort of hang around the house. I sometimes, very occasionally, go out shopping with my girlfriend. I do very little during the day and I'm very much aware that I'm doing nothing, which annoys me. Yet so far – we've been running sixteen weeks – I haven't actually done anything positive about it.'

For all his new-found self-awareness, Dudley seemed even more downbeat about his private life. He was living alone, he told Mavis, cohabiting with a cat called Stanley. 'I have a lot of aggression in me which I'm terrified of letting out because I feel it is destructive,' he said. 'But it's not really,' he added, somewhat plaintively. 'It's very creative in many ways.' Yet his piano playing had ground to a halt ('I don't really know why') which rather undermined this theory. 'Are you a depressed person?' Mavis asked him. 'Yes,' said Dudley, before embarking on a bit of psychobabble about how being depressed made him happy. Mavis told them that she'd enjoyed *Behind The Fridge*, but said how moody they'd both seemed onstage – a perceptive observation which had escaped the first-night critics.

PETER: My problem is onstage I tend not to concentrate. My mind can drift off. It's not that I can't help it because if I really concentrate I can do it.

DUDLEY: So why do you do it? Why do you in fact not concentrate for two performances in a row? Why do you make me get into this state?

PETER: I don't make you 'get into this state.'

DUDLEY: Yes, you do.

The summer of 1973 was marred by personal tragedy for Judy. First, Sean Kenny died suddenly, less than six months after their divorce, from a heart attack and brain haemorrhage, hastened by drink and drugs. He was only 42. Then, a few weeks later, Judy's father died after falling downstairs. Peter was also feeling unwell. He was throwing up, and when he brought up blood his doctor diagnosed hepatitis and an inflamed liver. He was advised to forsake alcohol for eighteen months but it wasn't long before he was drinking again. The last thing his liver needed was an American tour.

Dudley, Peter and Judy.

CHAPTER TWENTY ONE

GOOD EVENING

DUD: I wouldn't mind having ladies use me as a sexual object – having them satiate their lust upon my body.

PETE: But surely you'd rather be respected for your mind than your body.

DUD: No. Well, eventually, yes, but I'd like them to give my body a good going-over first.

('Women's Rights', *Good Evening*, Plymouth Theatre, New York, 1973)

Alexander Cohen saw *Behind The Fridge* during its first week at the Cambridge Theatre. On his way out, he bumped into Clive Barnes, the influential theatre critic of the *New York Times*. 'You're not thinking of bringing that to New York, are you?' [1] Barnes asked him. Having produced *Beyond The Fringe* on Broadway, Cohen was undeterred. He made Peter and Dudley an offer. Peter was eager to accept, but Dudley was wary. He was worried about Peter's drinking. The idea of accompanying Peter on a drunken tour of America seemed hellish. Initially he said no, but Cohen's subsequent offer was too good to turn down: $7,000 a week, plus a percentage of the box office. Dudley said yes. Despite Dudley's reservations, the prospect re-energised his partnership with Peter. As they planned their forthcoming trip, their recent fracas seemed to melt away.

Before he left for America, Peter moved again. He hadn't warmed to Denbigh Terrace. He wanted to be back in Hampstead. Judy found the perfect place, just around the corner from the house that Peter had shared with Wendy. It looked like a romantic folly, with little gothic windows, arched and latticed. Judy likened it to 'a small, enchanted castle.' [2] Peter was just as keen. 'I've bought a super Queen Anne coach house in Perrins Walk, which is a lovely cobbled mews at the back of Church Row,' he wrote to his parents. 'I'm very pleased and excited about it. I hope I never have to move again.' [3] After Ruston Mews and Kenwood Cottage, it was his fourth new address in four years.

On 25 September, Peter and Dudley flew to New York to prepare for their US tour. Judy stayed behind, to arrange the sale of Denbigh Terrace (it was snapped up by Richard Branson) and oversee the improvements to their new home. She'd arranged to fly over a few weeks later, in good time for their Broadway opening, but she was apprehensive about leaving Peter to his own devices in America. She knew he'd miss her, but she knew also that he'd be exposed to all sorts of temptations in the States.

On the plane to New York, Dudley laid it on the line. They'd won a Tony for Beyond The Fringe, he told Peter. They owed it to themselves to do just as well this time. Peter promised to stay off the sauce, but by the time they touched down he was so drunk that Dudley had to write out both their immigration forms while Peter sat crying in the corner. 'I don't know why he was crying,' said Dudley. 'He had a lot of angst but he didn't talk about it.' [4] A decade of psychotherapy might have given Dudley some understanding of his own troubles, but it had clearly given him scant insight into Peter's. In fact, it is perfectly easy to discern why Peter was so upset, even at a distance of forty years. He missed Judy. He missed his children. He was addicted to alcohol. And he knew that spending two years touring America would make all these things far worse. Peter's problems were intractable, but they were eminently practical. For all Dudley's fluent psychospeak, his own issues were actually far more unfathomable. 'We both gravitated towards being isolated,' said Dudley. 'His was an anxiety that was inexpressible.' [5] He could have been talking about himself.

Alexander Cohen liked *Behind The Fridge* but he didn't like the title. Peter suggested one of his favourite catchphrases, *Good Evening*, which he liked to repeat ad infinitum. At Cohen's request, they dropped their Ted Heath and Idi Amin sketches, replacing them with several old standards, a couple of which ('One Leg Too Few' and 'Sitting On The Bench') had featured in the Broadway run of *Beyond The Fringe*. This time, there was also a long tour ahead. After New York, they were due to travel on to Washington, Detroit, Toronto, Montreal, Philadelphia and Chicago, finally finishing up in Los Angeles. It would be the biggest tour they'd ever done.

Cohen liked Peter's new title. The American show was renamed *Good Evening*. He was less impressed with Peter's attitude to rehearsals. Dudley was as reliable as ever, but Peter often turned up late or asked to reschedule. He was enjoying meeting up with his old friends from *Beyond The Fringe*, most notably Jackie Onassis, previously Jacqueline Kennedy. Jackie was very pleased to see Peter again and introduced him to her sister, the glamorous socialite Lee Radziwill.

Dudley was also enjoying his social life in Manhattan. He was still involved with Lysie Hastings, but he now renewed his acquaintance with Tuesday Weld, a stunning actress with whom he'd had a brief fling ten years earlier, during the Broadway run of *Beyond The Fringe*. Intelligent and feisty, Weld had just turned thirty, having survived a childhood worthy of a Hollywood melodrama. A child model turned teenage film star, she made her first movie when she was thirteen, spent her high-school years on film sets, and had been linked with various stars, including Frank Sinatra and Elvis Presley. Talented but troubled, she'd made a few good movies (most notably *The Cincinnati Kid* with Steve McQueen) and a fair few bad ones. She might have been an even bigger star, if she hadn't turned down *True Grit*, *Bonnie and Clyde*, and the role she was born to play, *Lolita*. 'A screen actress of subtlety and considerable range, able to convey a deep well of experience and suffering through extraordinarily expressive eyes,' [6] wrote Dudley's first biographer, Paul Donovan. The archetypal wild child, she was now divorced, with a six-year-old daughter. Beautiful and unpredictable, she exuded a powerful allure, in person and on camera. As Judy put it, she sounded like a handful.

One night, calling from Boston, where Peter and Dudley had gone to perform the first previews of *Good Evening*, Peter told Judy that he'd spoken to Tuesday on the phone. Apparently, Tuesday had called the hotel to speak to Dudley and had been put through to his room instead. Judy didn't pay much attention, but there must have been something about the way he told her which lodged in her subconscious because a few nights later she dreamt that Peter had been to bed with Tuesday. The next time Peter phoned, Judy told him about her dream. There was a pregnant pause, and then Peter admitted that what she'd dreamt about had really happened. He told her it meant nothing. Judy recognised this as another instance of the intensive rivalry between Peter and Dudley. Peter wanted Judy, so Dudley wanted Judy. Dudley wanted Tuesday, so Peter wanted her too. Judy was devastated but she still missed Peter terribly. He asked her to fly over as soon as possible. She promised that she would.

Good Evening premiered in Boston on 12 October 1973. Dudley was apprehensive but he needn't have worried. They played to a full house and the audience lapped it up. Many punters were clearly familiar with *Beyond The Fringe*, and welcomed the reappearance of old favourites like 'One Leg Too Few' and 'Sitting On The Bench'. Peter's opening line ('I could have been a judge, but I never had the Latin') got a big round of applause. This first-night house was so familiar with this monologue – and so pleased to see it revived – that they even joined in on some of the punchlines. Usually, comedians are castigated for repeating old material. This audience was delighted to see Peter and Dudley reprise their greatest hits. Twenty years before the term became a cliché, Peter and Dudley had reinvented comedy as rock and roll. 'It was the best audience we've had since we left Australia,' [7] said Peter. When he fell into the orchestra pit, the punters thought it was a hoot. 'I lay there shouting, "Save me!"' said Peter. 'The audience just laughed, thinking it was part of the show.' [8]

Judy put a brave face on Peter's fling with Tuesday. But when she arrived in New York on 14 October, Peter had another unpleasant surprise in store. He told her that he'd also had a brief affair with Lee Radziwill. Judy was understandably upset that Peter had slept with two other women in the few weeks since she'd last seen him, but she tried hard not to show it. Looking hard for a silver lining, she told herself that if he'd been to bed with Lee he couldn't be that keen on Tuesday. Emotionally, she had no need to worry. Peter was in love with her. Like Oscar Wilde, he could resist everything except temptation. He was in no fit state to be left alone.

Despite his interest in Tuesday, Dudley had also been playing the field. A letter to his friend and former agent David Dearlove, written in 1980, summed up his attitude to the transient nature of most love affairs. 'It is never surprising for me to hear of the ending of relationships with people and never very shocking or painful either,' he wrote. 'It always seems to be for the best and something that is inevitable and to be accepted without drama.' [9] It was a pragmatic attitude, but it betrayed an element of detachment. Dudley would prove similarly dispassionate about his impending split with Peter.

Good Evening transferred to the Plymouth Theatre in New York on 29 October, opening on 10 November. The first night was a smash hit. The critics loved it. Clive Barnes said it was 'funny and truthful', which was ironic after what he'd told Cohen in London. Thanks to Cohen's input, the show was now much tighter, and the reception was a lot better than it had been in the West End. The *New York Post* called Peter and Dudley two of the funniest men in the world. Stars like Cary Grant, Charlton Heston and Walter Matthau came to see the show and went backstage to congratulate Peter and Dudley afterwards. Tennessee Williams dropped in, too. They even had a visit from Henry Kissinger. Groucho Marx invited them back to his house to perform the show for him in private – he was deaf, and hadn't been able to hear a word when he came to see the show at the theatre. He subsequently called them 'two of the funniest performers I have ever seen.' [10]

Offstage, Peter's life was more erratic. He shocked Judy by taking her to a peep show in Times Square, to ogle a naked woman on a turntable. Judy was even more shocked when Peter told her he'd been before. On his first visit, he'd gone through the wrong door and had ended up onstage. 'What I should have been doing was peeping in through a tiny window,'[11] he said. Instead, he found himself face to face with the naked woman on the turntable. He'd had a brief chat with her:

```
        PETER:  This must be rather a boring job.
NAKED WOMAN:  It is.
        PETER:  How long do you do it?
NAKED WOMAN:  About five hours at a time.
        PETER:  Do you just revolve?
NAKED WOMAN:  I occasionally yawn, but mainly I revolve.
        PETER:  This must be very tedious. How much do you
                get paid?
```

At this point, the bouncers arrived and threw him out. 'As I left I saw these feverish eyes peering through tiny windows, obviously thinking they were going to see something more than what they'd actually paid for,'[12] he said. On his return visit with Judy, a full hour passed before Peter finally agreed to leave.

Another time, when Judy was back in London for a few days, Peter phoned. He said he loved her. He said he missed her. At this point, a woman's voice came on the line. 'Get your arse out of here if you're going to call your wife on my phone.'[13] 'What am I going to do?'[14] Peter asked Judy. 'For goodness' sake, Peter, go back home to your apartment,'[15] she said. She knew that she should have been cross, but she couldn't help laughing. She was a woman in a million. Peter would do well to keep her.

What Peter needed, more than anything, was some sort of order in his daily life. He rented a splendid flat in the Apthorp, a popular apartment block for actors. His landlord was Tony Walton, a stage designer (and Radley old boy) who'd been married to Julie Andrews. With four bedrooms, three bathrooms and fantastic views over Manhattan, it was a lot better than being cooped up in a hotel. With Judy by his side, Peter was inclined to spurn the social whirl. 'Judy and I find New York rather dull,' he wrote to his parents, reassuringly. 'I haven't really seen much of the people I used to know here and we are leading a very quiet life.' [16] In her absence, it was a different story. 'He got a little pie-eyed during the New York run,' said Dudley, with considerable understatement. 'I certainly didn't like working with him in this way.' [17] Dudley could see the change in him – his delivery was becoming slower, which had a detrimental effect on both of them – but Peter was in denial. 'I'm fine,' he'd mouth to Dudley from the wings before they went on. 'I'm fine.'

One day, Peter failed to show up for the matinee. Cohen and his colleagues had to go round to his apartment and break down the door. They found Peter passed out on the sofa. They had to throw cold water over him to wake him, slap him round the face to bring him to his senses, drag him into a waiting car and drive him to the theatre. The audience were told he'd been held up by a traffic accident. Dudley had to go on alone for forty-five minutes and entertain the waiting punters on the piano. Finally, Peter arrived. 'He appeared in the wings like a ghost and gave me the thumbs-up,' said Dudley. 'I was so shocked I gave him an off-centre cue but he managed to pull it off.' [18] The show eventually started three-quarters of an hour late.

*

Somehow, Peter stumbled through the show. 'I think I was the only one who could tell,' [19] said Dudley. When he told his friend Francis Megahy, who'd seen the show, that Peter had been drunk, Megahy was amazed. 'He said it didn't show at all.' [20] But Cohen was not amused. 'He'd lost his ability to control himself,' he said. 'It was irresponsible and unprofessional – which is about the worst thing I can say about a human being.' [21] Dudley was also livid, and had an angry showdown with Peter straight afterwards. 'It was horrible,' [22] said Cohen. He must have wondered what he'd let himself in for.

It wasn't one-way traffic. There were resentments on both sides. Peter was cross that Dudley insisted on a joint writing credit for *Good Evening*. Dudley's input had grown considerably (from virtually nothing at the outset) but the bulk of the material was Peter's, particularly sketches like 'Sitting On The Bench' and 'One Leg Too Few', which he'd written before he teamed up with Dudley. Dudley was practically incapable of writing comedy on his own (music was another matter) but by now Peter also found it hard to write in isolation. The solitary virtuosity of his early years had faded. The writing was easier – and much better – with Dudley. Peter still wrote the lion's share – it was never fifty-fifty – but it was impossible to measure Dudley's contribution in crude percentage terms.

This simmering dispute summed up their codependence, and the mutual antagonism it engendered. Dudley didn't want to work with Peter and Peter couldn't work without him. Their stuttering social life replicated this unease. After the show Dudley would often disappear, without telling Peter where he was going. Peter would try to hunt him down, but when he caught up with him they'd often quarrel, like an unhappily married couple. Cohen had no illusions about why they continued to put up with each other. 'I was paying them a great deal of money.' [23] Peter respected Cohen, and tried to rebuild bridges with him. In a television interview he praised Cohen for improving the show since its US transfer, tactlessly belittling McGrath's contribution in the process. 'We did it rather lazily in the West End – we didn't work hard enough at it,' said Peter. 'It was a much, much better show on Broadway.' [24] This was quite true, but it was Peter's laziness, more than anything, which had made the show so much slacker in the West End. McGrath was understandably aggrieved.

As well as Peter's drinking, Judy was worried about his pill-popping – pep pills in the morning to wake him up, tranquillizers at night to calm him down. He was also smoking dope, supposedly to unwind after the show. He told Judy he wanted to use cannabis instead of alcohol. He ended up using both. 'He was terrified all the time that he was going to run out of pills,' said Joseph Heller, one of Peter's neighbours in the Apthorp. 'He had brought a supply of uppers and downers from London, but he only knew what they were called on his London prescription. He didn't know the generic name, or how to replenish his supply.' [25] Cohen recruited a young minder to try and keep Peter on the straight and narrow, but Peter was very persuasive. It wasn't long before his minder was joining in the fun.

Dudley's daily fix, conversely, was psychotherapy, which Peter treated with ill-concealed contempt. Dudley's friends were more polite, but they also doubted whether analysis was quite the cure-all that Dudley seemed to think it might be. 'How much is it costing you to go to analysis every morning?' [26] asked Bryan Forbes, who was in New York casting *The Stepford Wives*, with his wife, Nanette Newman. 'A hundred and fifty dollars an hour,' [27] replied Dudley. 'Why don't you pay me instead?' said Forbes. 'Nanette and I would be happy to talk to you, and we'll even cut the price.' [28] It was ironic that one of his most therapeutic friendships was with his ex-wife. 'It was lovely to see her,' wrote Dudley to his mother, after Suzy stopped off in New York to see him, on her way back to London from LA. 'We had a good time together and get on so much more easily now we are apart.' [29]

On 14 February, Valentine's Day, Peter and Judy got married. The venue they chose was Sardi's, their favourite restaurant in New York. Judy wore a white trouser suit. Peter wore his navy blue stage suit. He was completely sober, having resolved not to drink for three days before the wedding. Peter asked Alexander Cohen to be the best man. Cohen alerted the media, and Sardi's was besieged by journalists and camera crews, but Peter and Judy didn't mind. They knew he had a show to sell. Dudley wasn't invited, which made him most upset. But he would have wanted to bring Tuesday, and Judy didn't want Peter flirting with her at the wedding. There was no time for a honeymoon. Peter went straight on to a TV interview in the afternoon, and then to the Plymouth Theatre to do the show that evening. Judy and Peter were both extremely happy to be married, but there were more unwelcome revelations in store. One night, Peter told Judy that he and Dudley had shared a prostitute. Peter went first, then Dudley, then Peter went back 'to have a long meaningful talk with her about Dudley.' [30] Apparently, Peter spent an hour with her, discussing the intimate details of Dudley's visit. Peter wasn't shamefaced – on the contrary, he found it funny – but Judy was mortified. Peter reassured her that he hadn't had penetrative sex, but that was small consolation. Peter had crossed a moral rubicon. Having broken this taboo for the first time, breaking it again would be a lot easier.

Despite these offstage dramas, *Good Evening* became a Broadway sensation. It won a Tony and a Grammy. It broke the box-office record for the Plymouth Theatre before transferring to the Lunt-Fontanne Theatre, where it set a new record for Broadway's longest-running two-man show. The BBC sent over a camera crew to shoot an interview for a documentary, appropriately entitled *Success Story*. The interview was shot at Sardi's (union rules meant they couldn't shoot inside the theatre). By way of contrast with *Good Evening*, they were asked to recall their worst gigs. Performing with the Cambridge Footlights for the Great Yarmouth Young Conservatives, said Peter. 'I did cabaret in Manchester following wrestling and striptease,' said Dudley. 'They were excellent audiences but my material was very bad.' [31] 'Well, you weren't stripping or wrestling, were you?' [32] said Peter, as sharp as ever. The BBC were desperate for them to do some more *Not Only ... But Also*, but all they would commit to was some new links for a Christmas Special of old sketches, called *Pete & Dud in New York*. Jimmy Gilbert flew over to direct them – the American broadcast unions wouldn't let him film on US soil, so he had to shoot the scenes on an old tug moored in the Hudson. Gilbert set about putting together a greatest-hits compilation, only to discover that much of the material he'd planned to use had vanished. Peter and Dudley remained unaware that much of their finest work had been erased.

In spite of his transgressions, Peter clearly loved Judy deeply and missed her dreadfully when she was away. One Saturday, when she was in London, he flew home after the show, just to spend a few hours with her, knowing that he'd have to fly back to New York the next day. He was still just as funny, but as his old friend from Radley, Michael Bawtree, observed, his humour had become darker and more hurtful. It was as if he couldn't help himself. As Lysie Hastings recognised, he was almost too clever for his own good. Peter's comic imagination had always been like a runaway machine. Now, fuelled by drink and drugs, it was transporting him to more savage destinations. 'You know nothing,' he once said to Judy. 'Keep it to yourself.' [33] In a play, it would have been a priceless put-down. In real life, it was cruel and pointless. Peter was in pain, but by lashing out at the people closest to him he hurt himself as much as he hurt them. 'There was a separation, in the end, between the higher and lower aspects of his character,' [34] said Wendy, speaking for everyone who loved him, and everyone he'd ever loved. 'There was a good Peter Cook and a bad Peter Cook,' [35] concurred Cohen. The good Peter was a warm-hearted wit. The bad Peter was a vicious drunk. After *Good Evening* finished its Broadway run, their stage-manager-cum-director, Jerry Adler, threw a Christmas party in his New York home. Tuesday was there, with Dudley. 'How does it feel to be the only woman in town who's fucked the entire company of *Good Evening*?' [36] asked Peter, in full view of the other guests. He'd always pushed the envelope onstage. Now he was doing it in real life. In England, in certain quarters, he might have got away with it. Yet Americans tend to be more po-faced. Cohen was mortified. From that moment on, he lost all trust in Peter. And Dudley? 'You expect your best friend to shit on you,' he said. 'I was resigned to it and just licked my wounds in a corner, like a cat.' [37]

CHAPTER TWENTY TWO

ON THE ROAD

RUSSELL HARTY: Have you come back to England to
recharge your batteries?

PETER COOK: If I could find them, I'd recharge them. [1]

After the Broadway run of *Good Evening*, Peter and Dudley would both have been happy to call it a day. However, Edward Heath's Conservatives had been ousted by Harold Wilson's Labour Party, which had introduced a 90% tax band for Britain's highest earners. Peter and Dudley didn't relish the prospect of being squeezed until their pips squeaked. Financially, it made good sense to remain abroad for as long as possible. In February 1975, after a two-month break, they resumed their US tour in Washington DC.

Washington loved *Good Evening*. The show was a sell-out. But by now Peter and Dudley had been performing the same show, on several continents, for the best part of four years. They were weary of the material. They were weary of each other. Tethered together by contractual obligation and force of habit, they soldiered on. A transfer to Detroit didn't improve Peter's mood. 'This is the ugliest, most boring city I have ever visited,' [2] he wrote to his parents. They were there for five long weeks. 'I've never said a bad thing about any American city – apart from Detroit,' said Peter. 'It has 35% unemployment, it's freezing, nobody comes into the centre of the city because everybody who's got any money lives in the suburbs and you're inclined to get killed.' [3] Peter and Judy ended up lying on the bed in their hotel room, betting on the upward and downward passage of the elevators.

In Toronto they were joined by Tuesday, and the tension ratcheted up a notch. They were all staying in the same hotel. Dudley and Tuesday's suite was on the floor above, directly over Peter and Judy's. Tuesday was friendly towards Judy, but Judy wanted to maintain some distance. Dudley was cross that Judy wasn't being more sociable. Judy feared that he might want a foursome. She told Peter about her suspicions. Peter remained poker-faced. Dudley went cold on Judy. Upset that Peter seemed to be siding with Dudley instead of her, Judy decided to fly home. Her plane was already taxiing down the runway when a voice came over the intercom. 'Is there a Mrs Cook on board?' [4] 'Yes,' replied Judy. 'Your husband has requested that you come off the plane.' [5] The plane stopped, the doors opened and Peter walked down the aisle. 'Please come back,' he implored her. 'Don't go home.' [6] The other passengers stood up and applauded. Judy got off the plane.

Such dramatic gestures showed that, for all their travails, Peter and Judy were still very much in love. It was Peter's relationship with Dudley which was in real trouble. Dudley said that when the tour was over, he wanted to stay on in America and try to make it as an actor. Peter was shaken. He knew that if this happened their partnership would be over. He had no intention of remaining in the States. Their respective attitudes to the two countries encapsulated the differences between them. Peter liked living in London. Dudley was happy just to visit. Peter was fascinated by Fleet Street gossip.

Dudley was indifferent. Dudley hated football. Peter loved the game so much that he once feigned illness, cancelled a performance of *Good Evening*, and flew to London to see Spurs play at White Hart Lane. Peter missed Hampstead. He missed *Private Eye*. Most of all, he missed his daughters. Dudley had no such ties. 'I've spent the past seven months in hotel rooms and really rather enjoyed it,' he said. 'The anonymity of living like that appeals to me. I suppose I am rather like some cheap old whore being seduced by hotel after hotel.'[7]

Dudley felt liberated in America, where people said what they meant and meant what they said, and where you came from didn't matter. He'd always felt stifled by caustic, classbound Britain, with its sarcastic jokes and its snobbish obsession with what school you went to and who your parents were. 'There is still a sort of royal versus peasant kind of mentality which abounds in England,'[8] he said. Peter, on the other hand, didn't want to let it all hang out. His comedy was all about buttoned-up emotions, and the absurdity of the class system. It wasn't that he approved of it. It was simply the landscape of his life. As someone who preferred to keep his feelings under wraps, he felt at home in England. With his more expressive temperament, Dudley felt more relaxed in the States. 'Peter misses London,' he said, 'but I don't – not at all.'[9] In America, said Dudley, he felt safe from the things that had worried him when he was younger. The country nurtured him, in a way that England never could. Even when his marriages had broken down, even after his film career had died, even when he was dying, he would never leave America.

By the time the tour reached Philadelphia, Dudley had acquired a US agent who was putting him up for parts. Clearly, his plan was more than just a pipe dream. Roused into action, Peter tried to do some writing of his own. He even hired a secretary to help him with the admin. He started a screenplay, called *Dr Jekyll and Mrs Hyde*, about Queen Victoria's gynaecologist, inspired by Richard Ingrams whose grandfather had performed that regal role. It was a brilliant idea, but it remained unfinished. His drinking didn't help, but that was only part of it. It was a circular problem. Did the drink stop him writing, or did he drink because he couldn't write?

Touring also took its toll on Dudley's relationship with Tuesday. She decided to fly back to Los Angeles. Judy continued to shuttle between America and Britain, and while their respective partners were away Peter and Dudley abandoned any semblance of monogamy. 'Peter and Dudley had a ghastly rivalry between them to pull the birds,' said Judy. 'Dudley was very charming to all women and talked psychotherapy, wanting to know their real feelings and their problems. He would listen all night if necessary. It was a very seductive method. Peter could be insulting to women, and some women actually liked this.' [10] There was nothing jovial about this rivalry. Its intensity was revealed in an interview that they gave to *Penthouse* magazine, in which they bickered openly – and bitterly – about the relative merits of their contrasting chat-up lines:

PETER: The secret of success in the States, in my limited experience, is to be fucking rude. It's the only method. Kindness and civility and everything else is a waste of time. Tell them they're dirty fucking cows and stupid to boot. That's because the American male has spent the last fifteen years reappraising his role in society, and getting more and more nervous about how badly women have been treated.

DUDLEY: That doesn't seem to me to be true at all. I mean, your attitude seems to be quite exceptional. I

don't know many men who go up and say, 'You're a
dirty fucking cow,' and then except them to go to
bed with you. That wasn't my experience at all. [11]

The interview quickly degenerated into a fractious quarrel –
ostensibly about seduction techniques, in reality about their growing
antipathy to one another. It was more like a domestic dispute than a
conventional interview, as their shared sexual history increased the
bitterness of the debate:

PETER: If you go through your whole life history – this
tedious tale – also get into what star sign she
has, read their fucking palms, give them your
psychiatric history, then at about four o'clock in
the morning there's a possibility that you might
be able to meet her next weekend for a cosy tea.

DUDLEY: Speak for yourself. I've had no trouble. If the
only way you can get them into bed is by saying,
'You're a cunt ...'

PETER: Not the only way. It's the quickest.

DUDLEY: Speak for yourself, dear.

PETER: Who else would I be speaking for?

DUDLEY: Well, you're speaking to me about it. You're saying
it takes me until four in the morning, star signs
and telling them about my psychiatric treatment.
I don't know where you get all this fucking ...

PETER: Private detectives. [12]

Peter was talking tripe, of course – Dudley was the undisputed
champion at talking women into bed. Yet, as in any marital dispute,
the subject matter was irrelevant. Their public appearances were
becoming increasingly adversarial. As Dudley told the man from
Penthouse, as he struggled to get a word in edgeways, the atmosphere

was thickening like gravy.

The show moved on to Chicago where Peter awoke one morning to find two strange men in his hotel room, rummaging through his belongings. They dashed out when he woke up, which was fortunate, as there was no way he could have defended himself. 'I was fully armed with one soiled Kleenex,' [13] he said. Peter remained admirably calm, phoned reception with the robbers' descriptions, and gave a detailed statement to the police when they came to dust his room for fingerprints. But the experience had rattled him. At five o'clock that afternoon, after the police had gone, he fainted.

The tour finished in Los Angeles, with a six-week run at the Schubert Theatre. Dudley and Tuesday rented a house off Sunset Boulevard. Despite his infidelities, Dudley was still smitten. 'Tuesday's amazingly bright and honest, totally straightforward,' he said. 'She's taught me that you cannot hide things. Even if you fancy someone else you must say so. You mustn't smother it. Her honesty sometimes makes things difficult. But now I realise it's the only way to function. For years I lived my life like a burglar, creeping around.' [14] Peter rented a luxurious mansion on Roxbury Drive – one of LA's smartest streets, and a regular drive-by destination for tour groups and coach parties, on account of all the celebrities who lived nearby. It had five bedrooms, five bathrooms, a pool table, a table-tennis table and a spacious swimming pool. Yet despite these creature comforts, Peter didn't warm to LA. Even the sunshine brought him down. Dudley loved the weather. 'I've lived under stones for so long,' he said. 'It's nice to be in the sun.' [15]

Judy flew out to be with Peter and found that he was drinking even more heavily. 'Day had become night for Peter,' she said. 'He would sleep all day and eat just before he went onstage.' [16] He'd wake up around noon with a hangover, drink copious quantities of black coffee, eat lunch and then drink himself back to sleep again. He'd wake up again a few hours later and have a shower and a light meal before the chauffeur drove him to the show. After the show he'd often go out on the town, alone, until the small hours. Judy would wait in for him, unable to sleep until he got home. She was worried what he might be up to. She was worried that someone might break in. When Peter came home he was frequently off his face. He wouldn't tell Judy where he'd been. In the morning, when he'd sobered up, he'd be contrite and weepy. But then he'd have another drink, and it would start all over again.

Peter pulled himself together when his daughters flew out for a visit. He was amusing and affectionate and relatively sober. Lucy and Daisy had a great time. Peter and Judy took them to Disneyland. They swam in the pool every day. Yet, sadly, this was just a brief interlude. Peter's daily life was becoming increasingly sedentary and unhealthy. The drink made him impotent, which made him angry – with women in general and Judy in particular. 'Peter's impotency is not just sexual but in every aspect of his life,' reflected Judy, 'from dealing with his addictions to coping with Dudley's growing rejection.' [17] Dudley, for his part, felt rejected by Peter. 'I was conscious that he really wasn't with me,' said Dudley. 'He really didn't have any interest in what I was doing.' [18] Drink had become the other woman. Even when Peter wasn't pissed, Dudley knew his attention lay elsewhere.

Good Evening was still a hit, but friends and colleagues could detect a change in the partnership, onstage as well as off it. Having seen the show in London, Eric Idle saw it again in LA. 'What had happened was that Dudley had become the funny one,' said Idle. 'He was carrying Peter and that was terribly tragic, because Peter's alcoholism had stopped him being funny.' [19] For Idle it was like seeing the ventriloquist's doll controlling the ventriloquist. 'He's labouring,' thought Idle, as he watched Peter onstage. 'He's being held back by seeing people through a veil.' [20]

Peter was scared and angry about Dudley's decision to go solo, but he didn't want to talk about it. He preferred to blot it out with drink. He'd become virtually nocturnal, watching TV in bed all night, playing with the controls on their rotating bed. Unable to sleep beside him, Judy started sleeping in another room. She felt he'd lost control.

Judy flew home, to more bad news. A smear test revealed precancerous cells. She was told she'd need to return for six-monthly check-ups. She had to have a biopsy. Her fallopian tubes were blocked. She couldn't have a baby. Having terminated a pregnancy before they were married, this was an awful blow for her, and for Peter too. He was in tears when he heard the news. He'd been desperate for them to start a family. 'I believe Peter and I would have made brilliant parents,' [21] she reflected. She'd hoped that if they'd had a child together it might have helped to moderate his drinking.

Meanwhile, back in the USA, Dudley had been hit with a reproductive crisis of his own. Tuesday was pregnant. Dudley was appalled. He was worried that any child of his would inherit his disability. He asked her to have an abortion. She refused. 'I didn't know what to do,' he said. 'I was afraid of being tied to anyone for twenty-odd years.' [22] But he was still bewitched by Tuesday, and extremely fond of her daughter Natasha. 'It's not at all easy,' he said. 'We have some pretty headlong collisions. Terrible ups and downs when we decide it's all over. But each time it seems to advance our relationship a little further.' [23] Dudley duly asked Tuesday to marry him. After *Good Evening* finished its LA run, they drove out into the desert and were married in Las Vegas. They moved into a house in Bel Air, with Natasha. Dudley had made his own future. It was a future without Peter.

When the curtain came down on *Good Evening*, Peter had no plans. 'I just want to sit in a bar and drink,' he told Judy. 'I don't want to be here. I don't want to go back to London. I just want to sit here and drink.' [24] Yet Peter could still be enchanting company, as long as the circumstances were right. He and Judy went on holiday to Jamaica where they had a brilliant time. They stayed at the Sans Souci Hotel in the resort town of Ocho Rios, in a clapboard house with its own garden, backing onto a private beach. They smoked some of the local dope – a few times they got so stoned that they couldn't even find their way to the hotel restaurant. Peter cut back on his drinking – just a few beers and the odd glass of wine. Judy remembered why she loved him. 'At heart he is such a sweet man,' she reflected. 'It is just alcohol that causes all his terrible rages.' [25] They stayed for five weeks.

Midway through this idyllic break, Peter and Judy flew to New York. Peter and Dudley had been booked to appear with Chevy Chase on *Saturday Night Live*, alongside Neil Sedaka and the Muppets. They performed 'Frog and Peach' and 'One Leg Too Few', and did a send-up of Sonny and Cher singing 'I Got You, Babe'. It was billed as a farewell performance after their US tour, but as far as Dudley was concerned it was the final curtain. After the TV recording, the two men went their separate ways. Dudley returned to LA, and to Tuesday, while Peter and Judy flew back to Jamaica to resume their holiday. Peter was still in denial about Dudley's true intentions. They were merely having a rest from one another, he told the press. In fact, Dudley had vowed never to work with Peter again. 'It was like a knife wound to Peter,' said Judy. 'It was the end of their writing partnership. A light had gone from Peter's life and I never saw him so depressed.' [26]

Peter returned to Perrins Walk, and two years of unopened post. He didn't open any of it. The building work was finished, but now he had other headaches to contend with. Wendy had left Kenwood Cottage and had moved to Forest Row, a village in the Sussex countryside, so that Lucy and Daisy could attend the local Steiner school. The girls were very happy there, but it was several hours' drive from Hampstead. Reluctantly, Peter agreed to buy a house there, which Wendy and the girls would live in until Lucy and Daisy finished school. Before he could sell Kenwood Cottage there were squatters to deal with. After the listless limbo of touring, real life was rearing its ugly head again.

A few weeks after Peter and Judy got back to Perrins Walk, Dudley flew to London. He came and spent the afternoon at home with them. Dudley told Peter that he didn't want to work with him any more. He was willing to do the odd one-off – a personal appearance or a commercial. But he wasn't going to do any more shows together, whether on TV or in the theatre. He wanted to do some proper acting. He was tired of performing sketches. Most of all, however, he was tired of performing with Peter.

Peter put on a brave face, but deep down he was devastated. When Dudley departed, Judy saw her husband crumble before her eyes. Professionally (and in many ways emotionally) Dudley had been the love of Peter's life. 'He can't bear the fact that the man he thinks should always be there for him is walking away,' reflected Judy. 'Dudley has been his perfect workmate, and he knows he is irreplaceable.' [27] As well as the raw pain of rejection, there were financial implications, too. Peter hadn't made as much money from the US tour as he'd hoped he might. Without Dudley, he was worried about how he'd make a living. Judy had abandoned her own career to be with Peter. She too was terribly worried. When she cried, he'd hug her, and he'd end up crying too. But what Peter felt most of all was anger, the fury of a lover spurned. 'Perhaps in his heart Peter knows his drinking has caused their split, but he won't admit it,' wrote Judy in her autobiography. 'Instead, he insists Dudley has betrayed him. He becomes obsessed with him from the moment he gets up until he goes to bed.' [28]

In the weeks that followed, Peter talked about Dudley incessantly. He stayed up through the small hours and slept until lunchtime. He lost interest in his appearance. There were weeks when he didn't change his clothes, or wash his hair, or take a bath. He didn't want to go outside. He'd fly off the handle at the smallest things. His rage was hard to live with. Judy became afraid of him. He didn't hit her but he shouted at her. While he ate and ate, her weight fell to six stone. Peter was having a breakdown, he was dragging his wife down with him, and his former partner was thousands of miles away.

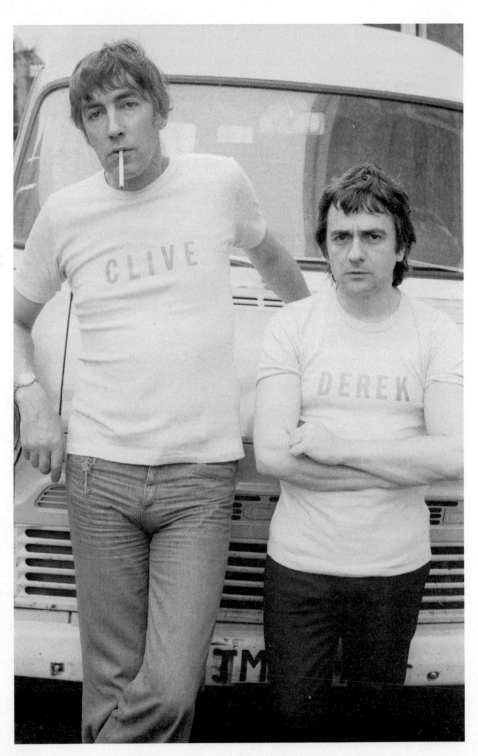

Peter and Dudley as Derek and Clive.

CHAPTER TWENTY THREE

DEREK & CLIVE (DEAD)

DUDLEY: We would like to be more blasphemous and
obscene. We'd both quite like to do a really
dirty show with a small audience in mind. [1]

In February 1976, after an emergency Caesarean, Tuesday gave birth to a baby boy. It was a difficult delivery – the umbilical cord became wrapped around his neck – but her child was perfectly healthy. He had no club foot, as his dad had feared. Dudley was ecstatic. At the age of forty, he'd become a father. He returned home in the small hours, went into the garage, where he'd parked his piano, and played triumphant music for an hour or more. Tuesday and Dudley named their son Patrick Havlin Moore: Havlin after Dudley's dad's original surname; Patrick after Patrick Garland, Dudley's friend from Oxford, whom he'd hardly seen since then. 'It's a very noble and touching tribute but I'm not sure if I deserve it,' [2] said Garland, modestly. A kindly man, he had no idea how much his kindness had meant to Dudley.

Dudley was a doting father, but monogamy was a bridge too far. Within a month of Patrick's birth, he was seeing other women. Tuesday intercepted various love letters and was understandably upset. Barely a month before his son was born, he'd had a fling on a trip to New York during a futile attempt to drum up some acting work. Now, with a newborn baby, he was playing the field again. As ever, Dudley sought refuge in his music, playing the piano in his Bel Air garage. He had no other work to distract him. His overtures to producers had so far come to nothing. *Good Evening* had been a huge hit but his track record in the movies was patchy, to say the least. Breaking out of a double act is a tricky business at the best of times, and in Hollywood forty is a ripe old age at which to try and forge a new career. 'I'm not really known in Los Angeles, despite the fact that we did our show here,' he said. 'Theatre doesn't make much impact here – only films. Tuesday can sit around and the phone will still ring with offers. But not for me.' [3]

Like Dudley, Peter was finding it hard to land decent solo work. He made another ill-advised foray into the movies, in a forgettable flop called *Find The Lady* – a lame comedy starring John Candy as a useless policeman. After the neglected brilliance of *Bedazzled*, and the heroic failure of *The Bed Sitting Room*, Peter's film career was starting to resemble a series of increasingly unsuccessful false starts. He tried to do some writing with Claude Harz, Tuesday's first husband, whom Peter had got to know in America when Harz started going out with Dudley's former girlfriend Lysie Hastings. Harz was a disciplined writer. He turned up on time, relished hard work and was happy to sit at the typewriter while Peter strode around improvising. He should have been the perfect writing partner for Peter, but the screenplay they wrote together (about a vacuum cleaner that conquers the world) was yet another wonderful idea – like *Dr Jekyll and Mrs Hyde* – which, sadly, came to nothing. As Harz said, Peter could still be very funny when he was drunk, but sometimes he was simply too drunk. As any drinker can confirm, drunken people are only funny if you're drinking with them. The only sign of promise, for Peter and for Dudley, came from a most unlikely quarter – an obscure recording they'd made in New York called Derek & Clive.

Derek & Clive had a curious – and completely accidental – conception. It all began with a monologue that Peter had been batting around since the early 1960s, simply to amuse himself and his friends at *Private Eye*. Back in 1962 Hollywood starlet Jayne Mansfield, famous for her ample bosom, was shipwrecked on a Bahamian island, clad only in her bikini. Apparently, she'd gone waterskiing and her speedboat had capsized. Thankfully, her PR man was on hand to save her, which was handy as she had a new film out. It was exactly the sort of silly story that tickled Peter's fancy, and as he speculated about the crustaceans that might have become entangled in her swimsuit, he gradually expanded this showbiz yarn into a routine called 'The Worst Job I Ever Had'. It was far too rude for broadcast or public performance, but it was extremely funny and Peter wanted to preserve it. In 1973, in New York, bored of performing *Good Evening*, evening after evening, he hired the Bell Sound Studios in New York and invited Dudley along. Peter told him he simply wanted to improvise, in the sweary style they often adopted to amuse each other on the road. The resultant recording was a comic classic, enhanced by the fact that Dudley didn't have a clue what was going on:

PETER: I'll tell you the worst job I ever had.

DUDLEY: What was that?

PETER: The worst job I ever had was with Jayne Mansfield. She's a fantastic bird – big tits, huge bum and everything like that – but I had the terrible job of retrieving lobsters from her bum.

DUDLEY: Really? Bloody hell! That must have been a task.

PETER: It's quite a task because she had a big bum and they were big lobsters …

There was no real creative role for Dudley. All Peter wanted from him were rudimentary prompts and responses. Indeed, when Dudley tried to interject a little humour of his own, Peter told him to shut up. In public, Dudley was replacing Peter as the dominant partner. This was a return to their early days, when Peter still took centre stage with Dudley as his feed and foil. So many of Peter's private routines vanished into the ether. It was a shame he never got around to recording a few more. 'It came out of nowhere,' said Dudley, unaware that Peter had been polishing this particular riff for ten years or more. 'I had to do a very hasty improvised response. It was all about picking up Winston Churchill's bogeys.' [4] It wasn't half as funny, but he hadn't had a decade in which to practise it.

Peter had only planned to record this one sketch, but he'd enjoyed himself and so had Dudley. So one night, a few weeks later, after a performance of *Good Evening*, they reconvened at the Electric Lady Studios 'armed with several bottles of wine' [5] to try out some more material. This time it really was off the cuff. 'We had no preconceived attitudes or intentions,' recalled Peter. 'What emerged, on the whole, was a shower of filth with no socially redeeming or artistic value.' [6] He was right, but there was something to it nonetheless. These sketches ranged from the surreal ('Squatter and The Ant') to the sinister ('Winky Wanky Woo') but at their best they had a crude and cheerful candour, as in 'This Bloke Came Up To Me', which consisted chiefly of Peter and Dudley calling each other 'You fucking cunt.' No big deal nowadays, of course, but in the 1970s swearing was still a big taboo, shocking people who would happily put up with any amount of sexist or racist banter. American comic George Carlin was hounded through the US courts for performing his stand-up routine, 'Seven Words You Can Never Say On Television' (Shit, Piss, Fuck, Cunt, Cocksucker, Motherfucker and Tits, since you ask) while Kenneth Tynan became notorious as the first person to say 'Fuck' on British TV. Bad language had become a battleground, and expletives were regarded in some quarters as totems of free expression. Of course, there was no higher purpose to Peter and Dudley's scatological excesses – they were simply having fun – but it does explain why language that's normal nowadays was considered sensational back then.

'We heard it back the next day and found it to be funny, but on the other hand we had no idea what to do with it,' recalled Peter. 'A few weeks later we decided to try out the same sort of rambling filth on a small audience.' [7] They hired a club called the Bottom Line in Greenwich Village, invited along a few friends, and repeated some of the same material, plus a couple of old sketches – Dudley's boogie-woogie number, 'Bo Duddley', from *Not Only ... But Also* and Peter's Establishment skit, 'Appeal on Behalf of the Blond'. 'Peter and Dudley mainly ad-libbed from a few notes they had written down,' recalled Judy. 'Peter used the opportunity to be as insulting, aggressive and barmy as he liked.' [8] They had no idea if anyone else would find it funny, but the invited audience laughed along. Clearly, this was more than just a private joke. To distinguish them from their more amiable alter egos Pete & Dud, they christened their foul-mouthed creations Derek & Clive.

In some respects, the differences between Pete & Dud and Derek & Clive weren't quite as pronounced as they appeared. 'When they were doing Pete & Dud it was Derek & Clive when we were rehearsing,' said

Joe McGrath. 'They never held back from using four-letter words.' [9] Peter also acknowledged some similarities, describing Derek & Clive as Pete & Dud on speed. Yet their attitudes were worlds apart. Pete & Dud were well-meaning idiots without an ounce of malice between them. Derek & Clive were far more malevolent. 'They are probably both mechanics, strongly Tory, like a drink, are embarrassed by women and like football,' declared Peter. 'They don't like poofs or having to pay taxes while the country goes down the toilet.' [10] These weren't Peter's opinions per se (he wasn't remotely homophobic) but they reflected his growing antipathy towards the world at large. Pete & Dud discussed fine art, religion and philosophy. Derek & Clive discussed violence and depravity, in depraved and violent terms. The industrial language was a side issue. Beneath the boisterous obscenity there was a nihilistic streak, particularly in Peter's fierce invective (Dudley's filthy contributions had more of a naughty-schoolboy flavour) which became more prominent as time went by. For the time being, however, Derek & Clive was just a jolly jape – a way of amusing a few friends and their favourite audience – each other. Dudley held his own, but Peter was a grandmaster. 'He had a genius for obscenity,' said Dudley. 'He wouldn't stop until he got a laugh. Never mind how much dross there was, he had to come up with a jewel.' [11]

Peter and Dudley had actually done something similar ten years earlier, during the Broadway run of *Beyond The Fringe*. Then as now, to allay the tedium of a long run, they'd made a series of recordings called *The Dead Sea Tapes* – a series of reminiscences from acquaintances of Jesus Christ that somehow never made it into the Bible. Unbroadcastable back then, these tapes have long since vanished. This time, Peter and Dudley were more resourceful. They sent the Derek &

Clive tapes to Peter's friend Christopher Blackwell, the boss of Island records. Blackwell also found them funny. He also had no idea what to do with them. Peter and Dudley set off on tour. Like *The Dead Sea Tapes*, Derek & Clive looked destined to be forgotten.

Yet as Peter and Dudley toured the States, they bumped into some of the world's biggest rock bands, such as The Who, Led Zeppelin and The Rolling Stones, and soon discovered that they'd become these superstars' favourite comics – not as a result of anything they'd done onstage, on TV or in the movies, but because of Derek & Clive. Blackwell had played the tapes to various people in the music business, studio technicians had run off pirate copies, and now no tour bus was complete without a bootleg of this unreleased recording. They became friends with some of these rock stars – particularly Keith Moon, who threw a surprise party for Peter (with a swimming pool full of bunny girls) and encouraged him to cut a single. Thankfully, the subsequent recording session finally cured Peter of any ambitions to become a pop star. 'All we got done in twelve hours was a three-chord backing track, because the musicians were all going off shooting up in the toilets, and I conclusively demonstrated that I could not hit a note,' [12] he said. Still, Derek & Clive's popularity with Moon & Co got Peter thinking. If these rock groups found the material funny, he concluded, their fans might find it funny too.

Peter was bang on the money. By the time he returned to England, Derek & Clive bootlegs were widely available on the black market. Copies even started cropping up for sale in small ads in the back of *Private Eye*. Other people were making money out of Derek & Clive but Peter and Dudley hadn't made a penny. When Dudley flew to England, the duo got together with Blackwell and listened to the tapes again. They still found them funny. They decided to put them out on an LP. *Derek & Clive (Live)* was released in August 1976. The only pity was that they didn't stick with the working title – *Derek & Clive (Dead)*. 'All of us had certain fears,' recalled Peter. 'Dudley and I because we thought it might destroy our "cuddly" image, and Christopher for legal reasons.' [13] Their worries were unfounded. The contrast with 'cuddly' Pete & Dud was part of what made the record so amusing and, despite its provocative content, the LP escaped prosecution. Derek & Clive were ready to roll.

This time it was Dudley who was forced to eat humble pie. Although he'd told Peter he didn't want to work with him again, this bizarre out-take from their Broadway run was the only job in his diary. In California, he'd discovered, English self-deprecation didn't pay. 'I tend to downgrade myself in front of people,' he said. 'Out here, if you do that, they believe you. You've simply got to walk around bursting with self-confidence, and that isn't easy for me to do.' [14] Tired of sitting around in Los Angeles waiting for the phone to ring, Dudley flew to London to help Peter promote the LP. His help was hardly needed. The record virtually sold itself. The BBC banned it, which was the best publicity they could have hoped for ('quite unacceptable' snorted the Beeb), Capitol Radio banned it too, and, bolstered by this endorsement, *Derek & Clive (Live)* quickly became a smash hit. In Britain it sold 50,000 copies in the first few weeks and 100,000 overall. It became Peter and Dudley's biggest-selling LP on both sides of the Atlantic, easily outselling their previous, more well-mannered recordings. In terms of pounds per hour, it was possibly the most lucrative work they ever did.

Even the cover was a masterpiece of slapdash understatement. In an era of gatefold sleeves adorned with intricate artwork, its untidy scrawl stood out in record racks like graffiti in an art gallery.

'Warning!' read a notice beneath the title. 'This record contains language of an explicit nature that may be offensive and should not be played in the presence of minors' (or miners, as Peter called them). Like the radio ban, this disclaimer served as an advertisement rather than a deterrent. The record became especially popular with adolescent boys, as Peter discovered when he was mobbed by a bunch of prepubescent fans at a football match. 'Instead of saying, as usual, "Where's your mate, Pete?" they were saying, "Here, Clive, you're a cunt,"' [15] he reported afterwards. From its ad-hoc beginnings as a private entertainment, Derek & Clive had become an anarchic (yet very lucrative) public joke.

Peter and Dudley had no problems defending this coarse but cheerful LP. 'I don't find it shocking,' said Peter. 'That sort of language is commonplace.' [16] 'Mozart had a very scatological sense of humour,' said Dudley. 'He was always talking about farting and cunts and arses.' [17] The reaction of the broadsheet press was actually fairly positive. 'The record does not rely on obscenities for its humour,' argued the *Sunday Times*. 'It is simply satirical about people who swear every other word.' [18] Dudley was more worried about what his mother might think. Judy also had reservations ('His deep well of anger could be recycled into something more upbeat and creative,' [19] she concluded) and Wendy felt similarly ill at ease. 'I just felt that it was completely not what he was about,' she said. 'Being the mother of young impressionable children at a Steiner school where it became a cult, I just found it incredibly distasteful.' [20] Unbeknown to Wendy, her young impressionable children were smuggling the record into their Steiner school for the amusement of their classmates. From football stadia to Steiner schools, Derek & Clive now enjoyed broad juvenile appeal.

Distasteful or not, *Derek & Clive (Live)* was incredibly influential, inspiring a new generation of entertainers. At a time when the most popular comedians on British TV were trad acts like Morecambe and Wise, it had an underground appeal that chimed with punk rock and anticipated alternative comedy – not bad going for two men who were several years older than the Beatles. Peter and Dudley had been in danger of becoming forty-something has-beens. Thanks to Derek & Clive, they now seemed young and edgy.

Back in fashion, Peter and Dudley landed a lucrative ad campaign, fronting a series of TV commercials for Guinness. The job necessitated a week's shooting in Amsterdam. Peter returned home drunk, and told Judy that he and Dudley had shared another prostitute. Despite this unwelcome revelation, relations remained cordial enough for Peter and Judy to join Dudley and Tuesday for dinner, to toast Dudley and Tuesday's first wedding anniversary. To Dudley's amazement, Peter even footed the three-figure bill.

Far better than making adverts (or sharing prostitutes) Peter and Dudley now landed the sort of movie deal they'd both been coveting for so long – the first feature film they'd been asked to write AND star in since *Bedazzled* a decade earlier. With such a tempting offer back in Britain and no offers forthcoming in the States, Dudley had little option but to backtrack on his earlier decision to terminate his partnership with Peter. He rented a house in Cheyne Walk, Chelsea, Tuesday flew over with Patrick, and Peter started coming round to write their new screenplay, a comic version of *The Hound of The Baskervilles*. (Very) loosely based on Sir Arthur Conan Doyle's story, and inspired by a sketch from *Goodbye Again*, in which Peter played Sherlock Holmes to Dudley's Doctor Watson, it had all the makings of a hit. 'We both thought it could be the funniest film ever,' [21] said Dudley.

Getting back together with Dudley galvanised Peter. He went on a diet, losing more than two stone, and cut back on his drinking. He even dyed his greying hair ('Peter's gone prematurely orange,' [22] observed Jonathan Miller's wife, Rachel). Dudley duly returned to LA – to avoid paying British taxes, he could only spend two months at a time in the UK – but they continued work on the screenplay, staying in touch by phone. Meanwhile, Peter started to write a weekly column for the *Daily Mail*, called 'Peter Cook's Monday Morning Feeling'. Despite the downbeat title, it found him in good spirits. 'This column is here on a strictly trial basis,' he wrote. 'If it disappears as suddenly and mysteriously as it has arrived, there will be three possible explanations: that it has been found to be insufferably tedious by all and sundry; that I have found the job too time-consuming and ill-rewarded; (and most likely) that there has been a massive walkout by other writers on the paper to protest against the "unfair competition" of the sustained brilliance of my contributions.' [23] Peter had every reason to be optimistic. With a hit record in the charts, and a movie in the pipeline, the double act was back on track.

Peter and Dudley in *The Hound of the Baskervilles*, with Kenneth Williams and Hamish.

CHAPTER TWENTY FOUR

THE HOUND OF THE BASKERVILLES

*'There's a film Dudley and I might be doing, a film of
The Hound of the Baskervilles, with me as Sherlock Holmes
and Dudley as the dog.'*

(Peter Cook) [1]

The omens for *The Hound of The Baskervilles* could hardly have been better. Spoofs of Hollywood classics were very much in vogue. Mel Brooks had scored two big successes in this field, sending up Westerns (*Blazing Saddles*) and horror films (*Young Frankenstein*). *The Hound of The Baskervilles* was backed by Michael White, who'd produced two of the funniest films of the decade, *The Rocky Horror Picture Show* and *Monty Python and The Holy Grail*. The director, however, was Paul Morrissey.

Morrissey was an unusual choice. He was a big fan of British comedy, particularly the *Carry On* films, but he'd made his name in America, directing art-house movies for Andy Warhol's Factory. After sitting in on some of Peter's initial meetings with the director, Judy felt uneasy. The two men hit it off, but she thought Morrissey was a bit too zany to bring out the best in Peter. She felt that he needed a firmer hand. She was also apprehensive about Morrissey's plan to crowbar some of Peter and Dudley's old sketches into the movie. Peter was worried, too. 'That was Paul's idea,' he told *The South Bank Show* when they came to shoot a documentary about the making of the movie. 'We said, "It will just look like we're rehashing old material," but he said, "No, it's stuff which works. If you look back to the Marx Brothers, they did stuff on film which they'd done on stage for years and years, and they did it on film because it worked." I hope he's right.' [2] Dudley was similarly pessimistic. The Marx Brothers might have recycled their old stage routines in the movies, but they hadn't already aired them on TV.

Morrissey cast Kenneth Williams, the king of *Carry On*, as Sir Henry Baskerville. On a personal level, Peter was glad to be reunited with Williams, who'd given him his first big break. Since they'd first met, when Peter was still a student, they'd stayed in touch and got along very well. Williams was virtually the only comedian to whom Peter was willing to defer. When Peter socialised with other entertainers, he tended to monopolise the conversation. When he socialised with Williams, he actually sat and listened. Yet although they enjoyed each other's company, their approach to comedy was poles apart. Williams's delivery was ornate, Peter's was understated. Williams's characters were hysterical, Peter's were reserved. Even in the West End revues that Peter had written for Williams nearly twenty years before, these contrasting playing styles had sometimes jarred.

Morrissey rewrote the script, shoehorning in some gobsmacking *Carry On*-style gags. The final script was full of groaners, but Williams didn't mind. 'It made me laugh out loud,' he wrote in his diary. 'Some of it is very funny.' [3] Funny or not, the screenplay was scuppered by Morrissey's step-pause-gag direction, which turned the film into a series of corny cameos. Even in their broadest sketches, Peter and Dudley had never been a slapstick act. The supporting cast was full of big names (Denholm Elliott, Roy Kinnear, Spike Milligan, Terry-Thomas, Max Wall) but this merely made matters worse, as comics and character actors queued up to perform their party pieces. In the *Carry Ons*, Williams was surrounded by straight men (and women). Here he was surrounded by music-hall turns. Cinema amplifies the subtlest nuance and exaggerates the slightest gesture. Yet Morrissey encouraged everyone involved to be as theatrical as possible. Dudley played Watson as a Welshman. Peter played Holmes as a Jew. In a short sketch, this would have been amusing. Spread across an entire feature film, it reduced their characters to cartoon cut-outs with no shade or subtlety whatsoever.

In public, Peter remained bullish. 'Dudley is still not quite sure how to play Watson,' he wrote in his *Daily Mail* column. 'I tell him that Dr Watson is basically a small, bumbling, ineffective fool, but Dudley has some objection to playing himself.' [4] But as soon as they started shooting he could sense that things had gone awry. 'Paul Morrissey has made me as grotesque as I've ever been, apart from in my private life,' he told *The South Bank Show*. 'It's been very hard to do a take which was over the top for him.'[5] Kenneth Williams adopted a completely different view. 'It's being played for absolute reality,' he told the papers. 'It's not a *Carry On*. Everything has to be sincere and every reaction has to be honest. That's what makes it so screamingly funny.' [6] He must have been watching a different movie. *The Hound of The Baskervilles* made the *Carry Ons* look like highbrow costume dramas. This was pantomime, without the laughs.

Peter did his best to minimise the damage. Despite his limitations as an actor, he knew that, on the big screen, less is more. 'Sir Henry must be very mild and vulnerable,' he told Williams. 'Be careful you don't get that edge into your voice.' [7] It was sound advice, but it fell on deaf ears. 'It's ludicrous the way he and Dudley talk about truth in characterisation the whole time,' wrote Williams in his diary. 'The seriousness with which everyone sits around discussing the merit of this word or that word for inclusion in this hotchpotch of rubbish is the sort of thing Cook would have ridiculed in his undergraduate days.' [8] Trying to give Williams direction was futile. He was famous for his flamboyant performances. Even if Morrissey hadn't been on board, he would have been loath to tone it down.

Powerless to improve the film, Peter hit the bottle. He was also taking uppers and downers, to get him going in the morning and help him sleep at night. He was due on the set at 7:30 a.m. A car would collect him from Perrins Walk at 6:30. The driver would hammer on the door, but Peter was usually sleeping off a heavy night so he sometimes wouldn't hear him. He'd often kept Judy up until late, so she'd be out for the count as well. The driver would have to dash to a local call box and phone the house to rouse them. On the journey to the set, Peter would drink a bottle of red wine and chain-smoke with the windows closed until the car was full of cigarette smoke. Doing a day's filming in such a state would have finished off a weaker man, but Peter would arrive home wired. Judy would make him supper – comfort food such as macaroni cheese – but often he wasn't hungry. Instead of winding down, he'd tell her endless jokes, as if he was performing for an audience. He'd be up until the small hours and then it would start all over again.

Ironically, the lack of laughs on camera contrasted with an abundance of laughter off it. When the cast broke for lunch, Williams was the life and soul of the party, entertaining everyone with luvvie yarns about Orson Welles and Richard Burton, and nearly flooring Peter with an energetic arabesque. Peter responded by dragging Williams into the stables where he stripped off half his clothes and commanded him to perform a love scene with Hamish, the Baskerville Hound. Sadly, hardly any of this comic mayhem found its way into the film. When he sat down to watch the first rushes, even Williams was underwhelmed. 'Critics will say "tired, laboured, unfunny, etc.,' he confided to his diary, 'but it don't matter.' [9] Maybe not to Williams, for whom this was just another potboiler, but to Peter and Dudley it mattered very much indeed. This was their big comeback, their make-or-break movie. If this film flopped, their career as a cinematic double act would be over.

Peter and Dudley made one last attempt to save the movie. They had a showdown with Morrissey. They spoke to the film's producer, John Goldstone. Peter spoke to Williams. 'John Goldstone and Dudley and I agree that Paul has made you do things which are over the top and bogus, and we must put this right,' he said. 'He was the only one at the rushes who was laughing at your stuff.' [10] It was a valiant effort, but it was too little too late. A week later, Morrissey went down with hepatitis. The shoot was suspended. The cast convened to view the footage – a mere 63 minutes so far. Williams was forced to admit defeat. None of it made him laugh, he conceded, and – as Peter and Dudley (and Judy) had feared – old sketches like 'One Leg Too Few' didn't belong in the film at all. Dudley described his own contribution as raucous and unfunny. It was a ruthlessly accurate self-assessment, which could have applied to the entire film.

For a movie which had promised so much, it was a bitter disappointment. Peter and Dudley laid most of the blame at the door of the director. 'Paul Morrissey frustrated us at every turn and we should have dumped the entire idea,' said Dudley. 'He wanted something comedic to happen whenever we did anything. It was an obsession with him, and it took all the fun out of doing it.' [11] 'Asking Paul Morrissey to direct English comedy – which he loves – is like asking me to direct an improvised movie about junkies in LA,' concurred Peter. 'The script is a very bad compromise between Dudley, myself and Paul.' [12] Peter and Dudley were so unhappy with Morrissey's edit that they edited another version themselves. Peter thought this cut was slightly better, but as he said himself, 'there's still no making it any good.' [13] The studio agreed. *The Hound of The Baskervilles* was postponed indefinitely. For Peter, it was like *The Rise And Rise of Michael Rimmer* all over again. Strictly speaking, Peter was right. With the benefit of hindsight, Morrissey had clearly been the wrong choice. Yet, overall, the problem wasn't Morrissey but Peter. Better directors had tried – and failed – to transfer his relationship with Dudley onto celluloid. Some of the other films had been near misses, this one had missed by a mile, yet none of the films he'd made with Dudley had really hit the mark – not even *Bedazzled*. Peter was simply not a movie actor. And nor, on current evidence, was Dudley.

The two men filled in time with a few Pete & Dud sketches for the American TV channel ABC, trudging round London's tourist traps for a Silver Jubilee tribute called *To the Queen! A Salute to Elizabeth II*. These sketches weren't quite as sycophantic as this cringeworthy title suggested, but to fans of Derek & Clive they must have seemed extremely tame. 'It was great fun working with network censorship,' wrote Peter in his *Daily Mail* column. 'For example, it was all right to say that you could buy inflatable life-sized Queens who wave their left arms when you let air out of their legs. It was also fine to talk about souvenir tights with the Queen on one leg, Prince Philip on the other, and a corgi somewhere else. But they drew the line at our joke allegations that, in his pre-photographic days, Tony Armstrong-Jones was an all-in wrestler known as Tony Strong-arm-Jones.' [14] For Dudley, these British jobs were just a sideshow. He'd decided to make his move to LA permanent. He applied for US residency. He found a house he loved, on an unspoilt beach at Marina del Rey near Santa Monica. He disposed of his British assets. He even arranged to make a Californian will, and buy a burial plot in California. By now Peter was resigned to losing him, but the bitterness still festered. If they made another film, Judy asked Peter, what role would he chose for Dudley? 'A murderer,' [15] said Peter. Judy thought that was an extraordinary thing to say.

Dudley had fallen for America, but America had yet to fall for him. With no US work forthcoming, he had agreed to appear with Peter on a second Derek & Clive album, called *Come Again*. This time Island Records weren't involved. Prompted by the success of *Derek & Clive (Live)* Peter had set up his own offshore company to publish the LP. CBS would distribute it. Richard Branson's Virgin Records would look after the release. Peter and Dudley met up at the CBS studios in Whitfield Street, in London's West End. They'd prepared nothing in advance. Peter was pissed. Dudley was sober. They recorded the entire album in a single day, and it showed.

Derek & Clive Come Again bore virtually no resemblance to the filthy, happy first LP. The rude good humour of *Derek & Clive (Live)* was replaced with spiteful rage, directed by Peter at his partner. Willie Donaldson called it a scream of pain. Dudley tried to be as rude as Peter (sometimes, he was even ruder) but what was most shocking wasn't Dudley's schoolboy smut but Peter's menopausal fury. Dudley had 'cancer of the knob' – Peter had 'cancer of the wife.' Dudley sang a filthy ditty about being sucked off by his mother – Peter sang a savage ditty about his father suffering from colon cancer (the disease that had recently killed Dudley's dad). 'It just became an arena for us to throw mud at each other,' said Dudley. 'He probably wanted to shock people and he did – there's no doubt he shocked me and that was, it seemed, his main source of pleasure.' [16] Virtually the only sketch with any wit was 'Joan Crawford', essentially a gynaecological variation on 'The Worst Job I Ever Had':

CLIVE: Up Joan Crawford's cunt there are fucking fleets of ships, light aircraft.

DEREK: Hamburger stands.

CLIVE: Hamburger stands, but no fucking hamburgers.

These flashes of crude inspiration were few and far between. Peter was like a gambler betting blind, flipping over cards at random, hoping to turn up a winning hand. He loved to improvise, and in the right circumstances he was brilliant at it, but he needed something to work with. Dudley hadn't learnt the script this time. There was no script for him to learn. *Derek & Clive (Live)* had some hilarious ad-hoc moments, but even on that LP the funniest sketches were the ones they'd prepared in advance.

In any case, *Come Again* was bound to be a completely different sort of album. *Derek & Clive (Live)* was made for Peter and Dudley's own amusement. Its mutation into a best-selling LP was almost entirely accidental. It felt like eavesdropping on a private joke. That was what gave it its bawdy charm. *Come Again*, on the other hand, was a commercial product from the start. Normally, that wouldn't have mattered, but with Derek & Clive it was fatal. Somehow, it was only really funny when they were doing it to amuse themselves.

By far the funniest thing about this record was the sleeve notes, which chronicled Derek & Clive's descent into celebrity madness. With its references to Derek's psychiatry and Clive's drug use, it was like a hallucinatory account of Peter and Dudley's last few years together:

Derek, always a sensitive soul, developed strange phobias. He locked himself in the toilet for weeks on end, watching reruns of *Emmerdale Farm*. He also had a morbid fear of germs and insisted on boiling his Peugeot before going for a drive. He also wanted to boil Clive, who rightly insisted that his mate should see a psychiatrist. Completely swathed in Bronco, Derek went to see Dr Fritz Leprechaun on Fifth Avenue. The consultation was a failure and the eminent doctor was found parboiled in his own fish tanks.

Cook and Moore finally persuaded the pair to do a six-week tour of North Korea, where they have a huge cult following. Unfortunately, one of the huge cults followed them back to their hotel and beat the shit out of them. Clive then turned to the twilight world of drugs. It seemed harmless at first. Just the occasional snort of Harpic, but this escalated and he soon reached the stage that he couldn't reach the stage without massive injections of Fairy Snow and Jeyes Fluid. In October of 1977 they got on what they thought was a Laker flight to Washington and found themselves in Amsterdam. This album was recorded immediately after their arrival. Despite their personal problems, their inherent wisdom and decency shine through once again. Will they ever work together again? Can they resolve their artistic differences? Has stardom claimed two more victims? We may never know. Derek collapsed after the recording and Clive was last seen at a crematorium asking to be burnt alive and have his ashes scattered over Gracie Fields.

Come Again was released on 18 November 1977. On 13 November, Peter and Dudley left the country, ostensibly to perform at a private function in Bermuda but also, as Peter admitted, in his column in the *Daily Mail*, to avoid any awkward questions about the record from the press. 'It is my belief that I was drugged by an employee of the notorious Virgin Record Company,' he wrote. 'Dudley claims to have no memory of having made the record at all. The last thing he remembers is that somebody handed him a walnut whirl.' [17] Peter was adept at parodying the po-faced indignation of the papers. 'I have listened to this disgusting record with genuine shock and horror. It is nothing but a stream of obscenities about unpleasant subjects,' he wrote. 'A learned Australian journalist who had heard the tapes had counted that there were 144 [Fucks] and 89 [Cunts] in the space of 60 minutes.' [18] Yet the objections didn't just come from journalists. After 40,000 copies had been sent to record shops, CBS decided to suspend distribution, having been advised that they'd be jointly liable if the LP was prosecuted for obscenity. EMI, Boots and WHSmith all refused to stock it. Undeterred, Virgin reps hawked the album round the stores themselves. Helpful publicity was provided by a practical joker at a mail-order company, who put 700 cassette tapes of *Come Again* into cases for *Black Beauty*, and 700 *Black Beauty* tapes into cassette cases for *Come Again*. The record reached number twelve in the album charts and grossed £100,000 in its first few months. Branson's Virgin Records duly commissioned a third album for the following year.

On his return from Bermuda, Peter turned forty. Judy gave him a skateboard for his birthday, which he loved. She threw a big birthday party for him at Perrins Walk with neighbours, friends and family plus a few celebs like Barry Humphries. Peter was in great form. He didn't overdo it. He'd cut back on his drinking, and things were better with Judy. However, work was another matter. On his fortieth birthday he phoned the *Daily Mail* and axed his weekly column. This was a shame. 'Monday Morning Feeling' was popular, and getting better all the time. The *Mail* were sorry to see it go. Crucially, it was something that Peter could do without Dudley. Dudley had agreed to do the third Derek & Clive album with Peter, but that was all.

A week after Peter's fortieth birthday, Judy gave a (very) frank interview to the *Daily Mail* about the ups and downs of her marriage. She told the paper she'd had an abortion. She talked in some detail about their quarrels. 'I had bronchitis recently. I was really ghastly, so I moved to the spare room and crawled into the bed. He came and shouted into my ear that if I was set on this course I had better pack all my things and be gone. I think Peter has some bitterness against women. One day he reduced me to silence for three days.' [19]

While Peter was skateboarding around Hampstead, Dudley was filming in San Francisco. After a year killing time, practising the piano in his garage, he'd finally landed a role in a US feature film. Chevy Chase had become a big star in *Saturday Night Live* and had been offered his first motion picture, called *Foul Play*. Chase was a fan of Peter and Dudley's work (particularly *Bedazzled*) and had worked with them the year before when they'd appeared on *Saturday Night*

Live. He liked Peter's performance, but he liked Dudley's even more. Chase phoned Dudley's American agent, Lou Pitt. 'I may be shooting myself in the foot,' said Chase, 'but I just have to have Dudley play a part.' [20] Dudley was suitably flattered, but once he'd read the script he turned it down. 'I thought it was bloody awful,' [21] he said.

Foul Play was a light romantic comedy and Dudley's part was only a cameo, playing a randy nincompoop – the sort of typecasting he wanted to put behind him. The film's director, Colin Higgins (who'd written the screenplay for *Harold and Maude*) asked him to reconsider, but Dudley wasn't swayed. Only when Higgins beefed up the part, rewriting Dudley's character as a conductor, did Dudley finally say yes. It was still only a supporting role, and Dudley was still uncertain. 'I didn't want to play another oversexed, undersized twit,' [22] he said. He was unhappy with his performance, but he did a very good job indeed. He only had three scenes but he sparkled in all of them, in his inept pursuit of the film's romantic lead, Goldie Hawn. 'He was one of the funniest people I've ever worked with,' [23] said Hawn. Chase was equally enthusiastic. 'I learned more from him than I'll ever know,' [24] he said. The contrast with *The Hound of The Baskervilles* could hardly have been more stark. Peter and Dudley's film was scheduled for release in April 1978. Fortunately for Dudley's Hollywood career, it was delayed until the autumn. Peter told journalists it had been postponed because of the World Cup. Valiantly, he continued to talk it up. 'The script was guided by celestial messages from Conan Doyle,' said Peter. 'There was many a table-tapping session in which he sent down his revisions of the errors he had made in the original. So this is the first really authentic version.' [25] Unfortunately, his jokes about the movie were funnier than anything in the actual film.

*

Foul Play premiered in San Francisco in July. It was a huge hit, taking over $70 million at the box office. Dudley was nominated for a Golden Globe. Yet his private life was still turbulent – he'd separated from Tuesday, though it would be three years before they divorced. Dudley sought consolation in group therapy, a marked contrast to his traditional one-to-one sessions with a shrink. 'We sit in a circle and just chat,' he said. 'We have a couple of film actresses, an architect, a script supervisor, a film director, a novelist and one total non-achiever who happens to be very rich. When I get weighed down by the gravity of the whole thing, I make the odd joke. Then there's the therapist who listens to us and takes the money.' [26] The film director was Blake Edwards, the man who would make Dudley a Hollywood star. This group-therapy session was the most important audition of Dudley's career.

Edwards was a man who understood the ups and downs of moviemaking. He'd directed classics like *Breakfast At Tiffany's*. He'd also had his fair share of flops. Unhappy with the way MGM had cut his film *The Carey Treatment*, he'd left Hollywood for Europe, where he'd revived Peter Sellers's career in the Pink Panther films. He'd admired Dudley from afar ever since *Bedazzled*. They'd met at a Hollywood party – Moore was doing a party piece about how people from different countries throw up – and they'd bonded during group therapy. Dudley was honest and amusing. Edwards liked what he saw. He also saw how much Dudley appealed to women in the group. He asked Dudley if he'd like to star in a series of films as The Ferret, a sort of espionage version of The Pink Panther, with Dudley as an inept spy. Dudley was delighted. He signed a contract for five movies. His Hollywood future seemed assured. There was just one thing. He couldn't start straight away. Edwards was already committed to another film, a romantic comedy called *10*, starring his wife, Julie Andrews, and George Segal. Dudley also had an outstanding commitment, his final obligation to Peter. In September he flew to London to record their third and final Derek & Clive LP, *Ad Nauseam*.

Dudley and Bo Derek in *10*.

CHAPTER TWENTY FIVE

10

PETER COOK:	There are storms. There are tantrums.
DUDLEY MOORE:	It's like a marriage.
MICHAEL PARKINSON:	How is it like a marriage?
PETER COOK:	We're getting divorced. [1]

The Hound of The Baskervilles was finally released in November 1978. The reviews were predictably awful. Barry Took called it one of the worst movies ever made. The punters voted with their feet. Fortunately for Dudley, the US release was delayed until further notice – it didn't reach American cinemas until 1980. Peter and Dudley went on *Parkinson* to promote the film and rounded off their appearance with a rendition of 'Goodbyee'. No one knew they were saying goodbye for good. *The Hound of The Baskervilles* had been their final shot. *Ad Nauseam* was their requiem. They never worked together again.

That autumn, Dudley finally got the big break that he'd been waiting for. Back in LA, the star of *10*, George Segal, had walked out. Orion Pictures sued Segal for damages. Segal countersued. Edwards had a cast and crew ready to roll and no leading man. He thought back to his group-therapy sessions with Dudley. 'There were so many things in his character that coincided with the character in *10*,' [2] said Edwards. He decided to offer Dudley the role. Dudley was in Dagenham, staying with his mum. Edwards sent the script to Dudley's agent, Lou Pitt. Pitt read it. He loved it. He called Dudley in London and told him he should do it. Dudley flew back to LA a few days later and said yes.

For Dudley it was a huge stroke of luck, catapulting him into the leading role in a major motion picture, a job he would have found extremely hard to get in normal circumstances, even with Edwards on his side. A Californian comedy of sexual manners about a menopausal man searching for the perfect woman, it was the perfect theme for Dudley – and his character, George Webber, was a perfect fit. Webber was a pianist and composer. He lived in a beachfront house in Malibu. He was even in psychoanalysis. It was hard to believe that the role wasn't written with Dudley in mind. '*10* really seemed to mirror my life,' he said. 'I didn't have to put on a voice or a funny walk, which I had always done in my other work.' [3] It was the kind of role he'd always wanted. He didn't have to get into character. He already *was* the character. Dudley told Edwards he wanted to play Webber dead straight.

Edwards directed Dudley with a light touch, letting him find his own way rather than talking him through every scene. He let Dudley play around with the dialogue, tweaking the colloquialisms in the script to suit him. His trust and tact paid off. Dudley regarded Edwards as the finest director he'd ever worked with, and Edwards teased out the finest performance of Dudley's film career. Dudley got along very well with Julie Andrews and Bo Derek (the 10/10 beauty of the title) and, as the shoot moved on to Acapulco and Hawaii, word began to get around that his performance was something special. From the beach to the bedroom, Dudley was a revelation, tackling everything from romance to knockabout with the same naturalistic charm. He knew how to be sincere. He knew how to get a laugh. He'd always been able to light up a theatre, or a TV studio, or a private party. Now, playing a libidinous musician on the brink of middle age, he'd finally found a way to project his puckish personality onto the big screen. He inhabited the part completely. It was impossible to imagine anyone else in the role.

Made before the onset of AIDS, against a backdrop of swingers in flares and mirrored shades, *10* was a Hollywood homage to late-1970s LA. A last waltz before the uptight 1980s, it captured the spirit of the age and became a worldwide hit – not least in Britain, where its West Coast hedonism felt like an exotic honeymoon after the Winter of Discontent. Bo Derek gave the movie sex appeal, Julie Andrews made it feel respectable despite its racy subject matter, and Dudley's warmth and humour gave it a funny, feel-good glow. *10* grossed $60 million from a $6 million budget. For Dudley, the only downside was that his $100,000 flat fee didn't include any share of future profits. But at the time that hardly mattered. His career prospects were transformed. A short, club-footed, forty-something comedian from Dagenham had suddenly become America's most unlikely sex symbol. The Hollywood Women's Press Club gave him their Golden Apple award for Male Discovery of the Year, ahead of Richard Gere. 'I wasn't surprised,' said Alan Bennett. 'My only surprise was that they hadn't got onto him sooner.' [4] Making a mark in his own right meant a lot to Dudley. 'He was always the second banana to Peter,' said Lou Pitt. 'Being accepted as a leading man all of a sudden was something I think he relished and cherished.' [5] What was more, he'd done it playing a realistic character rather than a sketch-show caricature. His decision to break up with Peter had been vindicated. He was his own man at last.

Back in Britain, watching Dudley metamorphose from stooge to superstar, Peter inevitably had mixed feelings. He would have been useless in a romcom like *10* – George Webber was the last role on Earth he could have played – yet he would have been less than human if Dudley's achievement hadn't rankled. Was he jealous? Who wouldn't be? Probably the best people to judge were Jonathan Miller and Alan Bennett, who'd become famous with Peter and Dudley in America a decade earlier. But even they couldn't quite agree. 'Peter wanted to be a movie star and envied Dudley that particular success,' [6] said Miller. 'He wanted to be a showbiz celebrity. It really mattered to him a great deal.' [7] Bennett didn't think that Peter resented Dudley's success, but he said that, of the four of them, Peter was the only one who really wanted to be famous. In a way, they were both right. Peter wanted fame, but on his own terms, not Dudley's. 'There's fame like Charles Manson and there's fame like Dudley,' he said. 'There has to be something between the two.' [8]

Virtually anyone who's seen a friend or business partner move on to bigger (though not necessarily better) things tends to feel a complex mixture of pride, admiration and sour grapes, and Peter was no exception. While Dudley was filming *10*, Peter stayed in touch. After it came out he didn't contact Dudley to congratulate him. He never even mentioned the film to him again.

'He must have been jealous,' said Dudley. 'He never said a word about any of my films – never even said he'd seen them.' [9] More than anything, however, Peter was simply saddened. He missed Dudley, he regretted the way things had gone awry and, although he still hoped they'd get back together, he could see that the more successful Dudley became in LA, the less likely that was to happen. Ironically, it was Lou Pitt, the architect of Dudley's Hollywood success, who put it best. 'The two of them spent a lot of time together, they wrote an awful lot of material, they made albums, so you get to know somebody really, really well,' said Pitt, 'so I'm sure he was disappointed and hurt.' [10]

The papers did their best to stoke it up. In public, for the most part, Peter remained polite. 'Of course I miss him,' he told the *Sun*. 'I'm really very fond of the little sod.' Indeed, while Dudley was filming *10*, he'd missed him so much that he'd even phoned his mother, Ada, in Dagenham, for a chat. But that was before the film came out. Afterwards, behind closed doors, at *Private Eye*, Peter was far more frank. 'It doesn't matter how much therapy Dudley goes to, how many psychiatrists he sees,' said Peter. 'He'll still be short and thick.' [11] 'He was cut up about Dudley's success,' said the *Eye*'s editor Richard Ingrams. 'He started talking about him in a disparaging way – calling him a deformed dwarf. There's no doubt that one of Peter's fantasies was to have been a Hollywood film star. It must have been very galling to him when Dudley succeeded. He was supposed to be the glamorous one of the two. Dudley was this comic figure from Dagenham. If you'd said, which of these two men is going to be a Hollywood sex symbol, we'd all have said Peter – and it didn't turn out like that.' [12]

Despite his public protestations to the contrary, Peter still had ambitions of his own, and Dudley's achievements, in whatever field, were bound to make his own setbacks more frustrating. After Dudley's departure to LA, Peter had been brilliant as the misanthropic host of ITV's new-wave music show, *Revolver*. Playing a grumpy nightclub proprietor, he'd poured scorn on the acts and the audience alike. The audience returned the compliment, treating Peter like a pantomime villain. This clever conceit worked a treat. It was a refreshing antidote to the cheesy DJs on *Top of The Pops*, who looked increasingly ridiculous introducing the punk bands who were storming the Top Forty. *Revolver* was the ideal forum for punk rock and Peter was the ideal host, yet the show was slammed by clueless TV critics, shunted around the schedules and terminated after seven weeks.

Plainly, Peter and Dudley's partnership was over. Yet a letter that Peter wrote to Dudley revealed that he was still in denial about Dudley's decision to bring down the curtain on their double act. 'When we manage to do another series,' wrote Peter, 'your mother should become a regular along with Dud and Pete. I don't want to press you when things are obviously going so well for you in the States. I like to think that when you become "hot" and "enormous" it will make it easier for us to do a decent movie together.' [13] It was hard to tell which of these two notions was more fanciful – that they'd ever do another TV series, or that they'd ever make another film. In 1978, in 1979 and again in 1980, Peter contacted the BBC to set up a fourth series of *Not Only ... But Also*. The press lapped it up, but none of these announcements had any substance. On none of these occasions had Dudley agreed to anything, so the fourth series never went ahead. If anything, the idea that they might make another film together was even more misguided. The contrasting fortunes of *10* and *The Hound of The Baskervilles* was proof enough that Dudley's future as a film star lay as far away from Peter as possible.

Written before *10* came out, Peter's heartfelt letter was full of affection for his former partner, stressing the similarities they shared and the ways in which Dudley had once followed his lead. 'I worry, you worry,' he wrote. 'I move to Hampstead, you move to Hampstead – I get divorced, you get divorced.' [14] Yet the creative gulf between them was underlined by Peter's optimistic assurances about *Derek & Clive Get The Horn*, the ill-conceived film of their fractious *Ad Nauseam* recording sessions, which Peter had arranged without Dudley's prior knowledge or consent. 'It works really well visually,' wrote Peter. 'Some of the stuff in the control room is hilarious.' [15] In fact, the film's visual appeal was virtually non-existent, and the sequences in the control room were particularly unfunny and unpleasant. Dudley had hated making *Ad Nauseam*. He hated the film even more. He didn't want it to be shown at all, and subsequently managed to block its release in the States. Not that there was much demand for *Derek & Clive Get The Horn* Stateside. 'Dudley wasn't too keen on it being released in America,' said Peter, 'but then America wasn't too keen on it being released there either.' [16] The LP of *Ad Nauseam* was released without any (helpful) controversy, and was met with a muted chorus of bewilderment and disappointment. In the *Sunday Times*, Stephen Pile said it went 'beyond humour or satire into abuse and cruelty'. 'Pete and Dud are settling for out-takes,' wrote Brian Case in the *Melody Maker*. 'Fine minds at the end of their tether,' was his verdict. It was hard to disagree.

As Dudley vanished into superstardom, Peter's futile attempts to bring out *Derek & Clive Get The Horn* toppled over into farce. First, the film was denied a certificate by the British Board of Film Censors. 'The point of this comic exercise is to be as offensive as possible, and to break every taboo the performers can think of, however outrageous,' wrote the board's James Ferman in a letter to the producers. 'Cutting would be pointless, although we believe that the sequence about Jesus Christ and the sexuality of the lower half of his body is probably blasphemous in the legal sense of the term. If this is so then this brief scene would have to be cut. The offensive references to the Pope and the Holocaust are not, in our view, illegal, though they will certainly prove deeply offensive to some people.' Undeterred, Peter pressed ahead with a video release, but several hundred copies were seized by James Anderton, the pious Chief Constable of Greater Manchester, and distribution was delayed while the legal process took its course. With no sales coming in to cover its costs, the distribution company went bust. All unsold copies of *Derek & Clive Get The Horn* were impounded as assets. Peter and Dudley's final film disappeared from public view until 1993. Its belated premiere would be their epilogue, but that was thirteen years away.

CHAPTER TWENTY SIX

THE TWO OF US

DAVID DIMBLEBY: That's all come to an end, your relationship with Dudley?

PETER COOK: No, his number-one priority at the moment is to make films, but there is no actual end to our partnership. We'd both like to do a series over here. We will, fairly soon, I hope. [1]

While Dudley seduced America, Peter finally confronted his drink problem. With Judy's encouragement and support, he joined the Hampstead branch of Alcoholics Anonymous. Friends like Alan Bennett feared he'd be unable to take the meetings seriously but, heroically, he remained teetotal for a year. But at the start of 1979 he started drinking again – Judy couldn't work out what triggered it – and his home life deteriorated rapidly. In March, Judy was granted an injunction, on grounds of mental cruelty, to stop Peter entering the spare bedroom where she was sleeping. No sooner had she returned home from court than the phone rang. It was a reporter. Someone had leaked the details to the *Sun*. The next morning the story was all over the papers, and for the next week or so the press besieged their house. Thankfully, for Peter it was a wake-up call. He started to get his life back together. He went back on the wagon, and his relationship with Judy and his work improved.

In June Peter appeared at *The Secret Policeman's Ball*, an Amnesty International benefit at Her Majesty's Theatre, in London, and brought the house down with a masterpiece of satirical invective called 'Entirely A Matter For You'. The week before, the leader of the Liberal Party, Jeremy Thorpe, and three others had been acquitted of all charges that they'd conspired to murder Norman Scott, a former male model who'd claimed to have had a homosexual relationship with Thorpe – a claim that Thorpe denied. In his summing-up, the judge, the Honourable Mr Justice Cantley, called Scott a 'sponger'. He called the chief prosecution witness a 'humbug'. He called Andrew Newton, who claimed he'd been hired to murder Scott, 'a chump'. 'The judge took it upon himself to destroy the good character of these three key witnesses,' [2] wrote Peter's *Private Eye* colleague Auberon Waugh. Peter delivered a merciless lampoon of Cantley's summing-up:

We have been forced to listen to the pitiful whining of Mr
Norma St John Scott – a scrounger, a parasite, a pervert, a
worm, a self-confessed player of the pink oboe, a man or woman
who by his or her own admission chews pillows. It would be
hard to imagine, ladies and gentlemen of the jury, a more
discredited and embittered man, a more unreliable witness
upon whose testimony to convict a man who you may rightly
think should have become Prime Minister of his country or
president of the world ... You will probably have noticed that
three of the defendants have very wisely chosen to exercise
their inalienable right not to go into the witness box to answer
a lot of impertinent questions. I will merely say that you are not

to infer from this anything other than that they consider the evidence against them so flimsy that it was scarcely worth their while to rise from their seats and waste their breath denying these ludicrous charge ... You are now to retire, as indeed should I, carefully to consider your verdict of Not Guilty.

It was a virtuoso display, as good as 'TVPM' or anything else in *Beyond The Fringe*. It showed that Peter could still do it, when he really wanted to, with Dudley or without him. Yet despite his hopeful announcements about their future plans, even Peter began to realise that it would have to be without him. In October Dudley flew to Britain to make a guest appearance on *The Muppet Show* and flew back to America without seeing Peter. In November, he began shooting a new movie, a biblical comedy called *Wholly Moses*. Doing another series of *Not Only ... But Also* was clearly the furthest thing from his mind. In Dudley's continued absence Peter started working on a one-hour TV special of his own, for London Weekend Television. It was a tacit acceptance that his other half wouldn't be coming back any time soon.

'Entirely A Matter For You' had given Peter a much needed fillip. Priggishly, the sketch was cut from ITV's Christmas broadcast of *The Secret Policeman's Ball* but it was released as a record and featured in a successful cinematic film of the live show, which went out the following year. Still teetotal, with his career and his marriage in better shape, Peter could see that his excesses of the past few years had been hard on those around him. 'I've made many, many mistakes,' he said. 'I know I've been destructive. What I do reflects the idiocy and chaos within myself.'[3] It was a brutally honest self-assessment, which boded well for the future. 'I do worry about what people think,'

431

he added. 'I don't want to be disliked. It's just that sometimes I put my foot in it.' [4] In February 1980 he flew to Los Angeles. Ostensibly, he was accepting an invitation from CBS to appear in a benefit show for Cambodian refugees. Actually, he was going to look for work.

Peter's visit to Los Angeles, in the footsteps of his former partner, began with an incident so symbolic of their divergent fortunes that even a Hollywood screenwriter might have been embarrassed to invent it. Landing in LA, Peter took a taxi into town and ended up in an awful traffic jam. Eventually the cab driver got out and went to see what had caused the trouble, leaving Peter in the cab. After a while he returned, agog, eager to tell Peter the reason for the gridlock. 'You'll never believe this,' said the star-struck cabbie. 'It's Dudley Moore up there!' [5]

LA was Dudley's town now, not Peter's and the papers weren't afraid to ask Peter all the usual leading questions. 'Yes, I would like to be a sex symbol,' he told the press, when Dudley's name came up. 'Who wouldn't?' [6] However, the part he landed wasn't that of a sex symbol but as a middle-aged butler in an American remake of a British sitcom called *Two's Company*.

Two's Company had enjoyed a successful run on ITV, running for four series from 1975 to 1979. It was about an American writer, played by Elaine Stritch, who hires an English butler to run her house in Chelsea. CBS had relocated the sitcom to America, with the butler as the foreigner rather than his boss. Renamed *The Two of Us*, the part first played by Stritch was rewritten for a younger woman – a glamorous chat-show host rather than a boring old writer. Peter was cast as her butler, a part originally played by Donald Sinden. Sinden probably would have done a better job, but in a part that didn't do too much to test his limitations as an actor Peter just about held his own. He still seemed aloof and awkward, but at least this time his character was *supposed* to be aloof and awkward. It was an imperfect fit, but it was close enough for him to busk it. 'This is not acting,' he said. 'I'm just being English. I don't have to dredge deep within my resources to be sardonic.'[7] CBS were happy with Peter's performance in the pilot – fortunately, Peter's mannered style seemed to fit their idea of what an English butler ought to be like. Peter was invited to return for more shooting in the autumn, once CBS had found a suitable co-star.

Peter spent the summer working on his LWT special for ITV. Sobriety had given him a new lease of life. 'I didn't have a drink problem,' he said, 'but a couple of years ago the doctor said that my liver was fine, but it could do with a rest. At first I thought I would give up drink for six months, but now I've become quite happy without it.'[8] Now that he'd dried out, the boozy notoriety of Derek & Clive had become a source of some regret. 'I make a couple of records and suddenly I'm supposed to swear wherever I go,' he said. 'It's got to the stage where people come up to me and say, "Peter Cook, isn't it? You're the one who goes [fuck] this and [fuck] that." It really isn't me at all.[9] There is a whole generation now who can only identify me with the "foul-mouthed" Derek & Clive records. I want to put that right.'[10]

Peter's LWT special steered away from Derek & Clive, harking back to the surreal world of E.L. Wisty, the world he'd inhabited before he'd teamed up with Dudley. Even the title, *Peter Cook & Co*, was tacit confirmation that Dudley was gone for good. Supported by an impressive cast, including Rowan Atkinson, John Cleese, Terry Jones and Beryl Reid, the show was a success. But although the sketches were entertaining, there was something missing. That something was Dudley, of course. Comedians like Cleese and Atkinson were too quirky for Peter's oblique comedy. Ordinary actors were too bland. Peter needed someone midway between a comic and a straight man to support him. Only Dudley's subtle stewardship could make his humour sing. Nevertheless, as the *Daily Mail* said, it was 'twice as fresh and twice as funny as the usual jaded junk.' The show did even better in the States, winning several awards. LWT offered Peter a series. Unfortunately he opted to return to America to do *The Two of Us*. Naturally, the money was tempting, but that was only part of it. As Cleese said, 'He started doing a number of things that were really to do with competing with Dudley rather than continuing to do what he was best at.' [11]

Dudley, meanwhile, had endured his first Hollywood setback when *Wholly Moses* flopped, inciting the righteous ire of various Jewish organisations in the process. 'I turned it down twice but allowed myself to be flattered into it,' [12] said Dudley. 'It is a piece of crap.' [13] But he soon bounced back. After a costly separation from Tuesday ('I love her and she loves me but we can't live together,' [14] he said) he got together with the American actress and model Susan Anton – one of the most important relationships of his life. She was blonde, slim, beautiful – and fifteen years his junior. She was almost as tall as Peter. 'A woman's height is all in the legs,' he said. 'Our bodies are about the same size.' [15] Invigorated by this new romance, Dudley started work on the most successful movie of his career.

At first glance, *Arthur* seemed a most unlikely prospect. The tale of a spoilt, drunken millionaire who falls for an impoverished shoplifter and stands to lose his inheritance if he marries her, it had already been turned down by James Caan, Richard Dreyfuss, Jack Nicholson and Al Pacino. 'Agents kept telling me nobody wants to see a picture about a rich drunk,' [16] said the film's writer and director, Steve Gordon. He hadn't written the character as an Englishman – he'd pictured Robert Redford, Ryan O'Neal or maybe Chevy Chase in the title role. 'Redford and the rest never read it,' said Gordon. 'Then I got a call to say Dudley had read it and liked it.' [17]

In Dudley, Gordon had found the one man who could make his hero lovable and believable. Dudley understood *Arthur* right from the start. 'I've just got to do this,' he told Lou Pitt, when he read the script. 'Who do I have to sleep with?' [18] He told his mother it was the funniest script he'd ever read. Dudley met Gordon over breakfast in the Polo Lounge of the Beverly Hills Hotel. He told Gordon he would walk out of the room and then walk back in as Arthur. That was exactly what he did. When Liza Minnelli heard that Dudley had got the part she signed up to play the female lead, having previously declined it before he was on board. The two of them hit it off, and proved a winning combination, carrying a storyline which contained a fair few duff notes. John Gielgud was cast as Dudley's English butler, at Dudley's insistence. 'I thought it was rather a smutty and a vulgar little film,' [19] said Gielgud. He initially refused it, and only came on board when the producers bumped up his fee. His participation proved crucial. His wit and gravitas transformed Arthur into a contemporary fairy tale.

In January 1981, Peter returned to Los Angeles to resume shooting *The Two of Us*. By now he'd been off the booze for nearly two years but Judy and his AA friends were anxious about what might happen to him, so far away from his support group. Rather than checking into a hotel, he stayed with the actress Brenda Vaccaro, a good friend. By now, pirate copies of *Derek & Clive Get The Horn* were knocking around LA – much like the pirate copies of *Derek & Clive (Live)* a few years earlier – and Vaccaro threw a Derek & Clive party in Peter's honour, with a special screening of the film. She invited all sorts of people including members of *Monty Python* – and Dudley. Despite Dudley's objections to releasing *Derek & Clive Get The Horn* on a commercial basis, he wasn't bothered about it being seen in private, and he was glad to see Peter. 'Dudley was so happy and proud to see him in such great condition, ready to go to work,' said Vaccaro. 'They were like brothers. There was a tremendous kindness between them – but more from Dudley, I think.' [20]

Peter's attitude to *The Two of Us* was paradoxical. Like all great English amateurs, he didn't want to look as if he'd been trying too hard. He told the press that he'd been offered the role while he was on holiday. He said he'd done the pilot never believing it would become a series. He said he hoped it would be cancelled after a few months so that he could go home to see his wife and daughters. On a personal level, this was quite true – Peter had no desire to spend the next five years in LA – but, on a professional level, he still wanted *The Two of Us* to succeed. 'He really wanted to make that work,' said Dick Clement, who went on from producing the second series of *Not Only ... But Also* to forge a successful career in Hollywood. 'I think he wanted success in America because Dudley had it.' [21] Initially, it looked as if Peter's professional hopes (and personal fears) would be fulfilled. He made two more pilots with two different co-stars. Mimi Kennedy was selected from the second one, and they shot four episodes together. These were broadcast in April, attracting a weekly audience of 30 million and great reviews. Twenty-four episodes were scheduled for the autumn. Peter flew home to Judy for the summer, ready to return to LA in the autumn.

While Peter was back in Britain, *Arthur* opened in America. The reviews were very mixed. Yet although the critics had reservations about the film itself, they were full of praise for Dudley. 'One of the things that makes it all work so well is Moore,' wrote the *Hollywood Reporter*. 'His great sense of comedy, including impeccable timing on delivery and reaction, gives the picture its momentum and style.' 'His timing is magical,' agreed the *New York Times*. 'Gordon's pacing is ragged, he has a pretty feeble sense of structure,' wrote the *New Yorker*. 'Considering that *Arthur* is a very thin comic construct, Moore does an amazing amount with the role.' 'The film is a gaudy, semi-precious setting with two crown jewels at its centre,' wrote the *Village Voice*. Those two jewels were John Gielgud and Dudley Moore. For Dudley, in only his third leading role, it was a critical triumph, but the box-office response exceeded all expectations. Audiences loved it. The film made more than $100 million. Dudley had been elevated from showbiz aristocracy to showbiz royalty.

Peter returned to Los Angeles in the autumn, as planned, to shoot the first series of *The Two of Us*. Fleet Street journalist Paul Callan was on assignment in Hollywood, and when he learned that Peter and Dudley were living a few miles apart he persuaded them to meet up at the Beverly Hills Hotel to do an impromptu session as Pete & Dud for the readers of the *Daily Mirror*. He even provided raincoats and flat caps, so that the *Mirror* photographer could get some pictures of them in costume. They ended up doing an impromptu update of their first ever Pete & Dud sketch, 'Film Stars', with Brooke Shields and Dolly Parton replacing Betty Grable and Greta Garbo. Yet beneath the laughter there was further proof that the balance of power had shifted, irrevocably, in Dudley's favour. It used to be Dud who asked the questions. Now it was Pete:

PETE: What aspects of the thespian arts are you
         currently engaged in, Dud? Or, to put it another
         way, what is a small, stunted, ugly Dagenham git
         like you doing here in the living temple to the
         likes of Gloria Swanson, Mary Pickford, Rudolph
         Valentino and Fatty Arbuckle?

DUD: I'm glad you asked me that question. I'm filling
         out my time being a multimillionaire, having
         earned a bit of pocket money for jumping up and
         down on top of Bo Derek in a film called *10* to the
         music of some bloke called Bolero.' [22]

The 'servile little creep' of *Not Only ... But Also* was no more. Their appearance in the bar of the Beverly Hills Hotel prompted a round of applause from the other drinkers. However, the applause was all for Dudley. 'They had no idea who Cook was – and he took it badly,' [23] wrote Callan.

For Peter, there were more misfortunes to come. In November London Weekend Television broadcast a tribute to Dudley on ITV. Dudley was in London at the time and Peter was still stuck in LA, so LWT set up a live satellite link and arranged for Peter to appear at the start of the programme, as a prelude to this cavalcade of adoration. 'Hollywood's newest screen sensation,' cooed the announcer. 'From humble beginnings in his home town of Dagenham he's stepped out to conquer the world of entertainment. Musician, composer, comedian and now international superstar, will you please welcome Mr Dudley Moore!' At the end of this sycophantic introduction, Peter was supposed to do a short piece to camera. He started bang on cue, describing Jayne Mansfield's aquatic complications with a starfish. But back in London the Dagenham Girl Pipers were waiting in the wings, eager to begin their march past. Someone on the studio floor cued them in too early, while Peter was still talking, and they made their noisy entrance to rapturous applause, rendering Peter utterly inaudible. The director had to cut him off in mid-flow and continue the show without him.

The first (and last) series of *The Two of Us* never matched the popularity of its spring previews. Having reached number four in the ratings back in April, it never even re-entered the top twenty. By Christmas it had dropped out of the top forty. Dudley put his finger on the problem. 'The trouble was, Peter was apologising all the time for being here, and it showed in his work,' [24] he said. Dudley loved America, and America returned the compliment. Peter, on the other hand, found many aspects of US life (especially Hollywood life) ridiculous. 'People are only interested in what you are doing, and they are always lying about what they are doing,' he said. 'The people who work on films go to bed early so they'll look good for early call in the morning. And those out of work don't go out in case anybody accuses them of not working.' [25] Even hiding behind a character who was supposed to share his contempt for Americana, you could tell that his heart wasn't in it.

Peter was working fifty hours a week, and this time he was alone in a hotel room. Tired and disillusioned, he flew back to England for Christmas. A chauffeur met him at Heathrow and drove him straight down to Judy's new home in Somerset. When he arrived he was completely pissed. He'd been drinking since he got on the plane in LA. Valiantly, he remained sober throughout his four-day stay (Judy kept no booze in the house) and then flew back to America. Yet there was no saving *The Two of Us*. In March the show was cancelled. In the same month Dudley was nominated for an Academy Award for best actor. It was no surprise that he didn't win (the winner, Henry Fonda,[26] was dying, and had never won an Oscar) but for Dudley, a relative newcomer, even a nomination was a huge accolade. In 1965 Peter had predicted that his partner would end up as 'Dudley Moore, the Cuddly Funster' playing the piano at the Edmonton Empire. Instead, he'd ended up at the Oscars, nominated for Hollywood's greatest prize. *Arthur* won two Academy Awards, one for the theme tune, 'Arthur's Song' (a suitably sentimental number, sung by Christopher Cross) and one for John Gielgud as best supporting actor. It was the cruellest of ironies. The great knight of the English stage had won an Oscar for playing Dudley's butler, at the same time that Peter's butler bit the dust. 'The star who was left behind when little Dud grew up into a giant,'[27] read the headline in the *Express*.

Returning to England, Peter's attitude to *The Two of Us* remained contradictory. On a personal level, he was happy to be out of it. He said he'd hated doing the show. He said he couldn't stand the snobbery and elitism of LA. Yet professionally, as his US agent confirmed, he was very disappointed. Implausibly, he told Clive James that he'd left of his own accord, because CBS hadn't stumped up the fee he wanted for a second series. Even more implausibly, he told friends he'd deliberately turned in a bad performance, hoping to scupper the show's chances (such a subtle act of sabotage would have been way beyond Peter's finite acting powers).

In fact, there was nothing unusual about a sitcom being cancelled after its first series, especially in America. The vast majority fall at the first few hurdles. Only a tiny minority survive. As Peter said himself, the chances of a pilot even making it to a first series were hundreds to one. *The Two of Us* had fared better than most sitcom pilots. It only looked like a failure compared to Dudley's film career. With its adult themes and X certificate, *10* had been something of a cult in Britain. *Arthur*, however, was everywhere – the must-see movie of the year. Dudley was now rated the third-biggest movie star in America, behind Clint Eastwood and Burt Reynolds. In the old days the papers had been more interested in Peter. Now they were more interested in what he had to say about Dudley.

Most of the time, Peter remained diplomatic about the man he still called his best and oldest friend. 'I'm delighted for Dudley,' he said. 'He's a brilliantly funny man and it couldn't have happened to a nicer guy.' [28] Yet after the umpteenth question, there were times when he lost his cool. 'Perhaps if I had been born with a club foot and a height problem I might have been as desperate as Dudley to become a star,' he told the *Sun*. 'That's all he ever wanted.' [29] This was said partly in jest. Peter had always taken the piss out of Dudley. 'I used to call him a club-footed dwarf and I think it was good for him,' he said. 'Everyone else used to pussyfoot around his problems.' [30] Dudley didn't see it quite that way. He'd never been entirely comfortable with Peter's ribbing. It stirred up painful memories of the bullies who used to call him 'Hopalong' at school. Peter's put-downs sounded harsher in print than they did in person, and reading them in Hollywood, where stars confined their comments about one another to bland eulogies, they seemed harsher still.

Dudley told reporters that he was upset by Peter's relentless cynicism. He called Peter to discuss it, but there was no answer. His message was not returned. 'It was a dismissive, juvenile put-down,' he retorted, when Peter's club-footed quip got back to him. 'Apart from anything else, it denies a whole area of ambition in Peter.' [31] But Peter had no ambition left. Far more revealing than any snide remark was Peter's admission that he hadn't seen *Arthur*. He'd decided to wait until it was on television, he said, but when it was shown on TV he'd decided to watch a football match on another channel instead. Maybe Peter was wise not to watch it. Years later, after Peter had finally seen the film, Peter and Dudley were together in a restaurant when they were collared by a fan. The fan asked Dudley where he'd got the inspiration for *Arthur*. Peter pointed at himself and Dudley realised he was right.

Dudley was playing himself in *Arthur*, but he was also playing Peter. When Peter and Judy saw the film, they both recognised Dudley's character. It was a role he'd played backstage, on tour, whenever Peter had been drinking. Dudley would imitate Peter, slurring his words in the way Peter did. Then it had been a private joke, a private coping strategy. Now he was sending up his former partner on the world's most public stage.

Dudley and Susan Anton.

CHAPTER TWENTY SEVEN

GET THE HORN

MAVIS NICHOLSON: Have you had a trial separation?

PETER COOK: No, an acrimonious divorce. [1]

In the summer of 1989, Dudley flew to England for his sister's sixtieth birthday. Emotionally, he was in fine fettle. Having split up with Susan Anton soon after his fiftieth birthday, he'd married for a third time, to the actress Brogan Lane. But his film career was on the wane. During the 1980s he'd made a dozen movies, for which he'd been paid a lot of money, yet none of them had matched the success of *10* or *Arthur*. A sequel, *Arthur 2 – On The Rocks*, had been a particular disappointment. The only person who liked it more than *Arthur* was Peter – or so he said.

Peter's film career had been even more undistinguished – bit parts, mainly, rather than leading roles like Dudley's. There had been a few bright moments: *Yellowbeard*, a daft pirate romp which he wrote with Graham Chapman and Bernard McKenna; *Mr Jolly Lives Next Door*, a black comedy with the Comic Strip crew, directed by Stephen Frears. Yet most of his film roles had been forgettable cameos in forgettable movies. His other work had been similarly sporadic – old sketches at benefit gigs, guest appearances on other people's programmes, but no stage show or series of his own.

Peter had been living apart from Judy since the early 1980s. She was living a peaceful rural life in the West Country, with her dogs and hens and horses. He was living a shambolic bachelor life in Perrins Walk. Visiting him at home in Hampstead, the journalist Hilary Bonner described a scene that had become typical of his daily routine. 'Peter Cook's eyes narrow as he slouches in his chair, gazing into the middle distance,' wrote Bonner. 'You're not sure if he'll tell a joke or fall asleep. He is wearing a crumpled but formal dark pin-stripe suit which seems right out of character. And soon you realise it was probably the closest garment to hand when he got out of bed.' [2]

Peter and Judy still loved each other. They talked on the telephone several times a day. They remained emotionally close, but Peter had various other girlfriends. This began to change after he met Lin Chong, an Oriental neighbour with a handicapped daughter. 'Why do you drink?' [3] she asked him. 'Despair, really,' [4] he told her. 'I just felt immensely sorry for him,' [5] she said. 'He seemed a very sad and lonely person and badly in need of a friend.' [6] At first, they were just good friends. Slowly, their relationship deepened. Slowly, she began to put his life in order. 'She's very good for me because she cares for me,' [7] said Peter, simply. Without Lin, it was quite possible that he wouldn't have lived to see fifty. She couldn't stop him drinking, but she helped him with virtually everything else.

After several years together, Lin wanted to put things on a firmer footing. 'As our relationship grew, no matter how much he said he loved me, I wasn't family,' she said. 'He said it didn't matter. But it hurt. I was not Lin Cook but Lin Chong. At the end of the day, I was looking after someone else's husband.' [8] 'If you love me enough to want to be with me all the time,' she told him, 'you have to accord me the dignity of being your wife.' [9] In 1988, Peter checked into Cedar Falls, a health farm near Judy's house in the West Country. Judy drove to Taunton station to meet his train. He'd put on a lot of weight since she'd last seen him. When he got into her car he started crying. He was drunk. Judy drove him to the health farm and helped him unpack. He was drinking from a bottle of Listerine. He had a bottle of vodka in his suitcase. He spent a week at Cedar Falls. Judy saw him every day. They still got on as well as ever, but Peter told Judy he had come to see her to get a divorce. 'Do you actually want a divorce?' [10] she asked him. 'No,' [11] he said. She said she didn't either. 'I agreed because although I still loved him, I knew I couldn't live with him and he couldn't function on his own.' [12]

In the spring of 1989 Judy arranged to go to Perrins Walk to talk through the financial settlement with Peter. On the table she saw a letter from his doctor, confirming that he had cirrhosis of the liver. In the two hours she spent with him he downed an entire bottle of vodka. It was the middle of the afternoon. On 5 April 1989 Peter and Judy were divorced. On 18 November 1989 Peter married Lin at a registry office in Torquay. He phoned Judy straight after the ceremony. 'Judes, I've just got married again,' [13] he told her. 'He didn't want me to read it in the papers first,' said Judy. 'It was typical Peter, that strange mix of sweetness and cruelty.' [14]

By the time that Peter met Lin, his relationship with Dudley had become distant. His statements about his former partner were a mixture of affection, resentment and regret. 'He's still selfish, vain and greedy – in other words, a fully rounded human being,' said Peter, nursing a ferocious hangover at home in Hampstead after a night out at Stringfellows. 'He did once complain to me that he is surrounded in Hollywood by fools and sycophants who laugh at everything he says. I reminded him that when he was living here he was surrounded by intelligent people who kept telling him what a little toad he was.' [15]

Dudley retaliated by damning Peter with faint praise. 'Cook? With a C? Who's he, then?' Dudley asked reporters, in the comfort of his MGM motor home on the set of his latest movie. 'Oh yes, Peter! I remember him. Sorry, Peter! Just joking. He says worse things about me. Much worse. It would be hard to do the sort of material I'm doing now with Peter. But we've always had a very loose arrangement. We've collided with each other from time to time to do various things and I'm sure we will again.' [16] Yet Dudley knew full well that this 'loose arrangement' had changed. Both of them had tried to make it on their own. Peter had failed. Dudley had succeeded. When Dudley came to London now he made no attempt to meet up with Peter. He flew in and flew out again, without contacting him. When pressed, he played down the prospect of them working together again. He said he found making films more satisfying than doing sketches. 'We're a little shifty with each other now,' he said. 'I don't know if we could ever go back to what we were before.' [17]

Lin could see how much Peter missed Dudley, and in 1986 she arranged a reconciliation. Ironically, it took place against the backdrop of the most humiliating assignment of Peter's career. The BBC had asked the American comedienne Joan Rivers to host her own talk show in Britain. She said she'd do it if Peter would be her 'second banana'. This was a familiar feature of US talk shows – a sort of straight man who has a brief chat with the host at the start of every episode, then sits in on the interviews, chipping in with the odd question or the occasional quip. It was a strictly subordinate role, requiring virtually no creative input beyond the ability to make harmless small talk. It was a job for someone who knew their place, who was happy to speak when they were spoken to and didn't mind playing second fiddle. It was completely wrong for Peter, but the BBC wanted Rivers and Rivers wanted Peter. With nothing else on the horizon, he said yes.

It might have worked if Rivers and Peter had been bosom pals, but Peter hardly knew her, and had no real chance to get to know her. To make matters even worse, the role of second banana was entirely unfamiliar in the UK. Consequently, the producers allowed insufficient time for Peter's backchat at the beginning of the show, and the viewers had no idea what he was doing there. Neither did Peter. While Rivers did her spiel, and the star guests came and went, he sat on the sofa and said next to nothing. Most of the Rivers guests ignored him, but Bernard Manning wasn't scared to stick the boot in. 'You used to be very funny,' he told Peter. 'He can't remember his lines,' he added, straight to camera. 'I work every night.'

The critics were even more unforgiving. The London *Daily News* called Peter 'a man with a great future behind him.' It was terribly unfair. When he'd fronted his own chat show, Peter's problems had been of his own making. Here, he'd done nothing wrong. There was nothing he could do. 'I was there to help Joan out if she got into trouble but she never thought she was in trouble, so I never helped her out,' [18] he said. It would have been bad enough for anyone, but to see the most inventive and influential comic of the 1960s reduced to a waxwork on a chat-show sofa was truly tragic. To make matters even worse, one of Joan's star guests was Dudley.

Thankfully, Dudley's visit gave Lin the opportunity for some deft diplomacy. She went to see him at Claridge's and told him how much Peter loved him. Shy and sincere, with none of Peter's acerbic humour, she was the ideal peacemaker. Peter and Dudley met up and got on well. Some of the old magic was still there. Later that year, when Dudley was the surprise subject of *This Is Your Life* – a rare return performance, filmed this time in America – Peter contributed a courteous tribute via satellite. It was a magnanimous gesture, after Dudley's first appearance on the programme had scuppered the dress rehearsal of *Behind The Fridge*. The guest list for the show underlined how far the focus of Dudley's life had shifted. When Dudley first appeared on *This Is Your Life* in 1973, most of the guests had been British. In 1987, they were mainly American: Chevy Chase, Bo Derek, Kenny Rogers, Robin Williams ... It was another indication that Dudley had left Britain (and Peter) far behind. In 1987, when Peter and Dudley performed together for the first time in more than ten years, it was in Los Angeles, not in London. Peter and Lin flew out to LA for a TV special in aid of Comic Relief. Peter and Dudley did 'One Leg Too Few', and afterwards they went out to dinner with Lin and Brogan. Peter apologised to Dudley for being so rude to him. After the froideur of the early 1980s, they were back on friendly terms.

However, friendship was one thing. Work was another matter. Peter was forever telling journalists that he'd love to work with Dudley again. When journalists asked Dudley the same question, he was positive but vague. 'We could work with each other tomorrow,' said Dudley. 'All one of us has to do is pick up the phone.' [19] Suitably encouraged, Alexander Cohen brought Peter and Dudley together to discuss the idea of a new stage show, but Dudley turned him down flat. 'I can't do it and I won't do it,' [20] he told Cohen. All he'd consider was the odd interview or charity show. He had no intention of working with Peter on anything else. He left a message on Peter's answerphone, telling him to focus on his own work rather than squandering his talent. Peter never mentioned the message to him. In 1988 Peter was interviewed by *Vanity Fair* for a profile of Dudley and made some disparaging (though very amusing) remarks about Dudley's new wife, Brogan. He said her home with Dudley was like Munchkinland. He said she looked like Mick Jagger. Dudley could see the funny side, but Brogan was upset, and he felt duty-bound to defend her. 'She thought it was quite evil,' [21] he said. 'I'm getting fucking tired of it.' [22] It was against this backdrop that Dudley flew into London for his sister's sixtieth-birthday bash, with his third wife by his side.

After Peter's comments about Brogan, Dudley was reluctant to mix business with pleasure but, after some energetic arm-twisting from John Cleese, he eventually agreed to appear with Peter in the latest Amnesty fund-raiser, *The Secret Policeman's Biggest Ball*. Brogan did not attend the show. The venue was London's Cambridge Theatre, where Peter and Dudley had performed *Behind The Fridge* all those years ago. There were a few old hands in the line-up, like Willie Rushton, but most of the cast were from the new wave of comedians who'd grown up admiring Peter and Dudley from afar. The duo joined Fry & Laurie, French & Saunders, Rory Bremner and Ben Elton at the Cambridge Theatre for four nights, from 30 August to 2 September. At the first *Secret Policeman's Ball*, ten years before, Peter had stolen the show with 'Entirely A Matter For You'. This time, he and Dudley merely reprised 'Frog & Peach' and 'One Leg Too Few'. The papers didn't mind. They were simply happy to see them together again. 'Good comedy never dies,' reported *The Times*. 'It simply gets recycled for the next generation.'

While Dudley was in London, Peter and Dudley gave an interview to Mavis Nicholson for her series *Mavis Catches Up*. They met at Villa Bianca, Peter's favourite restaurant, just around the corner from his Hampstead home. This interview was interspersed with footage from the interview she'd done with them in 1973, and the difference between their early 1970s and late 1980s incarnations was dramatic. Dudley's 'sex-thimble' days were behind him but he still looked slim and dapper. Peter's bloated frame was a shocking contrast with the svelte figure in the archive clips. Mavis asked him why he drank a lot. Was it to alleviate the boredom (as he'd said in their first interview)? 'No, it's because I like drinking a lot – that's the reason,' replied Peter. 'It's nothing to do with boredom, or anything else.'

Mavis asked Dudley why he'd emigrated to the USA. 'I felt that there was a certain friendliness there that I couldn't get hold of here,' he said. 'I didn't particularly like Los Angeles,' added Peter, explaining his short-lived attempt to follow him. 'It may have been my fault. I was in a bad mood when I was living there. I was doing something I didn't really want to do.'

'We never said we're never going to do this again, or we're never going to do that again,' said Dudley, explaining away their separation. 'We just drift in and out of each other's lives, don't we, Peter?' 'Yes, we do,' said Peter, but Mavis wasn't fooled. In 1973, when she'd first interviewed them, they'd been equal partners. Now Peter was the supporting player. Dudley was the leading man. It wasn't just a matter of public perception. The relationship between them had shifted, too. Now, when Peter spoke, Dudley wasn't scared to correct him. When Dudley spoke, Peter listened – more attentively than before:

DUDLEY: I always knew I could act. Anybody can act. I think people can act if they just relax. I don't think there's any mystique about it, really. I really don't. I'm sorry about that, actors everywhere, but it's true.

PETER: He's wrong about acting. I can't act. I feel very self-conscious, and I just feel a prat.

DUDLEY: You don't like saying other people's words.

PETER: Not very much, no.

MAVIS: What is it about you that makes you think you're a prat when you're so clever?

DUDLEY: He's a clever prat.

But there was tenderness between them, too. Partly, this was because Peter was less abrasive. Partly, it was because Dudley wasn't such a big star any more. 'When I first started and I did *10* it was wonderful,' said Dudley. 'It was my first big American role, so it was very exciting and glamorous. Now I don't have the same ambitions. I play the piano much more.' 'I think it must have been very difficult having a musical gift which was very obvious – and probably obvious from a very young age – and then on the whole being famous for comedy,' said Peter. 'I would guess that music would actually be your number one love.' In one sentence, he'd summed up the central dilemma of Dudley's life. Peter had never been this empathetic towards Dudley – not in public, at any rate. This was a side to him that TV viewers had never seen before.

'Comedy was something that I did from an early age and which I sort of took for granted,' agreed Dudley. 'I've just got different urgencies now.' And that urgency was music. 'It was certainly difficult to do what I wanted musically. I didn't quite know how to do it because I didn't have the patience or the confidence. Now I have the confidence.' And he had the patience, too. 'The important thing happened three or four years ago, when I started playing more. I had the patience to really be intimate with the music and practise it with some degree of calm, I guess, and that's a different motivation than I've had in the past.' Did he have any regrets about being sidetracked by comedy, asked Mavis. Did he wish he'd applied himself more rigorously to his music in the past? 'I regret not having done the pure kinetic work when I was a kid, learning things now that I should have learnt when I was five, but that's OK. I've never really had a teacher. I've always been very stubborn and obstinate that way and wanted to do things in my own time.' Mavis asked Dudley why he'd given up psychotherapy. 'I stopped about six years ago, and I feel fine,' he said. 'I think you get to a point where it really doesn't matter.' Now music was his psychotherapy, as it really always should have been. 'It's the great love of my life, really, playing the piano. I practise in a way that I didn't practise before.' This was his release, a release that Peter lacked.

PETER: People have said over the years, 'You really should take up an interest,' but I've never found an interest to take up.

DUDLEY: I remember you saying you'd read Pascal's *Pensées* [23] at the age of eighteen, and then you sort of gave up after that. Is that because it said everything and there was nothing more to be said?

PETER: I was just showing off, I think.

Peter and Lin subsequently met up for dinner with Dudley and Brogan. Brogan thought that Peter and Dudley seemed awkward and uncomfortable together, but Lin had no such doubts. 'It filled my heart with joy when I listened to the two of them,' [24] she said.

Peter and Lin saw each other every day but they didn't move in together. They remained in their separate houses, around the corner from one another. It was an unusual arrangement, but it suited Peter. Even in her own home, Lin's presence had a galvanising effect on his career. In 1990 Peter finally persuaded the BBC to bring out a video of *Not Only ... But Also*. Despite the Corporation's best efforts to eradicate his masterpiece, there was just about enough stuff left to fill a commercial video. Reviewing the surviving footage of himself with Dudley was a salutary experience. 'I had no idea I was so cruel to the little bugger,' [25] he said. Peter flew to LA to enlist Dudley's support. Dudley was happy to help and happy to see Peter. His marriage to Brogan Lane had run into the usual trouble, namely his innate inability to keep his trousers on. At Dudley's invitation they dropped some Ecstasy, and later cooked up a new Pete & Dud sketch for the VHS:

PETE: We have not spoken for twenty years and now we have broken the silence. Or rather I have broken the silence whereas you are sat there and not talking.

DUD: It's because I can't get a word in edgeways.

Dudley came to London to help to promote the video, and the six half-hour compilation programmes that the BBC had decided to broadcast alongside it under the suitably apologetic title, *The Best of What's Left of Not Only ... But Also*. They went on Wogan, supping pints – Dudley sipped his, Peter glugged his. 'He's an ambitious little bastard,' [26] said Peter of his partner, but now that Dudley's Hollywood star was waning Peter's jibes had a lot less bite. Dudley was refreshingly frank about the downturn in his film fortunes. 'Every dog has its day and I seem to have had mine,' he said. 'I am not being offered parts any more – not decent ones, anyway. The few scripts I am offered are so daft your brain falls out your ear just reading them. And they usually come with a note saying, "Robin Williams, Chevy Chase and Sylvester Stallone have all rejected this. Do you fancy it?"' [27]

Peter and Dudley stayed in touch and in 1993, when *Derek & Clive Get The Horn* finally secured a certificate, Dudley agreed to release the video. He still wasn't mad about the film – to put it mildly – but it no longer posed a threat to his dwindling film career. 'The thing about clowns is that as they get older they become more isolated,' [28] he said. '*Foul Play* and *10* came up, and then *Arthur*, but I was wrong about the rest of the films I did.' [29] When Dudley returned to London to promote his classical music series *Concerto!* he was happy to help Peter plug the VHS. When *Derek & Clive Get The Horn* was made, fifteen years before, their attitudes had been poles apart. Now Dudley was more sanguine and Peter was less defensive. 'It's only when I saw it through again that I realised what a bully I was,' said Peter. 'I had no idea I was so dreadful.' [30] 'I think we were scraping the bottom of several barrels,' [31] reflected Dudley. 'Not so much scraping the barrel,' added Peter, 'as incorporating the barrel into the material and going through the floor.' [32] The reviews were level-headed – the *NME* called it rubbish – and Peter did little to defend it. The promotional interviews were more amusing than the video itself. 'The Japs were jolly stern taskmasters,' said Peter, making Dudley corpse as they posed for photos for *Harpers & Queen*. 'When I started the war I was 93 stone, and by the time I finished that bridge I was down to three pounds four ounces – looked lovely in a swimming costume.' Interviewed by the *Mail on Sunday*, they slipped back into Pete & Dud:

PETE: I was on the bus the other day.

DUD: Course you were, Pete. I remember that.

PETE: As you rightly say, you remember that. I was picking up a woman, as buses are the best places to pick up women.

DUD: How's that then, Pete?

PETE: The trick is to play it very cool and ignore the woman completely. Ideally, get off two stops before her. Wait for the years to go by and she will then come running for you.

As Peter said, 'Meeting up again has given us a whole new lease of death.' [33]

The launch party for the video was the social swansong of Peter's life. A host of celebs packed into an upstairs room at the Cobden Working Men's Club in Kensal Road. The guest list was like a timeline of Peter's comedy career: from Roger Law to Ian Hislop, from Alan Bennett and Jonathan Miller to *Monty Python* and the Rolling Stones. As well as these old faces there was a new generation of comedians who'd grown up with his humour: Julian Clary, Rory McGrath, Paul Merton, Mel Smith and Griff Rhys Jones ... The place was so crowded that Bennett and Miller never even managed to say hello to him. Afterwards the party reconvened at Perrins Walk, and continued through the night. Peter accidentally set fire to his trousers and had to jump into the goldfish pond to put them out.

Peter was still keen to do some more sketches with Dudley, but Dudley was adamant. Those days were past. Now that their friendship was restored, Peter finally seemed ready to accept it. Fired up by the success of *Get The Horn*, he teamed up with two of the smartest comics in the country. Neither of them could match Dudley – and neither of them were daft enough to try – but they were two of Britain's best comedy brains, and they brought out the best in Peter.

The first of these collaborators was Clive Anderson, who'd established a reputation as Britain's cleverest talk-show host. A former president of the Cambridge Footlights who'd performed at the opening night of London's Comedy Store, Anderson straddled the two worlds of Peter's comedy – the tradition he came from and the new wave he'd inspired. In Dudley's absence, this barrister turned broadcaster was Peter's ideal foil. At a *Private Eye* party they hatched the bright idea of devoting an entire episode of Anderson's Channel 4 chat show to four fictional characters, all played by Peter. Rather than treating the concept as a joke, which would have spoilt it, Anderson's production team played the whole thing completely straight. Researchers were assigned to Peter's characters and interviewed them in advance, like real people, producing a conventional set of questions which Anderson delivered poker-faced. Anderson gave Peter the perfect forum and Peter rose to the challenge. He created four new comic characters, all as funny as each other: a biscuit-quality controller called Norman House who believes he's been abducted by aliens; a manic football manager called Alan Latchley, vaguely reminiscent of Brian Clough; a psychotic high-court judge called Sir James Beauchamp, and rock legend Eric Daley, formerly of The Corduroys, latterly of 1970s supergroup Ye Gods:

ERIC DALEY: I've just got out of the Henry Ford Clinic.

CLIVE ANDERSON: Not the Betty Ford Clinic?

ERIC DALEY: No, the Henry one is a much tougher regime. You have to build a car before you're allowed out.

Like all the best interviewers, Anderson was happy to take a back seat. He gave Peter room to breathe and the show was a triumph. Peter was in better form than he had been for years. Norman House and Sir James Beauchamp bore more than a passing resemblance to E.L. Wisty and Sir Arthur Streeb-Greebling – though they were none the worse for that – but Alan Latchley and Eric Daley were completely new, and could have spawned more sketches or even a series of their own. Peter's friends and fans all loved it. They were happy to have him back, doing what he did best. As well as a return to form, there was a depth and understanding which hadn't been there before. 'There is something new here – an insight and even a sympathy in the way in which Cook approaches his characters,' wrote John Bird. 'The comedy has become, not mellower necessarily, but more humane.' [34]

Well, up to a point. There were barbs that went unnoticed by most of Peter's fans and friends. Norman House's wife was called Wendy, in a routine that parodied some of Peter's first wife's alternative ideals. Likewise, Judy felt sure that Sir James Beauchamp's unflattering references to his wife were directed at her. She was too upset to really take in the rest of the show. 'Peter often slightly alters names and situations when he writes a sketch, but the person it is aimed at knows absolutely it is about them,' she reflected. 'I still care about him and I am sorry he feels angry that I won in court.' [35] Peter and

Judy's divorce had been a painful and expensive business. The judge had ordered Peter to pay Judy £230,000, plus the costs of the case. In court, under cross-examination by Judy's barrister, Peter had broken into tears and admitted his addictions to gambling, pornography, alcohol and cocaine.

In 1994, Peter made what would be his final series, for BBC Radio Three. Aptly, it was called *Why Bother?* Again, he found a brilliant partner in the iconoclastic young comedian Chris Morris. Most people who worked with Peter treated him with too much respect. Playing a pompous presenter, ignorant of his subject's reputation, Morris gave Peter something to bounce off and provided some rich humour of his own. *Why Bother?* returned to a subject that Peter had previously tackled in 1990 – a series of twelve five-minute programmes called *A Life In Pieces*, in which Ludovic Kennedy interviewed Sir Arthur Greeb-Streebling about his long and pointless life. By Peter's own admission it hadn't really worked. *Why Bother?* was bleaker and far funnier. Morris edited down eight hours of tape into five eight-minute programmes, and the results were very sharp:

CHRIS MORRIS: Why did you agree to these interviews?

SIR ARTHUR STREEB-GREEBLING: The reason is really very, very simple. I've lived a long time. I've been distorted, I've been misrepresented and I've been quoted accurately, which is perhaps the most appalling, and I thought in simple conversation with another human being I would get some things off my chest and onto other people's.

The mournful flavour was inevitable. Peter was near the end. He phoned Dudley in America and asked him, once more, to work with him again. He told Dudley that *Not Only ... But Also* was the only programme that he didn't feel ashamed of. Dudley said no. He was never coming back. In her interview with the two of them, in 1989, Mavis Nicholson had asked them where they thought they'd be in fifteen years' time. 'Hampstead Tube station, I think,' said Dudley. 'I shall be lying in a haze of morphine in a luxurious Swiss Hospital,' said Peter. In fact, they were both dead.

CHAPTER TWENTY EIGHT

GOODBYEE

DUDLEY: Now is the time to say goodbye.

PETER: Goodbye.

DUDLEY: Now is the time to yield a sigh.

PETER: Yield it, yield it.

DUDLEY: Now is the time to wend our way, until we meet
again, some sunny day.

('Goodbyee', Decca, 1965)

Why Bother? brought Peter more job offers, but it was too late. He was spent. 'Ambition fades,' [1] he told Dudley. His mother died in June 1994. He missed her terribly. Her death hit him for six. He'd been a loving and caring son, but for some reason he felt he'd let her down. His father had died ten years before, and although Peter was now in his mid-fifties he took to describing himself as an orphan. 'His mother's death completely crippled him emotionally,' said Lin. 'He couldn't cope with that grief.' [2] His father's death had prompted Peter to stay off the sauce, for a while. This time, however, he drank and drank. As his liver began to lose the battle he was admitted to hospital on a couple of occasions. Once he phoned the hospital himself, and asked to be admitted. He said he just wanted to lie down.

The previous summer Peter had appeared in a film of *Black Beauty*, where he was reunited with his old friend and fellow performer Eleanor Bron. They got on very well, and spent a lot of time talking in their trailers. 'He seemed more open than I had ever known him,' [3] observed Bron. They created a pair of comic characters, and talked about doing a stage show. A year later, Peter was still keen and called Bron to arrange some more improvising sessions, this time with a tape recorder. Sadly, it didn't come to anything. A second series of *A Life In Pieces* also failed to surface, despite the best efforts of Peter's writing partner Peter Fincham. One of Peter's last TV appearances was on the BBC's *Room 101*, where his list of pet hates included the countryside, one of the things that had come between him and Judy.

Peter's last substantial piece of work was a video called *Peter Cook Talks Golf Balls*, in which he played four bizarre golfing bores, including Major Titherly Gribble, a chauvinistic golf-club secretary with an unhealthy interest in young boys:

> 'I was in Morocco looking at the beaches. The fact that the beaches were covered with little boys in tiny bathing suits was nothing to do with my visit to Morocco. I was doing a brochure for the golf club because we wanted to see what kind of sand we were going to have in the bunkers and naturally I went off to see what sort of sand they should have and, erm, I saw some sand and all these little boys lying down on it. I said, "Well, when we get back to the club we'll take this sort of sand as a sample, and just because we've gone to all this expense, why not take a few of the boys in the bag as well?"'

Sadly, Peter's performance didn't match the quality of the material. For the first time in his career, this was a monologue which read better than it played:

> 'I see the future of golf this way – no particular sponsorship, just beautiful links courses with beautiful sunshine flooding down on them, onto which we can look out of the window from here in the Antler Room and see lissom young boys striding – naked if they wish, naked if I wish – all over the links, unencumbered by clubs or costume, or all that stupidity which surrounds the game.'

The last time Wendy saw Peter was at the wedding of their daughter Daisy in September 1994. Daisy wanted both her parents to be there. Peter came, without Lin, to give the bride away. He made a simple, sincere speech, unencumbered by silly voices. He made his peace with Wendy. 'I'm so happy I saw him,' [4] she said. Daisy was happy to see her parents together on her big day. 'It was fantastic to see them chortling together like old times,' [5] she said. His sister Sarah was there, too. 'Taking a break from the bopping and boozing, we sat in companionable silence in the drizzle on a tree stump in the Sussex countryside,' [6] she recalled. Of all the weddings he'd attended, he told her, this one was the most perfect.

Peter presented a mellow figure in the last months of his life. 'I'm a big softy,' he said in his final, tearful newspaper interview, in November 1994. 'I've curbed my tongue a bit. I don't like unpleasantness about other people. I get no pleasure out of other people's alleged failure, and comics are probably as bad as anyone else in the envy game. I've just got slightly nicer. Awful, isn't it?' [7] He looked back on *Not Only ... But Also* as the happiest part of his career. 'That was perfect,' he said.

'I can't imagine a comedy relationship being better. I adore Dudley. I would have been very happy for it to continue.' [8]

His attitude to his solo work was less sentimental. 'I've never attempted to achieve my potential,' he said in his last TV interview. 'What could be worse than achieving your potential so early in life?' Stephen Fry and Michael Palin were among the guests at Peter's 57th birthday party a fortnight later, but he missed *Private Eye*'s Christmas lunch. He was back in hospital. He came home for Christmas but on 3 January he returned to hospital again – this time in an ambulance, on a stretcher. He was coughing up blood. His body had lost the fight. He was admitted to intensive care at the Royal Free Hospital in Hampstead. The condition of his liver was critical. By the time his sisters and daughters arrived to say goodbye, he'd already lost consciousness.

Peter died on 9 January 1995 of a gastrointestinal haemorrhage – alcohol had damaged his liver beyond repair. Meanwhile, in Majorca, Wendy noticed that her watch had stopped. It was only later that she heard the news. Judy heard the news from a friend, who'd seen it on TV. She went into the kitchen to make a cup of tea, to calm her nerves, but she was so shaken that she poured boiling water over her hand and had to go to casualty.

When Judy had seen Peter on *Clive Anderson Talks Back* she'd been shocked by his appearance. She'd wondered how long he had left, but living quietly in the country she'd had no idea that he'd been in hospital. 'I would have loved to have held his hand and said to him that no matter what has happened I still love him,' she wrote in her moving memoir, *Loving Peter*. 'I so wish I could have said goodbye.' [9] She felt as if a light had gone out. She felt a hole had opened up. She remembered him as a poet, as well as a comedian. She called him the love of her life. She phoned Peter's answerphone, just to hear his voice again. Later, she learned that Dudley had done the same thing.

It was still the small hours in Los Angeles when Lin phoned Dudley. He was the first person she called. 'Oh God, the fucker's dead,' said Dudley to himself. 'There's a hole in the universe.' [10] It wasn't a complete surprise. Lin had phoned him when Peter went into hospital. By an odd coincidence, John Bassett, the man who'd brought Peter and Dudley together, half a lifetime earlier, was in LA and had arranged to see Dudley on the day that Peter died. He found Dudley tongue-tied and upset. 'He was the last of the Fringers I thought would go,' said Dudley. 'I thought it would probably be me.'[11]

As countless other entertainers queued up to smother Peter with superlatives, Dudley said all the right things. 'My life will never be the same because I felt so linked to him,' he said. 'I counted him among my friends, if not my best friend, in later years.' [12] However, he actually felt strangely muted. 'I felt hollow,' he admitted later on. 'I did not know how to respond.' [13] After the initial shock had subsided, he was a lot more dispassionate. 'I had a lot of problems with Peter,' he said. 'I still resent some of the things he said about me when we were no longer working together.' [14] Peter had been his best friend, he said, but he'd ended up looking like a beached whale, and the work they'd done together had been governed by the law of diminishing returns. Peter probably would have agreed with him. He'd said much the same thing himself, many times. And as someone who often called Dudley a club-footed dwarf, he probably would have laughed at that bit about the beached whale. Peter could dish it out, but he could take it too.

Peter was buried on 14 January 1995 at St John's Church in

Hampstead. His sisters and his daughters were there with Lin. Wendy and Judy were not invited. Lin subsequently arranged a memorial service, on 1 May, also at St John's. The guest list read like a roll-call of British comedy, an indication of the huge effect that Peter had had on several generations of entertainers: David Baddiel (*The Mary Whitehouse Experience*), Tim Brooke-Taylor (*The Goodies*), Ben Elton (*Blackadder*), David Frost (*That Was The Week That Was*), Ian Hislop and Paul Merton (*Have I Got News For You*), Richard Ingrams and Auberon Waugh (*Private Eye*), Clive Anderson, Eleanor Bron, Barry Cryer, Harry Enfield, Barry Humphries, Hugh Laurie, Jonathan Ross, Willie Rushton, Ned Sherrin, Barry Took, Terry Wogan, half of *Not The Nine O'Clock News*, most of *Monty Python* – and Dudley.

The Radley Clerkes, a choral group from Peter's old school, sang 'Love Me Tender' and 'Goodbyee', with Dudley at the piano. Dudley also played a piano skit inspired by Peter's Braille sketch, called 'Three Blonde Mice'. Auberon Waugh delivered an address. Richard Ingrams also spoke. Stephen Fry wrote a moving tribute in the order of service. John Cleese read from *The Tibetan Book of The Dead*. Peter's death hit Cleese very hard. He found it even more painful than the death of his comic partner Graham Chapman. It was what Peter represented, as well as who he was. 'This is a figure from the parables, a publican, a sinner but never a Pharisee,' said Alan Bennett, speaking at the service. 'In him morality is discovered far from its official haunts, the message of a character like Peter's being that a life of complete self-indulgence, if led with the whole heart, may also bring wisdom.' [15] It was left to Dudley to bring things back down to Earth. 'I think he would have been mildly embarrassed,' [16] he said, when reporters asked him what Peter would have made of it. The *Guardian*'s Maggie O'Kane had the bright idea of asking people what Peter would have done if he'd been there:

DAVE ALLEN:	He would have left for the bookmakers.
SPIKE MILLIGAN:	He'd have gone off halfway through.
DUDLEY MOORE:	He probably wouldn't have turned up.

Inevitably, the press focused on Peter's unfulfilled promise. 'Of course he fulfilled it,' countered Jonathan Ross. 'He fulfilled it when he was still young.' [17] Yet that didn't make it any easier to live with, as Jonathan Miller confirmed. 'A lot of comedians who write their own material reach a point at which they can't create any more and then I think life becomes absolutely desperate,' he said. 'One of the great tragedies of comedy is that it runs out. There are very few people who go on inventing, and when you don't have any more to say, if you haven't got anything else in your life, you're beached.' [18] Dudley wasn't beached. Dudley had his music. It was an outlet that kept him grounded. It was an outlet that Peter never had. Booze was his only respite from that funny voice inside his head. Dudley said Peter bludgeoned people with his comedy. He said he was relentless, but Peter had no choice. His comedy was instinctive and compulsive. 'Writing and performing and being funny was something we chose to do, did when required, then switched off,' observed Alan Bennett. 'For Peter, on the other hand, there was no switching off.' [19] As Bennett said, other comedians clocked in. Peter never clocked out. Michael Parkinson likened him to George Best, but Best never depended on a teammate the way Peter depended on Dudley.

Without Dudley, Peter's comedy retreated whence it came, into his private life. His was that precious sort of humour that happens with a group of friends more often than it happens on a film set, which is why so many of his best bons mots vanished into space. His humour was so original that the perfect format for it had yet to be invented. Significantly, when Stephen Fry was asked to write a compact memoir about Peter the most entertaining anecdote he came up with was about Peter inventing a wonderful poolside parlour game when they were on holiday together, complete with its own arcane rules and vocabulary. 'The thing I enjoy most is sitting around with some people and making up some jokes,' [20] said Peter. 'I don't much enjoy being on television. I'd rather do it for a few people socially, but it would be a bit rude to take up a collection after dinner.' [21]

While Dudley was around, it was another matter. 'He was so pernickety,' [22] said Peter. 'He always wanted to work out every minor detail and situation and explain it first.' [23] Yet that pedantic quality, that pianist's insistence on playing the right notes in the right order, was Dudley's greatest gift to him. His other gift was friendship. 'Dudley was the person Peter loved the most, but I think in the earlier years Dudley didn't realise how much Peter felt for him,' said Lin. 'Both of them had difficulty in expressing their love, and it was only in later years that Peter felt more able to express his emotions.' [24] Wendy put it more simply. 'Peter probably loved Dudley more than anybody in his life.' [25] And yet, in the end, that love remained largely unrequited. 'I was very surprised about how emotionless I was,' said Dudley after the memorial service, on his return to LA. 'I've been waiting for the emotion to kick in, and it just hasn't. I'm not sure why.' [26]

By the time Peter died, Dudley's Hollywood career had almost slowed to a standstill. Only in Britain was he still regarded as an A-list star. 'Look at the careers of most actors,' he said. 'If they're lucky, they're top banana for five years, no more. I was tops for around two years.

And then, one morning, you wake up and find you've been shifted onto another list. You're no longer an A-list actor. You're now on the B list, and falling.' [27] He appeared in two minor films that year – *The Disappearance of Kevin Johnson* and *Weekend In The Country*. They were the last two films he made.

In 1990, Dudley separated from his third wife, Brogan Lane. 'I am easy to get along with but bloody awful to live with,' [28] he said. 'I will never, ever get married again.' [29] In April 1994 he married Nicole Rothschild, a woman half his age. During a domestic quarrel on Oscar night, he and Nicole both called the police. Dudley was just another punter now, watching the ceremony at home on TV like the rest of us. The police turned up and arrested Dudley on suspicion of cohabitational abuse. Handcuffed, he spent two hours at the police station before being bailed for $50,000. In his mugshot he looked weary. The British press responded with that special brand of *Schadenfreude* reserved for ungrateful émigrés who've forsaken the UK for the States. The *Independent on Sunday* called him, 'part of that sad procession of has-beens, clinging to past, brief glories and diminishing wealth.' [30]

A week after his arrest, Dudley proposed to Nicole. The City Attorney's office dropped their charges against him, so long as the newly-weds agreed to see a marriage-guidance counsellor. It was an unusual start to married life. In June 1995 Nicole bore Dudley a second son, Nicholas Anthony Moore. She already had two children by her former husband, Charles Cleveland, who ended up living with them and sharing the parental duties. He was a colourful character, with a complicated personal life. Home life was lively, to say the least. When Dudley eventually filed for divorce, lurid tabloid tales emerged of him spending five-figure sums on drugs and prostitutes. Judy was shocked to hear about it. When she was around, Dudley had always disapproved of Peter taking drugs.

With his film career in decline and his personal life in tatters, Dudley focused on his first love: classical music. Even at the height of his fame he'd never abandoned the piano. He kept four pianos in his house in Marina del Rey, three nine-foot concert grands (a Yamaha, a Steinway and a Bosendorfer) and the upright he'd learned to play on as a child, which Brogan had shipped over from the UK. Bach's 48 Preludes and Fugues were his daily workout. He played them first thing every morning. 'They're so gorgeous and so optimistic,' [31] he said. He performed occasional recitals throughout the 1980s, at venues like Carnegie Hall and the Hollywood Bowl: Beethoven's Triple Piano Concerto; Gershwin's *Rhapsody In Blue* … 'I started life as a choirboy,' he'd say, before playing his first composition, 'Anxiety', which he wrote when he was eleven. It was, he'd tell his audience, 'a precursor of things to come'.

At first these recitals were sporadic respites from his film-making schedule but, as his stardom dwindled, the piano resumed its rightful place at the centre of his world. 'When I went up to Oxford in 1954, I thought music was going to be my life, the way I'd earn my living,' he said. 'Instead, I ended up in the theatre – and later, in television and film – and became intoxicated by the response of an audience. But now that my acting career has gone all quiet, classical music has become a way of earning my keep.' [32]

The woman who nurtured this renaissance was a concert pianist turned journalist called Rena Fruchter. Down-to-earth and maternal, she looked like an unlikely soulmate for a fading sex symbol, but they had more in common than first met the eye. She was a journalist by default. He was an actor by default. At heart, they were both musicians. Like him, she'd been a piano-playing prodigy. As a child, she had been even more precocious than Dudley. She made her debut as a soloist with the Philadelphia Orchestra when she was six, and went on to play with numerous first-class orchestras in America and Europe. When she reached adulthood she turned professional, and studied at the Royal College of Music in London. Like Dudley, music remained her first love, but like Dudley, she'd become better-known for her secondary career. When she met Dudley, in 1987, she was writing an arts column for the *New York Times* combining piano playing with journalism, among other things. She interviewed him before a concert. For Dudley, it was a relief to talk to someone about classical music rather than movies or his love life, or Peter. 'Everybody here is so busy getting tanned and blond,' he told her, of his life in LA. 'They don't seem to have the time to discuss Chopin.'[33]

Unlike so many of the women who'd come in and out of Dudley's life, Rena was happily married and happy to remain that way, and so their friendship developed and endured. When she founded Music For All Seasons (a charity dedicated to bringing music to people in confined facilities – from hospitals to prisons to children's homes) with her husband Brian Dallow, she asked Dudley if he'd be Honorary Chairman. Dudley said he'd only do it if he could play an active role. He became Advisory Board President instead, a role he maintained for the rest of his life.

Dudley threw himself into promotional work for Music For All Seasons. In 1994 he returned to Carnegie Hall to play Grieg's Piano Concerto in A minor. In 1995 his performance of this concerto was released as his first classical CD. As Dudley toured with Rena, playing solo and duo performances all around the world, as far afield as Australia and the Far East, it seemed that his career had come full circle. He could never make up for those lost years, but he practised hard – four hours every day – and the emotional empathy of his playing made up for any technical deficiencies. 'If I could force myself to do just four hours a day of composing and practising, everything else in my life would fall into place,' [34] he'd said, in 1965. Now, thirty years later, he was finally doing it. At last he was becoming something like the musician he might have been if *Beyond The Fringe* hadn't intervened. 'Music has certainly been a great friend to me,' he said. 'If I did not have music, I don't know what I would do.' [35] Now that friendship was about to be snatched away for good.

In 1995, after Peter died, Dudley began to have trouble with his memory. He told the journalist Giles Smith that he'd met a friend for lunch and found that he had no recollection of having met her for lunch the day before. That wasn't all. 'He spoke slowly, drawing the words out, inserting long, reflective pauses into which some of his sentences disappeared, never to emerge,' observed Smith. 'Occasionally, he would start an anecdote and let it dwindle into nothing, as if losing its thread.' [36] He started filming Barbra Streisand's *The Mirror Has Two Faces*, but struggled to remember his lines and was fired after the first day's shooting. 'I certainly don't hold a grudge against her,' said Dudley. 'I think I would have fired me if I were her.' [37] His replacement was George Segal, whom Dudley had replaced in *10*.

In 1996 Dudley began to notice a problem with one of his fingers. When he was playing the piano, it wouldn't do what he wanted it to do. Soon both his hands started playing up. 'My fingers feel like sausages,' [38] he told Rena. The problem began to spread. His speech became slurred. He became light-headed. Sometimes he toppled over backwards. Strangers assumed he'd been drinking, which upset him. He'd never had a drink problem – other problems, but never drink.

Narrating a performance of Prokofiev's *Peter and The Wolf*, he had to deliver all his lines sitting in an armchair. The performance only lasted half an hour, but he was scared of falling over. If he'd fallen over, people would have assumed that he was drunk. When his son Patrick met up with him, Patrick knew there was something wrong. His dad seemed drunk. He seemed brittle. He said the same thoughts kept going round and round inside his head in an endless loop. 'They say there's something wrong with me,' said Dudley, 'but they can't figure out what it is.' [39] It was the last time they met.

In 1999, after a long round of tests, Dudley announced that he was suffering from progressive supranuclear palsy, a rare neurological condition related to Parkinson's disease. Life expectancy was usually about five years, give or take a year or two. The disease was degenerative. There was no cure. As PSP progresses, sufferers find it increasingly hard to swallow. The most common cause of death is pneumonia caused by food particles and liquid in the lungs. The earlier symptoms are easy to mistake for drunkenness. 'I'm doomed to become Arthur in real life,' [40] Dudley told Rena. For the creator of Hollywood's happiest drunk, it was a sick joke of the blackest sort.

Dudley saved his best joke for the press release: 'I understand that one person in 100,000 suffers from this disease, and I am also aware that there are 100,000 members of my union, the Screen Actors Guild (SAG) who are working every day. I think, therefore, it is in some way considerate of me that I have taken on this disease for myself, thus protecting the remaining 99,999 SAG members from this fate.' People applauded his gallows humour, but the truth was darker than they knew. To his intense irritation, Dudley's statement had been sanitised. His preferred version was considered too depressing. This is how it should have read: 'I think, therefore, it is in some way considerate of me that I have taken on this disease for myself, thus protecting the remaining 99,999 SAG members from this fate worse than death.'

Dudley was anxious not to become a mere figurehead for PSP. 'This disease is dreadful,' he declared. 'I don't want anyone to go through what I am going through. But I want people to remember my music, my piano, my films, my humour – not primarily my illness.' [41] As he considered his final legacy, the word order was significant. For Dudley, comedy was secondary. Music came first.

Dudley agreed to be interviewed on TV by Barbara Walters, the doyenne of American TV interviewers, on ABC. 'I just want people to know the truth,' he said. 'I want them to know I'm going to die from this.' [42] At least the interview scotched the false rumours that he'd become a drunk:

BARBARA WALTERS: People thought you were Arthur. They took the character from the movie who was drunk and said, 'That's Dudley.'

DUDLEY MOORE: It's amazing that Arthur has affected my body to the point that I have become him.

BARBARA WALTERS: Your mind is intact, so you know very well what is happening to you?

DUDLEY MOORE: Yes, I know very well what is happening to me – particularly what people say and what they think.

BARBARA WALTERS: What do you most want people to know?

DUDLEY MOORE: I want people to know that I'm not intoxicated and I'm going through this disease as well as I can.

Inevitably, the papers were less sensitive. 'He used to be a heartbreaker, now Dudley is a broken man,' read one such report. 'Those Peter Pan features have been replaced by a bloated mask.'[43] There was a moralising tone to these articles, a superstitious inference that Dudley's disease was some sort of payback for his free-living, free-loving past. He started to use a walking stick. He switched to two canes, which he used like crutches. His speech became more slurred. In November 1999 he got back together with Julie Andrews, to narrate Saint-Saens' Carnival of the Animals. In previous performances, he'd played one of the piano parts (Rena played the other) and narrated from the keyboard, but now even the narration, no problem for him a few years before, was an enormous effort. This time Rena and her husband, Brian Dallow, played the two piano parts. It was Dudley's last performance.

By now he'd left LA and moved to a three-bedroom ranch house, next door to Rena's family. He brought his grand pianos with him but his playing was now deteriorating dramatically. Soon he could no longer play. 'My hands feel like strangers,' [44] he said. 'The messages are still going out from my brain but it's impossible to get the hands together. I just can't play the sounds I hear in my head.' [45] In private he was less matter-of-fact. 'Why me?' he asked Rena, tearfully. 'Why my music?' [46] Without the piano, he felt as if he was drowning. He described it as the ship that had carried him through his life. 'I don't know how I can go on without the piano,' he told her. 'You can put all the rest into a thimble. I would give up what's left of my legs, my balance, if I could play the piano again.' [47]

In April 2001 Dudley celebrated his 66th birthday, at a concert staged in his honour by Music for All Seasons at Carnegie Hall. Chevy Chase and Bo Derek were among the guests. A string quartet played a composition that Dudley had written when he was at Oxford. A piano and string quartet played a medley from some of his more recent compositions – *Songs Without Words* and the score he'd written for the film *Six Weeks*. Rena played the piano. Dudley was actively involved with the arrangement and preparation, despite his failing health. The Dudley Moore trio played too, with the pianist Benny Green standing in for Dudley. Rena played Dudley's mash-up of Beethoven and Tom Jones from *Not Only ... But Also*. And Eric Idle joined the American comedian Jimmy Fallon to perform 'One Leg Too Few'.

In November 2001, Dudley flew to London to receive his CBE. He could have received it at the British Embassy in Washington, or at the British consulate in New York. Yet, even though he was now confined to a wheelchair, he was determined to receive it at Buckingham Palace. Rena and Brian, and Dudley's sister Barbara and her husband Bernard, came too. They all knew that it was his last trip home. Dudley arrived at the Palace in a 1954 Rolls-Royce Silver Wraith, the same car he'd used in *Arthur*. 'Mr Dudley Moore, for services to television, film and theatre,' announced the Lord Steward. A page wheeled him up to the royal dais. 'From a grey, almost waxlike 66-year-old face, his dark eyes stared into the middle distance with angry intensity but no apparent focus,' wrote Robert Hardman in the *Daily Mail*. 'His mouth was fixed in a grimace. His pinstriped legs and leather Chelsea boots dangled aimlessly from the seat of his wheelchair. But as the Prince of Wales presented him with the insignia of Commander of the Most Excellent Order of the British Empire, we could suddenly see life – and, above all, happiness – flooding back into those features.' [48] He was too ill to talk to the media. It was left to Rena's husband, Brian Dallow, to speak for him. 'Dudley is absolutely thrilled,' he said. 'It's such a great honour from his home country.' [49] As an Englishman who'd emigrated to America, Dallow knew how Dudley felt.

Back home in New Jersey, Dudley's condition was now deteriorating rapidly. He fought off two bouts of bronchitis. 'You cannot continue to lose weight at this rate and remain alive,' [50] his doctor said. He was told that a feeding tube might extend his life for a short time but he refused it. 'This has been an incredible journey,' he told Rena. 'Do you think there will be music there, wherever I'm going?' [51] He died on 27 March 2002, of pneumonia, in the bosom of Rena's family. A recording of *Songs Without Words* was playing as he slipped away. 'What are you seeing?' Rena asked him, as he lay dying. 'I'm sitting at the piano, playing Bach,' [52] he whispered. 'I can feel the warmth of the music all around me.' [53] Those were his final words.

Like Peter's obituaries, seven years earlier, Dudley's British obits bemoaned Dudley's unfulfilled talent. 'For all his commercial success, there was a lingering sadness,' concluded the *Daily Telegraph*. 'His Faustian pact with Hollywood did no justice to his gifts.' [54] 'He was carried away by all the glamour,' said Jonathan Miller. 'I think in the end Hollywood did him a lot of harm. It was a terrible waste.' [55] Actually, compared to most Hollywood actors, Dudley's track record wasn't too bad – two classic movies, a few near misses and a lot of lucrative also-rans. It only felt like a waste compared to what he'd done before – with Jonathan Miller and Alan Bennett, and with Peter.

Two years after Dudley died, Rena took a book down from her bookshelf and found a scrap of paper tucked inside it. There was something written on it. She recognised Dudley's handwriting straight away. At first she struggled to read it. Eventually, she worked it out. 'Celebrate the journey rather than the destination,' he'd written. For Peter, Dudley was the destination of his life's work, a life that changed the course of British comedy. For Dudley, Peter was just one stop along the way.

...BUT ALSO

JOHN BASSETT

'A lot of women found his size very attractive.
I suppose the size means that you're no challenge.'

John Bassett was the man who brought Peter and Dudley together, when he formed the quartet that became *Beyond The Fringe*. I met him at The Flask, Peter's Hampstead local. Hidden down a quiet side street, it's a pretty, peaceful pub. You can see why Peter liked it. However, Bassett met Dudley long before he met Peter. He was at Oxford with Dudley. He was reading PPE at Wadham College but he spent more time in the Union Cellars, playing the trumpet with his jazz band. 'All the different clubs in the university used to have a small dance once a term,' he says, over a pub lunch. 'As there were sixty or seventy clubs, that meant there was a dance in the Union Cellars every evening.' By his own admission, Bassett was not a great musician but he was great at spotting and promoting talent. His band got paid a bit of beer money, and Bassett would put some aside to pay the fare for a professional musician to come up from London and sit in with them.

Bassett met Dudley in Magdalen College chapel in 1955. Bassett was in his first year. Dudley was in his second year. They'd been brought together by Anthony Page (who went on to become an eminent professional director) in his student production of *The Changeling*. Page asked Dudley to write the music. He asked Bassett to play the trumpet. Bassett was terrified – not of Dudley, but of the music that Dudley had written. Bassett couldn't play it. 'Oh, well,' said Dudley, 'just play anything and I'll follow you.' He climbed up into the organ loft, Bassett began to play and Dudley played along, perfectly. It was the beginning of a partnership that would transform both their lives. That evening, Dudley came to the Union Cellars and played the piano with Bassett's jazz band. Dudley was already besotted with the jazz pianist Erroll Garner but it was the first time he'd played jazz in an ensemble. After that, Dudley returned to play with Bassett's band virtually every night. When he took his bows at the end of his solos, he started larking around and getting laughs. Bassett believes this gave him the confidence to start doing cabaret. 'He owes his performing confidence to dear old jazz.'

Bassett and Dudley hit it off, as friends as well as musicians. Bassett could see straight away that his new friend had something special. 'His talent was overwhelming.' Although Dudley was self-conscious about his club foot, his talent gave him an aura that transcended his physical (and social) handicaps. By the time that Bassett met him, Dudley was very self-assured. 'If there is one thing you can do superbly well that nobody can take from you, it gives you a presence and a confidence.' For Dudley, that thing was music. 'He was five million light years better than anything I'd ever heard.'

While he was at Oxford, Bassett also came across a history student at Exeter College called Alan Bennett. He saw him at a student Smoker and found him very funny. Bassett's jazz band made some money playing debutante balls, and Bassett booked Bennett for some of these shows. But Bennett wasn't all that keen. 'I got a letter from Alan, while he was at Exeter, saying "please, please don't get me too many cabarets unless they're extremely well paid, because I really don't want to have anything to do with the theatre."' Bassett booked him anyway. He also booked a Cambridge graduate called Jonathan Miller, whom he knew through Miller's sister (they'd been at school together). By now, he'd found three-quarters of *Beyond The Fringe*.

When Bassett left Oxford he walked straight into a wonderful job, as Assistant to Robert Ponsonby, the Artistic Director of the Edinburgh Festival. Ponsonby told Bassett about his plan, to put on a cabaret that would be beyond the capabilities of any of the performers on the Festival Fringe, and asked Bassett to find four performers. Bassett already had a trio in mind. Miller told him the fourth member of the quartet had to be Peter. He'd seen Peter perform just once, but he had no doubt about his ability. Even in a sketch where he remained hidden behind a newspaper, Peter held the stage.

Half a century later, Bassett can still recall the first meeting he arranged for them, over lunch in an Italian restaurant around the corner from the hospital where Jonathan Miller was working. It was at this lunch that Bassett realised the difference between Dudley and the others. Peter, Alan and Jonathan were all reluctant to make a joke, in case the others didn't laugh. Dudley had no such qualms – he even followed the waitresses in and out of the kitchen, walking with a stooping gait like Groucho Marx's. That broke the ice. From then on, Bassett knew that he had a winner on his hands.

Bassett went up to Edinburgh and stayed with the cast in their flat in the Old Town, but the first time he saw the show was on the first night. They started with the curtain already up – considered rather daring in those days. Peter, Alan and Jonathan were all onstage, waiting for Dudley to come on and play the National Anthem. But there was no sign of him. Then came the sound of flushing water, from their dressing room on the fourth floor. This was followed by the noise of Dudley coming down four flights of stairs, humming nonchalantly all the way. The show, when it finally started, was sublime. 'It was absolutely wonderful,' says Bassett. 'The news spread like wildfire. It was booked solid the next day.' Every subsequent night was oversold, with three rows standing. They received more than a dozen offers from London managements for West End transfers.

They went to Cambridge to warm up before the West End run. There, in front of a student crowd, they brought the house down. The show ran for more than four hours. It was a different story in Brighton. They had a bad review in the local paper, a bad reception from the local punters, and Donald Albery withdrew his offer to put them in his Wyndham's Theatre, leaving them in the smaller Fortune Theatre. 'I suppose some of the jokes might have been lost in the caverns of Wyndham's,' says Bassett, 'but it would have made a lot more money – and a lot more people would have seen it.' Come the first night at the Fortune, he wasn't nervous, despite the poor reaction they'd had in Brighton. His confidence was fully vindicated. The show was a smash hit from the start. Bassett flew to America for the opening night in New York. Mort Sahl, Bob Hope and Frank Sinatra all saw the show on Broadway. Bassett's quartet had proved successful beyond his wildest dreams. 'It was being in the right place at the right time,' he says modestly.

MICHAEL BAWTREE

'He found everything ridiculous, but it was very
good-natured at Radley. He just found everything
irresistibly funny.'

Michael Bawtree met Peter at Radley when they were both thirteen, but it was during their last two years at school that they became close friends. 'We became heads of our houses, or Socials, as they're called at Radley, so we spent the last two or three terms sharing the school prefects' study, and being together a great deal, and having a wonderful time.'

Michael is a theatre director. He's lived in Canada since 1962 but he's often back in Britain. We're talking at his friend's house in London's Notting Hill. I ask him what he thought of Peter's acting, at Radley and thereafter. 'I never actually thought that he was a terribly good actor,' he tells me. 'I thought he was the most wonderful performer, and a brilliantly witty improviser, but he always seemed a little awkward as an actor.' For Michael, that never changed. 'He was not really capable of doing that magical thing that a fine actor does, of becoming someone else.' Still, Michael had no doubt that Peter was out of the ordinary. 'It was a funny mixture. He was self-conscious physically, but extremely self-assured.' Peter was impressive as Don Armado in *Love's Labours Lost*, but his finest performance was his private impersonation of Arthur Boylett, the school butler – the man who inspired E.L. Wisty. 'He had no personality of any kind whatsoever, and was absolutely literal in everything that he said or did,' says Michael. 'Peter made him into something which he wasn't at all.'

The theatrical finale of Michael's school career, and Peter's, was *Black & White Blues*, the puppet musical which they produced together in their final term, under the guiding hand of Radley's art master, Chris Ellis – an Old Etonian who'd won the George Medal for bomb disposal during the war. 'Chris was very much a believer in people teaching themselves,' says Michael. 'He was one of those people who gave pupils their chance.' Ellis's Marionette Society was the apotheosis of his philosophy. The society performed puppet versions of classics like *The Magic Flute* and *The Pirates of Penzance*. The boys made everything themselves, from scratch, from the puppets to the sets and lighting. 'I've spent most of my life being a stage director, but my first directing job was with puppets,' says Michael. His directorial debut was a puppet version of *The Beggar's Opera*. Ellis asked Peter and Michael to write a puppet musical together. Michael wrote the music and directed. Peter wrote the words and provided the voices for the leading roles. It was the first time that the society had produced an originally scripted show. Ellis asked Peter to write the book in rhyming couplets, but he gave him a free hand with the subject and Peter came up with a tale of a missionary jazz band converting cannibals in Africa. It was a huge hit.

After they left Radley, Peter and Michael set off with their schoolmates Jonathan Harlow and Noel Slocock on a picaresque camping trip to Shropshire, the New Forest and the Forest of Dean. 'We were young, we had the world before us, we'd all been accepted into university,' says Michael. 'We were tremendously happy.' Peter seemed particularly at ease. 'It was so wonderful to have Peter with us,' says Michael. 'I think he was almost as happy as he'd ever been. He didn't have to put on a show. We weren't just admirers. We were genuine friends.' Peter later described it as one of the happiest times of his life. And although he was under no obligation to entertain, he was terribly entertaining nonetheless. 'It was incredibly funny to be with him. He didn't do much. He was the court jester. He kept us laughing while we cooked the meals.' It was an idyllic interlude, a precious pastorale between childhood and adulthood. 'I think I'm playing the ukulele in one of these,' says Michael, showing me some photos of grinning young men sitting in the long grass around campfires. 'We camped everywhere we went. Sometimes we asked, sometimes we didn't. We just talked and laughed and had a lovely time.' Peter's humour was still a pastime, rather than a career plan. 'We knew he was going to make his way in the world, but we didn't quite know how.'

All too soon, Michael had to head off to do his National Service. He went to Cyprus with the army, and then up to Oxford to read English, but the two friends stayed in touch. By now, Peter's comic reputation had spread beyond Cambridge. When Michael invited him to Oxford, to do a half-hour revue together, his Oxford friends were impressed. 'By that time we were beginning to realise that he had something rather special.' And Peter was beginning to realise too. 'He'd done enough comedy to realise that he had a gift.' Michael went to see *Pieces of Eight*, the West End revue that Peter wrote for Kenneth Williams. 'It was a terrific success,' says Michael. 'It was one of the first things that made me realise he was on his way up.'

Michael's career took him to Canada, where he made his home (he meant to spend a year there – fifty years later, he's still there) and, by the time he saw *Beyond The Fringe* in Toronto, Peter had become a star. 'He enjoyed seeing me because he didn't have to perform,' says Michael. 'It had become a compulsive tic, almost, to be a comedian at all times and in all places.' Michael saw *Beyond The Fringe* again on Broadway, went to stay with the four Fringers in Alexander Cohen's country house in Connecticut, and got to know Alan, Jonathan and Dudley. A decent piano player, Michael was offered Dudley's part in a touring production of the show, but Peter talked him out of it. 'He said, "You're worth more than that. Don't do it."' Michael still can't decide whether it was the right decision.

On his return trips to England, Michael went to Peter's Establishment Club. 'You used to see people you recognised everywhere,' he says. 'You could hardly get a table – or a chair.' Michael saw Lenny Bruce perform there. 'Lenny was much darker and more terrifying than Peter ever was,' he says. 'Not poisonous exactly, but really toxic.' The night Michael saw him, there was a long – overlong – interval before Bruce returned for the second half. 'He wouldn't go back on unless I shot him up with heroin,' Peter told Michael. 'His whole arm was absolutely covered in puncture marks.' 'I can't do this,' Peter told Lenny. 'I'm not going to go on unless you do,' Lenny told Peter. 'Peter was very freaked out by that,' says Michael.

Michael stayed with Peter in his flat in Prince of Wales Drive in Battersea but, though they remained firm friends, their artistic tastes were diverging. 'I was beginning to realise that Peter's satire was not temperamentally my scene,' he says. 'I was maybe too much of a romantic, or too much of a believer in things – his satire really depended on not believing in anything very much, whether it was God or the Prime Minister. I didn't feel that I wanted to spend the rest of my life knocking things. I wanted to build things.'

Michael enjoyed Peter and Wendy's hospitality at their house in

Church Row, in Hampstead. Peter was very gregarious. It was almost as if he couldn't bear to be alone. 'Wendy was a terrific hostess, and she was a great cook,' he says. 'People would come round and they would expect Peter to amuse them and he did so.' But it was hard to get up close. 'For most people, he would be armoured against them by his comedy.' The last time Michael stayed with him in England, Peter and Wendy had split up, which made Michael very sad. 'I'm seeing a psychiatrist,' Peter told him. 'Why are you doing that?' asked Michael. 'I've been putting on so many funny voices that I don't know who I am,' he replied. 'As soon as he said that to me, I could understand it completely,' says Michael, 'that he had become a kind of machine of comedy, and that he had lost himself somewhere along the way.'

FRANCIS BENNETT

'You didn't converse with him. You listened,
and you laughed, and you were lucky.'

'I arrived at Radley in September 1955,' says the publisher Francis
Bennett. 'Houses were called Socials and the head of our Social was
Peter Cook.' Francis was thirteen. Peter was eighteen. 'He was very
tall and very thin. We had a communal bathroom. After games he
used to sit in the bath for hours, and all the voices and all the jokes
that we associate with him just poured out. It was non-stop, quite
extraordinary. I'd never in my whole life come across anybody like
this.' Francis couldn't stop laughing. 'I found it hysterical,' he says.
'I'd never heard anything like it before – I'd never met someone who
could invent, on a continuous basis. He'd start with an idea – I'm sure
with no idea where it would lead – yet something inside him pushed
him forward, drove him on. It wasn't one-liners. There were stories,
inventions, fantasies.' Peter wasn't a figure of fun. His personality
gave him authority. 'He was a wonderful head of house,' says Francis.
'Because he made everybody laugh, you did what he wanted.'

We're sitting in Francis's elegant flat in London. It's over fifty
years since he left Radley but his memories are still strong. 'When
you went to a public school like that, in those days, you had to pass
a new-boys test, and if you didn't you were beaten by the head of
house.' Francis failed, and was sent to Peter to be beaten. 'I went into
his study and I had in my hand a Penguin copy of *Jacobean Tragedies*,'

he says, 'so we started talking about that – and he never beat me.' A more conformist boy would have beaten him. A more nonconformist boy never would have become head of house. 'He was two people, in a way. I don't mean in a schizophrenic way. He was a very clever operator. If you talk to Peter Way's wife, Elizabeth, [1] about Peter Cook, "Very dull boy" is what she will say. And that's exactly how he appeared to the people he had to report up to. He gave them what they wanted. He knew exactly what he was doing. He was acting. And to us, down below, he gave the other Peter Cook. He was developing this extraordinary character.' Peter had an anarchic side, but it was always cunningly concealed.

'In those days, the food at Radley was indescribably awful. My mother used to send me monthly food parcels, to keep me going. We lived on toast.' Yet despite its various privations, Radley gave its pupils the time and freedom to cultivate interests of their own. 'It was a very laissez-faire school. It wasn't very intellectual, but there were some very intelligent, clever people there.' And Peter was one of them. 'Life was pretty tough there. The food wasn't good. The living conditions were – compared to today – very hard, in a way. It was bloody cold, I'll tell you that – we had cold baths every morning – but if you wanted to, you were able to make your own life there.'

Pupils were encouraged to pursue their own projects, and the project Francis can recall most vividly is *Black & White Blues*, the marionette musical that Peter wrote and performed with his friend and fellow pupil Michael Bawtree. 'It was absolutely wonderful,' says Francis. 'I'd never seen anything like it. It was incredibly funny and incredibly clever.' He enjoyed it so much that he went to see it a second time. Francis also took part in Peter's illicit (association) football matches. 'He was very approachable. I was thirteen and nobody and he was head of house, but he was a very approachable bloke.'

Francis lived in Cambridge – his father was a Don at the university. A few months before he went to Radley, his parents took him to see the Cambridge Footlights. 'Jonathan Miller appeared onstage wearing a pair of jeans, a blue shirt and no shoes. He was a naval rating on Nelson's ship, trying to draw Nelson's attention to the fact that the French were coming, and failing. I've never forgotten it. It was hysterical.' When Peter left Radley and went to Cambridge, Francis used to see him occasionally around town. He'd always stop and have a chat. He was still just as approachable.

When Francis left Radley he went on to Cambridge University, like Peter. Peter had already graduated, but he returned to Cambridge in *Beyond The Fringe*. Francis was in the audience. 'My only recollection is roaring with laughter, and feeling slightly embarrassed that I was doing so. Deference was so marked in those days. You didn't mock the Prime Minister. You didn't make a mockery of people who'd been in Spitfires fifteen years before. The war wasn't that long ago, so it was very challenging humour. My parents only enjoyed bits of it. They found some of it too much to take, which you can understand. They were brought up in a harder tradition than I was. All that's gone today, and Peter had a significant role in destroying deference, because that was what the 1960s was about. It was really an attempt to equalise society.'

Francis had seen Bamber Gascoigne's Footlights show, *Share My Lettuce*, a few years before. He'd enjoyed that show, but it had no satirical intent – it was just jokes. *Beyond The Fringe* was completely different. '*Share My Lettuce* was old-style revue and *Beyond The Fringe* was new-style revue,' he says. Francis was eighteen when he saw

Beyond The Fringe, in his first year at Cambridge, in 1960. Yet some of his fellow undergraduates were in their early twenties. They'd been abroad on National Service. 'They had a different view. Some of them, after all, had fired shots in anger, so there was a divide between the two.' *Beyond The Fringe* widened this divide. 'It threatened your way of life, the way you'd been brought up,' he says. 'We laughed, we felt shocked, we felt threatened – it was dangerous.' In his Macmillan parody, Francis saw a sharper edge to Peter's humour which he hadn't seen at school. 'He could be quite cruel.' Yet Peter's 'Sitting On The Bench' monologue was exactly the sort of thing that Francis had seen him doing in the bathtub. 'That's absolutely typical. That's a bath story.' And now there it was, onstage.

MICHAEL BILLINGTON

'In double acts, one person has pretensions,
which the other person squashes.'

'I first became aware of Dudley at Oxford in the summer of fifty-nine,' says the *Guardian*'s theatre critic Michael Billington, over a delicious lunch in his cosy house in Chiswick (his French wife is a superb cook). In 1959 Michael was an undergraduate at Oxford University. Dudley had already graduated, but he was still around. 'It was a production of Aristophanes' *The Birds*. It was quite brilliant. Dudley supplied the music, and out of that came "Strictly For The Birds".' That solo piano piece became Dudley's first single. His haunting score was the soundtrack of that magical Oxford summer. 'It was one of those golden experiences,' remembers Michael. He realised straight away what a phenomenal talent Dudley was.

Michael didn't meet Dudley until later that summer when the Experimental Theatre Club took Ben Jonson's *Bartholomew Fair* on a short tour, first to the Guildhall in Leicester and then on to Stratford-upon-Avon to perform outdoors, in a clearing called the Dell, a short walk from the main theatre. They rehearsed in Oxford over the vacation. 'Ken Loach, who co-directed the show with a guy called David Webster – who later became a judge – engaged Dudley to just roam through the production providing little musical interludes, as an itinerant peddler,' recalls Michael. When they got to Leicester they found themselves billeted in a huge open-plan dormitory, with the men at one end and the women at the other. There was a piano in the dorm. When they bedded down for the night, Dudley would sit down and improvise until the small hours. 'All the women in the company would gather round the piano and gaze adoringly at this musical genius,' says Michael. 'They became entranced by him.' Deprived of sleep (and female adulation), the men weren't so enamoured. Michael and a few others formed an anti-Dudley group. This 'rather po-faced faction' demanded alternative accommodation. They were duly given another room, safely out of earshot. A few years later, Michael switched on the TV to watch *Sunday Night At The London Palladium*. 'There was Dudley, doing much of the material he'd been trying out in Leicester. We had it all for free, but we didn't appreciate it at the time.'

Dudley's musical talent was inseparable from his sex appeal. 'His compulsive sexual urge was very strong – and pretty evident,' says Michael. 'He just had to attract all the women in the room – and he did. He was mischievous and twinkly and funny and engaging – and brilliant at the piano – and so all the women in the company were besotted by him.' A lot of the company were keen to pursue careers in the theatre or television – and a good many of them did so – but Dudley was always different. 'There was this wild card, this wild genius in our midst who, even then, was compulsive in his desire to amuse and entertain.' Yet with that compulsion came a certain distance. The rest of the cast would socialise together, sitting around in cafes or scouring the local bookshops. 'I don't remember Dudley ever being part of that. There was also a sort of solitude.' He only really came alive when the spotlight was on him. 'After midnight a different Dudley emerged, which was the jazz pianist, the comic. I don't remember him in the daytime at all.'

The show moved on to Stratford, full of big names that summer –
Laurence Olivier and Charles Laughton, plus rising stars like Albert
Finney, Vanessa Redgrave and Diana Rigg. 'Yet again, we were all
put into communal living quarters,' says Michael. 'And the same
thing happened all over again.' This time, there was no alternative
accommodation. They had to lump it. 'It was literally every night,'
says Michael, with a rueful chuckle. 'He never showed any remorse
or anxiety.' But Michael didn't hold a grudge. 'It was my insight into
how difficult it must be to live with anyone with a touch of genius.
While they have phenomenal gifts, they're not necessarily people
you'd want to share accommodation with.'

Michael was quick to spot Dudley's gifts but they were so eclectic,
straddling jazz and classical music and comedy, that he couldn't
quite see what Dudley would do with them. 'You wouldn't have said
this guy's going to become a comic actor or a Hollywood movie star.
That would have been inconceivable at that time – an idiosyncratic,
unclassifiable talent that didn't quite fit into any obvious niche. At
that stage, not many people were combining comedy and music.' And
then, in the summer of 1960, Michael went up to Edinburgh, as a
student critic, and saw the first night of a new revue called *Beyond
The Fringe*. Dudley had found his niche.

'It was unstoppably funny. It was also technically disastrous. They
hadn't had a technical run-through, so things started to go wrong.
The lights went out in the middle of Alan Bennett's sermon. But
this didn't matter a damn, because you knew you were witnessing
something unique.' Michael believes that *Beyond The Fringe* didn't
just change British humour. He believes it changed the face of
Britain. 'It wasn't *Look Back In Anger* that changed British life in 1956
– it was *Beyond The Fringe* in 1960,' he says. 'It was the moment when

automatic respect for authority in Britain died.'

Before *Beyond The Fringe*, the British Establishment had been regarded as above mockery. The Church, the Army, the Monarchy – now all these institutions were up for grabs. 'Anything became a legitimate target,' Michael says. 'The Establishment Club wouldn't have happened without it, *TW3* wouldn't have happened without it, *Private Eye* wouldn't have happened. It opened the door. It marked that moment when authority, hierarchy, all those things, were punctured – for good, it seemed to me. I think it was genuinely subversive, in that it infiltrated the values of a whole generation.'

Michael felt the four performers complemented each other perfectly. 'Every single member of the quartet had their own speciality – their own forte, their own style. They each brought something different to the mix. Jonathan Miller brought this surreal zaniness. Peter brought this ability to caricature Establishment types. Alan Bennett brought this peculiar, quaint English mix of satire and nostalgia, which I still think imbues his work. It's a strange mixture of sentimentality and subversiveness. Dudley was the jester in that foursome. The others were very good at representing authority figures, and lampooning them. Dudley could never be an authority figure.'

For Michael, it's no mystery that Dudley became a film star and Peter didn't, even though, at the outset, Peter looked like the one destined for stardom. 'Peter's genius was a verbal genius. His gifts, I thought, were predominantly linguistic, and that's not something that naturally transfers to film.' Likewise, his air of patrician authority, which worked so well onstage, wasn't something that worked so well on the big screen. 'Dudley, on the other hand, is always this imp of mischief – this sexy little satyr. There was obviously an ability to establish an instant rapport with an audience – to beguile women. That was always there in Dudley, and that seems to me to come across on-screen much better.' Where Peter scored more highly was as a writer. As Harold Pinter's biographer, Michael recognises some similarities between Pinter's work and Peter's. 'What Cook and Pinter shared was an awareness of the surreal possibilities of the English language,' he says. 'It's an alertness to the absurdities inherent within language.' Clearly, there are parallels between Pete & Dud and the dark double acts in Pinter plays like The Dumb Waiter and The Birthday Party. 'Both Pinter and Pete & Dud feed off that memory,' he says. 'They're drawing on a common tradition.'

Unlike Beyond The Fringe, Michael was rather underwhelmed by the first night of Behind The Fridge. 'I think I wrote a fairly caustic review, edged with disappointment,' he says. 'Something very strange happened the following morning. I was at home when the phone rang. It was Peter Cook, whom I'd never met, and he offered a slightly halting defence of the show.' To Michael, it had seemed as if Peter was propping up Dudley. He'd said as much in his review. In fact, it was the other way around. It was after that performance, and this review, that Dudley decided to end their partnership. Peter's phone call was an attempt to make amends with Dudley. 'I think what he was trying to do was redress the balance,' says Michael. 'He was suggesting it wasn't Dudley's fault that it hadn't worked. I think he was motivated by a genuine desire to set the record straight.'

GAYE BROWN

'It was a bit like the older brother and the younger
brother with those two. It was a bit like Cain and Abel
– the need to have each other's girls, the need to have
each other's careers. The only thing Peter couldn't do
was play a fucking piano.'

The actress Gaye Brown first met Peter at The Establishment. 'It was an open audition,' she says. 'They were looking for a singer.' She didn't get the job, but Peter's club became her favourite hangout. 'It was the place to go,' she remembers fondly. 'We used to go every night.' She worked behind the bar, serving rising stars like Terence Stamp and Michael Caine. She worked for *Scene*, the magazine that Peter set up with Nicholas Luard. Meanwhile, Dudley would be downstairs, playing the piano. She'd never known anything like it. It was unlike any other nightclub, before or since. 'It was very informal, and very exclusive.' It captured the spirit of the age.

'There was this huge influx of extraordinarily funny people,' recalls Gaye over dinner in an Italian restaurant in Covent Garden, after rehearsals for her latest West End show. She saw Lenny Bruce there, and Frankie Howerd, and Barry Humphries too. 'Nobody got it at all,' she says of the man who became Dame Edna. 'I knew it was good, but I didn't know why.' But it is Peter and Dudley who loom largest in her mind's eye. 'I loved him,' she says of Peter. 'He was very attractive and very funny.' He could be caustic, but maybe that was just shyness.

Dudley, on the other hand, was always kind and charming. 'I adored Dudley,' she says.

Gaye became friends with Peter's first wife, Wendy, and went to their house in Hampstead where Wendy held her celebrated dinner parties. 'She entertained royally,' says Gaye. 'She made it possible for him to do his shtick.' If Swinging London happened anywhere, it happened in that basement kitchen in Church Row. Peter usually held court, but when Dudley got going there was no stopping him. Gaye recalls an evening at the Ark, a trendy restaurant in Notting Hill, when Dudley suddenly went off on an absurd riff about the Nazis. Peter was funny too, but this time it was Dudley who set the pace. The entire restaurant was agog. 'It was an extraordinary twenty minutes,' recalls Gaye. If only she'd had a tape recorder.

Peter and Judy met at The Establishment, but they got together at one of Gaye's dinner parties. Gaye could sense that they were attracted to each other. 'She was nothing like Wendy,' says Gaye, of Judy. Wendy was a wife and mother, Judy was his lover. He loved his family. He was in love with Judy. He was bound to suffer heartbreak either way. 'Peter suffered a huge amount of guilt,' says Gaye. 'There was a huge amount of pain.'

The culmination of her friendship with the two of them was during the three weeks she spent in New York over Christmas, during the Broadway run of *Good Evening*. 'I got to know Peter very well,' she says. 'Peter and I spent a lot of time together, and Dudley and I also spent a lot of time together when I was there. Dudley wasn't very well. He was staying at the Algonquin. I used to go over there and have tea.' Judy was unwell too. She was back in London. Alone in New York, Peter dropped his guard with Gaye, but he was missing Judy and drink had wrought a change in him. 'For the first time I saw that really unpleasant streak.' She saw less of him after that.

She was appearing in a play in Bromley when she heard that Peter had died. 'I was very upset,' she says. She dedicated the show to him. 'I think he really wanted Dudley's career,' she says. 'Dudley was fine while he was still playing the piano. The moment he became an icon, doing those films, I think it was very hard for him.' After he went to Hollywood, she lost touch with Dudley too, but one year, out of the blue, she got a Christmas card from him. 'Do you remember me?' he'd written inside. 'I wonder where that's come from?' she thought. That was the last time she ever heard from him.

MICHAEL BURRELL

'Peter was the most difficult person in the world to
corpse. I managed it twice.'

The actor and director Michael Burrell met Peter during his second year at Cambridge. 'It was the spring term. I went into the college and got my mail. There was a card which said, "Could you come and see me at my digs in Clarendon Road at ten-thirty tomorrow morning, Peter Cook."' Michael knew all about Peter. So did everyone at Cambridge. He was President of Footlights. He had a show running in the West End. Michael was surprised to hear from Peter. Michael had done a lot of acting, but he wasn't in Footlights. At ten-thirty next morning he reported to Clarendon Road.

'I think he's still asleep,' said Peter's landlady. 'I've got an appointment,' said Michael. 'Well, you'd better go up,' she said. Michael went upstairs. Peter's landlady was right. Peter was still in bed, curtains drawn, fast asleep. He woke up when Michael came in. 'Would you like to do the Footlights Revue this summer?' Peter asked him, bleary-eyed. 'Yes,' said Michael. 'I'd love to. I'd better audition, then.' 'What for?' asked Peter. 'You have to audition to be a member of Footlights,' said Michael. 'Don't be a cunt,' said Peter, with a yawn. 'You're doing the Revue. You're in the Footlights.' And with that, he went back to sleep. Michael went away elated.

Michael was reading English at Peterhouse. He'd gone to a public school, as a day boy, on a scholarship. 'I went up intending to be a schoolmaster,' he says over lunch at the Liberal Club in London, 'until I found myself acting with Corin Redgrave, John Fortune, Ian McKellen, Derek Jacobi, John Bird, Eleanor Bron, Trevor Nunn ... The list goes on and on.'

Michael appeared with Peter in *Pop Goes Mrs Jessop*, mainly written by Peter and widely regarded as the funniest Footlights Revue ever staged. They performed several sketches together, including one of Peter's classics, 'Interesting Facts'. 'He was a genius and we were all aware of that,' says Michael. 'Everybody else was funnier when he was around.' But not as funny as Peter. One night, Michael changed the closing line of one of Peter's sketches. 'Of course it fell flat on its face.' As Michael came off, he found Peter waiting in the wings. 'Perhaps that'll teach you to do the script I wrote,' he said.

Pop Goes Mrs Jessop played to packed, ecstatic houses for two weeks in June. Two months later Peter was in Edinburgh, performing in *Beyond The Fringe*. He returned to Cambridge the following spring, with Alan, Jonathan and Dudley, to dust down the show in preparation for its transfer to the West End. Michael saw the preview. 'All four of them were superb,' he says. 'It was very much a quartet, although much of it was written by Peter.' Peter's comic eye, the way he saw the world, was already fully formed.

Like a lot of people who admired Peter and cared about him, Michael was saddened and frustrated by the false starts of Peter's later career. When he saw Peter's US sitcom, *The Two of Us*, he actually felt quite angry. 'What the hell are you doing?' he thought. 'You had a unique quality and a unique ability and you're coming out and doing crap.' 'It wasn't that the script was crap. It was the way he was doing it. He couldn't do it. He wasn't an actor. That wasn't what he should have been doing.' What he should have been doing was writing and performing with Dudley, but Dudley was long gone. 'It was a marriage in the way that Morecambe & Wise was a marriage,' says Michael. But Morecambe & Wise was a rarity. Most double acts don't last. 'You end up knowing far too much about each other,' says Michael. You could say the same about most marriages. And although Dudley became a star without Peter, he could never match Peter's creative flair. 'Dudley wasn't an originator in the way that Peter was. Peter was a creator – and he created a world.'

ELIZABETH COOK

'If a child gets sent away when they're really small, and there isn't anyone to turn to who loves them, that must create habits of containment of some kind.'

'I remember him leaping into the swimming pool in Nigeria,' says Elizabeth Cook, Peter's youngest sister, recalling her earliest memory of her big brother. 'I was floating around in this little inflatable rubber boat, and Peter leapt from the diving board and landed on the boat.' She was a toddler at the time. Her sister Sarah was seven years older. Peter was seven years older still. 'We come in seven-year instalments,' she says, over coffee in the kitchen of her terraced house in London's East End. 'It means we didn't really have childhoods together. Peter was nearly fifteen years older than me.' She was slightly closer in age to his eldest daughter, Lucy. 'We weren't all children together. Peter was nearly an adult when I was born.'

Elizabeth was born in Gibraltar, but her parents took her to Nigeria when she was still a baby. It was her father's second spell in Nigeria. Elizabeth loved it there, but her mother preferred Gibraltar. 'I know mum's heart sank when dad decided to go back to Nigeria. She didn't enjoy it very much.' Peter was boarding at Radley, and would only appear during the holidays. 'He was just this wonderful elder brother who would suddenly arrive.'

Peter and Sarah both went to boarding school when they were seven. Her parents were merely trying to do their best for them, but Sarah, in particular, didn't like being sent away. 'It was horrible for her,' says Elizabeth. 'I was fortunate because I went to boarding school and hated it and ran away, but I didn't go until I was twelve.'

By the time Elizabeth was old enough to really talk to him, Peter was at Cambridge. 'I remember him coming out to Libya, where our father was working for the United Nations,' she says. One of her most vivid memories was when Peter came for the vacation before his Finals, to revise. Peter got jaundice, and their mother had to return to England to tend to her dying father, leaving Elizabeth and her father to look after Peter. 'Me aged seven, a little nurse in my nurse's uniform, bustling around trying to look after him. I think we were fairly incompetent.' It's a moving image, all the same.

Their father, Alec, sounds like a gentle man. 'Quite eccentric, in a quiet way,' says Elizabeth. 'Not nearly as conventional as has been portrayed.' And not as posh. 'He wasn't in the Foreign Office,' she says. 'He was in the Colonial Service. His mother, I would say, was kind of distressed gentlefolk. Her husband died young. She ran a sort of boarding house in Southsea, and really struggled financially. We weren't a grand family at all, or a wealthy family.' As a political adolescent, Elizabeth was slightly hostile towards her father's work, but now she regards his career as rather idealistic, a bit like VSO today. 'It wasn't a fantastic way to make money – it was a really tough, and quite a lonely life.' Alec wasn't a diplomat. He worked in local government. 'A lot of responsibility, which he took very seriously. He really worried a lot, I think, about getting things right.' Elizabeth remembers their mother, Margaret, with equal fondness. 'She was very warm and made friends very easily.' She was also very bright. She'd read the whole of Dickens by the time she was twelve. 'She would have loved to have gone to university, but her parents couldn't afford it.' When Elizabeth got into Oxford to read English, Margaret was thrilled.

It was only after Alec's death that Peter discovered that Alec's father, Edward, had killed himself. 'It was a terrible discovery,' says Elizabeth. Alec's mother had kept it a secret throughout her life. The strain on her, and on Alec, must have been immense. 'I don't know how our dad would have responded had he known,' says Elizabeth, but deep down he must have sensed that something was awry. Though he never knew the truth, Elizabeth feels sure the tragedy must have affected him on some subconscious level. The eventual revelation was an awful shock for everyone. 'I felt as if I was meeting my grandfather and losing him all at once.' Peter found some newspaper cuttings, full of affectionate tributes to his grandad. Edward was Alec's middle name, and Peter's too.

Elizabeth adored her elder brother. 'He was very glamorous to me, and handsome and gorgeous and rarely seen, so when he wasn't at home I would try and piece together who he was, and go through his things. He lit up the house when he arrived. There was a general air of celebration when he was around. He made everybody laugh.' He wasn't the only one. 'As a family we communicated a lot by laughing,' says Elizabeth. They didn't tell each other jokes, as such. 'It was a way of being alive.'

Elizabeth spent her eighth birthday in Edinburgh, where she saw *Beyond The Fringe*. Her mother drove her up there, with her sister Sarah. 'It took ages,' she recalls. 'We kept stopping for the night at bed and breakfasts.' But the show was worth the trek. 'I was absolutely bursting with pride and excitement – I loved it,' she says. "And now Dudley Moore continues to play with himself."

I thought that was very funny. I had no idea what it meant.' She'd heard Kenneth Williams doing Peter's sketches, on the LPs of *Pieces of Eight* and *One Over The Eight*, but it was the first time she'd seen her brother perform. Elizabeth was very proud of him, as were Sarah and their parents. 'They didn't find the World War Two sketch that funny, because they'd recently lived through the war and it was not a laughing matter, but I don't think there was anything else that upset them. They thought most of it was terribly funny.'

It was in Edinburgh that they met Wendy for the first time. 'She was really nice to me. She was very good with small children. And she was very good when I was an adolescent.' Wendy used to lend Elizabeth her clothes. 'She was very groovy.' Wendy's relationship with Alec and Margaret was rather more restrained. 'I don't think they quite got each other.'

The success of *Beyond The Fringe* propelled Peter into a different orbit – first the West End, and then Broadway. 'That was really sad for me – for all of us, because we missed him.' Elizabeth was pleased when he returned to England, and set up home in Church Row with Wendy. Going to stay with them for a week or two was always the highlight of her school holidays. 'It was a beautiful house – it still is. I peered in the window with Daisy and Lucy once. It's still got the same William Morris wallpaper.' Peter and Wendy had an en-suite bedroom – still a novelty in those days, 'and a lovely kitchen in the basement, where Wendy cooked up a storm.'

And then there was Dudley. 'I adored Dudley. He wrote me a lovely letter when Peter and Wendy got married. I was stuck at school. It was very kind, very thoughtful. It was a funny letter as well.' Alec and Margaret had flown over for the wedding, but they couldn't afford to take Sarah or Elizabeth. Unprompted, Dudley took it upon himself to write to Elizabeth to cheer her up. When they got together as a double act, Elizabeth could see that Dudley brought out something special in Peter. 'It just seemed to be exactly the right kind of input – and lack of input. Dudley was more passive in their work together. It was the right sort of rhythm.'

When Elizabeth was away at school, she was allowed to watch Peter in *Not Only … But Also*, but only under strict supervision. 'I had to go into the house mistress's study and watch it with her. She wasn't filled with a sense of humour. She'd sit rather stony-faced next to me.' It would have made a splendid sketch. She did get along to the TV studios a few times, to see *Goodbye Again*, with Donovan and Ike & Tina Turner, and Peter's spat with Zsa Zsa Gabor on Eamonn Andrews's chat show.

Peter didn't mind the fame. 'He always got a kick out of it,' says Elizabeth. 'He always seemed to be quite tickled if the taxi driver recognised him. He liked the fact that he could be friends with the Rolling Stones – that was really fun – but it didn't go to his head.' Yet society was changing fast – changed in part by people like Peter. They were now in uncharted territory, and couples like Peter and Wendy paid a heavy price. 'I think it was a really heady way of living that they got into, which is probably not very good for any relationship.' Then Peter and Wendy split up, and Peter got together with Judy. 'I think probably, of his three wives, she was the one he liked best, and had most fun with – they made each other laugh. Judy was great with Lucy and Daisy. They were really very, very fond of her.' Yet that marriage also ended in divorce. 'I think, again, in a way, that probably fell victim to the whole atmosphere of too much booze and drugs.'

The other relationship that didn't last was Peter's partnership with Dudley. 'I always felt Peter missed Dudley very much. People have said that he was deeply envious of Dudley's success. I never saw a glimmer of that at all. I thought he was glad for Dudley and a bit amused by it. I think he thought it was a bit funny, Dudley being a film-star sex symbol. But I think mainly he missed him. There was no sense of envy at all.'

When Elizabeth was at Oxford, she'd go and stay with Peter and Judy, and saw he was drinking more and more. 'I'd try and keep up with him, as a way of being with him, which wasn't a very good idea,' she says. 'One component of his drinking was that he saw more than he could bear to see. He was so aware of the dynamics in the room going on between people. Sometimes it was very hard to see so much. He drank to simplify himself in a way, to coarsen himself, because he wasn't coarse at all.'

JUDY COOK

'It was never boring with Peter or Dudley. I couldn't have done it if I was older. I had to be young, beautiful and desirable to be in that situation. It was a very dangerous situation to be in. I'm not proud of all of it. A lot of things I do regret, because I would have liked to have had children, and been happily married, and all the rest of it. But for one reason or another, I was there at that time, and I was fascinated by it.'

'It's as light as a feather but as sharp as a sword, and yet it's got this abstract quality. It's not humour that punches you in the face. It almost slips past you.' I'm sitting in a quiet corner of the Castle Hotel in Taunton, sharing a pot of tea with Judy Cook, Peter's second wife, the central romance of his life. She's trying to describe his elusive wit, the wit that changed the course of British comedy. 'Just when you think, "That was just a little puff of wind," you suddenly die from it. You realise he's absolutely clobbered you.' Her eyes are bright with tears – tears of sadness, tears of laughter.

Judy shows me a card that Peter sent to her on her birthday. 'Hope You Have A Speedy Recovery,' it reads. 'May You Be Up And About Again Soon.' Peter has changed it to 'May You Be Down And Out.' The picture is of an old man, fishing on a riverbank. 'This is to remind you that it is your 87th birthday today,' he's written in his spidery scrawl.

Peter was generous with his humour. He never rationed it for a paying public. 'It was in the fabric of him,' says Judy. 'It wasn't something that got switched on because he was writing or performing. It was there all the time. If you went gently with it and you didn't put him under pressure there was no end to it.' She's talking about their relationship, but she could be talking about Peter's relationship with Dudley. 'Now, you tell me how I could ever leave him, in spite of all that went on.' She shows me one of his tender love letters. 'It drove me crazy at times. I thought, "I can't go on." But when I knew what was in him, the way he expressed himself, it was impossible not to love him at a very deep level.'

The first time Judy saw Peter was in *Beyond The Fringe*. Her parents took her to see the show at London's Fortune Theatre. She couldn't take her eyes off him. 'The way Peter performs, he's demanding your attention all the time. He's delivering the lines, to Dudley or Jonathan or Alan, but he's looking out into the audience, to get the audience's reaction – as if to say, "Aren't I just the best thing on this stage?" So you can't help but follow everything he's doing. Even though he may be ruining the line for someone else, he's making it for himself.' Judy was in a show called *The Lord Chamberlain Regrets*. 'Our show closed because of *Beyond The Fringe*. Ours was an old-fashioned revue.' Suddenly everything looked old-fashioned, compared with *Beyond The Fringe*. 'It was so funny and witty and new.' She found the other three fascinating too. 'They had the confidence, a laid-back confidence, at such a young age. They were so pleased with themselves. You just didn't expect that. It was marvellous to see. It was like watching something flower.'

The first time they met was at The Establishment. Judy was only nineteen. 'All the girls used to gather round the piano, listening to Dudley.' She remembers regulars like Michael Caine, but the biggest buzz was around Peter. 'Word would go round that he was dropping in that night. Maybe he was going to perform.' One night, he asked her to dance. 'That was quite a shock,' she says. 'I thought I'd be looked upon as just a silly deb.' But Peter was with Wendy, so things never went any further. At The Establishment Judy met Sean Kenny, who'd designed the place – and *Beyond The Fringe* – and married him. Peter and Judy didn't meet again for several years.

The next time they met was in Jermyn Street, in London's West End, where Peter went to have his silk shirts made. Wendy was in Majorca. 'I knew when I met him in Jermyn Street. I knew he was going to pick up the threads.' Then Judy's friend Gaye Brown invited them to the same dinner party. 'I didn't want to go because I thought it was dangerous. I was married. He was married.' But Judy's marriage wasn't happy. 'Things were pretty desperate with Sean. I was involved in something that was way out of my depth.' Sean Kenny was a binge drinker. 'He never had drink in the house. He went days without touching it, weeks without touching it. But when he did, he'd go out with people like Francis Bacon, for days on end, and come back absolutely smashed out of his head.' It wasn't just drink. 'He jumped out of a window, thinking he was Batman.'

After Gaye Brown's dinner party, Peter followed Judy home. He was in his battered Citroen. She was in her white open-top E-type Jaguar. He slept in her bed. She slept on the sofa. But it wasn't long until they became an item. 'I let him be him without asking him to perform, which is very important to someone.' It was especially important for Peter.

It was also important for Peter that Judy got along with Dudley. 'Dudley was like a brother to him. There was a deep connection. He wasn't just a working partner. He wanted to show me off to Dudley. He wanted Dudley to fancy me. He wanted Dudley to approve of me.

And he wanted to say, "Look what I've got!" All of that.' And on top of all that, he wanted them to be friends. 'He wanted all of that at once.'

However, when Dudley turned up at Peter and Judy's new home, Kenwood Cottage, Judy could tell that he had other ideas. 'I could tell from the twinkle in his eye that it was going to be a different kind of problem.' The problem was that Dudley wanted whatever Peter had. Yet, despite these complications, Peter wanted him around. 'Peter needed somebody who would feed him, and Dudley was the perfect person. He was the perfect wife, brother, everything. They did love each other. It was brotherly love.' Dudley's musicianship gave Peter's verbal abstractions a sense of structure. 'Dudley was fanatical about timing,' says Judy. 'He'd always stick to the script.' And then Peter would throw it up in the air and create absolute havoc. Peter could ad-lib and Dudley couldn't. That was the big difference. It was that fusion of contrasting talents which made them such a special team. They made comedy to amuse each other. The rest of us were just listening in.

Peter remained sober – while his partner was around. 'When he'd finished a day's work with Dudley, he'd hit the bottle.' It wasn't a big issue – yet – but Judy started to notice subtle changes. 'When he was frustrated with Dudley, and things weren't going right, he'd drink quite a lot of wine.' One morning Judy woke up to find that, overnight, Peter had polished off a bottle of cheap sherry, which she'd bought to make a trifle. 'Why do you need to drink a bottle of cooking sherry?' she asked. 'Oh, I couldn't sleep, and it was there,' he answered. 'Peter always had an answer,' she says.

Judy's mother was the first person to spot that Peter was an alcoholic. 'She should know. She was one.' Judy took Peter to visit her parents in Jersey. 'She got him totally rat-arsed after dinner. She just kept plying him with more brandy. She was flirting wildly with him. Like women of a certain age who shouldn't but do, when they're drunk. My mother could be very over the top.' 'He's a drunk, Judy,' her mother told her. 'He's a total alcoholic.' Well, you should know, thought Judy. 'I felt very angry, because she'd been plying him with drink all evening, and then telling him what he was.'

When Peter and Dudley were invited to tour Australia, in *Behind The Fridge*, Judy went with them. 'I'd been ill with peritonitis, so there was no way I could work. I couldn't do anything, even if I'd stayed in England. I was too weak. And he wanted me to go out, so I went.' Judy had been very ill indeed. Her weight had dropped to five stone. She needed some sunshine. She needed a change of scene. 'I had looked death in the face, and that does stay with you a bit. Once you've had that experience you're frightened that it's going to happen again.' Her health remained precarious, and Peter's promiscuity didn't help. 'I needed Peter to learn from that, and not go on giving me infections. But he did, because he was sleeping around. So he didn't grow as a man, and learn with me. He didn't learn from these things that happened to him. He thought it was still all out there on a plate.'

Peter drank more in Australia, in the evenings and at lunchtime. Often he'd crash out and Judy would be left alone with Dudley. 'If Peter was passed out on the bed, through drinking Australian wine, Dudley would just happen to walk past and knock on the door.' Dudley was the only person she could talk to about Peter's drinking, but he had another agenda. 'Dudley was wildly flirtatious,' she says. 'Peter had already warned me that Dudley had a devious side.' It was almost like Jekyll and Hyde. 'Dudley was incredibly charming, and yet there was this undertone all the time – that he was going to get me. A different atmosphere had crept into it. It was very dangerous. I could see that. I could not only have ruined my own life, but Peter's life, completely – and Dudley's.' She knew Peter never would have forgiven her. Thankfully, for all their sakes, Judy resisted Dudley's advances. 'I wasn't the pliable little girl that Dudley wanted me to be. I wouldn't go to bed with him. I wouldn't do what he wanted. He then turned against me, in the same way that he turned against Peter when Peter wouldn't do what Dudley wanted.' Yet there was no way out. She knew that if she walked out, it would have caused chaos. Peter would have been destroyed.

Back in London, doing *Behind The Fridge* in the West End, Judy took over as Peter and Dudley's dresser. By now, she knew the show inside out, and when she was backstage she could control Peter's boozing. 'He'd limit his drinking to two glasses of champagne and orange juice. I'd take it in on a tray.' 'Here's your limit for the night, while you're onstage,' she'd say. Peter would stick to it. After the fiasco of the first night, when Peter got completely bladdered, the show was now on safer ground, but offstage the relationship between the two men had become obsessive. 'Dudley wanted to know everything that Peter was doing,' she says. 'He'd ring up, and if Peter wasn't there he'd want to know what he'd had for breakfast, what he was wearing, where he was going. My whole brain was filled with what one or the other was doing.' At Dudley's instigation, they all went to the same psychiatrist. 'Where Dudley and Peter went, I went. What they did, I did. What they talked about, I talked about.' It was almost like an addiction. Other people seemed boring by comparison. 'I looked around and I didn't see anybody more interesting. Would you have thought any different?'

*

Then the show transferred to Broadway. 'I knew before they went to America that there would be trouble. Dudley was fed up with me, because I hadn't done what he wanted. And Peter was annoyed. I had flirted with someone else because I was angry with him, with his drinking. I knew he was going to pay me back.' When they left, Judy had a horrible feeling. She knew the whole dynamic was changing. 'What's going to happen now?' she thought. 'Who are they going to pull in now?' She was right to be concerned. Soon after Peter arrived in America he had a brief fling with Tuesday Weld. 'Some of it was so ludicrous. He and Dudley went to the same prostitute. And he was telling me what Dudley had told this prostitute.' Yet there was no way Judy could walk away. 'It was still interesting. It was almost like I couldn't believe I was part of it. It fascinated me, in a way.' It was like being stuck inside a movie. She had to know what would happen next.

America wasn't all bad. They got married in New York. Judy cut her hair short before the wedding and wore a white trouser suit. They would have liked a Las Vegas wedding, just the two of them, but Peter had to do the show that evening. 'I couldn't get away, he couldn't get away. We were trapped in that treadmill, of having to make the money. It's what gets you in the end.'

After the American tour, Peter and Judy came back to London, leaving Dudley in America. Dudley flew to London and came to Perrins Walk to tell Peter that the partnership was over. 'Peter was absolutely devastated by Dudley refusing to work with him any more. That was the end of his career. He had done everything with Dudley.' He knew Dudley gave him something he could never get elsewhere.

'He tried to work with other people but it was never the same as it was with Dudley,' says Judy. 'Dudley facilitated him in everything. Dudley knew how to sit down beside him, get him started, work with him, and just let it roll.' It was a unique way of working. Once it was gone, it was gone for good. The thing that replaced it was booze. 'He'd drink a bottle of vodka and then he'd chase it down with endless beers.' The effects were masked by the downers and uppers he took to kept him both laid-back and alert – barbiturates and slimming pills. 'He was mixing a lot of stuff,' she says. 'He thought he was invincible.'

Dudley's performance in *Arthur* rubbed salt in Peter's wounds. 'When he was angry with Peter for drinking he used to mimic Peter like Arthur. That was his dress rehearsal for *Arthur*. Dudley was doing Arthur in front of Peter long before he did the film. It was sending Peter up and Peter hated it.' No wonder Peter never saw it on the big screen. 'We were watching the film together in Perrins Walk and I just froze.'

Peter ended up in such a bad way that in the end Judy obtained an injunction. 'I got a court order restraining Peter from coming into the spare room at night and shouting at me.' She was in a bad way, too. 'I wasn't capable of leaving. I didn't have a job. I couldn't do anything. I was underweight, grotesquely thin. Sort of anorexic, almost. I didn't have any other home, and Peter had become my family and my life.' She still feels bad about it today, but she has no need to. It was an act of desperation. 'I still couldn't leave him, even if I'd gone somewhere to stay the night. Not that I could, because how can you explain that situation to anyone? How can you say, "This is how it's been with him. This is how it's come to this." People didn't believe me.'

Judy used to seek solace with a friendly shopkeeper. 'She used to let me go in and have coffee with her, and I just used to cry,' she says. 'I couldn't stop it, I couldn't control it. And by that time I was a codependant. I know that now, from reading books on alcoholism. I was stuck in it myself. I didn't know whether I was hindering him or helping him, because I was so dragged down by it.'

The injunction brought Peter to his senses. He started going to AA meetings. However, this valiant attempt to beat the bottle was undermined by his return to America, to appear as a butler in *The Two of Us*. This American remake of a British sitcom wasn't the best use of Peter's talents. It also pushed him off the wagon, and he never really got back on. 'He used to ring me up regularly,' says Judy. 'It was obvious, the state he was in. Peter was too addicted to stuff. It was never going to stop.'

Judy moved to Somerset. She needed to be connected to something natural. She got some dogs, chickens and horses. 'I just wanted to get out. Just ride.' Peter didn't move there with her – he remained, alone, in Hampstead – but he joined her for weekends. Judy hoped it was the start of something new. 'He was able to be quiet and relaxed. He could potter about in the garden and go where he liked.' Helping with the daily chores did him the world of good – mucking out the horses, taking the dogs for a walk. 'He didn't drink down there. He used to go on a sabbatical and drink orange juice.'

Sadly, a tabloid sexposé about Peter's life in London hurt Judy deeply. In the aftermath of these revelations she had a brief affair. 'My pride and vanity got the better of me.' Peter could hardly blame her – he'd had numerous liaisons – but even so it hit him terribly hard. 'He couldn't cope with it. He went to bits, and I went to bits because I'd pulled him to bits.' She wanted to go back to London to be with him, but she couldn't leave the animals. 'I didn't stick with it,' she says. 'If I'd just had a bit more faith ...' But she'd forgiven his countless affairs. 'Why couldn't he forgive me one?'

*

Eventually, Peter asked for a divorce. Judy went to their old home in Perrins Walk, to discuss it, and saw the letter from Peter's doctor telling him he had sclerosis of the liver. 'What are you going to do about it?' she asked him. 'I'm going on holiday,' he said. 'It just makes me want to drink more.' The last time they met was in court. They'd been unable to agree a settlement. 'I was on the stand for a day and a half, and I stood up to all that. When I got off the stand he shook my hand. I think it was more sarcastic than anything else, because I'd survived it. He was on the stand for about two hours, and he broke down.' It transpired that he was spending a lot of money on cocaine. 'He was forgetting a lot of stuff – serious stuff – and he was quite bemused. He was saying, "Did I do that?" I realised he was suffering from a form of dementia you get when you're drinking all the time.'

They spoke to each other on just two other occasions thereafter. Peter phoned Judy from Torquay, on the day of his wedding, to tell her that he'd married Lin. And then he phoned her again on his honeymoon, to ask her what she thought of Freddie Starr. 'I just went ballistic. I said, "How can you ring me up and ask me about Freddie Starr?"' Their relationship meant too much to her to reduce it all to trivia. She'd given the best years of her life to Peter. She wasn't prepared to become a comic cameo. 'My pride was not going to take that. I was furious, but that actually made it all the more funny.' If there is any moral to this sad story, it is that fame corrupts, and absolute fame corrupts absolutely. 'That's how he stayed regressed, in a sense. He didn't grow up, because he always got what he wanted.' So could the whole thing have worked out differently, I ask her. 'Yes, I think if I'd had children,' Judy says.

WENDY COOK

'I don't know about deeply in love – whether he was
capable of that, quite honestly. It was a very complicated
relationship and I think he didn't know how to love. I do
look to the childhood circumstances, his mother leaving
him when he was only months old to go and be with his
father – that's what wives did. He developed this strategy
for keeping the world at bay by laughing at it. This is what
humour does. If you laugh at something, it can't hurt you.'

Over lunch in a deserted restaurant in a grand old house in the West
Country I ask Peter's first wife, Wendy Cook, how she met the father
of her two children. 'I was an art student at Cambridge, I was eighteen
or nineteen, and I was friendly with a photographer – he was an
undergraduate, but he did most of the photographs for *Varsity*, the
university newspaper. He said, "I've got to find a pretty girl to be in a
photograph with Peter Cook," who already was a kind of character in
Cambridge – not only because he was a Footlights star, but because,
even by then, he'd written a revue for Kenneth Williams called *Pieces
of Eight*, so he'd got some glamour about him. I went up to the *Varsity*
office, and there was Peter. He was rather spotty. He had quite an
acne problem. He was extremely skinny. I had to drape myself across
his knee – I didn't have to, I could have refused – but he made it kind
of funny.' The photo shoot was for a feature about the forthcoming
May Ball. 'I borrowed a rather pretty blue and white ball gown.' She
didn't have one of her own. 'I felt he was terribly tense and rather full

of himself.' She went away and thought no more of it. Sometimes she saw him at parties. He'd wave and she'd wave back. 'I certainly didn't find him particularly attractive.'

Unlike a lot of students at the university, Wendy wasn't wealthy. She had to get jobs during the holidays. While she was working as a waitress in the Kenya Coffee Bar in Cambridge, Peter came in with a friend. 'Are you going to buy me a coffee?' Peter asked her. Wendy was gobsmacked. She had no shortage of suitors. 'How about you taking me to the pictures tomorrow?' he asked her as he left. She liked his cheek. She cancelled a date with her boyfriend, and she and Peter went to the cinema together. 'He was pretty fresh,' she says, 'but he made me laugh. I'm so intense, and laughter releases tension, so it was brilliant to be with somebody that actually made me laugh at myself.' Eventually, they became an item. 'Shakespeare's jesters have all the best lines, and when you get a good jester, who's not only making you laugh, but giving you insights – this is what Peter could do.'

When Peter went to visit his parents in Libya and contracted jaundice, he wrote Wendy some sweet letters, which deepened the bond between them. When he returned to Cambridge he was still ill. Wendy would go round to his rooms and grill bacon for him on his gas fire. In the end he moved into Wendy's digs, a converted pub called the Prince of Wales, which she shared with a shifting cast of fellow students. 'We'd stay up until two or three o'clock in the morning, having these deep discussions – what was happening in society, and the hypocrisy of this, that and the other.'

It was an extraordinary time to be in Cambridge. Derek Jacobi, Ian McKellen and Trevor Nunn were just a few of Wendy's contemporaries. 'I'd grown up in Bedfordshire, amongst the cabbage patches,' she says. 'To find that there was this amazing multicultural society only an hour away from where I lived!' Peter appeared onstage with friends like Eleanor Bron, but the shows were almost incidental. In a way, he was always acting. The other occupants of the Prince of Wales gave him a captive audience. 'He was a compulsive performer,' says Wendy. 'I'd make dinner every night and he'd just have everybody in stitches.' He never let up. He never let anybody else get a word in. If anyone else had been doing it, it might have been a terrific bore. 'He was so intelligent. It was incisive. It was rapier. But it was also warm – there was an affection there.'

They got engaged at the Edinburgh Festival, during the first run of *Beyond The Fringe*. 'I had a lovely green agate silver ring which we bought in Edinburgh.' In Edinburgh, and thereafter, she got to know Alan Bennett, Jonathan Miller and Dudley. 'Jonathan and Alan were very dismissive of Dudley and his jazz, and the women.' Wendy saw another side of him. 'I liked him a lot. He had real depth.' She wasn't the only one who felt that way. 'People loved him,' she says. 'He was very accessible.' And he made Peter's comedy accessible, too. Dudley had a lightness about him, which Wendy likens to champagne bubbles. It was Modern Languages meets Music. In the comedy they made together, Wendy could see Peter's knowledge of Proust and Goethe combine with Dudley's love of Bach.

'Dudley was affectionate, and Peter didn't know that. He didn't know about affection. He really didn't.' Public school had made him impeccably polite, but it hadn't been so good at giving him access to his emotions. 'The only time I saw Peter cry – well, a tear or two – was when the cat had to be put down,' she says. 'The whole thing is to take a young boy away from his mother, and subject him to more and more cruelty – the ability to be punished and to punish others, so he can go out into the military and lead, and be a warrior.' Dudley gave Peter access to part of his personality that boarding school had shut away. 'I think Peter loved Dudley more than anybody. I'm not saying it's a homosexual thing at all, but I think he really, really loved him. And yet he trashed it. Alcohol makes you trash things.'

When *Beyond The Fringe* transferred to London's West End, Peter's career found another level, and when he started the Establishment Club their social circle went stellar. 'There was Dudley downstairs with all the girls, and Peter upstairs with the politicians, the actors and the writers.' Nureyev dropped in, although Wendy was too shy to speak to him. 'I loved it. You wouldn't go to bed until four o'clock in the morning.' Yet her relationship paid a price. 'Peter and I were hardly ever alone.'

Wendy played a big part in Peter's newfound celebrity. She dressed him in the latest fashions. 'I spent a lot of time grooming him,' she says. 'He had no dress sense whatsoever.' Wendy had a good eye, and Peter was happy for her to choose his clothes. 'He enjoyed being a dandy.' The Establishment only lasted for a year or so before *Beyond The Fringe* transferred to Broadway. 'Peter took the team and left an empty room, and Nick Luard had not got the talent to be able to fill it, and that's when it went bankrupt.' Peter was a brilliant innovator, but he wasn't so good at sustaining things. 'He didn't really have a clue about managing things,' says Wendy. 'He was very compulsive.'

In New York, Wendy found a basement flat for them in Greenwich Village, which had been decorated like an Arabian tent by its homosexual owners. 'This wacky pad proved to be one block away from the Bowery, which is Skid Row, and one block away from the women's prison, where we'd hear them screaming at night.' Peter found it exhilarating. 'He was a high-adrenalin guy. But he took taxis everywhere. He didn't walk the streets.' They lived there together for nearly a year.

When they got back from Broadway, Wendy applied her aesthetic flair to the London homes they shared, first in Battersea and then in Hampstead. 'He was perfectly happy for me to make that contribution. It worked well.' Wendy fulfilled a deep need in Peter. 'He became very dependent on me as an organiser, kind of creating a scene that he could just be the clown in. I made homes. I made lovely meals. I enjoyed people. I knew who to invite together to be an electrical combination.' When they were in their house in Hampstead all sorts of people would drop in. 'Paul McCartney used to pop by with Martha, his lovely sheepdog, and have breakfast,' she says. 'We'd have Bernard Levin and Kenneth Tynan and Peter Ustinov round our dinner table.' It was like the greatest chat show on earth. 'We had amazing exchanges that went way into the night.'

Peter had always had a fascination with Faust and, once they were settled in Church Row, Wendy urged him to turn it into something concrete. 'He was almost obsessed by this struggle between light and darkness,' she says. 'I really encouraged him to make this into a film script.' Wendy had just given birth to Lucy, their first daughter. The first time she left her was to go to the cinema with Peter to see Cary Grant and Audrey Hepburn in *Charade*, directed by Stanley Donen. 'That's who you need,' she told Peter. 'He would do the right thing.' The following week, they were invited to dinner with Dirk Bogarde. Donen was there. Peter and Wendy invited him back to Church Row for dinner a week later, and he agreed to direct *Bedazzled*.

'Peter loved both little girls,' says Wendy, recalling their happy times together in Church Row. 'I think the change came when Daisy was born with severe asthma and eczema, and then this child needed a different environment, and I started getting worried about this atmosphere, to bring children up in.' She also felt that Peter had lost some of his early idealism. 'I fell for him because I knew he was going to change things. He was very idealistic, and very keen to slice away hypocrisy. He always said, "I would never do advertising."' Then one day he told her he'd signed a contract to do a beer advert for Watneys. Wendy was gutted. 'He doesn't need to do this,' she thought. It wasn't just the adverts. She could see that the comedy he did with Dudley was changing too. 'It was becoming decadent. Something else was creeping in which wasn't their true selves.'

Was Peter's growing wealth an unwelcome distraction? 'It wasn't so much the money. It was just the pace of life. When you've got two children, and the nights are disturbed, I just felt we needed a different kind of environment. And I hardly ever saw Peter. He was so busy.' Peter adored his daughters, but in those days (even) fewer men did their fair share of childcare. 'He never changed a nappy or took a baby out in a pram,' she says. 'Our marriage would have been very different if he had participated in that way.'

During this time, Dudley and his first wife Suzy Kendall were neighbours, and frequent guests. 'They chose exactly the same William Morris wallpaper.' None of Dudley's friends have a bad word to say about Suzy, or the marriage, so why didn't it last? 'Dudley had such problems with his own self-esteem,' says Wendy. 'He had to keep proving himself with women – and Peter too. He didn't have a deformed leg. He had a deformed personality.' Eventually, Wendy became involved with Simon Gough, the nephew of Robert Graves. 'Maybe I was the first person to break that tryst, within the marriage. We'd had six years of living together, and having a fairly open relationship – whatever that means. I don't think it's very positive.'

There was a sexual revolution going on, and a lot of marriages got swept away.

'I had depression. Maybe it was post-natal depression, but I got depressed. I think I got fed up, not being able to tackle any of the issues that I thought were important – life was just a merry-go-round.' The next movie, the next TV series ... 'I could see the way it was going, and it wasn't for me. I'm a country girl. I was depressed in the city, so I persuaded him to let us buy this farm in Majorca, and I spent a year learning the language and doing it up. I thought, "There's hope if we can actually have some proper family time together."' Peter and Wendy had some good times there. 'We had time away from all those distractions that showbiz brings.' However, Peter's work was back in London, and he could never bear to be alone. 'His affair with Judy Huxtable became very serious,' says Wendy. 'I miscalculated, I think, that you can leave a handsome and attractive man on his own, who's not going to go off with somebody. Men can't bear to be on their own – not the ones I know.' And so they split up, and Peter moved in with Judy. 'I think he thought that he could have both of us, and I probably reacted too quickly. My children suffered. It was a very crucial age for them. I wish I'd had a bit more wisdom.' The divorce was inevitably very painful. Peter took out an injunction which meant that Wendy had to bring Lucy and Daisy back to England. 'He tried to get custody of the children, which was devastating for me. He was pretty unsuccessful, but he had the money, he had the power.'

For Wendy, the night that Harold Macmillan came to see *Beyond The Fringe* was a turning point, in all sorts of ways. 'A young, recently graduated chap – he was only about twenty-four – strayed from the agreed script, and the Prime Minister of the day was imprisoned in his seat. What a cowardly thing to do, in a way.' But there was something very brave about it too. 'A deadly silence fell upon the whole thing – on the audience, and backstage.' Alan, Jonathan and Dudley watched from the wings, open-mouthed. 'The age of deference died on that night – respect for our politicians, for all the statesmen. I think we've gone too far now. This was the thing that started to make me come unstuck with Peter. It's all very well to tear things down, but you have to put something in their place – especially when you've got small children.' Pete & Dud was warm and benign, but she thought Derek & Clive was vicious. There was a pornographic deadness about Derek & Clive, a deadness fuelled by booze. 'Alcohol completely changes people.' Yet when they were together, Peter was never a big drinker. 'He could hold his drink,' she says. 'There were only two occasions when I remember him being drunk.'

Wendy's idealism was in tune with the changing times, but not with Peter's humour. 'I was looking for this spiritual life, where people had a very different set of values.' These were values which Peter found difficult to take seriously. 'He made fun of me. You see it in some of his sketches.' In the end, that made her depressed. Even at the best of times, living with a comic genius is never easy. 'They're living on a very different planet to yours – a different reality. In the end, you say, "What's real?"' Like a lot of creative people, Peter needed someone who would hold it all together. For a while, that someone was Wendy. 'The breaking-up of our marriage just turned him upside down. I'm a very earthy person. I'm a good manager. I'm a homemaker. Basically, everybody's looking for home in the end – especially somebody like him.' The last time she saw him was at their daughter Daisy's wedding. 'He was almost unrecognisable, and he smoked throughout the whole occasion, but there was a moment when we were in the Registry Office. He just gave me a look that said,

"You've done a good job," and that meant a lot to me.' On the day he died, her watch stopped. It wasn't the battery. 'I keep pondering on this whole question of genius,' she says. 'Is it possible to have genius and be a balanced person? For me, when I look around at the people who we call geniuses, living with them has been a nightmare, mostly, for their partners.' So was it a nightmare for Wendy? 'I left before it got to be a nightmare.' Yet there were lots of good times too. 'It was exciting. I can't regret that. Thank God I had it at a time that I don't yearn for it now.'

PETER CORK

'He was brilliant, absolutely brilliant, but he never did anything until the last minute.'

Peter Cork lives alone in a modest 1930s semi in Folkestone. The house belonged to his parents, both dead now. He shows me a photo of them. They look like gentle people. His father was a Baptist minister who'd been gassed in the trenches in the First World War. He'd played the cornet in a military band. Earl Haig presented him with a silver cornet. He lost it on the battlefield. Peter's father bought Peter an upright piano when he was eight years old. Peter was Dudley's music teacher at school in Dagenham. In his unassuming way, he helped shape the course of Dudley's life.

Peter trained as a teacher and served in the RAF during the Second World War. After the war, he studied composition at the Royal College of Music. He wanted to be a composer, but it was hard to make ends meet. He went into teaching out of necessity. At first he wasn't all that keen. He got a job as a music master at a grammar school in Dagenham, a place he'd never been to before. 'It's always held up as an example of how not to plan a housing estate,' he says. 'You could walk for miles and miles, and miles and miles, and it looks exactly the same. Even though I was there for seventeen years, I could still get lost.' Yet Dagenham High School was a revelation. 'It was a very happy school,' he says. 'It was an honour to be there.'

Like all the best schools, Dagenham High strived to make its pupils feel they could achieve anything they wanted to. 'It was a very good grammar school because it expanded people's horizons.' And the pupil with the widest horizons was a boy with a club foot called Dudley Moore. 'It was all there at the start,' he says. 'When all those wonderful things happened to him, later in his life, we weren't surprised.' Dudley was fifteen. He was studying for his Music O level. Straight away, Peter could see he had an incredible gift for music. 'You could put anything in front of him and he could read it at sight,' he says. 'He played the piano brilliantly, and played the organ as well.' He was incredibly charming, too. By the time Peter met him he'd learned to appease the bullies with his clowning. 'He's always said that when he was a youngster people were very unkind to him, but when I first met him I would have said he was one of the most popular boys in the school. Everybody loved him.' Especially the girls. Dudley's dramatic gifts were already evident. 'He was a very good actor,' says Peter. 'I'll always remember him in *She Stoops To Conquer*. He had a drinking scene, where he stood on a table with a tankard of ale.' His only weakness was procrastination. 'He would never get things in on time. He would always leave everything until the last possible moment.' But the results were always impeccable. 'I used to get so angry with him at times. He was an amazing man.'

Peter and Dudley had four happy years together, making music. When Peter conducted the school choir, Dudley was his accompanist. It was the beginning of a friendship that would last for life. 'We were very good friends,' says Peter. There were only eight years between them. He was more like an elder brother than a father figure. They went on a walking holiday in the Lake District, with another boy from school. 'Dudley's mother had sewn money into his jacket, which is the sort of thing they did in those days. I had a lovely three-part book with bass harmonies. We used to sing as we walked around.' They stayed in small guest houses. When Dudley spilled his Ribena on the tablecloth, Peter apologised to the proprietor on his behalf.

After Dudley went up to Oxford, the two men stayed in touch. Dudley came to stay with Peter in Folkestone. They took a bus into the countryside and went to evensong at a country church. Dudley returned his hospitality, inviting Peter to visit him at Magdalen. 'I love to hear the sound of high heels tip-tapping along these corridors,' said Dudley, as he showed him around the college. When Peter went to see *Beyond The Fringe* in the West End, Dudley slipped a reference to a 'Mrs Cork' into the show. To Peter, it was clear that Dudley was much more than just the pianist. 'His musicality, and what he could do with music, in many ways outshines the other three.'

Peter Cork met Peter Cook only once, in an edit suite in London. The duo were working on their ill-fated final feature film, *The Hound of The Baskervilles*, trying to salvage something from the wreckage. He sensed an element of bullying in the sketches. 'I've never been completely happy with what Peter Cook brought out in Dudley,' he says. 'I've often wondered, if Peter Cook hadn't been around, what would Dudley have done on his own?'

When Dudley went to America, he and Peter Cork inevitably saw less of one another, but they became pen pals instead. It was the height of Dudley's fame. Peter was amazed that he found time to write to him at all, but Dudley wrote frequent lengthy letters – thoughtful and reflective, the private, not the public, man. When

Dudley appeared on *This Is Your Life* in Los Angeles, Peter was flown out there to appear on the show alongside stars like Bo Derek. He sat next to Jackie Collins in the studio. He had to follow Robin Williams. Williams was supposed to do five minutes. 'He just went on and on and on,' says Peter. 'He went on for well over a quarter of an hour. I was standing behind the curtain.' Eventually, Williams finished and Peter came on and said his piece. Dudley was delighted to see him. He gave his old teacher a big hug. 'The next day, I spent all day with Dudley. That was lovely.' They went to Dudley's home, and his restaurant. He met Brogan Lane, Dudley's third wife. 'I liked her immensely. I think she really cared for him.'

Dudley helped Peter to realise his lifelong ambition. When he was fifty, Peter retired from teaching and became a full-time composer at last. Dudley made some introductions. Several years after Dudley died, Martine Avenue Productions published a collection of the letters that Dudley wrote to Peter between 1980 and 1994. 'Our positions as master and pupil were now absolutely reversed,' he wrote in a heartfelt introduction to the book. It was only after Dudley fell ill that the letters petered out. 'People thought he'd become like Arthur,' says his old music master, sadly.

Before I leave, I ask Peter if he'll play me a few of his compositions – on the piano where he and Dudley used to play together – so we step into his tidy drawing room where his beloved Broadwood grand has pride of place, and as he takes his seat the years fall away. Although he's old and stooped, he hasn't lost his youthful touch. As he plays for me, with the verve and brio of a youngster, I'm struck by the similarity between these wistful melodies and some of Dudley's later work – rooted in the classics, with just a hint of jazz. There's no suggestion of cross-fertilisation, or even overt influence – despite their prolific correspondence, they rarely played together after Dudley went away. No, these musical similarities must stem from something deeper – some common bond they've always shared, ever since their Dagenham days. Peter plays me four poignant pastorales – *Across The Valley*, *Stepping Stones*, *Deepest Woodlands* and *Summer By The Sea* – and though he says this suite is a homage to the landscape of his native Kent I can't help wondering whether it might also have been inspired by that walking holiday with Dudley in the Lake District, when Dudley was a teenager and Peter was a young man.

A few days later, Peter calls me up. He says there are a couple of things about Dudley which he'd forgotten to tell me. 'When I was first at Dagenham County High School I didn't have a flat of my own,' he says. 'I was in lodgings with a lovely lady called Mrs Nobbs. She had an upright piano and an enormous stock of old piano duets – Edwardian, mostly – the sort of thing you get in silent movies. I remember one called 'Flick & Flock – The Fireman's Gallop', lovely stuff – completely over the top. Dudley would come round and we'd really enjoy playing through them. I used to play the bass parts. He used to play the treble because he was a much better sight-reader.' Peter's other memory was from a lot later on, when Dudley was living in LA. 'He came back to do that Father Christmas film. [1] I asked him about his first son, with Tuesday Weld. [2] He would have been a teenager at the time. I remember him being a bit worried that he hadn't been a good enough father to him. "He wants to be an entertainer like me," he said. "What he doesn't understand is all the hard work. I had to work at it for years and years."'

Peter Cork died in September 2012. He was eighty-five years old. He hadn't been well before our interview. He'd had cancer. He'd been into hospital for an operation. He'd had to delay our meeting several times. Even so, he cooked me lunch and insisted on walking me back across the park, towards the station. During our brief time together, I caught a glimpse of why Dudley was so keen to stay in touch with this kind and modest man.

DAVID DEARLOVE

'I never met anybody who was a more natural comic,
but it wasn't just silly jokes. He was also highly articulate,
well educated and well read. There was always an edge
of intelligence, as well as sheer fun.'

Dudley's first agent, David Dearlove, lives at the very end of England, surrounded by sea and sky in Cornwall's most westerly port, Penzance. He meets me off the night train, and takes me home and makes me breakfast in his lovely little house, high above the beach, looking out across the ocean. 'We became close friends,' he says, of Dudley, over tea and toast and marmalade. 'I don't know any jazz pianist I enjoy listening to more.'

David had been working in the music business since the early 1950s. He wanted to be a songwriter, but he did a lot of other jobs as well. He wrote a West End musical called *Meet Me By Moonlight*, which ran for four months at the Aldwych. He worked at Associated Rediffusion during the early days of ITV. He met Dudley through the jazz musician John Dankworth. John and David were working on a musical together. Dudley was playing in John's jazz band. John and David decided to make a recording, to try and drum up a bit of interest. John borrowed a few musicians from his band for the recording. The pianist he borrowed was Dudley Moore.

David was impressed by Dudley's talent straight away. 'He was a superb accompanist – immensely sensitive, terrifically inventive, a wonderful sense of rhythm. He had everything. When I play the record now it gives me terrific pleasure to hear how beautifully it's done.' And it wasn't just the music. 'He was so funny all the time as well.' John and David decided to start an agency together. David left Associated Rediffusion and they rented an office in Denmark Street, London's Tin Pan Alley. They represented Dudley and John's wife, Cleo Laine. David introduced Dudley to George Martin at Parlophone. Martin cut Dudley's first record, 'Strictly For The Birds'.

'He was a lovely companion,' says David. 'Endlessly funny, always in a good mood. The flow of fun and obscenity from him was unstoppable.' David used to drive Dudley around. 'The window would be down and every pretty girl we passed – in those days with short Sixties skirts – he'd lean out of the window and scream, "Get 'em orf!" And the girls would roar with laughter.' How did he get away with it? 'The expression on his face was kindly and obviously clownish, rather than rapacious. Women found him unthreatening, though they found him very attractive.' They sensed his vulnerability, too. 'He limped,' says David. 'Because he was lame and very small he was a natural victim. While I knew him he was beaten up in the street.'

They had quite a lot in common. Their fathers were both railwaymen. David went to Oxford on a scholarship, like Dudley. They used to meet up virtually every day. They went to restaurants together, where David was struck by the enormous quantities of salt and sugar that Dudley sprinkled on his food. It was around this time that John Bassett got in touch and invited Dudley to join the cast of *Beyond The Fringe*. David went to Edinburgh to see the show. Straight away, he could sense it would become a big hit. 'I thought it was so funny and so original,' he says. 'Previous revues I'd seen were just silly or frivolous. It was the satirical element that made it different. It made fun of things like the War, and Shakespeare, and other things that people had previously taken seriously.' David met up with the four of them, and dined with them. It was a special time. 'I loved it. I felt excited by the fact that there were these people who were all doing creative and funny things.' Peter's off-the-cuff humour was particularly impressive. 'He was one of the funniest people I'd ever come across.' But Peter's wit was cutting and Alan's wit was dry. Jonathan was more analytical. Only Dudley's humour was really warm. He was the only one who had the music in him. 'He's just about one of the best jazz players I've ever come across. Terrific rhythm, interesting chords. He was academically trained. He knew everything about music.'

In 1961 David had a disagreement with John Dankworth. He was frustrated that their musical had never got anywhere. 'Bugger this,' he thought. 'I've spent ten years trying to be a songwriter, and nothing much has happened. I'm going to get out.' David decided to quit the rat race. He handed in his notice and put his home in London up for sale. 'I became a minicab driver as a fill-in job, and the very first thing I did was to take Dudley down to Oxford.' Dudley was doing cabaret at a college ball. It was David's first fare. David drove him to Oxford and waited while he did the show and then drove him back to London. When Dudley went to Broadway with *Beyond The Fringe* he stayed in touch with David, and when he returned from America he went to stay with David for a few days in his new home in Cornwall. 'He was very generous, wonderfully generous. He'd take us out and give us a really good dinner.'

David was disappointed by Dudley's subsequent film career. 'I've never found any of his films very good. I always feel embarrassed by the material he's working with. I thought it was an awful shame.

I didn't like *10*. I couldn't even sit through *Arthur*. I found myself getting embarrassed for him. I felt very sad. Not only was he not being used to his full comic potential, but it was overshadowing all the music. He was more intelligent than the vehicles he was in. I would have liked to have seen him in wittier, more intelligent comedies.' David would have loved to see Dudley in a Woody Allen film. 'He was offered money, fame and a glamorous place like Hollywood to pick up girls. It was a lure that not many people would resist.'

The disease that Dudley died from, progressive supranuclear palsy, is very rare, but by an odd, morbid coincidence David had another good friend who died from PSP. 'One by one, everything breaks down. Nothing works. Eventually the last thing goes and you die, but your intelligence is not affected by it. You know you're losing every sense – the ability to swallow, the ability to move, to stand up, to do anything.' Meanwhile, the person inside looks out, aghast, like a prisoner being bricked up inside a cell. 'Talk about a malevolent god. If there were a god, it would be sheer malevolence.'

ELEANOR FAZAN

'Revue always has to be written by the young.
It has to have that feeling to it.'

Eleanor Fazan came to Britain from Kenya when she was fifteen to become a dancer. 'I knew nothing, absolutely nothing,' she says over cake and coffee in her homely flat in London. It was 1945 and the Second World War was still raging. She sailed down the Nile, spent a month in Cairo trying to find a boat, and finally sailed to Britain on a troop ship from Alexandria, sharing a cabin with nine missionaries. By the time they docked in Glasgow, the Germans had surrendered. She studied at Sadler's Wells, and then at the Arts Educational School. When she was eighteen she went to work. Her first job was with music-hall legend George Robey, The Prime Minister of Mirth. Robey was nearly eighty and his best days were way behind him, but Eleanor didn't mind. 'I was so excited to be in the theatre.' She went on to work in variety and pantomime, with seasoned pros like Joan Sims and Tommy Trinder. She married the composer Stanley Myers (who went on to write the music for *The Deer Hunter*) and when she fell pregnant she had to stop dancing. She choreographed a summer season and directed a revue, which was how she came to the attention of the theatre proprietor Donald Albery. 'I got on well with Donald, and Donald didn't get on with very many people,' says Eleanor. 'He was a grandee. He didn't like mixing with actors.'

Eleanor directed numerous revues, including Bamber Gascoigne's

Share My Lettuce. She worked with up-and-coming writers like John Mortimer and Harold Pinter. She transformed a show of Albery's that had been a flop, which gave her a reputation as a fixer. Albery's friend, the young producer Willie Donaldson, asked her to help him with a new revue called *Here Is The News*, written by a young Cambridge graduate called John Bird. 'I got it better,' she says, 'but it wasn't good enough, and it never came into the West End.' Nevertheless, she got on well with Donaldson and her work impressed him, so when he bought up *Beyond The Fringe* he gave her a call. 'It's a very little job,' he told her. 'It's been this huge success. It's just seeing it into the West End.' 'I'll have to see it,' she told him. Willie persuaded the four performers to do a run-through in a church hall, just for him and Eleanor. What Eleanor didn't realise was that this was also the first time he'd seen it. 'He'd bought it sight unseen.'

'Willie, this isn't a small job,' she told him afterwards. 'It's a huge job.' She thought he'd get someone else to do it. On the contrary, he was delighted. 'I'm so pleased you think of it like that,' he said. 'I thought exactly the same.' Eleanor agreed to do it, but she still had reservations. She felt the cast were brilliant, but a bit superior. 'They were Oxbridge. There's a kind of superiority that goes with that which has disappeared, but then it was apparent.' She didn't know whether they'd be willing to do the necessary work. 'I thought each one of them was terrific. It's just that they were amateur. They were lolling about. It needed an awful lot of work.'

Eleanor set to work. 'They didn't want to be thought of as professionals, in any way. They didn't want to look professional.' They were gentlemen. Pros like her were players. 'I wasn't a highly educated person at all – far from it. I'd given up school at fifteen.' 'I've got one requirement,' she told them on the first day of rehearsal.

'Turn up. We'll work from ten to five-thirty. We'll do ordinary hours.' And they always did.

It was useful for the four Fringers to have an outsider to make the tough decisions. That way, they wouldn't end up arguing about which sketches to cut and which ones to save. Eleanor rationed them to one solo each in either half. The rest would be ensemble pieces, with an opening and closing number in each half. They rehearsed at her flat in Hampstead, where they wrote some new sketches, improvising into a tape recorder for Donaldson's secretary to transcribe. Creating these new ensemble numbers, Peter was in his element. 'He was an inspiration,' says Eleanor, 'and the others would pick up on it.' Dudley, on the other hand, found it very difficult. 'He couldn't think what to do. Jonathan really helped him. He knew about the Third Programme, and how to send it up. He was a sort of intellectual, which I wasn't at all.' This disparity was a big asset. Eleanor wasn't competing with them head-to-head. She was teaching them something they didn't know – how to put on a proper show. 'I had an instinct about those things.'

Right from the outset, Eleanor realised this show was something special. 'It was so funny. There were times when I would be doubled up with laughter.' And she knew it was unlike any previous revue. 'What was different about it was the plainness of it. There were no dancing girls or songs. I drew the set on my kitchen floor.' Eleanor created a set with several levels, giving the show a visual variety which it hadn't had in Edinburgh. She varied the length and pace of the sketches, giving the show a variety of different tempos. Yet despite her best efforts, at this stage Donaldson still hadn't found a West End theatre. He asked Eleanor if she'd bring in Donald Albery. She went to see him but he wasn't all that keen. West End revues were usually lavish affairs, with star names. Despite their success in Edinburgh, the four Fringers were still virtually unknown. Yet Eleanor was a fan, and she managed to persuade him. After a week in her Hampstead flat, they started rehearsing in the bar of one of Albery's West End theatres, the Prince of Wales.

Willie Donaldson was a constant source of support. 'I loved Willie,' says Eleanor. 'He was always encouraging. He never pushed too hard. He was a wonderful boss in that way.' Albery, conversely, was gloomy and pessimistic. When the show opened in Cambridge, he went there to see it for the first time and didn't really like it, even though it went down very well with the students there. 'Donald, I think you're going to like this show,' Eleanor told him over a drink afterwards. 'I think this is going to be fun.' 'Are you sure?' he asked. From Cambridge they transferred to the Theatre Royal, Brighton. The show didn't go down at all well there, but Eleanor wasn't fazed. 'It took them time to get going,' she says. 'They had to get used to it.' She'd seen lots of shows falter in provincial previews, then find their feet when they got to London. Her confidence was rewarded, for it was while they were in Brighton that they finally found a West End theatre.

The dress rehearsal at the Fortune Theatre was chaotic, as dress rehearsals of good shows often are. 'I don't know how you stand this,' the lighting director said to Eleanor. 'Don't worry,' she told him. 'They will be fine.' She was right. On the opening night she stood at the back of the stalls, to watch the audience as well as the performers. As soon as the show began, she knew they had a hit. 'The laughter was incredible,' she says. She was pleased, but not surprised. She'd always believed in it and now her faith had been vindicated. It was Donald Albery who was taken by surprise. 'He was not a fan of Beyond The Fringe. He was a businessman. He knew how to sell the show.'

RENA FRUCHTER

'He had no intention of becoming an American film star.
I think what he was doing with jazz was pretty natural for
him, and being part of *Beyond The Fringe* was natural
for him, because he always had that funny, quirky way
of looking at life. But as far as being a superstar – that
wasn't a goal of his. It surprised him as much as some of
the people around him.'

'I didn't really know anything about him being a musician – I knew that he played some jazz, but I didn't really know that he was a serious classical musician as well,' says Rena Fruchter, recalling how she got to know Dudley. We're talking in a Chinese restaurant in a hotel in central London. Rena lives in New Jersey with her husband, Brian Dallow, a fellow musician, and their family. As a classical musician and a music critic, Rena was uniquely placed to run the rule over Dudley's musical skills. Dudley was performing with the New Jersey Symphony Orchestra. Before the concert, she interviewed him on the telephone for the *New York Times*. They just talked about music. 'I was impressed with his knowledge of music. We talked about Beethoven for a long time, and other classical composers, and piano technique.' Rena wrote up the interview for the *New York Times*. She also reviewed the concert. 'He was still a little bit uneasy about his technique. His classical musicianship was solid but he wasn't doing a lot of concert playing at that point.' However, Rena liked the concert and Dudley liked her write-up. They still hadn't met up, face to face, but they stayed in touch by phone. They never discussed his personal life. They hardly ever discussed his acting. They only talked about music. A special friendship had begun.

They finally met in New York when Dudley was filming *Arthur 2 – On The Rocks*, the ill-fated sequel to his biggest Hollywood hit. Because their friendship was based on music, not showbiz, Rena wasn't remotely star-struck. 'I didn't treat him like a celebrity and I wasn't intimidated by him as a celebrity,' she says. 'I never dealt with Dudley as a movie star.' To her, he was a fellow musician. 'He was craving that,' she tells me. 'Music was at the core of everything he did. He would get up every morning and play Bach. That was his great love. He fell into the acting.' Music was his one constant, a source of discipline in a life that was becoming increasingly chaotic.

A few years later, when Rena was setting up her musical charity Music For All Seasons (which takes music into places where people are confined, from prisons to hospitals) she asked Dudley if he'd be Honorary Chairman. 'No,' said Dudley. 'If I'm going to be involved with an organisation that has such a fine purpose, I'm going to take an active role.' Dudley became a board member, and President of the Advisory Board. He helped bring some of his friends and colleagues on board. Meanwhile Dudley was doing some more piano concerts, with a full orchestra. He was finding it a stretch. Rena asked him if he'd like an extra pair of ears. Dudley said he would, so Rena went to some rehearsals. They talked about doing a benefit concert for Music For All Seasons. 'There's one concerto I've always wanted to play – the Grieg,' he told her. They talked about doing it in Carnegie Hall. 'It was totally crazy,' she says. At that time, Rena's charity was barely a year old, but Dudley was undeterred. 'Let's do it,' he said. So they booked Carnegie Hall. Rena went to LA to help Dudley prepare, playing the orchestral part on a second piano. They really enjoyed playing together. 'That's how we became a two-piano team.' They communicated through their music. The concert was a great success. 'It was something that was very close to his heart.'

So, as a classical pianist, just how good was Dudley? 'There was brilliance to his musicianship,' she says. 'He had great insight into the music. He struggled a little bit with technique. He couldn't always play what he wanted, because he hadn't practised steadily over the years. He played every day, but the solid work that you need as a child – he felt he hadn't had that.' Still, for someone who hadn't always practiced regularly, his musical facilities were remarkable. He was an excellent sight-reader, he got around the keyboard extremely well, and the music he wrote was sublime – timeless, pastoral and very English, reminiscent of Elgar or Vaughan Williams. He wasn't a great classical pianist, but he had something else which was unique. 'He heard things. Composers hear the works of other composers in a different way, and he had that.'

Rena and Dudley toured together, playing *Carnival of The Animals* by Saint-Saëns. 'It was a piece he was really comfortable with.' For Dudley, it was a renaissance. After all these years, his classical musicianship had finally begun to blossom. He played Gershwin's *Rhapsody In Blue*, and finished off with some of his old parodies. It was more than ten years since *Arthur*, and he hadn't had a big hit since, but he still got a hero's welcome. 'His public loved him. He could not do anything wrong.' As he ran into deeper problems with his fourth and final marriage, to Nicole Rothschild, the abstraction of classical music provided an escape and a release. 'When he sat down at the piano, he could play for hours. We would rehearse for four, five, six hours at a shot. I thought my concentration was good, but he had me beat.'

Living in New Jersey, not Los Angeles; a classical musician, not an actress; happily married with a growing family, not a free and easy singleton – Rena was the opposite of most of the women who came in and out of Dudley's life. She was a friend, not a fan. 'He felt secure in our friendship. There was never an ulterior motive. It was just based on music and that was where he was at that point in his life.' In time, Dudley became friends with all of Rena's family, especially her husband Brian – an English musician who, like Dudley, had made a new life in the States. Dudley relished his serious conversations with Rena. He didn't always want to be on show, but he enjoyed some aspects of celebrity. 'He liked being recognised. He liked people coming up and asking for his autograph.' The one thing he didn't like was people calling him Arthur. That sometimes used to happen when people saw him in the street.

It was during the time that Rena and Dudley were playing together that Peter died. 'It was strange for him because it was remote, and he wasn't reacting the way people thought he should react,' says Rena. 'He said he had mixed feelings. He was very sad, but he was also still angry and hurt, and he didn't know how to communicate that mixture of emotions. It was like a close friend, or a brother.'

Rena realised something was wrong with Dudley's health when he started shooting Barbra Streisand's film, *The Mirror Has Two Faces*, and was fired when he couldn't remember his lines. Dudley was confused and upset. He'd never had any problem learning lines before. 'People assumed he was drinking, which he wasn't,' she says.

'He didn't know what was wrong.' After Dudley and Rena toured Australia together, he started having problems with one of his fingers. 'We knew something needed to be checked.' His marriage was also becoming increasingly stormy. He asked if he could come and stay with Rena's family for a while, to take a break from his domestic life and sort out his health. After a few months, he asked if he could stay a while longer. He ended up living in Rena's house for two years. 'He'd been through so many things that ended – so many marriages that ended badly,' she says. 'We made it clear when he came to stay with us, he could pay for lunch, but we would not ever take money from him. That was our condition, because we didn't want this to be based on something superficial.'

It took more than a year to get to the bottom of Dudley's health problems. Check-ups revealed a blocked artery. He had open-heart surgery. The doctors thought that would fix things, but his health became even worse. He started falling over, often in public places, which led to tabloid speculation. 'It's my club foot coming home to roost,' he said. In the end, a doctor in New Jersey recognised his slow eye movement as a symptom of progressive supranuclear palsy. He diagnosed PSP straight away. Dudley had mixed feelings. 'He was tired of searching and searching and not knowing what was wrong, but it was pretty serious. He was told he could survive three to eight years.' There was no cure. There wasn't even any effective medication. PSP would attack the two things he held most dear – his ability to speak, and his ability to play the piano. 'He never got over that. He could never really come to terms with that.' To top it all, the early symptoms were akin to drunkenness, like Arthur or Peter.

Dudley wanted to go public about his condition. 'He wanted the public to know that he wasn't a drunk.' Inevitably, understandably, his Californian representatives weren't all that keen but eventually, about a year after his diagnosis, Barbara Walters offered him an opportunity to tell the world, via her TV show on ABC. What with Dudley's failing health, and the press attention that went with it, the burden on Rena's family became more intense, but now there was no question of Dudley going back to LA. 'We had to let him stay. He was part of the family.' Rena and her family cared for him, with growing support from professional nurses, as his condition grew worse and worse. One day, he toppled over the banisters, and Rena and Brian decided that it was no longer safe for him to get up and down the stairs. As luck would have it, the same day a three-bedroom ranch house right next door came up for sale, and so Dudley moved into it, with his three concert grand pianos. It was in this house that he saw out the remainder of his days.

During those final years, Dudley would sometimes talk about Peter. 'Even though they had kind of mended fences, he remained disturbed that Peter had been harsh and critical of him. I don't think he ever forgave him.' Dudley had some fond memories of Peter, but there was hurt amid the sadness. 'He objected to the fact that Peter was drunk onstage.' He liked quoting from old sketches like 'One Leg Too Few' but he had no nostalgia whatsoever for Derek & Clive. 'He hated that. He never expected that to get out.' When *Bedazzled* was remade (with Liz Hurley playing Lucifer) Rena and Dudley went to see it, incognito, in a cinema in New Jersey. Nobody recognised him. Dudley had fond memories of *Bedazzled*. He didn't like the remake. 'He was indignant. He thought they'd done the ultimate *Bedazzled*.' He was right. Thankfully, Dudley didn't live to see the remake of *Arthur*. 'I know he would have hated that.'

Dudley had long discussions with Rena about his thwarted attempts at fatherhood. 'He felt that he couldn't be a good father because his father hadn't been a good father, and he'd been distant. But you can change that. You can change how you act and what kind of a parent you are. It was an easy crutch for him.' His ability to bed so many women was an additional distraction. 'He enjoyed having that effect but it was meaningless after a while.' But now those days were long gone. 'He didn't like anything that made him feel trapped, so that was probably the problem with the marriages. His parents had a marriage that he felt was like a death sentence, and I think that was his image. He said every time he got that marriage licence in his hand, the marriage was already over.'

Eventually, during the last few months, even speaking became a struggle. 'Everything that was Dudley was still inside him – he just couldn't communicate it,' says Rena. 'Others, from the outside looking in, think that they don't know what's going on, but that's far from the truth – they completely know everything that's going on. He was thankful that we understood that.'

Dudley died in his New Jersey home, surrounded by Rena's family. 'They kind of set up a hospital for him at home, so he wouldn't have to be in an institution. We were there 24 hours a day.' Dudley listened to lots of piano music during those last few days. 'I felt at the heart of Dudley was music,' says Rena. 'Will there be music there?' he asked her, just before he died. His own composition, *Songs Without Words*, was playing when he passed away. 'He was like a family member to my whole family,' says Rena. 'There was nothing phoney about Dudley.' The media were on the doorstep within the hour.

'People wanted to take care of him – women wanted to mother him,' she says. 'There wasn't anything tough about Dudley ... He'd

551

get hurt by little things.' Things people said to him, or comments in the press. 'Little things became big things to him.' Hardly the best character trait if you were in a double act with Peter Cook. 'I'm actually surprised it went on as long as it did.'

JOHN GALE

'Most of the time I spent my career signing much bigger cheques to artists than I ever got for myself, but on the odd occasion when you do have a smash hit, then you do make more money than the actors.'

John Gale is a theatre producer. The culmination of his career was as Director of Chichester Festival Theatre (he built the Minerva Theatre) but one of the best bits of business he ever did was in 1960, when he invested £1,000 in a new revue called *Beyond The Fringe*. Sadly, only £100 of that £1,000 was his. 'I laid off £900 of my £1,000 and kept £100 for myself,' he says over lunch in his idyllic rural home, with his wife Liselotte by his side. 'That £100 turned into £18,000 profit.' If only he'd hung onto the entire £1,000, he'd have made £180,000.

'It was a triumphant first night,' he says of the West End opening at the Fortune Theatre. 'The audience loved it. They laughed and laughed.' He knew then it'd be a big success, but he had no idea how big. 'It's unusual. People don't realise how rare the real smash hits are in London. The plays that open and sell every seat at every performance are very few and far between.' He'd seen a preview at RIBA (the Royal Institute of British Architects) which he'd liked enough to put in some money, but this was something else. 'They'd turned it from a little cabaret performance into a big smash hit West End revue.'

John had a hundred quid at stake, but he wasn't really thinking about the money. 'I don't think any of us had any idea that it would be the success it was. This is a phenomenon. This isn't just a run-of-the-mill smash-hit show. This is something that's once in a lifetime.' His wife Liselotte was there that night. She thought it was amazing, but she didn't find it shocking. 'They were intellectuals who made you think about things.' 'They they were incredibly clever,' concurs John. 'It was the first intellectual revue that there had ever been.'

Yet despite its West End success, John remained pessimistic about the show's New York prospects. 'I never thought it would work on Broadway,' he says. He was pleased to be proved wrong. 'Show business is full of people making mistakes and saying daft things.' Nor did he ever imagine that Dudley would become a Hollywood sex symbol. 'Never. He was practically a dwarf. I can't imagine Dudley Moore being a heart-throb, but that's what he became.' And Peter? 'Well, Peter had a drink problem,' says John. 'It's a terrible waste of a life.'

NICHOLAS GARLAND

'There sometimes seemed no gear change between what
Peter was like offstage and what he was like onstage, or
what he was like with a written piece and what he was
like just chatting, talking, making you laugh.'

'You can judge somebody partly by the influence they've had, and
Peter influenced British comedy to an extraordinary extent,' says
Nicholas Garland over coffee in the living room of his handsome
town house in Camden. 'Up until then British comedy had been
extremely safe.' Most of the comedy that came before had been kind
and gentle, harmless and good-natured, comics like Frank Muir
and Denis Norden. 'There was a kind of membrane between how
performers were and what their lives were like. Peter – and Dudley
to some extent – seemed, in a funny way, to break that down.'

Nicholas had been an art student at The Slade. He subsequently
became a stage manager. He was working at the Royal Court
when he met Dudley. The Royal Court was staging N.F. Simpson's
absurdist play, *A Resounding Tinkle*, in which (among many other
things) a man tries to teach some weighing machines to sing the
Hallelujah Chorus. The cast and crew did a recording. Dudley came
in to direct them. Nicholas found him charming. He wore his talent
lightly. 'There were sometimes people in the theatre who could be
a bit hoity-toity. It was a very hierarchical system in those days.
Dudley manifested none of that.' The recording was great fun for

everyone. Everybody liked him. There was no bullshit about him. He had no side.

When *Beyond The Fringe* came to play the Theatre Royal, Brighton, before its West End run, Nicholas was also working on a show in Brighton. He'd known Jonathan Miller since they were children – their mothers were good friends. Jonathan invited him to have dinner with the cast. That was where Nicholas first met Alan Bennett, and Peter. 'They were a glamorous bunch,' he says. 'I was tremendously impressed by them. I thought they were absolutely great, so it was terrific fun to meet them and hang out with them.'

Nicholas first saw the show in London, at the Fortune Theatre. 'By the time I saw *Beyond The Fringe* it was already a massive hit. I remember the audience roaring.' Nicholas was roaring too. 'Christ, they're good!' he kept thinking. 'That's so beautifully done. That joke's so unexpected. It came out of nowhere and it's brilliant.' He found it terribly amusing, but he was full of admiration too. 'There was a real excitement that came from being in the presence of something being done so brilliantly. I'd never seen anything like it. It was so funny and it was so extraordinary. Going to the theatre, usually people had make-up on, they had costumes, there were lighting effects, there were sets ... This wasn't like that. They were just wearing grey flannel trousers and jerseys and shirts.' The humour wasn't iconoclastic. 'It was good-natured,' he says. 'It wasn't damaging.' But it was the thin end of the wedge.

At the Royal Court, Nicholas also met John Bird, who was working there as a director. When Bird joined Peter at The Establishment Club, Nicholas went to help to direct and stage-manage the cabaret. 'I adored Peter and admired him enormously,' says Nicholas. 'He seemed to be doing everything – publishing *Private Eye*, running

The Establishment Club, starring in *Beyond The Fringe*, talking about television shows, making movies. He knew everybody. It seemed effortless.' Humour seemed to pour out of him. 'Jonathan would make jokes,' he says. 'Peter would just start talking.' One time, Peter and Nicholas and their respective wives went on holiday to Brittany. After dinner, Peter and Nicholas went for a walk. Peter set off on a riff. 'He was talking about an enormous black boxer, who was terrifying, and a bee. And the commentator was describing the opening of this fight, and the question was would the bee be able to actually get up into the ring. He never made it. Peter was just talking. Sometimes he was the commentator, sometimes he was the bee, sometimes he was people watching, and he was bemusing himself. He was laughing while he was doing it, almost as if he didn't quite know where it was going to go.' Eventually, Nicholas had to ask him to stop. He was laughing too much. 'It's what he did. It's what he was like. In some strange, generous, uninhibited way, this comedy just came out of him, in the form of a long, wild monologue.' It was a bit like E.L. Wisty, but Wisty was mournful, low and thoughtful. This was just as rambling, but more upbeat. 'It wasn't like anybody else I'd ever known.'

When the cast of The Establishment went to America, Nicholas went with them. It was the first time he'd been to the States. By now, *Beyond The Fringe* was on Broadway, and Nicholas and his wife Harriet spent a lot of time with Peter and his first wife, Wendy, in Manhattan. The four of them became firm friends. Nicholas looked up to Peter. There was a lot to look up to. 'I sort of worshipped him, really,' he says. 'I was so pleased that we were friends, and so delighted in his company.' Back in Britain, Nicholas would often visit Peter and Wendy in their flat in Battersea. 'She was kind and she was pretty and she was amused by Peter and also looked after him.' When they bought a house in Hampstead, Nicholas would visit them there too. 'They were very close. It seemed a very happy marriage. They had two lovely little children.' Nicholas recalls the pleasure Peter took in watching his children learn to walk. Peter and Nicholas loved playing tennis together. Once, after a tipsy evening together, they tried to play by moonlight, in the middle of the night. 'I could hear him at the other end of the court, but I couldn't really see him. He served and he said, "Was that in?" I said, "Was what in?"'

Nicholas was a guest at some of Wendy's legendary dinner parties. He recalls an evening when they were joined by Barry Humphries, John Lennon and Lennon's first wife, Cynthia. 'Those three men – Barry, John Lennon and Peter – began a funny sort of bantering. Not being themselves, but sort of exaggerated characters of themselves, somehow. And the bantering got more and more intense, until they were basically insulting each other.' In a way, it was just a joke. But there was a serious side to it, too. 'Something that had started off as something light-hearted was getting darker.' It was almost as if they were about to start physically threatening each other. 'I was beginning to feel quite nervous.' Nicholas and Harriet's baby daughter was in a carrycot in the room. 'I don't want one of them tumbling over and falling on the baby,' he thought.

Nicholas knew Barry Humphries pretty well. He didn't know John Lennon. 'John Lennon is fantastic at this,' he thought. 'He is every bit as good as they are.' Not many people were. Most people who tangled with Peter, or with Barry Humphries, came off second-best. Not Lennon. 'It really was impressive,' says Nicholas. 'I didn't expect him to have that talent. It got to a stage when suddenly Cynthia said, quite sharply, "John, John, stop it! Stop it!"' It was as if someone had switched a light on. The three men sat down. 'The conversation became normal again. It was a curious moment.' Nicholas felt as though he'd been put in his proper place. 'I wasn't one of them. I wouldn't have dreamt of joining in.'

In 1966, Nicholas left the theatre and started working as a cartoonist. Peter introduced him to Barry Humphries, and encouraged them to collaborate on *The Adventures of Barry McKenzie* for *Private Eye*. 'He kept coming up with new ideas: new publishing ideas; new ideas for sketches; new ideas for movies or television programmes.' *Barry McKenzie* was just one of these. 'It was great fun,' says Nicholas. It was a great success, as well. However, when Nicholas joined the *Daily Telegraph* his daily life became more journalistic. 'My life changed. I had a job. I had a deadline.' Inevitably, he saw a lot less of his theatrical friends after that. He became very close friends with Jonathan, but he lost touch with most of the others.

'There was a funny side of Peter which I don't understand, and I've never seen it written about or discussed,' says Nicholas. 'There was a certain kind of fame, a sort of popular fame, like a rock star's fame, that I think he wanted. He was very famous, and he was very successful, and he was much admired.' But there was a form of fame he coveted which remained forever out of reach. 'A particular kind of being famous – in, say, the way the Beatles were famous, or even the way that Dudley became famous.' People acknowledged Peter's talent, but there was a part of him that wanted more. 'He used to love to pretend to be a rock star. He just loved the glamour and the fun of being a superstar, and he never was. In a way, he was something much more than that. He was an immensely influential, revered artist of some kind – but he wasn't Elvis Presley. He wasn't Buddy Holly, or whoever the equivalent would have been, and he sort of hankered for it, in a way. And I think when Dudley did become it that was quite difficult for him.'

However, most of the movies that Peter made were a waste of his talents, and of his time. 'It was a different medium, and he didn't slip easily into it. I do remember him talking about Tony Hancock, and saying, in effect, that it was difficult to see a guy who was so good, and so much on top of his game, and so far ahead of everybody else, struggling so hard now to find his feet, and doing rubbishy things, because Tony Hancock also went into a terrible decline. Maybe he was aware that he was also beginning to struggle a little bit. That energy he had, and that easy access to success – the ability to just charm his way through anything, riding the wave, surfing on approval – he began to lose that. He lost it, somehow. He changed.' And the change was colossal. 'There was something terribly sad about it.'

PATRICK GARLAND

'He wasn't really a womaniser. He was very successful
with women, which is something different.'

The theatre and film director Patrick Garland met Dudley when they
were both at Oxford University. 'I met him in the high street,' recalls
Patrick, over lunch in a cafe near his rural home where he runs an
animal sanctuary with his wife, the actress Alexandra Bastedo. 'He
was at Magdelen and I was up the road in St Edmund Hall.' Patrick was
a freshman. Dudley was in his second year. He was already renowned
as a musician and a composer. Student directors were always asking
him to write music for their plays. 'Dudley would always say yes,
because he could do it so effortlessly.' When other students talked
about the latest undergraduate production, they always used to say,
'It's got this wonderful score by Dudley Moore.'

Dudley made an immediate impression on Patrick, as a comedian
as well as a musician. 'He was obviously a comic personality, with
enormous imaginative gifts. He made it all up on the spot. He wasn't
a person who just told anecdotes. He was his own natural comedic
self.' Patrick recalls something that Jonathan Miller once said. 'He
said that, in his experience, Dudley was the one person who never
changed, from the first day he saw him. It was true. He was always
like that. He was always funny. He always pulled these funny faces,
which were natural to him – not contrived.' This lack of artifice was
a big part of Dudley's sex appeal, but the biggest part by far was his

sense of fun. 'He was always very attractive to women,' says Patrick. 'I never regarded him particularly – in the pejorative sense – as a womaniser. He made women laugh.' Eventually it became a bore. 'He got a bit fed up at Oxford,' says Patrick. 'When he came to a party they'd all be sitting in a circle round him, ready for him to entertain them. He used to get fed up with that. He used to feel this obligation to come in and be the funny man.'

At the end of Patrick's first year, Patrick and Dudley went to the Edinburgh Festival together, in a student production of a new play called *The Disciplines of War*. [1] Kenneth Tynan said it was the best thing on the Fringe. They all slept in one big dormitory. That was where they really got to know each other. Patrick played the leading role, and played it well, but Dudley stole the show. People used to stop him in the street, and say how much they'd enjoyed watching him. 'We thought you were wonderful,' they'd tell him. And he was. 'What was quite new at that point was this comic personality allied to these very good looks. You didn't have comics like that – comics looked like comics.' Most were clowns like Frankie Howerd, with misshapen faces to match their humour. Dudley had the body of a clown and the face of a matinee idol. 'It was difficult for him because he had this very handsome face and a lot of women fell in love with him.' It was fun while it lasted, but it was difficult to build something solid which would endure.

Patrick was full of admiration for *Beyond The Fringe* ('there was no humour like it') but as he made a career in straight theatre, and Dudley became a TV star and then a film star, they ended up in different worlds. The last time he saw Dudley onstage was in *Behind The Fridge*, with Peter, at London's Cambridge Theatre. 'It was terrific,' he recalls. 'They were at the top of their form.' The classic combination of wit and clown had never been better. Patrick likens it to Jacques and Touchstone in *As You Like It*. Perhaps such classic double acts can't last, because the two comics are always pulling in different directions. For a while, these opposing forces create a dramatic tension, but in the end they're bound to pull apart.

Patrick kept in touch with Dudley, but he saw even less of him after *Behind The Fridge*, so he was astonished when Dudley told him that he'd named his first child after him. Patrick felt honoured, but it was a big surprise. They'd been good friends at Oxford but they were never intimate. Dudley never talked about his club foot, and Patrick knew not to ask. By the time Dudley became a father, their friendship was mainly in the past. Patrick had assumed that Dudley must have had closer friends, but maybe Dudley wasn't all that close to any man (women were another matter). 'I didn't really know Dudley all that well, but none of his other friends that spoke of him knew him very much better than I did.' Maybe the friendship they shared was the closest Dudley ever came to befriending another man. [2]

VERA GRIGG

'I still have it in my head that he should have gone into jazz. He should have been a musician.'

Vera Grigg lived on Monmouth Road in Dagenham, the same road as Dudley. Like Dudley's family, her family were bombed out during the war. Dudley's family escaped unharmed. Sadly, Vera's family weren't so lucky. Vera's father was killed. She was in the house when it happened. She was ten years old. When she was eleven, she started at Dagenham County High School.

She'd been at the school for a few years when Dudley arrived. The first time she noticed him was when she went into assembly one September morning and saw a small boy sitting at the piano. Dudley had only been at the school for a few weeks. He was only eleven. He looked even younger. 'We were appalled!' remembers Vera. 'What was this little first-year doing, playing the piano? How dreadful!' But as soon as he started playing she changed her mind. All her classmates were amazed. 'It made a tremendous impact on us,' she says. 'We realised he was something special.'

Dudley played the piano at most assemblies thereafter, and at countless concerts, throughout the rest of his school career. Over the few years that followed, Vera heard him play all sorts of things, from J.S. Bach to jazz. His technical expertise was impressive, but what impressed Vera most was his musicality. 'Musicality means putting your soul into the music,' she explains. Dudley put his heart and soul into each performance. 'He made us listen to his music. And from that very first time, we always did.'

Dagenham County High was a beacon of opportunity. 'It was a very good school,' says Vera over a cup of coffee in the conservatory of her tidy Home Counties home. 'The teachers were very good. For example, I don't think you'd recognise any Dagenham accent in me. That was because of our English teacher, Miss Darby, who told us – quite firmly – that you can only get on in the world if people are going to listen to you.' Back then, that meant speaking the Queen's English – or Received Pronunciation, as it was called in those days. Her English teacher taught Vera and her classmates to converse in the neutral dialect of the Southern English middle classes. 'She told us to listen, and to speak properly. She taught us about grammar.' Dudley left Dagenham County High School having shed his Dagenham accent, too.

Vera's English teacher didn't just teach her pupils to speak proper. 'She took us to the theatre. I'd never been to the theatre before.' At the end of her first term, Vera and her classmates put on a school production of Shakespeare's *A Midsummer Night's Dream*. 'We were putting on plays all the time.' Music was equally prominent. Vera remembers Dudley's music master, Peter Cork, very well. 'He was a very impressive teacher. He was a very impressive person.' When it was raining, he'd let them sit inside and listen to records of classical music. These formative influences lasted Vera a lifetime. They lasted Dudley a lifetime too. 'We had teachers who were very aware that these were Dagenham children with working-class backgrounds, but that they had the ability to get on.' And many of them did. 'They introduced us to a different world. They told us, "You come from a working-class background, but you can do anything in this world if you really want to."'

Vera became a teacher. She ended up as a deputy head, and a university lecturer too. She did several degrees. 'The school was the making of so many of us,' she says. 'The most socially inclusive schools are the grammar schools.' And this culture of self-improvement wasn't confined to the classroom. It was an intrinsic feature of the place where people like Dudley and her grew up. 'The people who went to Dagenham, who got places on the housing estate, were called the upper working class. To get a house in Dagenham, you had to be in work, you had to have no debts, and you had to be an active participant in a church or chapel.' You had to keep your garden tidy. You had to wash your windows every week. But Vera's family weren't complaining. They came from the East End. After the rented rooms they'd been living in, these new council houses were luxurious. 'It was just fantastic to get into a house with a garden and a bathroom. It was incredible.'

JONATHAN HARLOW

*'If you do your best work, not sitting by a lamp with
a pen but with people around you to sparkle off, then
what do you do when there ain't no people around
you to sparkle off?'*

When Jonathan Harlow first met Peter, when they were both new boys at Radley, the thing that really struck him was Peter's cynicism – his cynical demeanour, his cynical tone of voice. They were both thirteen. Jonathan is a teacher. His wife is a doctor. They live in Gloucestershire. 'He didn't strike me as terribly funny,' he says over a pub lunch in his local. 'For a long time he was a friend, but I don't think we thought, "That's the chap who's going to remake British comedy."'

Peter was caustic, but he was no rebel. At Radley, any rebellion, however mild, was quickly quashed. 'If you were subversive you got points, and if you got enough points you got beaten. Peter only got beaten once.' That was at Henley, when Peter and Jonathan were caught smuggling beer into their punt. The school was resolutely conservative, with a small 'c' and a big 'c'. When Radley held a mock election, the boy who stood as a Labour candidate was an object of outright ridicule. The only time Jonathan can remember Peter expressing a political opinion was when he lampooned a Labour MP. This was not the exception. It was the norm. 'If we mocked a master, we were more likely to mock one who we suspected of working-class origins and speech.'

The school butler, Arthur Boylett, who waited at the high table, was more working-class than most. Peter's mockery of him was affectionate, but patronising nonetheless. 'His was the first voice that Peter reproduced and amplified. If there was a moment when Peter became a comic, it was when Boylett swept some crumbs into a prefect's lap and told him, "Well, they were your crumbs," by way of explanation. From that time on, when any of us were at the high table, the great thing was to draw him into conversation.' Was Boylett mad? 'No, he was very sane – but very prosaic and very simple.'

Peter was a superb mimic, but it took him several years to find his feet. Jonathan marvelled at his unique ability 'to take a tiny motif and build it up into a whole movement, a whole symphony of idiocy. He was wonderful, but I don't think any of us detected this in the first three years.' It was only in his last two years at Radley that his humour blossomed. He impressed Jonathan as Don Armado in *Love's Labours Lost*. 'He'd found a vehicle,' says Jonathan. 'Don Armado is fantastical.' And fantastic, rather than naturalistic, characters were what Peter always played best. 'He was not an actor in the sense that he could subdue himself to whatever part had been written for him. He was a performer.'

After they left Radley they all set off, with several friends, on a couple of camping trips, to the Forest of Dean, and the Lake District. 'We sorted it out as we went along, where we'd go and where we'd stop.' It sounds idyllic. Jonathan went off to do his National Service, in Cyprus. When he'd done his two years, he went up to Cambridge to read English. Here he was reunited with Peter, who'd escaped National Service on account of his allergy to feathers and was now in his final year. Jonathan visited him in his rooms at Pembroke College, where Peter introduced him to Jonathan Miller. Jonathan Miller was a West End star, and Jonathan Harlow was just a fresher, but Peter's manners were impeccable. He treated both Jonathans just the same. Peter now had his own show in the West End, but he hadn't changed. 'He never made a big thing of being Peter Cook.' Jonathan was still at Cambridge when he saw Peter in *Beyond The Fringe*. In Peter's 'Sitting On The Bench' monologue he could hear the echo of Arthur Boylett. Peter's private jokes had gone public. 'I know where this started,' thought Jonathan remembering his childhood friend.

TONY HOLE

'Peter was not a bad influence in any way – very much
the opposite. He was an influence for good.'

Tony Hole was at Radley with Peter. He started there in January 1951, aged thirteen. Peter arrived that September. Tony remembers Radley very fondly. 'I was so happy from the moment I arrived,' he tells me over coffee in his tidy house in Dorking. 'I really don't remember an unhappy day at Radley.' Nonetheless, by today's standards, the daily routine was austere. 'It was pretty bleak,' he says. 'We were meant to have a cold shower in the morning.' Meals were served in the main hall. 'The food was ordinary but not unpleasant. I think we were all pretty hungry, so we didn't mind too much.' There was fagging, but Tony didn't find it too oppressive. He took his turn as a fag, making toast and suchlike. A natural sportsman, he eventually became captain of rugby, hockey and cricket. 'I had a wonderful time in my little world.'

Peter was not subversive. 'He was very much part of the Establishment.' Eventually, Tony and Peter both became prefects. Peter was Head of his House (or Social). Tony was Head of his Social and also Head Boy. Prefects were allowed to beat younger boys. Like most prefects, Tony did so once or twice, but the Dons didn't take it lightly. 'I remember going to one of the Social Tutors and asking for permission to beat some boy and he talked me out of it.'

Tony has vivid memories of Arthur Boylett, the school butler who inspired Peter's comedic alter ego. 'He was quite small, no great weight but looking rather flabby, and not really very bright.' He struck Tony as rather feeble. 'He did look quite absurd. He'd wear this tail coat, so he'd look as though he was at the Savoy or somewhere, but he was so ordinary that he couldn't carry that off very well.' Despite this formal attire, he always looked scruffy. 'He was completely incompetent – pretty unintelligent, I would say. I don't remember ever having a proper conversation with him about anything, because I think he was a very simple soul, but Peter's eye could see the absurdity of it.' Boylett only waited at the high table, where the masters and prefects dined together. If Peter had been more of a rebel, he might never have encountered him at all.

Like Peter, Tony went to Cambridge, but unlike Peter he did his National Service before he went up, as an infantry officer in Germany. Therefore, by the time he went up to university – to read Law at Trinity Hall – Peter was already a finalist. 'He was very much then in the Footlights world.' Most of Tony's friends were from the army. Tony followed Peter's subsequent career with great interest, but as an outsider, not an insider. He went to see *Beyond The Fringe* and thoroughly enjoyed it. He went to The Establishment once, but he felt his face didn't fit and left pretty quickly. 'I clearly wasn't in the set.' In a way, he never was, but that's what makes him such a useful witness. He knew Peter as a fellow prefect, when they were both part of the Establishment at public school.

BARRY HUMPHRIES

'It was difficult for him to take anything seriously,
let alone his self-destruction. It was happening to the
last person in the world you would have thought
would sabotage his life.'

Barry Humphries first met Dudley during the London run of *Beyond The Fringe*. Humphries was appearing in *Oliver!* at the New Theatre, alongside 'a gorgeous girl' called Anna Leroy. Dudley was her boyfriend. When the cast went for drinks at the Lamb and Flag, a pub in Covent Garden, Dudley used to come and join them. 'I was looking for a way out,' says the man behind Dame Edna Everage in the drawing room of his London home, a handsome town house full of paintings. 'I always felt that I'd like to do more of my own thing, and so I was rather envious of this group of young university people, roughly my age, for having this great success at the Fortune Theatre.' Humphries met Peter a little later, through *Private Eye*. 'Peter was rather a remote figure,' he says. 'He was very languid in his manner, aloof, and I think – in retrospect – rather shy. He felt it necessary – all his life – to keep up a constantly jocular flow of conversation. In a way, it was a sort of defence against intimacy. Nothing was serious. Everything was a joke.'

When *Beyond The Fringe* transferred to Broadway, Peter and Dudley left for New York. When *Oliver!* transferred to Broadway, Humphries followed them to America and ended up living near Peter. They spent a lot of time together. They went to the Apollo Theatre in Harlem to see the Supremes. 'He was a fellow spirit,' says Humphries, yet there were a lot of interests they didn't share: Humphries couldn't reciprocate Peter's love of sport; Peter was uninterested in literature; Peter liked rock music and pop music, but classical music left him cold. Yet his humour was incredibly sophisticated. 'Peter could take an idea and transform it and develop it. In that sense, he was probably the most original comedian of his time.'

Peter had heard some recordings that Humphries had made in Australia, featuring one of Humphries's comic characters, a sad suburban bore called Sandy Stone. 'The absurdity was his earnestness, and the dullness of his life.' Peter loved these recordings. 'You must do a show at my new club,' he said when Humphries returned to London. That club was The Establishment. 'I was wary before I went,' says Humphries. 'It was *the* place in London. It was full of dolly birds and journalists.' As a private members' club, it was allowed to serve alcohol after the pubs closed – a rare attraction in those days. All in all, it was entirely the wrong forum for Humphries's subtle, downbeat characters – even his Edna Everage was a lot more dowdy in those days. 'The material at The Establishment was very political,' he says. 'My show was a terrible flop.' Reluctantly, Peter's business partner, Nicholas Luard, paid him off. Happily, Peter harboured no hard feelings and subsequently asked him to write a comic strip for *Private Eye*. He introduced him to Nicholas Garland, who drew the pictures. The strip was *The Adventures of Barry McKenzie*, featuring a cheerful lager-swilling Australian cutting a boozy swathe through British society. 'Peter loved it,' says Humphries. Eventually, the Barry McKenzie character became the basis for a feature film, adapted from the strip by Humphries's friend, Bruce Beresford. Beresford gave Peter a part, but by now Peter was drinking. 'He was not sober at any time during the making of the film,' says Humphries. 'Peter was very good in the McKenzie movie, but clearly not well.'

When Peter wrote a movie of his own, *Bedazzled*, he asked Humphries to play one of the Seven Deadly Sins. 'I played the role of Envy, which I felt was a good role for me, because I was so envious of Peter.' Humphries wore a splendid pair of green pyjamas, with an E (for Envy) on the breast pocket. He thought the film was brilliant, but he found Peter's performance nervous and uncomfortable. There was an uneasiness about him. 'He was much better on the small screen, much more relaxed.'

Humphries had already worked on the small screen with Peter and Dudley, in *Not Only ... But Also*. He was amazed how well they worked together. 'In spite of the sophistication of much of the material, which delights in paradox, they were an old-fashioned music-hall team, not so far away from Morecambe and Wise.' So why did the relationship burn out? 'I think a lot of it had to do with Dudley's success in America, and Peter's resentment of that success. He was not a selfish man, but I think he just felt that some of the success should have been his. He didn't understand that he was unwell.'

'I've given up drinking,' Humphries told Peter. 'It's marvellous. It's as if I've been driving with the handbrake on all these years. I'm full of energy. I think you should think about it.' They went to some meetings together, but Peter seemed subdued and slightly resentful. 'Peter never really got the message that abstinence wasn't such a bad alternative to what was happening,' says Humphries. 'His sense of the ridiculous was too highly developed. Nothing was serious enough, not even, it seems, his own life. But he was capable of great generosity to other people. He was very generous to me. He helped me in my early days a lot.' But he couldn't help himself. 'He couldn't envisage life without vodka, and that was really very tragic.' Some people find their problems are masked by a few drinks. This process becomes a habit, and then it becomes a necessity. 'It's a very insidious process,' says Humphries. 'This hugely common, fatal illness is still not fully understood.'

The last time Humphries saw Dudley was when he returned to London to collect his CBE. Dudley was already very ill. He was staying in a hotel in Leicester Square. Humphries went to visit him, with Dudley's friend and colleague, the cellist Steven Isserlis. Isserlis played the cello for Dudley in his hotel bedroom. 'It was a wonderful moment,' says Humphries. It was forty years since they'd met.

SUZY KENDALL

'I miss him. He was someone who made my life better from knowing him. The world is a sadder place without his music and his laughter.'

Dudley was more than anything else a kind person. He never wanted to hurt anyone, even verbally. When he teased, he was fast to say 'not true, not true' before anybody could be hurt in any way – very different from Peter, who took great delight in teasing, which could result in the recipient being very bruised. I had a healthy respect for Peter's tongue and thankfully he never used it in my direction.

Dudley and I met at a restaurant and club called The White Elephant. Dudley had done *Beyond the Fringe* and started *Not Only ... But Also*, neither of which I had seen as I had been working abroad. I had no idea what he did. I had been asked to a photo shoot for a magazine about the 'in' people in London. I was an 'up-and-coming actress.' Vidal Sassoon was on my left and this very funny person, Dudley, was on my right. After the photo shoot I stayed on at the restaurant for dinner with Ronnie Carroll, the singer, another 'in' person. I was entranced later to hear Dudley play as the club's entertainment. He knew Ronnie and joined us for coffee after he had finished his set.

Dudley had the most handsome face I had ever seen – tousled hair, twinkling mischievous eyes and a smile to light up the room. He was a wonderful listener, a hilarious mimic and truly, honestly kind. Add all this to the funniest person I had ever met – not to mention that to hear him play was quite simply glorious. I was on my way to falling in love. He asked me out for the following evening and so began my lifelong love for him as a person, talented comedian and musician.

The most significant thing in forming Dudley's character was his club foot and withered leg. He was deeply embarrassed by it and had spent most of his childhood in and out of hospital having surgery to correct it as much as possible. Early on in his life he made fun of himself to stop the bullies tormenting him and to make them laugh. By the time we met he had learnt to live with his disability and had special shoes made so that he could play the organ.

What he would not do was to undress on the beach. He knew I loved the sun and sunbathing and took me on holiday to Corsica where he sat fully clothed on the seafront. I tried to persuade him to undress by sitting stubbornly, equally fully clothed, pouring sweat beside him, until he put a swimsuit on. He finally gave way and had the courage to show the world (or at least the beach) his leg. I felt his leg and foot made him the kind and sympathetic person I knew. Also because of it, even in spite of the obvious adoration he had from women, he never truly believed he was attractive.

Dudley was a perfectionist with the music he wrote – writing, rewriting and never satisfied. When he was doing the score for the film we did together, *Thirty Is A Dangerous Age, Cynthia* – a film he had written loosely about our lives – I had to drive him to the studio so that he could scribble away making last-minute changes whilst the full orchestra waited to grab the scores out of his hand. He wrote two songs for me, "Waltz for Suzy", which was my theme tune from the film, and "Sooz Blooz", a delicious thumping sexy melody. He always called me Sooz and spelt my name that way.

We bought a house in Hampstead which by coincidence was not

far from Peter Cook. Peter was married to the exotically beautiful Wendy, who was an incredible chef and homemaker. We spent many happy evenings in their kitchen around the big table with the most amazing selection of interesting people. I have to admit to pinching a few design ideas from Wendy's home but could never equal her cooking. She was an exceptional hostess and created an incredibly supportive home environment for Peter.

Dudley and I wanted children but I had to have fertility treatment which over the years became very difficult and our relationship suffered. The stress and disappointment at failure was hard to live with for both of us. After a number of miscarriages, when I still wanted to have a child Dudley felt I would love the child, should I have one, more than him and became reluctant to be a father. We divorced because I knew I would not be happy unless I at least tried to have a child.

Thankfully we didn't row but our love turned into a loving friendship. He became for me the brother I had never had. Throughout his life he was always there for me and for the daughter I eventually had. He became my daughter Elodie's godfather.

Peter and Dudley's relationship was complex. Dudley was in awe of Peter's way with words and Peter was in awe of Dudley's musical talent. Peter would have loved to have been a pop star, Elvis Presley in particular. He never missed an opportunity to leap up sing and gyrate his hips when Dudley played.

One year Dudley gave a concert at the Albert Hall and arranged for Peter, my daughter Elodie and myself to have a box to watch the show. At the interval Peter was full of praise for Dudley and said that he could never entertain the Albert Hall on his own for a whole show. He had a great fondness and respect for Dudley. That was never more apparent than in Peter's will. He had left Dudley his precious Tiffany lamp. It is sad that Dudley, because of his kind heart, never received it. His widow asked Dudley not to take it, saying that she could not bear to be parted from it. Dudley said of course she could keep it.

Peter was much harsher in his wit and dealing with people, often putting Dudley down with sarcastic humour which did not please Dudley. However, he took it in his stride, because I think he could always eventually see the funny side and use it in some sketch at a later time. Peter and Dudley had a healthy respect for each other's talents and best of all they made each other laugh. It was a privilege to be around when Peter came to the house to work on the scripts for *Not Only ... But Also*. The pair of them would come out with more and more outrageous ideas, making each other howl with laughter. They worked with a tape recorder so that they had a script for the show but, as many guest stars were to find out, they would often both go off at a tangent as the spirit took them. They were great at ad-libbing, which often resulted in them corpsing and made the show even funnier.

There came a time, though, when they no longer worked well together. They were doing a tour in Australia and Peter was drinking heavily to the extent that Dudley never knew what Peter was going to say or even if he would come on stage. When there are only two of you on stage this is an impossible situation. Peter was with Judy Huxtable at the time and I am sure she found his drinking difficult too. Dudley and I had separated by now but he rang me up and asked if he could send me a ticket to come to Australia. Judy was understandably very emotional and leaning heavily on Dudley's friendship, going to him for support and a shoulder to cry on. This made Peter jealous and made him drink even more. Dudley did not know how to handle the situation and thought my presence might calm them both down. Unfortunately nothing could change the situation on stage, which was chaos. I saw a lot of Australia, but sadly Dudley came to the conclusion that he could never again be on stage with Peter.

I think it was difficult for Peter when Dudley left for America, but Dudley loved it there and did not want to come back and live in England. He had a huge success there and his life became more than he could ever have imagined whilst living in a council house in Dagenham. He had a successful film career, was the toast of Hollywood and the ladies adored him. For a long time he was very happy there.

I still lived very near to Peter and he would spend time with me, my husband and our daughter Elodie. His wit was just as sharp but drink had taken hold of him. He had achieved so much in his life, written a West End show at the age of eighteen, become a household name and earned the respect for his wonderful work from every comedian and writer. He talked often of Dudley and dearly wanted to work with him again. I think he missed that fantastic productive time of their youth.

After a concert in Australia, Rena Fruchter, the pianist who was performing with Dudley and a close friend of his, rang to say Dudley was in trouble and could he come and live with me and my family for a while. I was worried when he arrived as he was certainly not himself. I booked him into a London clinic to get him off all the medication he had been prescribed over the years. It was devastating to find after a scan that some parts of his brain were damaged and the doctors did not know the cause. It took a number of years before we got the diagnosis of progressive supranuclear palsy.

This hideous disease progresses very slowly, taking the balance away and slurring the voice and eventually trapping the mind in a body that no longer functions. Dudley would fall down without his body giving him any warning. It was a terrible time for him, culminating in him not being able to remember his lines for a Barbra Streisand film and then, in the later stages, no longer being able to play his beloved piano. It was a horrendous time for him, especially as the press had taken to saying he was drunk. Vicious people also began making money from spreading false stories to the press which have never been corrected.

It was a cruel twist that Nigel Dempster, the journalist, and a friend of ours, died of the same disease. When Nigel was ill, he said that he realised he had not understood Dudley's illness and was sorry for stories his paper had published. It is a terrible disease which strikes for no reason and it is very sad that they both suffered so much from it.

Dudley died in America, but with the help of Rena, Dudley's Oxford College and the generosity of the BBC who funded it, we had a beautiful memorial service in Magdalen College chapel, where Dudley played the organ during his time at university there. His friends and colleagues gave wonderful speeches, but I will always be grateful to Michael Parkinson, who put my thoughts into words. If only I had been able to express them so well. He was talking about the obituaries about Dudley and how he did not recognise the Dudley he knew. This is what Michael said at the service: 'One writer put it, "Success took the place of achievement." The assumption being, of course, that the two are incompatible. Dudley, they suggested, died a man unfulfilled. Well, who knows about that except Dudley? But if it be so, I can't think of anyone who had a better time being unfulfilled than Dudley did. Unfulfilled? Well, he was a great jazz player. His musical satires of Benjamin Britten and Beethoven were brilliant. He was one quarter of a group that redefined British humour in the Sixties. He was one half of a comedy partnership on television which still inspires comedians and audiences forty years on. And then he became a film star. Maybe that was his problem – a box-office success, a sex symbol – or sex thimble, as he called himself. Unfulfilled? I don't think he had the time to be unfulfilled. He couldn't be bothered with all of that."

CHRIS LANGHAM

'Comic genius is a form of disability, because no one
knows how to say to you, "So, how are things?"'

Chris Langham first met Peter in America in the early 1960s, when
he was in his mid-teens. His mother was an actress. His father was a
theatre director who'd worked with Alexander Cohen, the Broadway
producer of *Beyond The Fringe*. Chris's parents were staying at
Cohen's country home, in Connecticut. It was the school holidays,
so Chris was with them. Peter came over for the day. He was doing
Beyond The Fringe on Broadway. 'I got introduced to lots of famous
people through my parents,' Chris says, 'but because Peter was
funny, it was a relationship I wanted to cultivate.'

Chris was a pupil at St Paul's, one of London's top public schools.
He had the LP of *Beyond The Fringe*, and he asked Peter if he could
perform one of his monologues when he went back to school. Chris
was particularly keen to do 'Sitting On The Bench'. ('I could have
been a judge, but I never had the Latin ...') Peter said he could. Chris
had done some acting, but this was the first time he'd done any
comedy, or anything on his own. 'It was like heroin,' he says, sitting
on a bench in the garden of his rural abode in the Home Counties.
'It was completely seductive.' It was the start of his career as a comic
actor. 'I can't wait to do this again,' he thought.

Chris was still at school when Peter and Dudley started doing
Not Only ... But Also on TV. 'I really loved that show,' he says. 'I

loved the fact that they made comedy out of two people having a conversation.' He loved the fact that it had no proper punchlines. 'It had a dramatic legitimacy,' he says. 'It was genuinely funny.' He could see that Peter and Dudley gave each other something special. 'What breaks the sound barrier,' he explains, 'is that they found each other very funny. That's why it really cooked.'

Chris didn't cross paths with Peter again until the late 1970s when they ended up with the same agent, David Wilkinson. Wilkinson would invite Chris and Peter along to Lords, where Peter kept Chris entertained with his absurdist commentary about slow bowlers impaling themselves on cricket stumps, and so forth. 'He was quite egoless,' says Chris. 'The stuff just came out of him. He wasn't career-driven, in the way that Dudley was at that point. There was a kind of carelessness about his life.' Chris and Peter were both drinking but, even blurred by booze, Peter's comic faculties were remarkable. 'I was in awe of him because he was so brilliant. I always felt like a bit of a passenger in conversations with him, because it was hard to keep up. I'm capable of being funny but I'm slow. It takes me a long time to write stuff. He was in the air. He was in the moment, and I admired and feared that about him. I feared that standing next to him, my lack of talent and lack of ability and lack of eloquence really got shown up.'

One day Chris got a message from Peter, recommending a clinic in Chelsea to treat his drinking. 'This would be a really good idea for you,' he said. 'Because Peter was famous and witty and clever and cool, it kind of made it all right for me to go to treatment,' says Chris. 'I agreed to go into treatment when the show that I was in closed, and prayed for it to run for as long as it possibly could. About nine months later, I ended up going into treatment, by which time Peter was out and drinking again.' The treatment didn't really work for Chris, either. 'It didn't really have much effect, apart from chewing up a lot of my dad's money, but it introduced me to AA.'

Chris and Peter became friends. 'We had similar interests – which were basically alcohol and cocaine,' he says. 'We were both people who were trying to be in recovery and failing. I'd go up to his place in Perrins Walk, and we'd just spend the afternoon chewing the fat. This happened a lot, days and days of just hanging out, Peter and I, on our own, amusing each other. Sometimes we would end up doing things we shouldn't do, and sometimes we'd end up going to AA meetings together.' 'That is better than any comedy show I've ever been to,' Peter told Chris, after one such meeting. 'That's the best bit of comedy I've ever experienced.' 'It was a guy talking about his suicide attempts,' says Chris, 'and the meeting was rocking.' People were in stitches. They were falling off their chairs.

Their friendship wasn't just about getting wasted, or trying not to get wasted. With Chris, Peter really opened up. 'I think he did find it hard to talk about himself. I think the conversations that we had, long into the night, were unusual for him. He told me stuff about himself that I've never heard from anybody else, so I guess it's stuff he didn't tell anyone.'

Peter dried out several times, but he never achieved lasting sobriety. 'He really wanted it, but he didn't see the point of having a life. He just didn't see the point of having a life. I completely identified with that. He was a kindred spirit for me at that time.' As someone once said of Chris, Peter was trapped in a box and the instructions on how to get out were written on the outside. 'It's hard to see why anybody would want to be sober, when you're drinking,' he says. 'It's a cruel thing. It's a horrible illness.'

585

Attending Alcoholics Anonymous meetings with Peter was a profound illustration of Peter's curse, his comedic Midas Touch. 'He'd say, "It's been rather a trying week," and everybody would laugh, because he's funny. He's Peter Cook. And then he'd say something else that was just a direct statement, not a performance, and they'd laugh even more, and eventually he'd end up just doing a set, because he was in a club with an audience. He was in the room with the solution, and he wasn't allowed to have it.' So how come Chris survived and Peter didn't? Was it because Peter was funnier than Chris? 'Yes,' says Chris. 'Thank God for my lack of talent. If that's what it comes down to, I'll take whatever it takes. If it takes me not being as talented as Peter Cook, that's a fair price to pay.'

Was Peter always an alcoholic? Was it an accident waiting to happen? Or did he become an alcoholic at some specific point in his life? 'I used to hear people say in AA meetings, "I was an alcoholic long before I drank." I used to think, How's that possible? You catch alcoholism by drinking. I didn't really understand what alcoholism was. I associated it with drinking too much. As time went by, I began to realise that I was an alcoholic long before I drank. All through my childhood, I was frightened. I did a lot of funny stuff. I was a funny child, because it was my way of getting you to like me. I remember Peter saying he understood why people thought he was funny, because he thought he was really good at what he did. He thought he was really funny, and he completely accepted that he had a gift. He said the thing that used to flummox him was why people liked him. Now that's not something you catch from a bottle of Scotch. That's something that comes from childhood. That's why these people in AA meetings would say, "I was an alcoholic long before I drank." They felt this way and then when they drank they didn't feel that way any more. Alcohol cured their alcoholism.' It was a slow form of suicide. 'We talked about suicide a lot,' says Chris. 'There's certainly a genetic component to alcoholism. Is there a genetic component to suicide?' The two things certainly go together. 'It's a major component of alcoholism,' says Chris. 'Preferable to stopping drinking.'

Peter couldn't help himself, but he was always ready to help Chris. 'Are you getting to AA meetings?' Peter asked him one day, when Chris went to visit him in Perrins Walk. 'It's hard to get to meetings, because I don't have a car,' said Chris ('I couldn't get on public transport to save my life but I would have done anything for a bottle or a bag of coke'). 'I've got a car,' said Peter. 'You can have it.' (In fact it was Judy's car. She'd given it to Peter, but he'd never changed the paperwork. It had been sitting outside his house for years.) Peter gave Chris the keys. The leather interior was covered with moss – the dashboard, even the steering wheel. 'It won't start,' said Peter. 'You'll have to call the AA' (the Automobile Association, not Alcoholics Anonymous). The AA came and started it, and Chris and his wife drove it up the hill to Hampstead High Street. 'As we hit the incline, about five gallons of brackish water fell out of the ventilation ducts, full of dead leaves and dead birds and things.' Thanks to Peter's generosity, (and Judy's, inadvertently) Chris no longer had any excuse for missing meetings. 'He was amazingly generous to me, with his time and his support,' he says. 'I never did anything for him to justify the kindness he bestowed on me.' Sadly, not all of Peter's friends were quite so sensitive. 'People who are now considered national treasures would turn up at his house and try and persuade him to do some coke. It was tough to watch.'

So why didn't Peter beat the bottle? 'Most of us don't,' says Chris. 'For any alcoholic, to be sober is a statistical anomaly. Why Peter didn't get it is because he's an alcoholic, and most alcoholics don't get it. I go to the funerals. You watch people get sober, and their lives come back together, and their families get healed, and they have a relationship with their children that they never had, and then they drink and they die.' Chris says AA is by far the most successful recovery programme in the world, yet only six per cent of people who do it stay sober for ten years. 'One in ten of the population experience a degree of self-centred fear,' says Chris. 'That subset of the population will drink to the point of destruction.' Peter was part of that subset, and his sense of humour was no help to him. 'One of the reasons I can't get sober is because I keep getting the slogans wrong,' he told Chris. 'You know that AA slogan, Easy Does It But Do It? I keep thinking it says Take It Easy But Take It.' 'There was this secret landscape inside him,' says Chris. 'He did actually have feelings. He just didn't know how to get them from in there to out here.'

The last time Chris saw Peter was when they worked together on *The Twelve Days of Christmas*, the series that Peter made for BBC2 as Sir Arthur Greeb-Streebling in 1990. Chris had been away in LA. He'd been sober for four years. It was a long time since they'd seen each other. He found Peter very changed. 'Alcoholism is a progressive illness,' says Chris. 'It only gets worse.' The show was not a success. 'He was not funny,' says Chris. 'It was really, really sad. Nothing I'm saying is against Peter. He was a guy in the grip of a condition that he never chose to have. No one goes to the careers master at school and says, "I'd like to be an alcoholic, please." It wasn't that he was drunk. It was alcoholism. He was unreachable.' Chris calls it Wet Brain. 'What was so frightening about *Twelve Days of Christmas* was that he seemed to be on the edge of that,' says Chris. 'You don't come back from that.' Maybe the most powerful drug in Peter's life wasn't alcohol, but the entertainment industry itself. 'It attracts alcoholics and addicts – it doesn't turn people into alcoholics and addicts – because in the entertainment industry is available one of the headiest narcotics known to man: approval.'

Peter died four years later. Chris wasn't surprised. He was surprised that Peter hadn't died sooner. 'His internal organs exploded, basically,' says Chris. 'It's what happens to us. He died a down-and-out's death. That's how down-and-outs die – massive internal haemorrhage as a result of alcohol consumption.' Chris calls it a textbook case. 'In a funny sort of way, I kind of saw the best and the worst of him. And by the best, I don't mean a glittering evening when he was hilarious at the Groucho Club. I mean a guy sitting in his room talking honestly about how difficult it is being alive.' And the worst? 'He died from a massive internal haemorrhage because he went to meetings and asked for help and people thought it was hilarious.' In the end, no one was to blame. 'If he'd really, really wanted it, he could have got it,' says Chris. 'He just didn't think his life was that important.'

But it was. '*Beyond The Fringe*, The Establishment and *Private Eye* changed the face of what was acceptable in comedy. Suddenly, we were allowed to make jokes about the headmaster.' The first joke about the headmaster was Peter's send-up of Harold Macmillan in *Beyond The Fringe*. 'It was absolutely shocking to have someone impersonating the Prime Minister,' says Chris. 'In those days it was considered sort of sacrilegious to be actually poking fun, personally, at our leaders.' So what gave Peter the confidence to do it? 'The amazing thing about Peter was that he was unbelievably honest,' says Chris. 'He liked to prick the bubble of pomposity, and that is the purpose of satire.' But he also opened a Pandora's box. 'Satire, which used to be about taking on powerful people and reminding us that everybody's human, has now become a sort of industry,' says Chris, sadly. 'These things could only prosper because of repression. Without repression they didn't have any fuel.'

ROGER LAW

'The time was right and none of us knew it, but
everything seemed possible. I don't quite know why.'

Roger Law was an art student in Cambridge when he met Peter. He
met Wendy first. They were in the same year at art school. 'Wendy
was very pretty,' he says, over lunch at the Academy Club in Soho. 'I
was her boyfriend – for about five minutes. There were six men for
every girl in Cambridge, so if you were pretty you got invited out.'

Roger made the most of Cambridge. He borrowed a gown and
went along to lectures at the university. He became art director of
Granta magazine (edited by Mark Boxer, then by David Frost). He
worked to supplement his grant. 'I waited table at Trinity,' he says.
'In fact, Peter Fluck and I were responsible for turning it into self-
service.' Fluck became his creative partner. Together, as Fluck & Law,
they went on to create *Spitting Image*.

Roger heard of Peter long before they met. 'You were aware of
him because everybody you went and got pissed with had all these
funny voices.' 'What the fuck are they going on about?' he thought.
He found out when Wendy started going out with Peter. The first
time Roger met him, Peter made a big impression. 'Most of it went
over my head, but you realised he had something special, because
his flights of fancy were extraordinary.' As the writer of a West End
show, Peter was already making money, and it showed. 'He was like a
Regency Buck,' says Roger. 'He was a local celebrity.' But he was hard

to get to know. He didn't like to talk about himself. If you asked him how he was or how he felt, he'd always deflect it with a joke. Roger realised that Peter's humour was compulsive and instinctive. 'I'm a good draughtsman,' he says. 'I had some ability in that direction, but I needed to go to art school. I needed to be taught. I never felt that with him. When I worked with him, it was a fucking nightmare, because he never sat down and did regular hours. He'd do it in the taxi on the way to the theatre. Some of the things he came up with in the taxi are now in the *Oxford Book of Quotations*.'

Roger was eventually expelled from art school ('for shagging, basically') but by then he'd begun his artistic career – with some generous support from Peter. Peter provided the premises for East Anglian Artists, Fluck & Law's first venture as an artistic double act. When Peter and Wendy moved to London, to a flat in Prince of Wales Drive in Battersea, Roger was a frequent guest. Peter and Roger collaborated on a column for the *Observer*. 'I wasn't going to lose contact with Cook, because whenever you got involved with Cook you could do what you wanted,' says Roger. 'You could take your cartoon, which no one would publish, to *Private Eye*, and they'd publish it.' When Peter started The Establishment, he hired Roger to draw a weekly cartoon, on a long strip of wallpaper, which he hung above the bar. 'You could put stuff on the wall that you couldn't publish. That was a huge attraction, because you were free. You didn't have to edit it. You could do what you liked.' In a roundabout way, The Establishment inspired *Spitting Image*. 'Cook made things possible for a lot of people,' says Roger. People like Barry Humphries, Frankie Howerd and Lenny Bruce.

Roger saw all three of them at The Establishment. 'Frankie Howerd was just fucking funny – he took the piss out of the audience,' he says.

'Lenny Bruce could be absolutely brilliant or dead boring. He used to go on about his court cases.' It could get quite rowdy, too. 'I was quite violent when I was young,' says Roger. 'I used to like to fight.' One night, on the dance floor, he got into a scuffle with a couple of heavy characters. 'The whole place erupted,' he recalls. 'I thought, "I'd better get out of here."' As Roger fled the basement, the two men chased him up the stairs. One of them had a cut-throat razor. He took a few swipes at Roger and just missed him. At the top of the stairs there was a table. 'As they came up after me, I got the table and ran down, and they went over. Then I ran up again, and out. I had a friend there that night who was a racing-car driver. We got into his van. He certainly knew how to drive. They chased us but we lost them. We were laughing about it. Then I took my coat off. It was like a Chinese lantern. It had been shredded by the razor blade. I didn't go back to The Establishment after that. I used to send my strip in.'

Peter had a more laid-back way of dealing with the heavies. 'He was renovating the place when they came round for protection money. Cook was at the bar. There was a big canvas on the floor because they'd taken up the floorboards. Cook just sat there. They came across to talk to him, without saying anything, in that sinister way, and just disappeared down into the fucking basement. And then of course they left, because they'd lost so much face.'

Roger doesn't remember Peter as a big drinker. 'When I knew him in the early years in London, that didn't seem to be a huge problem. He was onstage every night. You can't do that if you're pissed all the time.' So what changed? Perhaps it had something to do with the supreme ease with which Peter created comedy. 'I know if I go back to work, to draw, it'll take me a month to get to the point where what I'm doing is acceptable to me, to the standard that I want. It's not something that just flows out of the end of your fingers. But it seemed to me, when Cook was young he had that ability to be funny, on the spot, to order, whenever he fucking felt like it. Now, if you've got no structure … He didn't need to discipline himself when he started, and then you get to the point when it's too late.' As always, the way in is easy, but the way out is hard. 'It's very difficult, once you're addicted to alcohol, to get off it,' says Roger. 'If you don't have something that you want to do more, ultimately you won't get off it.' It seems that Peter didn't. So how did he get started? 'If you drink enough, you'll be addicted. If you drink on a regular basis, you will be addicted. It's that fucking simple.'

ELISABETH LUARD

'Dangerous men are never easy, but most of all they're
a danger to themselves.'[1]

'The Establishment was full of the Establishment,' says the writer
Elisabeth Luard over lunch in a busy West End restaurant, a short
walk away from the former premises of Peter's famous club. 'The
whole of the Establishment was in there, along with various villains
and bent policemen.' And there were artists, too. 'In those days,
worlds were not as divided as they are now. There were writers, there
were poets, there were painters.' There was nowhere else like it. Not
then. Not now. 'Most of that generation were born in the war. That
must have detached us a bit from society. A lot of us had lost our
fathers, or the marriages had split up, so we got a bit wild.'

Elisabeth met Peter when she was working for *Private Eye*. 'Typist,
bookkeeper, dogsbody – nothing intellectual.'[2] She met her husband,
Nicholas Luard, when Peter and Nicholas took over the *Eye*. When
Lenny Bruce played The Establishment, he stayed with the Luards
in their flat beside Hyde Park. 'I think he was on methadone at that
time.' Was Bruce a good house guest? 'No, of course he wasn't –
he was absolutely appalling!' she laughs. 'His character was highly
dangerous and highly unpredictable. It was quite a relief when he got
onstage. You didn't have to deal with anything else that was going
on. He could be incredibly boring onstage, incredibly repetitive –
and unbelievably illuminating.' She calls The Establishment 'a little

centre of subversion', and at that time Bruce was the most subversive comedian in the western world. She saw Frankie Howerd play there, too. So what was he like? 'Smelly. Probably drunk. He used to get up whenever I came into the room, on the grounds that I looked like the Queen. He was funny but very damaged – there was a lot of damage.'

She first saw Peter onstage, at the Fortune Theatre, in *Beyond The Fringe*. 'He was the man with the sharp instrument,' she says. Peter's instrument was his sharp wit. '*Beyond The Fringe* did change things,' she says. 'It was incredibly funny, incredibly irreverent, and completely mirrored what I was feeling. They articulated what you'd been feeling. You didn't know there was anybody else feeling things like that.' When she met him face to face, Peter was already a star. 'He was quite scary,' she says. 'He was definitely not easy to get close to.' When Elisabeth saw him at parties, he seemed like more of an observer than a participant. He was presenting a front, and it was hard to get behind it. 'He was acting for an audience,' she says. 'He didn't talk about himself.'

Beyond The Fringe ushered in a period of tremendous change. Elisabeth's marriage to Nicholas Luard survived the social upheavals of the 1960s. Peter's marriage to Wendy was one of many marriages that didn't. 'Open marriages were not at all unusual, and advocated by quite a lot of psychiatrists at the time. Amphetamines were quite readily supplied, sometimes in the form of slimming pills, and that must have altered people's consciousness.' But it was alcohol that killed Peter. 'It was the drink that got him,' she says. 'Everybody was drinking then. That was the drug of choice. Everybody sat up drinking from the middle of the day right until the end of the day, right up until four in the morning. So what does that do? You can sustain it for quite a bit. Some people drink all their lives and don't die of drink. Other people drink all their lives and do.' Metabolism played a part. There was an element of pot luck, like Russian Roulette. 'The women are still on the planet, most of us. It's the men who've gone.'

'The drink took over,' Elisabeth says as we sip our coffee. 'Drink makes you miserable. There's no such thing as a happy drunk.' As Richard Ingrams said, alcohol made Peter muddy. 'It wasn't that he lost his talent. It was that he just didn't use it.' Yet in the short time that he used it, his talent had a catalytic effect on an entire generation. 'I think his life was spectacular,' says Elisabeth. 'Maybe it's not a happy thing, being a catalyst.' And where did Dudley fit into all of this? 'He obviously did something for Peter that got lost when he went. Peter was fantastic, Dudley went to Hollywood, and nothing much happened afterwards. It probably was a marriage, and off it went.'

GILLIAN LYNNE

'He was intrinsically nice. It's a horrible word, nice – but it also means something. Lots of people aren't nice. I think inside him was a real untroubled nice person – but that got pushed aside by the whole Hollywood thing.'

Gillian Lynne first met Dudley when she was commissioned to choreograph a new ballet called *Collages*. She was thrilled to hear that he'd been hired to write the music. She'd already seen him in *Beyond The Fringe*. *Collages* was a blend of classical and jazz, which was just right for Gillian's style of dance – and for Dudley's style of music. 'We were made to work with one another,' she says, a lithe and elfin figure even today, in her eighties. 'We hit it off immediately. He was so easy and friendly and lovely – very naughty. Always very naughty.'

Collages was a huge hit. 'It was all about Dudley's feelings – and mine – about how impossible it is to find the right person at the right moment,' she says. 'Dudley and I had been through the mill emotionally – both of us – and we poured it all into this ballet.' We're sitting in her handsome home in North London. The room is adorned with discreet mementos of her successes as a choreographer. She was already a successful dancer when she met Dudley but, as a choreographer, doing *Collages* with Dudley was her first big break. She's sad that Dudley's subsequent career overshadowed his achievements as a musician. 'I think it's a shame,' she says. 'He did some wonderful films, which made him a lot of money, and made him a household name. He also hid his main talent.' When he played, it was like someone speaking. 'This is why it's such a tragedy, in a way, that he became a film star.'

Half a century later, she's still grateful for his generosity, sending her money to mount *Collages* in Edinburgh while he was performing *Beyond The Fringe* on Broadway. He kept sending her cheques. She kept sending them back. 'If you send this to me again I shall tear it up and wipe my bum with it and then send it back,' he told her. He used to send her tapes of the score as he wrote it, with bawdy introductions: 'This is my feelings about cunnilingus in the style of Mozart.' He'd pay for her to fly to New York, to work together on the ballet. She'd stay in his apartment, and see the 'curiously unripe blondes' leaving his room in the morning. 'Darling, when are you going to get someone who puts their arms round you and hugs you close and it doesn't matter a damn what they look like?' she'd ask him.

Gillian believes that Dudley's womanising had a lot to do with his disability. 'He had this thing about this wretched club foot.' One day, when they were hard at work at the piano, she took off his left boot. 'Let's look at this foot which is giving you so much trouble,' she said. 'What d'you mean?' he said. 'It's giving you trouble because you feel you've got to compensate,' she told him. 'It's the sweetest little foot I've ever seen. You don't have to compensate for that at all.' And then she kissed it. 'Everybody loves you,' she told him. 'You can't have everything in life. You don't need these statuesque women with no heart. You need someone with heart. There are plenty of attractive people with heart.' But those people can be hard to find, when other women are always falling at your feet. 'I think it was a mixed blessing,' she says of Dudley's extraordinary powers of attraction. 'He was devastatingly attractive in the most unusual way. He was a brilliant comic actor, and on the other side was this marvellous composer and performer. He played brilliantly. Dudley taught me to play with rhythms. I hear rhythms that other people don't hear, and that's entirely due to my work with Dudley.'

It wasn't only a working relationship. 'We were really very close friends – I miss him badly. Once he went to live in Venice Beach, we all lost him a bit, because LA is such a strange place.' Another thing that separated him from his English friends was his interest in psychotherapy. 'He'd got far too deeply into psychiatry, like everybody seems to in America.' Gillian recalls one particular discussion when they were together on Broadway. 'I've just come back from my shrink,' said Dudley. For Gillian, this felt like a slap across the face. She was that angry. 'Do you really need that?' she asked him. 'I don't think you do.' 'She's working on getting my aggression out,' he said. 'What are you talking about?' said Gillian. 'How much do you pay this person? I'll give you a class for nothing. That'll get your aggression out.' 'Lots of people find it very difficult to open up about themselves,' she says. 'I think women find it much easier.' Dudley didn't take her up on her offer. Maybe paying a stranger was easier than opening up to a close friend.

'By that time, something had got hold of him,' she says. 'I don't mean someone. I mean a way of life – the whole Hollywood bit, the whole West Coast bit.' As John Updike said, fame is a mask that eats into the face. 'It was that bloody film, 10, that did it. He probably thought it was the best thing in the world. In retrospect, knowing all the other talents, I don't think so.' Amid all that adulation, the musician got forgotten. As she says, if you're a little man with a club foot and you're suddenly acclaimed as a Hollywood sex symbol, it's easy to be distracted from doing what you ought to do.

'He never found the right person,' says Gillian. This, she believes, is the reason for the aching melancholy in his music. The last time she saw him was over lunch in LA. Dudley was about to get married, for the fourth and final time. 'I don't know whether to get married or not,' he told her. 'Dudley, if you have to ask me the question, then naturally you shouldn't do it,' she told him. 'If you're asking me, "Should I or shouldn't I?" you know the answer in your deepest heart.' 'But I'm in so deep now,' he said. 'You're not in that deep,' she said. 'You haven't signed a legal document.' 'No,' he said, 'but you know what it's like.' 'No, I don't,' she said. 'It's a serious thing, getting married, and if you don't want to marry someone you must not do it. Darling, please, I beg you not to do it.' She knew he wouldn't listen. 'He had a weakness,' she says. 'He kept having these women who were utterly wrong for him.'

DAVID MACLAREN WEBSTER

Sally Mclaren: You didn't have heart-to-hearts with Dudley.

David Maclaren Webster: His heart-to-hearts were through
the piano.

David MacLaren Webster first met Dudley at Oxford in a student
production of *The Changeling*. It was David's first term, reading
English at Christchurch College. 'There was a huge confidence in the
air then, and an innocence,' he says, over lunch in his lovely house in
Wiltshire.

David and Dudley subsequently performed together in several
student plays, in a company that included Ken Loach and Patrick
Garland. They went to the Edinburgh Festival together, and to
Leicester and Stratford-upon-Avon with *Bartholomew Fair*. They
slept in dormitories, about a dozen to a dorm. Dudley kept everyone
awake, reciting obscene limericks. Dudley only had a walk-on part,
but he still brought the house down. He never played a leading role.
He didn't need to. He could get a laugh just by wiggling his eyebrows.
'Cameos were his forte,' says David.

'Everybody loved Dudley,' says David's wife Sally, whom David
met at Oxford. 'There was nothing nasty about him.' Yet there was
something slightly remote, almost unknowable about him. 'He was
very self-effacing,' she says. 'At cast parties he'd just sit down at the
piano. I suppose it was a kind of escape for him. He didn't have to
talk to anybody. He'd just play jazz – improvise endlessly, all night.'

JOE McGRATH

'If the audience didn't laugh, it was the audience's fault.
They knew what they were doing was funny.'

Joe McGrath first met Dudley when he went to see the Johnny
Dankworth Orchestra. Dudley was playing the piano. Afterwards,
Joe and Dudley got talking. They found they had a lot in common.
Dudley's dad was Scots, like Joe. Joe's dad had been a music-hall
comic. Joe found Dudley easy company. He always treated Joe like
an equal.

Joe was working for Associated Rediffusion as a graphic designer.
He'd written a couple of short sketches for one of their comedy
programmes, a one-off show called *Just For Men*. One of Joe's
sketches featured a drunken toff. He asked Dudley if he'd play the
part – a role Dudley would later reprise in *Arthur* ('I think you were
rehearsing me for that part,' he told Joe, years later). 'If you're going
to play a drunk, you've got to be a likeable drunk, and he was very
likeable,' says Joe over breakfast in a cafe in Swiss Cottage. 'Dudley
was a clown, and I mean that as a compliment.'

Joe would have loved for them to have done more stuff together,
but Dudley had other plans. 'I've got to go to Edinburgh to do this
show,' he said. The next time they met was when Dudley invited
Joe to come and see the same show at the Fortune Theatre. *Beyond
The Fringe* had become a hit, and Dudley had become a star. Joe was
now working as a TV director for ABC, on an arts programme called

Tempo with Kenneth Tynan. Tynan told Joe he had to see *Beyond The Fringe*. Joe enjoyed the show. It was the first time he'd seen Alan or Jonathan, or Peter. He thought they were all very good, but he thought Dudley added something special. 'He was likeable in a way none of the rest of them were,' says Joe. 'I recognised at that moment that he was a good actor, a much better actor than Peter Cook would ever be.'

Joe subsequently moved from ABC to the BBC. He can still recall how *Not Only ... But Also* came about. 'Have you got any ideas for a comedy special?' his boss, Bill Cotton, asked him. 'Yes,' said Joe. 'Let's do a comedy special with Dudley Moore.' 'Will you produce and direct it?' asked Cotton. 'Yes,' said Joe. And that was it. The budget was fixed, but otherwise he was given an entirely free hand. 'We won't have any scenery,' he decided. 'We'll do it in an empty studio.' They rehearsed in Sulgrave Boys' Club, on Goldhawk Road. There was no heating. It was freezing cold. 'We were all wearing heavy coats and hats and scarves.' Peter and Dudley told Joe they had a couple of ideas for things they could do together. Joe was all ears. The two ideas they showed him were Peter's debut as Sir Arthur Streeb-Greebling and Peter and Dudley's debut as Pete & Dud. Joe knew they were onto a winner when they did these sketches in front of the technical crew. 'When it came to Arthur Streeb-Greebling, the crew erupted with hysteria. And then we put on the caps and plastic macs and sat them down, and it just went out of control. In rehearsal, it ran for something like four minutes. When we did it in front of an audience, it ran for about eight.' Afterwards, Joe was in the BBC bar when Bill Cotton came up to him. 'I hear you've got a very, very funny show,' said Cotton. 'Who told you?' asked Joe. 'The crew,' said Cotton. 'They came into the bar and said, "Wait until you see this."'

'The first series of *Not Only ... But Also* was possibly the happiest time of my life,' says Joe. 'It was just joyous.' Behind the scenes, beyond the spotlight, he strived to make it even better. Audaciously, he asked John Lennon to do a guest spot. Lennon was such a big fan of *Beyond The Fringe* that he said he'd do it for nothing. The Beatles' manager, Brian Epstein, told Joe the BBC would have to pay him, to make it a proper contract. 'Oh God,' said Joe. 'How much?' 'Five pounds,' said Epstein. 'Peter became enamoured of John Lennon, and became a great friend of his,' remembers Joe. 'Peter's heroes were rock-and-roll stars, yet he couldn't sing a note.' Joe and Dudley used to laugh about it. 'Stop him singing!' Dudley would tell Joe. 'Don't let him sing!' Even when they did 'Goodbyee', Dudley told Joe to make sure Peter spoke the words, rather than trying to sing them. If there was a mike on the set, Peter would grab it and start swinging it around and warbling. 'You can't do it,' Dudley used to tell him. 'You don't have rhythm. You're like some upper-class guy at a hunt ball.'

With his bold use of film, Joe took Peter and Dudley out of the studio. He made their humour more dramatic, persuading Peter to visualise his verbal gags. When Peter came up with a sketch about the Leaping Order of St Beryl, Joe said they had to see nuns leaping, rather than just hearing Peter talk about it. The resultant sketch, 'Tramponuns', prompted a fan letter from Graham Greene. Greene said it was the funniest thing he'd ever seen on TV. He said the creators must be lapsed Catholics. He was partly right, at least. Peter and Dudley were lapsed C of E, but Joe was raised a Catholic.

Peter's growing reliance on idiot boards didn't help his acting, but as a comic he was fearless. One night, as they were about to record an episode, the news broke that Churchill had died, just as the studio audience were filing in. 'Nobody knows about it yet,' said Joe. 'Don't tell them. It'll kill the atmosphere.' Peter stepped forward. 'I've got an announcement to make,' he said. 'Winston Churchill's died.' The show went down a storm.

The next time Joe worked with Peter and Dudley was when they asked him to direct the London run of their two-man stage show, *Behind The Fridge*. The preparations went well enough so, for Joe, Peter's drunkenness on the first night came as a complete surprise. Joe kept the West End run on track, but after the show transferred to America, and Peter decided not to take Joe along, he lost touch with Peter. He never lost touch with Dudley, though. They remained good friends for life.

The last time Joe saw Dudley was after he'd been diagnosed with PSP. 'He'd been onstage and when he came off someone told him he'd sat there for two minutes doing nothing, and he couldn't remember it.' Yet when he came to stay with Joe, his faculties were mercifully unimpaired. 'Do you mind if I play your piano?' Dudley asked him. 'Please do,' said Joe. Dudley sat and played for three hours, non-stop. When he'd finished playing, they went out for a walk. Dudley said he was getting divorced again. He'd left LA in a hurry. He hadn't packed enough clothes. He needed to buy some shirts. They went into a men's outfitters, but none of Dudley's credit cards worked. His told Joe his wife had stopped them. Joe bought the shirts.

Joe never saw Peter again, but his wife is an art director and quite by chance she ended up on one of Peter's final projects, *Peter Cook Talks Golf Balls*. 'I never see Joe now,' Peter told her. 'Maybe we could meet up and have dinner and get to know each other again?' 'OK,' she said. 'I'll tell him.' There was just one other thing. 'You couldn't get me a glass of brandy, could you?' he said.

BARBARA MOORE

'Put the lad in front of a piano, put him in a concert hall,
put him in front of people – the minute he went in and
sat down at a piano and smiled at the ladies, that was
enough. And the men loved him as well.'

'I could actually play you the tune that started it all off,' says Barbara Moore (no relation) remembering the first time she met Dudley. We're sitting in the vast conservatory of her beautiful home in Bognor Regis, where she lives with her grand piano. She's a pianist and a composer, just like Dudley. She's also a singer, which Dudley never was. It was as a singer that she was hired by ITV, to record a demo, to help an actress learn a song. The recording studio was in Holborn. Inside the studio was a piano. 'It was small upright piano, and seated at it was a small upright little chap.' That small upright chap was Dudley.

'Hi, I'm Dud,' he said. 'I'm Barb,' she said. They shook hands. The song was 'Stranger In Paradise'. 'It's a bit classical for me,' she thought, 'but I'll do my best.' On the first take, she saw Dudley's shoulders twitching. She realised that he was giggling. They tried it half a dozen different ways, getting sillier every time. They ended up doing it like 'My Old Man's A Dustman'. By the end, they were both in fits. 'Call yourselves professionals?' said the producer. 'For God's sake, give me a decent straight version!' Somehow they managed one straight version without corpsing. 'My name's Dudley Moore,' said Dudley, when they got outside. 'My name's Barbara Moore,' said Barbara. 'Gosh, that's my sister's name,' he said. 'That was a gas.' They both started laughing. They kept laughing all the way to the nearest pub. 'I'm just down from Oxford,' said Dudley over a lemonade (he never was much of a drinker). 'I've done an organ scholarship and I'm now starting rehearsals with three other guys on a revue called *Beyond The Fringe*. I have to write all the music and I have to play a few numbers – send-ups, a bit like the ones we were just doing. I've got a nice bedsit in Notting Hill, but there's only one hang-up. I haven't got a piano.' Barbara had split up from her husband. She was living with her five-year-old daughter at her mother's house in Ealing. They had a piano. She invited him to come round and practise. 'Can I bring my bass player?' he asked.

'Every Sunday, for three glorious months, my Yorkshire mother would make one of her famous Sunday lunches, and Dudley and his bass player, Hugo Boyd, would come over and rehearse.' Barbara would listen to them making the music for *Beyond The Fringe*. She'd grown up with music, but she was amazed by his harmonic progressions. 'Give him a little theme to play and he'd play it in ten different ways.' Dudley must have been impressed by Barbara's musicianship as well. When his trio got bookings he'd ask her to sing with them. He only made a pass at her once, after a gig they did at Brasenose College, at Oxford University. There was a mirror in the room. Barbara took him by the shoulders and turned his head to face it. In her high heels, she towered over him. 'I'm sorry,' she said. 'I don't fancy little men. I always like the tall ones.' At first he seemed deeply hurt – but then suddenly he roared with laughter. 'He never ever made a pass at me again, but he gave me something far more precious,' she says. 'He gave me a lifelong friendship.' If they'd slept together, she doubts the friendship would have lasted. 'I would have been just another tick on the list of Birds What I Have Conquered.'

'I saw so many of those rehearsals,' she says, of *Beyond The Fringe*. 'I knew every line of every sketch.' That was when she met Peter. She felt that Peter patronised Dudley, despite the warmth and humanity that Dudley brought to this wordy, cerebral show. 'It was wonderful the way he could act from a piano. It was like a part of him. His hands and the keys were conjoined.' Even in rehearsals, Barbara had no doubt that the show would be a hit. 'Everything in it was a new way of looking at things.' She went up to Edinburgh for the opening night. 'The audience were literally on their feet. There was an incredible response. It was the beginning of pure satire. They took the mickey out of just about everything that was current.'

After their first night in the West End, at the Fortune Theatre, Barbara went backstage and found the cast hobnobbing with their families. All except Dudley. 'Where are your mum and dad?' she asked him. 'Oh, they don't like this kind of affair,' he said. He'd told them to wait outside. 'You bastard!' she said. 'You snob!' She went out to fetch them. 'Dudley wants you to come in and have a drink,' she told them. 'That's the only time I ever saw Dudley do anything that was even remotely inconsiderate,' she says. 'He was ashamed of them.' But she couldn't remain cross with Dudley for long. 'He had charisma in every sense of the word,' she says. 'He brought out a bit of the maternal that's in all of us. You wanted to protect him.' When *Beyond The Fringe* was at the Fortune, she would often go for supper with the cast after the show. She didn't get much chance to speak, and nor did Dudley. Peter and Jonathan would monopolise the conversation. Alan was more cagey. He was always the first to leave the table. He always seemed to be on his own. He was kinder to Dudley. That was a class thing, as much as anything.

During the West End run, Barbara took her daughter to the South of France on holiday. Dudley's bass player, Hugo Boyd, was also on holiday in France, driving his Lamborghini around the Riviera. He offered to pick them up and drive them back to London. When he didn't show up, Barbara brought her daughter home by train. It was only when she got home that she heard he'd been killed in a car crash, on his way to collect them. 'I thought of Dudley, going on to do a comedy show that night,' she says. 'He still had to go on and make people laugh.' She went to the theatre that night, and went backstage to comfort him. They were sitting in his dressing room, both crying their eyes out, when there was a knock on the door. Barbara opened the door to tell whoever it was to go away. It was Charlton Heston. He'd seen the show and had come backstage to say how much he'd enjoyed it. When she told him what had happened, he left them alone.

When *Beyond The Fringe* transferred to Broadway, Barbara went out to New York for a while. She saw a lot of Dudley. One day she washed his feet, and he told her that he was worried what his girlfriend, Celia Hammond, would think of his club foot when she saw it. 'She's going to think it's the most ugly foot she's ever seen in her life,' she said, and he laughed. 'This foot, my dear, is part of you – it's part of your persona. How many other men have a foot like this?' Dudley was smitten with Celia Hammond. He was heartbroken when she left him. He had no shortage of female company thereafter, but Barbara detected an enduring sadness in his music. 'His cadences, his harmonic sequences, keep going down a semitone.' When he went to Hollywood they kept in touch and saw each other when they could.

He seemed a little sadder every time. Dudley enjoyed being famous. It didn't change him but it did distract him from his main calling, which was music. 'I think he would have composed some fabulous things. He would have been a latter-day Gershwin.' He promised he'd marry Barbara's daughter. He was only joking, but it says something about the depth of their friendship, all the same.

When his fourth marriage was breaking down, Dudley came to England for a rest, to escape the trauma and the US media. He stayed with Suzy Kendall, his first wife, who had become a second sister to him. He was already very ill. Suzy phoned Barbara. 'I'm very worried about Dudley,' she told Barbara. 'He can hardly move and hardly speak, but one thing he keeps saying is, "Ba, Ba." I know what he's saying. He's saying, "Barbara, Barbara."' 'No, he's not,' said Barbara. 'He's saying, "Bastard! Bastard!" That little man inside, that spirit, is fighting away. He knows he can't move, he knows he can't speak, but he is still who he is inside that head of his.'

Dudley came to Bognor to stay with Barbara. He insisted on coming by train. She met him at the station. Someone had to help him down the steps. Despite his club foot, this was the first time she'd seen him limping. Barbara took him home, to her daughter and her granddaughter. 'We literally carried him out of the taxi,' she says. 'He looked like a little doll.' In the evening she brought him downstairs to play the piano, but he was too ill. He couldn't even speak. 'It was horrific. It was worse than I'd imagined.' His face was like a mask, but his eyes were still alive. She took him to Chichester Cathedral. She had to push him round in a wheelchair. When the time came for him to leave, it was awful. 'He couldn't say goodbye.' They carried him into the limousine and then Barbara got in and put her arms around him and kissed him on the cheek. 'I knew it was the last time I would ever see him.'

Barbara went to his memorial service in Oxford, at the college chapel where he used to play. She shared a taxi with Jonathan Miller. George Martin, Joe McGrath, Michael Parkinson and Eric Sykes read tributes. The college choir sang 'He Who Would Valiant Be'. The music included Bach's Preludes – the music that Dudley loved to play every day, by his favourite composer. His friend Rena Fruchter played selections from one of his favourite compositions, Songs Without Words. The service finished with Goodbyee. 'As he would have said, there wasn't a dry seat in the house,' she says. 'I was honoured to have known him. I'm good at friends, good at friendship, but he was the one that I loved the most.'

ROBERT PONSONBY

'Of course I dearly wish that I'd had one per cent of the income of the show, but that's not the business of the artistic director of an arts festival. You aren't in it to make money out of it.'

Educated at Eton and Trinity College Oxford, where he read English, Robert Ponsonby's credentials as Artistic Director of the Edinburgh Festival were impeccably conservative – which makes it all the more remarkable that he came up with the idea for *Beyond The Fringe*. 'It was a complete departure,' he says over a pint in a pub in Baker Street. 'What really irked me at that time was that our thunder was constantly stolen by the Fringe.' But it never would have come together if Louis Armstrong, whom he'd planned to book for the Lyceum Theatre, hadn't dropped out when his agent failed to put together a British tour. 'It was all very accidental,' he says. 'I didn't know what to do.' What he decided to do was to instruct his assistant, John Bassett, to assemble a troupe of comic graduates to do a revue that would be beyond anything that the undergraduate comics on the Fringe could muster.

When Bassett brought Alan, Jonathan, Peter and Dudley along to meet him, in his London office, Robert was impressed. 'It was quite clear that they were characters. I suppose Peter was the most obviously entertaining, spontaneous person. He was extremely funny.' Jonathan seemed more donnish. 'Dudley was sparky and fun. Alan didn't make much of a mark. He was quite quiet.' Robert gave them carte blanche. 'Do what you like,' he told them. 'Go as far as you like.' Robert was still only 34, but he'd been assistant director for five years, and then artistic director for five. This was his last year. He'd already resigned. He'd decided it was time to do something new.

Robert didn't see the show until the ad hoc dress rehearsal. 'The dress rehearsal was a disaster,' he says. 'They corpsed, they broke down, they forgot their lines.' Yet he could see that they had something. After booking Flanders & Swann the year before, he knew there was an appetite for revue, but this was something new. 'It had a tang and an outrageousness which I had never heard before. Flanders & Swann were genteel by comparison.' The fact that the cast were well spoken and well educated gave their material an added frisson. 'It made it all the more telling,' he says. 'It was coming from the very people you wouldn't have expected it to come from.'

The first night calmed Robert's nerves. 'There was a lot of laughter.' The theatre was far from full but it was full every night thereafter. 'There was a huge buzz,' he tells me. 'It took off in a very big way.' A few weeks later, Robert and the cast went their separate ways. 'It was a prodigiously gifted ensemble,' he says, 'but I claim no credit for realising this at the time. It just looked like it was going to be a good show – if I was lucky.' He *was* lucky, but winners make their own luck. Almost by accident, he caught the zeitgeist. 'If Louis Armstrong hadn't called it off, none of this would have happened.' Today the Edinburgh Festival is the biggest comedy festival in the world.

PETER RABY

'I never remember Peter being unkind. All my memories
are of him being generous and humane.'

Peter Raby and Peter Cook were in the same boarding house
at Radley. From the start, Raby had a sense that Peter Cook was
different. He was slightly aloof, slightly detached. He seemed more
sophisticated, more mature. 'He didn't stand out because he was
rebellious. He wasn't particularly sporty.' It was the quality of his
intellect that set him apart.

Raby is an academic. We're talking in his college common room
at Cambridge University. 'Radley at that time was a relatively
happy place,' he says. 'It was quite a civilised place.' Even so, there
was fagging, corporal punishment and a compulsory cadet corps, a
foretaste of National Service. Some of the teachers (or Dons, as they
were called at Radley) were quite eccentric – regarded with affection,
but somewhat absurd figures nonetheless. Laughter was a survival
technique. 'There was a strain of mockery,' he says.

Raby first saw Peter perform in Ben Jonson's *The Alchemist* as the
prostitute Dol Common, and as the lovelorn Spaniard Don Armado
in *Love's Labours Lost*. 'There was a lot of theatre – the senior play, the
junior play, the house plays.' They acted together in Peter Ustinov's
The Love of Four Colonels, but the performance that impressed him
most was a sketch that Peter wrote and performed with a fellow pupil
called Paul Butters, sending up the two luvvie thespians who'd come

to judge the house-drama competition. 'The whole school recognised it immediately,' remembers Raby. It was a revelation that such a subject could be mocked.

Raby went up to Cambridge a couple of years after Peter. Peter was a finalist when Raby arrived. He saw Peter in Smokers, at Pembroke College and at Footlights. He recognised Peter's impression of the Radley school butler, Arthur Boylett, straight away. 'I hadn't realised how good he was until I came to Cambridge. When I saw him in the Footlights, in a slightly wider world, then I realised how distinctive he was.' Yet in some senses, this world was only slightly wider than Radley. 'We had to be in college by eleven. If you wanted to be later than eleven, you had to have a note from your tutor. You had to wear gowns in the street.'

Raby saw *Beyond The Fringe* in London, at the Fortune Theatre. 'I found it quite shocking,' he says. 'I'd never seen anything like it before.' Peter's impression of Harold Macmillan was particularly arresting. 'It did strike me as a bit cruel,' he says. 'There was something slightly decayed about it.' Fifty years later, the show still resonates. 'Here was something very distilled and very pure and very simple. Nobody had chucked a lot of money at it. It was pure intellect and performance brio. That was a brilliant conjunction of people.' Clever people, in a country where the word 'clever' is often a backhanded insult. 'It isn't a self-congratulatory cleverness. It's a cleverness of people who have a breadth of interests.' Back then, Peter's interests were exceptionally broad. It was only later, after he lost touch with his friends from Radley, that they began to narrow.

SARAH SEYMOUR

'I told Peter to leave his Tiffany lamp to me, but he didn't. He left it to Dudley. To me, that means he had great affection for him.'

'It was a very happy time,' says Peter's sister, Sarah Seymour, recalling her childhood in Gibraltar. She went there when she was only one year old. Peter was seven years older. He stayed in England, where he went to school – a day school in Torquay, then prep school in Eastbourne – but he spent school holidays with Sarah and their parents, Alec and Margaret. Despite the age gap, he was always good company, as were her mum and dad. 'Although they were quite reserved people in some ways they weren't stuffy,' she says. 'They liked a bit of fun.'

We're sitting in the sunlit living room of Sarah's terraced house in a leafy suburb of Newcastle. She shows me some early letters from Peter. It was 1944. The Second World War was still raging. Peter was only six years old:

> Dear Mummy
> How are you? I am very well and I have grown at least three inches. I wonder what you are doing. We had straw-berries for tea last Friday. I am getting on well at school. I was seventh out of fourteen last week. There are five new boys this term. I am going to have a guinea pig.
> Love from Peter

Dear Mummy
We caught a mole yesterday and took it to school in a box.
We kept it in the prefect's study. The guinea pigs are coming
on Saturday. We have made a hutch for them.
Love from Peter

Even in these early letters, Peter's passion for creepy-crawlies was already evident. Sarah always wrote exactly the same reply to her big brother every time:

Dear Peter
I hope you are well. I am very well.
Love from Sarah

Even though she was seven years younger, Peter was always happy to play with his kid sister. They went fishing for tiddlers together. They found some terrapins in a river bed and put them in their garden pond. 'It was a lovely climate, and when dad was on leave we all went home. We drove all the way through Spain and France, which was an adventure.' Their mother, Margaret had hated her husband's previous posting, in Nigeria. She was much happier in Gibraltar. She was very gregarious. She played second violin in the Gibraltar Symphony Orchestra. There were plenty of picnics and dinner parties. 'Spain wasn't touristy then. It was very poor, but lovely empty beaches.' 'Margaret, come and have a cocktail,' her neighbour would shout over the garden wall.

Sarah shows me a photo of her paternal grandmother who was widowed, with two young children, when her husband Edward killed himself in Kuala Lumpur. 'I find that picture terribly sad, because I know what happened. I think how brave she must have been to keep this secret. She was always cheerful.' She never remarried. 'My father never knew. He used to occasionally come in with this one photograph that he had, saying, "My father was a good-looking chap and I never knew him, and I always wonder about him."' His death remained a mystery, until Peter traced the family history through Debrett's and found lots of newspaper cuttings from Malaysia. 'I just felt this great surge of sympathy for this poor man,' she says. 'He'd been given some more responsibility in his job, he was worried about it and he wasn't sleeping properly. His family were back home. He was all on his own. I don't think people want to die. I think they just want to stop what's happening now, which has become unbearable.' The note he left behind said, 'I must get some rest.'

Edward's son, Alec, their father, followed his father into the Colonial Service. 'He said to me that when he was at university, the choices were to go into business or to go to the colonies, and that the colonies was an idealistic choice. You were off to do good for the world. He cared deeply about the job. He was terribly conscientious.' He also had a sense of humour. 'My mum and I were driving down into the town, and there was the most enormous bang, like a bomb going off. A ship loaded with ammunition had blown up in the bay. When Dad got home that evening, he said that he and his colleagues had all hidden under the table and played bears. Or maybe he just made that up for me.' Alec was a witty man. 'And quite sarcastic. This is also a family trait that can get us into trouble – all of us, me included. I have a sharp tongue on occasions, and so did Dad and so did Peter.' Their familial wit was echoed in the books they read: P.G. Wodehouse, Molesworth, Lewis Carroll, Edward Lear, *1066 And All That*, and *Ruthless Rhymes For Heartless Homes*. 'It's absolutely wonderful. It's terribly bleak and macabre.'

'When grandmamma fell off the boat, and couldn't swim and
wouldn't float,
Matilda just stood there and smiled – I almost could have
smacked the child'

'To me, it's the acknowledgement that life is awful and dangerous, and can only end badly. It's in the face of that that we laugh and create these silly stories because it is so awful. It's laughing to stay afloat.'

When Sarah was seven, Alec and Margaret returned to Nigeria, and Sarah was sent away to boarding school in England. Her younger sister Elizabeth was born just before they left. Sarah shows me a letter she wrote from boarding school, when she was about ten:

Darling Mummy & Daddy
We had quite a nice maths exam yesterday ...

'That's a ridiculous thing to say,' says Sarah. 'I failed Maths O level twice. Our maths teacher used to chain-smoke and throw things at us and swear. He was terrifying.'

... Thank you very much for your letter. I've just finished reading *Jane Eyre*. I think it is one of the nicest books that I have ever read. I can't find a friend now. Nobody will play with me and it is jolly lonely. Nobody seems to want to play with me. I'm sorry that my writing is so awful, but my pencil is so awfully blunt. Ah, somebody has lent me their pen. There isn't really any news.
Lots of love from
Sarah

Their mother was so disturbed by Sarah's letter that she telephoned the headmistress. 'Nonsense!' said the headmistress. 'Sarah's got lots of friends.'

*

The first time Sarah saw Peter perform was in Edinburgh, in *Beyond The Fringe*. She was fourteen. 'That was wonderful,' she says. 'We drove up from Eastbourne, which was where my grandfather lived. I wasn't a very questioning child, because Granny Mayo lived in Torquay and Grandfather Mayo lived in Eastbourne, and I didn't ask why they lived in different towns.' In Edinburgh, Sarah met the rest of the cast. 'I remember Dudley being very friendly and Alan being very friendly and Jonathan being a bit stand-offish. I suppose he was much more grown-up.' She was also introduced to Wendy. 'We stayed in a funny little guest house. I had a big clunky tape recorder, which was so exciting – my brand new toy – and I persuaded Wendy and Elizabeth to record an excerpt from *The Importance of Being Earnest*, for some unknown reason. I was Miss Prism and Wendy was Lady Bracknell.' Sarah saw the show several times. 'I'm sure Elizabeth and I didn't get half the jokes but it was very funny – Dudley was very funny, so physically funny.' She loved the confusion of the opening sketch, 'Steppes In The Right Direction', in which Dudley played the National Anthem. 'People didn't know whether to stand or not.' Her mother enjoyed it too – the only thing she was a bit uneasy about was 'The Aftermyth of War'. 'People could take that sketch the wrong way. It's not belittling anybody who took part in the war. It's belittling the crap people talked about it.' The show turned Peter into a household name. 'I think I had a bit of a crisis in my late teens and early twenties, feeling very inadequate by comparison. But then I decided that brilliant people need an audience, so an audience has a worthwhile function as well.'

'I don't remember Peter being a drinker until much later in his life,' Sarah says. 'I think perhaps drink creeps up on people.' Sarah didn't see so much of him in those later years. 'When he wasn't in touch, I just thought he didn't want to inflict himself on people when he was depressed. I know that feeling. I think it's very sad. I sort of thought he was so tough physically that he would survive anything. You have to do a lot to damage your liver. The liver's a big organ, isn't it? It can renew itself quite well. I just thought he was strong, physically, and he could survive – that it wouldn't do him in.'

Yet Peter was a source of strength to those around him, even in those later years. When their father Alec became ill with Parkinson's disease and was put into a hospital, Peter arranged to bring him home, and paid for nurses to look after him. 'During this time, between us, there was this fictional character called Auntie Flo, who we used to talk about on the phone,' Sarah says. 'It was a kind of light relief.' She shows me a letter from Peter, all about her:

> Sarah Dearest
>
> Very nice for some people, swanning up to London and ducking their responsibilities. Our Auntie Flo never had a swan, let alone a duck. They did once leave her alone with a duck, but then they took it away again. Just the same as the man who stole her heart away, and broke it into the bargain. Auntie Flo never even had a bargain to be broken in. Mind you, they never broke her in, but they did saddle her with a lot. Not that that lot ever allowed her a lot. At least Lot's wife was turned into a pillar of salt. He was a tower of strength, that man. Auntie Flo just ebbed. She never even had a pinch of salt, let alone a pillar. And of course, they took her with a pinch of salt and threw her on the cold ham with a lot of pepper. She couldn't bear pepper, Auntie Flo, let alone children. She was as barren as they come. Not that they ever did, and so on, ad nauseam. Seriously though, Dad was delighted to be back home ...
>
> Much love
>
> Peter

Peter was a splendid son to his mother, too. In 1992, Margaret Cook went into hospital in Exeter. Peter travelled down from London to see her. 'He walked onto the ward – and she was very, very ill – and he said, "Mum, you look so pretty!" And she just beamed. She was a pretty woman – even when she was ill – so he wasn't faking it. It was genuine. She just lit up. That was totally spontaneous – not planned, not scripted – but it was just perfect.' Her death, in June 1994, hit Peter terribly hard. 'I think that was part of the real decline, somehow. It was just so awful for him.' Sarah shows me a photo of Peter at his daughter Daisy's wedding, a few months before he died. Daisy looks a lot like him. 'He was very proud of his gorgeous daughter,' says Sarah. 'She's got the sticky-out ears. Dad had it as well. That's a genetic thing. You can't help your ears.'

The last time that Sarah saw her brother was at his home in Perrins Walk, a few weeks before he died. She went with Liz to deliver some Christmas presents. Peter had just come out of hospital. He was very quiet, uncharacteristically quiet. They only stayed for fifteen minutes. 'I don't know how well you ever know anybody. I think everybody's a mystery. I really do think that. However much you know them or love them or whatever, at the end I don't think we can ever be fully understood by another person.'

BARBARA STEVENS

'I don't think I was quite so studious as Dudley –
or as clever.'

Dudley's elder sister, Barbara, lives in a nursing home in the Cotswolds. It's a beautiful building, hewn from the local honeyed stone. Her husband, Bernard Stevens, lives in a pretty little cottage right next door. Sadly, Barbara is too infirm for them to live under the same roof any more – she needs round-the-clock care – but Dudley's generosity has given them the next best thing. In a few minutes, Bernard can be out of his bedroom and into hers. Although they live in separate houses, they seem inseparable, like newly-weds. They see each other all the time. They've been married nearly sixty years. Bernard takes me to her room, but then he leaves me with her. It's a generous and trusting gesture. Talking to her, in her cosy room, the years and miles melt away, and we're back in Dagenham again. Even though she's frail and elderly, Barbara is still as bright as a button. She's got Dudley's dark good looks. Like him, she could be Jewish, even Romany. 'My father's sisters were very dark,' she says. You can see a lot of Dudley in her – and it's not just the way she looks. She also shares his wit and charm. There's one big difference. At five foot eight, she always used to tower over him. Even though she has to conduct this interview lying down, her mind and memory are as sharp as ever, and she's anxious to make me feel at home. 'Could we have some biscuits for Mr Cook, please?' she asks the nurse. 'Would you like a sherry?' I warm to her straight away.

'This is an absolute myth, all these operations – he just had one, when he was about seven,' she says. 'He was in a ward full of wounded soldiers. He was the only child in the ward. And then he went away to a convalescent home in Hertfordshire.' His club foot never held him back. 'At school, he played cricket and tennis and he swam.' Barbara recalls the day she was evacuated, with her mum and Dudley, in the Blitz. She wasn't scared. 'We walked down to Dagenham docks, got on a boat there and went round to Yarmouth, stayed in a hotel for three days. On the Monday morning we were collected by bus and went out into the Norfolk countryside. We sat outside in the churchyard and people from the village would come along and get you. We had a very nice couple, Captain and Mrs Coltart. We were very happy there. We stayed there eight months.' Back in Dagenham, rationing dragged on, long after the war, but Barbara doesn't remember those times as hard times. She made some good friends. She's still in touch with a few of them. 'We were all in the same boat.'

There was a marked contrast between the two sides of the family. 'My father was very quiet – not an emotional father at all. He never put his arm round you or anything like that.' He was very religious. 'My father was at church all the time,' she recalls. 'He went to two services a day – or even three.' Her mother's family were more extrovert. 'My mother had a big family and so I had lots of aunts and uncles, and that was terrific – Christmases at my grandparents in Hornchurch.' It was this side of the family which was musical, but nothing out of the ordinary, nothing like Dudley. 'My mother's eldest brother played the violin and the organ, and then there was another brother who played the violin. My mother played the piano but no one else in the family played.' Barbara and Dudley both started learning the piano when they were seven. They shared the same piano teacher, a kindly spinster with a terrible stutter. The lessons cost a shilling a time. Even though Barbara was four years ahead, her younger brother soon overtook her. 'He won a scholarship to the Guildhall School of Music and he used to go there every Saturday morning. I worked in the City, and on Saturdays, when I was working there, I used to walk down to the Guildhall and we used to go home together – or sometimes go to a concert at the Albert Hall. There were Winter Proms in those days.' Barbara pursued the same career as her mother. 'She was a shorthand typist and bookkeeper in the City, like me.'

Dudley went up to Oxford the year that Barbara married Bernard. She used to sing in an operatic society in Hornchurch with Bernard's sister. Bernard had just come back from Iraq, where he'd been serving with the RAF. She visited Dudley on his twenty-first birthday in Oxford. 'He had a room on the ground floor, overlooking the Deer Park.' But it was *Beyond The Fringe* that really changed things. She'd seen the rave reviews in the papers, but she didn't know what to expect. '*Beyond The Fringe* was wonderful.' She wasn't surprised by Dudley's success – 'I think it was always there' – but she thought music would be his forte. 'The show came to London in 1961 and we saw it, and then the next year they were off to America and then I didn't see Dudley for four years, because the next year we went to Singapore for three years, and didn't get back until 1966.' By then, her brother was a star.

Dudley stayed in touch, but inevitably the remainder of their relationship was played out at long distance. Barbara met his first three wives – Suzy, Tuesday and Brogan – but not his fourth wife,

Nicole. 'I saw the premiere of *Arthur* in 1981 and about a fortnight after that my mother died,' she says. 'I preferred watching him on TV rather than in films.' In 1987 she was flown to LA to appear on *This Is Your Life* with Dudley. 'Unfortunately it wasn't a direct flight. First stop was Chicago, then St Louis, and I was absolutely exhausted by the time I got to Los Angeles. But it was a lovely evening.' She only met Peter a few times. The last time was in 1992, at Dudley's concert at the Albert Hall. 'He was there with his wife Lin.'

'It was round about 1997, he phoned me up from America and said he'd got this PSP, and I'd never heard of it, and I didn't realise how bad it was, and then, in 1998, Rena and her husband brought Dudley to lunch at our home in Upminster. He was bad then.' When Barbara and Bernard moved out here, to the Cotswolds, Rena brought Dudley here to see them. By now he was even worse. 'The next time I saw him was in 2001, when he received the CBE at Buckingham Palace, and I could see then how very bad he was.' Dudley and Barbara were both in wheelchairs, but Dudley, the kid brother, was in far worse shape than his big sister. 'He was like a graven image. You couldn't really tell if he was looking at you or not. He really was bad then. The next day, we had lunch at my daughter's house in Hertfordshire. That was the last time I saw him.' When Dudley died, it was Bernard who broke the news to her. 'I was very upset.' Barbara and Bernard have two daughters and two grandsons. 'They're both at university. The oldest one got a First Class Honours degree. Now he's doing his Doctor of Philosophy.' When Dudley went to university, it was seen as an extraordinary achievement. Now it's a family tradition.

BERNARD STEVENS

'There's been so many people drinking champagne on
my brother-in-law's back for so many years.'

'My sister was married to a guy and they were both in an operatic
society, and so was Barbara – that's how I met her,' says Bernard
Stevens. 'She lived in Dagenham. My parents lived in Hornchurch.'
We're sitting in the tidy sitting room of his pretty Cotswold cottage,
next door to the nursing home where his wife Barbara now stays. For
nearly sixty years she's been Barbara Stevens, but when Bernard met
her she was Barbara Moore, and Dudley was her kid brother. 'Barbara
was living in Dagenham, on the Becontree council estate. I was born
on the Becontree council estate. My parents moved to Hornchurch
when I was five. That's where I was brought up.' Bernard was a pilot
in the RAF. 'When I finished my tour in the Middle East I came home
and I went to my parents' home for leave.' That was when he met
Barbara.

Bernard had cousins in the road where Barbara lived, with her
parents Jock and Ada, and Dudley. So how has Dagenham changed
since he met Barbara, sixty years ago? 'You know what Dagenham's
like – narrow roads and broad pavements. That's because they were
only meant for the milkman's horse and cart. There were broad
pavements for the kids to play on. Now the pavements are covered
in cars.' It was all very different back in 1951. 'It's not so much the
place, it's the time. England was a grey place to be. I'd been stationed

in the Suez Canal Zone and Iraq and they were pretty grubby places, but England was so dull and grey.' Food was still rationed, and lots of other things besides. 'I'd already had my name down for a new car for three years, and I never got it. There was nothing. Nobody had any money. You went everywhere on public transport. Everybody did, and that was normal.' It was hard to imagine things any other way. When Bernard was 25 and Barbara was 24, they got married. Dudley was at the wedding. 'I couldn't get married before I was 25. The Air Force wouldn't allow it.'

So what are his recollections of Dudley? 'Dudley was a grammar-school boy, clearly a very bright one,' he says. 'A fine musician – no question about that.' In his memories of that time and place, Dudley's mother Ada looms large. 'His mother wanted him to be an organ player,' he says. 'He earned as much pocket money at the weekend as his father did in a week, playing at weddings.' Bernard speaks as he finds. 'I've read an awful lot about the relationship between Dudley and his mother and every word of it is bullshit,' he says. 'My mother-in-law thought the sun shone out of Dudley's arse. She would have walked over Barbara, trampled Jock into the dirt, just so as not to inconvenience Dudley.' Jock and Ada said Bernard could marry Barbara, but they said they wouldn't pay for the wedding. 'They weren't a well-off family. Fair enough. When I asked why they weren't prepared to do anything for Barbara, they said that everything they had was for Dudley's education.' Bernard's parents picked up the bill. 'It was just that they preferred Dudley to Barbara.'

Barbara was devoted to Dudley. 'She was his number one fan. She was very proud of him. There's no question about that.' And there's also no question that her parents favoured her younger brother. 'It's very difficult as a parent not to have favourites,' says Bernard, 'but the Moores did it in spades. It was open, it was blatant. It was almost honest, in as much as they made no secret of it.' Bernard respected Ada ('she could make a hundred and ten pence out of every pound that you gave her') but she was absolutely brazen about her favouritism for Dudley. 'It was wrong, but she wasn't going to hide it.' It's a sad old story. Mozart's elder sister Nannerl was a talented musician, but their father Leopold favoured little Wolfgang and decided that his son would be the genius of the family, not his daughter. For Nannerl, read Barbara. 'She was a good pianist, Barbara, which was tragic.' So what if Jock and Ada had got behind Barbara and encouraged her to fulfil her potential, like they did with Dudley? 'Life wasn't like that then,' says Bernard. Sisters were encouraged to get married and start their own families in those days.

Jock and Ada were very private people. 'I wouldn't say my parents-in-law were antisocial. They were asocial, if there's such a word.' After Jock died, with Dudley away in America, life became even more solitary for Ada. 'She didn't have any friends. She was a very lonely woman.' She lived in the same council house until she died. When she died, and Dudley came to Dagenham with Susan Anton for the funeral, Bernard and Susan stood outside the house together, keeping the reporters and photographers at bay. 'Susan was great. She was intelligent, she was very nice, she fitted in very well.' Of all the women in Dudley's life, she was Bernard's favourite. 'Barbara and I cleared the house by hand. I took the keys round to the rent office.'

Bernard always thought Dudley would become a musician, not an actor. 'That's what he wanted – that's what he should have been. I don't think he could act his way out of a paper bag. He was just a ham. The idea that he got nominated for an Oscar is ridiculous.' Bernard isn't afraid to call a spade a shovel. 'I heard him say once that he thought they were all mad in Hollywood, but if they were going to offer him three million dollars to act in a film, he'd go and do it. I could see the sense in that, but I don't think he believed it himself.' Music was another matter. 'There is no question that he was a supreme musician.' That's what Bernard admires most.

The last time Bernard saw Dudley was when he came to collect his CBE from Buckingham Palace. 'Dudley was quite unconscious – he didn't know where he was,' says Bernard. 'His face never changed. His eyes never moved. We took him outside in his wheelchair and the photographer propped his arm up, put the hat in his hand, took the photograph, and it all fell apart.' The next day they all went to Bernard and Barbara's daughter's house in Hertfordshire. 'Barbara held his hand. I spoke to him. There was absolutely no reaction. Dudley wasn't there. He couldn't move his facial muscles, he couldn't move his eyes. He had to be fed with a spoon, he had to be toileted like a child. He was gone. There was no Dudley. It was a dreadful occasion, one of the worst days of my life.' Looking back, he describes Dudley as a very intelligent and very stupid man. 'Once you get past a certain level, where money and material things are just there, then what is there? For people like Dudley, it's public adulation.' But Dudley made sure he shared the rewards of that adulation with his sister. His generosity has allowed her to live out the autumn of her life in peace and comfort, with her husband by her side.

PETER WAY

'A question addressed to the Warden as to whether or
not he thought acting and the productions of plays had
a useful place in an adolescent's education was met with
an emphatic "No!"' [1]

I'm sitting with Peter Way and his wife Elizabeth in their lovely
house in the Cotswolds. Peter Way was Peter Cook's drama master.
He's nearly ninety, but there's something wonderfully youthful
about him. His frame is fragile, but his voice is strong and his boyish
eyes still sparkle. Maybe that's what comes of spending your career
teaching boys at Radley.

Peter Way went to Radley College as a pupil when he was thirteen,
in 1936, the year before Peter Cook was born. Then as now, the school
was renowned for its rowing, but drama was what he particularly
enjoyed. He must have been a fine actor. His fellow pupils could still
recall his performances half a century later. Way played Mrs Candour
in *School For Scandal* and Mark Antony in *Julius Caesar*. He was very
happy. He ended up as Head Boy. He left school in 1941, when he was
eighteen, and went straight into the army. 'A whole lot of us went
from public schools,' he says. 'Our regiment had had rather a bad
time at Calais – lost a lot of people there.' He trained as an officer,
and served in North Africa and then in Italy. He fought at Anzio and
entered Rome on D-Day. He was wounded, recovered, and entered
Austria on VE Day. In 1946 he went up to Oxford to read English. He

married Elizabeth, whom he'd met in Italy, the same year. At Oxford he won the Newdigate Prize for Poetry, following in the footsteps of Oscar Wilde. After he came down he became a teacher. In 1952 he returned to Radley, to teach English and Drama. In 1954 he directed a boy called Peter Cook.

'I produced him in *The Alchemist* by Ben Jonson,' says Way. 'He was Dol Common.' It's a funny part, and Peter was very funny in it. At Radley in those days, as in Jonson's day, the women were played by boys. Peter, with his long eyelashes, was often cast in female roles. Elizabeth was helping out backstage. Peter was the only performer she remembers. 'He blacked his tooth,' she recalls. 'It was really quite a shock.' 'Who told you to do that?' she asked him. 'Nobody,' he replied. 'I decided to do it myself.'

In 1956, Way produced *Love's Labours Lost* and cast Peter as Don Adriano de Armado. 'He was wonderful – frightfully good,' says Way. 'He was very, very amusing. It's a good part and he made it his own.' He shows me some photographs of Peter, looking very dashing as Don Armado. Way didn't think Peter was destined to become a professional performer, but there was something unique about him. 'He was different,' says Way.

Way also saw Peter's dramatic tour de force at Radley – the puppet musical that Peter wrote with Michael Bawtree, *Black & White Blues*. 'It was great satire,' says Way. With its cannibals and missionaries, and subtle send-up of the headmaster, Warden Milligan, it almost sounds like a schoolboy version of Evelyn Waugh's *Black Mischief*. 'I think he suspected drama,' says Way, of the Warden. 'He suspected relationships between boys to develop in an unsuitable way.' Peter Way taught at Radley until he retired, in 1983. Along the way, he taught the future Poet Laureate, Andrew Motion. Like Way, Motion became Head Boy, and went on to win the Newdigate. Way played no further part in Peter Cook's life, but he was there at the end of it. In 1995 he was at Peter's memorial service in Hampstead, where The Radley Clerkes, a group of Radley pupils, sang 'Love Me Tender' and 'Goodbyee'.

TERESA WELLS

'I suspect they were both quite jealous of each other and quite prickly.'

Teresa Wells is John Wells's widow. She still lives in London, in the house they used to share. She met Peter through her husband, when John was working for *Private Eye*. 'I think both Dudley and Peter could see the comic possibility of almost anything,' she says over coffee, at her kitchen table. 'They amused each other very much, and that's very amusing to watch.'

Teresa hardly knew Dudley, but she knew Peter for thirty years. The man she remembers was generous and gentle. The way she describes him, he sounds ill-equipped for mainstream fame. 'Peter was always nice to people who were uneasy or unhappy,' she says. 'He would have loved to have been a film star. But that would have been a pathetic career, wouldn't it, really? I mean, anyone can be a film star.' Well, maybe anyone apart from him. 'I expect Peter wouldn't have really actually tried to be a film star, would he? And Dudley probably did try very hard and succeeded. I can't imagine Peter in Los Angeles or in Hollywood. He would have been miserable.' She's quite right. He was.

'I did love him – he was very lovable,' says Teresa, as we say goodbye. 'He couldn't help being funny,' she adds, almost as an afterthought. 'Whenever he opened his mouth he said something funny.' But was that a blessing or a curse?

Next morning, I pack up a parcel of Peter and Dudley's scripts to send to Teresa. I'm about to set off for the post office, when the phone rings. It's Teresa. We talk a bit about Peter, and the book, and Peter's widow Lin, of whom Teresa is very fond. 'He was really very conventional, underneath it all,' she says of Peter, and I wonder if this throwaway remark isn't actually more revealing than anything she told me yesterday.

NORMA WINSTONE

'The first time I saw him, he smiled at somebody – not me. It was in the canteen at school. He walked in and somebody called him and he looked round and he smiled at them. He had a fantastic smile. That's when I noticed him. It really was as if the room lit up.'

The jazz singer Norma Winstone is sitting in her seafront home on the South Coast. She's showing me her autograph album. One signature has pride of place. 'Dudley Moore' it reads. Dudley wasn't famous when he wrote it. He wrote it back in 1954, when he was still at school. Norma had to pluck up the courage to go up to him in the playground and ask him. She was in the first year. Dudley was in the sixth form. Even though he was still a schoolboy, to her he was a star. 'I had a big crush on him,' she says. 'I fell in love with him on sight.' She bought a photo of him in his school blazer, from a classmate with a camera. It cost her sixpence. 'He was incredibly good-looking,' she says. 'People say, "He was so short," but so was I – I still am.' She was captivated by his piano playing – in assembly and with the school choir. During the lunch hour she'd stand outside the fire doors and listen to him practising in the hall. One day she crept inside and hid behind a pillar. 'He was singing,' she remembers. 'I hadn't realised he sang as well.'

Even when he wasn't performing, Dudley was an entertainer. 'They had a prefects-against-teachers rounders match, and I can remember him putting his coat and cap on back to front and running round, just being funny.' Yet he couldn't run quite like other boys. 'When he ran, he'd slightly drag his leg.' Norma's friends told her that he had a club foot, but she didn't know what a club foot was until she saw him in the local swimming pool. 'Went swimming,' she wrote in her diary. 'Dudley was there. Saw his poor little leg.' She felt sorry for him, but it didn't change the way she felt about him.

Norma was born in Bow, in London's East End, which makes her a proper cockney. 'Our playgrounds were bomb sites.' The terraced house she grew up in didn't have a bathroom. The loo was in the backyard. After eight years on the waiting list her mother got a council house in Dagenham. They moved there when Norma was ten. She lived there until she was twenty-one. It felt like moving to the country. For the first time, they had a garden where they could grow their own fruit and veg. 'Now virtually all the houses are owner-occupied. When I lived there it was council property, so all the houses looked exactly the same.' Despite its enormity and uniformity, the Becontree Estate felt like a friendly place. Hardly anyone had a car, so people got to know their neighbours. The children played in the street. 'It looked absolutely anonymous,' she says, 'but I was excited by it, compared to Bow. I went to a school where I had a teacher who played the piano. She recognised that I was musical.' Even though Norma hadn't had any piano lessons for several years, her new teacher encouraged her to apply for a music scholarship to Trinity College in Central London. She gave Norma free piano lessons, after school, to prepare her for the exam. Norma passed, and started travelling there every Saturday. 'I'm sure I'd never have done anything like that in Bow.'

Unbeknown to her, Dudley had been doing much the same thing at the Guildhall. 'I remember getting on the train at Dagenham Heathway. It got to Barking and suddenly Dudley got on, with his violin, and sat right opposite me. Of course I had this terrible crush on him. I didn't have many clothes, so I was wearing my school blazer. He smiled at me. I smiled back and then tried not to look at him for the rest of the journey, which was quite difficult because he was sat right opposite me. I didn't dare speak to him. I mean, what would I have said, at that age? He seemed like a grown-up. He was seventeen or eighteen. I was eleven or twelve.' Norma went to Trinity to learn the piano. When she was invited to learn a second instrument, she chose the organ. Why? 'Because Dudley played the organ.' A friend of Norma's had an older brother who was friends with Dudley. 'You'll never guess the latest thing that he's saying he wants to do,' she told Norma. 'Write film music!' And she burst out laughing. 'What's funny about that?' said Norma. 'If he wants to write film music, I'll bet he'll do it.' And he did.

Norma kept her sixpenny photo of Dudley in her wallet for years. One day a boyfriend found it. 'Who's this?' he asked. 'Oh, I don't know,' she said. 'You don't want it, do you?' he asked her. 'No,' she told him, as she ripped it up. 'I had to do it,' she says, sadly. 'I've never seen one like it since. Two weeks later, I was reading the *Melody Maker*. It said, "Dankworth Piano Gets An Oxford Accent." I read the article. It said this guy from Oxford had joined the Dankworth band. I thought, "That's him!" I wasn't surprised.' Within a few years, he was on telly. 'I always had the feeling that, deep down, there was a slight melancholy in him. But what you saw of him in *Not Only ... But Also* was just what I remembered seeing of him at school.'

IN HEAVEN

DUD: In the midst of life, Pete, we are in death, as the poet says.

PETE: No, he didn't say that. You're thinking of Coleridge. What he said was 'In the midst of life we are in debt,' referring to his own financial plight, brought about by spending too much on opium, what he took intravenously to do his poems.

DUD: Oh, I see, yeah. But what I was meaning, Pete, was – are we really alive, you know? Or are we merely figments of our own imagination? But if we're not alive, then we haven't got no imagination – so whose figments are we, then? I don't like the idea of being someone else's figment, boy. Or are we, in fact, merely a reflection of ourselves, as seen in a pool at twilight?

PETE: What you're saying is if the imagination of an imagined being imagines that life itself is imaginary, how can the imagined life of the being who is himself imagined be imagined by the being who is imagining himself through a glass darkly. That's what you mean, isn't it?

DUD: Yeah. That's it, yeah – of course.

('In Heaven', *Not Only ... But Also*, BBC2, 1966)

BIBLIOGRAPHY

Every biographer follows in the footsteps of their predecessors and I am grateful to the authors of all the books below, who trod this ground before me. If you enjoyed this book, do seek them out. You're bound to enjoy them too. The second part of this book is compiled from primary sources, but secondary sources were crucial in the compilation of the first part of this book. As well as copious newspaper reports, cross-referenced in the footnotes, several TV documentaries have been invaluable, especially *Some Interesting Facts About Peter Cook* (BBC1, 1995) and *Peter Cook – At A Slight Angle To The Universe* (BBC2, 2002). Of the books, all of the following were useful, but some are absolutely indispensable and warrant a special mention: Harry Thompson's definitive biography of Peter Cook; Barbra Paskin's authorised biography of Dudley Moore; Wendy Cook and Judy Cook's brave and honest memoirs of their marriages to Peter, and Rena Fruchter's heartfelt account of Dudley's final years. Humphrey Carpenter's clever survey of 1960s satire, and Roger Wilmut's meticulous history of post-war British comedy were also extremely helpful, as was Alexander Games's perceptive joint biography *Pete & Dud*. Without those titles it would have been impossible to write this book and I am indebted to the people who wrote them.

Turned Out Nice Again – The Story of British Light Entertainment by Louis Barfe (Atlantic Books, 2008)

In Two Minds – A Biography of Jonathan Miller by Kate Bassett (Oberon Books, 2012)

Beyond The Fringe … And Beyond by Ronald Bergan (Virgin Books, 1989)

State of the Nation – British Theatre Since 1945 by Michael Billington (Faber & Faber, 2007)

You Cannot Live As I Have Lived and Not End Up Like This – The Thoroughly Disgraceful Life and Times of Willie Donaldson by Terence Blacker (Ebury, 2007)

How To Talk Dirty and Influence People by Lenny Bruce, with an introduction by Kenneth Tynan (Peter Owen, 1966)

That Was Satire That Was – The Satire Boom of the 1960s by Humphrey Carpenter (Victor Gollancz, 2000)

Spike Milligan – The Biography by Humphrey Carpenter (Hodder & Stoughton, 2003)

Loving Peter – My Life With Peter Cook and Dudley Moore by Judy Cook with Angela Levin (Piatkus, 2008)

Something Like Fire – Peter Cook Remembered, edited by Lin Cook (Methuen, 1996)

So Farewell Then, Peter Cook – The Untold Life of Peter Cook by Wendy E. Cook (HarperCollins, 2006)

The Comedy Store – The Club That Changed British Comedy by William Cook (Little Brown, 2001)

Tragically I Was An Only Twin – The Complete Peter Cook, edited by William Cook (Century, 2002)

Goodbye Again – The Definitive Peter Cook and Dudley Moore, edited by William Cook (Century, 2004)

Letters From Dudley, edited by Peter Cork (Martine Avenue Productions, 2006)

How To Go To The Movies by Quentin Crisp (St Martin's Press, 1984)

The Kenneth Williams Diaries, edited by Russell Davies (HarperCollins, 1993)

The Kenneth Williams Letters, edited by Russell Davies (HarperCollins, 1995)

Beyond A Joke – Inside The Dark World of Stand-Up Comedy by Bruce Dessau (Preface, 2011)

Dudley by Paul Donovan (W.H. Allen, 1988)

Kenneth Williams – A Biography by Michael Freedland (Weidenfeld & Nicolson, 1990)

Dudley Moore – An Intimate Portrait by Rena Fruchter (Ebury Press, 2006)

I'm Chevy Chase ... And You're Not – The Authorised Biography by Rena Fruchter (Virgin Books, 2007)

Pete & Dud – An Illustrated Biography by Alexander Games (Chameleon, 1999)

No Ordinary Place – Radley College and the Public School System by Christopher Hibbert (John Murray, 1997)

Comic Inquisition by John Hind (Virgin Books, 1991)

More, Please – An Autobiography by Barry Humphries (Viking Penguin, 1992)

My Life As Me – A Memoir by Barry Humphries (Viking Penguin, 2002)

Prick Up Your Ears – The Biography of Joe Orton by John Lahr (Allen Lane, 1978)

Automatic Vaudeville by John Lahr (Methuen, 1984)

The Orton Diaries, edited by John Lahr (Methuen, 1986)

The Diaries of Kenneth Tynan, edited by John Lahr (Bloomsbury, 2001)

Still Spitting At Sixty by Roger Law (HarperCollins, 2005)

The Pendulum Years – Britain and The Sixties by Bernard Levin (Jonathan Cape, 1970)

The Life And Death of Peter Sellers by Roger Lewis (Century, 1994)

Just The One – The Wives And Times of Jeffrey Bernard by Graham Lord (Sinclair-Stevenson, 1992)

David Tennant and The Gargoyle Years by Michael Luke (Weidenfeld & Nicolson, 1991)

Private Eye – The First Fifty Years by Adam MacQueen (Private Eye, 2011)

Frankie Howerd – Stand-Up Comic by Graham McCann (Fourth Estate, 2004)

The Private Eye Story by Patrick Marnham (André Deutsch, 1982)

Parky – My Autobiography by Michael Parkinson (Hodder & Stoughton, 2008)

Parky's People by Michael Parkinson (Hodder & Stoughton, 2010)

Dudley Moore – The Authorised Biography by Barbra Paskin (Sidgwick & Jackson, 1997)

A Small Thing – Like An Earthquake by Ned Sherrin (Weidenfeld & Nicolson, 1983)

Born Brilliant – The Life of Kenneth Williams by Christopher Stevens (John Murray, 2010)

Dudley Moore – On The Couch by Douglas Thompson (Little, Brown, 1996)

Richard Ingrams – Lord of the Gnomes by Harry Thompson (William Heinemann, 1994)

Peter Cook – A Biography by Harry Thompson (Hodder & Stoughton, 1997)

The Life of Kenneth Tynan by Kathleen Tynan (Weidenfeld & Nicolson, 1987)

Will This Do? An Autobiography by Auberon Waugh (Century, 1991)

From Fringe to Flying Circus by Roger Wilmut (Methuen, 1980)

The Complete Beyond The Fringe, edited by Roger Wilmut (Methuen, 1987)

NOTES

CHAPTER ONE – AD NAUSEAM

1. Derek & Clive – *Ad Nauseam* (Virgin, 1979)
2. *Melody Maker*, 2 December 1978
3. *Time Out*, 30 January 1991
4. *Loving Peter* by Judy Cook with Angela Levin (Little, Brown, 2008)
5. Ibid.

CHAPTER TWO – DAGENHAM

1. *Parky's People* by Michael Parkinson (Hodder & Stoughton, 2010)
2. *Dudley Moore – On The Couch* by Douglas Thompson (Little, Brown, 1996)
3. Ibid.
4. *Observer*, 9 December, 1979
5. *Dudley Moore – On The Couch* by Douglas Thompson (Little, Brown, 1996)
6. Ibid.
7. Ibid.
8. Ibid.
9. *Letters From Dudley* edited by Peter Cork (Martine Avenue Productions, 2006)
10. *Observer*, 9 December 1979
11. *The Times*, 12 June 1993
12. *Dudley Moore – On The Couch* by Douglas Thompson (Little, Brown, 1996)
13. *Letters From Dudley* edited by Peter Cork (Martine Avenue Productions, 2006)
14. *Dudley Moore*, Antelope Productions for ITV, 1994
15. *Dudley Moore – On The Couch* by Douglas Thompson (Little, Brown, 1996)
16. Ibid.
17. *Dudley Moore – The Authorised Biography* by Barbra Paskin (Sidgwick & Jackson, 1997)
18. *Observer*, 9 December, 1979
19. *Dudley Moore*, Antelope Productions for ITV, 1994
20. *Dudley Moore – The Authorised Biography* by Barbra Paskin (Sidgwick & Jackson, 1997)
21. Ibid.

22. Ibid.
23. Ibid.
24. *Dudley Moore*, Antelope Productions for ITV, 1994
25. *Sun*, 28 May 1965
26. *Dudley Moore*, Antelope Productions for ITV, 1994
27. *The Times*, 12 June 1993
28. *Newsday*, 1980
29. *Sunday Express*, 25 September 1966
30. *Dudley Moore – On The Couch* by Douglas Thompson (Little, Brown, 1996)
31. *Dudley Moore*, Antelope Productions for ITV, 1994
32. *Letters From Dudley* edited by Peter Cork (Martine Avenue Productions, 2006)
33. Ibid.
34. *Dudley Moore's World of Jazz*, BBC Radio 2, 20 March 2012
35. *Daily Mirror*, 5 December 1983
36. *Jazz Professional*, 1966
37. *The Times*, 11 March 1992
38. *Dudley Moore – On The Couch* by Douglas Thompson (Little, Brown, 1996)
39. Ibid.
40. Ibid.
41. *Dudley Moore – The Authorised Biography* by Barbra Paskin (Sidgwick & Jackson, 1997)
42. *Letters From Dudley* edited by Peter Cork (Martine Avenue Productions, 2006)
43. *Dudley Moore*, Antelope Productions for ITV, 1994
44. Ibid.
45. *Dudley Moore – On The Couch* by Douglas Thompson (Little, Brown, 1996)
46. *Dudley Moore*, Antelope Productions for ITV, 1994
47. Ibid.
48. Ibid.
49. *Mavis Catches Up*, Thames TV, 22 November 1989

CHAPTER THREE – RADLEY

1. *Parkinson*, BBC1, 1977
2. *No Ordinary Place – Radley College and The Public School System* by Christopher Hibbert (John Murray, 1997)
3. *Peter, My Beautiful Brother* by Sarah Seymour, *Guardian*, 15 October 1996
4. Ibid.
5. *Comic Inquisition* by John Hind (Virgin Books, 1991)
6. *Peter Cook – A Biography* by Harry Thompson (Hodder & Stoughton, 1997)

7. One of the many Peter Cook projects that never quite materialised was a screenplay of Evelyn Waugh's *Scoop*, written with John Bird.
8. *Peter Cook – A Biography* by Harry Thompson (Hodder & Stoughton, 1997)
9. 'Some Interesting Facts About Peter Cook', *Omnibus*, BBC1, 1995
10. Ibid.
11. *Radio Times*, 23 December 1978
12. *Sunday People*, 3 February 1968
13. *Independent*, 14 December 1993
14. John Bird in *Something Like Fire – Peter Cook Remembered*, edited by Lin Cook (Methuen, 1996)
15. 'Some Interesting Facts About Peter Cook', *Omnibus*, BBC1, 1995
16. *Peter, My Beautiful Brother* by Sarah Seymour, *Guardian*, 15 October 1996
17. Ibid.
18. *Good Afternoon*, Thames Television, 19 April 1973
19. Ibid.
20. Jonathan Harlow in *Something Like Fire – Peter Cook Remembered*, edited by Lin Cook (Methuen, 1996)
21. Ibid.
22. *From Fringe to Flying Circus* by Roger Wilmut (Methuen, 1980)
23. Historically, Peter's preference for soccer was actually conservative rather than progressive. After abandoning Radley rules (the school's own brand of football) in 1881, Radley had played Association Football for more than thirty years, only switching to Rugby Union in 1913.
24. *Parkinson*, BBC1, 19 February 1977
25. 'Not only a splendid cricketer, he was also a fine golfer, a first-class rackets player, a brilliant fly half on the rugger field; and, without any particular training, he won the hundred yards and quarter mile at Radley, breaking the school records for both events.' *No Ordinary Place – Radley College and The Public School System* by Christopher Hibbert (John Murray, 1997)
26. Henley Regatta, about twenty miles downstream on the Thames, was the highlight of Radley's social and sporting calendar. After Eton, Radley traditionally entered one of the strongest rowing teams.
27. *Parkinson*, BBC1, 19 February 1977. Peter's drinking at the Henley Regatta was hardly unusual for Radley. 'Many Radley boys were to be seen reeling drunkenly in the streets,' an Old Radleian (1947–52) told the school's historian, Christopher Hibbert, 'and the vandalism on the special train was worthy of the worst soccer hooligans.'
28. It was ever thus at Radley, even in the nineteenth century. 'Political topics discussed in the Debating Society were never very lively since few boys could ever be found to present other than Conservative views,' wrote Christopher Hibbert of Radley in the 1880s in *No*

Ordinary Place – Radley College and The Public School System (John Murray, 1997). 'When a motion such as "Should the lower classes be educated?" was proposed in the Society it was almost a foregone conclusion that the consensus of opinion would be strongly against it.' In a poll conducted by *The Radleian* in 1957, the year Peter went up to Cambridge, 82% of pupils approved of fagging, only 27% preferred co-education and 55% would have banned the *Daily Worker*.

29. Jonathan Harlow in *Something Like Fire – Peter Cook Remembered*, edited by Lin Cook (Methuen, 1996)
30. *From Fringe to Flying Circus* by Roger Wilmut (Methuen, 1980)
31. Jonathan Harlow in *Something Like Fire – Peter Cook Remembered*, edited by Lin Cook (Methuen, 1996)
32. Ibid.
33. Michael Bawtree in *Something Like Fire – Peter Cook Remembered*, edited by Lin Cook (Methuen, 1996)
34. Ibid.
35. Nicholas Luard in *Something Like Fire – Peter Cook Remembered*, edited by Lin Cook (Methuen, 1996)
36. Peter Way was the third of four Old Radleians (so far) to win the Newdigate Prize for poetry. The fourth was Andrew Motion, whom Way had taught at Radley, and who subsequently became Poet Laureate. Other notable winners include John Ruskin, John Buchan and Oscar Wilde.
37. 'Some Interesting Facts About Peter Cook', *Omnibus*, BBC1, 1995
38. *Good Afternoon*, Thames Television, 19 April 1973
39. Ibid.
40. *Parkinson*, BBC1, 1977
41. 'Some Interesting Facts About Peter Cook', *Omnibus*, BBC1, 1995
42. *No Ordinary Place – Radley College and The Public School System* by Christopher Hibbert (John Murray, 1997)
43. *Dudley Moore – On The Couch* by Douglas Thompson (Little, Brown, 1996)
44. *From Fringe to Flying Circus* by Roger Wilmut (Methuen, 1980)
45. *Person To Person*, David Dimbleby, BBC, 1979
46. Sleeve notes, *Not Only Peter Cook ... But Also Dudley Moore* (Decca, 1965)
47. *Junkin's Jokers*, BBC Radio 2, 19 October 1993

CHAPTER FOUR – OXFORD

1. *Dudley Moore – An Intimate Portrait* by Rena Fruchter (Ebury Press, 2006)
2. *Dudley Moore*, Antelope Productions for ITV, 1994
3. *Observer*, 9 December 1979
4. *Dudley Moore*, Antelope Productions for ITV, 1994
5. Ibid.

6. *Sunday Express*, 25 September 1966
7. *Good Afternoon*, Thames Television, 19 April 1973
8. *Dudley Moore*, Antelope Productions for ITV, 1994
9. Ibid.
10. *Dudley Moore – The Authorised Biography* by Barbra Paskin (Sidgwick & Jackson, 1997)
11. *Dudley* by Paul Donovan (W.H. Allen, 1988)
12. *Dudley Moore – The Authorised Biography* by Barbra Paskin (Sidgwick & Jackson, 1997)
13. *Dudley Moore*, Antelope Productions for ITV, 1994
14. *Dudley Moore – The Authorised Biography* by Barbra Paskin (Sidgwick & Jackson, 1997)
15. *Guardian*, 18 June 1998
16. *Dudley Moore – The Authorised Biography* by Barbra Paskin (Sidgwick & Jackson, 1997)
17. Ibid.
18. *Sunday Times*, 31 March 2002
19. *Dudley Moore – On The Couch* by Douglas Thompson (Little, Brown, 1996)
20. *Dudley Moore*, Antelope Productions for ITV, 1994
21. *Dudley* by Paul Donovan (W.H. Allen, 1988)
22. *Dudley Moore*, Antelope Productions for ITV, 1994
23. *Parky's People* by Michael Parkinson (Hodder & Stoughton, 2010)
24. *Dudley Moore – An Intimate Portrait* by Rena Fruchter (Ebury Press, 2006)
25. Ibid.
26. *Dudley* by Paul Donovan (W.H. Allen, 1988)
27. *Dudley Moore – The Authorised Biography* by Barbra Paskin (Sidgwick & Jackson, 1997)
28. Ibid.
29. *Dudley Moore's World of Jazz*, BBC Radio 2, 20 March 2012
30. Ibid.
31. Ibid.
32. Ibid.
33. Ibid.
34. Ibid.
35. Ibid.
36. *Dudley Moore – The Authorised Biography* by Barbra Paskin (Sidgwick & Jackson, 1997)
37. *Dudley* by Paul Donovan (W.H. Allen, 1988)
38. Ibid.
39. *Dudley Moore – The Authorised Biography* by Barbra Paskin (Sidgwick & Jackson, 1997)
40. Ibid.
41. *Dudley Moore – On The Couch* by Douglas Thompson (Little, Brown, 1996)

42. Ibid.
43. *Dudley Moore – The Authorised Biography* by Barbra Paskin (Sidgwick & Jackson, 1997)
44. *Dudley Moore – On The Couch* by Douglas Thompson (Little, Brown, 1996)
45. *Dudley Moore – The Authorised Biography* by Barbra Paskin (Sidgwick & Jackson, 1997)

CHAPTER FIVE – CAMBRIDGE

1. New Court was built in 1881 by Sir George Gilbert Scott, whose pupil, Sir Thomas Graham Jackson, built a good deal of Radley.
2. *News of the World*, 29 May 1966
3. *Independent*, 14 December 1993
4. Ibid.
5. *Daily Mail*, 12 November 1994
6. *Sunday People*, 4 February 1968
7. *Still Spitting At Sixty* by Roger Law (HarperCollins, 2005)
8. *Peter Cook – At A Slight Angle To The Universe*, BBC2, 2002
9. Established in 1855, Cambridge University's Amateur Dramatic Club was the oldest, biggest and most prestigious student drama society in the country. During Peter's time at Cambridge, it produced Derek Jacobi, Ian McKellen, Trevor Nunn and Eleanor Bron.
10. Adrian Slade in *Something Like Fire – Peter Cook Remembered*, edited by Lin Cook (Methuen, 1996)
11. Ibid.
12. *Still Spitting At Sixty* by Roger Law (HarperCollins, 2005)
13. Peter Bellwood in *Something Like Fire – Peter Cook Remembered*, edited by Lin Cook (Methuen, 1996)
14. John Bird in *Something Like Fire – Peter Cook Remembered*, edited by Lin Cook (Methuen, 1996)
15. Ibid.
16. *So Farewell Then, Peter Cook* by Wendy E. Cook (HarperCollins, 2006)
17. *That Was Satire That Was – The Satire Boom of the 1960s* by Humphrey Carpenter (Victor Gollancz, 2000)
18. *From Fringe to Flying Circus* by Roger Wilmut (Methuen, 1980)
19. (Manchester) *Guardian*, 10 June 1959
20. Ibid.
21. *That Was Satire That Was – The Satire Boom of the 1960s* by Humphrey Carpenter (Victor Gollancz, 2000)
22. Ibid.
23. *Ramblings of An Actress* by Sheila Hancock (Hutchinson, 1987)
24. *From Fringe to Flying Circus* by Roger Wilmut (Methuen, 1980)
25. Ibid.
26. *Still Spitting At Sixty* by Roger Law (HarperCollins, 2005)
27. *Guardian*, 10 January 1995

28. 'Some Interesting Facts About Peter Cook', *Omnibus*, BBC1, 1995

29. *Peter Cook – At A Slight Angle To The Universe*, BBC2, 2002

30. *Person To Person*, BBC TV, 1979

31. 'Some Interesting Facts About Peter Cook', *Omnibus*, BBC1, 1995

32. *From Fringe to Flying Circus* by Roger Wilmut (Methuen, 1980)

33. *Peter Cook – A Biography* by Harry Thompson (Hodder & Stoughton, 1997)

34. *Mail on Sunday*, 4 May 2003

35. *So Farewell Then, Peter Cook* by Wendy E. Cook (HarperCollins, 2006)

36. Ibid.

37. *Mail on Sunday*, 4 May 2003

38. *So Farewell Then, Peter Cook* by Wendy E. Cook (HarperCollins, 2006)

39. Ibid.

40. *Peter Cook – A Biography* by Harry Thompson (Hodder & Stoughton, 1997)

41. *So Farewell Then, Peter Cook* by Wendy E. Cook (HarperCollins, 2006)

42. Ibid.

43. Ibid.

44. *Peter Cook – A Biography* by Harry Thompson (Hodder & Stoughton, 1997)

45. Ibid.

46. *Junkin's Jokers*, BBC Radio Two, 19 October 1993

47. *Peter Cook – A Biography* by Harry Thompson (Hodder & Stoughton, 1997)

48. *Peter Cook – At A Slight Angle To The Universe*, BBC2, 2002

49. 'Some Interesting Facts About Peter Cook', *Omnibus*, BBC1, 1995

50. *Still Spitting At Sixty* by Roger Law (HarperCollins, 2005)

51. *Peter Cook – At A Slight Angle To The Universe*, BBC2, 2002

52. 'Some Interesting Facts About Peter Cook', *Omnibus*, BBC1, 1995

53. *Friday Night, Saturday Morning*, BBC TV, 16 November 1979

54. *Person To Person*, BBC TV, 1979

55. *Peter Cook – A Biography* by Harry Thompson (Hodder & Stoughton, 1997)

CHAPTER SIX – BEFORE THE FRINGE

1. *Beyond The Fringe ... And Beyond* by Ronald Bergan (Virgin Books, 1989)

2. Michael Flanders and Donald Swann wrote and performed witty songs together. Flanders composed the music and played the piano. Swann, who wrote the lyrics, had been confined to a wheelchair by polio.

3. *That Was Satire That Was* by Humphrey Carpenter (Victor Gollancz, 2000)

4. These two worlds of comedy were so separate that they could coexist

without any contact or cross-fertilisation whatsoever. Eric Morecambe met his wife Joan while performing in variety with Ernie Wise at the Edinburgh Empire (now renamed the Festival Theatre) but he never played the Edinburgh Festival, or its unofficial Fringe.

5. *That Was Satire That Was* by Humphrey Carpenter (Victor Gollancz, 2000)

6. *Beyond The Fringe ... And Beyond* by Ronald Bergan (Virgin Books, 1989)

7. *Yorkshire Post*, 7 May 1977

8. *Writing Home* by Alan Bennett (Faber & Faber, 1994)

9. 'The Poet of Embarrassment' by Stephen Schiff, *New Yorker*, 6 September 1993

10. *Beyond The Fringe ... And Beyond* by Ronald Bergan (Virgin Books, 1989)

11. *That Was Satire That Was* by Humphrey Carpenter (Victor Gollancz, 2000)

12. *Beyond The Fringe ... And Beyond* by Ronald Bergan (Virgin Books, 1989)

13. *Sunday Times*, 11 November 1954

14. *Daily Telegraph*, 7 June 1955

15. Bassett and Collet both went to Bedales, a progressive co-education boarding school in Hampshire. More recent alumni include Daniel Day-Lewis, Sophie Dahl and Lily Allen.

16. *A Profile of Jonathan Miller* by Michel Romain (Cambridge University Press, 1992)

17. *The Sun*, 28 October 1989

18. *From Fringe to Flying Circus* by Roger Wilmut (Methuen, 1980)

19. 'Some Interesting Facts About Peter Cook', *Omnibus*, BBC1, 1995

20. *So Farewell Then, Peter Cook* by Wendy E. Cook (HarperCollins, 2006)

21. 'Some Interesting Facts About Peter Cook', *Omnibus*, BBC1, 1995

22. *So Farewell Then, Peter Cook* by Wendy E. Cook (HarperCollins, 2006)

23. *From Fringe to Flying Circus* by Roger Wilmut (Methuen, 1980)

24. 'Some Interesting Facts About Peter Cook', *Omnibus*, BBC1, 1995

25. Alan Bennett, from an Address at Peter Cook's Memorial Service at Hampstead Parish Church, 1 May 1995, subsequently published in the *London Review of Books*, 25 May 1995.

26. *From Fringe to Flying Circus* by Roger Wilmut (Methuen, 1980)

27. Dudley Moore postscript, *The Complete Beyond The Fringe*, edited by Roger Wilmut (Methuen, 1987)

28. 'Some Interesting Facts About Peter Cook', *Omnibus*, BBC1, 1995

29. *Beyond The Fringe ... And Beyond* by Ronald Bergan (Virgin Books, 1989)

30. *Junkin's Jokers*, BBC Radio 2, 19 October 1993

31. *Beyond The Fringe ... And Beyond* by Ronald Bergan (Virgin Books, 1989)

32. Ibid.

33. *Dudley Moore – The Authorised Biography* by Barbra Paskin (Sidgwick & Jackson, 1997)
34. Dudley Moore postscript, *The Complete Beyond The Fringe*, edited by Roger Wilmut (Methuen, 1987)
35. Ibid.
36. *Beyond The Fringe ... And Beyond* by Ronald Bergan (Virgin Books, 1989)
37. *Dudley Moore – The Authorised Biography* by Barbra Paskin (Sidgwick & Jackson, 1997)
38. 'Some Interesting Facts About Peter Cook', *Omnibus*, BBC1, 1995

CHAPTER SEVEN – EDINBURGH AND AFTER

1. *That Was Satire That Was* by Humphrey Carpenter (Victor Gollancz, 2000)
2. *Beyond The Fringe ... And Beyond* by Ronald Bergan (Virgin Books, 1989)
3. *That Was Satire That Was* by Humphrey Carpenter (Victor Gollancz, 2000)
4. Monday, 22 August, 1960
5. *That Was Satire That Was* by Humphrey Carpenter (Victor Gollancz, 2000)
6. Ibid.
7. Ibid.
8. *Dudley Moore*, Antelope Productions for ITV, 1994
9. Ibid.
10. *That Was Satire That Was* by Humphrey Carpenter (Victor Gollancz, 2000)
11. 'Some Interesting Facts About Peter Cook', *Omnibus*, BBC1, 1995
12. *Dudley Moore – The Authorised Biography* by Barbra Paskin (Sidgwick & Jackson, 1997)
13. John Wells in *Something Like Fire – Peter Cook Remembered*, edited by Lin Cook (Methuen, 1996)
14. *Beyond The Fringe ... And Beyond* by Ronald Bergan (Virgin Books, 1989)
15. *That Was Satire That Was* by Humphrey Carpenter (Victor Gollancz, 2000)
16. *Daily Mail*, 2 March 1962
17. Eric Idle in *Something Like Fire – Peter Cook Remembered*, edited by Lin Cook (Methuen, 1996)
18. *London Review of Books*, 25 June 1995
19. *So Farewell Then, Peter Cook – The Untold Life of Peter Cook* by Wendy E. Cook (HarperCollins, 2006)
20. *That Was Satire That Was* by Humphrey Carpenter (Victor Gollancz, 2000)

21. *Guardian*, 18 June 1998
22. Michael Palin in *Something Like Fire – Peter Cook Remembered*, edited by Lin Cook (Methuen, 1996)
23. *From Fringe to Flying Circus* by Roger Wilmut (Methuen, 1980)
24. *Dudley Moore – The Authorised Biography* by Barbra Paskin (Sidgwick & Jackson, 1997)
25. *Observer*, 28 August 1960
26. *Daily Mail*, 24 August 1960
27. *That Was Satire That Was* by Humphrey Carpenter (Victor Gollancz, 2000)
28. Ibid.
29. Ibid.
30. Ibid.
31. *Peter Cook – A Biography* by Harry Thompson (Hodder & Stoughton, 1997)
32. *From Fringe to Flying Circus* by Roger Wilmut (Methuen, 1980)
33. *Peter Cook – A Biography* by Harry Thompson (Hodder & Stoughton, 1997)
34. Ibid.
35. *You Cannot Live As I Have Lived And Not End Up Like This – The Thoroughly Disgraceful Life And Times of Willie Donaldson* by Terence Blacker (Ebury, 2007)
36. Ibid.
37. Peter Cook postscript, *The Complete Beyond The Fringe*, edited by Roger Wilmut (Methuen, 1987)
38. *Peter Cook – A Biography* by Harry Thompson (Hodder & Stoughton, 1997)
39. *So Farewell Then, Peter Cook – The Untold Life of Peter Cook* by Wendy E. Cook (HarperCollins, 2006)
40. Ibid.
41. Bassett told Wendy that they actually got £180 a week, plus a ½% royalty.
42. *Peter Cook – A Biography* by Harry Thompson (Hodder & Stoughton, 1997)
43. Alan Bennett postscript, *The Complete Beyond The Fringe*, edited by Roger Wilmut (Methuen, 1987)
44. Ibid.
45. Ibid.
46. *You Cannot Live As I Have Lived and Not End Up Like This – The Thoroughly Disgraceful Life and Times of Willie Donaldson* by Terence Blacker (Ebury, 2007)
47. Ibid.

CHAPTER EIGHT – BRIGHTON OR BUST

1. *The Ascent of Man*, BBC (1973)
2. *So Farewell Then, Peter Cook* by Wendy E. Cook (HarperCollins, 2006)
3. Ibid.
4. *Peter Cook – A Biography* by Harry Thompson (Hodder & Stoughton, 1997)
5. Eric Idle in *Something Like Fire – Peter Cook Remembered*, edited by Lin Cook (Methuen, 1996)
6. *Daily Mail*, 6 April 1961
7. *Beyond The Fringe* by Eleanor Fazan, quoted in *You Cannot Live As I Have Lived And Not End Up Like This – The Thoroughly Disgraceful Life And Times of Willie Donaldson* by Terence Blacker (Ebury, 2007)
8. *William Donaldson* by Eleanor Fazan, quoted in *You Cannot Live As I Have Lived And Not End Up Like This – The Thoroughly Disgraceful Life And Times of Willie Donaldson* by Terence Blacker (Ebury, 2007)
9. *London Review of Books*, 5 January 2006
10. *Beyond The Fringe* by Eleanor Fazan, quoted in *You Cannot Live As I Have Lived And Not End Up Like This – The Thoroughly Disgraceful Life And Times of Willie Donaldson* by Terence Blacker (Ebury, 2007)
11. *That Was Satire That Was* by Humphrey Carpenter (Victor Gollancz, 2000)
12. *Heroes of Comedy – Peter Cook*, Thames Television for Channel 4, 19 January 1998
13. *A Profile of Jonathan Miller* by Michel Romain (Cambridge University Press, 1992)
14. *Vanity Fair*, December 1995
15. *Beyond The Fringe ... And Beyond* by Ronald Bergan (Virgin Books, 1989)
16. *Writing Home* by Alan Bennett (Faber & Faber, 1994)
17. 1 May 1961
18. *Writing Home* by Alan Bennett (Faber & Faber, 1994)
19. *Peter Cook – A Biography* by Harry Thompson (Hodder & Stoughton, 1997)
20. *Junkin's Jokers*, BBC Radio 2, 19 October 1993
21. *Brighton & Hove Herald*, 6 May 1961
22. *So Farewell Then, Peter Cook* by Wendy E. Cook (HarperCollins, 2006)
23. *Brighton & Hove Herald*, 6 May 1961
24. Ibid.
25. *From Fringe to Flying Circus* by Roger Wilmut (Methuen, 1980)
26. *Writing Home* by Alan Bennett (Faber & Faber, 1994)
27. Predictably, there has always been some disagreement about who suggested this pornographic outing. Donaldson always denied that it was his idea, though he certainly organised it. Fazan reckoned the cast requested it, though Ronald Bergan, in his history of *Beyond The Fringe*, notes that Bennett was none too keen.
28. *Beyond The Fringe ... And Beyond* by Ronald Bergan (Virgin Books, 1989)

29. *So Farewell Then, Peter Cook* by Wendy E. Cook (HarperCollins, 2006)
30. The contraceptive pill arrived in 1959, Beatlemania in 1963.

CHAPTER NINE – BEYOND THE FRINGE

1. *Daily Express*, 11 May 1961
2. Ibid.
3. Ibid.
4. Ibid.
5. Ibid.
6. *Dudley Moore*, Antelope Productions for ITV, 1994
7. Michael Frayn introduction, *The Complete Beyond The Fringe*, edited by Roger Wilmut (Methuen, 1987)
8. Ibid.
9. *Daily Mail*, 11 May 1961
10. Preface to *Kenneth Tynan – Profiles* (Nick Hern Books, 1990)
11. *Sunday Times*, 14 May 1961
12. *Observer*, 14 May 1961
13. Ibid.
14. *From Fringe to Flying Circus* by Roger Wilmut (Methuen, 1980)
15. *Peter Cook – At A Slight Angle To The Universe*, BBC2, 2002
16. *Dudley Moore – The Authorised Biography* by Barbra Paskin (Sidgwick & Jackson, 1997)
17. *Daily Herald*, 13 May 1961
18. Michael Palin in *Something Like Fire – Peter Cook Remembered*, edited by Lin Cook (Methuen, 1996)
19. *Vanity Fair*, December 1995
20. *From Winchester To This* by Willie Donaldson (Peter Owen, 1998)
21. *Peter Cook – A Biography* by Harry Thompson (Hodder & Stoughton, 1997)
22. Ibid.
23. *From Fringe to Flying Circus* by Roger Wilmut (Methuen, 1980)
24. *Peter Cook – At A Slight Angle To The Universe*, BBC2, 2002
25. *Sunday Pictorial*, 18 February 1962
26. *Observer*, 1 October 1961
27. Ibid.
28. *The Pendulum Years – Britain and The Sixties* by Bernard Levin (Jonathan Cape, 1970)
29. *From Fringe to Flying Circus* by Roger Wilmut (Methuen, 1980)
30. Ibid.
31. *Daily Mail*, 1 March 1962
32. *Dudley Moore – The Authorised Biography* by Barbra Paskin (Sidgwick & Jackson, 1997)
33. Alan Bennett in *Something Like Fire – Peter Cook Remembered*, edited by Lin Cook (Methuen, 1996)

34. *Beyond The Fringe ... And Beyond* by Ronald Bergan (Virgin Books, 1989)
35. *Dudley* by Paul Donovan (W.H. Allen, 1988)
36. *Dudley Moore*, Antelope Productions for ITV, 1994
37. *Dudley Moore – The Authorised Biography* by Barbra Paskin (Sidgwick & Jackson, 1997)
38. Ibid.
39. *Dudley Moore – On The Couch* by Douglas Thompson (Little, Brown, 1996)
40. Ibid.
41. Eric Idle, foreword to *Dudley Moore – An Intimate Portrait* by Rena Fruchter (Ebury Press, 2006)

CHAPTER TEN – THE ESTABLISHMENT

1. *Russell Harty Plus*, LWT for ITV, October 1975
2. *Peter Cook – At A Slight Angle To The Universe*, BBC2, 2002
3. *From Fringe to Flying Circus* by Roger Wilmut (Methuen, 1980)
4. *Observer*, 1 October 1961
5. Ibid.
6. Nicholas Luard in *Something Like Fire – Peter Cook Remembered*, edited by Lin Cook (Methuen, 1996)
7. *From Fringe to Flying Circus* by Roger Wilmut (Methuen, 1980)
8. *Evening Standard*, 4 October 1961
9. John Wells in *Something Like Fire – Peter Cook Remembered*, edited by Lin Cook (Methuen, 1996)
10. *Evening Standard*, 10 January 1995
11. *Evening Standard*, 4 October 1961
12. *Richard Ingrams – Lord of the Gnomes* by Harry Thompson (William Heinemann, 1994)
13. *Daily Express*, 5 October 1961
14. *Postcard From London*, Clive James, BBC1, 31 July 1991
15. *Scotsman*, 25 September 1965
16. Ibid.
17. Ibid.
18. *Observer*, 8 October 1961
19. *Sunday Times*, 8 October 1961
20. 'Some Interesting Facts About Peter Cook', *Omnibus*, BBC1, 1995
21. John Bird in *Something Like Fire – Peter Cook Remembered*, edited by Lin Cook (Methuen, 1996)
22. *Peter Cook – At A Slight Angle To The Universe*, BBC2, 2002
23. *From Fringe to Flying Circus* by Roger Wilmut (Methuen, 1980)
24. *Observer*, 14 January 1962
25. Ibid.
26. *Dudley Moore – On The Couch* by Douglas Thompson (Little, Brown, 1996)

27. *Friday Night, Saturday Morning*, BBC2, 16 November 1979
28. Ibid.
29. Ibid.
30. *So Farewell Then, Peter Cook* by Wendy E. Cook (HarperCollins, 2006)
31. *That Was Satire That Was – The Satire Boom of the 1960s* by Humphrey Carpenter (Victor Gollancz, 2000)
32. *Peter Cook – A Biography* by Harry Thompson (Hodder & Stoughton, 1997)
33. *How To Talk Dirty and Influence People* by Lenny Bruce (Peter Owen, 1966), with an introduction by Kenneth Tynan
34. Ibid.
35. Ibid.
36. *Postcard From London*, Clive James, BBC1, 31 July 1991
37. *Peter Cook – A Biography* by Harry Thompson (Hodder & Stoughton, 1997)
38. *Postcard From London*, Clive James, BBC1, 31 July 1991
39. Ibid.
40. *How To Talk Dirty and Influence People* by Lenny Bruce (Peter Owen, 1966), with an introduction by Kenneth Tynan
41. *This Is Your Life*, Thames TV, 27 February 1976
42. *Frankie Howerd – Stand-Up Comic* by Graham McCann (Fourth Estate, 2004)
43. *This Is Your Life*, Thames TV, 27 February 1976
44. Sleeve notes, *Theme From Beyond The Fringe And All That Jazz* (Atlantic Records, 1962)
45. *Dudley Moore – The Authorised Biography* by Barbra Paskin (Sidgwick & Jackson, 1997)
46. Ibid.
47. Ibid.

CHAPTER ELEVEN – ON BROADWAY

1. *Daily Mail*, 2 March 1962
2. *From Fringe to Flying Circus* by Roger Wilmut (Methuen, 1980)
3. Barry Humphries interview, *Bedazzled* DVD (Second Sight, 2005)
4. Ibid.
5. *Peter Cook – A Biography* by Harry Thompson (Hodder & Stoughton, 1997)
6. *Dudley Moore – The Authorised Biography* by Barbra Paskin (Sidgwick & Jackson, 1997)
7. *So Farewell Then, Peter Cook* by Wendy E. Cook (HarperCollins, 2006)
8. *Guardian*, 29 October 1962
9. *From Fringe to Flying Circus* by Roger Wilmut (Methuen, 1980)
10. *Dudley* by Paul Donovan (W.H. Allen, 1988)

11. *Peter Cook – A Biography* by Harry Thompson (Hodder & Stoughton, 1997)
12. Ibid.
13. Christopher Hitchens and Joseph Heller in *Something Like Fire – Peter Cook Remembered*, edited by Lin Cook (Methuen, 1996)
14. *Peter Cook – A Biography* by Harry Thompson (Hodder & Stoughton, 1997)
15. Alan Bennett in *Something Like Fire – Peter Cook Remembered*, edited by Lin Cook (Methuen, 1996)
16. *So Farewell Then, Peter Cook* by Wendy E. Cook (HarperCollins, 2006)
17. Ibid.
18. Barry Humphries interview, *Bedazzled* DVD (Second Sight, 2005)
19. Ibid.
20. *Observer*, 4 June 1967
21. *Dudley Moore – On The Couch* by Douglas Thompson (Little, Brown, 1996)
22. *Dudley Moore – The Authorised Biography* by Barbra Paskin (Sidgwick & Jackson, 1997)
23. Ibid.
24. *So Farewell Then, Peter Cook* by Wendy E. Cook (HarperCollins, 2006)
25. *That Was Satire That Was – The Satire Boom of the 1960s* by Humphrey Carpenter (Victor Gollancz, 2000)
26. Ibid.
27. *A Small Thing – Like An Earthquake* by Ned Sherrin (Weidenfeld & Nicolson, 1983)
28. *Facing The Nation* by Grace Wyndham Goldie (Bodley Head, 1977)
29. *A Small Thing – Like An Earthquake* by Ned Sherrin (Weidenfeld & Nicolson, 1983)
30. *From Fringe to Flying Circus* by Roger Wilmut (Methuen, 1980)
31. *Varsity*, 12 October 1963
32. *So Farewell Then, Peter Cook* by Wendy E. Cook (HarperCollins, 2006)
33. 'Some Interesting Facts About Peter Cook', *Omnibus*, BBC1, 1995
34. Ibid.
35. *Evening Standard*, 9 May 1968
36. 'Some Interesting Facts About Peter Cook', *Omnibus*, BBC1, 1995
37. *So Farewell Then, Peter Cook* by Wendy E. Cook (HarperCollins, 2006)
38. Ibid.
39. Ibid.
40. Ibid.
41. Ibid.
42. *Peter Cook – A Biography* by Harry Thompson (Hodder & Stoughton, 1997)
43. *So Farewell Then, Peter Cook* by Wendy E. Cook (HarperCollins, 2006)
44. *From Fringe to Flying Circus* by Roger Wilmut (Methuen, 1980)
45. *So Farewell Then, Peter Cook* by Wendy E. Cook (HarperCollins, 2006)

46. *The Complete Beyond The Fringe*, edited by Roger Wilmut (Methuen, 1987)
47. Ibid.
48. Christopher Hitchens and Dudley Moore in *Something Like Fire – Peter Cook Remembered*, edited by Lin Cook (Methuen, 1996)
49. *Junkin's Jokers*, BBC Radio 2, 19 October 1993
50. *The Complete Beyond The Fringe*, edited by Roger Wilmut (Methuen, 1987)
51. *Dudley Moore – The Authorised Biography* by Barbra Paskin (Sidgwick & Jackson, 1997)
52. Ibid.
53. Ibid.
54. *Parkinson*, BBC1, 18 November 1972
55. *In Two Minds – A Biography of Jonathan Miller* by Kate Bassett (Oberon Books, 2012)
56. *Beyond The Fringe ... And Beyond* by Ronald Bergan (Virgin Books, 1989)
57. *Peter Cook – A Biography* by Harry Thompson (Hodder & Stoughton, 1997)
58. Christopher Hitchens and Dudley Moore in *Something Like Fire – Peter Cook Remembered*, edited by Lin Cook (Methuen, 1996)
59. *Peter Cook – A Biography* by Harry Thompson (Hodder & Stoughton, 1997)
60. *Evening News*, 2 October 1972
61. Ibid.

CHAPTER TWELVE – HOMEWARD BOUND

1. *Parkinson*, BBC1, 1977
2. *Peter Cook – At A Slight Angle To The Universe*, BBC2, 2002
3. *Mail on Sunday*, 12 November 1994
4. Nicholas Luard in *Something Like Fire – Peter Cook Remembered*, edited by Lin Cook (Methuen, 1996)
5. *So Farewell Then, Peter Cook* by Wendy E. Cook (HarperCollins, 2006)
6. *Scotsman*, 25 September 1965
7. *Daily Mail*, 24 September 1963
8. *Peter Cook – A Biography* by Harry Thompson (Hodder & Stoughton, 1997)
9. *Richard Ingrams – Lord of the Gnomes* by Harry Thompson (William Heinemann, 1994)
10. *Mail on Sunday*, 12 November 1994
11. *Richard Ingrams – Lord of the Gnomes* by Harry Thompson (William Heinemann, 1994)
12. Ibid.

13. *Richard Ingrams – Lord of the Gnomes* by Harry Thompson (William Heinemann, 1994)
14. 'Some Interesting Facts About Peter Cook', *Omnibus*, BBC1, 1995
15. *The Very Best of Goodbye Again*, Granada Television, 2004
16. *Richard Ingrams – Lord of the Gnomes* by Harry Thompson (William Heinemann, 1994)
17. *Private Eye*, South Bank Show for LWT, ITV 15 September 1991
18. 'Some Interesting Facts About Peter Cook', *Omnibus*, BBC1, 1995
19. Barry Humphries interview, *Bedazzled* DVD (Second Sight, 2005)
20. *My Life As Me – A Memoir* by Barry Humphries (Viking Penguin, 2002)
21. *Junkin's Jokers*, BBC Radio 2, 19 October 1993
22. *The Very Best of Goodbye Again*, Granada Television, 2004
23. *So Farewell Then, Peter Cook* by Wendy E. Cook (HarperCollins, 2006)
24. *Sunday Times*, 31 October 1965
25. *Good Afternoon With Mavis Nicholson*, Thames TV, 9 March 1973
26. *Daily Express*, 7 February 1967
27. Ibid.
28. *The Harvard Crimson*, 7 August 1964

CHAPTER THIRTEEN – NOT ONLY ... BUT ALSO

1. Joe McGrath, letter to the author, 3 November 2011
2. *Dudley Moore – The Authorised Biography* by Barbra Paskin (Sidgwick & Jackson, 1997)
3. *From Fringe to Flying Circus* by Roger Wilmut (Methuen, 1980)
4. *Beyond The Fringe ... And Beyond* by Ronald Bergan (Virgin Books, 1989)
5. *Dudley Moore – The Authorised Biography* by Barbra Paskin (Sidgwick & Jackson, 1997)
6. *Dudley Moore – On The Couch* by Douglas Thompson (Little, Brown, 1996)
7. *From Fringe to Flying Circus* by Roger Wilmut (Methuen, 1980)
8. *Time Out*, 30 January 1991
9. *Success Story*, BBC, May 1974
10. *Offensive – The Real Derek & Clive*, Channel 4, 2002
11. *Peter Cook – At A Slight Angle To The Universe*, BBC2, 2002
12. *Dudley Moore – The Authorised Biography* by Barbra Paskin (Sidgwick & Jackson, 1997)
13. *Peter Cook – A Biography* by Harry Thompson (Hodder & Stoughton, 1997)
14. Ibid.
15. *Peter Cook – At A Slight Angle To The Universe*, BBC2, 2002

16. *Daily Mail*, 28 February 1966
17. *Peter Cook – At A Slight Angle To The Universe*, BBC2, 2002
18. *Dudley Moore – The Authorised Biography* by Barbra Paskin (Sidgwick & Jackson, 1997)
19. 'Some Interesting Facts About Peter Cook', *Omnibus*, BBC1, 1995
20. *The Very Best of Goodbye Again*, Granada Television, 2004
21. *Junkin's Jokers*, BBC Radio 2, 19 October 1993
22. *Dudley Moore*, Antelope Productions for ITV, 1994
23. Ibid.
24. *Peter Cook – A Biography* by Harry Thompson (Hodder & Stoughton, 1997)
25. Ibid.
26. *From Fringe to Flying Circus* by Roger Wilmut (Methuen, 1980)
27. *Peter Cook – At A Slight Angle To The Universe*, BBC2, 2002
28. *Peter Cook – A Biography* by Harry Thompson (Hodder & Stoughton, 1997)
29. *Sunday Times*, 31 October 1965
30. *Dagenham Post*, 3 November 1965
31. *Sun*, 1 March 1965

CHAPTER FOURTEEN – THE WRONG BOX

1. *Sunday Times*, 31 October 1965
2. *Peter Cook – At A Slight Angle To The Universe*, BBC2, 2002
3. *So Farewell Then, Peter Cook* by Wendy E. Cook (HarperCollins, 2006)
4. *Dudley Moore – On The Couch* by Douglas Thompson (Little, Brown, 1996)
5. Elisabeth Luard in *Something Like Fire – Peter Cook Remembered*, edited by Lin Cook (Methuen, 1996)
6. *Evening Standard*, 9 May 1968
7. Elisabeth Luard in *Something Like Fire – Peter Cook Remembered*, edited by Lin Cook (Methuen, 1996)
8. *Peter Cook – At A Slight Angle To The Universe*, BBC2, 2002
9. *So Farewell Then, Peter Cook* by Wendy E. Cook (HarperCollins, 2006)
10. Ibid.
11. Ibid.
12. *Peter Cook – A Biography* by Harry Thompson (Hodder & Stoughton, 1997)
13. Ibid.
14. Ibid.
15. *Sunday Times*, 31 October 1965
16. *Dudley Moore – The Authorised Biography* by Barbra Paskin (Sidgwick & Jackson, 1977)
17. Ibid.
18. Ibid.

19. *Film Commentary*, November-December 1979
20. *Dudley Moore – The Authorised Biography* by Barbra Paskin (Sidgwick & Jackson, 1977)
21. *Dudley* by Paul Donovan (W.H. Allen, 1988)
22. *So Farewell Then, Peter Cook* by Wendy E. Cook (HarperCollins, 2006)
23. Ibid.
24. *Peter Cook – At A Slight Angle To The Universe*, BBC2, 2002
25. *So Farewell Then, Peter Cook* by Wendy E. Cook (HarperCollins, 2006)
26. *Sun*, 29 September 1965
27. *Dudley Moore – The Authorised Biography* by Barbra Paskin (Sidgwick & Jackson, 1977)
28. *Pete & Dud – An Illustrated Biography* by Alexander Games (Chameleon, 1999)
29. *Peter Cook – At A Slight Angle To The Universe*, BBC2, 2002
30. *Dudley Moore – The Authorised Biography* by Barbra Paskin (Sidgwick & Jackson, 1977)
31. *Peter Cook – At A Slight Angle To The Universe*, BBC2, 2002
32. *Pete & Dud – An Illustrated Biography* by Alexander Games (Chameleon, 1999)
33. *So Farewell Then, Peter Cook* by Wendy E. Cook (HarperCollins, 2006)
34. *News of The World*, 10 September 1967
35. *The Times*, 18 November, 1972
36. *Dudley Moore – The Authorised Biography* by Barbra Paskin (Sidgwick & Jackson, 1977)
37. *Funny Business*, BBC TV, 6 December 1992
38. *Pete & Dud – An Illustrated Biography* by Alexander Games (Chameleon, 1999)

CHAPTER FIFTEEN – BEDAZZLED

1. *Sunday Times*, 31 October 1965
2. *Peter Cook – A Biography* by Harry Thompson (Hodder & Stoughton, 1997)
3. Ibid.
4. 'Some Interesting Facts About Peter Cook', *Omnibus*, BBC1, 1995
5. *Dudley Moore – The Authorised Biography* by Barbra Paskin (Sidgwick & Jackson, 1977)
6. *Peter Cook – A Biography* by Harry Thompson (Hodder & Stoughton, 1997)
7. Barry Humphries, *Bedazzled* DVD (Second Sight, 2005)
8. Ibid.
9. *So Farewell Then, Peter Cook* by Wendy E. Cook (HarperCollins, 2006)
10. Ibid.
11. Ibid.
12. *Daily Mail*, 24 November 1977

13. Ibid.
14. Ibid.
15. *Daily Mail*, 24 November 1977
16. *Mail on Sunday*, 5 December 2004
17. *Peter Cook – A Biography* by Harry Thompson (Hodder & Stoughton, 1997)
18. Included as a special feature on the Second Sight DVD of *Bedazzled*.
19. Bernard Braden died in 1993, aged 76. His *Now & Then* interviews with Peter Cook, Richard Lester and Spike Milligan all feature on the BFI's DVD of *The Bed Sitting Room*.
20. *Daily Mail*, 21 December 1967
21. *From Fringe To Flying Circus* by Roger Wilmut (Methuen, 1980)
22. Ibid.
23. Christopher Hitchens & Dudley Moore in *Something Like Fire – Peter Cook Remembered*, edited by Lin Cook (Methuen, 1996)
24. *Peter Cook – A Biography* by Harry Thompson (Hodder & Stoughton, 1997)
25. Barry Humphries, *Bedazzled* DVD (Second Sight, 2005)
26. *How To Go To The Movies* by Quentin Crisp (St Martin's Press, 1984)
27. *Sunday Express*, 14 January 1968
28. Ibid.
29. *Sunday People*, 4 February 1968

CHAPTER SIXTEEN – GOODBYE AGAIN

1. *Film Commentary*, November-December 1979
2. *Beyond The Fringe ... And Beyond* by Ronald Bergan (Virgin Books, 1989)
3. *Dudley Moore – The Authorised Biography* by Barbra Paskin (Sidgwick & Jackson, 1997)
4. Ibid.
5. Ibid.
6. Ibid.
7. *Beyond The Fringe ... And Beyond* by Ronald Bergan (Virgin Books, 1989)
8. *Dudley Moore –The Authorised Biography* by Barbra Paskin (Sidgwick & Jackson, 1977)
9. Ibid.
10. Ibid.
11. Ibid.
12. Ibid.
13. Ibid.
14. *From Fringe to Flying Circus* by Roger Wilmut (Methuen, 1980)
15. *The Orton Diaries*, edited by John Lahr (Methuen, 1986)
16. *Prick Up Your Ears – The Biography of Joe Orton* by John Lahr (Allen Lane, 1978)

17. *Observer*, 18 February 1962
18. Richard Lester interviewed by Bernard Braden, *Now & Then*, 3 November 1967
19. *Dudley* by Paul Donovan (W.H. Allen, 1988)
20. Richard Lester interviewed by Bernard Braden, *Now & Then*, 3 November 1967
21. *From Fringe to Flying Circus* by Roger Wilmut (Methuen, 1980)
22. *Film Commentary*, November-December 1979
23. *Dudley Moore – The Authorised Biography* by Barbra Paskin (Sidgwick & Jackson, 1997)
24. Richard Lester interviewed by Bernard Braden, *Now & Then*, 3 November 1967
25. *The Bed Sitting Room* by Michael Brooke, British Film Institute, 2009
26. *Dudley Moore – The Authorised Biography* by Barbra Paskin (Sidgwick & Jackson, 1997)
27. *Peter Cook – A Biography* by Harry Thompson (Hodder & Stoughton, 1997)
28. *Dudley Moore*, Antelope Productions for ITV, 1994
29. *So Farewell Then, Peter Cook* by Wendy E. Cook (HarperCollins, 2006)
30. Ibid.
31. Ibid.
32. Ibid.
33. *Peter Cook – A Biography* by Harry Thompson (Hodder & Stoughton, 1997)
34. *Mail on Sunday*, 12 November 1994
35. *Dudley Moore – The Authorised Biography* by Barbra Paskin (Sidgwick & Jackson, 1997)
36. Ibid.
37. Ibid.

CHAPTER SEVENTEEN – POETS CORNERED

1. *So Farewell Then, Peter Cook* by Wendy E. Cook (HarperCollins, 2006)
2. *Daily Mail*, 24 November 1977
3. *Loving Peter* by Judy Cook with Angela Levin (Little, Brown, 2008)
4. Ibid.
5. *Evening Standard*, 31 October 1970
6. *Beyond The Fringe ... And Beyond* by Ronald Bergan (Virgin Books, 1989)
7. *Peter Cook – At A Slight Angle To The Universe*, BBC2, 2002
8. *Peter Cook – Bedazzled* by John Lahr, *The New Yorker*, 23 January 1995
9. 'Some Interesting Facts About Peter Cook', *Omnibus*, BBC1, 1995
10. *Beyond The Fringe ... And Beyond* by Ronald Bergan (Virgin Books, 1989)

11. Ibid.
12. *Evening Standard*, 31 October 1970
13. *Beyond The Fringe ... And Beyond* by Ronald Bergan (Virgin Books, 1989)
14. *Dudley Moore – On The Couch* by Douglas Thompson (Little, Brown, 1996)
15. *Loving Peter* by Judy Cook with Angela Levin (Little, Brown, 2008)
16. *Peter Cook – A Biography* by Harry Thompson (Hodder & Stoughton, 1997)
17. *From Fringe to Flying Circus* by Roger Wilmut (Methuen, 1980)
18. *Peter Cook – A Biography* by Harry Thompson (Hodder & Stoughton, 1997)
19. *Dudley Moore – On The Couch* by Douglas Thompson (Little, Brown, 1996)
20. *Peter Cook – A Biography* by Harry Thompson (Hodder & Stoughton, 1997)
21. *The Times*, 18 November 1972
22. *Daily Telegraph*, 28 March 2002
23. *Peter Cook – A Biography* by Harry Thompson (Hodder & Stoughton, 1997)
24. Ibid.
25. *So Farewell Then, Peter Cook* by Wendy E. Cook (HarperCollins, 2006)
26. *Dudley Moore – The Authorised Biography* by Barbra Paskin (Sidgwick & Jackson, 1997)

CHAPTER EIGHTEEN – WHERE DO I SIT?

1. *Daily Mail*, 17 February 1970
2. *The Times*, 3 November 1973
3. *So Farewell Then, Peter Cook* by Wendy E. Cook (HarperCollins, 2006)
4. Ibid.
5. *Daily Mail*, 28 September 1996
6. *Daily Mail*, 10 November 1970
7. *Loving Peter* by Judy Cook with Angela Levin (Little, Brown, 2008)
8. *So Farewell Then, Peter Cook* by Wendy E. Cook (HarperCollins, 2006)
9. Ibid.
10. Ibid.
11. 'Some Interesting Facts About Peter Cook', *Omnibus*, BBC1, 1995
12. *Evening Standard*, 31 October 1970
13. Ibid.
14. *Beyond The Fringe ... And Beyond* by Ronald Bergan (Virgin Books, 1989)
15. *Russell Harty*, London Weekend Television for ITV, 9 October 1975
16. *Peter Cook – A Biography* by Harry Thompson (Hodder & Stoughton, 1997)

17. *Loving Peter* by Judy Cook with Angela Levin (Little, Brown, 2008)
18. Ibid.
19. Auberon Waugh in *Something Like Fire – Peter Cook Remembered*, edited by Lin Cook (Methuen, 1996)
20. *Peter Cook – A Biography* by Harry Thompson (Hodder & Stoughton, 1997)
21. *The Times*, 20 February 1971
22. Ibid.
23. *Turned Out Nice Again – The Story of British Light Entertainment* by Louis Barfe (Atlantic Books, 2008)
24. *Daily Mail*, 8 March 1971
25. *Russell Harty*, London Weekend Television for ITV, 9 October 1975
26. *Beyond The Fringe ... And Beyond* by Ronald Bergan (Virgin Books, 1989)
27. *Turned Out Nice Again – The Story of British Light Entertainment* by Louis Barfe (Atlantic Books, 2008)
28. *Beyond The Fringe ... And Beyond* by Ronald Bergan (Virgin Books, 1989)
29. Ibid.
30. 'Some Interesting Facts About Peter Cook', *Omnibus*, BBC1, 1995
31. *Dudley Moore – The Authorised Biography* by Barbra Paskin (Sidgwick & Jackson, 1997)
32. Ibid.
33. Ibid.
34. Ibid.
35. Ibid.

CHAPTER NINETEEN – DOWN UNDER

1. *Dudley Moore – On The Couch* by Douglas Thompson (Little, Brown, 1996)
2. *Sunday Times*, 8 October 1972
3. *Good Afternoon With Mavis Nicholson*, Thames Television for ITV, 9 March 1973
4. *Peter Cook – A Biography* by Harry Thompson (Hodder & Stoughton, 1997)
5. Ibid.
6. Shane Maloney in *Something Like Fire – Peter Cook Remembered*, edited by Lin Cook (Methuen, 1996)
7. *Peter Cook – A Biography* by Harry Thompson (Hodder & Stoughton, 1997)
8. *The Times*, 18 November, 1972
9. *Loving Peter* by Judy Cook with Angela Levin (Little, Brown, 2008)
10. *Dudley Moore – The Authorised Biography* by Barbra Paskin (Sidgwick & Jackson, 1997)

11. *Peter Cook – A Biography* by Harry Thompson (Hodder & Stoughton, 1997)
12. Christopher Hitchens and Dudley Moore in *Something Like Fire – Peter Cook Remembered*, edited by Lin Cook (Methuen, 1996)
13. *Dudley Moore – The Authorised Biography* by Barbra Paskin (Sidgwick & Jackson, 1997)
14. Christopher Hitchens and Dudley Moore in *Something Like Fire – Peter Cook Remembered*, edited by Lin Cook (Methuen, 1996)
15. 'Some Interesting Facts About Peter Cook', *Omnibus*, BBC1, 1995
16. *Parky – My Autobiography* by Michael Parkinson (Hodder & Stoughton, 2008)
17. *Peter Cook – A Biography* by Harry Thompson (Hodder & Stoughton, 1997)
18. Ibid.
19. *Peter Cook – At A Slight Angle To The Universe*, BBC2, 2002
20. Lewis Morley in *Something Like Fire – Peter Cook Remembered*, edited by Lin Cook (Methuen, 1996)
21. Ibid.
22. *News of the World*, 7 July 1988
23. *Loving Peter* by Judy Cook with Angela Levin (Little, Brown, 2008)
24. Ibid.
25. *Dudley Moore – On The Couch* by Douglas Thompson (Little, Brown, 1996)
26. *Loving Peter* by Judy Cook with Angela Levin (Little, Brown, 2008)
27. *Loving Peter* by Judy Cook with Angela Levin (Little, Brown, 2008)
28. Ibid.
29. Ibid.
30. Ibid.
31. Ibid.

CHAPTER TWENTY – BEHIND THE FRIDGE

1. *The Times*, 3 November 1973
2. *Peter Cook – A Biography* by Harry Thompson (Hodder & Stoughton, 1997)
3. *My Life As Me – A Memoir* by Barry Humphries (Viking Penguin, 2002)
4. *Peter Cook – A Biography* by Harry Thompson (Hodder & Stoughton, 1997)
5. *The Diaries of Kenneth Tynan*, edited by John Lahr (Bloomsbury, 2001)
6. Ibid.
7. *That Was Satire That Was – The Satire Boom of the 1960s* by Humphrey Carpenter (Victor Gollancz, 2000)
8. *So Farewell Then, Peter Cook* by Wendy E. Cook (HarperCollins, 2006)

9. *Loving Peter* by Judy Cook with Angela Levin (Little, Brown, 2008)
10. Ibid.
11. *Dudley* by Paul Donovan (W.H. Allen, 1988)
12. *Dudley Moore – The Authorised Biography* by Barbra Paskin (Sidgwick & Jackson, 1997)
13. Ibid.
14. *Dudley Moore – On The Couch* by Douglas Thompson (Little, Brown, 1996)
15. *The Times*, 18 November 1972
16. Joe McGrath in *Something Like Fire – Peter Cook Remembered*, edited by Lin Cook (Methuen, 1996)
17. *Peter Cook – A Biography* by Harry Thompson (Hodder & Stoughton, 1997)
18. *Peter Cook – At A Slight Angle To The Universe*, BBC2, 2002
19. *Peter Cook – A Biography* by Harry Thompson (Hodder & Stoughton, 1997)
20. Ibid.
21. Ibid.
22. *Dudley Moore – The Authorised Biography* by Barbra Paskin (Sidgwick & Jackson, 1997)
23. John Wells in *Something Like Fire – Peter Cook Remembered*, edited by Lin Cook (Methuen, 1996)
24. *Peter Cook – A Biography* by Harry Thompson (Hodder & Stoughton, 1997)
25. *Dudley Moore – The Authorised Biography* by Barbra Paskin (Sidgwick & Jackson, 1997)
26. *Peter Cook – At A Slight Angle To The Universe*, BBC2, 2002
27. Ibid.
28. *Dudley Moore – The Authorised Biography* by Barbra Paskin (Sidgwick & Jackson, 1997)
29. Ibid.
30. *Peter Cook – A Biography* by Harry Thompson (Hodder & Stoughton, 1997)
31. *Good Afternoon*, Thames Television, 19 April 1973

CHAPTER TWENTY ONE – GOOD EVENING

1. *Dudley Moore – The Authorised Biography* by Barbra Paskin (Sidgwick & Jackson, 1997)
2. *Loving Peter* by Judy Cook with Angela Levin (Little, Brown, 2008)
3. *Peter Cook – A Biography* by Harry Thompson (Hodder & Stoughton, 1997)
4. *Dudley Moore – The Authorised Biography* by Barbra Paskin (Sidgwick & Jackson, 1997)

5. Ibid.
6. *Dudley* by Paul Donovan (W.H. Allen, 1988)
7. *The Times*, 3 November 1973
8. Ibid.
9. Dudley Moore, letter to David Dearlove, 19 June 1980
10. *Dudley Moore – On The Couch* by Douglas Thompson (Little, Brown, 1996)
11. *Parky's People* by Michael Parkinson (Hodder & Stoughton, 2010)
12. Ibid.
13. *Loving Peter* by Judy Cook with Angela Levin (Little, Brown, 2008)
14. Ibid.
15. Ibid.
16. *Peter Cook – A Biography* by Harry Thompson (Hodder & Stoughton, 1997)
17. 'Some Interesting Facts About Peter Cook', *Omnibus*, BBC1, 1995
18. Christopher Hitchens and Dudley Moore in *Something Like Fire – Peter Cook Remembered*, edited by Lin Cook (Methuen, 1996)
19. Ibid.
20. Ibid.
21. *Dudley Moore – The Authorised Biography* by Barbra Paskin (Sidgwick & Jackson, 1997)
22. Ibid.
23. Ibid.
24. *From Fringe to Flying Circus* by Roger Wilmut (Methuen, 1980)
25. Christopher Hitchens and Joseph Heller *in Something Like Fire – Peter Cook Remembered*, edited by Lin Cook (Methuen, 1996)
26. *Dudley Moore – The Authorised Biography* by Barbra Paskin (Sidgwick & Jackson, 1997)
27. Ibid.
28. Ibid.
29. Ibid.
30. *Loving Peter* by Judy Cook with Angela Levin (Little, Brown, 2008)
31. *Success Story*, BBC, May 1974
32. Ibid.
33. *Russell Harty*, LWT for ITV, 9 October 1975
34. *Peter Cook – At A Slight Angle To The Universe*, BBC2, 2002
35. *Dudley Moore – The Authorised Biography* by Barbra Paskin (Sidgwick & Jackson, 1997)
36. Ibid.
37. Ibid.

CHAPTER TWENTY TWO – ON THE ROAD

1. *Russell Harty Plus*, LWT for ITV, October 1975
2. *Peter Cook – A Biography* by Harry Thompson (Hodder & Stoughton, 1997)

3. *Parky's People* by Michael Parkinson (Hodder & Stoughton, 2010)
4. *Loving Peter* by Judy Cook with Angela Levin (Little, Brown, 2008)
5. Ibid.
6. Ibid.
7. *Sunday Express*, 17 August 1975
8. *The Times*, 12 June 1993
9. *Dudley Moore – On The Couch* by Douglas Thompson (Little, Brown, 1996)
10. *Peter Cook – A Biography* by Harry Thompson (Hodder & Stoughton, 1997)
11. *Penthouse*, Volume Eleven, Number Nine
12. Ibid.
13. *Parky's People* by Michael Parkinson (Hodder & Stoughton, 2010)
14. *Sunday Express*, 17 August 1975
15. *Dudley Moore – On The Couch* by Douglas Thompson (Little, Brown, 1996)
16. *Peter Cook – A Biography* by Harry Thompson (Hodder & Stoughton, 1997)
17. *Loving Peter* by Judy Cook with Angela Levin (Little, Brown, 2008)
18. *Dudley Moore – The Authorised Biography* by Barbra Paskin (Sidgwick & Jackson, 1997)
19. *Peter Cook – At A Slight Angle To The Universe*, BBC2, 2002
20. Ibid.
21. *Loving Peter* by Judy Cook with Angela Levin (Little, Brown, 2008)
22. *Dudley Moore – The Authorised Biography* by Barbra Paskin (Sidgwick & Jackson, 1997)
23. *Sunday Express*, 17 August 1975
24. *Peter Cook – A Biography* by Harry Thompson (Hodder & Stoughton, 1997)
25. *Loving Peter* by Judy Cook with Angela Levin (Little, Brown, 2008)
26. *Mail on Sunday*, 5 December 2004
27. *Loving Peter* by Judy Cook with Angela Levin (Little, Brown, 2008)
28. Ibid.

CHAPTER TWENTY THREE – DEREK & CLIVE (DEAD)

1. *Success Story*, BBC, May 1974
2. *Dudley Moore – The Authorised Biography* by Barbra Paskin (Sidgwick & Jackson, 1997)
3. *Sunday Express*, 6 February 1977
4. Christopher Hitchens and Dudley Moore in *Something Like Fire – Peter Cook Remembered*, edited by Lin Cook (Methuen, 1996)
5. *Sheffield & North Derbyshire Spectator*, 1976
6. Ibid.
7. Ibid.

8. *Loving Peter* by Judy Cook with Angela Levin (Little, Brown, 2008)
9. *Offensive – The Real Derek & Clive*, Channel 4, 2002
10. *Sheffield & North Derbyshire Spectator*, 1976
11. 'Some Interesting Facts About Peter Cook', *Omnibus*, BBC1, 1995
12. *Penthouse*, Volume Eleven, Number Nine
13. *Sheffield & North Derbyshire Spectator*, 1976
14. *Sunday Express*, 6 February 1977
15. *Penthouse*, Volume Eleven, Number Nine
16. *Guardian*, 20 August 1976
17. *Dudley Moore – The Authorised Biography* by Barbra Paskin (Sidgwick & Jackson, 1997)
18. *Sunday Times*, 22 August 1976
19. *Loving Peter* by Judy Cook with Angela Levin (Little, Brown, 2008)
20. *Peter Cook – A Biography* by Harry Thompson (Hodder & Stoughton, 1997)
21. *Dudley Moore – The Authorised Biography* by Barbra Paskin (Sidgwick & Jackson, 1997)
22. *Peter Cook – A Biography* by Harry Thompson (Hodder & Stoughton, 1997)

23. *Daily Mail*, 31 January 1977

CHAPTER TWENTY FOUR – THE HOUND OF THE BASKERVILLES

1. *Parkinson*, BBC1, 21 February 1976
2. *The South Bank Show*, LWT for ITV, 8 April 1978
3. *The Kenneth Williams Diaries*, edited by Russell Davies (HarperCollins, 1993)
4. *Daily Mail*, 27 June 1977
5. *The South Bank Show*, LWT for ITV, 8 April 1978
6. *Evening Standard*, 29 July 1977
7. *The Kenneth Williams Diaries*, edited by Russell Davies (HarperCollins, 1993)
8. Ibid.
9. Ibid.
10. Ibid.
11. *Dudley Moore – The Authorised Biography* by Barbra Paskin (Sidgwick & Jackson, 1997)
12. *From Fringe to Flying Circus* by Roger Wilmut (Methuen, 1980)
13. Ibid.
14. Daily Mail, 6 June 1977. The photographer Antony Armstrong-Jones was created Earl of Snowden upon his marriage to Princess Margaret in 1961. The couple divorced in 1978.
15. *Loving Peter* by Judy Cook with Angela Levin (Little, Brown, 2008)
16. 'Some Interesting Facts About Peter Cook', *Omnibus*, BBC1, 1995

17. *Daily Mail*, 14 November 1977
18. Ibid.
19. *Daily Mail*, 24 November 1977
20. *Dudley Moore – The Authorised Biography* by Barbra Paskin (Sidgwick & Jackson, 1997)
21. *Mail on Sunday*, 1 October 1995
22. *Peter Cook – A Biography* by Harry Thompson (Hodder & Stoughton, 1997)
23. *Dudley Moore – The Authorised Biography* by Barbra Paskin (Sidgwick & Jackson, 1997)
24. *Beyond The Fringe ... And Beyond* by Ronald Bergan (Virgin Books, 1989)
25. *Evening News*, 26 May 1978
26. *Observer*, 9 December 1979
27. *Independent on Sunday*, 6 June 1993

CHAPTER TWENTY FIVE – 10

1. *Parkinson*, BBC1, 16 September 1978
2. *Daily Mirror*, 18 January 1980
3. *Beyond The Fringe ... And Beyond* by Ronald Bergan (Virgin Books, 1989)
4. *Dudley Moore – The Authorised Biography* by Barbra Paskin (Sidgwick & Jackson, 1997)
5. *Fame, Set & Match – Beyond The Fringe*, BBC2, 23 November 2002
6. *Dudley Moore – The Authorised Biography* by Barbra Paskin (Sidgwick & Jackson, 1997)
7. *Heroes of Comedy – Peter Cook*, Thames Television for Channel 4, 19 January 1998
8. *Dudley Moore – The Authorised Biography* by Barbra Paskin (Sidgwick & Jackson, 1997)
9. Ibid.
10. Christopher Hitchens and Dudley Moore in *Something Like Fire – Peter Cook Remembered*, edited by Lin Cook (Methuen, 1996)
11. *Dudley Moore – The Authorised Biography* by Barbra Paskin (Sidgwick & Jackson, 1997)
12. *Peter Cook – A Biography* by Harry Thompson (Hodder & Stoughton, 1997)
13. Ibid.
14. Peter Cook to Dudley Moore, quoted in *Dudley Moore – The Authorised Biography* by Barbra Paskin (Sidgwick & Jackson, 1997)
15. Ibid.
16. Ibid.

CHAPTER TWENTY SIX – THE TWO OF US

1. *Person To Person*, BBC1, 2 August 1979
2. *The Last Word – An Eye Witness Account of The Thorpe Trial* by Auberon Waugh (Michael Joseph, 1980)
3. *News of the World*, 2 December 1979
4. Ibid.
5. *Peter Cook – A Biography* by Harry Thompson (Hodder & Stoughton, 1997)
6. *Daily Mail*, 28 February 1980
7. *Beyond The Fringe … And Beyond* by Ronald Bergan (Virgin Books, 1989)
8. *Sun*, 2 August 1980
9. *News of the World*, 2 December 1979
10. *Daily Mirror*, 22 August 1980
11. *Peter Cook – At A Slight Angle To The Universe*, BBC2, 2002
12. *Evening Standard*, 13 March 1981
13. *Dudley Moore – An Intimate Portrait* by Rena Fruchter (Ebury Press, 2006)
14. *Observer*, 9 December 1979
15. *Dudley* by Paul Donovan (W.H. Allen, 1988)
16. *Sunday Times*, 13 December 1981
17. Ibid.
18. *Dudley Moore – The Authorised Biography* by Barbra Paskin (Sidgwick & Jackson, 1997)
19. Ibid.
20. Ibid.
21. *Peter Cook – At A Slight Angle To The Universe*, BBC2, 2002
22. *Daily Mirror*, 26 October 1981
23. *Daily Express*, 21 December 2004
24. *Beyond The Fringe … And Beyond* by Ronald Bergan (Virgin Books, 1989)
25. *Sunday Express*, 12 September 1982
26. Henry Fonda won the Academy Award for Best Actor for his performance in *On Golden Pond*.
27. *Daily Express*, 15 March 1982
28. *Sunday Express*, 12 September 1982
29. *The Sun*, 17 March 1982
30. Ibid.
31. *Sunday Telegraph*, 17 November 1985

CHAPTER TWENTY SEVEN – GET THE HORN

1. *Mavis Catches Up*, Thames TV, 22 November 1989
2. *Mail on Sunday*, 29 July 1984

3. *Heroes of Comedy – Peter Cook*, Thames Television for Channel 4, 19 January 1998
4. Ibid.
5. Ibid.
6. *Daily Telegraph*, 17 September 2002
7. *Daily Mail*, 10 January 1995
8. *Daily Telegraph*, 14 October 1996
9. Ibid.
10. *Peter Cook – A Biography* by Harry Thompson (Hodder & Stoughton, 1997)
11. *Loving Peter* by Judy Cook with Angela Levin (Little, Brown, 2008)
12. *Mail on Sunday*, 5 December 2004
13. *Sunday Express*, 15 January 1995
14. *Mail on Sunday*, 5 December 2004
15. *Sun*, 20 November 1984
16. *Mail on Sunday*, 30 January 1983
17. *Sunday Express*, 8 December 1985
18. *The Times*, 27 February 1987
19. *TV Times*, 18 November 1989
20. *Dudley Moore – The Authorised Biography* by Barbra Paskin (Sidgwick & Jackson, 1997)
21. *Illustrated London News*, December 1988
22. *Dudley Moore – On The Couch* by Douglas Thompson (Little, Brown, 1996)
23. Pascal's *Pensées* constitute a philosophical defence of Christianity – Pascal's Wager sets out the logical case for believing in God. 'Pascal didn't have too many hints for seducing eighteen-year-old girls,' Peter told the journalist John Hind, 'but he did tell me a little about getting them drunk.' (*Comic Inquisition*, Virgin Books, 1991)
24. *Peter Cook – A Biography* by Harry Thompson (Hodder & Stoughton, 1997)
25. John Wells in *Something Like Fire – Peter Cook Remembered*, edited by Lin Cook (Methuen, 1996)
26. *Guardian*, 27 December 1990
27. *Daily Mail*, 6 November 1990
28. *Daily Telegraph*, 6 August 1993
29. *Daily Mail*, 10 August 1993
30. *Today*, 4 September 1993
31. Ibid.
32. Ibid.
33. *Mail on Sunday*, 15 August 1993
34. John Bird in *Something Like Fire – Peter Cook Remembered*, edited by Lin Cook (Methuen, 1996)
35. *Loving Peter* by Judy Cook with Angela Levin (Little, Brown, 2008)

CHAPTER TWENTY EIGHT – GOODBYEE

1. *Daily Telegraph*, 29 May 1995
2. *Hampstead & Highgate Express*, 20 December 1996
3. Eleanor Bron in *Something Like Fire – Peter Cook Remembered*, edited by Lin Cook (Methuen, 1996)
4. *Daily Mail*, 10 January 1995
5. *Daily Mail*, 26 May 2001
6. *Peter, My Beautiful Brother* by Sarah Seymour, *Guardian*, 15 October 1996
7. *Daily Mail*, 12 November 1994
8. Ibid.
9. *Loving Peter* by Judy Cook with Angela Levin (Little, Brown, 2008)
10. 'Peter Cook – Bedazzled' by John Lahr, *The New Yorker*, 23 January 1995, reprinted in *Light Fantastic – Adventures in Theatre* by John Lahr (Bloomsbury, 1996)
11. *Mail on Sunday*, 24 September 1995
12. *Daily Mail*, 10 January 1995
13. *Independent*, 14 October 1995
14. *Dudley Moore – An Intimate Portrait* by Rena Fruchter (Ebury Press, 2006)
15. *London Review of Books*, 25 May 1995
16. *The Times*, 2 May 1995
17. *Sunday Times*, 15 January 1995
18. *Heroes of Comedy – Peter Cook*, Thames Television for Channel 4, 19 January 1998
19. Alan Bennett in *Something Like Fire – Peter Cook Remembered*, edited by Lin Cook (Methuen, 1996)
20. *Mavis Catches Up*, Thames TV, 22 November 1989
21. *Daily Mail*, 12 November 1994
22. *Guardian*, 22 August 1980
23. *Sun*, 20 November 1984
24. *Dudley Moore – The Authorised Biography* by Barbra Paskin (Sidgwick & Jackson, 1997)
25. *Peter Cook – At A Slight Angle To The Universe*, BBC2, 2002
26. *Daily Telegraph*, 6 August 1993
27. *Mail on Sunday*, 1 October
28. *Today*, 22 January 1992
29. *Daily Telegraph*, 6 August 1993
30. *Independent on Sunday*, 27 March 1994
31. *Observer*, 16 February 1992
32. *Mail on Sunday*, 1 October 1995
33. *Dudley Moore – An Intimate Portrait* by Rena Fruchter (Ebury Press, 2006)
34. *Sun*, 28 May 1965

35. *Independent*, 14 October 1995
36. *Daily Telegraph*, 6 January 1995
37. *Dudley Moore – On The Couch* by Douglas Thompson (Little, Brown, 1996)
38. *Dudley Moore – An Intimate Portrait* by Rena Fruchter (Ebury Press, 2006)
39. Ibid.
40. Ibid.
41. Ibid.
42. Ibid.
43. *The Express*, 16 December 1998
44. *Dudley Moore – An Intimate Portrait* by Rena Fruchter (Ebury Press, 2006)
45. *Sunday Times*, 31 March 2002
46. *Dudley Moore – An Intimate Portrait* by Rena Fruchter (Ebury Press, 2006)
47. Ibid.
48. *Daily Mail*, 17 November 2001
49. Ibid.
50. *Dudley Moore – An Intimate Portrait* by Rena Fruchter (Ebury Press, 2006)
51. Ibid.
52. Ibid.
53. Ibid.
54. *Daily Telegraph*, 28 March 2002
55. *Sunday Times*, 31 March 2002

INTERVIEWS

FRANCIS BENNETT

1. Peter Way was Peter Cook's drama master. Elizabeth is Way's wife.

PETER CORK

1. *Santa Claus* (Rank, 1985) produced by Ilya & Alexander Salkind and Pierre Spengler, directed by Jeannot Szwarc.
2. Patrick Havlin Moore, born 1976, named after Dudley's university friend from Oxford, Patrick Garland. Dudley's father was born John Havlin.

PATRICK GARLAND

1. *The Disciplines of War* was subsequently renamed *The Long And The Short And The Tall*. Patrick played the part later played by Peter O'Toole.

2. Patrick Garland died in 2013, shortly before the publication of this book.

ELISABETH LUARD

1. Elisabeth Luard, Preface to *So Farewell Then, Peter Cook* by Wendy E. Cook (HarperCollins 2006)
2. Ibid.

PETER WAY

1. *No Ordinary Place – Radley College and The Public School System* by Christopher Hibbert (John Murray, 1997)

PICTURE CREDITS

Introduction: © Philip Jackson / Daily Mail / Rex Features

Dudley by Peter: © Redferns / Getty Images

Peter by Dudley: © Everett Collection / Rex Features

Chapter One – © Condé Nast Archives / Corbis

Chapter Two – Dagenham: Courtesy of Rena Fruchter

Chapter Three – Radley: Courtesy of Sarah Seymour

Chapter Four – Oxford: © Courtesy of Rena Fruchter

Chapter Five – Cambridge: Courtesy of Sarah Seymour and Elizabeth Cook

Chapter Six – Before The Fringe: © John Bulmer

Chapter Seven – Edinburgh & After: © Courtesy of Sarah Seymour, Elizabeth Cook and Wendy Cook

Chapter Eight – Brighton or Bust: © Lewis Morley Archive / National Portrait Gallery, London

Chapter Nine – Beyond The Fringe: © Terry Disney / Hulton Archive / Getty Images

Chapter Nine – The Establishment: © Lewis Morley Archive / National Portrait Gallery, London

Chapter Eleven – On Broadway: © Ivan Keeman / Redferns / Getty Images

Chapter Twelve – Brighton or Bust: Courtesy of Rena Fruchter

Chapter Thirteen – Not Only ... But Also: © Photoshot / Hulton Archive / Getty Images

Chapter Fourteen – The Wrong Box: © Keystone / Hulton Archive / Getty Images. Courtesy of Wendy Cook

Chapter Fifteen – Bedazzled: © Gamma-Keystone / Getty Images

Chapter Sixteen – Goodbye Again: Courtesy of Suzy Kendall, taken by Chiara Samugheo

Chapter Seventeen – Poets Cornered: © Michael Putland / Hulton Archive / Getty Images

Chapter Eighteen – Where Do I Sit?: © Bill Johnson / Rex Features

Chapter Nineteen – Down Under: © Aubrey Hart / Evening News / Rex Features

Chapter Twenty – Behind The Fridge: © Express Newspapers / Hulton Archive / Getty Images

Chapter Twenty One – Good Evening: © Ron Galella / WireImage / Getty Images

Chapter Twenty Two – On The Road: © NBC Universal / Getty Images

Chapter Twenty Three – Derek & Clive (Dead): © Estate Of Keith Morris / Redferns / Getty Images

Chapter Twenty Four – The Hound of The Baskervilles: Evening Standard / Hulton Archive / Getty Images

Chapter Twenty Five – 10: © SNAP / Rex Features

Chapter Twenty Six – The Two of Us: © Hulton Archive / Getty Images

Chapter Twenty Seven – Get The Horn: © Mike Hollist / Associated Newspapers / Rex Features

Chapter Twenty Eight – Goodbyee: © Time & Life Pictures / Getty Images

In Heaven: © Nils Jorgensen / Rex Features

TEXT PERMISSIONS

INDEX